Planets in Transit

Other Books by Robert Hand:

Essays on Astrology
Horoscope Symbols
Planets in Composite: Analyzing Human Relationships
Planets in Youth: Patterns of Early Development

Robert Hand

Planets in Transit

Life Cycles for Living

A division of Schiffer Publishing, Ltd.
77 Lower Valley Road, Atglen, PA 19310 USA

Published by Whitford Press

A Division of Schiffer Publishing, Ltd.
77 Lower Valley Road
Atglen, PA 19310
Please write for a free catalog.
This book may be purchased from the publisher.
Please include $2.95 postage.

Planets in Transit: Life Cycles for Living
by Robert Hand

Library of Congress Catalog Card Number: 76-12759
ISBN: 0-914918-24-9

Edited by Margaret E. Anderson
Typeset in 10 pt. Paladium on Compugraphic ACM 9000
Composition by Hieratic Typesetting Co., Inc.
Printed on 55-pound SRT II Paper

Manufactured in the United States of America

To my father, Wilfred Hand,
who started me on this road

Contents

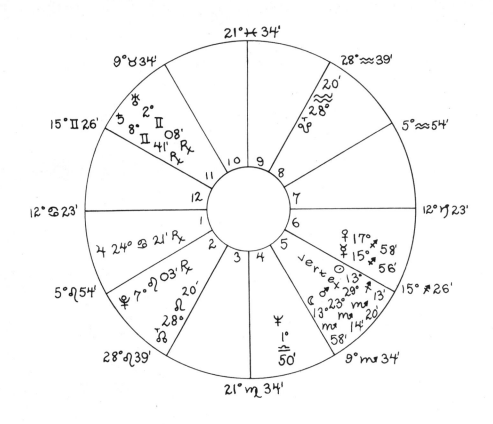

Natal Chart of Robert Hand

Birthdate: December 5, 1942
           Plainfield, New Jersey
           Longitude 74° W 25'
           Latitude 40° N 37'

Birthtime: 7:30:11 pm Eastern War Time
           23:30:11 Universal Time
           23:29:01 Sidereal Time

Ascendant calculated for geographic latitude

Birthplace houses

Foreword

The interpretation of a natal horoscope is an art that requires considerable skill. To interpret that horoscope as it moves and unfolds through time calls for even more skill. This is why a good book that takes up the subject of astrological timing is so valuable to us all.

Broadly speaking, there are four methods of astrological timing: progressions and directions, postnatal epochs, solar and lunar returns, and transits. Progressions and directions are sporadic but discontinuous. They do not occur at regular intervals, and there are times when the bodies are not in orb of aspect. The postnatal epochs that Eleanor Hesseltine and I have discovered are also sporadic because they are timed by progressions or directions, but their effects continue until death. Continuity of effect is also apparent in solar and lunar returns, whether in the tropical or sidereal zodiac. They occur periodically, however, not sporadically as postnatal epochs do. Each solar return is effective for a year. The fourth and most basic form of timing is transits, which are periodic and discontinuous in nature.

It is really surprising that there have been so few good books on the subject of transits. Grant Lewi's *Astrology for the Millions* has been the best book until now, but it is written at a very elementary level. Thus Robert Hand's *Planets in Transit: Life Cycles for Living* fills a really enormous hole in the literature of astrology and does it very well indeed. Quantitatively, it is a large and very complete book, but certainly not larger than necessary for the enlightenment it provides on a complex subject. In this book everyone from the novice to the seasoned professional will find complete coverage of all phases of timing by transit. Its organization and arrangement make it very easy to find what you need.

The main problem in modern astrology, however, is not quantitative but qualitative. Astrology is highly popular, and an enormous amount of material is surfacing in books, magazines, classes and lectures. Unfortunately, much of this material is inferior, for there is still only a small number of experienced, top-flight astrologers. Many of us value Charles Carter's book on aspects, but it is not a very large book. What is remarkable about *Planets in Transit* is its sustained high quality. Robert Hand's clarity of expression contrasts sharply with the work of some of our leading contemporary astrologers, who are very hard to read.

The ability to interpret a planetary combination, whether statically in a radical chart or dynamically by transit or progression, depends on two things. It depends first on knowledge of the contributions made by the best of one's predecessors and colleagues and second on extensive personal empirical observation of the many combinations. If an author relies solely on other people's experience, his book will be derivative, as are the majority of books now being published. The experienced astrologer will recognize that this book is based on personal observation and that it is also consonant with the main findings of the majority of astrologers concerning transits. One very good reason for this is that Robert Hand has been doing astrology since he was very young.

Perhaps the main challenge in the art of interpretation is integrating a number of factors. Overemphasis on any one factor gives a lopsided picture, as is the case with simultaneous or nearly simultaneous transits. It is noteworthy that this book deals with this problem very thoroughly and clearly. Indeed, I would suggest that the reader should study the first part of the book very carefully, for it deals with many essential matters that are skipped in most books on transits. Advocates of a sidereal zodiac will be delighted to find that a correction for the precession is recognized as giving more precise timing than can be found with conventional tropical zodiac positions.

The following example shows a basic phase of transits that is seldom covered. Let us say that you were born with Saturn square your Sun and that transiting Saturn comes to the trine of that Sun. How do we interpret this? Does that natal square affect the meaning of the transit? It does, of course, although too many astrologers seem not to realize this The author of this book notes that a natal or radical aspect is of primary importance and can seriously modify any aspect by transit or progression. Robert Hand has covered all the bases in this, the first book on transits that really does so. The series of books published by Para Research, commencing with Robert Pelletier's *Planets in Aspect*, bids fair to become a major addition to the literature of astrology.

Finally something should be said about the underlying philosophy that permeates the book. There is a definite emphasis on a psychological approach. Among their other notable contributions to astrology, Dane Rudhyar and Dr. Zipporah Dobyns have made an important advance by removing astrology from the fear-ridden fortune-telling tradition. (However, I feel that Dane Rudhyar has gone too far in the other direction, almost completely eschewing the importance of events.) Yet certainly their approach and that of Robert Hand has had a salutary corrective influence. *Planets in Transit* teaches you not to fear some oncoming transit, but rather to think of it as an opportunity for more growth and seasoning. It is not too much to say that in the annals of astrology the name of Robert Hand will be writ large, not only for this book and his authoritative *Planets in Composite*, but also for those yet to come. His is a rising star!

Charles A. Jayne

Introduction

A transit occurs whenever a planet, moving in its orbit during your lifetime, forms an aspect to a planet, the Sun, Moon or any of the house cusps in your natal horoscope. Also, whenever a planet passes through the part of the zodiac occupied by a house in your natal chart, we say that the planet is transiting the house.

The study of transits is one of the most fundamental techniques in astrology. That transits indicate important trends and issues in your life is one of the few points upon which all astrologers agree. Along with directions and progressions, they are basic to the astrologer's predictive methodology. Yet there is not a single, detailed one-volume text that gives you an idea of what to expect from each transit. Nor is there much literature on how to integrate transits into a larger view of the development of your life as a whole. This text is designed to fill that gap.

Here you will find extensive delineations of the transits of the Sun, Moon and planets to all of the major factors in the horoscope by conjunction, sextile, square, trine and opposition, with some introductory notes on the minor aspects. Some readers will note that the transiting node of the Moon is not included. Although I believe that the Moon's node has an effect, at this point I am not sure enough of its meaning to speak about it with confidence.

While these descriptions are not totally complete — that would be an impossible goal to realize — they do provide an in-depth account of the significance of each transit. You will learn what you are most likely to experience, emotionally, psychologically and circumstantially, under each transit. The delineations differ from those in earlier texts because they are written primarily in psychological terms rather than in terms of events. In the past, most texts have been oriented primarily to predicting the events that will happen *to* you. This tends to support the older view of astrology as a fortune-telling system, which almost everyone now agrees is at best a debased form of the art.

The purpose of astrology really should be to give you an understanding of your place in the universe and the kinds of energies that are flowing through you and through the physical universe. Astrology should not try to make up your mind but instead provide information upon which you can make an intelligent decision. Obviously, transits indicate times that are appropriate for certain kinds of actions and inappropriate for others, and certain kinds of events often do occur with particular transits. But transits should never be viewed as signifying events that will inevitably come to pass, with you as a helpless observer.

A very common theory about the different roles of transits, directions and progressions is that transits indicate circumstances that you must face in the outer world, while directions and progressions indicate your inner psychological evolution. In this theory, transits tell what you must face, and directions and progressions tell what inner resources you have to face it with. However, I do not support this idea for several reasons.

First of all, this system does not accord with my experiences as an astrologer. I have found both transits and directions indicating both events and psychological changes, and I cannot find any clear set of criteria to distinguish between the roles of these two major predictive systems. The only real distinction is that by their very nature progressions indicate longer-term effects than transits. In fact one astrologer of my acquaintance, who is unusually competent and experienced in these matters, has reversed the traditional roles and has declared that transits indicate psychological growth, while progressions and directions indicate events. The fact that astrologers can disagree so widely indicates how unclear the distinction is. In particular, solar arc directions, which are derived from progressions, are used by most practitioners to forecast events.

It has been my experience that there are two distinct types of people. One type experiences transits and directions primarily as major emotional and psychological changes, which may or may not be accompanied by a clear pattern of events. At best, it is very unclear whether events cause psychological change, or vice versa. The other type of person experiences both transits and progressions as events that seem to come out of the blue and happen to him. It is my opinion that this type of person is simply less aware of the dynamics of his life than the first type.

The astrologer R. C. Davison of Great Britain has arrived at a view that I consider the correct one. In his book *The Technique of Prediction* (L. N. Fowler and Co. Ltd., London, 1955), Davison suggests that in the same way that progressions are derived by substituting one day for each year of a person's life, a transit can be regarded as a progression based upon one day for each day of life. This notion makes it clear that there is no real distinction between the two techniques; rather, they are two forms of the same idea. Even astrologers who adhere to the conventional distinction in meaning between transits and progressions will not hesitate to use progressions to rectify a chart based on *events*.

Transits as Symbols of Intentions

I believe that the conventional view is based upon a false distinction shared by many astrologers as well as many scientists. In their view the universe consists of individual subjects, who are clearly distinct and separate from the outer, physical universe. The individual ends at the skin, and the physical universe begins there. This view also holds that events in the physical universe are absolutely real and independent of any observer, whereas events or changes that take place within oneself exist on a lesser order of reality, because only the individual can experience them.

But what really happens? Let us suppose that an event occurs in the physical universe that many people can perceive or experience. We know very well that each person who perceives that event will have a somewhat different experience of it. If we get together to discuss our experiences, we may try to eliminate those elements that not everyone experienced, in order to arrive at a compromise that we can all agree upon without violating our integrity. Usually after going through this process, we quite effectively censor our memory to eliminate the purely personal elements of our experience, or we relegate them to the status of subjective or imaginary. Now if another observer of the event comes along, and his experience isn't too different from ours, we accept his experience, again subject to certain compromises, and modify our view slightly. If his experience is too different, we reject it entirely, classifying it as totally subjective or imaginary. In extreme cases we declare him mad.

The point is that what we call an objective description is nothing more than a collective subjective experience. There may be an absolute reality outside of anyone's experience, but it is quite irrelevant to our daily life. We act upon our universe, and we receive reactions from it in a continuous field of consciousness. There is no clear boundary line between ourselves and the world, and the observer always plays a creative role in the observation. We do not live in the physical universe so much as in a universe of agreements, conventions and concepts that we create with others. And because of the limitations of language, each of us lives in a much more private universe than we realize. Most events have no significance beyond what we have agreed on or been trained to give to them. Very little really happens *to* you, with yourself as only a passive observer.

It is my belief, which I cannot "prove" here, that within each of us is a creative core that actively creates the universe, either by making up each part out of nothing or by agreeing in advance, prior to our physical incarnation, to play a certain game with certain rules. In this scheme your horoscope becomes a symbol of your intentions, not a record of what is going to *happen* to you. As astrologer Zipporah Dobyns likes to say, character is destiny.

Both transits and progressions indicate the working out of various phases of this original intention. Although I frequently lapse into causal vocabulary in this book, I do not believe that the planets "cause" anything. They are merely signs of the manifestation of the original intention, part of which is experienced as flowing through you as will. This is the intention that you are aware of. Part of the intention is experienced as coming from without; you may call it fate, destiny or circumstances beyond your control. But this, too, comes from within you, and you need only raise your consciousness to know it. Part of the function of astrology is to raise the individual's consciousness in just this way.

One factor that may cause trouble for you is the inner turbulence that arises whenever an intention of yours comes into conflict with your conscious belief about what is right, moral or correct. In order to work out your particular intentions (or if you prefer, karma), you must have a certain kind of experience, but you cannot simply go out and have that experience because your belief system or ethical system forbids it. In that case you experience the event as something that happens *to* you, rather than as something that you bring about. Thus you succeed in having the experience without having the responsibility, by which we usually really mean guilt. Astrology helps to disclose your real intentions and thus forces you to take responsibility again. You will notice that this position is quite different from that of people who say that astrology takes away responsibility. When we do not take responsibility, we project the energy outward and become victims of circumstance. When we take responsibility, we are consciously in control again.

Here is how we should use transits. Your natal horoscope makes a statement about the kinds of intentions with which you come into your life. But because the "language" of astrology contains the flaw inherent in all languages, whether of words or symbols, we cannot specifically designate the level at which the intentions will work themselves out. A given set of astrological symbols can manifest themselves in many ways. Transits indicate how the symbolism of your life unfolds in time, exactly as do progressions, although transits give greater detail over the short range. The progressions indicate a more general structure over a longer time.

gift of self- validation virtue of ME

Transits do signify events, but only if we expand the conventional notion of an event. An event can occur totally within yourself as a psychological change, or as an interchange between yourself and another, or as a change totally outside yourself in the material and social universe. It is my contention that ultimately transits signify changes totally within the self — psychological changes, to be sure, but only if you expand what is normally meant by psychological. However, you may experience these inward changes either as psychological changes in the conventional sense, as social interactions, or as events totally outside of yourself. An "event" may also be felt as an illness. These are projections through which your inner energies are experienced at various different levels of life. This is an important idea to understand, because if you do not understand how you are involved in causing a particular event, it means that you are operating unconsciously and are therefore not in control of the circumstances.

Here is a typical example. Uranus in the seventh house of your natal chart is an indication that you seek freedom in the context of relationships. Often this is manifested as a desire for nonmarital affairs or for a very open marriage in which love is permitted with other people besides your partner. But if you are brought up to believe that such affairs are wrong, there will be a conflict between the energy of the seventh-house Uranus and your belief system. You will refuse to recognize this energy within yourself but will attract a partner of the opposite sex who demands that same kind of freedom. Meanwhile you continue to play the game of wanting a "normal" respectable relationship in which the two of you love only each other. Your partner, feeling trapped, then leaves you in order to seek freedom elsewhere. The tragedy here is that both of you want the same thing, but one of you cannot admit it. Thus you project your need for freedom onto someone else and become the "victim" of a series of unreliable lovers. But if you are exposed to the idea that you really need freedom in relationships and that it is all right to seek it, then it becomes possible for you to have satisfactory relationships that embody your real needs.

Similarly with transits, "bad" events often happen to you because you are unwilling to deal with an inner dilemma. Or they may happen because a course of action that you have taken really gets in the way of your long-range intentions. Physical ailments also are usually the result of energy that you have repressed rather than successfully adapted to. The repressed energy surfaces in your physical body as an illness that has the same symbolism as the energy involved. In astrology all illnesses are ultimately psychosomatic, although nonetheless real.

Thus in this text I have stressed the psychological significance of transits, because you have to know what a transit signifies about your inner being and how that may lead to an external event. A transit always signifies at least a psychological event, which may or may not surface in the physical world. Where appropriate, I have indicated the kinds of external events that a given set of energies is likely to produce if manifested that way. Please note that the events are caused by the psychological energies signified by the planets, not by the planets themselves. Psychological energies are your real intentions, the actual effects of your true will operating. These determine your world. Or, more correctly, you determine your world.

Astrology has too often dealt only with the superficial and external significance of astrological indications. I have attempted to give you an understanding of each transit's inner significance. Do not expect this book to uncover every possible event in the outer world that can be associated with a transit. I do not even claim to have begun to exhaust the psychological significance of transits. But no matter how thorough or spotty the interpretations in this book are, ultimately you must base your knowledge of transits on your own experience. Intellectual knowledge alone is insufficient. You don't really know astrology until you know it in your gut.

Text and Calculations by Computer

There are two ways to find out what your transits are at any given time. One is to cast your natal horoscope, or have someone cast it for you, and then, using an ephemeris, compare the positions of the planets on the day in question with their positions at the time of your birth. This is a fairly simple procedure once you have your correct natal chart, especially if you do it regularly and get to know roughly where the planets are all the time. Calculating when a given transit is going to occur is mathematically more difficult but it can be done.

The other way is to have all your transits calculated for you by computer. The Astral Guide, a computerized transit calendar based on your exact time and place of birth, is available from Para Research. Your Astral Guide gives every transit to the planets in your natal chart that will occur in the next twelve months, with the date it enters one degree of orb, the date it becomes exact, and text delineating the meaning of the transit for your life. The text is based on the text in this book but is necessarily more condensed. The Astral Guide consists of one 19 by 22-inch page for each month, suitable for wall hanging, with the outer-planet transits and delineations printed at the top and the inner-planet transits plus key-word interpretations given on the dates they become exact.

For information on how to order your Astral Guide see page 530.

Chapter One

Interpreting Transits

Traditionally there were only two kinds of transits, good ones and bad ones. The bad ones made everything go wrong, as if you were a helpless tool of malevolent fate. The good ones made everything go smoothly and ensured the success of any enterprise begun under their influence. The bad transits were the oppositions, squares and about half of the conjunctions, while the good ones were the trines, sextiles and the other conjunctions. But in modern astrology this notion has largely been abandoned. In theory at least, all transits are strictly neutral and merely represent qualitatively different combinations of the planetary influences of the natal and transiting planets.

I say "in theory" because it is still true that certain combinations of planets are usually experienced as difficult while others are usually easy. And it is also true that if you are going to exhibit the negative characteristics of a transit, it will usually be on the old "bad" aspects, the oppositions, squares and difficult conjunctions. But some squares and oppositions are usually easy and quite pleasant, and it is quite possible to have negative results with trines and sextiles. Thus there was some truth in the traditional view, although the modern view is closer to reality. The so-called bad transits bring difficulties because the particular planets do not combine readily; either they are contradictory in nature or they are totally unrelated to each other. The only reason that the trines and sextiles of these planets are less difficult is that these aspects are inherently less dynamic than the conjunctions, oppositions and squares.

Remembering that none of these are irrevocably bad, the following combinations are usually the most difficult, particularly in the square and opposition aspects. The trine and sextile as well as some of the conjunctions may be handled more easily or may have two decidedly different outcomes. See the individual entries for more complete information.

Difficult Transits

Sun-Saturn, Sun-Uranus (square and opposition), Sun-Neptune, Moon-Mars, Moon-Saturn, Moon-Uranus, Moon-Neptune, Moon-Pluto, Mercury-Neptune, Venus-Neptune (square and opposition), Mars-Saturn, Mars-Uranus, Mars-Neptune, Mars-Pluto, Jupiter-Saturn (square and opposition), Saturn-Uranus, Saturn-Neptune, Saturn-Pluto, Uranus-Neptune (square and opposition).

It must be said, however, that these are not usually destructive transits. They do not indicate sudden spurts of bad luck that will afflict you from heaven high in ways totally beyond your control, as the older astrologers actually suggested. Most people go through most of these transits without any appreciable trouble. They are destructive to you only if they signify an issue in your life that you cannot handle; it is not the planetary transit that is destructive, but your own weakness. The transit only signifies the moment when you will raise the issues that you cannot handle. In the largest sense, transits do not signify what happens to you, they signify either what you do directly or what you unconsciously program your environment to do to you. From the standpoint of higher consciousness, this includes sickness and accidents as well as the actions of other people.

The so-called difficult transits are those that test the way you have put your life together. And this is not a wholly negative process; it does not mean that if you have put your life together badly in some respect the transit will cause destruction. In fact the transit will probably change the weak area of your life, often through a significant purifying process that leaves you revitalized and renewed, although that may not be immediately obvious. The "difficult" transits clear away the refuse from one's life. The only persons who experience continuous, severe problems from difficult transits are those who resolutely continue on the wrong course despite all the evidence that they should change direction. These transits are difficult mainly in that they are frequently unpleasant because they disrupt our cherished ways of living. We try to cling doggedly to our negative traits. These transits are difficult also in that they usually signify the expenditure of a great deal of energy.

On the other hand, if the part of your life signified by the transit is not in bad shape, the "difficult" transit may catapult you to new levels of success and fortune. This may seem to be a disruption at first, but you will quickly realize that it has opened the way for new opportunities.

The easy transits — the trines, sextiles and several conjunctions — are easy primarily in that they are not unpleasant and do not require any special outpouring of energy. Also they do not test your weak points. But they may reinforce your weak points, simply because they denote periods of equilibrium and ease in which you tend to continue in whatever direction you have been taking. To react this way is a waste, however. Although these influences do not impel you to action, you can act more easily with them because the energies of the universe seem to flow with you. The significant challenge of these transits is to find your own weak spots and then change them voluntarily. But the usual reaction is to do nothing, because nothing cries out to be done. Some people even become totally lethargic. As a result, these transits can do even more damage than the so-called difficult ones, although that is not usually apparent until the next difficult transit of those two planets.

The following is a list of the generally easy transits. Those not listed in this list or the "difficult" list should be considered neutral, that is, likely to go either way. This list refers to sextiles and trines, except where it is noted that the other aspects are also easy.

Easy Transits

Sun-Moon, Sun-Mercury, Sun-Venus (all transits), Sun-Jupiter (all transits), Moon-Venus (all transits), Moon-Jupiter (all transits), Venus-Mars, Venus-Jupiter (all transits), Mars-Jupiter. The trine and sextile combinations not listed here are considered neutral. They are usually quite easy but not as universally as the ones listed above.

I repeat this point because it cannot be stressed enough: the transits in themselves do not cause either good or bad happenings. In fact they do not cause anything; they are just signs that you will have to confront certain issues in your life at a particular time. The ease or difficulty of a particular transit comes from your inner makeup. General indications about various activities being favored or inhibited under a particular transit are based on the average person. Various personal strengths may enable you to overcome any negative indication. Similarly, your weaknesses may make a mess out of the most favorable transit. Watch your reaction to the transits as a sign of what you need in order to grow as an individual. Also it must be pointed out that you need to have a thorough understanding of the natal chart in order to get a clear idea of how someone will react to a given transit. For example, a person whose natal chart is filled with trines and has no squares or oppositions may vegetate through transiting trines and sextiles, getting nothing out of them at all.

Models for Transit Interpretation

In the interpretations of transits, the planets have pretty much the same meaning that they have in the natal chart. This is true of the aspects also, but transiting aspects have certain characteristics that make it necessary to discuss them at greater length. Because they are moving aspects and in a constant state of change, their character is dynamic or cyclical. This is true in the natal chart, but it is harder to distinguish. Also, most existing textbooks give no detailed descriptions of the bases of aspect delineation except for the division into good and bad. The exceptions to this statement are in the works of Dane Rudhyar and the other Humanistic astrologers.

For this reason I believe that students will be helped by a detailed explanation of the bases, philosophical and otherwise, of the aspect interpretations. These bases fall into three categories, three different ways of looking at the aspects, each of which contributes something to our whole understanding of them. These three ways of looking at transits are the theory of harmonics, the dynamic cycle approach and the house relationship approach. No one of these approaches is correct to the exclusion of the others, although the harmonics theory is perhaps the most fundamental and the basis for the others. We will discuss each theory in detail and then give a synthesis of the three approaches for each aspect.

Harmonics

This relatively new way of looking at aspects stems largely from the work of John Addey of Britain and his associates, although the roots of his approach go back to Pythagoras of Samos and can also be found more recently in the writings of Johannes Kepler.

This theory is based on the nature of the aspects themselves, and the signs and the houses. In fact this type of approach bids fair to become the basis of all other systems, for it appears that signs, houses and aspects are all rooted in harmonics.

Briefly, the theory of harmonics comes from the division of the circle of 360° by small whole numbers, which gives rise to what is called a harmonic series, thus:

$$\frac{360°}{1}, \quad \frac{360°}{2}, \quad \frac{360°}{3} \quad \frac{360°}{4} \quad \frac{360°}{5}, \quad \frac{360°}{6}, \quad \frac{360°}{7}, \quad \frac{360°}{8},$$

and so forth.

When these indicated divisions are performed, we get the values 360°, 180°, 120°, 90°, 72°, 60°, 51° 25′ 43″ and 45°. Except for the next to last figure, which comes from dividing the circle by seven, these numbers should look familiar, for they are the angles of the aspects — conjunction, opposition, trine, square, quintile, sextile and semisquare. The division by seven is often called the septile. It is not commonly used, but may be quite significant. The signs and houses are based on the division by twelve.

None of this appears very earth-shaking until one discovers from Addey's work that there is hard, empirical evidence based on massive statistical samples that the meaning of each aspect is clearly related to the symbolism of the number by which the circle is divided to produce the aspect. The conjunction is related to the meaning of unity, the opposition to two, the trine to three and so forth. It is becoming clear that astrology is nothing more than a complex manifestation of the principles of number, that it is really a very elaborate form of numerology. This also enables us to predict the meanings of aspects based on the division of the zodiac by numbers that have hitherto not been used, such as eleven and thirteen.

Actually this whole approach has been used implicitly in Hindu astrology, which uses aspects based on nine, seven and other divisions that are unusual to us. Their method of handling aspects is different from ours, but the more unusual harmonics are being used.

The reader who is interested in this approach to astrology should see John Addey's works for a more thorough explanation than can be given here, particularly a new book, *Harmonics in Astrology*, introducing the whole subject. Back issues of the *Astrological Journal*, published by the Astrological Association of Britain, contain many articles on the subject.

Most of the smaller aspects generated by harmonic theory are not relevant to the basics of transit study, except under conditions that will be discussed later in Chapter 2, beginning on page 27. For our purposes at this point it will be sufficient to discuss the major aspects only — the conjunction, opposition, trine, square and sextile, which arise from the division of the circle by one, two, three, four and six, respectively.

One: the conjunction. The first harmonic symbolizes union and perfect togetherness.

It is the number of beginnings. There is no polarization and therefore no conflict between the principles. However, if a conjunction occurs between two planets that are not basically easy to combine, the result will not be easy. The difficulty does not arise because of a conflict between the principles, but because the union is difficult. As all things in metaphysics proceed from the ONE, so the conjunction carries within it the seeds of all other aspects, and therefore one can expect a considerable variation in the effects of conjunctions. Remember that a conjunction is 2 × 180°, 3 × 120° and so forth. Thus it is that some conjunction transits are more like trines or sextiles, and others are more like squares or oppositions.

Two: the opposition. This is the number of polarity, of confrontation between two principles, and it is inherently connected with conflict. But it is also the symbol of I and Thou, of the interaction between Self and Other, without which there can be no consciousness at all. There can be no awareness prior to the operation of the number two. It is not more objective than one, it is the actual issue of the subjective versus objective.

Three: the trine. This number symbolizes the resolution of polarity and conflict through an intermediary. It is also a state of equilibrium and balance. There may be a great deal of activity associated with the number three, but it always consists of a series of complementary processes that balance out so that there is no net change. This is a symbol of creative, unresisting flow with the universal energies.

Four: the square. Four is the first composite number of the series, the first number that is a multiple of a number other than one; that is, $2 = 2 \times 1$, $3 = 3 \times 1$, but $4 = 2 \times 2$. Because it is the product of two times two, it shares much of the nature of the opposition. It is a number of dynamic change and instability. But on its own it is associated with ego-consciousness and the notion of material reality. It is related to Saturn somewhat in this regard. Four symbolizes situations in which there is resistance to some force, and the force is challenged to prove itself against the demands of the material universe.

Five: the quintile. This number is not important in basic transit study, but does become very important in certain situations that will be discussed later on.

Six: the sextile. Like four, this is a composite number, the product of two times three. It can be regarded as the opposition of the trine series. It connotes a state of balance somewhat like three, but it serves to sharpen consciousness and heighten awareness, which requires a certain degree of initiative. It is not possible to remain passive to a sextile the way you often can with a trine. Six is a number of activity within a state of balance, so structures can be built relatively easily. From this comes the sextile's traditional association with opportunity.

As mentioned earlier, the higher harmonics are significant, but they do not usually operate except in association with other, more potent transits. We are concerned here only with those harmonics whose aspects work at least to some extent in single transits. It must be said, however, that a single transit by sextile will often go by without much notice.

Dynamic Cycle Approach

This approach is clearly related to the harmonics, but the cycle as a whole is taken into consideration, with each transit in the series treated as part of the whole. For some reason, although the cyclical approach must work with all transit cycles, it is more obvious in some than in others. It is particularly worthwhile for the transits of Saturn by the various aspects to the planets and houses. It is also quite evident in the cycles of the Sun. The advantage of this approach is that it enables the chart reader to get an overview of the native's life cycles, and it clarifies the meaning of a long period of years of the native's life taken as a whole.

Below is a description of the archetypal cycle. Credit should be given to Dane Rudhyar, who first pointed out the nature of the general cycle and the meanings of the individual aspects within it.

Stage One: the conjunction. With the transit by conjunction of one planet over another planet or over a house cusp, there is an event either within yourself or between you and the world that begins a process or a series of developments. The nature of this process is in accordance with the nature of the planets involved; the transiting planet imposes its energy expression upon that of the transited planet. Thus Saturn on Venus, for example, would signify that the reaching out for love or affection proceeds in a saturnian manner. There is considerable evidence that if one casts a chart for the exact moment of the conjunction transit that the chart will describe the whole cycle in a general way. Unfortunately, to do this for the outer planets would require ephemerides that are considerably more accurate than those we currently possess. But this is the rationale for the already highly developed techniques of solar and lunar returns. The conjunction transit is often unconscious in its effects. You know that something is happening, but you often have to wait until later to know exactly what.

Stage Two: the separating sextile. The process that began with the conjunction is now on a stable path and functioning pretty well. Now you can see what happened at the conjunction, and you should examine it and see how well it works. If it is not working well, this is the time to make adjustments. Necessary changes that are left undone will have an unfortunate effect at the next stage, the transit by square. Success at the time of the sextile does not guarantee anything without this process of scrutiny.

Stage Three: the separating square. It should be noted that this approach to transits makes a distinction between a separating aspect by transit, in which the transiting planet is moving away from the last conjunction toward the opposition, and the approaching aspect by transit, in which the transiting planet is moving back toward the next conjunction away from the last opposition. In this text, the distinction is made only when the cyclical nature of the transit is very clear, as with Saturn. To make this distinction consistently would make an already lengthy text too long.

At any rate, the separating square is a time of crisis, hence its unsavory reputation in the old books. But crisis does not mean disaster, and this can actually be an extremely productive time. The process that began at the last conjunction now undergoes a period of testing to determine its weak points and to find out if the course of events should be continued. If you learn that the process is improper for you and your life, events will occur or changes will take place that make it impossible for you to continue along this path. Remember that a psychological change within you is an event. Unfortunately you will not always realize that a failure has occurred. You may be able to piece together a structure that is basically not viable in your life and keep it working for a time. In such a case the denouement will come at the opposition. But if you can, it is better to be as realistic as possible now, write off any effort that has failed and begin looking about for a new course to follow. If you do, the next opposition will be a time of new beginning, just as if it were a conjunction.

Of course, if you succeed in overcoming the challenges signified by the square, then this will be a time of great forward motion leading to the culmination of your efforts, which will come at the next opposition.

Stage Four: the separating trine. This trine is like the sextile in that it is a time of relative ease when you should scan the whole series of events in this cycle. If you have overcome the crisis of the square, you should get everything into shape for the culmination of the cycle at the opposition. On the other hand, if the square showed that your efforts have been pointless or harmful, you should take this time to think about what has happened and learn as much as you can from it, so that when the opposition comes you will be able to make a new start. The danger of this trine is that if you have managed to keep going at something that is basically not a good idea, you will persist in it now, convinced that you have managed to save yourself or what you are doing. But the opposition will show you that you have not won by bringing about a more complete downfall.

Stage Five: the opposition. As has been made clear from the foregoing, a number of things can occur during this transit. If the process has gone well, this is the time when your affairs reach a culmination, and you begin to reap the reward of your efforts. Also you should begin a transition phase in which you gradually begin to adapt and change what you have done so that you can move onto a new level. You should not be content with staying at this level, even though success makes it tempting to do so. Also be happy to accept the rewards for what you have done. The future beckons, and a new stage of development is about to begin.

But if you managed to patch together a basically unfavorable situation at the last square and convinced yourself at the last trine that everything was all right, the opposition will probably prove you wrong. Challenges that were not really successfully withstood at the last square will have their most devastating consequences at this time, especially in a Saturn cycle. Only if you faced your difficulties honestly at the last square, changed course and prepared a new direction on the last trine, will you be able to make the best use of this stage of the transit cycle. If the square defeated the course of action you were taking then, this is the time for a new beginning, and from here on the cycle will continue as if it started at the opposition rather than the conjunction, and the aspects that follow will be like the earlier stages in the transit cycle. In fact, the Saturn-Sun cycle, with Saturn transiting natal Sun, usually seems to follow this backward course, starting with the opposition rather than the conjunction, although it sometimes goes the other way as well. It probably depends on the period of your life when the Saturn-Sun conjunction or opposition occurs.

Stage Six: the approaching trine. We are now in the second half of the cycle, and usually this is the second reaping and transforming stage of the cycle. This transit is analogous to the separating sextile rather than the separating trine, because it is the first easy state of equilibrium after the initial crisis symbolized by the opposition. Now you should look about and see how you can adapt to meet the needs of the changing future. If everything went well at the last opposition there is a great temptation to sit on your laurels now, because everything seems to be running very smoothly and nothing needs to be done. That is true, but it does not mean that you should not provide for the time when something does need to be done. See what kinds of changing roles you can play in the time to come, and do not be satisfied to go on as you have. If you began a new phase of activity at the opposition, this stage is equivalent in every way to the separating sextile at stage two.

Stage Seven: the approaching square. The challenge now is quite different from that of the separating square. You may suddenly be forced to adapt to a new situation, for nothing is ever so good that it can go on forever, although most people try to do just that. Even the most successful creation reaches a peak merely to give rise to another phase of activity. That is what is happening now. If you adapt and change to allow the birth of the next phase in the final stages of this cycle, events will proceed smoothly. Otherwise you will bring about a crisis that will lead to total collapse at the next conjunction. Then you will truly have to start over again, with nothing. The first square was a crisis in building up some structure, while this one is a crisis in letting go of it. If you cannot detach yourself from it or assist creatively in changing it, you will destroy it. For those who began a new cycle at the last opposition, the function of this square is identical to that of the separating square.

Stage Eight: the approaching sextile. Its function is related to the separating trine in that it represents a period of equilibrium just after a square. If everything has gone well at the last square, this sextile is a time for making final preparations for the changes that will come at the beginning of the next cycle. You should be making an effort to fit yourself into the new order that is taking shape now. If you do this well, you will be able to take advantage of the burst of creative energy that will occur at the conjunction transit.

It is quite possible and even highly advisable to divide this cycle into more parts, but this division is the best place to start from. It is a relatively simple way of looking at the cycle, and even when more parts are included, as some authors do, the basic structure is the same. The transits that are usually added are the semisextile or 30°, the semisquare or 45°, the sesquiquadrate or 135° and the quincunx or 150°. These transits are important but their meanings are not as clearly evident as the major parts of the cycle that have been described here.

The House Approach

This method of analyzing aspects by transit is especially popular among followers of a very traditional interpretation and is the main form of aspect analysis used in India. In this scheme the aspect is discussed in relation to the houses to which its angle corresponds. The conjunction is considered to be a first-house aspect; the sextile, a third-house, eleventh-house aspect; the square, a fourth-house, tenth-house aspect; the trine, a fifth-house, ninth-house aspect, and the opposition a seventh-house aspect. This mode of description has considerable merit if it isn't carried too far. Not every sextile affects neighbors, friends and communications, for example, nor does every trine portend the possibility of a long journey. The opposition, on the other hand, corresponds quite consistently to the symbolism of the seventh house. This is because the seventh house contains the symbolism of the number two very thoroughly, as does the opposition, which is the second harmonic.

The relationship of the houses to the aspects is completely valid as long as one realizes that the houses themselves are merely superficial meanings derived from much more basic principles. The usual assignments between the houses and the aspects is at the most profound level of symbolism, because both are based on harmonics. Therefore you can derive valid insights into the meaning of the aspects by looking at the houses to which they correspond. Also, in most cases a trine, for example, will be in the fifth or the ninth house from the house occupied by the natal planet, which emphasizes the fifth-house, ninth-house flavor of the trine.

But it is important not to go too far with this method unless the house symbolism of the aspects is reinforced by the planets involved. For example, a trine by transiting Jupiter may indicate traveling, not only because the trine is a ninth-house aspect but also because Jupiter has an inherent connection with travel. Below are the meanings of the aspects in terms of the houses to which they are related. Readers who are familiar with the traditional meanings of the houses will notice that these delineations are not precisely the same as those of the houses but are derived from the abstract principles upon which the houses are based.

Conjunction: the first-house aspect. Beginnings, the way one expresses oneself to others, oneself taken by oneself in one's own terms. Often rather unconscious in its actions.

Sextile: the third-house, eleventh-house aspect. Relationships with groups, integration of the self with immediate surroundings, contacts with those surroundings.

Square: the fourth-house, tenth-house aspect. The expression of the ego in the world and within one's personal sphere, challenges and confrontations in those two worlds.

Trine: the fifth-house, ninth-house aspect. Creative flow of the life energies that allow for easy self-expression, the ability to expand one's experience of the world and to grow in knowledge.

Opposition: the seventh-house aspect. Confrontation and partnership, the self as experienced through others, the conflict between one's personal world and the external world.

If you try to expand these definitions to include all of the affairs signified by a particular house, you will create two problems. First, your predictions will probably be inaccurate except in rare cases. And second, a given transit will signify so many possibilities that it will become completely unintelligible to the person whose chart you are reading. Readings in which every transit has a million possibilities are not worth much.

Summary

At this point it will be helpful to synthesize everything that has been discussed about each aspect so that you can easily find the general signification of each aspect in transits.

Conjunction:
Beginning of a new cycle; matters involving the self alone or in conjunction with its most intimate surroundings; the birth of a new phase of life; the culmination of the process that began at the last opposition transit involving the same two planets.

Sextile:
Matters involving your relationship to groups; interaction with your immediate surroundings; a time of balance, when you can and should take the initiative; a time for reviewing recent events and seeing what needs to be changed; changes involving relatively little effort; a time when you can act with little resistance from outside circumstances.

Square:
Challenges from circumstances or others that force you to prove yourself or to make necessary changes; a time when a course of action proves incorrect or, if the challenge is withstood, a time of new initiative and active forward motion; a challenge to your self-expression, which may force changes in your way of relating to others or may inaugurate a period of new effectiveness.

Trine:
A period of easy energy flow and relative lack of stress, when you can make creative changes but are tempted to just flow along; a time when your experience and self-expression expand to make you wiser and more effective; a period of little change, even when there is considerable activity; little resistance to your efforts, with matters often working out with little effort on your part.

Opposition:
A time of confrontation with others; the culmination of your affairs in some way or the total collapse of some area of your life that has not worked successfully; events that increase self-consciousness through meetings with others; interaction between your inner and outer worlds; a time of dynamic changes.

Chapter Two

Timing Transits

One of the most difficult problems in applying the theory of transits is timing, that is, finding when the influences associated with the transit reach a peak. Precisely when will an event concerning the outside world happen? At first, this might not appear to be a problem, because you would expect the influence to peak and the event to occur at the precise moment when the transit becomes most exact. But this is seldom the case, because each event in your life, whether it involves purely internal, psychological changes or external events, is usually related to several factors operating simultaneously. We will discuss those factors in this section.

Let us begin by taking the simplest case, in which only one transit is operative at the time. In such a case, you would rightly expect the occurrence to coincide with the exact time of the transit, but even here you cannot count on it completely. First of all, if there really is only one operative transit at a given time, there probably will not be a noticeable event; whatever happens will be too subtle to notice. Very few important changes in life are ever marked by a single transit. If you pay attention only to the transits of the outer planets, it may seem that they indicate important events, but in fact you will find that there are simultaneous transits by the inner planets that reinforce the outer-planet transits. Or there are very significant transits to midpoints, which reinforce the outer-planet transits. Midpoint transits are very important and will be discussed in detail further on in this section.

You will often find that the arc of an inner-planet transit is closer than that of the outer-planet transit that it accompanies. But the event cannot be described without reference to the outer-planet transit. This is quite a common occurrence and elucidates the first principle of transit analysis.

> Rule 1. An outer-planet transit is usually accurately timed by an inner-planet transit that approximately coincides with it and reinforces the nature of the outer-planet transit.

Often more than one inner-planet transit is doing this, which considerably complicates the timing. In this case other methods have to be incorporated, as will be discussed later on in this chapter. However, for the present we can say that the event will occur in the space of time between or among the times of the various inner-planet transits. The Sun and Mars most often perform this timing function, although sometimes Mercury will be important in indicating when an event becomes known to you consciously. Now we will introduce a second principle that many people will find somewhat different from what they have been taught.

Rule 2. Strictly speaking, there is no such thing as an "orb" of influence concerning a transit.

The term orb usually means an area in which events concerning a transit occur. It is measured in space and considered to be so many degrees along the ecliptic. Space can be converted into time, because the transiting planet is moving, so an orb of so many degrees and minutes indicates the length of time in which a transit is likely to indicate an event.

The problem is that one cannot speak of the length of time that a single transit will be in effect without referring to the transits, both of inner and outer planets, that are occurring around it or without referring to the nature of the events and processes symbolized by the transit. Some internal events or psychological changes take a great deal of time to build up to a climax and then more time to develop their consequences. The length of time involved is a function of the events, not of the transits.

The best that we can hope to do is locate the center point of the entire process, which will occur closest to the transits that signify it, although other factors described in this chapter may deflect the event from the apparent time of the closest transit. But again I emphasize that this is not because of an orb effect, but because the event is associated with a number of different transiting factors. In my experience, if you take into consideration all of the various transits that may affect the timing of the process, and combine their effects correctly, you will get very close to the exact time of the event. It should be pointed out that the methods described in this chapter may result in more than one possible time for a given event during a larger span of time, but each of the possible times will be very precisely defined. It is not that an event will take place sometime over the course of several days or even months, but that there are certain clearly defined times when the event may occur.

Admittedly, this process is much easier to carry out after ai. event than before, but the principles are still theoretically correct. Whenever an event has apparently not corresponded with the times of maximum planetary influence, I have always found that I have overlooked some factor. The indeterminacy in the timing of a transit results simply from the difficulty of taking into account all of the factors, not from an actual orb or zone of equal probability in the transit.

Rule 3. When a number of transits describe an event, the time of the event will be closest to the time when the average orb of all the transiting planets approaches zero.

This principle is applied with regard to Nixon's resignation in the case study of Nixon and Watergate. It is most applicable when several planets are transiting one point in the chart. The technique is to find the distance between the transiting planet and the point of exact transit. Until the planet reaches the point of transit, the angle is considered negative. After the planet has reached the point of transit, the angle is positive. Of course, the signs of the angles can be reversed, as long as the approaching and separating angles to a transit are given opposite algebraic signs.

After calculating all of the angles between the transiting planets and the point of transit, add them algebraically; in other words, add the positive numbers together and then subtract the negative ones from the sum. If the sum of the negative values is greater than the sum of the positive values, subtract the positive sum from the negative sum and call the result negative.

For example, let us suppose that we have a natal Sun at 12° ♌ 00'. Uranus, coming to a square from Taurus, has the longitude 11° ♉ 15'. The transiting Jupiter is at 16° ♏ 00', and the transiting Mars is at 11° ♌ 25'. We see that each transit has an angle of separation between it and exactitude. Uranus square natal Sun = −45'. Jupiter square natal Sun = +4°00'. Mars conjunct natal Sun = −35'. We change the 4°00' figure to the equivalent figure of 240', then add the positive figures to each other and the negatives to each other. The positives add up to 240', since there is only the one positive angle, while the negatives add up to −80'.

$$240' + (-80') = 240' - 80' = 160'$$

That sum represents the total angle of separation. We divide that sum by the number of transiting planets, which in this case is three. 160'/3 = 53.33333', which is the average, or mean, angle of the transit at this time. Since the mean is positive, we can see that the combined strength of the three transits is beyond its peak.

This computation can be done in another way if all of the transiting angles are multiples of thirty degrees or if they have the same sign. This is usually the case, except if there are a number of semisquares or sesquiquadrates. Just add the position of each transiting planet for the particular time in terms of its sign, rather than in 360° notation. Here is the calculation for our example.

$$11° 15' + 16° 00' + 11° 25' = 38° 40'$$

We then divide this value by three, the number of transiting planets, to get 12° 53.33333'. This method, using the average position of the transiting planets within their own signs, also shows that the combined influence of the three planets is 53.33333' beyond its peak. The major defect with this method is the difficulty of dividing into a number that is made up of degrees and minutes. Here is the method.

1. To divide 38° 40' by 3, first divide 3 into 38°.

$$38° \div 3 = 12° \text{ remainder}: 2°$$

2. Convert the degree remainder into minutes by multiplying it by 60.

$$2° \times 60 = 120'$$

3. Combine this converted degree remainder with the 40' of the original figure, 38° 40'.

$$120' + 40' = 160'$$

4. Divide the minutes sum by 3.

$$160' \div 3 = 53.33333'$$

Thus we get the final answer of 12° 53.33333'.

> Rule 4. If two planets that are in aspect in a natal chart are being
> transited, the influence leading up to an event will peak and thereby
> time the event when the transiting planet contacts each of the two
> natal planets exactly and also when it is exactly halfway between the
> two transits in arc.

This is another situation in which the mean orb of the transits approaches zero, but
here there are two natal factors and one transiting factor. As an example, let us say
that we have a trine from 1° ♈ 05' to 4° ♌ 56' and a transiting planet in early
Gemini. There will be three peaks of influence. The first occurs at the exact transit by
sextile from 1 ♊ 05', and the third is at 4 ♊ 56', but there is also a peak at 3 ♊ 01',
because the angles between the transiting factor and the earlier natal factor are equal
but opposite in sign. This peak is often the strongest of the three! Aslo note that this
point represents the exact transit to the point halfway between the two natal factors,
usually called the midpoint or halfsum. In this case, the reader can readily see that the
transiting factor is conjunct the midpoint of the two natal factors.

In this connection, it is important to note that the transits between the transiting
factor and the first and second natal factors were sextiles, but the transit to the
midpoint is a conjunction, and it acts like a conjunction rather than a sextile.
Similarly, if a transiting factor forms simultaneous trines to planets in a natal trine, it
completes a grand trine for the duration of the transit. In this case the trines do not
act like trines; instead, the influence is like that of an opposition.

At this point I would like to discuss the method for calculating midpoints, which is
quite simple. First of all, convert the longitudes of the two natal planets in question to
360° notation; that is, measure their angular position in the zodiac from 0° Aries
rather than from the beginning of the sign. This is done by adding the appropriate
values derived from the following table to the longitudes expressed in terms of the
sign. To convert the value 23° ♑ 36' to 360° notation, we add 30° to 23° 36',
obtaining 53° 36'.

Now let us take another factor at 17° ♏ 19' and calculate the midpoint between it and
the factor at 23° ♑ 36'. We already have the value for the first position.

0°	Aries	180°	Libra
30°	Taurus	210°	Scorpio
60°	Gemini	240°	Sagittarius
90°	Cancer	270°	Capricorn
120°	Leo	300°	Aquarius
150°	Virgo	330°	Pisces

Table 1

To calculate the value for the second position, we look up Scorpio in the table and find 210°. We add 210° to 17° 19', obtaining 227° 19', and then add the two values.

$$227° \ 19' + 53° \ 36' = 280° \ 55'$$

To get the midpoint we divide this sum by 2; hence the term halfsum.

$$280° \ 55' \div 2 = 140° \ 27.5' \text{ or } 140° \ 28', \text{ rounded}$$
off to the nearest minute.

This is equal to 20° ♌ 28'.

Sometimes this technique gives an answer that seems to be exactly 180° degrees off. It is not actually off, it is the midpoint taken along the longer of the two arcs between the two planets. In this case, simply substitute the sign opposite the position that you have obtained. The midpoint of the shorter arc is usually preferred, although for the purposes of timing it makes no difference.

Sometimes an event seems to appear out of thin air with no significant corresponding transits. This is almost always a mistake resulting from checking the transits carelessly. As I have stated, events are usually timed broadly by long-term outer-planet transits and more precisely by inner-planet transits. Usually an inner-planet transit by itself is not sufficient to signify an important event, except in the following case.

> Rule 5. On a certain date a group of transiting planets, perhaps all inner planets, may form a complex of aspects among themselves. If that complex transits a natal planet, an event will occur in the native's life that bears the symbolism of the natal planet combined with that of the transiting planets.

Even the transiting Moon, whose effects are so fleeting, can enter into such a combination. The important point to note here is that no outer-planet transit is required to bring about the effect, and the event can be quite significant. One example of this principle, which all astrologers are familiar with, is the transiting eclipse, which is generally considered quite significant when it occurs conjunct or opposite a natal factor, even though solar and lunar transits by themselves are not usually considered critical.

Another related principle can also cause events to happen seemingly out of thin air when there are no apparent corresponding transits.

> Rule 6. If several planets simultaneously transit the natal chart by the same minor aspect, an event will occur that is appropriate to the nature of that aspect and to the planets involved.

In this text I have not delineated the meanings of the transits by minor aspects. Such aspects include the quintile, 72°; the semisquare, 45°; the sesquiquadrate, 135°; the semisextile, 30°; the quincunx, 150°; the biquintile, 144°; the septile, 51° 25' 42.9";

and other minor subdivisions of the circle. Several of these are quite significant in natal charts, but do not appear to have much significance in transits. A single transit by an aspect such as the semisquare, even by a slow-moving outer planet to a natal planet or to the Midheaven or Ascendant, usually does not signify much and will often go by without any notice. However, the exception to this principle occurs whenever several of these transits happen at the same time. Even if the transiting planets do not form any aspects among themselves, there will be significant occurrences related to the symbolism of the transiting planets combined with the symbolism of the natal planets.

These compound transits can be a source of some difficulty to the practicing astrologer because they are so easily overlooked, especially if the planets transit by one of the minor aspects that are not easily recognized, such as the quintile or septile. When looking over an event after the fact, the astrologer can very often find patterns of this type that had been overlooked before the event. However, there is a device that can assist in finding these transits in advance. Most astrologers know it as a mechanical aspectarian, or simply as a 360° dial, which is a wheel marked with the complete 360° of the zodiac, and the aspects, both major and minor, indicated at the appropriate spots. In order to use the wheel for our purpose, it is necessary to use it also when drawing the chart, so that the planets and house cusps are shown in their real angular relationship along the ecliptic. This is different from the common English and American practice of simply writing the positions into a schematic chart in which the twelve houses are represented as equal 30° divisions of the circle.

Having erected a chart with the aspectarian, you then place the pointer of the dial on the degree of each transiting planet and note all the transiting aspects. If the minor aspects are not indicated on the dial, it is easy enough to put them in. With the standard chart blank used by most astrologers in this country, it is hopeless to keep track of these minor transits unless you do a great deal of calculating. The beginning student can ignore these transits for the present, but eventually you will encounter an event that is signified entirely by a complex multiple transit by minor aspects. To help you deal with these, I give here a list of the meanings that are commonly assigned to these aspects.

Semisextile (30°). This aspect seems to create some tension, because it bridges the two adjacent signs, which have no connection with each other symbolically. Adjacent signs are of different elements, quadruplicity and polarity. The semisextile generates a sense of discomfort about the issues signified by the planets or houses involved in the transit.

Semisquare (45°) and *sesquiquadrate* (135°). These aspects are discussed together because they are quite similar in nature, being much like the square but less strong. They represent a dynamic link between the planetary energies that is likely to produce change and tension, if one is unable to go along with the changes involved. Experience has shown that these aspects are quite significant in transit, but only when several occur at once or when one occurs in connection with a major transit.

Septile (51° 25′ 42.9″). Also check the various multiples of this angle. This aspect relates to hidden inner changes that often affect one's psychological state. Sometimes it also signifies events that cause radical changes in perception and consciousness. The septile is often described as being related to "occult" phenomena, but this is not a very meaningful characterization. This aspect is most significant in a transit to planets that are related to each other by septile.

Quintile (72°) and *biquintile* (144°). These may not be minor so much as misunderstood. They relate to forces that combine to bring about metamorphoses or fundamental changes in one's life. Usually these are very creative energies, but they may be destructive if blocked. Their symbolism has qualities of both Venus and Pluto, in that they can create new structures and destroy old ones.

Quincunx (150°). Many astrologers might object to placing the quincunx among the minor aspects, but by transit it is usually less significant than the aspects described at length in this book. Transits by quincunx relate to situations that seem to arise spontaneously in the environment and that force one to make a fateful change that affects one's later life. Many investigators have noticed that they coincide with health crises as well as accidents.

There are other minor aspects, but they are completely beyond the scope of this book. As we come to understand them better, I hope that they will become the subjects of specialized works.

Precession Correction

Another issue that should be considered in trying to predict when transit patterns will reach their maximum influence is the matter of precession. Most astrologers are aware that the vernal equinox, otherwise known as the first point of Aries, does not remain stationary with respect to the fixed stars but moves backward through them at the rate of approximately 50.25 seconds per year. This is because of the effects of the gravitational pull of the Moon and planets upon the rotational cycle of the Earth on its axis. This movement has caused the signs of the zodiac and the constellations of the same name to slip out of alignment with each other by about 25°, depending upon how one measures the constellations. Because of this problem, one group of astrologers has abandoned the signs based on the vernal equinox, called the "tropical" zodiac, and adopted a zodiac that is fixed with respect to the stars, called the "sidereal zodiac."

The problem for us is not which zodiac to use, but that the timing of transits taken in the two zodiacs begins to differ significantly as a person gets older. This effect begins to be noticeable by your late twenties, and when you are seventy-two years old, there will be a difference of one degree between the two positions, which significantly affects the timing of outer-planet transits. Even more important, this problem almost immediately begins to affect return charts, that is, charts cast for the moment of the Sun's or Moon's return to its exact natal position. By the age of thirty-six, one's tropical solar return differs from one's sidereal solar return by twelve hours, which completely alters the positions of the planets in the houses.

I personally feel that the signs of the tropical zodiac give interpretive results that are more useful than those of the sidereal, but I recognize that it is possible to treat the tropical zodiac as if it were moving. In other words, one should treat the natal positions of the planets as if they were fixed stars. Since the vernal equinox moves backward, the positions of the fixed stars move forward in the tropical zodiac. Opinion differs on this point, but many astrologers agree that at the very least, determining the positions of the natal chart corrected for precession helps significantly in timing events. Examples of this are given in the case study of Nixon and Watergate.

My own experience has been that in timing an event the corrected positions are more accurate than the uncorrected ones, especially if you follow the rules given earlier in this chapter for transit timing. Sometimes it may appear that uncorrected transits give close results, but that is only because you are not applying the principles explained in this chapter. If an event is signified by several transits, one of them is very likely to be close using uncorrected positions, but the average orb is usually greater. Occasionally, no amount of explanation will make the precession-corrected transits time an event more closely than the uncorrected positions, but this is not usually the case. And frequently no amount of juggling can make the uncorrected positions time an event closely.

Alexander Marr of Germany believes that both positions are valid but for different purposes, and that certainly is a possibility. For the present I would suggest keeping track of both positions, until you have a feeling for what works best for you. In astrology there is the perennial problem that on many matters different astrologers have different experiences. To settle this particular dispute, more elaborate tests will have to be devised. But for the present I will explain how to make the precession correction so that you can judge for yourself.

Take the person's age in years at the time of the transit and multiply by five, then divide by six and round off to the nearest minute. The resulting correction should then be added to all natal positions or subtracted from all transiting positions, these being equivalent. What this does in effect is to convert all planetary positions, both natal and transiting, from the equinox of one's birth to the equinox of the transiting date, or vice versa. Here is an example. Let us say that the person's age is twenty-seven years and six months, or 27.5 years. The calculations proceed as follows:

$$27.5 \times 5 = 137.5 \qquad 137.5 \div 6 = 22.9$$

Rounded off to the nearest minute, the answer is 23'. This value is then added to all natal positions for the time of the transit or subtracted from the transiting positions, which is equivalent. Just don't add the correction to the natal positions *and* subtract it from the transiting positions, for that would double the precession correction. To facilitate this procedure, Table 2 gives the appropriate values to add or subtract for any age.

This table is based on the mean rate of 50,2675 seconds per year as of 1950, but it can be used for transit timing at any date in modern history. However, it would not be applicable to any chart that required a measure of precession between two dates that is precise to the nearest second of arc. Such a chart would be a solar return cast for the moment that the Sun transits its natal position with precession added. The reader

Age in Years	Value	Age in Years	Value	Age in Years	Value	Age in Years	Value
1	0′ 50.2″	21	17′ 35.6″	41	34′ 20.9″	61	51′ 6.3″
2	1′ 40.5″	22	18′ 25.8″	42	35′ 11.2″	62	51′ 56.5″
3	2′ 30.8″	23	19′ 16.1″	43	36′ 1.5″	63	52′ 46.8″
4	3′ 21.0″	24	20′ 6.4″	44	36′ 51.7″	64	53′ 37.1″
5	4′ 11.3″	25	20′ 56.6″	45	37′ 42.0″	65	54′ 27.3″
6	5′ 1.6″	26	21′ 46.9″	46	38′ 32.3″	66	55′ 17.6″
7	5′ 51.8″	27	22′ 37.2″	47	39′ 22.5″	67	56′ 7.9″
8	6′ 42.1″	28	23′ 27.4″	48	40′ 12.8″	68	56′ 58.1″
9	7′ 32.4″	29	24′ 17.7″	49	41′ 3.1″	69	57′ 48.4″
10	8′ 22.6″	30	25′ 8.0″	50	41′ 53.3″	70	58′ 38.7″
11	9′ 12.9″	31	25′ 58.2″	51	42′ 43.6″	71	59′ 28.9″
12	10′ 3.2″	32	26′ 48.5″	52	43′ 33.9″	72	1° 0′ 19.2″
13	10′ 53.4″	33	27′ 38.8″	53	44′ 24.1″	73	1° 1′ 9.5″
14	11′ 43.7″	34	28′ 29.0″	54	45′ 14.4″	74	1° 1′ 59.7″
15	12′ 34.0″	35	29′ 19.3″	55	46′ 4.7″	75	1° 2′ 50.0″
16	13′ 24.2″	36	30′ 9.6″	56	46′ 54.9″	76	1° 3′ 40.3″
17	14′ 14.5″	37	30′ 59.8″	57	47′ 45.2″	77	1° 4′ 30.5″
18	15′ 4.8″	38	31′ 50.1″	58	48′ 35.5″	78	1° 5′ 20.8″
19	15′ 55.0″	39	32′ 40.4″	59	49′ 25.7″	79	1° 6′ 11.1″
20	16′ 45.3″	40	33′ 30.6″	60	50′ 16.0″	80	1° 7′ 1.3″

Table 2
Precession Correction Values

is referred to the writings of the siderealists, especially Donald Bradley, *Solar and Lunar Returns* (Llewellyn, 1948) for the precise method of casting these charts. The general procedure is to follow the rules for casting a sidereal solar return and then convert back to the tropical zodiac. The problem is that precession does not move at a constant rate, but wobbles slightly. The tables given by the siderealists enable one to correct for this wobble, known as *nutation*.

The Problem of Triple Transits

One complication that often makes it difficult to identify the time of maximum stress indicated by a transit is that very often an outer planet will cross the same degree three times — forward, then retrograde and once more forward. At which of the three times will the significant event occur?

This is not an easy question to answer, for it sometimes appears that the event can occur at any one of the three times. Many astrologers have claimed to have exact schemes for how to analyze such situations, but most of these schemes break down in practice. However, two basic patterns do seem to apply most of the time.

The first pattern applies whenever the triple transit seems to relate to a long-term process rather than to a single event. In this case the first contact indicates the beginning of the process, the second is a culmination or a crisis, and the third indicates the concluding events in the process. Often this effect is quite subtle, but if you look carefully you will usually see events that relate to the first and last contacts of the transiting planet. It is usually harder to understand the connection of the middle or retrograde transit.

In the second pattern, one of the three transits will signify an issue for you to handle, often arising from a single event that is not repeated at the other two transits. If you handle that issue properly, the other transits may go by without any notice. If you do not, another issue will arise that attacks the same problem from a different angle, and this will continue to happen until the problem is taken care of. Favorable or "benefic" transits, to use the older term, usually seem to conform to the first pattern. But a difficult transit that comes three times may present one major event or three, depending upon how you handle the first transit. Needless to say, if you do not handle the issue during the first transit, by the third time you will probably be so tired of the problem that you will do whatever is necessary to take care of it.

When a transiting planet goes stationary on a natal planet, it is possible to have a double transit. Under this condition, a Mars transit will last an entire month and thereby become a major transit. A planet that makes a station, direct or retrograde, while transiting a natal planet is very significant, and whatever event is signified by the transit will usually happen at that time rather than during the swifter direct transit that takes place either before or after the stationary transit.

Eclipses

Since whole books have been written about eclipses, I will not go into great detail about them here, but I would like to mention some of the basic principles of eclipses as they affect a natal chart.

An eclipse is a special kind of transit, because as the Sun and Moon are conjoined they both transit a natal planet. An eclipse seems to be most effective when it either conjoins or opposes a natal planet, but other aspects may have a weaker effect. Authorities differ on this point. But if an eclipse transits a planet or an angle by opposition or conjunction, it puts that planet or angle into a high-energy state in which its capacity to generate action is increased, either for both good or bad. Eclipses are often said to be difficult, but that is not necessarily so. The difficulty of the eclipse depends more upon the condition of the natal planet as indicated by house position and aspects to it from other natal planets.

Thus activated, the natal planet is more likely to signify a major event later when transited by another planet (most frequently Mars or the Sun) that acts as a trigger and signifies the time of release of the stored-up energy. Thus the events related to the eclipse seldom coincide with it; in fact it may occur up to several months later. However, I am not among those who believe that an eclipse may have a great effect years later, unless it is reinforced by more recent transiting events, which in my experience are usually sufficient to explain the event. But oddly enough, the triggering transit sometimes *precedes* the eclipse by a couple of months. This may seem peculiar at first, until you realize that an eclipse indicates the close of a major cycle between the transiting Sun and Moon, and that the cycle operates all the time, not just when the Sun and Moon actually eclipse each other.

Chapter Three

Case Study: Nixon and Watergate

The purpose of this chapter is to demonstrate the techniques described in the last chapter. For our case study we will use the chart of Richard M. Nixon, who at the time of the Watergate scandals was president of the United States.

First we will examine Nixon's natal chart (shown on next page) to see what aspects and other indications there are for some occurrence like the Watergate scandal. Nixon was born in Yorba Linda, California, 33°N 53', 117°W 49', on January 9, 1913. The birth time recorded by the attending nurse was 9:35 pm P.S.T. The chart shows that Nixon has a Sun-Neptune opposition from the fifth house to the eleventh house, an indication of a poorly developed reality standard; that is, he is capable of deluding either himself or others. Note that Neptune is in the eleventh house of friends, indicating that he might be likely to attract deceptive friends or be deceived by his friends.

Remember, however, that this opposition is equally likely to manifest itself as a highly spiritual personality capable of extremely altruistic acts. Nixon got caught in a web of intrigue because he worked out the opposition between Neptune and the Sun in the worst possible way. Neptune as a planetary symbol denies the normal demands of the ego. If a person with this aspect tries to get ahead in the usual manner, following relatively normal ego drives, he will run into obstacles in his way. Usually this aspect denotes a severe lack of confidence at some level and the belief that direct confrontation tactics will not work. Consequently, such natives often resort to devious tactics or try to throw dust in other people's eyes.

By itself, this aspect does not explain how Nixon got into the Watergate situation. Most persons with this aspect would simply be very unassertive and avoid confrontations. However, Nixon also has the signs of a very strong ego drive, as indicated by the complex of planets consisting of Pluto in the tenth house opposed by a triple conjunction of Mars, Mercury and Jupiter in the fourth house. Any Mars-Pluto combination indicates a strong ego drive, and with the addition of Mercury and Jupiter it shows that he would bend every bit of mental effort to getting ahead. Combine this drive with the fear of direct confrontation indicated by the Sun-Neptune opposition, and you have an explanation for the tactics that led to Watergate.

Again I repeat that these planetary combinations did not make Watergate inevitable. They merely indicate a type of person who would employ these tactics if he were pushed to the wall or if he were operating at a relatively low level of self-awareness.

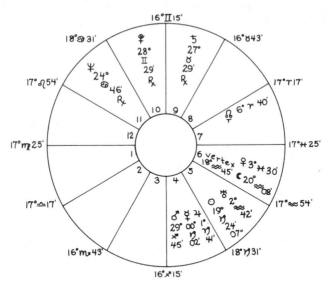

Natal Chart of Richard M. Nixon
Houses: Koch (Birthplace)

Nixon is probably not really aware of this side of his personality, or else he refuses to face it. I feel that Nixon was sincere in denying that he was a crook, that is, he did not see himself as one.

Now let us look at the long-range transiting pattern at the time of the Watergate break-in and subsequent crisis. This period extends from June 17, 1972, to August 9, 1974, when Nixon finally resigned. The background for this period is set by the transits of the outer planets through the houses.

Examining an ephemeris, we learn that at the time of the break-in Saturn was about to enter the tenth house, which it did in late July. For the rest of this period Saturn remained in that house. In this text I have chosen to use the M.C., Ascendant and house cusps of Nixon's recorded birth time, but many astrologers who have worked with Nixon's chart feel that he was born a little earlier. The most popular of these amended charts give an M.C. of about 13° ♓. This would make Saturn's entry into the tenth very close to the time of the Watergate break-in. But even accepting the time that was recorded by his nurse immediately at his birth, the Watergate crisis is clearly tied to the transit of Saturn through the tenth house.

This transit normally represents a peak in one's career, and in fact Nixon's career did peak during this time. He was reelected by one of the largest majorities in this country's history, and he traveled to Moscow and Peking. The fact that this period also saw his complete fall from power is typical of the effects of a tenth-house Saturn transit if, as the text warns, the native has taken drastic shortcuts in his efforts to reach the top or has broken the rules seriously. The transit of Saturn through the tenth is a time when one reaps the rewards and consequences of one's life efforts to accomplish something. Whatever Nixon's role in the practical planning of the

Watergate break-in, the tactics used by his men reflect his style of campaigning throughout his career, a fact amply attested to by several independent sources. Also an afflicted Pluto in the tenth house, which Nixon has, is likely to mean a sudden fall from power, especially if the native has resorted to devious tactics in the past.

During this period Jupiter was at first transiting his fourth house and then moved through his fifth and sixth houses. These transits are not especially relevant, but Jupiter's transits to specific planets during this period helped Nixon keep the lid on Watergate as long as he did. We will look at these transits shortly.

Uranus began in the first house, but for most of the time it was transiting the second house. Uranus in the second often denotes uncertainty in income, a change in income sources or rapid fluctuations in income. Nixon has experienced all of these effects since Watergate, although it took a couple of years for them to appear. More important than this transit is the series of transits that Uranus made to Nixon's Sun-Neptune opposition during this time, a series that ultimately timed his fall from power with remarkable precision. We will look more closely at that situation shortly.

Neptune was transiting his third house and made no important planetary transits except a square to Venus, which I suspect is not relevant to Watergate.

At this time Pluto was transiting Nixon's first house, as it had since the time when he had come back from defeat in the 1962 gubernatorial race in California. This transit, which continued right through his first term in office and the Watergate scandal of his second term, denotes his strong push for power. During the actual Watergate crisis, transiting Pluto squared his natal Pluto, which quite accurately timed an important event, the Watergate break-in itself.

Now let us examine the charts and transits of the more important events in the Watergate crisis and see how their timing is affected by various factors.

First is the break-in itself. The planetary positions here are given for 2:00 am E.D.T., June 17, 1972. Sun 26° ♓ 08′; Moon 10° ♍ 02′; Mercury 10° ♋ 21′; Venus 26° ♓ 45′R; Mars 22° ♋ 45′; Jupiter 4° ♉ 25′R; Saturn 12° ♓ 09′; Uranus 14° ♎ 12′; Neptune 3° ♐ 17′; Pluto 29° ♍ 20′; mean node 27° ♉ 43′; true node corrected for the various aberrations in the Moon's orbit, 26°. ♉ 25′. The time is not accurate enough to justify a set of house cusps.

As we examine the transits, we see that Mars is in a wide-orbed conjunction with natal Neptune and a wide-orbed opposition to the natal Sun. This is such an appropriate pair of transits for a secret action like the break-in that it seems odd that the orbs are so wide. Let's see if they really are that great.

Remember that if a transiting planet affects more than one factor (planet or house cusp) at a time, the event signified by this transit will occur at the time when the average orb of transit to all of the natal planets is closest to zero, allowing for some small error due to circumstances that we don't thoroughly understand. This principle of zero average orb is more an ideal than a realizable fact, but by using this principle we can certainly reduce the orb from what it appears to be.

The average position of the natal Sun and Neptune is 22° ♎ 06', which is also the midpoint of the two planets. The only difference between the midpoint and the average point is that although you can have an average position for more than two planets, it is difficult to apply the midpoint principle to more than two. Considering the average point of the Sun and Neptune to be 22° ♎ 06' reduces the orb of the transiting Mars to 39'. This isn't bad, but it can be reduced still further by applying another principle that was referred to in Chapter 2, the principle of precession correction. The natal positions are moved forward 5' for every six years of life. Referring to the table of precession correction in Chapter 2, we find that the correction is 50' of arc. If we add 50' to the average position of the natal Sun and Neptune, we get 22° ♎ 56'. This makes the transiting Mars only 10' short of being an exact transit at the time of the break-in and represents the few hours that it would have taken for Nixon to learn that something had gone wrong. Mars transiting Sun and Neptune is a sign of vigorous, secretive action that may result in defeat.

When we look at the transiting Pluto, we see that it is approaching the natal Pluto-Mercury-Jupiter-Mars complex and squaring that axis. But the orbs are rather large, and none of the transits seems very precise. Pluto had been in this position for some time, and here we have the problem of triple transits — that is, we could not tell which one of the three transits of Pluto would trigger the event. This problem was discussed in Chapter 2. In looking over the charts, there is also some possible confusion as to which of the natal factors — Mercury, Mars, Pluto or Jupiter — squared by transiting Pluto would time the event. One would be justified in thinking that Pluto could be squaring Mars, squaring Pluto or squaring the average position of Mars and Pluto. The average position of Mars and Pluto is 29° 07' mutables, which is the closest position to the transiting Pluto without precession correction. The orb is 13' of arc. However, if we apply the precession correction of 50', we find that the corrected Pluto is 29° ♓ 19', an orb of one minute of arc from an exact square with transiting Pluto. Like all squares, that of transiting Pluto to natal Pluto denotes a crisis in which the person is tested in some way. With Pluto, the test is about power. It should be said that this event could have occurred on any of the contacts between Pluto and the natal Mars or Pluto or their average position. Mars aspecting his natal Sun and Neptune served to time the event more precisely, which is typical. In most cases either the Sun or Mars plays this role.

Transiting Neptune is square Nixon's natal Venus, but it is difficult to determine exactly what this means in relation to Watergate. It is more likely to indicate something in his personal life that we know nothing about. Neptune does square Venus in the sixth, so this transit could indicate a disappointment in the area of work, although this is not appropriate to the symbolism of the transit. A health problem would be more likely, and it is probable that his phlebitis problem first flared up at that time, since Venus has to do with the blood system.

One of the most remarkable aspects of the whole Watergate scandal was that in the months after the break-in and during the campaign, Nixon did such a good job of hushing up Watergate and convincing the country that it was nothing more than "a second-rate burglary attempt," that it implied nothing significant about his conduct of the presidency. Most people considered the Democrats' allusions to it simply as campaign rhetoric and refused to take the matter seriously.

Obviously something in Nixon's chart should indicate this period of favorable luck or delay of the inevitable, depending on how you look at it. And there is such an indication. Throughout the period preceding the Watergate break-in, transiting Jupiter was going retrograde back to late Sagittarius. In the months after Watergate, Jupiter went stationary directly opposition Pluto and conjunct Nixon's fourth-house triple conjunction. It moved very slowly forward through September and only really moved off the conjunction at the end of October, 1972. This easing off of pressure is a typical effect of Jupiter transits. Jupiter opposition Pluto represented the height of Nixon's personal Jupiter-Pluto cycle, which among other things is the drive for personal success and power. Under any other circumstances this would have been the supreme peak in his life, and actually it was, except that Nixon did not take advantage of it as he should have. With such powerful energies in his favor, he could have been much more open about Watergate, and he would have been able to totally defuse the whole issue. He couldn't have been totally open about it, because he was guilty of participating in the cover up conspiracy, as later events revealed. But Nixon chose to act in a way that is appropriate to an unconscious Sun-Neptune opposition type, for he was afraid of direct confrontation.

The pressure began to build again in earnest in early 1973. In January the Watergate trial began, but it involved only the burglars, McCord and Liddy, who refused to implicate anyone higher up. However, suddenly on March 23, 1973, Judge John Sirica announced that he had received a letter from McCord clearly indicating that persons higher in the administration were responsible for Watergate and that they were trying to cover up the scandal. During this same period, the Senate created the special Watergate investigating committee headed by Sam Ervin. The first of these two developments, the letter from McCord, extended the life of the Watergate grand jury, which otherwise would probably have folded up its operations and gone home. The creation of the Senate committee, on the other hand, led to the single most important event in the whole Watergate investigation, the revelation of Nixon's system of secretly taping all conversations in his office.

As a result of these activities, pressure began to build against the administration. Prior to that time most Americans had agreed with Nixon's characterization of the Watergate as a second-rate burglary. But at this point many people began to realize that something more serious was happening.

In the administration, John Dean began to have doubts about the wisdom of continuing his role in the coverup. He warned Nixon about the seriousness of the matter and informed him of the burglars' demands for hush money and executive clemency. These events in turn led to the resignations of Dean, Ehrlichman and Haldeman in April. Clearly, the benevolent and protective effects of Nixon's Jupiter transit were gone. What was happening in his chart?

First of all, transiting Saturn, which had retrograded back across his M.C. into the ninth house, was coming back again for the third pass. This was Saturn's final entry into Nixon's tenth house. Thus we could reasonably expect the beginning of the harvest of consequences, both negative and positive, of Nixon's preparation for this point in life. Remember that this transit does not have to be all that difficult, if the person is well prepared. But Nixon's preparation apparently had too many weak points to withstand the pressure that this transit placed him under.

The second important event was the return of transiting Uranus for a retrograde pass to Nixon's Sun-Neptune opposition. This had happened the first time during his reelection, but then it was largely offset by the benevolent transit of Jupiter already referred to. This time, however, there was no protection. Also there was a semisquare between transiting Uranus and transiting Neptune, so that every time one of these planets transited Nixon's chart, the other did also. Whether or not you apply the precession correction to Nixon's natal positions, these transits encompass the hottest period for him in the spring of 1973.

Of major importance during this period were the resignations of Dean, Ehrlichman and Haldeman, which were announced on the evening of April 30, 1973. The positions for midnight G.M.T. of May 1 were as follows: Sun 10° ♉ 29'; Moon 14° ♈ 48'; Mercury 20° ♈ 54'; Venus 16° ♉ 00'; Mars 24° ♒ 56'; Jupiter 10° ♒ 45'; Saturn 18° ♊ 29'; Uranus 20° ♎ 12'; Neptune 6° ♐ 45'; Pluto 2° ♎ 07'.

We can see immediately that Uranus at this time was closely square the Sun in Nixon's chart. In fact, if we add 50', the correction for precession to Nixon's Sun, we get the position 20° ♉ 14', only two minutes of arc off the exact transit as of midnight on May 1, 1973. The transit had been exact within the last twenty-four hours. Also we can see that transiting Saturn was very closely exact square Nixon's Ascendant. Nixon's precession-corrected Ascendant is 18° ♏ 15', only fourteen minutes from the transiting Saturn square. Remember that even with the most accurately recorded birth date, it is common to find an error this large in the M.C. and Ascendant. In fact, this is a good argument for the accuracy of Nixon's recorded birth time.

Let us digress a moment to ask a question. Granted that Nixon's Sun-Neptune opposition is a significant aspect, why was it so especially critical for him? Many people go through life without anywhere near the problems that Nixon had to contend with. Granted also that his problems were largely self-created, or at least self-exacerbated, we still have to account for the peculiar power of this aspect. One would expect the transits to Nixon's Mercury-Pluto-Mars-Jupiter complex to be the more important influence in timing the major events of this period. At the time, I thought so too, and predicted that Nixon's fall from power would come in June, 1974, instead of August, as actually happened.

The answer lies at least partly in the locality chart, a technique to which I was not paying enough attention at the time. The locality chart is the native's birthchart erected as if he were born at a place of residence other than the actual birth place. The same G.M.T. is used in erecting this chart, but a correction is made for the new L.M.T. Therefore the planets are the same, but the houses are different. Since Nixon was born in California, the locality chart for Washington D.C. would be quite different from his natal chart. Here is the method in brief. Take a copy of Dernay's *Longitudes and Latitudes in the United States* and look at the last column, which is headed, "To obtain G.M.T., add to L.M.T." for the place of birth. Add this figure to the S.T. of the birthchart. If the place isn't in Dernay, this figure is gotten by dividing the longitude in arc by 15. If the longitude is east, subtract the figure from the natal

S.T., then look up the same value for the new place of residence. If the longitude is west, subtract the figure from the previous result. If the longitude is east, add the figure. This new value is the resulting S.T. for the locality chart at the new residence. Nixon's locality chart for Washington D.C. is shown below.

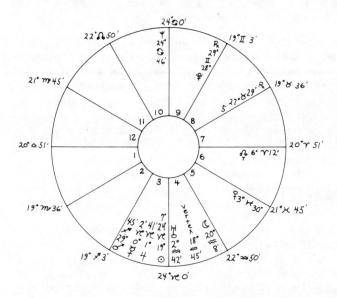

Locality Chart of Richard M. Nixon for Washington, D.C.
Houses: Koch (Birthplace)

In the locality chart, Neptune is precisely on the M.C. by longitude, and the Sun is close to the I.C. in the third house. Moving to Washington put this aspect in Nixon's natal chart right on the most powerful place in the horoscope. And even for advocates of equal house division, this is a strong figure, for the opposition is also square the Ascendant. The meaning of this change is that Nixon's move to Washington D.C. made his Sun-Neptune attributes most powerful. Note that the transiting Uranus was going back and forth over the locality Ascendant. It is my opinion that the natal M.C. and Ascendant always take precedence over locality cusps, but in this case the locality cusps give additional information, helping to explain events that are otherwise difficult to understand.

In the months after his aides resigned, the pressure continued to build up against Nixon. Astrologically, we find that not only did Uranus continue to afflict the Sun-Neptune axis in his chart and the locality M.C. and Ascendant, but in addition Saturn came in for its first pass over the Pluto-Mercury-Jupiter-Mars complex.

On July 16, 1973, the largest single bomb was dropped concerning the Watergate affair when Herbert Butterfield stated in testimony before the Senate Watergate committee that a White House taping system had recorded every conversation in Nixon's office. Prior to this time, the issue was Dean's testimony and that of a few others against the word of the president and his other aides. It was the tapes that eventually brought Nixon's career down. Although the tape system had been mentioned in closed session a couple of days before, the public announcement was made on July 16, shortly after 2:00 pm E.D.T. Here are the positions at that time: Sun 24° ♋ 02'; Moon 7° ♒ 57'; Mercury 29° ♋. 44'R; Venus 19° ♑ 54'; Mars 16° ♈ 08'; Jupiter 8° ♒ 57'; Saturn 28° ♓ 07'; Uranus 19° ♎ 07'; Neptune 4° ♐ 55'; Pluto 2° ♎ 00'; nodes (true) 7° ♏ 39'.

The most outstanding transits are the simultaneous assault upon Nixon's Sun-Neptune opposition by transiting Mars, Sun, Uranus and Mercury. Some of these orbs may seem rather large, but if you calculate the average position of these four planets in the cardinal signs, simply by adding up the positions and dividing by four, you will find that the average of these four positions is 22° cardinals 15'. Nixon's Sun-Neptune average position is 22° ♎ 05'! This array of simultaneous transits is an example of the principle that an event of great significance will not be triggered by just one transit. In this case the positions that are not precession-corrected give the more accurate time. Work at this time seems to indicate that both the precession-corrected and the noncorrected positions have to be taken into consideration in such cases, although the precession-corrected ones seem to have a higher success average.

Two other powerful transits at this time, transiting Saturn and Pluto, are hitting Nixon's Mercury-Mars-Jupiter-Pluto axis. The average position of this axis in Nixon's natal chart is 29° 59' of the mutable signs. The average point of the transiting Saturn-Pluto is 0° 04' of the cardinals. Here again, the uncorrected orb is smaller. If you check the delineations for all of these transits, namely Saturn transiting conjunct natal Pluto and opposition natal Mercury, Mars and Jupiter, you will have a good description of the crisis. The other transit complex, consisting of transiting Mercury, Mars, Sun and Uranus to Nixon's natal Sun and Neptune, is most clearly relevant when it is viewed as a whole. Mercury rules communications and announcements; Uranus, suddenness; Neptune concerns deceptions. Mars serves simply to reinforce the disruptive nature of the transit. The transiting and natal Suns demonstrate the importance of this transit, and the transiting Sun also acts as a timing factor. The reader will also note that the locality M.C. and Ascendant are powerfully involved in this collection of transits.

After early August, the Senate committee recessed until September, which quieted things down for awhile and took the heat off Nixon. The committee continued to be a powerful force in the investigation, but not to the extent that it had been.

During the fall, several other matters took the heat off Nixon, the first being the Mideast crises and the resulting oil embargo. Second, there was the Agnew affair, which culminated in Agnew's resignation from the position of vice-president. But on October 20, the heaviest storm thus far broke when Nixon fired Archibald Cox and William Ruckelshaus, while Elliot Richardson resigned in protest, the famous "Saturday Night Massacre." This was the action that led to the beginning of impeachment proceedings. The main transits in effect on that day were the Sun and Uranus hitting Nixon's Neptune. The average position of the transiting Sun and Uranus is 25° cardinals 34'. The precession-corrected natal Neptune is 25° ♋ 36'. Of course, these are not the positions for the exact moment of firing, since that time is unknown. The important fact is that when Uranus again hit the Sun-Neptune axis the heat began to build again for Nixon.

Also, Mars and Jupiter were simultaneously affecting Nixon's natal Uranus and his Ascendant, an example of a minor aspect by transit producing a significant result. The reason is that both Mars and Jupiter hit the Ascendant by sesquiquadrate (135°), but on opposite sides. Thus the Ascendant in Nixon's chart splits the transiting square of Mars and Jupiter. Squares and oppositions to Mars and Jupiter are characterized by impulsive actions. Transiting Mars was at 2° ♑ 58', and Jupiter was at 3° ♒ 06'. Their average position is 3° 02' of the fixed signs. Nixon's natal Ascendant is 17° ♍ 25', with precession correction 18° ♍ 15', which is very close to the exact sesquiquadrate to the average Mars and Jupiter, especially since the actual firings took place before 0:00 hours G.M.T., the time for which these positions are given.

There were several other significant events during that period, but let us turn now to Nixon's resignation speech. It can be used to demonstrate particularly well the principles of transit timing that have been described in this book because it can be timed precisely. The speech was given on August 8, 1974 at the White House, Washington, D.C., 38° N 54', 77° W 02'. Watching on live television, I timed the beginning of the speech at 9:05 E.D.S.T. The chart of that moment is shown below.

Here again the natal Sun-Neptune opposition is the point that is under attack by the transits. Nixon's natal Sun-Neptune midpoint is 22° ♎ 05'. When we examine the transits to his natal chart, we find the following transits to the Sun-Neptune midpoint: Moon by opposition, orb −34'; Neptune by semisquare, orb −13'; Venus by square, orb +41'; Mars by semisquare, orb +45'; and Uranus by conjunction, orb +2° 12'. The two semisquares are very important because they are on opposite sides of

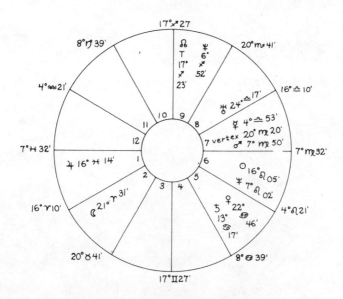

Chart of the Beginning of Nixon's Resignation Speech
Houses: Koch (Birthplace)

43

the natal Sun-Neptune midpoint such that their midpoint is conjunct natal Sun-Neptune. This is similar to the situation at the time of the Saturday Night Massacre, with the transiting Mars-Jupiter square.

In this case we shall calculate the average transiting orbs instead of the average positions, because the semisquares are not multiples of 30°. (See Chapter 2 on transit timing, page 21.) We add together all of the orbs, getting a total of 171'. This is divided by the number of transiting planets, which is five, to get an average orb of +33'. This is quite close, considering that the transiting Moon is part of this pattern, and if we add 50', the precession correction to the natal Sun-Neptune midpoint, this orb is converted from +33 to −18. During the course of the speech, the transiting Moon would move enough to reduce that figure to 0'. Thus the resignation actually did occur at the peak of combined energy of all the transits, as described in Chapter 2.

The most curious factor in this event is the role of Venus. Obviously, if you take the Venus transit out of context of the other transits, the results would not make much sense. But with the other transits, it simply indicates an event that affected Nixon's overall happiness and his relationships in general, not necessarily just sexual relationships.

Admittedly it is difficult to use the techniques for transit timing in advance of an event. However, with the dawn of the computer age, it is possible that we will be able to work out precise techniques for transit timing, based on the principles described in this text.

Chapter Four

Sun

Significance of Transiting Sun

The transiting Sun is quite important in predictive astrology, because the energy source of the solar system is also the energy source of the horoscope. The sign of and aspects to the natal Sun have more influence over the general condition of the horoscope than any other planet, except possibly the Moon. And the transiting Sun's changing relationship to the natal Sun determines how you react to the annual solar rhythm, a cycle that is exceeded in importance only by the diurnal rhythm, which depends upon the apparent revolution of the Sun around the Earth every twenty-four hours.

Physically, the Sun rules the basic energy of the body and the body as an energy system. Consequently the transiting Sun can have a great effect on feelings of health and vigor.

Psychologically, the Sun rules the energy of the psyche, what Jung called the "libido" or the basic drive to be. When the transiting Sun afflicts the natal chart, you can expect crises in which your will comes into conflict with someone else's. You may be challenged to assert yourself and stand up for your rights. The area of your natal chart affected by the transiting Sun points out the area of your life in which you must express yourself at the time. If you allow yourself to be unnecessarily defeated during a solar transit, the effects may be psychologically quite negative. In extreme cases, afflictions from the transiting Sun can indicate health problems.

The transiting Sun also has to do with men in general whom you may encounter and persons in authority of either sex. Afflictions from the transiting Sun often indicate problems with authorities or men.

However, the triggering function of the transiting Sun is even more important, and it works as follows. Long-term transits by the outer planets are often in effective range of natal planets for weeks, so it is often difficult to tell when an event related to the transit will occur. However, if the Sun transits the natal planet that is being transited by the outer planet and thereby aspects the transiting planet, you can expect the decisive event to occur at that time. The Sun brings into focus the issues related to the house or planet it transits. And if the natal planet is being transited by another planet at the same time, the Sun brings the other planetary transit into focus. A transit that is not also involved with the transiting Sun may not register at all. Therefore, when you have a transit of the Sun to your natal horoscope, see whether the planet transited by the Sun is also transited by another planet. If it is, that should be a significant day. Transits of the Sun alone without another simultaneous transit signify events of lesser importance.

Sun in the First House

At this time of year, for approximately one month, you will be able to recharge yourself, so to speak, for the year to come. You will become more concerned with personal matters and less with the world at large. This period is self-centered in a positive sense in that it is born not of selfishness, but of a real need to look at yourself and find out what you need for further progress.

Because the Sun is the source of all energy in the horoscope and because the first house is the projection of your personality, this transit indicates a time when you can project yourself with more forcefulness than usual. It is an excellent time for making an impression on others, but you must be careful because you will not be especially sensitive to their needs. This is because of the self-centeredness mentioned above. You are wrapped up primarily in your own concerns and are likely to have a very subjective viewpoint on most matters. For this reason, you may find it difficult to work with others during this transit. If your efforts to work on projects with others don't seem to get anywhere now, perhaps you should defer them until later. First you should take care of the proper business of this transit, which is to experience yourself in a subjective frame of reference.

Under certain conditions this transit may also result in marital problems, but only if there are other, more serious transits. Nevertheless, this is not one of the best times for resolving marital conflicts.

You have a great need to express yourself now, and it is a valid need. No purpose will be served by denying all your own needs in favor of a misguided concept of duty. There are times, and this is one of them, when your first duty is to yourself, and if you don't fulfill that duty, you will be of little use to anyone else.

Sun in the Second House

At this time you should reflect upon your values and the things that you value. Traditionally the second house is the house of money and of moveable property, as opposed to real estate. In modern times we refer to it as the house of resources in general and of what we value, both abstract values and material objects. During this month-long transit you should examine your relationship to the resources of your life. Do they serve your needs, or do you serve theirs? Many people, out of a misguided need for security, become so involved with their possessions that they cannot act freely for fear of damaging their own interests, that is, property interests. At this time you need to express yourself through your material and nonmaterial resources, using them to define you to yourself and others. For example, you may feel like having a party or other celebration so that your material resources can give pleasure and amusement to your friends. You may want to show off something you own to others, because you take so much pleasure in it yourself. Obviously this can be carried too far, so that your behavior is obnoxious to others, but it can also be a source of good times for you and your friends.

More than any other time, you now want to have greater control of your life through the things that you value. On the material level this may mean that you will acquire possessions in order to gain more control over your own life or over other people. On the psychological level it indicates a need to assert your value system. But remember that others have a right to their own values. You should stand up for your own, but not by obliterating someone else's.

Sun in the Third House

The Sun in this house turns your attention toward your immediate surroundings and increases your interaction with friends, neighbors, relatives and business associates — the people you deal with every day. It is a good time to look at how you handle these casual relationships that are so important for your life. Often we develop unfortunate little habits in communicating with these people, which undermine our effectiveness and our ability to communicate with them. In fact, clear communication should be one of the goals of this period. With the Sun in this house there is a temptation to pour out energy and take none in. But try to avoid this. Instead of always being the active agent in communication, be the passive one, too — in other words, listen!

This is also a time of year when the tempo of your life accelerates. There is more activity, more moving around and even a sense of restlessness that can be assuaged only by getting out and doing something new and different. You might take up the study of a subject that you have never encountered before, or you might take a series of short trips. Taking a vacation at this time will work out, but you might find it difficult to break away from the patterns of your everyday life while on vacation. You should integrate traveling into your routine at this time, instead of using it to get away from your everyday life.

This is an especially good time to tell someone clearly how you feel about some subject. If others have been confused as to what you are doing or thinking in some area, you should be able now to communicate your real thoughts and intentions. Don't leave people in the dark about yourself. Your mental processes should be relatively clear now, and you can use this ability to get through to others. If you don't feel clear yourself, this is a good time to consider your own position and make it clear. For you, this is the natural time of year to do this.

Sun in the Fourth House

At this time of year you focus your concerns upon your most intimate personal life and the people who affect it most, your family and parents. You will want to be in familiar surroundings now and feel that you have some kind of center or place where you can build a solid base for your activities. For most people this means a home. Although you should continue to live up to the demands of the outer world, because your personal life is interdependent with it, you should focus most of your attention inward. Not only inward to your personal life, but also inward in a psychological sense. Even more than the Sun's transit through the first house, this is a time of subjective consciousness, of feeling exactly where you are with respect to the world and getting in touch with your own deepest levels. If necessary, go off by yourself and spend time in contemplation or meditation.

Events that occurred in the past may come back to you now through memories and through consequences of those events that continue to affect you now. It is often wise to find out what effects your past, your upbringing and the experience of your family have had upon you. You may want to call in another person, perhaps even a professional counselor, to help you examine the role of the past in your present life. You may find that the past has generated behavior patterns that are completely inappropriate for your life now and that such patterns are a major source of tension for you. At this time of year, psychological self-evaluation can be of enormous help in your personal growth.

Sun in the Fifth House

According to tradition, the Sun is happiest in the fifth house. With the Sun here, you feel most free to express yourself and to be yourself. Your primary drive is to do what you want and as much as possible to set your own priorities. You are not especially interested in dominating others, although you may be capable of it at this time, but you will vigorously oppose anyone who tries to prevent you from doing what you want to do.

The fifth house is often described as the house of amusement and recreation. Therefore you have a strong drive to get out and have a good time, and there is no reason why you shouldn't, as long as you make some effort to meet your daily obligations and restrictions. But the free-spirited drive of the fifth-house Sun may not want to do this, which can be a problem. At any rate you will feel lighter than usual throughout this period.

You may have great concern with children now, although this does not mean that you will have problems with them. It only means that your emotional involvement is great. If you have children, this is a good time to examine your relationship with them. Also you could combine two of the activities associated with this house and take your children out to have fun with them.

Your attitude toward your relationships is much lighter at this time, almost as if you saw your relationships as a stage upon which you can perform. At any rate, you favor more than usual the relationships that are fun. This same drive may lead you to a new love relationship with the opposite sex, although that is more likely if this trend is confirmed by other transits.

But don't get so wrapped up in yourself and your enjoyments that you forget to examine yourself. This is the time to be yourself, but it also is the time to become conscious of who you are. It is one thing to be yourself; it is another to know yourself. You can use this time for both.

Sun in the Sixth House

This transit is quite different from the immediately preceding one. Now is the time to examine the problem of how you should manage your life and what duties and responsibilities that entails. This is a house of work, of tasks that need to be done, which may necessitate postponing immediate gratification. Your focus should be on efficiency and effectiveness. Strive to make every action as much to the point as possible. In your work this is a good time to examine and refine your techniques and procedures, for your mind can work clearly and sharply to discover the best way of doing things.

The only problem you may have to contend with at this time is that you will probably not be on top of the heap. That is, you will probably have to work according to someone else's wishes or needs. But because of this, you can find out whether you can lower your ego drives when the situation requires it. If you cannot, you are likely to encounter quite a bit of discomfort and conflict at this time. This is the house of service, and you cannot spend all your efforts getting your own way now. Even if you are your own boss, your actions will be dictated by someone else's needs, such as a client's or a customer's. Or your sense of obligation may be internal. You may have to live up to your own high standards of self-control.

Nevertheless, this doesn't have to be a time of repression and self-denial, without satisfaction. You can derive quite a bit of satisfaction from doing things well, and that will mean more to you now than any other kind of satisfaction.

This transit also concerns physical efficiency. This is a house of health, but that does not mean that your physical health will necessarily be worse than usual. However, you will be more inclined to look at your body and to see how its functioning can be improved. You may be unusually concerned with health and hygiene, which can be quite beneficial, as long as you don't get wrapped up in it to the point of obsession.

Sun in the Seventh House

At this time of year you should learn more about yourself through intimate one-to-one encounters with others. You will form working units with other people for various purposes, and through these units you will understand more about the effects that you have upon others. Already existing relationships of this sort will serve the same purpose, as you become more conscious of how you operate within them.

One of the most important such relationship is marriage, whether or not it is a legalized arrangement. If you are married, use this time to examine your relationship with your spouse and to discover what needs this relationship does and does not fill in your life. Try to discover how well you fill your spouse's needs as well. In any seventh-house relationship, whether it is a marriage, business partnership or other kind of partner-ship, you and your partner function as a unit, either in a specific area, as with a business partner, or in all areas, as with a spouse. For your own benefit, you must be as good for your partner as he or she is for you.

This is not a time of the year when you should try to go it alone in any type of activity. You should try to work with someone else, or at least seek out the opinion of another person in an advisory capacity. In business this is a good time to consult experts in whatever field you are involved in. A consultant, lawyer or other specialist may fit the requirements. The same applies to your personal life, where you may benefit from some type of counseling, if you have not been able to solve certain problems. You might consult a doctor, lawyer, psychologist, psychiatrist or even an astrologer. Such people can give you an independent perspective against which to measure your own views of the situation.

Sometimes the one-to-one encounter may take the form of a conflict. Conflict can be creative, because it forces you to examine your own position more thoroughly and thus become more aware of yourself. You and your opponent form a pair, just as you and a partner do. For this reason, the seventh house is connected with conflicts at law, and this could be a time when you have legal dealings of this sort, although this would have to be confirmed by other indications in your chart.

Sun in the Eighth House

You may feel the influence of this transit on a number of different levels. But in general you will consciously direct your attention to the subtler aspects of your psyche, your feelings and emotions and your general psychological health. Often this transit is an indication that you are much more in touch with this part of your being than usual, and it would be very good to take a look at your inner self. The activities of the everyday world do not always permit this, and you can become quite miserable by getting totally out of touch with your inner self.

One sign of this need that you may notice now is a sense of strong psychological compulsions surfacing and perhaps leading to behavior that you do not understand. At their most powerful, these compulsions can force considerable changes in your life, which are most disturbing if you do not try to get in touch with them.

Fortunately, with this transit you will have a strong desire to experience life on a feeling level, and this is just what you need. Intellectual understanding is not likely to be enough. Each time this transit occurs (it lasts for about one month every year), you will undergo a significant psychological transformation. Traditionally this is the house of death, usually meaning the death of some aspect of yourself or your life rather than the death of a person. Under rare conditions, with many other indications, this transit can mean an actual death, but that is not a prospect to worry about in most cases.

One very real possibility at this time is that an encounter with someone will produce the need for very searching psychological self-inquiry or will force very powerful changes in your life. This person may challenge your value structure, or there may be a powerful intermeshing of your personalities.

On the material plane, this transit can be a time of great concern about finances or resources held jointly with another person, such as a spouse or business partner. By itself, this is neither a good nor a bad indication; it simply makes the issue important. You may also be worried about trying to borrow money or get financial backing from a bank.

Sun in the Ninth House

During this time of year you should attempt to broaden your horizons in every way possible — through study, new and unfamiliar experiences, travel or by meeting people from totally different backgrounds who can reveal another aspect of the world. Strive to make even the most trivial encounter a positive learning experience.

This is an extremely favorable time to undertake a new course of study, a new hobby or intellectual discipline. It doesn't matter whether you are studying for a practical purpose or for enjoyment as long as it stimulates your intellect and gives you a broader perspective on the universe.

The same function can be served by doing things that are different from your normal routine. This is not the time to retreat to your home, except for reading or study, as mentioned. If you cannot get interested in a new mental activity, recognize that you are still eager for new understanding and satisfy this need by breaking out of your everyday mold and getting out into the broader world. Travel would be a good way to do this, if you can arrange for it at this time of year. But a trip should not be for purely recreational purposes. You should go somewhere where you can learn something.

On another level, this transit can indicate involvement or concern with the law, although probably you will not be directly involved in a legal case yourself. More likely you would have to investigate a principle of law in connection with your everyday activities or business.

This transit may also indicate metaphysical, religious and spiritual concerns in general. Certainly you are more than usually receptive to these aspects of life.

Sun in the Tenth House

This is a time of year when you should turn your attention to the most outward aspects of your life — your career, your role in the larger society and your standing and reputation within the community. You should also take this time to examine your life as a whole and see if you are going in the direction you want and making adequate progress in your life. The tenth house relates to the manifestation of your ego drives within a social context. Not as personal as other houses, it affects most strongly the most external areas of your life, which are nevertheless extremely important.

One possible effect of the Sun in this house is to put you in the limelight, either on a small or a large scale, depending upon the normal course of your life. You may be called upon to take over the direction of a task or project in which you would have considerable power, but take note that the responsibility will be equally great. It is extremely important to approach such an opportunity with proper knowledge of your strengths and weaknesses. At this time you do not have to be super strong or competent to succeed, because the natural flow of energies is with you. But you should know as much as possible about your real capabilities. Do not pretend to be something you are not, because the truth will eventually come out, and if you have misrepresented yourself, you will be damaged.

The tenth house also relates to one's parents, so this transit could indicate that your interaction with them is very important.

This transit is future oriented rather than past oriented. You may have to deal with elements of your past, but only to make corrections so that you can plan more intelligently for the future. The only real danger of this transit is that if you have done something wrong or in a slipshod fashion it may be exposed now and trip you up in unpleasant ways. It would be a very good idea to look over your life and correct any situations that might give you problems in this way. You can confine your concern to nonpersonal situations, although family problems may sometimes create difficulty in public at this time. This difficulty is usually indicated by a simultaneous transit by another planet that affects the tenth house.

Sun in the Eleventh House

At this time of year your attention is turned toward the groups you belong to, both formally and otherwise, to their values and ideals and your relationship to those values and ideals as well as your own. Friendships and other relationships are important to you now, and you are examining the role they play in your life. What kinds of interaction do you have with others and how well do you fulfill each other's needs? No one can live in a vacuum, and the function of this transit is to find out what that means for you as an individual.

At this time it is usually best to work and cooperate with other people. At other times you have found it necessary to be alone in order to find out who you are and the chief purposes of your life. Now you must ask these same questions in conjunction with others. Engaging in group efforts and projects in your personal and professional life will be the most effective way to accomplish this aim. Socialize extensively and study the people you associate with, for they are a reflection of yourself. What is true of your friends is also true of you, for the most part.

Among your friends, strive to establish who you are. Without becoming domineering, you should let them know what kind of person you are, so that you can fit into the group dynamic without violating your integrity. This is a time for team efforts, which can be effective only if everyone on the team is a fully realized individual.

Your idealism is aroused at this time, but it is personal rather than abstract idealism. It is your recognition of what you want your life to be, so follow that ideal.

Sun in the Twelfth House

At this time you have to get in touch with your own subconscious mind, to find out how it directs your life in ways that you aren't aware of. Try to see how your actions may run counter to your conscious intentions. We all broadcast two kinds of signals to the outer world. One kind is what we think we are trying to do. The other kind, which are unconscious signals, tell people what we are really trying to do. If these two sets of signals do not coincide, it is not because you are intentionally trying to deceive, but you may confuse people or, even worse, cause them to lose faith in what you are trying to do.

Particularly deadly are childhood behavior patterns that have long outlived their usefulness. They originated as a childish response to pressures that you could not understand at the time. Now that you are older and presumably more understanding, these patterns are quite inappropriate. The only way to handle them is to recognize and experience them with full and detached consciousness. That is, you must allow these emotions and feelings to exist, but recognize that they are not relevant to your adult life. This is a task that you can perform effectively at this time.

In a way, your year is ending, the year established by the transit of the Sun through your natal houses. This is a good time to look back over the year and see how well you have managed the art of living. It may be necessary to be alone now so that you can reflect in peace and quiet. But there is one danger. You must be prepared to evaluate with complete honesty all your behavior and ways of dealing with the world. Anything you refuse to face will continue to be a part of your unconscious mind and will work against you when you least expect it. This is not a time to be wrapped up in your ego. You must be prepared to acknowledge your faults and your virtues without fear or self-recrimination. And you must be able to do this with regard to others as well.

Unintentionally, your actions may have caused others to work against you. Sometimes these people are not even aware that they are working against you. If you can honestly acknowledge the less effective aspects of your personality, however, you will also lessen the effects these aspects have on others.

Sun Conjunct Sun

Today is your real birthday, even though it may be a day or two different from your calendar birthday. However, this is the date when the Sun returns to the position it was in when you were born, completing a full circuit around the ecliptic. Of course it is really the Earth that has moved, but we see our own motion as the apparent motion of the Sun.

As would seem appropriate with this transit, today is a day of new beginnings. A new year in your own personal calendar has begun, and the influences you feel today will affect the entire year to come. This does not mean that the whole year will be dis-appointing if today doesn't work out exactly as planned, but the planetary influences in effect today will have great meaning for the year as a whole. Many astrologers find that the chart cast for the exact minute and second that the Sun returns to its birth position provides a significant forecast for the year ahead.

The energies you feel today may not be very dynamic, but you do feel as though you ought to be the center of attention in some way. This is a natural effect of a powerful Sun transit and is not just because this occurs on or near your birthday. Nevertheless, despite the subtlety of the energy, this is a day when you should in fact make new beginnings. You are receiving a new impulse from the energy center within you, as symbolized by the Sun. Therefore any new venture that you start at this time will ride the crest of this new energy and will very likely come to an acceptable conclusion. Whatever you do or begin today will bear the stamp of your individuality more than anything else. This is the day to assert yourself anew. Plan to let the world know who you are, not arrogantly or smugly, but so that everyone knows you are here. You have needs and wants like everyone else, as well as something to contribute to the world.

Sun Sextile Sun

This transit occurs twice a year, roughly two months before and two months after your birthday. It is a time when you should strive to integrate your energies with those of the people around you — your friends, neighbors and the groups that you identify with. You will be able to work very effectively with others now, and your goals and objectives will harmonize with those of the people you associate with. You will do this without any loss of identity; in fact, you will feel that what you do affirms your identity.

This is a good time for socializing with others. You will enjoy people's company and derive much benefit from being with them. Even the company of people whom you consider to be above you will be easy and pleasant as well as beneficial to your overall development.

On the transit two months after your birthday, you should examine how far you have gotten in realizing the goals that you have set for this year. Don't be caught in the illusion that you can be unconscious of what you are doing this year. If you choose to remain unaware, about thirty days from now you will be challenged in ways that you won't understand. Inexplicable conflicts with others may erupt, forcing you to improvise solutions to problems that you have not thought about in advance. Now is the time to ascertain what has to be done, at least for the time being, and to put all your endeavors into reasonable order.

On the transit two months prior to your birthday, check to see how well this current cycle of the Sun has served you. Find out what you have succeeded in doing and what has failed and prepare for your birthday, when the next cycle will begin.

You will not be forced by any kind of cosmic energy to do these things, but this opportunity is too good to waste.

Sun Square Sun

This transit occurs roughly three months after and three months before your birthday. In both cases it is a transit of challenge and crisis. The seriousness of the crisis varies tremendously from person to person, but in any case you needn't fear this transit. However, you should watch for circumstances that will test you and the validity of whatever you are doing.

Very often this crisis occurs in the form of persons who are working at cross-purposes to your efforts. They may or may not oppose you intentionally, but the thrust of their actions forces you to prove that what you are doing is worthwhile. You may be very angry at these people, feeling that they are motivated by nothing but malice. In fact their motives are the same as yours, which you must learn to understand.

On the square three months after your birthday, the challenges may occur in connection with your efforts to build something up, to create a material structure or to get a project going. Or they may occur as a test of some new aspect of your personality that has recently come into being. It is as if some aspect of yourself or your life is struggling to get out into the light, but the world is demanding that this aspect prove itself before being allowed to enter. Both your successes and your failures at this time will bear fruit in about three months, when the Sun transits opposition your natal Sun.

At the square three months before your birthday, you will be challenged in your efforts to complete various projects and to reap their rewards or other consequences. You are already beginning to turn your attention to the next phase of development, even though circumstances are forcefully reminding you that this phase is not over yet. The challenges at this time are often related to events that occurred three months ago, at the Sun's opposition transit to the natal Sun.

Sun Trine Sun

This transit occurs twice a year, about four months before and four months after your birthday. It represents a time of balance and equilibrium in your life, when you can be yourself with the fewest obstacles from people or circumstances. Your energy level will be higher than usual, and you will be able to do whatever you want, either at work or at play, with great zest and energy. In fact this is a perfectly good time to take a vacation, if it is an appropriate time of year for you.

Various affairs in your life will hum along very nicely now, and you may be tempted to think that they will always go this well. But in fact this is the time to firm up your affairs and make sure that they are strong enough to withstand troubles that may come later on. Because the stress level in your life is low now, you can accomplish this with a minimum of difficulty.

On the trine four months after your birthday, you should examine the projects that have worked out well in the last few months and prepare them for a time in the near future when they will reach a critical culmination. Success in these matters is almost at hand, and you should use this time to prepare for it. If you are not ready, whatever success you gain will be wasted.

Also examine any matters that have not worked out so well to see whether you should cut your losses and prepare for a new start. You may have some difficulty in determining which projects are worth saving and which are not, but if you work at it you will be able to tell. Those that are worth saving will feel better subjectively than the others.

On the trine four months before your birthday, you should stop and survey your recent achievements. Decide how you can use them to prepare for the future and find out what you can get out of them that will have lasting value. But don't make the mistake of thinking that your striving is over, because you still have challenges to face.

Also examine those matters that clearly have not worked out. By now you should have made new beginnings in these areas, so you can tell how your new tack is working out. If you haven't taken a new tack, don't waste time with regrets but put all your energies into clearing up the remains and salvaging what you can. The quiet pace of a trine will assist you in this process.

Sun Opposition Sun

This transit occurs six months after your birthday and signifies a time when energies in your life are reaching a culmination. Now is the time to try to bring your affairs to a climax, but do not expect to escape opposition from other people, for others have ambitions that may be in conflict with yours. Be particularly careful with superiors and persons in authority. If you are not careful, you may provoke their opposition, which would be difficult to withstand.

You may find it difficult to make everything work out right, but if you have prepared properly for this time, you will succeed. You must avoid feeling smug, arrogant and superior. These attitudes just might undo all the progress you have made until this time.

Sometimes this can be a time of failure, when you realize that certain efforts have not worked out and that you must start over. But failures at this time should not be the occasion for feeling defeated. Instead you should feel that a "life experiment" has not worked out. With the information you have gained, you can launch a whole new enterprise that will avoid the flaws of the one that failed. Very often the failure itself has occurred several months earlier, but the truth about it has just become clear to you now, so this is the time when you are most likely to become discouraged. This may result in a period of low energy, although sometimes the "failure" may be manifested only as a state of tension leading to fatigue.

Psychologically speaking, events now take place in such a way as to make your individual life stand out in relief against your surroundings and other people. Thus the transit can serve to heighten consciousness and self-awareness. All kinds of personal interaction are extremely important now, and you will gain nothing by withdrawing from others. You probably won't even be able to.

Even with those aspects of your life that have been working out well and are now reaching a climax, you are not yet past the critical point. To achieve is one thing, but to incorporate these achievements into your life and make them part of your personal growth is something else. You have built structures and organized your life in various ways, and now you will experience the consequences of these structures as they begin to react and influence your life. Yet you still have the creative power to determine how your own creations will recreate you.

Sun Conjunct Moon

This transit brings your personal, domestic and emotional life to prominence. All the symbolic power of the solar energy is infused into your emotions, bringing them to the surface where you can observe and learn to understand them. But you needn't worry; this transit will not be especially turbulent. In fact you will feel more integrated and at one with yourself in many ways now than at any other time. And your relationships with other people, especially women, should be more harmonious as well. This is because you approach everything as a total person, with no loose ends hanging out to signify divided intentions.

The only problems with this manifestation will arise if you are afraid of your feelings. Then this transit can be turbulent and uncomfortable, for you will be confronting an aspect of yourself that you do not like. But disliking your emotions is the problem, not the emotions themselves. If you find this transit disturbing, you should examine your attitude toward your emotions. Chances are it is not a very healthy attitude, and you are missing out on a part of life that could make you feel more alive.

This transit will bring out all your unconscious attitudes, so take a long look at what comes up today. This can be a time of great discovery.

On a more practical level, this is a good day to consider your personal life, domestic situation and close family relationships. Events today will bring them into focus. You might want to make some changes, from something as simple as rearranging your furniture to having a long talk with a loved one about making changes in your relationship. This is a time of new beginnings in your inner life, a sort of personal "new Moon." All these areas of your life are in a state of flux, so it is easier to make changes now than at any other time of the year. (This transit always occurs at the same time of year.)

Don't pay so much attention to getting ahead in life just now. The areas of your life that are ruled by the Moon can actually make or break all your other efforts, because they are related to the deepest and most fundamental roots of your existence. If there is weakness here, there will be weakness everywhere, however much you try to ignore the fact. But if the innermost parts of your psychological being and your personal life are together and well ordered, not very much can really disturb you.

Sun Sextile Moon

This is a time of psychological and emotional equilibrium, when the different aspects of your personality are in tune with each other. You can face your daily life with less effort than usual, which is bound to have some consequences in your material universe as well.

Relations with friends and close neighbors will be very harmonious, and you may make some new friends. People will be at ease with you today because you are at ease with yourself. The routine discussions, negotiations and transactions of everyday existence will offer no obstacles.

Obviously this is a good time to be with others, if at all possible. Have friends come to your house — your home life will be more peaceful and serene than usual, and you may want to share this mood.

Relations with the opposite sex are also smoother than usual. Everyone carries within themselves an ideal image of the opposite sex, which is symbolized by the sign and aspects of the Sun, in women's charts, and the sign and aspects of the Moon, in men's charts. The sextile between the Sun and Moon, being a harmonious aspect, creates harmony between men and women as well as within yourself. Friendships and love affairs can result, although a major love affair would require additional impetus from another transit.

This is an especially good time to think about your personal and emotional life. Strains in that area can be corrected now, because you are relatively at peace with yourself and with others, and communications about personal matters should be easy. If you choose to avoid confronting these problems now, when it is relatively easy, you will have more serious confrontations later that will be more difficult. This is especially true if the transiting Sun is separating from the natal Moon in longitude. If the transiting Sun is approaching the natal Moon, confrontations are not quite so important, because you are basically taking a rest now, reaping the consequences of your immediate past actions and preparing for a new cycle of activity in your personal and domestic life. However, it would still be a good idea to examine yourself.

Sun Square Moon

This can be a rather tense time, but it also has the potential for much stimulation. If you have been bottling up pressures from your job, your home, your family or any other source, they will become very difficult to bear now, especially if you have not been willing to face them in the recent past. Your conscious actions may be impulsive and ill-thought-out today, as your emotions come into conflict with your conscious will.

In facing your problems, you may feel that you are split into two personalities who are working at cross-purposes to each other. One of these "persons" you can readily understand. It is your conscious personality, the one that you recognize as "yourself." If you were to describe yourself to someone else, this is the personality you would describe. But you have another personality, which appears in your unconscious compulsions, unbidden emotions and habits. Other people can see this side of you without difficulty, but you are usually unaware of it. This personality is not negative, it is only different from the more conscious part of you. The first personality is represented by the Sun, either natal or transiting, while the second is represented by the Moon. The square between the transiting Sun and natal Moon is expressed as irritability, proneness to upset or excessive emotionalism.

Unfortunately, this inward turmoil can also affect your outer world adversely. Aside from the obvious problems that can arise if you are too touchy with everyone, there are also problems arising from the more external aspects of this symbolism. For example, the Sun rules authority figures. You may react against bosses and other authority figures in a completely emotional way and have great difficulty dealing with them. Or your home life may be unusually upsetting today, with members of your family quarreling with each other or with you.

When this happens, you should try to find out whether you have been avoiding a problem that has brought about this situation. Days like this may be annoying, but they do bring hidden tensions out into the open so that you can do something about them, hopefully. However, it might not be a bad idea to let the dust settle first.

But this transit is not necessarily so difficult, depending on how well you have been handling your emotions. If you are in good shape emotionally, this can be an energizing transit that gives you both the emotional drive and the physical energy to get moving. Whatever you do under this influence will be done with complete emotional conviction as well as strong intentions. Remember, the source of most people's problems with this transit is keeping the balance between your will and your emotions so that you can operate consciously and also be involved in what you do. If you can keep this balance, you will act with great conviction.

Sun Trine Moon

Like the sextile, the trine transit of the Sun to the Moon is a time of inner peace and balance. You have the serenity to look into yourself and come to a deeper understanding of what you want, what you need and how you should go about getting it. Under this influence your approach to life is balanced. You try to live through your feelings as well as your intellect, and you communicate with others at both levels. Since you understand your own moods and feelings so well today, you are also in a good position to assist others in understanding themselves. Through your relationships, particularly those with the opposite sex, you will come to know yourself better than at most other times.

Since this is a time of balance and equilibrium, you should study your personal life and find out what you need to do to correct any misunderstandings and difficulties with other people that have created tensions between you. Today you are able to make the compromises necessary to getting along with others.

A trine formed by the transiting Sun separating from the natal Moon indicates that you should prepare any areas of your life that are approaching a climax. Soon you will be in a period of creative tension when the pressures will be so great that it will be difficult to evaluate the situation and make changes that will help everything work more smoothly. So make these changes now, when you're feeling calm.

If the transiting Sun is approaching the natal Moon, you have just passed a period of climax and tension, and you are in a good position to evaluate what has happened, its meaning and consequences for you. Use this time to take inventory and begin preparations for the future, when you will have to incorporate what you have learned into your innermost life. If the last few months have been a period of breakdown rather than creative climax, learn how to pick up the pieces and make a new start, particularly with events in your personal life.

Friendships and love relationships that start under this transit will have important consequences for your future life and may have a strong effect on your attitudes toward life in general.

Sun Opposition Moon

This may be a tense day, but it is an important one. Events today may show how well you cope with the daily and routine aspects of your life and how well you can use your inner energies to make your life work as you want it to.

You will probably encounter tension today between your personal needs and your public and professional duties. You may feel that you are being pulled in two different directions that are almost impossible to pursue simultaneously. Events that happen today emphasize the polarity in your life, so that you have to distinguish continually between "myself" and "them," subjective and objective, conscious intention and unconscious impulses, public and private. At its worst, this transit can be quite difficult, and you may feel as though everything were breaking down. The degree of difficulty depends upon how much you have deemphasized emotion and feeling in favor of rational intellect. If you are out of touch with your inner self, this day will become very tense.

On the other hand, this can also be a day of high energy and achievement. If you have been unified in purpose, that is, if your feelings and your conscious intentions have taken the same direction, this will be a day of successful endeavor.

Your personal life, especially relationships with your spouse and family, are the areas where tensions may become particularly heavy. You may act under emotional compulsions that cause you to react to others in a way that you do not understand. If you have this problem, it may be quite difficult explaining to yourself and others what happened today.

Your emotional nature will come out in one way or another. If you have been in touch with your feelings and made them part of your normal dealing with the world, you will go through the day with a feeling of complete unity. You will live in your guts and emotions as well as in your conscious mind.

Sun Conjunct Mercury

This transit emphasizes the areas of your life ruled by Mercury. There are several of these areas, and which you emphasize most depends upon your personal nature. First of all, you are likely to have many more conversations with people. Certainly this is an opportunity to get your point of view across to others, and you may be more inclined to talk than to listen, because like all conjunctions, this one makes you take the initiative and start things. You may be much more involved in sending or receiving letters. This is also a good time to take care of routine paperwork, because your mind will be clearer than usual and you should have little difficulty concentrating.

This is an excellent day for starting a new business venture. Mercury rules commerce and favors the rapid interchange of ideas and plans that is necessary in business activity. Here again you will be helped by the sharpness of mind conferred by this transit.

The nature of this transit makes you most concerned with matters that apply directly to yourself or that speak to you through your personal experience. You are more involved in examining yourself, stating your position with respect to others and anouncing your intentions than in examining the world. You are the active agent with respect to the world at large. You initiate communication, you talk to others and you express your point of view. Nevertheless, it is important to have a thorough understanding of the people and conditions you live with. Being excessively involved in yourself and your own ideas will weaken the effectiveness of what you do today. If your mind is filled with only your own thoughts, intentions and what you plan to say, you will miss important cues from others concerning your own plans.

This is a good time to make plans for the future. You have a good understanding of your needs now, and you can plan intelligently to achieve what you want, as long as you aren't too preoccupied with yourself.

You may also travel today, for an activated Mercury creates a restless tension within you that makes you want to move around. Try to go out and experience as much of the world as possible; you will be able to take in quite a bit.

Sun Sextile Mercury

This will be a very favorable day for all kinds of communications and personal interchange with others. Even routine connections with friends and neighbors will be very fruitful, for you will be able to get through to each other with greater clarity.

This is an excellent day for communicating something important to another person, in which it is necessary to be precisely clear. If you have to present the views of a group and your ideas must be in tune with theirs, this will be a favorable time.

But this is also a good day to examine your own goals and expectations. How well are you working to attain them? Can you change your tactics if necessary? What kind of aid can you enlist from others? People may give you opportunities and assistance without your requesting it, but you will have to recognize the value of these opportunities and be quick enough to take them up. This transit favors all types of commercial transactions, buying and selling or negotiating deals favorably.

Today is fine for traveling for any purpose, although you will be best served if it stimulates your mind or has an educational purpose. For example, it is good for going to a museum or for attending a concert or lecture. This is an excellent transit for all kinds of study, because you are alert and ready to receive all types of input.

Sun Square Mercury

This will be a mentally active day for you, because ideas and communications will come at you very quickly, and you will have to understand not only the surface communication but also the underlying meaning. In talking with others, be particularly aware of any hints they may drop about their motivations. This transit tends to produce interactions with others that test the clarity of your thinking and force you to prove the validity of what you say.

As with most squares, there is the potential here for conflict with people who are not actually opposed to your intentions, but who unknowingly have taken a position that conflicts with yours. Now is a good time to listen to others and find out how to reconcile possible conflicts. Also find the weak points in your own thinking and make whatever corrections are necessary. This is not the time to assume blindly that you know wherein all truth lies. Try not to be overwhelmed by the power of your own thought. It would be a good idea to be self-critical now, before others get the chance to tear your ideas apart. Avoid becoming totally wrapped up in your own concerns.

What you do today will serve to make people aware of your ideas and opinions. If you present them competently now, you will be able to handle the situation later when others really challenge your position. Like all squares, this one is a time of testing.

But you will have a lot of mental energy today, and you will be able to present yourself forcefully if you have to. You certainly will not consider this a boring day. Unless your thinking and communications are very poorly thought out, you should be able to accomplish whatever you set out to. The only problem that should concern you is the possibility of arousing opposition to your purposes and ideas that could become very intense later on. That is why it is so important to listen as well as to put forth your ideas.

Sun Trine Mercury

Under this transit you can increase your understanding of yourself and your goals, as well as of others and their goals. Certainly this is the time to communicate to others anything that is important to you. Your mind is functioning clearly now, and you should be able to get your point across. But you are not concerned with just making your own point, you are also genuinely interested in the other person's point of view. You are aware that your thinking and ideas have made an impact on others, and you want to find out how you have affected them.

This is a good time for all kinds of studying and learning. Your mind is quick and receptive, and you are eager to expand your knowledge in any area you encounter. You can put this curiosity and eagerness to know to your advantage, and you will quickly discover that the more you understand about a situation, the better able you will be to handle any problems that arise.

Your mind is relatively tranquil now, which makes this a good time to look over your general situation and make any necessary adjustments. Your present clarity of thinking and ability to see the overall picture makes it easy to understand everything you need to know about yourself.

This is an excellent transit for beginning a trip for recreational or business purposes, especially the latter.

Sun Opposition Mercury

This transit is a powerful stimulus to the mind and to all kinds of communication and interchange with others. You will be engaged in an almost continuous dialogue with others today, which should tell you exactly how you stand with respect to them and how they are reacting to you. This is not the time to tell everyone about yourself or your views, unless you also listen carefully to them. It is extremely important that you be receptive to anything that is presented to you. If your thinking is dominated by concern with yourself and your own position, to the point that you cannot hear what anyone else is saying, this is likely to be a day of argument and unconstructive dispute. But if you are receptive, you will be able to learn much. At the same time you can promote your own ideas by making it clear to others that your ideas are not a threat to theirs and that you are willing to work with them as a team.

Sometimes it is not possible to be compromising, however, and only an out-and-out confrontation will suffice. The trick that you must master is to know when this is really true. You may want to think that it is time for a confrontation when it is not. Above all else, objectivity is important now.

Normally this is not a time to go off in a new direction. What is happening is that you are learning the results of the directions you have taken previously. If it becomes clear that they have not worked out, plan new strategies, but don't put them into practice just yet. Wait until all the results are in.

Sometimes under this transit you may have to consult another person to get a clear picture of what is happening in your life. Needless to say, this will be useful only if you are completely willing to listen to what he or she has to say and can disregard your own point of view for a while. Look at your life as it is, not as you would like it to be. You should be able to obtain valuable information in this regard today.

You may have to travel about quite a bit under this transit, probably for business rather than for pleasure.

On the physical level, try to avoid situations that make excessive demands on your nervous energies. You will exhaust yourself quite easily and get keyed up and over-wrought about nothing.

Sun Conjunct Venus

The central issue today is self-expression through creativity and relationships. You will be assertive, but only in order to gain the attention of those whom you love or would like to love. You want people to pay attention to you, and you are willing to give love and attention in return. Sometimes this transit can bring a new love interest into your life.

This is a good time to get out and socialize, to make new contacts and friendships. You will attract people today, because you put so much personal energy into being warm and friendly, and others are bound to respond to you. If you feel like having a party, this is a good transit for it. The attractive power of Venus may bring you money and material possessions as well as friends. This is usually a favorable transit for all kinds of financial activities, but you should be careful not to be extravagant or self-indulgent. You could easily fritter your money away on impulse purchases that don't really mean that much to you.

This brings us to the only negative effect of this transit, which is for the most part very pleasant and gratifying. But there is a tendency to luxuriate and to be excessively indulgent now. You may flatter yourself that you are the most fascinating and interesting person in the world, which will only make others think that you are a vain fool. This attitude is not likely to have any unpleasant consequences now, but it could in months to come.

You should try to surround yourself with as much beauty and art as possible today. You have a greater than usual appreciation for beautiful objects, and you will get real benefit from them, as long as you don't overdo on buying things. Your physical health and vitality should be above average today.

Sun Sextile Venus

You feel good today and affectionate toward just about everyone around you. You should spend time with friends and even try to make new ones, if the opportunity arises. Think about your relationships and appreciate exactly how much love you give to and receive from others. If there are tensions in any of your relationships, this is a good time to work at smoothing them over.

Probably you will be quite popular today, and you should use the positive energies you are putting out to make a good impression on the people you want to impress. However, don't be phony about it, because you will not be very effective in the long run. The point is that the good impression you make will be because of the person you actually are, not the person you think others want you to be.

Friendships will be quite important to you, and opportunities of some sort may arise from a friendship today. But even more important, you need the love and reinforcement that only a friend can give, and you will be able to return these feelings to your friend. You will fit in well with a group and feel that their interests are yours, for you are not inclined to be especially individualistic now.

Work to remove unpleasantness in your immediate surroundings today by beautifying your home, your neighborhood or some other part of your environment.

This is a good transit for most financial matters, especially for negotiating new financial arrangements for a project that has already been begun. Firm up any loose financial situations in your life.

Sun Square Venus

This is not a typical square transit in that it is usually quite pleasant and easy to handle. The dynamic influence of the square makes you actively seek out pleasure, beauty, love and harmony. But you will probably not feel especially aggressive, because under the influence of Venus you may prefer to take it easy. Certainly you will avoid conflict as much as possible.

The positive side of this transit is that you will feel quite loving and affectionate to almost everyone around you. There may even be a new love relationship. Or you may feel like doing creative work, perhaps arts or crafts.

The negative side of this transit is that you may be inclined to seek self-gratification in excess, that is, in a total undisciplined manner, or you may seek it at the expense of a loved one. This is not one of the more serious or difficult transits, but it can reveal hidden strains within your relationships and show you where you need to make some changes. The problem is that you probably won't feel like doing anything that requires much effort today, so perhaps you should wait until you are in a more active mood. Avoid spending money to gratify foolish whims or momentary desires. You may have regrets in more sober moments.

Be careful also of a tendency toward passivity, sitting around and waiting for something to happen or for someone else to take the first step. With the attractive power of Venus stimulated by the transiting Sun, you hope that things will come to you without any effort. This may happen, but what comes may not be worth much. However, unless terribly severe demands are being made on you, today will be very enjoyable, easy, relaxed and pleasant. This is a good day for enjoying yourself.

Sun Trine Venus

This is a very positive transit, which makes you feel good physically and emotionally. It symbolizes your desire for complete self-expression through creative activity, love and good times. The influence of this transit is so light-hearted that you will find it difficult to get involved in any serious projects. If you don't have to work today, just enjoy yourself. This is a recreational transit.

You will have great sensitivity to beauty today and an appreciation of lovely and well-made objects. This is a good transit for buying clothing and art objects or for planning to redecorate your home. You have a strong desire to gratify your senses, but not to the point of being compulsive or foolish about spending. If you spend a lot of money on something that you want, the chances are it will be a good investment. In fact the best purchases to make today would be objects that will increase in value as they get older, such as jewelry or antiques.

Your relationships should be very positively affected by this transit, and you might even start a new romantic interest. However, it is much more likely that you will have a good time with someone with no long-range consequences.

You will be very affectionate, possibly even romantic, with the loved ones in your life, even if your relationship has gone beyond the romantic stage, as often happens in a marriage. This is a good time to smooth out any difficulties you are having with another person, because he or she will see that you have no interest in scoring points, that you only want peace between you.

This is a good day to go out with friends and have a good time. If you choose to be alone, you will feel very lonely.

Sun Opposition Venus

This transit brings all relationships into focus. Usually it is a rather easy and pleasant time, but it can release the hidden tensions in your relationships and force them out into the open where you will have to deal with them.

This transit signifies that you will encounter yourself through your different relationships. The good ones will remain good, but the bad ones will become unstable and difficult. If you study your reactions and your handling of these situations, you should learn a great deal about yourself.

In particular you may notice that you don't want to be alone and that you cannot operate without a close relationship with a lover, a friend or even someone whom you consult about a problem. Today is a good day to talk to another person, perhaps a counselor, about anything that is on your mind. You should not try to go it alone today; instead you should try, through everyone you meet, to learn more about how you operate with people. This transit is about consciousness, the awareness of relationship.

Its effects can range from relatively insignificant to highly significant, depending on a lot of background conditions that cannot be taken into consideration here, such conditions as are symbolized by outer-planet transits.

In your personal relationships, this transit should make you very aware of how much you need your loved ones. Usually this is a good transit in that you feel much love and tenderness toward those close to you. It is difficult only if there are problems that you haven't handled very well.

Sun Conjunct Mars

This is an excellent day for starting a new project, particularly one that you can work on by yourself, without having to take orders or coordinate other people's actions. You feel very vigorous and have a high level of physical energy, so you really need to be physically active today. One of the worst ways to handle this transit is to work quietly at a desk. You would quickly become itchy and irritable as your repressed energies try to find an outlet. Mental work will not be satisfactory unless it involves a great deal of physical activity as well.

It is important that you can identify with whatever you do today. Your ego energies are high, and you demand to be recognized as an individual. If you are not given this recognition, you are likely to become angry and easily involved in disputes. There is no question that unless you are totally occupied, you will be much more irritable than usual today. Other people may find you quite disruptive, which could get you into trouble with your employer or other persons in authority.

But the burst of energy within you today is useful and can be used for creative expression as well as for less constructive purposes. This transit can help you find out whether you are satisfied with your life situation and how you feel about yourself. The more insecure you are, the more likely you are to express this transit in a negative way.

Along with the tendency toward arguing, you should be careful of another form of excess energy. This energy can be expressed physically through accidents or illnesses. Inflammations, infections and fevers are characteristic of the physical action of Mars. Accidents occur if you act on reckless impulses to release energy that is not being expressed adequately through what you are doing. Be careful of sharp metal objects and machinery.

Sun Sextile Mars

This is an excellent time for accomplishing all kinds of work. Your energy is high, and you have faith in your ability to achieve. Usually your health is quite good now, and this influence is extremely favorable for all kinds of physical activity. In fact it would be very bad not to be physically active, because these energies must have an outlet. If they do not, they can cause problems even when they are basically positive, as with this transit.

You are able to work well with others now too, because your ego energies are well balanced, so you can derive personal satisfaction and gratification through group activity. At other times, others may be a threat to your security and sense of well-being, but that is not the case now. In fact you may have to work in a group in order to be most effective.

Nevertheless you are in a self-assertive mood today. If you have to fight with someone to maintain your position in any matter, you will be able to do it effectively. You are not inclined to back down, although you will seek out a common ground where the two of you can agree, if there is any.

You may unknowingly create for yourself an opportunity to take control or authority over others, to be a leader or director. Keep in mind that under this transit you will derive the most satisfaction through expressing the needs and desires of the people you work with. This is not the time to go off on a purely personal tangent. That opportunity will come shortly, as the Sun moves toward opposition with your natal Mars.

Sun Square Mars

This is a day when you will have to be very conscious of yourself and your motivations. You are likely to have serious ego conflicts with others today, especially if you allow your actions to be dictated by subconsciously motivated energies. As with all squares, this transit tests the validity of a position that you took or a statement that you made, either literally or figuratively, about six months ago. Circumstances as well as other people will be looking for chinks in your armor, flaws in your preparation, errors to challenge you with. If you consciously know what you are doing, you will be better prepared to handle that challenge as well as your experience of your own energies.

Your energy level will be high, perhaps too high if you are not careful. Watch for signs of irritable impatience with others whenever things do not go exactly as you planned.

Be assertive only when the situation calls for it, not whenever you feel like it. Also watch out for baseless conflicts with others, which you may not necessarily instigate yourself. The effects of any transit may be projected, that is, they may seem to originate with someone else. In this case you may not feel at all belligerent, but nevertheless you are attracting belligerence from others.

Because the Sun indicates persons or structures that are centers of energy, power and authority, you should be particularly careful of conflicts with authorities. Voice your complaints if they are legitimate, but expect a certain amount of hostile reaction to them. Also be careful that the tone of your complaint does not aggravate this hostility. What you get is usually a function of the energies that you put out.

On the physical level, try to find an outlet for your vigorous energies. Do something that requires a lot of hard work and gives your aggressions a satisfactory outlet. Frustrated personal energies can lead to illness or accidents if the energy turns inward. In fact if you feel no aggressive energies at all under this transit, you ought to be concerned, because you have probably sublimated the energy and may experience it through illness or accident. Or you may have projected it, so that you attract angry and difficult people. If used consciously and intentionally, this energy is positive and can help you accomplish considerable work and establish yourself in any position you want.

Sun Trine Mars

Today you will find it easy to be yourself. However, you should work alone and for your own benefit. It is not that you are feeling hostile or resentful of others becoming involved in your work, but that you do not want to be dependent upon others for support or encouragement.

Since you feel physically vigorous under this influence, physical activity is recommended, not only because it is good for your body, but because it also reinforces your mind and spirit at this time.

Your life is no doubt filled with projects that you have begun at various times. You may not always be aware of their significance, and you may be acting quite unconsciously in some ways, but these projects are important nevertheless. Now is a good time to take stock of them and to examine what state they are in. Or if you are not clear about what you are doing, try to find out. What motivates you? What are you trying to accomplish? In the near future you will have confrontations, so the more you understand about what you are doing, the better. Decide what projects you are trying to bring to a climax soon, or what you have accomplished recently when there was a climax. You should strive not only to be yourself, but also to know who "yourself" is.

If you must make new beginnings in your life to adjust imbalances that have developed, this is the time to do it. Otherwise put most of your energy into firming up the activities you are presently involved in. Look to your own criteria and needs rather than to other people's and try to make them work meaningfully in your life.

Sun Opposition Mars

This is a time of critical culminations, when many activities and projects will come to a climax in your life. Now it will become clear whether you have conducted these activities skillfully and intelligently. It is particularly important that you have worked with complete knowledge and understanding of what you were trying to accomplish. A Mars-Sun transit is most disruptive when the ego energies aroused by it are allowed to operate at an unconscious level. When they do, your actions are characterized by a blindly self-assertive energy that only arouses opposition from others. Sometimes your response takes the form of irritability and small aggressive actions against others, which weaken your relations with them.

Even under the best of circumstances, you will confront others at this time. They may be teammates, people whom you have won over to your well-thought-out and planned position, or they may be opponents who are fighting you in order to maintain their position. Any position that you have taken or "ego-statement" you have made will be sharpened and refined, or possibly invalidated, by a confrontation with others at this time.

This transit may also increase your self-awareness, because whatever makes you angry today is something that you have identified your ego with. That is, on a very real and practical level you are unconsciously regarding it as part of yourself, and you defend it as you would defend your physical body. Thus your behavior is determined by unconscious identifications that you may not even be aware that you have made. This transit can be this way, if you choose, but it need not be. Notice your anger and irritation and ask yourself what these emotions tell about your attitudes. You may find that what makes you mad is quite unimportant to you, once you recognize it.

For most people the area of greatest unconsciousness in this regard is that of close personal relationships, as with family and spouse. In these relationships you are most likely to experience the negative effects of this transit in the form of arguments and conflict. If you are in such a conflict, look carefully to see what is really at stake, if anything, and try to arrive at a workable compromise.

Yet you must deal with the hostility and aggression that may come with this transit in such a way that your feelings are truly relieved. Do not merely suppress them, for this can cause the energy to turn inward, either in the form of self-destructive behavior that can lead to accidents or, even more subtly, to illness.

Sun Conjunct Jupiter

On the purely mundane level, you will feel very good, physically and psychologically, today. Jupiter combined with the Sun provides optimism and a positive outlook on life. Even at its least constructive, this transit will give you a good day, but you can use this energy in ways that will make it work most positively both today and in the long run.

The symbolism of this transit suggests that, consciously or unconsciously, you want to include as much in your life as possible today. You desire experience and activity.

It will not be enough to stay in exactly the same place you have been. But instead of making you dissatisfied, as might be expected, this desire makes you go after what you want, with complete optimism that you will get it.

On the intellectual level, this transit can signify study or other mind-expanding inquiry. You have a strong desire to understand and know, even about ideas that you normally consider to be beyond your understanding.

On the physical level, you want to have all kinds of new experiences. The thrust of these energies is to broaden your life and enlarge the experience of living.

But just as there are two sides to the Jupiter energy, this transit also has a potential negative side. It can be large-hearted, magnanimous and generous, but it can also be arrogant and domineering, depending on your subconscious orientation to others. If you believe subconsciously that your own personal growth takes place at others' expense, then you will exhibit the negative side of this energy. If you believe that your personal growth comes about through the inclusion of others into your life, you will exhibit the positive side.

The drive to include and incorporate, which is inherent in Jupiter, may lead you to act in excess. That is, you may take on projects that are beyond your ability to handle. It is very important today that you act with a firm sense of discipline and not simply indulge every compulsive whim that comes along. Take on the projects that you can handle plus a little extra, but not very much extra. Handle your resources intelligently and be careful not to invest unwisely because of foolish optimism.

Nevertheless, despite the above warnings, today is likely to be an extremely positive experience with potential for future growth.

Sun Sextile Jupiter

This is an extremely positive transit that will be a useful aid in almost any kind of activity. Traditionally it is one of the transits regarded as "lucky," but actually it gives you the positive frame of mind that is at the root of most success. Almost anything you want to do today should work out as planned, unless there is some overwhelming influence to the contrary from other planets.

This is an excellent day to be with friends. You have a strong desire to be included in something larger than yourself, to participate in group consciousness and activities. Today you are able to work harmoniously with others, because you see that your own benefit is derived from that of the group. This orientation also extends to professional activities; this is an excellent transit for holding group conferences because of your ability to make them run smoothly.

This is also a good time to reflect on your life and to examine your goals and ideals. Your idealism will probably be strong with this transit, but instead of blindly assuming that everything will work out ideally, you should make a general review of your plans for the future, working very carefully toward attaining your ideals. Also you can put all the disparate parts of your life together into a complete picture, so that you can understand the whole.

Your relationship with persons in authority is usually good under this transit. An inner desire to be at one and in tune with the sources of energy in the universe can be expressed on the mundane level as a desire to get along with those in power. This is not usually a self-seeking desire, although with some people it will be. It is a recognition that you can learn something from them, gain more experience and improve the lot of those around you as well as your own.

Sun Square Jupiter

This is an extremely useful square, because it gives you energy to get ahead in almost any way that you desire, provided that you are disciplined and avoid obvious excess.

The difficulty with this transit is that it spurs you on to do more than you can handle, to involve yourself in projects that require more energy than you have or to extend yourself beyond your resources. But this same tendency can lift you to attempt and succeed at tasks you would not usually consider possible, especially if you have been acting rather conservatively. It all depends upon whether you are naturally cautious or naturally overoptimistic and exuberant.

Similarly this transit can make you generous or extravagant, depending upon your previous attitudes. Any tendency that is positive when exercised with restraint will work positively under this influence, and any that is negative when done to excess will be negative.

You can expect some difficulties with other people under this influence, but you should be able to handle them and even win them over to your side, unless you proceed from a position of arrogant self-righteousness. Be very careful to examine the other person's point of view and try to find a common ground for cooperation between you. Unfortunately one of the negative aspects of the Jupiter symbolism is self-righteousness and unwillingness to look at the other's point of view. But Jupiter is also compassionate, and that is the attitude you should work for today.

Sun Trine Jupiter

According to both tradition and modern experience, this is one of the most positive transits. Unless there is some powerful negative influence operating at the same time, this transit assures a day of good feelings, peace and harmony with others. But you should try to use its energy to accomplish something good and useful for yourself. The temptation is to enjoy the good feelings and let the day slip by without paying any special attention. This transit can indicate quite lazy feelings, but to sleep through it, figuratively speaking, would be a waste.

The enthusiasm, optimism and buoyancy associated with this transit will enable you to project energies into the environment that will help your affairs work out as you want. This may appear to be luck, but it is not really. Consciously or unconsciously, in your daily routine you operate with great understanding of the overall patterns, and you act with more foresight and consideration than usual. If you do benefit from "dumb luck," it is a consequence of something you have done in the recent past.

You should use this ability to see your life as a whole, to take stock of what you are doing and to see how it fits your real needs. Because you are in a positive frame of mind, you can make changes in any area of your life without feeling a great sense of loss. So often in our unhappiness, we cling to something we really don't need because we feel insecure.

Your mind is eager for new experience under this influence. Try out new activities; expand your mind; take a trip. Or use this energy to study philosophy or some other broad topic that interests you. You will be very attracted to any subject that helps you understand the workings of the world as a whole. And since you are cognizant of the universal order at some level, this day should go quite well.

Sun Opposition Jupiter

As with all transits by opposition, this one has a double potential. But in this case the positive side is more easily activated than with some other oppositions. Probably you will react to it by feeling quite good. Your mood is cheerful and optimistic, and you may feel as though nothing can go wrong with your world today. Obviously this can have both good and bad points.

All that is necessary for this transit to work well is to avoid going overboard on any matter, but that is precisely what can happen at this time. You may spend too much money, overindulge in luxuries or be wasteful. On the other hand, you may feel courageous enough to do something you have never done before. This transit can really build up your self-confidence, but be sure to stop short of arrogance. Any negative energies that you put out will become the source of conflicts with others. If you overstep your bounds, you will step on other people, and they will tell you so. Leave them alone, and resist the urge to instruct and edify people beyond what they are ready to hear. Even if what you have to say is worthwhile, your manner of presenting it today, unless you are very careful, will detract from its virtue. Your superiors might particularly resent behavior that seems out of place or above your position. You may feel that your actions are justified, and they may be, but do not expect to avoid the consequences as they react to you.

But if you control the tendency to be overweening or self-righteous, you will be able to project positive energies, which can help you considerably. Especially if you are usually rather retiring, others will see you now as a person worthy of respect.

As with other oppositions, this transit signifies energies coming to a head, reaching a culmination in several areas of your life. Your task now is to keep these energies under control and not allow them to run away with you. Do not overextend yourself or make commitments that you cannot keep. If you can do this, you will be able to succeed in many areas of your life.

Sun Conjunct Saturn

On this day you will turn your attention to your duties and responsibilities, to those tasks that you may not want to do but feel that you must in order to fulfill your obligations to others. These duties may be more imagined than real, but unfortunately they are often real. One element of the mastery of life is to be able to tell which are real and which are not. Many people assume that the demands of Saturn will deny you satisfaction and gratification today, but this isn't necessarily so. In fact what you accomplish today may have more lasting significance than could be attained under any other energy. Professional advancement may come under this transit; at the very least you will be most concerned with this dimension of your life. This transit often brings new responsibilities or reminds you of unfinished matters from the past that have to be finished now.

This transit is excellent for all kinds of organizing and planning. You are very concerned with form and order and want to incorporate it into your life as much as possible. This tendency may extend to organizing the people around you as well as ordering the material aspects of your life. You should be careful not to restrict other people unnecessarily.

Physically this transit can signify a time of low energy, which means you should concentrate your energies on the tasks that really must be done. You will have ample energy for those tasks, and if you leave them undone, you are quite likely to feel depressed and dispirited. Even worse, the sense of tasks left undone will press down upon you.

Emotionally, you may find it hard to relate to people under this influence. You feel isolated and alone. Saturn is concerned with objective reality, with real and tangible objects that can be manipulated in practical ways. Everything is distinct and isolated, in contrast to the affective function, through which you relate to others and feel in harmony with them, as symbolized by Venus and the Moon. Do not dwell on feelings of loneliness or depression. Instead, go to work, for that is where your concerns lie today.

Sun Sextile Saturn

This is an excellent transit for getting things done. You are in an orderly state of mind and have a strong sense of self-discipline. You carefully consider every move before acting. You make plans at a very concrete level and insist that it be possible to execute them in the practical universe. You are not interested in idealistic speculations or abstract considerations that cannot be applied in daily life.

All matters relating to work or your profession are favored by this transit, precisely because of your orderly mental state. Any tasks that you do today will be very carefully done with no loose ends. If you have work that requires great concentration or attention to detail, today is the day to do it. It is possible that your serious and attentive attitude to your work will attract the attention of your employer or other persons in authority whom you encounter.

This is also an excellent time to seek advice from an older person or someone whose wisdom and experience you respect. The combination of the Sun and Saturn relates to father figures, that is, people who can give you guidance concerning the larger world. You want to understand as much as possible about what the world expects of you and how you can do your duty.

Obviously this is not the day to relax and have a good time, because you are not in the proper frame of mind. If you don't work, you will spend your time reflecting upon serious matters.

In all of your actions you are willing to defer present gratification and wait until another day for your reward, if any. You are not interested in indulging yourself or wasting time in frivolity. Take advantage of this energy while it lasts, for you will not always feel this disciplined.

Sun Square Saturn

This can be quite a difficult transit, even though it is a short-term one. The problem is not that it is inherently difficult or "unlucky," as many people feel, but that it raises issues that most people find hard to handle. But these are issues that must be handled. The two questions you must resolve are: how much self-gratification do you owe yourself, and what duties and responsibilities do you owe to others? Today will be characterized by conflict between these two poles, duty and self-gratification.

On one hand, today may seem depressing and restrictive. You may want to break out of your rut but find that you cannot, because some barrier is holding you back from going out and being yourself. You may wish that you didn't have to go to work or school or be with people you would prefer not to be with. You feel that circumstances require you to be something other than what you really are, and you resent it. Other people seem to get in your way and interfere with what you are doing. But has it occurred to you to talk to somebody about this, or to ask if you are really required to do what you don't want? Often under this influence we make assumptions without checking whether they are true.

Relations with authority figures are not good under this transit, unless you can convert your impatience with restriction into self-discipline. Usually others are not holding you back; you are holding yourself back. But you may be projecting negative energies onto the people who have power over you, thereby creating difficult times with them.

Physically and psychologically, your energies are low at this time. You may feel that the weight of the world is too heavy, but you don't expect help because you have not asked for it. But remember, you have made that choice yourself. Your experience of life has not forced you to it. You reinforce the very circumstances that make you feel lonely and isolated. What you must do is break out of this vicious circle and take a good look at the world and the people around you. Even though you are having some problems with them today, the situation will improve rapidly.

The events of the day will show up the chinks in your ego structure. The purpose of discouragement is to reveal the weaknesses in your conception of yourself and to show where you must work to gain greater confidence in yourself.

Sun Trine Saturn

This transit signifies a great opportunity to know yourself through your relationship with and effect upon your environment. You are highly disciplined and able to channel all your energies toward any objective you wish to attain. There is a close relationship between who you are and what you do. So take this opportunity to examine your life and the structures you have built into it. Look at your habits, your home situation, your work or anything else that is important to you and find out how they work on a very practical level. Do not try to be abstract or intellectual.

On a more mundane level, this is a good day for work that requires discipline and self-control. You will derive great satisfaction and fulfillment from doing such work. Others may be impressed by your self-denial, but it will seem completely reasonable to you and will meet your needs.

Today you can organize and make an overall plan for the way you would like to order your affairs and then arrange them accordingly. Because you work very thoroughly and meticulously under this influence, your efforts will achieve lasting results. This is also a good time to undertake any intellectual discipline or technique that requires concentration and attention to detail.

Study your surroundings to see what you can conserve. You are bothered by waste and want to make the maximum use of every resource available to you.

Sun Opposition Saturn

Under this influence you will become very conscious of the limitations imposed on you by circumstances and other people. Your task today is to not let yourself be over-whelmed by them. One effect of this transit is a sense of loneliness or inability to communicate with others. You feel that there is a gulf between you and others that you can't possibly cross. What you are experiencing is the real gulf that always exists between people. The problem is that in your present frame of mind, if you aren't careful, you may let it overwhelm you. There is a point beyond which we cannot know each other or experience each other's feelings. But there is no need to let that truth drag you down.

You may not feel this effect psychologically, as described above. Instead you may find that you are actually unable to communicate with people, or that others constantly get in your way and hold you back. There seems to be a real conflict between your need for self-expression and your need for relationships. This may have' a strong effect on your close personal relationships today. Try to find a balance between your needs and your obligations, for neither can be allowed to win out at the expense of the other. If duty wins out to the point of extinguishing all self-expression, so that you do only what is expected, you will feel restless, inhibited and unfilfilled. But if you ignore your obligations and do only whatever you choose, you will be in great conflict with others, which will prevent you from deriving any real satisfaction from your activities. You have to make compromises. If you are honest in expressing your needs to others and ask that they do the same, you should be able to work it out.

Psychologically, the feeling of isolation and loneliness may be the most difficult to handle. Your energies are rather low, and you may not even make the effort to come out of yourself and communicate. But avoid this passive response. Find something rewarding to do that requires concentration. For the present, it might be best not to work closely with others, because your feeling of alienation may interfere with the work.

Sun Conjunct Uranus

Today may be surprising to you, or your actions may surprise others. The second manifestation indicates that you are more in tune with your inner self, because the fundamental meaning of this transit is that you have a strong drive to seek release from your usual routine of activity and consciousness. The everyday patterns of your life will not adequately satisfy your needs today, and you will act in ways that are completely out of accord with your habits. The function of this transit is to introduce the element of liveliness on the everyday level in order to keep your life from settling down into a dreary, lifeless routine.

However, you may not react positively to this transit. Unfortunately, most of us are wedded to our usual routines and normal conditions, and we resent and fear any departure from them, no matter how badly we need it. Consequently you may experience this transit, not as an exciting inner drive to be different but as a time when nothing goes as planned, with many annoying little upsets. Truly a Uranus-Sun combination requires flexibility, but it is a flexibility that you should cultivate.

At its best, this transit can signify a day when every event is electric, exciting and different. In fact you should plan to do something different, rather than waiting for it to come along. But even if you don't plan for it, surprises may crop up.

Uranus is also a planet of rebellion, and if you feel its energies, you may strike out against restrictions that you can no longer bear. This may lead to disputes with others, especially authority figures. Actions directed at breaking free are not a bad thing, as long as you are really trying to liberate yourself, but if this tendency is carried to excess you may be simply headstrong, impulsive and rash. You will find it very difficult to determine whether you are working to give yourself needed freedom or whether you are being unreasonably rash and impulsive. Only you can decide, and you must take the responsibility for your decision. Other people will certainly believe that you are acting rashly.

If you are afraid to express this energy overtly, it can take the sublimated form of impulsive behavior that makes you accident prone. To avoid this, try to be always conscious of your real moods. If you feel jittery, nervous or excited, avoid dangerous situations or activities in which there is heavy potential for accidents.

Sun Sextile Uranus

This transit can make your life today much more interesting, but not in a frightening or terribly disruptive way. In fact this transit will make your everyday encounters much more interesting and allow you to have very illuminating and enlightening experiences·

in the course of your normal routine. Through activities with friends and neighbors, you may encounter new experiences that will give you greater insight into the world around you.

On the mental level this transit serves to stimulate your curiosity and imagination. You feel alert, quick-witted and very lively. You catch on to ideas more quickly than usual, and having caught on at one level you want to proceed to the next. This is an excellent day to participate in any creative intellectual activity.

On another level, you will find it relatively easy to act freely today. You are not very tolerant of restrictions under this influence, and you will look for ways to get away from them. As a result, you are not very self-disciplined, but this is not a serious loss, because whatever you do now is more important than keeping your "nose to the grindstone." You feel that keeping your individuality is more important than living up to other people's expectations, and you let others know this. This is ultimately to your advantage, since you must be yourself in whatever you do.

Use this influence to make changes in your immediate surroundings. Chances are, your situation has become too ordered and static anyway. Reform the elements in your life that need to be reformed. This is an aspect of creative change.

Sun Square Uranus

This can be a somewhat disruptive transit, during which you are subject to sudden upsets or to behavior that is upsetting to others. Under this influence it is quite likely that you will not follow your normal routine as on other days. This disruption could be an automobile breaking down unexpectedly, a sudden argument or an unexpected separation from someone. The main point is that you can expect the unexpected today.

Relationships with others may be difficult today, either because you have difficulty in contending with the restrictions others place on you, or because they have difficulty contending with the restrictions you place upon them. This transit can indicate ego conflicts and disagreements.

As with other Uranus-Sun energies, you are striving to break down your everyday routine, and it would be best to find ways of doing this intentionally, rather than waiting for it to happen. Let the restless spirit within you express itself. You need new air! You may very well discover a valuable aspect of yourself that you never knew existed, because you were afraid to let it come out.

Unfortunately there is some danger that you will be accident prone with this transit, if you do not express its energy consciously. Without an outlet, the radical energies within you turn back onto you and set you up for the kind of behavior that leads to an accident. In this case it is important to realize that the accident is not happening to you; rather, you are creating the accident. Express your impulses to do something free, "wild" and different as much as possible without making a total shambles of your life. Do not expect to be able to contend with the everyday grind in a disciplined and patient manner. Nor will you be able to put up with other people patiently. Instead, find out what is really bothering you and whether you can make changes in your life that will eliminate these factors.

Sun Trine Uranus

This is an excellent transit for engaging in new activities and for making discoveries about yourself and the world around you. Your life now has an exciting quality that is not always present. Take advantage of this excitement to learn about yourself in ways that are not usually possible. Your heightened perception of your world will help you make changes with a complete understanding of how the various parts of your life are interrelated.

No aspect of yourself is hidden today, for you are quite frank about who you are. The people around you will see that you are much more interested in being yourself, and your liveliness will attract others.

This is a good transit for studying any discipline that can reveal new and stimulating aspects of the universe. It favors the study of science, technical disciplines, astrology or other branches of the occult. You want to broaden your understanding, and the more exciting your study, the more actively you will pursue it. Therefore this influence is not so good for any routine drill that requires great discipline. It would be better to take up a new field altogether. Days when Uranus is less prominent in your life will be better for the more disciplined, intensive kinds of study.

This is not a good time to sit around and relax, for you will be too energetic and restless. Use that energy as it is intended, to expand your life and experience through new encounters.

Sun Opposition Uranus

All one-to-one encounters and close intimate relationships will be occasions for surprising events today. Exactly what will happen is hard to say, except that it will be quite different from the norm, whatever your norm may be.

For example, in a close relationship as with your spouse, one or the other partner may be extremely restless. In this case, there is something in the relationship that one of you is impatient with and unwilling to put up with. This feeling may lead to an argument. Or perhaps one of you will do something radically different and startling that will disrupt the relationship or force you to encounter a new aspect of it. In a business or professional partnership, you may have to make a radical revision because of some unexpected factor.

The Uranian influence can also enter your life through persons you do not know who present you with a surprise or upset. The general function of this transit is to show you that you have not fully considered certain elements of your interaction with the world. These elements are related to parts of yourself that you have not adequately expressed before. Take heed of the restless feelings within yourself, and try to find out what it is that you want. It doesn't matter whether or not it is practical to go after it. All you need to do now is to determine what you want. Later you can deal with the question of whether it is attainable.

As with other Uranus-Sun contacts, if the energies involved are not allowed conscious expression, they may come out through accident-prone behavior.

Sun Conjunct Neptune

This transit has two distinct sides, and it is very difficult to know in advance which will be more prominent. Therefore you should examine both possibilities and watch for one, the other or even both to surface.

First of all, this transit greatly stimulates your awareness, often in ways that are difficult to understand rationally. You are more sensitive to other people, and you seem to know how they feel intuitively. At the same time, you are more concerned with their benefit and less with your own. Something about this transit enables you to identify with other people so much that you are more concerned for them than you are for yourself. It is as if you became them somehow. Therefore this transit is good for any activity in which you help people, whether as an individual or through an institution or charity.

A related effect of this transit is that it may arouse your interest in occult and spiritual activities. You are more concerned now about the deeper truths hidden behind the appearances of the everyday world.

But unfortunately this transit also has a difficult side. The ego-denying quality that enables you to identify with and help others may also manifest itself as a feeling of psychological weariness and inability to cope with the world. You may want to flee the everyday universe and go off into some private world of your own. A relatively harmless manifestation of this is daydreaming, but it can also surface as a full-scale effort to evade reality. Avoid taking drugs or alcohol under this transit, for you may find it difficult to control your use of them. Also your body is much more sensitive than usual, and you may react badly to drugs, even prescribed drugs. Allergies can kick up with this transit.

If you feel the need to withdraw from routine confrontation with the real world, you would get the most benefit from going off by yourself to meditate or contemplate.

Sun Sextile Neptune

This transit enables you to sense energies in the people and circumstances around you more keenly than usual. You are more aware of others' needs and more willing to help them out. This is because the Neptune-Sun combination lowers the demands of your own ego and makes it easier to receive input from other people. Others will be aware of your receptivity, and friends and neighbors may ask you for assistance. But you will not find this irksome, because service to others is a satisfactory form of self-expression for you now. You want to do it and you will do it. Consequently you may become involved in charitable activities or in working for the underprivileged or other disadvantaged persons.

Spiritual and mystical concerns are likely to claim your attention much more than usual. Today it is not enough to understand what something is; you also have to know what it means. This is an excellent day to withdraw from your normal routine and meditate upon the concerns that are important to you. Your physical energy level may be somewhat lowered, so it is not the best day to begin some colossal new effort. On other days you will feel more energetic. Use this day to gain greater understanding and to improve your spiritual well-being.

Sun Square Neptune

Your energy level may be decidedly lower than usual today, even to the point that you feel tired and unable to handle the normal demands of your everyday life. If this happens, do not be concerned. It is simply a sign that your body needs the day off. Take it easy if you can, and certainly, if you know of this transit in advance, don't put off until today any task that you can do some other time.

The effect can also be psychological; that is, you will tend to feel discouraged and beaten down by circumstances. Again do not take this mood seriously, for it is just a passing phase. However, these feelings should make it clear that this is not a good day for work that requires great self-confidence and courage. You just won't have it. And if you do take on an ambitious project, you may later discover that your objectives were totally unrealistic and impossible to attain.

Sometimes your feelings of inadequacy or futility may tempt you to avoid direct confrontations with people and even to take more devious courses of action than usual. The responsibility for such tactics lies directly on your head, so don't be surprised if they work against your best interests. You are probably not clear-headed enough to pull off a convincing deception. Also it is important to be careful about exactly what others tell you, for they might try to deceive you as well.

It is possible that this transit will stimulate your innate idealism, which is by no means bad and could produce a beautiful moment in your life today. But it could also make you want to reach for unrealizable goals, which is particularly discouraging in view of the low energies you probably feel. Use your common sense even about ideals, and above all, deal with the real world as it is, not as you would like it to be. You can work to make it what you want, but don't assume that it already is. Don't be discouraged by the gap between your ideals and reality.

Sun Trine Neptune

This transit arouses your inner idealism and gives you a strong desire to understand a deeper, more spiritual level of reality, both emotionally and intellectually. It is a good time to go off by yourself to think or meditate. Try to use today to get a clearer idea of where you are in your life and how well you have fulfilled your spiritual and material needs. It is a good day for quiet study, especially of metaphysical or spiritual subjects.

In various ways your ideals will be appealed to today. Someone may request your help, or you may be called upon to work for others, with no direct or immediate benefit to you except for the satisfaction of doing good work. A kind of idealistic romanticism may be a factor in your relationships today, which is perfectly all right if it enables you to experience beauty. But do not let your idealism convince you that your loved ones are any more than ordinary humans. You are inclined to give way to others' demands and to put your own needs in second place. Make certain that the persons for whom you do this are worthy of your self-sacrifice.

On another level entirely, this transit can increase your sensitivity to the subtler aspects of the world around you. Under certain conditions it can bring on a flash of ESP or some other mystical experience. Certainly any type of religious experience will be heightened by this transit.

Sun Opposition Neptune

This may be a day of considerable confusion and uncertainty. On the other hand, you may gain new awareness of and sensitivity to others and their needs and how they relate to your own. But be on the lookout for several pitfalls.

Your encounters with others today may be demoralizing or confusing. Your ego energies are not very high, and you are not in a self-assertive mood for vigorous competition. If someone comes at you aggressively, your natural inclination today is to avoid the confrontation. You might withdraw, or pretend to agree with the person just to avoid a contest. You are afraid that asserting yourself might accomplish nothing, and this fear may tempt you to act surreptitiously rather than out in the open. Avoid doing that, however, because it will demoralize you further.

This same energy pattern may lead you to surrender to another person, even though you have a perfectly good reason for standing up to him or her. Avoid playing a victim or martyr role under this influence. If you feel that you cannot assert yourself now, put off the confrontation until you have had time to reflect upon it. By that time this transit will have passed. Use this time to reflect on your life.

Relations with others may be confusing, and there may even be outright deception. Certainly this is a poor time to negotiate or make a contractual arrangement. You are simply not clear enough about your own needs to proceed intelligently.

Your relationships may show you a side of yourself or of your partner that is very difficult to understand at this time. Instead of trying to understand it now, reflect on what you have learned, and eventually it will begin to make sense.

At its highest, this transit allows you to experience a spirituality and depth of feeling in relationships that is quite magnificent. You and your partner may find that you have great sympathy and understanding for each other, with the potential for a real "soul-union." However, it would be best not to commit yourself to such a relationship today, because you should have the chance to see it in a different light after this transit has passed. It may be as good as it seems right now, but it may not be. Your power of discrimination in such matters is not at its highest today.

Sun Conjunct Pluto

This transit can have a variety of effects, but in general it indicates intense experiences that do not allow you to stay at the level of surface manifestations. You will really have to get involved in whatever you do today, and the results may be quite powerful. Pluto relates to the forces underlying all experience and leading to fundamental evolutionary changes from within. The inevitable power of these changes produces the major occurrences in the world — growth, evolution, decay and death, as well as rebirth and regeneration. Because this is not a major long-term transit, you are not likely to encounter any of these effects on a terribly profound level but rather as they occur in day-to-day life.

At the practical level, you may be concerned today with repairing something that has broken down, such as an automobile or an appliance. Or you may have to deal with a situation that has broken down to the point that it must change radically in order to continue, even along completely new lines.

You may have to contend with a person who is trying to exert unreasonable power over you today, forcing you to defend your right to do things your way. The person may feel that he or she is doing this for your own good, but that is not usually the case. True Plutonian energy does not manifest itself through someone's ego drives. It is a transpersonal flow of creative or destructive energy.

Under rare circumstances you may come into contact with someone who embodies the Plutonian energies within society, such as a person in power or someone who represents hidden elements of change and/or decay, such as a person living in poverty, a tramp, a criminal, or someone who is associated with a radical movement for social change. Avoid contact with criminals and do not go into areas where you are likely to encounter street crime. Under this transit it is just possible that you might have an unfortunate encounter.

Sun Sextile Pluto

Under this transit you will be able to make changes in your immediate environment and to reform circumstances that you have been unhappily contending with for some time. You should seize any opportunities that come today to wield creative power for the good. However, it is very important to realize that these energies must be used for the improvement of all and the general good. Only incidentally should this power benefit your purely personal ends.

On a very mundane level, this is a good influence for cleaning up a situation that has become disordered and confused, such as cleaning house or even clearing up a difficult personal situation.

Today you will probably have to confront the power of a group or collective that you deal with every day. But the results are not likely to be disadvantageous. You will have to realign your own intentions with the collective intentions of the group — friends, neighbors or business associates — but this will probably work to your advantage.

This transit also signifies a concern with deep thinking, a feeling that the superficial aspects of life are not adequate. You want to get to the bottom of whatever problem you are working on. You will work carefully and investigate with thoroughness and depth, leaving no stone unturned. Subjects such as psychology, the occult, yoga or other techniques of personal transformation will attract you. And they would be good for you at this time.

Sun Square Pluto

This is a day when you may have to encounter and even oppose powerful pressures and forces exerted upon you, both from without and from within. The way you live and exert your energies will be tested today, perhaps forcing you to make radical changes in the areas of your life that you find are not working very well. The best way to use this influence is to let go of old patterns of behavior that today's events demonstrate to be invalid. Holding on to them will only make your life more difficult, and if you give them up, you will have room for the positive creative changes that can take place now. In fact one manifestation of this transit can be a powerful sense of having purged something from your life.

It may be difficult to contend with persons in authority today. They may demand that you be able to account for yourself and your actions. If you can, you will have no serious problems with these people. But they may call you to account for work you have left undone or done poorly. Then again, such persons may give you problems just because they are wielding, and thereby abusing, naked power.

As with other Sun-Pluto combinations, with this one you may have to contend with the breakdown of machines or situations. Anything that tends not to function very smoothly will work very poorly today. It is time to straighten out the situation or fix up the mechanical problem.

You will derive satisfaction from those aspects of yourself that prove themselves by being challenged today. These are the parts of your life that you are handling well; they will be a source of strength in the future.

Sun Trine Pluto

This transit signifies that you need very intense and powerful experiences today so that you can learn everything possible about the inner workings of the world in general and your life in particular. This is an excellent transit for taking up any kind of investigation or study. Look within yourself to determine what motivates you, what you are seeking in life and what changes you should make so that your life will run more smoothly. Decide what parts of your life should be reformed, and then reform them. The transformative energies in your life now allow you to make changes rather easily and to derive great satisfaction from making them.

In your contacts with others you can, if you choose, express yourself forcefully and with considerable impact. This is a good time to make an impression on someone, if you need to, but do not use this energy for ruthless or selfish purposes. If you do, you will set into action powerful and hard-to-resist forces that will try to drag you down. Instead, use this energy to make your life evolve and grow upward.

You feel quite forceful, and you want to get things done today, so go ahead. This is an excellent time for exerting yourself through work that must be done. And in doing it, you will gain more experience and knowledge of yourself, which you can put to good use later on.

Sun Opposition Pluto

This transit indicates rather intense encounters with other persons and circumstances, which will reveal many aspects of your life that you may not have understood or may have chosen to ignore. In particular, this transit signifies that you may have power struggles with others, especially persons in authority, in which you will be forced to stand up for your position. On the other hand, you must avoid being overweening and domineering, because such an attitude will only create conflicts that you will probably lose, one way or another.

You may encounter breakdowns in your relationships such that you have to face the other person directly and forthrightly in order to get the difficulty out into the open. Only by thoroughly airing all grievances and making everything very clear will it be possible for the two of you to get past your grievances and establish a new beginning to your relationship.

As with other Sun-Pluto contacts, objects and machinery may break down under this transit, and you will have to stop and repair them. Many aspects of your life that have been limping along will now have to be fixed completely. Patching up will not suffice.

On the other hand, this transit is by no means all difficult or bad. It can be a time when your ambitions and the forces for creative change in your life reach a culmination. You will be able to make many sweeping and fundamental changes that you did not have the power to make before. Just make sure that the changes you are trying to bring about are for the larger good beyond your own and that you seek the aid of others in bringing them about. This is not a good time to go it alone, because you would be likely to encounter more opposition than you can handle.

Be careful not to place yourself in situations where you could be subjected to force or violence. Avoid places with high crime rates, or take precautions if you must go into such areas. Sometimes you can inadvertently draw violence into your life without knowing why.

Sun Conjunct Midheaven

This is a day when you should put all of your attention and energy into getting ahead and attaining your ambitions. More than any other transit, this one signifies ego-expression and expressing your will. You are inclined to be more strong-willed than usual today, to the point that you may not make compromises even when you should. Pursue your own objectives, but don't be so willful that you alienate others unnecessarily.

In your dealings with superiors, this transit has a double-sided significance. You may alienate your superiors because they see your actions as a threat to themselves, or you may win their regard and support. It all depends upon your relationship with them and your attitude toward authority figures in general. This transit indicates only that you will have extensive dealings with people in power.

Events today may further your reputation, depending upon what you are trying to do. Certainly if you have been trying to get public attention, this transit will help out. Neither malefic nor benefic, this transit serves to trigger issues in your life and bring them to the fore. For this reason, it could also signify damage to your reputation, if you have been laying a framework that could have that result.

Put as much positive energy into your work as possible today, for your work is likely to be noticed. Your home life may take a weak second position to your public life, so don't plan to stay at home and relax. Circumstances will probably prevent your doing so.

Sun Sextile Midheaven

Today you will focus your attention on getting ahead in some way. You feel strong, vigorous and confident. Your relationship with your superiors is good, and they may grant you some favor that will assist you in your efforts.

Nevertheless you do not feel dependent upon anyone now, nor do you feel that you need recognition from others. Instead you draw satisfaction from knowing inside yourself what you can do. You go about your work quietly and thoroughly and feel no desire to demonstrate your abilities to anyone. The ironic result of this, however, is that it may bring you recognition from others anyway. If so, you can be certain that you really deserve it, because it is based on your actions alone. Even if you have been trying to get recognition, it is still your actions that have brought it about — real deeds, not ones done for show.

This is a good time to plan your future course of action. You have a good understanding of yourself, and the calmness that usually goes along with this transit enables you to plan with a cool head. If you have already decided where you want to go, this transit will assist you in getting there.

Your personal and family life are also benefited by this transit, because your personal strength is coupled with a sense of responsibility and the knowledge that you don't have to take away anything from your loved ones in order to get ahead. You give them everything you have, which furthers your own ends, because your life is in order.

Sun Square Midheaven

This transit usually signifies a day of great activity in several areas of your life. You feel a great need to exercise your will and to determine where you are going and what you are doing. Often this is a day of hard work in your profession, and you can achieve great accomplishments. But you will be motivated by tasks that relate to your own personal objectives. To a great extent you are wrapped up in your own purposes, and you may not be very considerate of others. Therefore this transit can also signify conflict with others, arising from what they consider your selfishness and excessive self-involvement. Or as you pursue your own goals you may come into conflict with another whose goals are not in harmony with yours.

No matter which of these alternatives you encounter, this is a time for enlightened self-interest. But you must continually remember the people around you and be very careful not to alienate them any more than necessary. Although you probably do not feel like being a team player under this influence, you cannot be "anti-team" either. Even if you don't want to work with others, don't act in ways that cause them to work against you. And if you do get into a dispute with someone, make an effort to rise above your own point of view and look at the situation from a detached perspective. From that point of view, you may see whether you are right or wrong, and you can modify your position accordingly. You can do a lot under this influence, so do not let your desire to achieve get in your way.

Sun Trine Midheaven

With this transit you again have a clear idea of what you are doing and where you are headed. You feel that you know who you are and are therefore confident that you can achieve your objectives. But with this transit also comes a knowledge of and mastery over the necessary material resources and techniques for achieving your ends. You need more than mere self-confidence to achieve anything, as you are well aware. So you will work diligently at whatever task you set yourself today, paying great attention to detail and making thorough use of all the material that will help you accomplish your task. You feel pride in knowing that you have done good work as well as in knowing that you have moved one step closer to your goals.

As with the sextile, you do not feel the need to be dependent upon anyone else, and you don't feel that anyone else is a threat to you, either. Thus you proceed with a sense of equanimity that you may not otherwise feel. Others sense this confidence and know that they can rely upon you. As a result they may look to you for leadership today, but you may be reluctant to take it, especially if you cannot see how it would serve your purposes. You are not irresponsible or antisocial, but you are concerned primarily with your own ends. You are not willing to subordinate them to collective ends or to other people's purposes. On the other hand, if you can see the connection between your own purposes and what others are trying to do, you will accept the role of leader. Either way you will gain the respect of others today.

Sun Opposition Midheaven

Today you should attend to domestic affairs, your personal life, and family matters. Also it is a good day to withdraw into yourself and think things over. There are times when nothing is more important than getting in touch with yourself and your personal work. Now is the time to do this.

This is not the best time to make a great surge out into the world. Professional matters will not interest you as much as personal affairs, and you may not have the energy to carry them off well. Of course, if there is something that must be done in your profession, go ahead and do it. But don't get involved any more than necessary in that area. You may also have troublesome problems with persons who are opposed to your efforts in professional matters.

Demoralizing ego defeats are quite likely with this transit, if you concern yourself with matters that are not related to your real, inner needs and concerns. That is why it is so important for you to be alone or with your closest loved ones in your personal world. This is the only way to determine what your real needs are and how you should satisfy them.

On the other hand, within your personal sphere you can have very satisfying experiences that will prepare you for the time when you should make a new thrust out into the external world of your profession and the general public.

Sun Conjunct Ascendant

This transit is often felt as your second birthday, because the Ascendant is as vital as the Sun in your horoscope. When the Sun conjoins the Ascendant, you feel as if you have received a sudden burst of energy and enthusiasm. This will substantially renew your confidence in facing the world, and you will look forward to the season of the year when this transit occurs.

Today you will be able to project yourself with vigor and energy and to impress others with the force of your personality. Your general feeling of well-being enables you to get a lot of work done, if you choose, or to have a very good time just being yourself, if that is what you want.

Your approach to your environment is positive and active. Instead of waiting for someone else to initiate action, you do it yourself. You take control of whatever situation you are involved in and make it work the way you want it to. Of course, you may encounter opposition, but if you handle it diplomatically, you should be able to win people over to your side.

Above all with this transit, you will want to be uncompromisingly yourself. You don't want to play games with people, and you demand that other people be honest with you as well. This transit represents a new start for the year, just as your actual birthday does, so make as good a start as possible.

Sun Sextile Ascendant

During this transit you will seek recognition from your friends and the people you associate with every day. In little or big ways, you will try to let your immediate world know that you are a person with individual needs and wants and that you want recognition. If you are working with a group today, you may actively seek a leadership role or at least a role of independent authority. With this transit, however, it is usually better to work with others, because your own drives will be satisfied in the context of gratifying group needs, even though that may be difficult to understand.

Usually this transit makes you feel very social. You enjoy being with your friends and neighbors, talking and exchanging news with them. You may feel a little like showing off, which cannot do any harm in moderation. But whatever you try to show others about your strength, independence and ability to lead, it is clear that today you do need others, and you are quite aware of it. Do not try to delude other people about that. They will respect you for being honest, and of course, people like to feel needed. The old line that "No man is an island" has real meaning for you today. If nothing else, you need others to "show off" to, and you needn't fear that showing off will alienate people. Unless you are an insufferable braggart to begin with, it will not have that effect at all.

Sun Square Ascendant

During this transit you will display a great deal of energy in your dealings with other people. However, the problem lies in how you use that energy, for you may try to dominate others. Or you may encounter others who try to dominate you. Do not be so concerned with your own desires that your actions are out of harmony with the people around you. Do not be so willful that you actually get in the way of your own intentions.

You may encounter people today whose purposes and desires are at cross-purposes with your own. There is nothing to be done about this at the moment except to honestly evaluate your own intentions and fight for them if they are valid. if you know they are not valid, fighting for them will be harmful to you. This is one of the dangers of this transit. You may become so involved in getting your own way that you don't even stop to ask whether what you want is good for you in the long run. You must be very self-aware under this influence.

On the other hand, if you are self-aware, this transit can help you, because it enables you to make your mark on the people around you, so that they accept you and let you lead or help lead them. But you must be sure that you are right and that others really are willing to accept your leadership. Otherwise you will only create needless conflict that will bring you nothing.

For all of these reasons, if you are not aware of what you are doing and why, relations with superiors are likely to be bad today. They may see you as a threat or at least as a source of disturbance. If you are young, this may happen in your relationship with your parents.

Sun Trine Ascendant

Under this transit you are likely to feel quite good about yourself in a positive way. Also you will want to be with other people, particularly to have a good time. You do not want to attend to anything that is not immediately enjoyable and gratifying. It is a good day for play, although you can get work done if you really enjoy your work. But if you work only in order to get by, you will not put very much into it today.

With this influence you also seek to expand your daily routine. Today you won't be satisfied to do what you usually do. You would like to learn more about yourself, the world and other people. This is a good transit for beginning a trip, especially a vacation. It is a time to relax from the rigors of everyday life and enjoy yourself.

Despite your present casual approach to life, in your encounters with others you are able to make an impression. Your energies are strong, and even without trying you appear to be showing off to people. However, this is not likely to cause problems because your showing off is a performance, which most people enjoy, especially if the performer is having a good time.

Your relations with superiors should be good today, unless your attitude toward work prevents you from doing a good job. But if you enjoy your work, you will also get recognition for it from those above you.

Sun Opposition Ascendant

Today you will be chiefly concerned with all kinds of encounters with others. Psychologically, you will learn about yourself through the way you experience and affect other people. Therefore you must be very conscious of all your dealings with others today. There is no danger in not being conscious, but you would miss a great opportunity to learn more about yourself. Also some events that may occur with this transit are much more unpleasant if you don't understand them.

There is great likelihood of ego conflicts with others today, because the pressure of circumstances will draw you closer to others now than at almost any other time. That is, you have to work with them! You have little or no choice in the matter. Obviously, anyone whom you tend to have difficulty with will be a source of trouble today, because you cannot escape the confrontation. In fact it is a good idea to have it out and get your problems into the open so that perhaps you can clear it up.

You will be involved in partnership situations with people you are compatible with, and this will work out very well. Today you will work either with people or against them.

This is a good time to consult a lawyer, psychologist, psychiatrist, doctor or any other professional expert or consultant. The basic theme is working with a consultant personality, not with a particular type of consultant. It may even be a close friend whom you bring more closely into your intimate space for some reason.

The point is that you will not derive much benefit from keeping to yourself today. Even if your only encounter with another person is unpleasant, it will be useful to you in the long run. If you withdraw, the initiative will be taken out of your own hands and placed in the environment, where you have little control over it. And you will still have the confrontation.

Chapter Five

Moon

Significance of Transiting Moon

The significance of the transiting Moon is very transient, because the Moon moves so fast. Even though the natal Moon is one of the most powerful points in your horoscope, its transits may go by without too much notice. When it is transiting natal planets its effects are felt for a couple of hours at the most. Transits of the Moon through the houses last a couple of days. Exceptions to this rule occur whenever there is a major change of phase — new Moon, full Moon, etc. — upon a natal planet. Under these circumstances, you may feel the influence for one to four weeks. The effect of an eclipse on a natal planet may be felt up to several months. For the most part, these transits emphasize the nature of the natal planet that is being transited at the time of the lunation, eclipse, full Moon, or whatever. The natal planet's energy in your life is "set off," so to speak.

But by itself the transiting Moon is felt mostly as changes of mood, transient encounters with others, and passing feelings. Often you may not even be conscious of its effects, because they may occur unconsciously. But even though these effects are not visible to you, others can see them. Or you may see the results in unconsciously motivated actions on your part.

In traditional astrology, the Moon signifies women, and even in this day of blurring sexual identity, this is still largely true. Transits of the Moon may indicate various kinds of encounters with women, but the real purpose of these encounters, especially if you are male, is to make you experience your own unconscious attitudes toward yourself and toward aspects of your personality that, rightly or wrongly, you usually hide.

The traditional female attribute of being very changeable and unpredictable — which I do not agree with totally — exists because the Moon rules femininity. In both sexes the unconscious mind has a certain feminine cast, while the conscious mind is somewhat more masculine. Evidence of this is that patients of both sexes in mental institutions behave in cyclical patterns that are related to the position of the Moon. The only people who don't understand this are the scientists who never bother to look for something once they have decided that it is impossible.

The transits of the Moon through the houses of your birth chart signify the areas of your life to which you should turn your greatest attention. But you might not always be aware of this, for the Moon usually expresses itself through habitual behavior and unconscious reactions, especially concerning events from your past. Wherever the Moon is in your chart on a particular day, look to the area of your life ruled by that part to find out where you are most emotionally in tune. But if you have trouble dealing with that area of your life, your resistance will emerge through unconscious actions, habits and a general lack of conscious control.

When planning any kind of social occasion from your own point of view, avoid nights when the Moon seriously afflicts certain planets, as noted in the following descriptions.

Moon in the First House

This is a two-day period when personal and subjective considerations will override everything else, but it need not be difficult. First of all, you feel a great need to belong and to relate to your friends or loved ones. This need turns on your emotional sensors and makes you very sensitive to the feelings and moods of the people around you, because you want to fall in with their rhythms and become sympathetic with them. This is the unconscious sign of relating to a group. Thus you are emotionally right there whenever someone needs your sympathy, warmth and understanding.

Obviously there are two sides to this. On the one hand you can be very emotionally giving to those around you, but on the other hand you can be very emotionally demanding, especially if you feel inadequate in some way. Be careful that you do not demand more nurturing and support than you can give, or at least be ready to make up at another time for what you take now.

You are very concerned about yourself, which is fine, but don't distort this into a state of mind in which you cannot see anybody else's point of view. Objectivity, especially in dealing with others, may be difficult to come by now.

Moon in the Second House

This is a time when you emotionally identify with your possessions or whatever you value. This can lead to a very strong attachment to material objects and a general attitude of possessiveness about them, which can be a problem if someone needs to borrow something of yours, for instance. You may be less willing than usual to part with it now. Or, on a more psychological level, you may unconsciously identify with your own value system to such an extent that you feel every challenge to it as a direct challenge to yourself. You may have to defend yourself in areas where you really have nothing at stake.

During this time you probably will feel best when surrounded by familiar objects that have meaning for you from your past. Each of your possessions is more than the object itself; it is also the symbol of an important experience, emotion or idea. It is very important that you recognize this and understand that it is not the object that is really important to you but its emotional content. That you can never lose, even though material objects may be destroyed or lost.

Traditionally this transit is considered to be a bad time to spend money. The reason for this is that your attitudes toward possessions are so conditioned by unconscious drives, impulses and old thought patterns that you are not likely to make an intelligent decision about buying something based upon your real needs.

Moon in the Third House

During this period your communications with others are likely to be very subjective, colored by personal considerations and not always factually accurate. On the other hand, you are concerned with a very "gut" level of communication, that is, matters of great importance to you communicated through feelings and emotions. Your usually casual conversations with others have an emotional depth that can make these discussions very important now. You are not satisfied with the superficial face that other people show you, nor are you likely to show them a shallow side of yourself. So if you can keep conscious control of your emotions and not lose your objectivity, this can be a time of really meaningful communications.

Another danger of this transit is that your thinking may be unduly influenced by past experiences, habits and reactions to subtle stimuli put out by others. The third house is the house of our everyday world, which we generally take for granted and which is therefore very subject to automatic behavior. Usually you can get away with this, but there is a danger now that you will make a bad impression upon someone by reacting automatically instead of thinking about the demands of the moment. This is a problem especially with casual acquaintances and relatives.

Female relatives may play an important role in your life at this time, and one of them may conceivably be able to teach you something about yourself.

Moon in the Fourth House

This is a good time to retire by yourself to your own private place. You seek and need comfort from the demands of the outside world, and having a pleasant relaxing time at home is probably the best way to accomplish this.

Also this is a good time to go inside yourself and look at your attitudes, feelings and emotional orientation toward the world around you. You could do this by trying to bring out into the open those elements of yourself that usually remain hidden within you. But you could possibly become so overwhelmed by these elements that nothing of value will be accomplished. This is not so likely to happen, however, if you make the effort to look inside yourself consciously. That which is unconscious and unknown ultimately gains control.

One thing that may become really obvious to you at this time is how habits or past conditioning controls your life now. This realization may occur through a confrontation with another in which you suddenly understand that your words or actions are entirely inappropriate to the situation. Such an event may be dismaying, but what you learn from it can be of real value.

You will probably feel emotionally more possessive, both of things and in intimate relationships. Under this influence there is a strong fear of being alone or alienated, which makes you hold on even more tightly. However, this can lead only to losing the very thing you are holding onto. If you adopt a freer attitude toward what you are afraid of losing, you will be less likely to lose it.

Moon in the Fifth House

At this time it is very difficult to conceal your feelings from others, and you shouldn't try. You need to be yourself now and to feel what you really are. In your relations with others, you will project much more emotionally than usual, and if some people do not like this side of you it may be necessary to reconsider your friendship with them.

In love relationships, you will experience greater emotional depth than usual, and consequently your experience with a lover will be much more intense. The only danger to watch out for here is that you may be too possessive of the other person. Also you may be so wrapped up in your own feelings that you are unaware of the other's feelings.

Relations with women in general are improved by this transit. Regardless of your own sex, your experiences with them will very likely show you a great deal about yourself in a positive way.

Sometimes this transit can arouse your protective and nurturing instincts, so that you have a strong desire to take care of someone. You may be involved with children more than usually, or this effect may be expressed in your relationship with a loved one. Just be sure that your desire to protect does not deprive someone of his or her individual responsibility. The Moon can be overprotective.

Moon in the Sixth House

This is a time when you are inclined to put emotional considerations second to the immediate necessities, as you see them, in your life. There is a contradictory energy in this transit, because the Moon's need for personal and emotional contact is out of accord with the self-denying and abstemious nature of the sixth house. Emotional repression of one kind or another is a probable consequence of this transit.

On the other hand, this transit can also signify turning your attention to home crafts, personal hygiene, home care or a general reorganization of personal aspects of your life. This is a healthier expression of this energy than that described above.

If you do react to this transit with emotional repression, you may become hypercritical, which is really the expression of a repressed feeling, usually of resentment toward someone. Another negative expression of this transit is the "martyr game," a tactic of pretending that something is all right with you while subtly signaling that it is not and possibly trying to make others feel guilty for their behavior. Often this is done quite unconsciously. It is much better to put your feelings on the line, even if they don't seem to fit the situation.

Although this transit by itself is usually too fleeting to signify an illness, it can signify a time when the issue of personal health occupies your attention. This is fine as long as you don't allow it to become hypochondria.

Moon in the Seventh House

While the Moon is in this house you turn your attention to your most.personal relationships, in which you express yourself in a much more emotional manner than usual. This transit will affect a marriage, relationships with opponents, or any other inherently emotional confrontation. Loved ones and partners are much more important to you than usual, for they provide you with a feeling of security and support. And to be fair, you have the same interest in providing these elements for your loved ones. But if you are in a negative emotional state now, this transit will tend to make you excessively jealous and possessive, or you may act unconsciously or automatically with your loved ones.

Conflicts with others will be much more emotional, and you will find it difficult to maintain any degree of detachment and objectivity. This makes it easy for an opponent to control you by manipulating your feelings. Be careful that you don't react in an automatic, "knee-jerk" fashion to a given stimulus without conscious thought.

Confrontations with women, both positive and negative, are likely to be more intense than those with men. But no matter whom you confront now, you should look upon this transit as an opportunity to see parts of yourself that you are not usually conscious of. These will be brought out in the confrontations you encounter. It is your responsibility to remain conscious enough to see them.

Moon in the Eighth House

During this transit your emotional experiences are much more intense than usual, which is reflected in the kinds of people and situations that you are drawn to. For example, you may draw in unusually intense or powerful people who have a strong effect upon you. Very often through your emotional encounters with these people, you experience moods and feelings that are quite different from your "normal" self. You may ask if this is really you, it seems so different. This effect is most readily observable during a longer transit that also affects you psychologically. In ordinary months, this transit may go by with little fanfare.

You may also experience some of the effects associated with the transit through the second house, such as feeling overly possessive about property or liking to be surrounded by old and familiar things that hold memories from your past. But here there is the added danger of conflict, because this is the house of joint possessions and the possessions of other people. Thus you may desire something that belongs to someone else, or you may desire greater control over something that is both yours and another's. In either case you must recognize that your attachment serves no real purpose and that it is a potential source of trouble.

Moon in the Ninth House

At this time you may feel a strong urge to get away from the daily routine and go off somewhere, and you may not be entirely conscious of the reasons behind this drive. It is a mood, a restlessness that is hard to pin down. But there is more than one way to get away; for example it can be done in the mind as well as in the physical world. There is some contradiction in the energies of this transit, because the Moon naturally clings to the familiar and the comfortable, while the ninth house symbolizes taking you away from all that. Therefore this transit, although not a very severe one, is difficult to smooth out. Travel may be beneficial as long as the break from your routine isn't too radical. You are not really interested in getting totally away from it all, you are just bored with your everyday life.

Study or mental journeys may be more useful, because you can remain in familiar surroundings supported by the comforts of your normal world. Yet at the same time you can expose yourself to ideas and concepts that are both revolutionary and liberating. Thus you can have some of the excitement that you crave.

This is also a time when you may meet new friends from a foreign country or from a background that is very different from yours. However, since this transit occurs once each month, you obviously should not expect this to happen every time.

Moon in the Tenth House

This transit brings professional and business concerns into focus, but in a way that will test you. The symbolism of this transit is such that your most intimate and personal life is on public display more than usual now, and you may find it difficult to hide certain facts about yourself. Obviously you are best off if you have nothing to hide. Even if you usually have reservations about emotional display in public, you are likely to indulge in such displays now. For example, you might have a public argument with a loved one or spouse, or you might have a public outburst of good emotions.

This tendency can stand you in good stead in your career, for you display more emotional sensitivity and empathy toward the people you work with, and thus you can win them over. Perhaps you will want to help someone whom you know through your job and make the relationship something more than professional. But if it is to your disadvantage to blur the distinction between professional and personal relationships, be careful, because you will tend to do this.

In working with a group you are more sensitive and responsive to the general mood and therefore able to control your relationship with the group. This transit is good for any kind of public relations work or sales.

Moon in the Eleventh House

This transit can signify any one of several different effects. It can indicate a time when emotional contact with friends is very important to you. If you or your friend has something very personal to say, something that touches either of you at a deeper emotional level than usual, this is a good time to say it. Contact between yourself and friends is much deeper than usual now. A related effect of this transit is to bring a female friend or friends into prominence in your life, and in general you should find it easier to get along with them now.

In friendships you will probably feel more protective and supportive than usual, or you will attract someone who gives you needed emotional support. However, if you are not constantly conscious of your attitudes, you may become excessively possessive of a friend and try to restrict his or her freedom in some way because of insecurity. Childish as it may seem, you may become jealous when a friend pays more attention to someone else. If you are feeling depressed or otherwise unhappy, negative emotional patterns left over from childhood may adversely affect your relationship with a friend.

Examine your overall goals in life at this time. It is important that they be a real expression of yourself and not simply the product of emotional attitudes and unconscious drives from an earlier time that no longer apply to your present situation.

Moon in the Twelfth House

At this time you may be tempted to withdraw and keep your feelings secret, especially if you are at all insecure about your inner self. Perhaps you, like many people, have always felt that if others really knew you, they wouldn't like you. So you keep your entire emotional life secret. This can cause serious problems in your life, however, because whatever you hide from others, you will also hide from yourself. And whatever you hide from yourself can control you without your being aware of it. This is a time when your unconscious attitudes and fears can be very difficult. You need to communicate your deep inner feelings to another person, preferably someone you can trust. Inability to trust others may be part of your problem, however.

During this time relations with women can be difficult, usually because you don't understand each other very well. Here again communication is the only answer.

Probably you will not feel much like socializing now. And in fact it is a good time to be alone and face any aspect of yourself that you are reluctant to face. It is probably not really all that bad.

This is an excellent time for any kind of mystical or spiritual discipline, for you can understand these teachings not only with your mind but also with your emotions, that is, at the gut level.

Moon Conjunct Sun

This transit is like your personal "new Moon," a time when your mind and body are recharged for the month ahead. Your feelings at this time may be very strongly influenced by the larger emotional patterns that dominate your life.

Usually this transit is felt as a burst of energy in which will, physical vitality and emotions all work together harmoniously. The split between mind and feelings that often plagues us all is not noticeable now, and your relations with others, particularly with the opposite sex, will probably work more smoothly than usual. This is an outward reflection of your inner harmony.

Group efforts are very favorably affected by this transit, because it gives you greater sensitivity to the feelings of people around you. This is a good time for conferences or any other situation in which you and others have to come to some conclusion.

However, if you are not feeling very good emotionally because of a longer-range transit, you may have very little energy right now. If this is the case, take some time off to allow your energy to build up slowly. Otherwise the whole month may be deficient in this regard. In general this is probably not a good time to have major surgery. At the very least, take extra precautions and especially avoid surgery on that part of the body ruled by your Sun sign.

Moon Sextile Sun

This is a time of inner and outer equanimity. You can stop and take stock of yourself without feeling completely caught up in the usual turmoil and rush of events. Even if your affairs are not going too smoothly, this transit will provide a breathing space. If you have been feeling harried, you now have at least a brief opportunity to take it easy. And if you are relaxed, you will feel even better now.

Your relationships with groups and friends are quite good under this transit. You are able to understand other people's needs without losing sight of your own desires for fulfillment. Whether you are a leader or a follower, being with others will benefit you at this time.

As with the other easy Sun-Moon contacts, your relations with the opposite sex are good. You are able to make friends and establish a real emotional communion with others.

Opportunities may arise from unexpected corners that will improve your life in small ways at least. These may very well come about through friends. In general you will benefit from being out in the world today and having as much contact with others as possible.

Moon Square Sun

This transit usually represents some sort of challenge to the structure of your daily life, that is, your home life, intimate relations, routine daily contacts and so forth. All of us have hidden tensions that cause us to operate in ways that we do not understand. The effect of this transit is to bring these tensions to the surface. Thus you may feel ill at ease within yourself and have a bit more difficulty in getting along with others, particularly with the opposite sex. You may be a bit more irritable than usual and find other people's eccentricities harder to take.

This transit can also indicate that several small areas of your life simultaneously reach a crisis, not usually serious, but one that forces you to pay more attention to what is happening. This is especially likely to happen with situations or persons that you have been taking for granted. You should take the time to correct little problems as they arise and give them the attention that they require.

If everything is running smoothly in your life, you may feel this transit simply as a burst of emotional and physical energy that you can use creatively in any way you want.

Moon Trine Sun

Others things being equal, this is usually a very pleasant transit. Psychologically you feel very much in harmony with yourself and able to do whatever you have to do single-mindedly. Your energies flow with less resistance, and life seems to be easier now. As a consequence, you can relate to people more easily, for others perceive your inward harmony and are drawn to you because of it. Obviously this is a good time for any kind of group activity. You are able to relate your own interests to the interests of any group you are working with, so that everyone will gain from what you do.

Relations with the opposite sex are also improved for the same reasons. A marriage will be especially harmonious now, for this is a time of real understanding.

On the physical level this harmony is expressed as a feeling of vitality. You may not feel driven to accomplish a great deal of work, however. That is determined more by your innate character than by this transit, but whether or not you respond with a burst of energy, you will feel very good.

Moon Opposition Sun

At this time of the month, certain energies are at a high level. Probably you will feel quite physically energetic and want to accomplish a great deal. However, your energies may not be working very smoothly, because different areas of your life are working against each other now. You will have to work hard to develop harmony between your home and professional life, your conscious and unconscious personality, and your mind and feelings. You can accomplish a great deal as long as you don't get carried away by conflicts in these areas. In truth, for your life to work smoothly now, both sides of the areas mentioned above must be working together.

Discordant moods can create difficulties in relationships at this time, especially if you are having any kind of internal emotional struggle. You may have problems with persons of the opposite sex.

But on quite a different level, this transit can cause a passing attraction to a person of the opposite sex who seems quite different from you. And that difference is the very source of the attraction. But be careful about any relationship that starts at this time, because although interesting, it might not be very stable.

Moon Conjunct Moon

It is hard to generalize about the effects of this transit, which signifies the beginning of a major emotional cycle. A chart cast for the exact moment of the conjunction is a very common predictive tool in astrology because the prevailing influences in that chart seem to affect the entire month. So it is possible to say that your feelings now are likely to be the dominant theme of the month.

Certainly, emotional attitudes figure more prominently than usual at this time. You should be careful not to lose your objectivity in a discussion or lose your sense of perspective. But you will not feel particularly good or bad with this transit; rather, you will feel any emotion more strongly.

Sometimes there is a tendency to attract things to you at this time. Attracting things is a lunar or *yin* function, and this transit is a very *yin* time in the month. Women may also be more important to you than usual.

Objects, persons and places that are familiar to you are very important at this time because you need emotional reassurance from your surroundings. You may try to withdraw from others or from confrontations with unfamiliar or strange situations. This is not a negative condition; it arises out of a need to be by yourself for awhile.

Moon Sextile Moon

This is a time of deep feelings. You want to be surrounded by familiar people and objects that remind you of pleasant past experiences. It is a good time to be with relatives and family and to go over old times with them. Or you may feel like doing nothing more adventurous than staying home and curling up with a good book.

With this transit there is a great need for intimacy, which you wish to share with the people you are in contact with today. Superficial meetings and acquaintances will not satisfy your emotional needs. Regardless of your own sex, you will probably find the company of women more satisfactory, although men with great emotional sensitivity and understanding will fulfill the same function.

When you are with a group or before the public under this influence, you are able to establish a good rapport, and others will respond to you because you have responded to them. This is a good transit for making any kind of public presentation.

Friends, especially female friends, are important to you at this time. You have the ability to sit with them, listen to their troubles and offer a sympathetic ear, as well as good advice.

Moon Square Moon

This transit, although not long lasting, can provide some moments of difficulty and irritation. Your emotions are discordant, and you may be more inclined to get into disagreements with others. This will probably have the greatest effect in your most personal life and domestic situation. Consequently you should watch out for unnecessary conflicts with loved ones. If there are real tensions between you and someone else, they will surface at this time, but probably in a form that requires you to go below superficial appearances and analyze more deeply. But this is not the right time to try to do that, because you will be so wrapped in the issues that your perspective will be warped.

In a group, you will not feel that your interests are in accord with the others' interests. It is not a good time to work with people or to make any kind of public appearance, if peace and harmony is your goal. However, if you are trying to stir people up about some issue or call their attention to circumstances that must be dealt with, this transit can be quite helpful, although the others may not appreciate your role in this.

Your relations with women may not be very smooth at this time, but you will learn a great deal about your own inner emotional workings through encounters with them.

Moon Trine Moon

During this period you should have a very strong sense of well-being. Your inner self is functioning harmoniously, and you do not feel emotional turmoil or strife. Your relationships with others also function smoothly, reflecting this feeling.

At the same time you are most contented with the familiar elements of your life. You enjoy being at home with relatives and friends, and you like being surrounded by the objects you are used to. You are not in the mood for adventures, challenges and major changes, nor is it necessary to be so. There will be other times for adventure. Now you should restore and rejuvenate yourself in peace and quiet. Physical comfort is especially important to you at this time, but it doesn't have to be lavish. Your need is for a comfortable environment that seems supportive. You want to be surrounded by whatever you feel protects you.

On the other hand, assuming that these needs are met, you will also be able to offer aid and emotional support to others. You will feel like taking care of another person, and doing so will reinforce your sense of emotional security. If you are a parent, your children will be very important to you at this time. Otherwise you will be concerned with any group that you belong to. Relations with women are usually very good at this time.

Moon Opposition Moon

At this time your moods are quite deep and your emotions powerful. If you are aware, all your contacts at this time will show you how your emotional state affects other people. This can be either good or bad, but the growth in consciousness is usually very beneficial.

One problem with this transit, however, is that you find it difficult to see any point of view but your own. So if difficulties arise in a relationship because of an emotional conflict, you may be inclined to place all of the blame on the other person. Also, in dealings with a group there is a danger that you will feel that your own interests and desires are opposed to theirs, thus creating more potential for disagreement. You must learn to detach yourself somewhat in order to observe your feelings in action. Otherwise you will not be able afterward to evaluate what you saw.

If you are a person who has difficulties expressing or relating to your own emotions, this is likely to be an uncomfortable time. It is not that the feelings you are exposed to are negative, but that they are too strong for you. Men often project this problem onto the women in their life and experience this transit as difficulties with them. Women may also project, but they are more likely to feel dissatisfied with themselves.

Moon Conjunct Mercury

For a few hours your rational and logical mind is going to be strongly influenced by your moods, which could be either positive or negative, depending on other factors. For this reason it is not the best time to make a decision. But it is a good time to gather information that you can later base a decision on, especially information on how you really feel about some matter.

This is a good time to talk about your feelings. At other times you may find it difficult to express your emotions, but under this influence it should be relatively easy. Communications with women are usually very good now.

Sometimes your thinking may be overwhelmed by small issues, matters that seem very important to you at the moment but are of little real significance. "Thinking small" can be a real problem. Trivial talk and conversation may take your attention away from important matters.

Moods in general change very rapidly at this time, but it is not possible to specify the kinds of changes. This transit has no particular "good" or "bad" effect upon the emotions.

Moon Sextile Mercury

This transit is likely to increase the tempo of your social intercourse for awhile. You will spend a great deal of time talking with friends, acquaintances and neighbors about matters that affect you all. The conversation is not likely to be very profound or significant and it may even be gossip. But it will bind you all together and give everyone the sense of having something in common.

At another level this Moon-Mercury combination, like most of the others, makes it relatively easy to verbalize your feelings. If you have a problem or situation that you cannot handle, this is a good time to take it to a sympathetic friend. Getting another viewpoint will help you. And, of course, you may do the same for someone else.

Often this time is filled with news from friends or with letters and phone calls. Actually you are attracting communication from every conceivable corner of your life. This is a good time to write letters to the people you feel strongly about. But some people under this transit become so passive that it is difficult to take such an initiative. Their tendency is to allow others to take the initiative.

Whatever you say to people at this time will be characterized by sensitivity and awareness of the other person's feelings, which will be much appreciated by those around you.

Moon Square Mercury

This transit can signify a critical time in your communications with the people around you, particularly those with whom you are intimately involved. The danger is that your feelings and emotions will overwhelm your rational intellect, making your thinking so subjective that no one else will be able to relate to what you say. Nevertheless you have a strong need to communicate about your emotions. If you have a problem with someone, do not hold it back, for that will only make the problem worse. Then you will behave toward that person in subtle but irritating ways that you may not even be aware of but that can produce even more negative feelings between you. And on top of that, communication becomes even worse.

Others may also feel compelled to express the problems they are having with you, so don't expect to enjoy everything you hear today. But keep in mind that this is a time when tensions can and should be released. It is a time of psychological and emotional readjustment, and the best way to handle it is to just allow it to happen.

You should avoid dealing with controversy by changing your own views every time someone disagrees with them. You will tend now to change your views according to the prevailing wind, but this may result in compromising yourself if the people you have "agreed" with compare viewpoints. However, it is natural for your opinions to be in a state of flux at this time. Just be honest about admitting it.

Moon Trine Mercury

At this time you are in touch with your feelings to an unusual extent and are more able to express them to others. You probably lack the psychological tension that usually drives people to talk about their feelings, but you can listen most sympathetically to other people's problems now. The insight into your own feelings and the psychological equilibrium that you have now may enable you to offer effective help to others.

This transit also signifies a state of balance between your feelings and your rational intellect. That is, you are able to think with great emotional sensitivity but still remain logical in your thought processes.

You may receive information about your past or your family under this transit, or other matters concerning them will be important to you. You may feel rather sentimental during this period, but you will not be maudlin.

This is a good time to tell your loved ones how you feel about them, because your words will easily convey the depth of your feelings. Likewise it is a good time to write letters to friends.

Communication with women will be easy and quite favorable at this time, regardless of your own sex. And encounters with women may be quite informative in a positive way.

Moon Opposition Mercury

This transit has two potentials. On the one hand, you may experience a real conflict between feelings and reason. But on the other, you may have a very fruitful dialogue about the state of your soul, either internally or with another person.

In the first instance, the effect of the transiting Moon is to erase all the fine logical distinctions that you make in your everyday thinking. You are likely to lump people into categories, usually categories that you don't like very much, rather than regarding them as individuals. You might take a dislike to someone just because of his or her looks or clothes. Old habits, prejudices and childhood patterns of thought are very likely to take precedence over what you usually consider reasonable.

Obviously this is not a good time to enter into delicate negotiations with someone or to engage in an important discussion that requires clarity and logic. It might not be possible.

If you experience the second potential of this transit, this is a good time to withdraw by yourself or with another person and get in touch with your own feelings. As long as you recognize that your emotions are emotions rather than rational judgments, you will not have trouble with this transit. In fact, you can learn a great deal about yourself, because your feelings are very clear.

Moon Conjunct Venus

This is a good time to go out and socialize, because you feel quite cheerful and gregarious. You radiate warmth and emotion toward other people, so they enjoy being with you. This is a very good time to go to a party, for example.

Your relations with loved ones are usually good under this influence, and you may feel quite amorous. Usually this influence is too fleeting to indicate the beginning of a major relationship, but it does help existing ones. If there is a longer-range transit that suggests a new relationship, this transit may indicate the hour when it begins.

This is a favorable transit for undertaking any activity connected with beautifying your home and making it more pleasant. It is also a good time to entertain at home.

In shopping now, you may spend more money than you originally intended, and if you must stay within a budget, you would be well advised to postpone shopping until later. This is a reflection of the general tendency toward overindulgence under this transit, which applies to drinking and eating as well.

Moon Sextile Venus

Under this transit you want to be with your friends and the people you love. It also helps to ensure that you will have a reasonably pleasant time with them. Feelings of love and friendship may build in all areas of your life now, and you feel that life is richer and a little more rewarding.

Love relationships are usually aided by this transit, and it is a good time to go out with someone, because there will be a good rapport between you. If another transit indicates any kind of problem in a love relationship now, this transit can give the two of you a breathing space in which to restore emotional communication and perhaps straighten things out.

It is a good time to have friends come to your home for entertainment. You are able to make them feel good, and they will appreciate it, for you make it clear that you care about them. In general, your home situation and immediate environment will be the sources of your greatest satisfaction during this period. Your light and cheerful mood will be picked up by everyone around you, too.

However, because of the doubly passive nature of the Moon-Venus combination, you should be careful not to become passive yourself. There is a tendency to expect others to bring you things or do errands for you, or to expect circumstances to take care of you. This transit has a self-indulgent side that could conceivably undo all its usually positive effects.

Moon Square Venus

This is usually a very pleasant, light-feeling transit. You enjoy being with others and find all social contacts interesting, especially purely social ones whose only purpose is getting to know people. The Moon and Venus, even in square, are very sympathetic planets, and therefore this combination does not create problems as other squares do.

Most people feel very affectionate toward loved ones under this transit, and there is a strong desire to support and protect those people who are important to you. But be careful not to act too possessive or to try to limit anyone's freedom. If you behave in this manner, you will experience this transit discordantly and will have trouble with your loved ones.

You may feel very sentimental with this transit, for it tends to reawaken memories of the past and causes you to feel very attached to them. You enjoy being surrounded by persons and things that remind you of the past. The only problem is that if you go too far in this direction, you may not pay enough attention to the demands of the present.

As with other combinations of these two planets, you should beware of any tendency to overindulge in food or drink. Discipline is not one of the strong points of this transit.

Moon Trine Venus

This transit brings about pleasant feelings between you and everyone around you. It is a good time for being with friends or out having a good time. You enjoy everyone around you and they enjoy you.

Similarly you will enjoy good food and drink now, but be careful not to overdo it. With this transit you will tend to take things into yourself, so it is easy to overindulge. This is not a good time for getting very much work done, because it often brings out a lazy streak.

One exception to this is that you may feel like working to beautify or otherwise improve your home. You need beautiful surroundings, and you will work to get them.

Obviously, with these two planets this is a good time for love relationships. This transit by itself is too fleeting to start a major relationship, but it certainly is a help. Between you and your loved one there will be an easy flow of feelings. You will feel very protective of your loved one but not excessively possessive or smothering. The combination of Moon and Venus is related to motherhood, and the positive aspects of mothering will be evident in your feelings for others.

Moon Opposition Venus

This is usually quite a pleasant time, but you should be careful not to overindulge in rich foods or drink. Also you may believe that you will get everything you want from others without making any effort yourself.

Aside from that, the principal effect of this transit is a desire for strong emotional contact with others. You want to be involved in relationships at this time, and you don't care whether or not they are perfectly smooth. What is important to you now is the intensity of feeling and the interchange with another person. For this reason, relations with loved ones can be either smooth or rough with this transit. In fact, they are usually good, but if you are feeling negative for some other reason, this transit will not improve matters. On the other hand, even discordant contact with a loved one is likely to do more good than harm now, because it releases hidden tensions so that afterward you can feel better about each other.

Be careful of a tendency toward extravagance, which is closely linked with the self-indulgence mentioned above. You might buy something because of a passing fancy and question your own taste later.

Except for these possible negative effects, you should enjoy this transit. Use it to learn something about your relationships and your attitudes toward them.

Moon Conjunct Mars

Under this transit you may feel briefly irritable. Therefore it is not a good time to discuss any issues that are critical to you, because you will find it difficult to maintain your equilibrium and not fly off the handle. On the other hand, if someone challenges you unjustifiably, you certainly won't back down without a fight. The main problem is that your sense of perspective may be so distorted that you cannot tell the important issues from the trivial ones and will defend both with equal vigor.

There is also the risk that you will act hastily on many matters, impulsively and without foresight or planning. All you seem to care about is exercising your will and getting your own way. Obviously with this transit, you must try to calm down and be willing to compromise on any issue that is not really central to you. Also avoid quarrelsome people, whom you may attract even though you are not conscious of the discordant energies within you.

These same effects can be used for good. If you can control yourself, you will be able to take initiatives that would be difficult at other times. What seems like foolhardiness can also be bravery; it is all a matter of control. You have the will and the strength now to break down otherwise formidable barriers.

Moon Sextile Mars

At this time you have the capacity to work either with others or alone. If you work with others you will have to have a lot of independence or some kind of leadership role in order to feel that you have been given an adequate chance. Probably you will get that chance. You have a much greater desire than usual to take the initiative and much stronger feelings of courage and self-reliance.

In working with others, you will be able to give them the feeling that your aims are theirs, so that they will work with you more willingly. If you have to defend your point of view when challenged, you will not back down but will argue your case with vigor and passion. Others will respect you for this even when they do not agree.

In communicating with others, you express your feelings openly and sincerely. You leave no doubt about where you stand, but you do not offend others needlessly. You do not feel any need to make unwarranted attacks in order to maintain yourself.

In emotional relationships, you attract persons who are strong and have the courage of their convictions. You attract what you respect. If you are a man, you may seek the company of a strong-minded woman, but that characteristic is likely to be attractive to you.

Moon Square Mars

Under this transit there is a real danger of needless disputes, irritability, emotionalism, rash action and hastiness, which may result in harm or inconvenience later. You will find it difficult to handle other people for awhile. Fortunately this is a rather brief transit. One of its challenges is to successfully let off steam without making an unnecessary shambles. Also you have real tensions and grievances, which you should express, as well as little annoyances that are not worth getting upset over. But you may get involved with the annoyance in order to avoid the real grievances that you do not wish to face.

If you frequently feel somewhat discouraged about yourself, you should be especially careful with this transit. You may see everything that comes your way as a threat and react much too defensively. Or you may draw in people who seem to attack you for no reason. Are they really attacking you, or are you just being oversensitive and insecure?

If you have a bolder and more self-confident temperament, you may be inclined to act too quickly, to be hasty and overcritical of others. Or you may be accident prone. With this transit, you are not as careful as you should be, and you might hurt yourself. Be especially careful of sharp metal objects. Domestic accidents are especially likely unless you take pains to act calmly and deliberately. Make sure that you express any hidden aggressions against their proper objects and not against yourself.

Moon Trine Mars

Under this transit you can assert yourself in a positive manner and stand your ground if necessary. You feel more courage and confidence than usual, which you express by taking the initiative in making emotional contacts with others. You speak very directly and forcefully, but without being offensive, which others will respect you for.

This is a good time to work as a leader with groups of people. You understand what is needed, and you can unify your objectives and theirs, usually by talking them around to your point of view. Whenever you talk with others, you radiate an inner excitement, as if you were ready for immediate action.

Under this transit you have the capacity to start projects, although you should keep in mind that this is a short transit and its effects will not last long. If you want to start a project that will continue for some time, there should be another influence backing up this one. In fact there is a real danger at this time that you will start projects and never finish them.

Physically, your energy level is high, and you will want to do something that involves physical labor or exercise. Fortunately, with this Moon-Mars combination there is not the same tendency to rash action that characterizes several of the others.

Moon Opposition Mars

This transit is brief in its effects, but you should be careful because its energies are quite discordant and could create trouble in your personal life. The problem is that you are rather emotionally excitable and easily irritated or angered now. With other people you are far less tolerant of individual quirks, and little things irritate you. You may also be in such a contentious mood that no outside aggravation is needed to set you off. Be wary of arguing just for the sake of arguing. But on the other hand, if you feel real anger, you should release the energy; don't hold it in.

Although accidents are not usually triggered by such a fast-moving transit, your present tendency toward hasty actions and impulsive movements may be the last straw in bringing about an accident, if you are not careful. Try to check any sudden movements that might catch other people by surprise.

Your domestic scene may not be very peaceful under this transit, but try to remain calm, no matter how difficult it is. Relations with women may be especially difficult. If you have trouble at home at this time, it is probably a reflection of a problem that has been boiling under the surface for some time. Right now is not the time to try to smooth it out, but you should do so as soon as possible afterward.

Moon Conjunct Jupiter

This transit usually denotes a brief period of good feelings and generosity toward others. You feel that everything is all right, and you have nothing to fear. You express your self-confidence by being above petty irritations. Not easily angered, you tolerate even the most harsh behavior from other people. But you probably won't have to contend with "harsh behavior," because the energy of this transit does not arouse it in those around you. You will get what you give — kindness, friendship and nurturing support.

Your relations with females are very good at this time. You are able to help the women you know, and they will do the same for you.

This transit can also awaken your concern for the deeper aspects of life. You may seek metaphysical and spiritual insights, but with your heart rather than your mind. Rational knowledge is not likely to satisfy you at this time.

If you have to deal with the public or with large groups of people during these hours, you should do very well. You can build such a strong rapport with a group that everyone knows you understand each other on a deep intuitive level.

Moon Sextile Jupiter

Under this transit you usually feel quite good, and you enjoy being with congenial people. Probably it would be best to be with old friends whom you know well and with whom you have already established strong emotional ties. But you will not be closed to new acquaintances. You make it clear to those around you that you are concerned for their welfare and that you will help them out if they ever need it. And the chances are that they feel the same way about you. This transit denotes a time when you and your friends support each other and feel that you belong together.

This is a good time for any sort of group activity, because by working together you all will feel that it is a group effort from which everyone will benefit equally. And this is true.

If you have to persuade others, as in sales or public relations, this transit can be very useful. It enables you to project to the group the feeling that you understand their needs. Fortunately, with this transit you are concerned enough about others that you do understand their needs.

Regardless of your own sex, relations with women are usually good with this transit, and you may encounter someone who can show you a great deal about yourself in a positive sense.

Moon Square Jupiter

This is usually a very positive transit, making you feel very benevolent and generous toward those around you. Your spirit is inclined toward contemplation of the loftier aspects of life. You are not concerned with the nasty little details that make life less than it should be, although you are aware of them. But you simply cannot see any point in paying any attention to them. Emotionally you feel quite good, for this transit promotes optimism and positive thinking.

Often your attention will turn to religion, philosophy or other subjects that encompass life as a whole on an intellectual level. And in this area this transit can create problems, because at times it indicates self-righteousness and smug arrogance, as if you considered yourself as the embodiment of social truth and wisdom. This attitude may not be entirely conscious on your part, but it may be subtly evident in your phrasing or in an unspoken attitude toward others. In any case, people may suddenly react to you as if they are put off. Be sure to watch other people's reactions very carefully and then examine your attitudes as well.

Aside from this area, you should have very good feelings with this transit, which should indicate a very positive time for you.

Moon Trine Jupiter

It is unfortunate that this transit is so brief, because it gives you such a pleasant sense of well-being. You feel very warm and friendly to the people around you, and you are willing to offer emotional or physical support to anyone who needs it. You are generous and giving.

People will warm to you, and you should get from others exactly what you give, that is, warmth and affection. You are likely to attract basically happy and positive people with whom you will have an enjoyable time. This is not the result of a "Pollyanna" view of reality that refuses to recognize trouble and pain in the world, but of a real sense of belonging and oneness with others. In a very important sense you feel that helping others helps you.

On another level this transit indicates a concern with the general welfare, that is, beyond your immediate circle. But because the influence of this transit is so short-lived, by itself it is not likely to get you involved with any large-scale work for social reform. But you will be more concerned for people's welfare, even that of strangers.

This same concern leads to an interest in the meaning of life itself. You are not interested in abstract metaphysical answers, but in real experiences of the body and emotions.

Moon Opposition Jupiter

You usually feel quite good under this transit, but it does present some challenges if you are to make the best use of it. Usually you feel quite benevolent toward others, willing to be very generous and to help when necessary. But this help has to be voluntary and come from your own initiative. If others try to compel you to be generous by appealing to your sense of responsibility or duty, you are not likely to respond.

This transit stimulates your drive for personal freedom, and if you feel free and unencumbered, you will probably behave quite responsibly in other people's eyes. The more you feel that people are trying to hold you back or make you toe the line, the more you will resist.

The same applies to relationships. If your partner in a love relationship tries to be possessive or limit your freedom, you will resist. And a dispute could arise from your assertion of freedom.

On a very different level, this transit can manifest itself as a feeling of spiritual disquiet, a mood in which you question your fundamental goals and aspirations. And, indeed this is a good time to look at your life in this way. What you learn will be very important to you.

Moon Conjunct Saturn

At this time you are inclined to keep your feelings and innermost thoughts to yourself. A sense of loneliness or isolation frequently accompanies this transit, or depression and a general sense of pessimism. However, you should recognize that life probably looks much worse now than it really is, so don't take your negative feelings too seriously.

Domestic problems may also accompany this transit, usually because you feel that in some way your domestic life is not giving you what it should. This is part of a larger feeling that you are not getting support or assistance from anyone or anything, which may or may not be true.

Your real problem is either that you are cut off from your emotions or that your emotions are too unpleasant to deal with. This transit may force you to briefly experience what you consider to be your negative side. Thus there is a strong conflict between what you think of yourself and what you think you should be.

In some cases this transit can activate a sense of guilt about some past event, particularly if you are around a person who plays on that kind of feeling.

Regardless of your sex, relations with women will probably be difficult. If you are a man, this is because you are having difficulty with the unconscious feminine aspects of yourself, and if you are a woman it is a more conscious feeling of discontent. This is not a good transit for making decisions that affect your emotional life.

Moon Sextile Saturn

Under this influence you may feel like being alone with your thoughts and feelings. Your mood is not usually bad or depressed, you simply desire to be calm and reflective. But you are probably not in the mood for frivolity. You prefer the company of serious people, if any, and you want the conversation to be about important topics. Under this transit you may feel the need to consult an older, wiser person, someone whose higher vantage point you respect.

Under this transit you are able to balance your emotional needs with your sense of duty and obligation. While you are aware of your feelings, you do not let them overwhelm you. In all proceedings you are thrifty and careful. You may have to take care of someone else at this time.

You are very careful and thorough in your approach to any kind of work now. It is not likely that you will have to do any task over, nor will anyone else have to clean up after you.

Moon Square Saturn

This transit can indicate a period of fleeting depression. You are inclined to feel lonely and out of touch with others. Sometimes you have a pronounced sense that no one loves you, whether or not it is true. It is very important to realize that your moods and sensations under this transit often do not reflect reality, even though they seem to. Life usually looks worse than it is.

One area where you can have real trouble is in relationships. You will find it unusually difficult to relate emotionally to another person during this transit. Either you are caught up in internal negativism, or you feel so cold and insensitive that you do not register signals from other people very well. This is turn leads to failures of communication and genuine misunderstandings. Obviously this is not a good time to become involved in an emotionally delicate situation. Separations may occur now, although this transit is too fleeting by itself to indicate a very significant separation in your life. Such an event would be accompanied by a longer-range transit of similar meaning.

For persons of both sexes this transit can signify separations from women or difficulties with women.

You should be very careful about falling into negative thinking about yourself. You are very inclined to downgrade yourself under this transit and to think that you are inadequate. Or you may start to dwell endlessly on negative experiences from your past. The important thing to realize is that your perspective is distorted now, and everything will look better shortly.

Moon Trine Saturn

At this time you will keep your emotions under control, not in a repressive, negative manner, but in a way that enables you to take a more sober and realistic view of life.

You are able to put up with considerable adversity and strain under this influence because it gives you patience and reserve strength. You feel that you can stand alone against whatever difficulties may come, and even if none do, you will feel an inner strength and security. This transit by itself will not *make* any difficulty occur.

While you are not inclined to talk about your feelings to just anyone, you do not evade them in yourself. You may very well go off by yourself at this time to think about and evaluate your development.

If you have a problem, seek out an older person whose wisdom you respect, who can offer emotional support and suggest practical and immediate answers. You need common-sense answers now that can be applied directly.

At this time the past has a strong attraction for you. You feel rather conservative and not very experimental, inclined to follow the old answers that have always worked in the past. They probably will work now too. You will feel more secure if you are surrounded by whatever you are used to and whatever has supported you in the past.

Moon Opposition Saturn

This transit, although brief, can have a disruptive effect on your relationships. The problem is that it tends to make you feel very lonely and isolated, as if there is no one you can communicate with. And this can be a self-fulfilling prophecy. Perhaps unconsciously you send out signals to others declaring that you do not want to be bothered, that you would like to be alone. You may get into a depressed mood that baffles the people around you, so they give up on you for the time being and stop trying to help you. There is a strong tendency to look on the dark side of life and to react much more strongly to disappointments and failures than to reinforcement from others and success. Thus you plummet down into depression for no reason at all.

The best way to handle such feelings is to do nothing. Don't take them seriously and don't make any decisions based on the way you feel now. Your perspective is not very good, but in a short time you will feel much better and be able to make much more intelligent observations.

You may feel quite cold and unfeeling with this transit, but this too shall pass. It may be necessary later to explain to people that you were just in a bad mood, but everyone gets into such moods from time to time, and most people understand that.

Moon Conjunct Uranus

Under this transit you often feel impulsive and willing to act rashly. Your moods change so quickly that you surprise yourself as well as others. You may be with someone else who is like this, usually a woman. Probably you will be impatient with your normal routine and want to do something completely different. Assuming that the "something different" is within reason, it is probably all right to go ahead. In fact you might as well not bother trying to be disciplined and responsible for the next few hours. If you have work to do that requires great concentration, you won't be able to keep your mind on it, or you will do a sloppy job.

Usually this is not a sign of conflict, but if someone is trying to hold you back from expressing your impulses, you may get angry at him or her and get into a fight. At this time you are not very patient with people who tell you what you ought to be doing.

The danger here is that you may do something that you will regret very soon. Remember that this transit is only a few hours long and that its effects will soon wear off. Thus you could easily be stuck with the consequences of an action that you would not have taken in a more sober frame of mind. But these acts are not always negative. Sometimes they can clear the air and bring out tensions that should surface.

Moon Sextile Uranus

This transit gives you a pleasant feeling of restlessness, a desire for excitement but not to the point of disruption. You may feel like shaking up the people around you and jolting them out of their seeming lethargy. Or if you are not conscious of this desire in yourself, you may attract someone who shakes you up. Under any circumstances you want to be with exciting and stimulating companions.

In your home and other close surroundings you are not willing to accept the same old situation. You may try to find ways to change your circumstances or at least provide some temporary excitement.

It is possible that you will meet a new and exciting friend today, or an old friend will come back into your life unexpectedly. Friends may provide opportunities for advancement or for getting away from your usual scene for awhile. Female friends are especially likely to play this role.

Your desire for new experiences extends to ideas as well. You want to encounter new ways of thinking that arouse your fancy. You may be attracted to technical subjects that require a great deal of technical understanding, but unless another transit signifies this interest also, you may lack the discipline to follow through.

Moon Square Uranus

With this transit you should be very careful not to be hasty, jump to conclusions or react negatively to anything that is said to you. This transit arouses an independent and rebellious spirit in just about everyone. You are inclined to do exactly the opposite of what someone suggests and to reject whatever others say simply because they said it. For the same reasons you are impatient with restraints, duties and responsibilities. There is a great need to be free and to do something very different, maybe even a little bit wild.

You have a strong craving for excitement with this transit, and you may act in ways that you would never consider in a more sober mood. This could be either good or bad, of course, depending on how conservative you usually are and how unusual or outrageous the action. For some people this can be a very liberating influence. For others it is a bit too much.

At the deepest level there is an emotional unrest within you that is likely to disturb your own peace of mind as well as your relations with others, especially those who make emotional demands upon you. You may want to make many changes in your life now, but remember that this is a very fleeting transit.

Some persons will not experience the psychological effects of this transit directly but will encounter its symbolism through others or through events. Thus you may experience unexpected emotional upsets or the arrival of erratic and upsetting persons in your life.

Moon Trine Uranus

At this time you are likely to crave emotional excitement, something that departs from the routine of your daily life. You are likely to seek out people who are different from those you usually meet. You might spend the day or evening in very different surroundings. And while you may feel a bit impulsive, these impulses make you feel more alive rather than inclined to act rashly or stupidly.

On a more quiet level, you may use this energy to make needed changes in your immediate personal life or your domestic environment. While others may seem startled by your apparently sudden moves, these changes should be constructive, and the people in your life will accept them.

If you have to deal with groups of people or with the general public, you will advocate change and new policies. You may have to assume a leadership role in order to bring this about, so be sure you have the energy and inclination to follow through with this on the long haul. This transit by itself does not supply enough stamina for a continuing effort, because its effects are short-lived.

Sometimes this transit coincides with an unexpected surprise, usually not pleasant, that will change your plans for the next period of time. Don't count on having your expectations fulfilled today, although you will have the chance to make whatever happens work out favorably for you.

Moon Opposition Uranus

You will have to be quite careful for a while, because you are emotionally excitable and impulsive at this time. You may leap to unwarranted conclusions, especially about matters involving your emotional life, so you should avoid making any decisive moves at this time.

In your contacts with others you will seek excitement and stimulation, and thus you may attract people who are quite different from your usual crowd. You may even be quite upset by these new people, but you should realize that they are filling a real need in your life now. Or you may act disruptively in your current relationships. It is not exactly that you are trying to start a fight, but in talking with someone you may stir up feelings that cause a fight to begin unintentionally. Consequently this can be a stormy period in relationships.

It is also possible that you will have some sort of emotional surprise. For example, you may receive news that upsets you, or you may just feel very edgy and upset for no particular reason for several hours.

If anyone tries to restrict you, your reaction will be very negative, even if the restrictions are in your best interests. Your immediate response to any restriction is to break away and rebel. If someone asserts a point of view strongly, you may disagree out of pure contrariness. Obviously some caution is necessary, because you may react simply for the sake of reacting and thereby do yourself a disservice.

Moon Conjunct Neptune

The influence of this transit is subtle but not weak. Your sensitivity to your surroundings is greatly increased, as is your empathy with those around you. At this time you may listen to a friend's problems, or you may discuss your own problems with a friend.

You will be likely to pick up the mood of the people around you, as if you were an emotional "sponge." Therefore you should be careful about being with negative people who are not willing to discuss their emotional problems in a rational manner.

On another level, this transit can stimulate your fantasies amazingly. You may feel like just sitting down and drifting off into your own private world. On the negative side, this influence makes drinking or drug taking dangerous, because you may have difficulty controlling the amount you take. Sometimes with this transit you just feel sleepy.

Unfortunately, communications with others may be difficult now. Your thoughts are not very clear, and your experiences are difficult to reduce to words. Poetry and art, especially escapist art or literature, appeal to you greatly at this time.

Your relationships under this influence are dubious. You are very likely to misinterpret someone or be misinterpreted, which may lead to thinking about the situation very unrealistically. Beware of self-delusion.

Moon Sextile Neptune

This transit makes you extremely sensitive to other people's moods, and if you are at all psychic you will be more sensitive in this regard as well. But with this sensitivity, you have to be careful about the people you are with. Negative people or those who have destructive energies will exhaust you and make you feel bad.

On the other hand, it is good to be with friends whom you are devoted to. This combination can signify selflessness and genuinely caring for others without regard for your own needs. And this is not done in a martyred spirit. You feel great sympathy and compassion for those who are in need, and you are willing to help either personally or through working with a charitable group.

This transit may also arouse your daydreaming tendencies. You may wish to be by yourself and retire into your own private inner world, or you may wish to talk about your daydreams with friends. Sometimes it is good to discuss your fantasies, because even though they cannot be taken at face value, they do have meaning, which you should try to find out about now.

If you are at all interested in the occult or in spiritual or mystical matters, your interest will be especially great at this time. You are able to relax your mind in such a way that insights and truths come quite readily. You may discover that you know things that you weren't aware of knowing.

Moon Square Neptune

During this transit you are likely to fall into a dreamy state of mind in which fancies and illusions become more important than reality. With some people this takes the form of simple daydreams, which are not likely to be a problem. After all, daydreaming is quite harmless. Or you may appear to be in touch with reality and think that you are, although you are operating under a serious delusion about some matter. This is not a good time to make decisions or to embark upon a course of action that requires clear thinking.

Subconscious influences are often very strong with this transit, and they can distort your views in just about any area. Old points of view, habits picked up in childhood, prejudices — all can mislead you under this influence.

This transit also increases your sensitivity to environmental influences, but it is not always easy to understand the meaning of what you see. With some people this is a very psychic influence, but remember that you cannot take what you see at face value. You will probably have to spend much time reinterpreting it later, when your rational faculties are clearer. Often there is an inclination to study mystical or supernatural phenomena.

People with an alcohol or drug problem may have difficulty with this transit. It gives everyone a strong desire to leave the real world, which strengthens some people's dependence on drinking or drug taking.

Moon Trine Neptune

This transit will bring forth your innermost subconscious fantasies. You may spend considerable time daydreaming and not accomplish very much, but you will probably feel that it has been worth it. Dreams can be very refreshing to the spirit. At times we all need to withdraw a bit from the real world and encounter our inner selves.

Actually this transit can be quite useful even in a mundane sense, because it is very stimulating to the imagination. Just make sure that you can separate your fantasies from reality. But for any kind of artistic work or creative effort, this influence can be very useful.

Under this transit you have great sympathy for others. You are able to put yourself in their place and know exactly how you would feel in such a situation. You want to help others, with little thought of any benefit to yourself, and this is one of those influences that makes you truly selfless, not merely in appearance. You may work to help people whom you consider less fortunate than yourself.

On another level, you are very sensitive to other people's moods. You pick up impressions readily, and if you are not careful you could get into the same mood as the people around you, whether good or bad. So it is important to avoid persons who are in a negative mood who will not be helped by your positive input.

There is often a strong interest in psychic or spiritual subjects under this transit.

Moon Opposition Neptune

This can be a time of very strange moods. You are very sensitive emotionally, but the impressions you receive through your sensitivity may not be very accurate. You have vague feelings about the circumstances and people around you, and you may feel very confused, because you aren't sure whether you are being realistic or unduly suspicious and fearful. Under this transit misunderstandings with others are very likely, because you tend to feel that others have unfairly criticized or hurt you, although they have done nothing of the sort. Or you may feel that someone dislikes you for the flimsiest reasons. The source of the problem is that this transit activates your subconscious complexes, which take over your moods and perceptions. Instead of reacting to the reality of what you see, you react automatically to the subconscious process set off by what you see.

Another possible problem with this transit is that you may have feelings of inferiority or guilt, usually for no reason. Thus you are easily discouraged by circumstances and withdraw into your own private world. This may cause you to miss an opportunity to assert yourself when you should.

Avoid the use of drugs or alcohol, because they will reinforce the negative aspects of this transit and hasten your withdrawal from reality, which will further cloud the real issues of your life. Allergic reactions to foods and beverages are also likely at this time, which is another reason to be careful about what you consume.

Moon Conjunct Pluto

This transit can bring about very intense emotional experiences, because it tends to bring energies to the surface from the deepest part of your psyche. It is the sort of transit that could make for a very fruitful session with one's analyst. Even if you are not in any kind of therapy, however, you are likely to have some kind of self-analytic interaction with another person. Events that take place now may allow you to learn about your real feelings.

This transit can indicate strong feelings that completely overwhelm you for a time and take away your sense of perspective. Be very careful not to overestimate the short-range significance of your present feelings; they may be significant in the long run, but you cannot take the mood itself at face value. It is likely to symbolize a deeper emotion that really is significant. A closely related effect of this transit is its power to produce an obsession, an idea you cannot get out of your mind that seems to be running you. It will probably pass as soon as the transit is out of orb, but it can be uncomfortable for the time being.

Relations with women will be unusually intense now, and in a love relationship this transit signifies deep emotional experiences that can be either positive or negative. Be careful about games in which you and your partner manipulate emotions to gain power over each other. Also be careful about feelings of possessiveness and jealousy, which are likely at this time.

Moon Sextile Pluto

This transit arouses deep feelings and emotions. You desire experience at a very profound level and do not like superficial encounters. With friends and loved ones you seek the true meaning of your feelings for each other. Under this transit, deep-rooted feelings in a relationship are often brought to the surface so that you can deal with them. This has a therapeutic effect on most relationships, for it releases hidden energies that may be weakening the ties between you.

On another level this transit awakens a love of the mysterious. This can range from simply reading a good mystery novel to delving into the mysterious, occult and hidden. The study of psychology, astrology, magic or other supernatural phenomena may satisfy such a desire.

Often this transit signifies a desire to make changes in your personal and domestic sphere. These are usually short-term changes, such as cleaning, repairing and reorganizing things in your home.

Under this transit you should be careful not to set an objective for yourself and then become so obsessed by it that you lose track of everything else. Even this rather mild transit can result in a one-track mind and compulsive behavior. If this happens, it is a sign that hidden in this compulsion is a psychological energy that you should try to understand, because it could control some part of your life.

Moon Square Pluto

This transit can have many different effects, some of which you should be quite careful of. To begin with, it encourages compulsive behavior; your emotions acquire so much momentum that it is difficult not to give in to sudden urges and impulses that may not be good for you in the long run, particularly if you have been trying to suppress your feelings. This transit is least difficult if you deal with your feelings honestly and do not try to hide them from yourself.

On the plus side, however, this transit allows you to go inside yourself and find out what you really want in any situation. Emotional self-analysis is very effective now, as long as you are willing to be honest. Encounters with others may also force an emotional self-confrontation which is useful, even though possibly unpleasant.

This transit may take the more negative form of emotional power struggles with others. You may play the role of either perpetrator or victim. What happens is that you or another person uses or manipulates feelings and emotions in order to force the other to do something that he or she does not wish to do. Guilt, jealousy and other subversive techniques are characteristic of this process and may be used to manipulate someone's behavior. But this in turn may provoke a really nasty response from the victim, whether it be you or the other person.

Moon Trine Pluto

This transit makes your feelings and emotions much more intense, but at the same time it stimulates your sensitivity. You feel everything much more powerfully than usual, and you are not likely to take your feelings or anyone else's lightly. This transit puts you in a serious mood and makes you seek the most powerful and intimate encounters with another. Sexual relationships may be considerably enriched, because this transit enables you to get past the superficial levels of communication that may have been driving you and your loved one apart. In this way you can again feel as one.

Even with this relatively mild Moon-Pluto combination, there is a danger of obsessive thinking, of allowing one idea, objective or mood to dominate your mind. Don't let your emotions run your life at this time, but don't repress them and keep them from being expressed either.

Persons whom you encounter at this time may exhibit a similar intensity. When you meet them, there will be a great deal of feeling and soul evident, but you may find such a meeting exhausting. Moon-Pluto combinations release energies that demand much of your energy.

In general, life will call you to approach it with some passion and feeling. And if you can respond, it can be a very rich and rewarding experience in which you learn much about your feelings.

Moon Opposition Pluto

At this time your emotions are likely to be very profound and not always harmonious. There is a whole series of typical emotional conflicts that may occur in relationships, as well as conflicts within yourself.

First of all, you can expect intense encounters with others, chiefly those with whom you are very emotionally involved. The deepest and most powerful forces within your subconscious mind are influencing your actions now, and often it is difficult to avoid acting impulsively. Guilt, jealousy, overpossessiveness or simply the desire to control another's emotions can take possession of you, or you may experience these feelings through someone else. You can be sure that any conflicts between you and another person will reveal a great deal about the inner workings of you both. If you can view such conflicts dispassionately and in a calmer light later on, you may derive some benefit from this transit. Otherwise, these encounters are likely to be fruitless and irritating.

With this transit it is often hard to see your life clearly at the time. It stirs up subconscious forces that may influence your perception so much that you can't see anything as it really is. Like several other Moon opposition transits, this is not a good time for reaching a conclusion. On the other hand, if you experience a feeling that is so powerful it must be expressed, go ahead and express it. You will gain nothing by holding it in except to give it more unconscious power over you.

Moon Conjunct Midheaven

At this time you may display great sensitivity and feeling in front of or when dealing with others. Or you may allow your thinking to be entirely overcome by personal and subjective considerations so that no one can communicate with you or understand you. This transit can go either way.

On the positive side, it enables you to feel out the mood of a group of people so that you can appeal to their deepest emotional concerns. This is very good if you are acting in any kind of leadership role or if you have to make a presentation before a group.

But on the negative side, this transit may make you shy away from groups or from people in general. The same energy that enables you to feel out moods also makes you feel vulnerable and exposed with others. If you feel this way, you should withdraw from public view and stay in your own personal world. Thinking and decision-making are not favored by this transit, because your mind is dominated by personal fears, habits, the desire to protect yourself and petty personal motives that cannot go beyond your immediate psychological necessities. Obviously your own sense of inner security will determine which of these two paths you will follow.

Moon Sextile Midheaven

This transit normally indicates a period of unusually intense feelings. You will have a strong desire to know yourself and to experience life largely through the emotions. This is probably not the best time for work that requires a completely clear and dispassionate state of consciousness, but you will not feel like doing that kind of work anyway. You will want to engage your emotions in whatever you do, and you will experience a richness of feeling and inner life that is satisfying in itself.

But on another level, you may tend to react automatically and according to habit during this transit. You will be attracted to familiar surroundings and avoid situations that you are not used to. This is not necessarily a problem unless you carry it too far. You may react to others unconsciously and project aspects of yourself that you had no intention of projecting. This is particularly likely to occur if you have difficulty with your emotions in general. If you are generally at ease with your feelings, you will experience the more positive manifestations described above. Most people will encounter these, along with the inclination to retire to familiar surroundings.

This transit is good for any business matters concerning the general public or for any situation in which you have to appear before the public or a large group. Otherwise it is not a transit that stimulates drive and ambition.

Moon Square Midheaven

This transit is likely to signify rapidly changing moods, which may interfere with clear perception of your goals, especially if your goals have been set without much regard for your personal needs. If your goals are purely professional or make excessive demands on your personal and domestic life, this transit will be somewhat disruptive. You may feel dissatisfied with your progress, or you may feel that no matter how much you accomplish, there is always something lacking. This transit sometimes signifies tensions in your domestic life.

All of these feelings signify that you need to readjust or at least reexamine your priorities with regard to career and family. Which is more important to you in the long run, and which should be? There are no standard answers to these questions, but you should try to find your personal answers.

If you have handled this matter well, you should encounter the more positive side of this transit and be able to go about your business with a remarkable sense of wholeness. You will feel that your activities are satisfying, both professionally and personally, and that your inner and outer needs are being met. Thus you will have a great deal more emotional sensitivity in your business and personal life and will be able to relate to a situation emotionally as well as intellectually. Under any circumstances your emotions are unusually strong with this transit, and you will react to any situation much more emotionally than usual.

Moon Trine Midheaven

At this time your personal needs and career needs are balanced, and there will not be as much tension between them as at other times. Also your emotions are in tune with your intentions so that you can go about your business with complete oneness. There is less of the feeling that two sides of you are struggling for mastery over the whole.

Under this transit you have a great ability to relate to others on an emotional level, because you feel your emotions so richly yourself. You are sensitive to others' needs, and you understand how you can use their moods and sensitivities for positive ends. It is not likely that you will manipulate people's feelings in negative ways, but you can sway others to your point of view on any matter.

On the other hand, you may choose to retire into your own personal world, either within your own mind or in your home and family sphere. The richness of feeling and emotion that this transit brings may make you feel like being alone or with only your closest loved ones. It is a contemplative time, when quiet seems to be the highest virtue. But this feeling doesn't come from a desire to retreat from a confrontation with the world. It is a positive desire to be quiet and appreciate the higher beauties of existence. It is a time of recharging, which we all need to take from time to time. If you feel this way now, don't deny yourself the satisfaction of this need.

Moon Opposition Midheaven

At this time you will feel like going inside yourself and getting more in touch with your feelings and moods. If you have to be with people, you prefer to be with close loved ones or someone with whom you feel at ease and for whom you need not put on a social front.

This is a time when you would like to be at home with your immediate family. It is not a good time to have to put yourself on display, show off a talent or make a presentation to others. But if you can bring someone into your immediate circle, that is, into your most intimate environment, you will feel that it is easier to deal with him or her. You feel a strong need to be on "your own turf."

However, this transit does present an opportunity for you to be alone and to decide how you really feel about various matters. Your own feelings will be so strong and will influence your perception so much that it will be hard for you to escape them. Obviously your subjective concerns will take precedence over the demands of the outside world now, but this is as it should be. This is a time to recharge and build up energy for times to come.

Moon Conjunct Ascendant

For a few hours you will feel much more emotional than usual. This, of course, can be either good or bad, depending upon how you normally relate to your emotions. If you are ill at ease with your feelings, you will not consciously be aware of them. But you will relate to people in automatic ways, conditioned by habit. You will respond unconsciously to small cues put out by other persons that neither you nor they are aware of. The problem here is that you are unable to see each new moment and person afresh. You become nothing more than the product of your past, and your behavior can be quite inappropriate to the needs of the moment.

On the other hand, if you can handle the emotions that are aroused, you will be able to relate to others with great feeling and empathy. This transit is excellent for occasions when you and another person must relate at a very deep, intense level, when you communicate not only with your rational mind but with your subliminal senses as well. Even a casual encounter may have this quality of emotional depth.

Women may be very important to you today, and you should observe your reactions to them. Do not allow your unconscious mind to run away with you.

Moon Sextile Ascendant

This transit increases your desire to be with people whom you are emotionally close to. Friends, especially female friends, and relatives with whom you have shared many past experiences are very important to you now. You may spend this time talking over old times or engaging in a sentimental reverie.

But you are also very sensitive to other people's moods and can judge them quickly. You lend a sympathetic and friendly ear to people's problems, for you have a strong desire to protect and support your friends emotionally. Peace and harmony in your personal world are very important to you at this time, and you are not willing to deal with someone else's harsh feelings, except to try to smooth them over.

Your sensitivity to other people also enables you to deal easily with groups. You respond to the group's changes of mood and are able to fit your communication to that mood. Thus this is a good time for any sort of public appearance or situation in which you have to sell something to a group or persuade them of a point of view. You are able to make others feel that you are one of them.

Your emotions are strong at this time, and you are primarily concerned with relating to people emotionally. Your contacts with others may not always be characterized by strictly rational thinking or behavior at this time, but they will be warm.

Moon Square Ascendant

Under this transit your emotions are strong when dealing with others, which can be either good or bad, depending on how you handle it. On the plus side, it gives you a great deal of sensitivity toward others. You can feel their moods immediately and respond to them so that you are able to fit into any group you are with. You value emotional contacts at this time, and you project feeling, warmth and concern to others.

But on the negative side, this transit can also signify that you are so wrapped up in your moods that you can't get out of yourself and relate to anyone else. This transit can be a sign of destructive subjectivity in which you see only what you want to see.

In either case your moods are likely to fluctuate rather rapidly, so do not take your emotions too seriously at this time. You should make an effort to be with others, because forcing yourself to relate will bring out the better side of this transit.

Any task that requires much reason and clear thinking is not likely to work out very well under this transit, even at best. You are oriented to feeling rather than to logical thinking. Your judgments are likely to be impressionistic, based on the mood of the moment rather than on reason. Later, when that mood has passed, you may not be able to understand why you made a certain decision.

Moon Trine Ascendant

This transit is good for all kinds of relationships in that all your contacts with others are warm and emotional. You do not choose superficial or formal contacts but instead desire to make a personal connection with everyone you meet. At the same time you feel a strong need to protect and nurture those whom you are close to. There is something of the maternal instinct in the way you care for others. You are also very sensitive to people's emotional needs and wants, which enables you to respond to them at a very deep level of understanding.

Often this transit signifies being with women, and certainly you will be able to get along with women very well. You may even receive some benefit from a female acquaintance, regardless of your own sex. Even with male friends, you will relate on a very emotional level.

You will have a great need to feel that you belong to any group that you associate with at this time. Fortunately you will also be able to make others feel that they belong with you. Your sensitivity to others enables you to understand the moods of groups and of the general public, so this is a good time for any kind of public encounter.

One facet of this transit is that it can enable you to understand more about your emotional nature and the nature of your personal relationships, and it does so without being upsetting. Your emotions are so much closer to the surface of your being that you can see them clearly.

Moon Opposition Ascendant

During this transit your closest contacts will take on a more emotional tone. You will be able to communicate your feelings more easily to your spouse, a close working partner or anyone else whom you encounter on an intimate level. Quite frequently this transit is also a sign that you will be closely involved with a woman, although the nature of the involvement is not specified.

Although the effects of this transit are not very difficult to deal with, you should be aware that you are likely to be so emotional and subjective in your relations with others that you may have difficulty seeing someone else's point of view. This is not an especially good time for delicate negotiations or discussions in which you must think clearly and objectively. However, this transit favors situations in which you have to be sensitive to another's feelings or in which someone else has to be sensitive to yours.

In your contacts with others you will seek warmth, support and nurture, and you will be equally capable of giving these to others when necessary. You are very sensitive to this need in yourself and others, and if you do not receive it, you feel quite badly. You may be somewhat less self-reliant than usual now, for this is one of those times when interaction and needing others is more important.

Chapter Six

Mercury

Significance of Transiting Mercury

The transiting Mercury is not one of the most powerful indicators in the horoscope, but it does indicate shifts of mental focus and attention as it transits the houses and planets. Also it indicates the kinds of communications you have with other people throughout the year. Sometimes it is an indicator of travel, usually short trips that do not seriously alter your everyday routine.

On another level, Mercury *is* the everyday routine, in that it signifies the nature of your casual interchange with the world around you. But casual does not mean unimportant; it means simply something we are so used to that we do not see its effects. Nevertheless, being conscious of the "Mercury function" in your life can be enormously valuable. Most of us go through our lives without ever really being conscious of how our words affect other people; instead we are too caught up in reacting to their words. We are reacting to them reacting to us reacting to them, and so on. Obviously if you can become conscious of this process, you can learn to control it and thereby control many situations as well. Thus it is extremely important to study your Mercury transits and see how they operate for you. Even though their effects are subtle, the knowledge that you gain from them can be extremely useful.

On another level, Mercury relates to communications received as well as given. During a busy Mercury period you may receive a lot of mail or many telephone calls as well as unexpected visits. The pace of your interchange with others increases when Mercury is active in your horoscope, and it can sometimes be a very busy and exciting time. You can usually count on not being bored by Mercury, but again it is important to note that Mercury usually intensifies the daily routine rather than disrupts it.

Sometimes a Mercury transit represents a time when you should just sit and think. Mercury rules the rational mind, and in many of its transits, your mind is unusually clear. So it may be a good idea to get away from it all and be alone with your thoughts, even though Mercury usually likes to be around others.

Mercury in the First House

This is a good time for expressing your point of view to people. You are able to put a great deal of yourself into whatever you say, so it is somehow more authentically yourself speaking. At the same time, you have the capacity to examine yourself with somewhat greater objectivity and detachment than usual. Your mind will be more active, and it is important to keep it occupied with useful projects, because you can accomplish a great deal with your mind at this time.

One effect of Mercury is that your mind and consciousness jumps from issue to issue very rapidly, which may confuse the people around you a bit. You aren't trying to be deceptive, but your mind is likely to move so fast under this influence that you seem to be constantly changing. Again it is really the focus of your attention that changes. Mercury does not settle on any one issue for very long, which is one of the greater deficiencies of this energy, because it never really gets into an issue deeply. Try to control this tendency, for it can be a waste of energy.

If Mercury transits planets that are afflicted in your natal first house, or if Mercury is afflicted by another transiting planet while it is transiting a planet in this house, you may react with nervousness or anxiety. This usually means that you are becoming too involved in some mental problem. Try to relax and get your mind away from serious subjects to something light and entertaining.

Often with this transit you will have a strong urge to get out and travel, although not usually for long distances. This is fine if it is convenient and you feel like doing this. You could encounter a rather profitable and interesting experience in your travels. Usually this is a good time to be involved in negotiations or contract discussions of any kind. Your mind will be quite clear, if you keep it from running too quickly and if you know what you want.

Mercury in the Second House

At this time your attention naturally turns to whatever you value in life, whether it be material, intellectual or spiritual. You will think about and plan for these elements much more than usual now, and you may enter into negotiations with others concerning property or money. Or you may have to define your sense of values to another person so that he or she knows where you stand on an issue.

On the mundane level, this transit often signifies that you are much more concerned with business and commercial affairs than usual. This can cover a broad range of activity, from shopping much more than usual to entering into an important business negotiation. The important point here is that whatever you do in this area, you will put a great deal of planning and consideration into it, and transactions will be more important and elaborate than usual. As a result you should be able to make the situation work out the way you want.

There is an exception to this, however, if you have serious afflictions to planets in the house natally or if Mercury is afflicted while it is transiting a natal planet in this house. It is best to avoid significant financial or property transactions on such days. Check the transits of Mercury to your natal planets for this information. Your mind is likely to be cloudy or unclear then, so you will not see all the issues involved and may be misled accidentally or intentionally by another person.

Mercury in the Third House

Mercury is in its own house here. This means that its action is intensified, and you will feel its energies much more strongly than usual. You will have many group discussions and conversations with others; you will meet new people, possibly travel quite a bit and certainly have more contact with relatives and immediate neighbors. It is as if the electricity were suddenly turned on in your mind, and you feel that you have to communicate with as many people as possible.

This is a very good time for all kinds of intellectual activities, assuming that in your natal horoscope there are no serious afflictions to this house. It is also a good time to speak to others and listen to them.

It is not a good time to try to settle down and relax. The tempo of events in your environment is likely to be too fast, and it will be difficult to avoid getting caught up in it. Nevertheless you should try sometimes to disconnect yourself from this frantic pace, because it may get to the point that you are continually distracted and unable to think properly. For this reason it is not the best time to try to reach a conclusion on some matter. Wait until the tempo slows down so you can look over what you have learned with some perspective about the whole process. Use this time to gather information rather than to reach conclusions. In dealings with others, contract negotiations or business deals, it is wise to use this period to make everyone's position clear and to discuss possibilities rather than to reach final conclusions. Keep your mind flexible now and be ready for any new experiences that may come along. Do not allow your point of view or your opinions to harden.

Mercury in the Fourth House

This is a time of intellectual withdrawal, but not in a negative way. You aren't withdrawing to avoid a confrontation with reality but to reflect and think about all the ideas you have encountered recently. It is a good time to examine your personal and domestic life and to make plans or evaluate whether it is meeting your needs. This is an excellent transit for discussions with your immediate family about matters that are important to all of you. You are able to voice your innermost thoughts at this time, and you should if you feel that something must be said. Do not allow pressures to build up within you that you do not express toward the people around you. This will only lead to disturbances in your thinking later on. Besides, your mental focus is on this part of your life now, and it is easier than usual to express your innermost feelings and emotions.

Your thoughts may drift continually back to events that occurred in the past, and you may wonder why you cannot focus on the concerns of the present. This is an indication that some aspect of those past events is affecting the present and that your subconscious mind is drawing attention to it so that you can handle it in some way. In other words, look for a link between the events of the past that are on your mind and the matters that concern you today. Finding that link could enable you to solve a current problem.

You may have to communicate with one of your parents in order to find out more about the past event that is bothering you. And in any case, having a discussion with them or communicating via letters may prove extremely helpful to you in some way.

Mercury in the Fifth House

This is a good time for expressing your thoughts to yourself and for communicating them to others. In this respect it is rather like the transit of Mercury through the first house. You can make clear to people your stand on any matter and explain very effectively any issue that is on your mind. You will also be inclined to use your mind for amusement, that is, for reading, writing and playing games that require mental agility. These activities will be more attractive than usual during this time.

Often the ideas that come into your head now will have no special function except that they are fun to play with. Just be careful not to transfer this playful spirit to your communications with others to the extent that you play with people for your own amusement. Astrologers often fail to recognize that Mercury is the planet of pranks, and in this house it is very likely to make you feel prankish. The danger is that with this house you are more inclined to release your inner energy outward than to allow energy input to come from others. Thus you may be rather insensitive to people's needs if you are not careful. This is particularly important to remember if you feel like playing a joke on someone. Also, in conversations with others you may be a very poor listener at this time.

On the other hand, pursuing mental activities for their own sake, such as games or reading as mentioned above, can enlarge your mind even if that is not your intention. You may very well inadvertently educate yourself in ways that will later prove useful. Do not feel that you have to justify everything you do now with some practical motive. Later experience will no doubt show you the usefulness of these activities, but don't worry about that now.

Mercury in the Sixth House

Two different areas of manifestation — health and work — may be connected with this transit. Let us look at the work dimension first.

This is an excellent time for all kinds of mental work. You are much more attentive to detail than usual and especially concerned about using the best techniques available. You want everything you do to be as perfect as possible, so you plan carefully and work out every detail in advance. In that way you will not be caught by surprise. At the same time, your planning has a great sense of purpose. You feel that there is practical work to be done, and you are willing to devote your attention to getting it done properly.

This attitude toward doing a job well will enable you to get along well with employers and with employees. It is a good time to sit down with either of these groups and talk over any problems that exist. There is far less ego involvement than usual in your discussion, so you can take whatever steps are necessary, without your personal affairs getting in the way.

One problem to be careful about is criticizing others. This transit may sharpen your critical ability, and while you are less concerned with your own ego needs, you may also be rather careless of other people's ego needs. Even in the interests of what you consider to be "objective" truth, try not to trample on others' feelings.

If you experience the health aspect of this transit, it is most likely to be negative. If there are afflictions to this house in your natal horoscope or if Mercury is afflicted while transiting a planet in this house, you may feel nervous or anxious about some matter. The cause of your anxiety is most likely not a rational fear, and you should not take it seriously except that it is an unnecessary strain upon the body.

You may also become more concerned with your health and interested in improving your hygiene. It is not that this concern is especially necessary now, but that your attention is being drawn to this aspect of your life. If you do start to improve your diet now, be sure that you continue this program consistently as Mercury transits the other houses.

Mercury in the Seventh House

This is a good time to clarify and explain an issue to someone with whom you are intimately associated in daily life, such as your spouse or business partner. It is also good for consulting a specialist on any matter that concerns you. You should not think and plan alone or unassisted today. You need another person's consciousness and response to your ideas and statements in order to get a clear perspective on your thoughts. Also, finding out your partner's thoughts will help him or her to clarify them. Together you will be able to accomplish much more than either of you could separately.

It is also a good time to discuss any difficulties that have come up in your intimate relationships. You are capable of taking a much more detached view than usual, and you can reach conclusions objectively, which might be difficult at other times. Your communication concerning such matters is also unusually clear.

In all your encounters today, you will seek intellectual stimulation and conversation, ranging from cheerful banter to spirited debate. You are looking for mental encounters today, and even argument and controversy are interesting, certainly preferable to no stimulation at all.

This is a good transit for making contracts or entering into negotiations about any matter, if Mercury is not transiting a planet that is afflicted in your seventh house or if Mercury is not afflicted during its transit by another transiting planet. In such a case it would be wise to avoid all types of negotiations.

Mercury in the Eighth House

At this time it is good to look inward and reflect upon deep psychological truths within yourself. In many ways your rational intellect is closer now to the areas of your being that are usually hidden even from yourself. You can use this time to get more in touch with these hidden aspects.

This transit often signifies conversations and intellectual encounters that have a profound effect upon your mind, causing you to go deep within yourself and make changes in your point of view or ways of thinking. Or you may have this effect on someone else. In some cases you and another person may be amazed that you have a tremendous hold over each other's mind and can affect each other greatly. Even though all your communication is verbal, another kind of energy seems to be operating that is harder to fathom, that goes down to the deepest roots of your being.

This transit is conducive to very deep thinking, sometimes including thoughts about your own and your loved ones' mortality. Reflecting upon these matters from time to time in moderation can help to keep your life in perspective, but don't get too carried away by thoughts of death, because this can draw you away from the here and now.

On a mundane level, this transit can coincide with discussions and negotiations concerning finances or property, particularly those that you hold jointly with someone else. Unless you have serious afflictions to planets in this house or the transiting Mercury is itself afflicted, this should be a very favorable time for such negotiations.

Mercury in the Ninth House

This is a good time for any kind of study and education, because you are intellectually eager for knowledge and new experiences. You want to take a larger view of life in order to see how the various parts fit together to make up the whole. Any new and interesting phenomenon from a world outside your own is likely to attract your attention at this time. Subjects relating to foreign places, the law, philosophy or higher knowledge of any kind will engage your attention. It is possible that you may have some dealings with officials connected with the law, although you should not fear this possibility particularly.

Although this transit is not very long, it is a good time to travel. Your curiosity makes travel very interesting to you. But to get the most from the experience, you should expose yourself to a life as different from your own as possible. You are quite open to alternative lifestyles at this time, so try to encounter as many different ways of living as you can.

This transit is good for all kinds of conversation and communication with others, especially about rather abstract ideas, general philosophy and approaches to life. It is easier now to make your position in these areas clear to others. Also you will be inclined to listen more carefully to what others have to say about these ideas; and you will be especially interested if their beliefs differ from your own. Consequently you are much more tolerant than usual of different opinions.

Mercury in the Tenth House

Under this influence you should make plans concerning your professional life or the equivalent area of your life. Even if you do not have a profession, you doubtless have some activity that you pursue as a form of ego expression within your larger society, such as working in a club or organization. Think about what you have been doing along these lines and whether or not it is working out as you want it to. If necessary, plan to make changes that will improve it for you.

This is a good time to undertake new studies that might help your career — learning new techniques, for example, or studying your job in order to gain greater mastery over it.

This is also a favorable time to talk to superiors, bosses or employers about your work and how you may advance in your job. This may or may not be a good time for actually trying to get a promotion, depending on other factors. But you can use this time to find the best way to go about getting a promotion.

Communications on the job may assume greater importance than usual under this influence, but be careful not to get all tangled up in red tape. This transit can make you so concerned with petty procedural aspects of the job — paper work, filling out forms and so forth — that you don't have time for the important and rewarding aspects of your work.

On the other hand, you may become involved with the part of your business that involves communicating with the outside world, either through advertising or through contract negotiations. This should work out quite favorably, assuming that an afflicted planet in the tenth house of your chart is not being transited by another planet at the same time.

Mercury in the Eleventh House

Mercury in this transit inclines you to think about your goals and expectations in life. You will examine your ideals to find out exactly how well they have served you and to what extent you have attained them. You should also think about whether your goals are really your own or whether they are in part other people's goals that you have adopted for yourself. In the latter case, decide whether these goals are appropriate for you.

This is the house of group ideals and standards and also the house of your position in groups generally. You should examine your attitudes toward these groups. At this time you need and will have more verbal and intellectual exchanges with friends and with other groups that you are associated with. Talking over your problems with friends will be especially helpful in reaching an objective viewpoint. But keep in mind that talking things over with friends cannot free you from prejudices and preconceptions that are held by the entire group.

Another characteristic of this transit is that you may encounter younger people in your immediate circle of friends, which can give you a new and freer point of view about yourself and about life in general. This is a time of increased communication and social intercourse.

Mercury in the Twelfth House

There are two sides of this transit. On the one hand, you may be inclined to keep your opinions to yourself and not communicate them to others, even when you should. But at the same time you may be more in touch with the hidden sides of your own personality, your unconscious drives and compulsions than at most other times. The first of these two effects may be undesirable or inappropriate, but the ability to get at hidden areas of your character can be quite useful.

The problem here is that you may feel that others will hold anything you say against you. And this may be true, especially if your words are motivated by petty ego concerns. But it is even more likely that what you don't say will be held against you, so it is very important at this time to say everything that has to be said. Eliminate all doubt and uncertainty both from other people's minds and from your own. Keeping secrets will only undermine others' confidence in you.

You may feel like going off by yourself to think or study at this time, and that should work out quite well. You may also feel like withdrawing into yourself and meditating. Mercury in this house is often a sign of greater concern with spiritual and religious matters and increased ability to deal with nonrational aspects of reality.

On another level, this is a good time for doing research by yourself. You work and think best alone at this time, and you should not be afraid to do so. It is not inappropriate to go off to think or to be by yourself, but it is a poor thing to retreat from fear of confrontation. If necessary, confront someone and don't be afraid of that. If you keep the situation out in the open, it is less likely to work against you. But if you feel that quiet and peace would be beneficial, by all means seek them out.

Mercury Conjunct Sun

At this time you must express yourself and your thinking in every possible way. Your mind is clearer than usual, and you feel more alert and mentally sharp. At the same time you are very conscious of your purpose in any project you are engaged in, which enables you to express that purpose clearly to others. Just be careful that you aren't putting so much energy into communicating with others that you aren't allowing their communication to come back in to you. Also don't let your own subjective point of view blind you to others' points of view.

You are able to express yourself with considerable vigor and make an impression upon others if you need to. Even when the opposition gets heavy, you will stand up for your point of view, which will undoubtedly win the respect of even those whom you disagree with.

On a more trivial level, this day will be crowded with communications, whether by letters, telephone calls or personal conversation. And you will initiate most of these.

Sometimes this transit gives the day an electric quality that makes you eager to get out and travel. You may feel restless and unwilling to stay in one place. Your mind wants to capture as much new material as possible, so travel if you can. You will learn more quickly during this transit than at almost any other time.

Your eager mind may also attract the attention of someone above you, who will get in touch with you about some matter that is important to you. In general this transit favors communication with men rather than with women, but all communication is improved.

Mercury Sextile Sun

Under this transit you will have a rather busy but mentally stimulating day. You should have no difficulty keeping amused, because your mind is sharp, alive and ready for all kinds of experiences. Even in the ordinary, everyday aspects of your world you see the possibilities for new knowledge and understanding. You have great curiosity.

Quite frequently this transit indicates one of those days when the telephone never seems to stop ringing. It seems as if everyone wants to get in touch with you, and you have to contact many people too. Important communications from others may very well come by mail, telephone or personal conversation. And you will speak your mind with everyone. It is very important with this transit to let people know exactly where you stand on every issue. Your honesty and forthrightness in what you say will command the respect of others.

This is an excellent time for any kind of group discussion in which you have to work together to arrive at a common decision. It is also good if you have to report to a group about some activity that you have been involved in. Probably you will function as the head of such a group in some way.

Very often this transit is associated with travel. You may not have to go very far, but you will probably get around a lot more than usual today, most likely in the course of normal business. But as with other aspects of your life today, the tempo of your business traveling will be accelerated.

Mercury Square Sun

This is not an especially difficult square. It indicates a day of busy mental activity and many communications with others. You will be busier than usual with letter writing, paper work and group conferences, which should run smoothly, although under certain circumstances there could be problems. Be especially careful not to speak or otherwise communicate from purely egotistic motives. Make your point and let it go at that, because chances are your statement will have enough energy to be effective without making a controversy of it. If you do turn it into a controversy, you will encounter opposition from people who are similarly inclined, and communication will grind to a halt.

Of course, others may try to stir up controversy with you. In particular you may have problems with persons in authority today. The best way to get around this is to wait until a day when your communications can be more tranquil.

If the tempo of daily affairs becomes too fast, as indeed it might under this influence, you could become very nervous. But it is very important not to get too agitated, because that will make you sloppy and careless in your work. It isn't that you don't care about what you are doing, but you are "vibrating" so that it is difficult to keep everything straight. Obviously this is a relatively beneficial transit for people whose mental pace is rather slow and stable, and not so good for those who are inherently somewhat nervous.

Your thinking will be tested today on several levels. Consider it from that point of view and try to learn from your mistakes. Do not try to defend any ideas that are clearly shown to be invalid.

Mercury Trine Sun

This is a favorable transit for all kinds of mental work and communication with others. Your mind should be unusually clear, and you should have a very good idea of what you want in any instance. Also you are able to state your case forcefully before others if you have to. Any mental work requiring a broad overview of the situation is favored.

Spend the day getting rid of any backlog of paperwork, writing letters or making necessary phone calls. Even if you don't make many calls, you will probably receive quite a few. This is also a favorable time for all kinds of group discussions and negotiations, at least from your point of view. Any kind of business negotiation will work out well because you can spell out all the requirements in detail. No one should be able to claim that they were not clearly informed.

This is a good day for organizing yourself, another person or a group, again because of the clear-headedness indicated by this transit. The easy relationship between your natal Sun and transiting Mercury will help you balance your own individual ego needs with those of others. They will feel that you are giving them a fair shake.

Your great curiosity today should enable you to pursue any kind of study very effectively, especially if it is new and interesting to you. You can also do routine mental work with this transit, but that is not favored as strongly as the study of a new subject.

Mercury Opposition Sun

Usually this transit increases the flow of communication and ideas between yourself and other people. However, it can also indicate serious ego conflicts and conflicts of will expressed verbally or through other means of communication. Like all oppositions, this is a high-energy transit; that is, if you are not careful how you use it, you will encounter turbulence and difficulty. You may feel that you have an urgent message to deliver today, and you may find it difficult to wait for the chance to express yourself. When you have said what you wanted to say, others may be strongly opposed to it. A compromise may be necessary, but it will not be easy to bring about except by introducing a third party into the discussion. Just be careful that the third party is really neutral and that both you and your opponent are convinced of that.

You can count on one result of this transit. Whatever your reaction to others or their reaction to you, each side will get through to the other. Communications are reasonably clear under this influence, though not necessarily harmonious.

Negotiations and contract discussions or other business dealings conducted now may not reach a successful conclusion immediately. Use this time to get a clear understanding of each other's position. Instead of reacting emotionally to what others say, simply let them say it. When the mood becomes more peaceful, you will be able to come to an agreement.

Sometimes this transit signifies communications between yourself and persons whom you usually have difficulty communicating with. This transit seems to give both sides an extra charge that gets you talking.

Don't hesitate to discuss important issues with others now, but be prepared for energies running high in the discussion. What you bring into the open at this time could really help you in the future.

Mercury Conjunct Moon

This is the best possible time to express your feelings and emotions, but it is not so favorable for reasoned logical communication. You may be quite capable of reasoning well under this influence, but pure reason and logic alone cannot communicate all that you want to express. With this transit you have to communicate on all levels, not just with your mind.

At times, your thinking may be so influenced by your feelings that it will be difficult to think through a situation from an objective position. This is not usually a great problem, but it will make it difficult to share your state of mind with anyone who doesn't happen to be in the same mood. If you are also upset, which is not indicated by this transit alone, others will find you very difficult to deal with, because you will be unable to see any position except your own.

On the other hand, if you are in a reasonably tranquil state of mind now, you will be a much better listener than usual. Your mind is receptive to the point that you receive not only words but also another person's moods and feelings. You can listen very sympathetically, because you can literally feel with the other person. Traditionally this kind of sensitivity is thought to favor communication with women, but actually this transit favors discussion with anyone who communicates with feelings as well as words.

It is quite likely that you will want to talk about matters that are personally important to you that have affected your life at the most personal level — your own history, your family, your home. You will favor those who have shared similar experiences. And if you have to counsel someone, you will seek out the familiar elements in that person's history in order to show that he or she is not alone.

Logical distinctions do not interest you very much at this time. You are more concerned with the elements that bind categories together rather than those that isolate them. For example, you want to know what people have in common rather than what makes them different, and you will seek an understanding that you can share with everyone.

Mercury Sextile Moon

This transit puts you much more in touch with your own feelings and with the feelings of the people you encounter. You are able to sense others' moods and to shape your communications so that what you say fits in with their feelings. And you can do this without being dishonest or unfaithful to what you have to say. This is because you are more aware of the feeling side of communication than usual, and you understand its relationship to the rational.

This ability is particularly useful when dealing with groups of people. This is an excellent transit for talking to groups and trying to persuade them of your point of view. But it is important to be honest in what you are saying, because people will pick up the real meaning behind what you seem to be saying if there is a discrepancy. Sometimes this transit can give you the ability to charm groups of people.

Like other Mercury-Moon contacts, this transit is a good time to look into yourself and examine your psychological state. You are able to communicate your emotions to yourself as well as to others, which is important because we often lose track of our real feelings in the course of the day. If you have a problem that you cannot solve within yourself, this is a good time to talk it over with someone else.

By the same token, you will listen unusually well to other people's problems. Others will sense your interest and may call on you to help them with their problems. But that will not bother you, because you are very concerned with experiencing emotional richness in your communications with others, especially by helping someone in this way.

Mercury Square Moon

At the very least you will be in touch with your feelings today. In fact you should use this day to find out exactly how you feel about every matter that comes up. It will not all be pleasant, but it should not be totally unpleasant either. Your thinking will be unusually influenced by your feelings, and your communication with others may be so colored by unconscious compulsions that you will have difficulties. Psychological patterns from your past will be reactivated today, so be on the watch for inappropriate habits of speech and patterns of thinking as well as other forms of behavior that might run counter to your needs and intentions. Examine the attitudes you have inherited from your parents and continually ask yourself, "Have I experienced the truth of this point of view directly, or is it a dogma I was taught to believe in childhood?" It is impossible to root out every belief that makes up one's prejudices, but you should make a start, and this is a good time to do so.

Because women are so often the targets of one's unconscious projections (no matter whether you are male or female), this transit is often associated with arguments with women. However, anyone who activates an unconscious belief or thought pattern will be a source of difficulty for you at this time.

On the other hand, you can use this time to express your feelings to someone, as long as you don't pretend that you are expressing your rational side. Your feelings have their own logic and validity, which is not helped by rationalization. Learn about your unconscious mind and emotions, so that you no longer hold others responsible for the problems you have had in life. This transit gives you the opportunity to understand how you have contributed to your difficulties and to do something about them.

Mercury Trine Moon

The effect of this transit is to enliven your routine everyday world, which you usually don't think much about. It will be more interesting than usual and the scene of fascinating exchanges between you and others. The tempo of your everyday existence will speed up some, but not to the point that you feel that your energies are being scattered.

At the same time you are more in touch with your feelings than usual, and you show greater emotional sensitivity in your interactions with others. It may be good to talk about your feelings with someone today. In fact the richness of everyday experience, as referred to above, results from the fact that you feel more and put more of yourself into your experience.

This feeling quality makes you a good listener today. You are eager for input, and you would much rather listen to others than have to take the initiative yourself to start a conversation or make the connection that brings you together. When others talk to you, they will perceive your interest, sympathy and concern. They will realize that you aren't playing ego games with them.

The Moon signifies relations with women, and this transit helps to improve communications with them, especially if you are a man who usually has trouble with women. However, this effect also applies to women, since communication between two women (or between two men) often needs help.

Mercury Opposition Moon

The difficulty with this transit is that you will find it hard to keep emotional issues from clouding your communication with others. You may be expressing your unconscious drives and impulses more than communicating a logical message, but that is not all bad. If you are subject to such compulsions, it is good to express the energy that lies behind them and bring it out into the open. However, you may say something that you didn't want to say.

Under this transit you may encounter another problem in communication. Although you are not consciously aware of it, everything you say is conditioned by the habits and patterns of speech and thought ingrained from childhood. While this is always true to some degree, now it is likely to come out as an inappropriate message or one that doesn't apply to the present moment. Try to be conscious of exactly what you are saying and why you are saying it, and be aware of these patterns in your mind before you speak. If you are under emotional stress, as may very well be the case with this transit, be especially careful. If you allow your feelings to take over, what you say won't be worth much except to a psychologist.

Old thought patterns, attitudes from the past, and unconsciousness about your present situation all endanger your mental effectiveness today. It would be best not to try to reach any important conclusions now. If you do, you will probably have to change them tomorrow. Luckily, Mercury's influence usually doesn't last very long.

Mercury Conjunct Mercury

This transit is favorable for all types of mental activity and communication with others. Your intellect is sharpened, and you can clearly formulate and articulate ideas that you might otherwise have difficulty with, so that others can easily understand your meaning. Your power of reasoning is also improved, enabling you to follow any complex argument that someone else presents. Because you are able to see the flaws in people's reasoning, you are not likely to be taken in by specious arguments.

At the same time your curiosity is aroused. You are interested in finding out about unfamiliar facts and new ideas. Puzzles fascinate you as a mental exercise that you will make every effort to solve. Obviously this is a favorable influence for beginning the study of any new subject or discipline. If you are in school or taking some other type of course, this should be a very successful day.

Try to take advantage of the energy that Mercury provides for communicating with others. Today you have an opportunity to talk to people about matters that are really important to you, even matters that are usually too emotionally charged to discuss easily. Mercury on Mercury provides a greater sense of detachment and objectivity, so you can keep your emotional involvement in an issue down to a reasonable level for discussion. However, under this transit's influence you could simply fritter your time away in idle chatter. That is why you should make a conscious effort to communicate about matters that are important to you. Unless you make the effort, Mercury's communication is not necessarily about anything significant.

Your interaction with others will be much more lively today, and you will have many opportunities to get through to other people. After this transit has passed, you will realize that you have had many more contacts than usual and that much has been said. Make that communication useful.

This transit sometimes indicates travel, usually in the course of your everyday routine rather than to strange and faraway places. These will be short trips unless you routinely travel long distances, as some businessmen do.

Mercury Sextile Mercury

This transit favors all forms of mental work and planning. Your mind is quite clear now, and you are able to handle the details of intricate mental work. Work with figures and tasks that require close attention to detail should work out very well. The only thing to watch out for, however, is that you may not find such work interesting enough to want to do it. This is a matter of individual temperament. Some people get restless under this influence when confronted with any routine work, but others handle their routine much more effectively. Certainly if you have the discipline to stick with such work today, you will be able to do it well.

This is also a good day for all types of communications, especially if you have to present a detailed and intricate argument or discussion to someone. The clarity of mind conferred by this transit is a great help in such cases. Also your ability to keep track of details makes this a good transit for any business negotiations or other similarly complicated discussions. A contract or deal that you agree upon today will undoubtedly work out quite well, and you will be quite sure that you included everything important in the agreement.

Your intellectual curiosity is strong, so this is a good time to begin the study of a new subject. Amost any subject will be fine as long as it is entertaining and challenging. Reading purely for fun is also a good way to spend a day like this.

Like many other Mercury transits, this one may signify traveling over short distances much more than usual in the course of the day. For example, you might hurry around from one appointment to another or do something else that makes you feel you have covered a lot of ground.

Mercury Square Mercury

This is not a difficult square, but it does indicate a challenge to some of your basic beliefs. This should not be regarded as a threat, however, because the adjustments you must make in your thinking now could prove quite valuable later on. You will have quite a lot of communication with others today through conversations, letters, phone calls and so forth. Use this interchange to test out your ideas and see how people react to them. If you have made such a strong commitment to a particular position that you are unwilling to see it challenged, you may be quite upset by some of the reactions. But that would be a poor attitude to take. You can correct your thinking on a number of issues without too much difficulty now, while later you may be so committed that you cannot change. Be flexible.

Even with the best intentions, however, you may run into quite a bit of disagreement today. This does not necessarily mean that you are wrong but that you should reexamine your position. If you find that it is difficult to reach compromises, delay any negotiations or discussions until another day. These matters may go quite well, however, if you have prepared well for today. Then this transit should assist you. This is a critical day, when you must handle your affairs very carefully with perceptiveness and insight. And if you can remain flexible, you will have little difficulty.

If you are not careful, the brisk tempo of activity today could cause you to feel scattered and throw you into a nervous frenzy. Your mental tempo will be high enough that you should try to avoid noisy, disruptive environments. As much as possible, try to find harmonious surroundings where your mind can work peacefully and efficiently with a minimum of outside disruption.

Mercury Trine Mercury

This is an excellent transit for making plans, thinking things over or communicating in any way with others. A sign of mental equilibrium, this transit assists your mind in everything it has to do. Your thinking is clear and precise.

This transit should also arouse your curiosity about the world around you and make you want to learn about a new subject, either through study or direct encounter. You might want to spend the day reading, or you might go out to a museum, art exhibit or other event that will stimulate your mind. Even a conversation with friends could be the source of a new idea that your mind can latch onto.

As with other Mercury trines, this is a good time to get a point across to others, although your primary motive will probably be to communicate rather than to score debate points. Your attitude is much more objective than at other times, and you only want to get at the facts. If you have something important to say to someone, this is a good time to say it.

This transit favors traveling, especially to see something new, as described above. Mercury usually indicates traveling in your immediate area and getting in touch with local surroundings, rather than long trips. If you are planning to travel any distance, however, this is an excellent time to start.

As with other Mercury transits, this one favors all business and commercial transactions, especially where clear communication is vital to the success of the enterprise.

Mercury Opposition Mercury

Like most Mercury transits, this one will stimulate the flow of ideas and communication in your life. If you are out in the world today, you will meet many people and have many important conversations. Even if you are alone, your mind will be very active. This transit is favorable for thinking about and reviewing the past as well as for planning and looking toward the future. But it would be better to be out with people today, because this transit favors interaction with others more than solitary cogitation.

Try out your ideas on others today to find out what they think. Their feedback could be extremely valuable to you in adjusting your thinking. Don't get so wrapped up in your own ideas that you feel you must defend all your opinions with your life. That will take away the flexibility you need so badly at this time. Even if you get involved in a verbal argument with someone today, look at it as a test of your ideas and do not be afraid to change your thinking.

On the more negative side, watch out for signs that your mind is racing too fast. Sometimes this transit indicates nervous strain and tension, which can create a tendency to sloppy thinking and rash statements when you are talking with others. It can also lead to impulsive decisions and rash actions. In some of the older books, this transit is considered dangerous for travel because of the sloppy, rash energies it sometimes signifies. Pay very close attention to whatever you are doing today, and don't let your subconscious mind run the show. Consider everything carefully and thoroughly, and if you have to make any decisions today, leave yourself lots of room to maneuver later. You may have to make important changes after this transit passes. Above all, do not leave others out of your thinking processes, even though you may be inclined to argue with them. Everything you do will be much more effective if you work with others rather than alone.

Mercury Conjunct Venus

This transit can have a variety of effects. First of all, it can stimulate your appreciation of beauty, your interest in art, music or poetry. It may also indicate that you will tell someone that you love him or her or that you will discuss your relationship with someone. On a very abstract level, this transit can enable you to see the patterns running through your perception and experience that help tie everything together so that you can understand your life as a whole.

This is a mental transit; that is, it works primarily upon the mind rather than the feelings and is often expressed as an intellectual appreciation of beauty. However, to a considerable extent this transit also removes the distinctions between mental and emotional. You may experience concepts with great emotional feeling or express emotions in an intellectual manner. The area in which feeling and intellect can best be synthesized is in the arts. Thus you are much more receptive than usual to experiences through art.

On the personal level, this combination of feeling dominated by intellect enables you to communicate your feelings of love and affection for someone. If you usually have trouble talking about your feelings for another person, this transit will pave the way and even make you quite articulate. In an existing relationship the two of you will be able to discuss various aspects of your relationship and improve it by making certain that you really understand each other.

On the most abstract level, Venus relates to elements that unify. Consequently this transit gives you a greater ability to understand the qualities shared by seemingly unrelated aspects of reality. You can see the patterns inherent in the universe and appreciate them aesthetically. This is an excellent quality for doing any kind of scientific research.

Traditionally this transit is supposed to be favorable for all financial and business dealings.

Mercury Sextile Venus

This is not a very intense transit. It will have a lighthearted influence on the day, unless a heavier influence from another planet overwhelms the effect. It inclines you to use your mind for leisure pursuits, such as reading for amusement, going to an art exhibit or concert or chatting with friends. Even though these activities seem somewhat trivial, they are an important part of your life, because they give you a chance to rest between heavier concerns. Do not hesitate to take the day off if you can, and simply relax and enjoy it.

This transit is important in another way, for it puts you in touch with your feelings, especially those of love and friendship. It is important to know that these feelings are present in your life. In other words, even though days like today do not seem very significant, these are the times that justify all the other more difficult ones. That is why they are important.

Under this transit you may tell someone that you love him or her. As with other Mercury-Venus contacts, you are able to verbalize feelings that at other times you might be too shy to discuss or that you couldn't find the right words for.

Your appreciation of beauty is great today, so surround yourself with as much beauty as possible. This will greatly improve your spirits. This is a day for appreciating lovely objects that have no purpose except to be what they are. This is what art is all about.

Another appropriate activity today would be taking a short drive in the country or somewhere that is particularly lovely.

Mercury Square Venus

This transit does not make you mentally aggressive, but you will probably feel quite good. The only area of tension will be your personal relationships. Use this energy to have a discussion with a loved one about the state of your relationship. You may discover that the two of you do not agree in as many ways as you thought. But if you speak in a spirit of compromise, you should have little difficulty in reaching a working agreement. If you proceed from a position of inflexible righteousness, there will be disagreement and discord in your relationship that could sever communications for some time. Your attitude is very important.

Elsewhere in your life this transit will signify a time of good feelings and perhaps some self-indulgence. This is not likely to do much harm, but stay away from stores selling expensive goodies that you would like to have but don't really need and cannot afford. You would be inclined to buy, and you might regret these transactions later, when you feel more disciplined.

If you attend a social gathering, have a good time, but exercise restraint. Take note of how much you have indulged yourself and call a halt at a reasonable time.

In other encounters, be careful that you don't give ground too easily and thereby compromise yourself just to avoid unpleasant controversy. You really must hold on to your beliefs, standards and ideals, but today you might be inclined to give way before another person.

Mercury Trine Venus

This is a very agreeable transit that makes you feel quite positive and friendly toward everyone you meet. You are so anxious to have good feelings all around that you avoid saying anything unpleasant. Therefore this is a good day to smooth over any ruffled feelings that may have cropped up in your relationships. Also you are in tune with your feelings, and you speak with considerable sensitivity. This is a good time to meet new people, because you can project the most agreeable side of your personality. If you like to make sweet talk, this is the transit for it.

Get together with friends and have a good time today, for you will be as receptive to their good feelings as they are to yours. This is a good day to go out to a show, a movie or some other amusement.

On another level, you have a very strong aesthetic appreciation of beauty with this transit. You enjoy seeing beautiful objects and being surrounded with artistic creations. You will want to avoid noisy and unpleasant environments, so a drive into the country would accord well with your mood.

Of course this is an excellent time to talk with someone about your feelings of love and friendship, for it will be easier than usual to talk about these feelings. Often embarrassment or shyness prevents you from doing this, but that should not be a problem now.

In general, your approach to life today will be lighthearted, and you should enjoy the day very much. You may find it difficult to adopt a serious attitude about anything, however.

Mercury Opposition Venus

This transit can go by without very much effect unless you are watching for it. You might notice that you feel a bit better than usual, and your mind will naturally turn to light subjects. The people you meet will seem more pleasant than usual and you will have many pleasant conversations. You are likely to be involved in a social event that will turn out quite pleasantly.

In your personal relationships you will be inclined to compromise and to meet the other person halfway, especially if you are having a disagreement. You are not feeling very combative or argumentative, and you may even give ground on issues that you would otherwise stand up and fight for. But you may regret it later if you give in about something important.

This is not a very favorable transit for any difficult mental work that requires great discipline. You feel like enjoying yourself and having a good time instead of making a significant effort. For the same reason, you will avoid talking about difficult or serious subjects. You will quickly change the subject to something lighter.

Be careful of being too concerned with yourself or self-indulgent at this time. You are not likely to do anything dreadful that would be difficult to fix up later, but certain tendencies could be a bit of a problem. You might be inclined to buy luxurious trinkets that you don't really need or otherwise squander your valuable and limited resources.

On the positive side, you can use this time to tell someone that you love him or her. Although you may not feel like going into a melodramatic, heavy relationship, you do enjoy making another person feel happy about the two of you, and you may have very amorous thoughts.

Mercury Conjunct Mars

The influence of this transit must be handled with care, but it can prove quite useful if you exercise some restraint. On the plus side it confers a tremendous intellectual and mental energy. You can work with your mind much longer than usual and thereby accomplish quite a bit. At the same time you will feel intellectually competitive and fond of debating with others. You will present your position clearly and skillfully, defend it ably and find quite a bit of satisfaction in doing so.

The negative side of this transit is obvious from what has been said about the positive side. If you take yourself and your ego too seriously, you may speak and act during this transit as if you were spoiling for a fight. You may feel quite irritable and even be set off by rather trivial incidents. Often you will act defensively on issues that you have no real stake in at all. One problem with this transit may be that you will find difficult to determine when it is necessary to defend your position. You tend to identify your ego with everything you think, say and believe. Needless to say, this creates conflicts all over the place, most of which are entirely needless.

You may possibly encounter this problem in projected form; that is, someone else will act defensively toward you. When this happens, think about whether you have something real to defend before you decide to fight. Certainly you should not run away from defending a valid position.

The important point is to determine where your real concerns are, intellectually speaking. What ideas do you really have to defend in order to maintain your integrity? When you have worked out the answers to this question, you should have no trouble curbing the negative manifestations of this transit as they arise within you. Then this can be an extremely useful transit indeed.

Mercury Sextile Mars

Today you are likely to be extremely busy. You will work very hard mentally to advance any project that you are personally interested in. But you will not be so diligent about working purely for someone else's benefit. In fact, you may even resent such work. You should take any opportunities that arise today to display individual initiative. You may get the chance to take over and direct a project. However, the people around you will not be up to your level of hard work today, so you would be better off in a work situation in which you have to depend only upon yourself. It isn't that other people aren't dependable but that you are more energetic than usual.

Very likely you will have to convince someone of something today. This will probably not be an argument, but rather a situation in which you have to present your case with vigor and energy. But if someone tries to talk you into something, you will defend your own position vehemently and successfully. This transit is not as argumentative as it sounds. People will not see you as spoiling for a fight, nor will they be particularly likely to pick a fight. Instead they will respect you for taking a stand for your own beliefs. You may find yourself enjoying a good argument, but more in the spirit of competition than because of negative energies within you.

Your inner confidence in your ideas and beliefs will help you initiate and take advantage of the opportunities that come your way. Do not be reluctant to use them. Under the influence of this transit you should be successful.

Mercury Square Mars

This transit can be quite difficult. You are inclined to feel touchy and irritable and to regard almost any communication from another person as a challenge. And you will make this attitude so clear to people that they may even tread lightly around you for fear of setting you off. Anyone who crosses you will be told off in no uncertain terms.

Of course this transit has a milder side. It may mean that you will have to defend your ideas or beliefs against someone else. This could be anything from a simple debate to an out-and-out fight. The worst way to handle this, but what you are most likely to do, is to identify your own ego with what you believe or think. This will make you act as if your very life were threatened, which of course it is not. If you have to fight for your beliefs, this transit can be a help, but don't look for a battle or create an issue where none exists.

As with most transits, you may experience this one in projected form; that is, you may have to contend with another person who is acting touchy or defensive. Be careful that you have not been unconsciously sending out subtle signals that draw such persons to you.

This transit can indicate accident-prone behavior. If you are not careful, there is a real danger of accidents through burns, especially to the arms and legs, or while walking or driving. But these will probably not occur without warning. Most frequently, you will have a feeling of repressed rage, as if some kind of energy inside you is struggling to break free. If you find that you are acting impulsively for no reason at all, try to avoid driving and other forms of travel in which you are in control. Also be very careful with hot objects or anything sharp. Accidents under this transit are not caused by "bad luck" but by repressed hostility and aggressiveness. Lacking an external expression, they turn inward against you.

Mercury Trine Mars

This is a good time for all kinds of hard mental work. You have more energy than usual, and you are willing to tackle difficult problems. You will not be easily discouraged by apparent obstacles and may even regard them as a challenge, spurring you on to solve the problems you are facing.

Also you will want to speak your mind, not to start a fight but to get your views out into the open. You feel quite confident of your beliefs and not fearful of letting others know where you stand. This is an excellent time for taking some action that depends on impressing someone with your ability and confidence. For example, it is a good time to ask for a raise, because you communicate positively and with confidence, which others will respect. Even if you don't choose to assert yourself, you will defend yourself and your views to anyone who criticizes you or tries to tear you down.

This is a good transit for public speaking, because stage fright is less of a problem than usual. You feel that you have something to say and nothing to hide, which are prerequisites for any kind of public appearance.

The plans you make today will be much bolder and more innovative than usual. You are able to dare more and to take greater chances, not only with your words but also with your thoughts. Use this transit to advance a notion that you have previously been shy about. In any kind of negotiations you will get right to the heart of the matter and settle it very quickly. Your perceptiveness is no greater than usual, but you are more willing to believe in what you see.

Mercury Opposition Mars

Under this influence a certain amount of caution is advisable, precisely because it is likely to be missing in your speech and behavior. You feel like telling everyone you encounter exactly what you think of them, whether or not it is flattering. You are likely to be in a combative mood, which may cause other people to start a fight. Quite often this combativeness is well buried in your subconscious mind, and the only way you know it is there is because people seem to come out of the woodwork to start an argument. You may feel like the totally innocent victim of someone else's aggressiveness, and it may appear that way to a neutral observer, but nevertheless you have been sending out hostile signals at a very subtle level. At this time it is better to be conscious of your feelings of aggression, hostility and resentment toward others than to try to ignore them. At least you will have some control over them.

Even at its worst, this transit signifies that you are able to release buried ego energies. But also you can use this time constructively to get feedback from others about your effectiveness in any activity that you are engaged in. Just don't kid yourself! Make sure you are really prepared to hear some constructive criticism. If you are, you will learn about yourself in ways that can really help you grow. You can also use this time to make statements to others about your position on any matter. Unless you really want a fight, however, don't hit people over the head with your opinions.

Under some conditions, which are hard to analyze in advance, this transit can signify an accident, especially burns involving your arms or legs or an accident while traveling. Be very careful today, particularly when handling anything that could be dangerous. Watch out for signs of rash and impulsive behavior, because this is usually a warning of an accident within you looking for a place to happen. If you find that you tend toward sudden impulsive actions today, stop doing anything dangerous and look within yourself or your relationships for the hidden anger that is at the root of this behavior.

Mercury Conjunct Jupiter

This is an extremely useful transit that can be of great assistance to you in many ways. Psychologically, it broadens your comprehension of any issue that you are interested in and your understanding of life in general as you encounter it today. You are concerned with the largest, most comprehensive possible view, and you are eager to incorporate new information into your way of looking at the world.

At the same time you are intellectually more tolerant of other viewpoints, seeing them not as a threat to your views, but as a way of enlarging them. Even beliefs that are quite different from your own, which you might usually react to with hostility, seem interesting.

Your ability to see the larger view today enables you to plan with foresight. Where others see only confusion, you can see a pattern and come up with insights that will amaze others. In business or social activities you are able to organize very effectively, grouping people together so they can work most efficiently.

For these reasons this transit favors all forms of business and commercial activity. Often you will perceive the most advantageous course of action without even understanding its logical basis immediately. This is a result of the speeding-up of mental processes conferred by the combination of Mercury and Jupiter.

One problem you should watch out for, however, is that the broadness of Jupiter's vision can make you overlook details. Be careful not to get so carried away by enthusiasm that your thinking becomes sloppy. Use your ability to see the overall pattern, but do not overlook the individual exceptions to the pattern that could trip up your planning. Also do not fall victim to the delusion that you cannot be wrong about anything. Being overconfident about your ideas now is as foolish as at any other time. Also avoid being self-righteous, because your moral viewpoints are fallible.

However, in general this is an excellent transit, and with the enthusiasm and optimism it confers, you should be able to accomplish much more than usual.

Mercury Sextile Jupiter

Under this transit your attention turns to the larger issues in your life, and you will spend some time considering your overall plans for the future. Your hopes and wishes are much more important today, for the daily concerns of your life do not seem to satisfy your desire for significance. Today it is not enough to meet the demands of the day; you want to understand how they fit into an overall pattern.

At the same time you have a good understanding of the overall patterns of your life. Your mind is clear, sharp and alert to all possibilities today, and your optimistic and positive attitude will help you attain your objectives.

Being clear about what you want out of life will help you greatly in your dealings with other people. This is a very favorable transit for all business negotiations, commercial transactions and contract discussions. It is also favorable for dealings with the law. And all of this is because of your self-understanding today, helped by a certain generosity of feeling toward others. You recognize that you can get what you want most effectively by working with others and helping them get what they need as well. You are very conscious of group values and needs at this time.

This transit arouses your intellectual curiosity, so it is a good time to study any subject that gives you a greater comprehension of the world as a whole. Philosophical and religious subjects will attract you particularly, as well as information about strange and faraway places. You recognize that your immediate world is not the only one. And this realization makes you more than usually tolerant of other people and their differences.

Travel is sometimes indicated by this transit, and it is certainly a good time to start a trip, unless there are strong negative indications.

Mercury Square Jupiter

This is usually a fortunate transit, in that it makes you feel optimistic and positive about life. You are inclined to make big plans and set long-range goals under this influence as well as to examine the goals you already have. The advantage you have now is your ability to see the whole picture and to think in terms of large structures. You are more inclined to think in ideal, abstract terms. But also your foresight and planning ability make this a favorable time for most commercial transactions and business deals.

There is a negative side to this transit that is easily seen, but it can be destructive if you are not aware of it. You are sloppy about details and inclined to overlook any elements that don't fit neatly into your grand vision. Also there is a danger that in communicating with others you may adopt an arrogant or self-righteous tone that will alienate them and set them working against you. Your ability to think in large terms is the strength of this transit, but the tendency to speak arrogantly and overlook or despise the small is its weakness.

Try very hard to plan everything carefully and not overlook details. Recognize that every structure consists of parts integrated into the whole, which can be disrupted by an out-of-place part. Remain flexible in your point of view and do not assume that you have all the answers. In business transactions or in buying, be careful that you have all the facts straight and avoid plunging ahead precipitously. Don't overdo your optimism.

The nature of this transit makes it quite easy to correct these faults if you are aware of them. In fact, making the effort to correct them can make this transit an even more powerful force for good in your day.

Mercury Trine Jupiter

This is an excellent transit for making plans for the future and creating organizational systems, as well as for all other intellectual and mental efforts. As with other Mercury-Jupiter combinations, however, there is a tendency to avoid really difficult mental or intellectual problems, taking the easy way out instead. However, if you can create the proper sense of discipline, you should be able to overcome these negative effects and make this a day of very creative mental activity.

On a more mundane plane, this transit favors all forms of business and commercial activity. This is an excellent transit under which to sign a contract or conclude a deal. Also buying and selling should work out very well under this influence.

But you should be aware that these favorable effects do not happen through luck in the usual sense. Rather, this transit opens up and sharpens your mind so that you see, even if subliminally, all the possibilities inherent in a situation. This enables you to turn it to your best advantage. Also this transit gives you a well-founded feeling of optimism, which in turn creates the well-known "power of positive thinking." In fact that is probably the most important reason for the favorableness of this transit.

This transit also enlarges your mental scope. You are eager to be exposed to much more new information than usual, and new ideas don't bother you. In fact you are fascinated by them because they broaden your understanding of the world around you.

This transit is good for studying law, philosophy, religion and other subjects that deal with high-level thought. If you have to have dealings with the law today, this transit, or rather your own positive mind-set, will help make them work out favorably.

Mercury Opposition Jupiter

This transit frequently coincides with a period of good feeling and an optimistic outlook on life. It is definitely one of the more pleasant oppositions. And if you exercise some care, it will be very helpful for all kinds of contractual negotiations, conferences, planning sessions and discussions. However, it is important to be careful. Like all combinations of Mercury and Jupiter, this one gives a tendency to grand thinking, to seeing the whole more clearly than the parts. With this transit you often lose precision and clarity about details, so be very careful about fine points, and read every word of the small print in all your dealings. Make sure that you have covered all the various angles. You can be careful and very successful if you are thorough at the same time. Avoid the temptation of thinking that the small details are beneath the lofty concerns of the day. The whole may be more than the parts, but the parts still determine the effectiveness of the whole.

In communications with others, try not to give an impression of cocksureness or arrogance. Remain open to others' point of view and flexible enough that you can adjust your own. You may enjoy the feeling of engaging in an intellectual joust or friendly debate at this time, but don't take the debate too seriously. Avoid being smug and self-righteous, no matter how sure you are that you are right.

With reasonable care, you can count on being able to make accurate and perceptive judgments. The plans you make now as well as plans made previously and executed now will be furthered by this influence.

Mercury Conjunct Saturn

During this period you are likely to proceed with considerable caution, which has both good and difficult effects. You are much more conscious than usual of the distinctions between things, making it hard to see the "forest for the trees." This extends to your attitudes toward others, so that you may be inclined to concentrate on people's negative characteristics and to overlook their positive traits. Under this transit you may have to say farewell to someone who is leaving your life now, and this may leave a mark on you for some time to come.

On the positive side, this transit can give you great intellectual precision. If you have to do any work that requires extreme precision of thought and planning, now is the time. It will work especially well if you have previously outlined the general plan and left the detailed planning until now. On the other hand, this is not a good time to make plans that require a broad overall view. Your viewpoint is likely to be too cautious and narrow at this time.

Your critical faculty is extremely sharp, and you can immediately see the flaws in other people's arguments as well as your own. But be sure you use this insight constructively to correct these flaws rather than to undermine your own or another person's confidence in the ideas put forth.

At its worst, this transit can make communication with others quite difficult. Certain elements of your personality that you are afraid to expose seem so close to the surface now that everything you say is affected by them. You are afraid that you might give something away by speaking, so you say nothing. But because of the negative thinking that often accompanies this transit, this is precisely the time when you must speak. What you don't say now can certainly hurt someone.

And of course you should deal with the problem of negative thinking at this time. You are so conscious of the flaws, the bad and difficult aspects of life, that you may not be able to see the underlying unity in any structure. Do not take your gloomy viewpoint too seriously today except as a check to any overly optimistic thinking at other times.

Mercury Sextile Saturn

This is a good time to look around with a critical eye and see what needs to be changed or corrected in your environment. You are very conscious of the flaws in everything you look at, but you are not so overwhelmed that you cannot see the good as well. You are concerned with making the situation better, not simply with being a carping critic. Your mind is on serious concerns, and although you are not likely to feel depressed or to have other negative feelings, you are not attracted to frivolity or lightheartedness either.

In this mood you can be either a teacher or one who is taught, perhaps in a formal classroom situation or just in an informal discussion among friends. You respect people who have more experience than you do, and you are likely to turn to them for advice. Or someone else may cast you in this role and come to you for help. Older people, especially, are likely to be of service in this way.

Today you will work very carefully on any necessary mental task that requires precise thinking and concentration. But it is best to avoid any work that requires great breadth and scope of vision. You are much more concerned with details than with overall patterns, and in dealing with larger structures you may be overwhelmed by the fine points. In other words, you may not be able to see the forest for the trees.

While your serious concern for the practical aspects of life is laudable, don't carry it too far. This is not usually a depression transit, but you can make it one by working too hard and being too little concerned with the light side of life. This is especially likely if you have a tendency toward depression in the first place. Loneliness, whether justified or not, is a danger of this transit, because you may mentally isolate yourself from other people.

Mercury Square Saturn

This is a good transit for heavy mental work and for tasks that require disciplined thinking. Your critical faculties are sharp and your standards are high. However, you won't find it easy to communicate with others; either you will have difficulty being understood, or you will give a more negative impression than you intended. This is not a good time for important negotiations or business transactions because communications between you and the other parties will probably be delayed or misinterpreted so as to cause a delay. Also it will be difficult to make the right kind of positive impression in such a situation, so delay personal contact until another day.

Similarly, your present concern with criticism may make you dwell upon heavy or difficult thoughts, which can lead to depression or pessimism. It is often difficult to think positively with this transit. There is a strong tendency to feel lonely or even to withdraw into yourself rather than confront someone with whom you need to communicate. Instead of patching up your difficulties, you may say goodbye or at least think about doing so.

In order to lessen the negative side of this transit, you have to recognize that it is making you see the dark side of life, the imperfections and flaws, rather than the positive side. Saturn has the effect of making you think you are seeing the whole truth and that it is gloomy. But once you realize that you are seeing only part of the truth, you can make corrections for that.

Your ability to think practically is a positive effect of this transit, but it could be perverted to a negative result. No matter what kind of plan anyone proposes, you always want to know precisely how they are going to implement it. And you make this same demand of yourself — everything must be spelled out in detail. Do not let this practicality turn into narrow-mindedness or a total lack of vision. Certainly it would be better to work out the practical details of a project today than to lay down the general plan of a new one.

Mercury Trine Saturn

This is a day for serious thinking and important concerns. You feel you must deal with practical matters and keep your mind at work. You are not inclined to play at games or trivial amusements, not because you are depressed, only serious. Your mind works quite well under this influence, and you will be able to keep at a task until you have solved all its problems. You are also able to concentrate on mental work that requires great attention to detail. Your eye is sharp for the little pieces that make up the whole, and you are as concerned about them as you are about the whole structure. As a result, the work you do today will be done very carefully and thoroughly. You won't have to go over it again and check for mistakes, because your initial approach is methodical and painstaking.

This is a good time to organize yourself and your environment, especially if the organization has to be detailed and involved. Your critical faculty is sharp, and you can see very quickly what must be done to make an organization work. On the other hand, although you are very good at details, you may not have the overall view and scope that some situations require. Also, your approach is rather conservative and cautious today. Mercury-Jupiter transits are better for working out fine points.

You will not be very interested in abstract ideas today. You will want to know what practical purpose everything serves, and if it isn't useful, you will turn your attention to something else. Just be careful that you don't miss an important idea as a result.

You may be rather reserved with people, not because you are afraid or unwilling to communicate, but because you don't feel like saying very much unless it is important. You may prefer to be alone with your thoughts. However, this is a very good time to seek counsel from an older person who might have more experience than you in some area. This is the kind of discussion you will feel comfortable in today.

Mercury Opposition Saturn

This transit inclines you to very serious thinking. You are concerned with your relationship to the world and your place in it rather than with meaningless philosophical abstractions. You want to know how to meet your practical needs.

However, you are concerned with one area that others might consider rather abstract, and that is your identity. Under this transit you tend to dwell on your sense of personal isolation, loneliness, difficulties in relationships and other depressing thoughts. Clearly you need a dose of positive thinking and cheering up. It is important to remember that your troubles are probably more apparent than real, no matter how real or significant they seem. They may be just a product of negative thinking and looking at the gloomy side. Of course, they may be real difficulties, but dwelling on them will be of little help.

Under this transit you may say goodbye to a loved one or think about separating from a relationship. But it is not a good idea to actually do so now because of the distorted perspective conferred by this transit.

Assuming that you can control your negative thinking, this transit does give you the advantage of a sharp, critical eye. You can see what is wrong with a situation immediately and make the necessary changes to correct it then and there. But don't dwell on the flaws, just note and correct them.

This transit is a good time to do any heavy mental work that requires a great deal of discipline. But even though you can work very hard, be sure to take frequent breaks and really relax. Otherwise the work will begin to drag your mood down.

If you feel the need to talk with someone, seek out an authority you respect, not merely someone whom others consider an authority figure, unless you happen to agree with them. You need someone, usually but not necessarily an older person, who can talk to you like a father.

Mercury Conjunct Uranus

This can be a very exciting transit, for it creates a fast tempo in your thinking and communicating with others that makes every encounter interesting and stimulating. However, if you are not careful or if your mind is sensitive in this way, it can also signify scattered and hasty thinking. Much depends upon your normal mental speed, which is not the same as intelligence.

On the positive side, this transit indicates that your thinking will be greatly speeded up today. Your intuition is so active that you seem to be getting insights out of the air. This is extremely good for any mental work that requires originality and cleverness. Your inventive faculty is very much stimulated by this influence, which especially favors mathematical, technical and scientific work, as well as astrology and other branches of the occult. Puzzles and mysteries fascinate you, and you have the quickness of wit to solve them.

On the other hand, try to avoid jumping to conclusions. Test your insights to make sure that they can stand up to more rigorous analysis. Don't be afraid to experiment with new ideas, but don't accept them uncritically either. You may be so fascinated by newness that you accept it automatically, especially since you are rather tired of the old routine.

Sometimes the pace of thinking may become so fast that you really cannot handle it. Your mind leaps from idea to idea so fast that it can't settle down and allow you to get a handle on one idea. Thus, even though you may expend a lot of intellectual energy, you may accomplish nothing of value. This is especially likely if your normal mental speed is quite fast.

This transit can also manifest itself as nervousness if your nervous system is overstrained by the high-speed input. If this happens, all you can do is try to relax and let the time pass. Probably you wouldn't accomplish much if you continued to try to work.

When you travel, especially if you are driving or otherwise in control, be very careful. Your rapid and possibly confused pace of thinking may lead to an error in judgment that could result in an accident. Be cautious, and if you find that you are acting impulsively, stop altogether.

Mercury Sextile Uranus

This transit signifies a day when you will make new discoveries, encounter new people and generally have a sense of excitement and interest. And you won't have to go out of your way to experience these effects, for your immediate environment will present all the interest you need. Don't worry about being unpleasantly surprised, because the influence of this transit is mild and not usually disruptive. If you do find this day disruptive, examine your attitudes and ask yourself if you are being too rigid. Rigidity and unwillingness to allow anything to deviate from a prescribed plan will make this transit more difficult to handle.

This is a good day to tackle old problems that you have not been able to resolve in the past. Perhaps you were trying the same solutions over and over again, even though they didn't fit the situation. This transit will help you see fresh solutions, and you may be able to work these problems through at last. You have a great interest in new problems now, seeing them as a challenge rather than a threat. And this gives the day some of its exciting quality.

You will not want to spend the day in your usual routine, and you shouldn't. Do something different and leave room for total spontaneity. Very often with this transit you will start out in one direction but wind up somewhere completely different.

In your communications with others, even with old friends whom you think you know completely, startling new ideas will come up. All around you, new aspects of life will be opened up for you to experience.

This is also a good day for the study of certain subjects that can give you new insights into the world. Learning about math, science, technology and certain branches of the occult, such as astrology, would be very profitable today.

Mercury Square Uranus

Your mind will be very stimulated today. You are fascinated by every new phenomenon that you encounter and eager for more. If you are relatively flexible, this need for excitement means that you may get bored more easily than usual. If you are not flexible, this could be a very nerve-wracking day, full of little surprises and upsets that overtax your nerves. The plans you have made for the day may not work out at all, and the more you are counting on precisely one set of conditions to be fulfilled, the more upsetting this transit will be.

Either way, the day's tempo will be brisk. Thoughts will flash through your head at such an amazing speed that it will be difficult to keep track of them. Perhaps you should keep a tape recorder handy in order to record your ideas before they disappear. Sometimes under this influence you may think that you are positively inspired. If you can keep up with the pace, your thinking seems sharp, clear and very fast. However, it is also inclined to be sloppy, so tomorrow be sure to check out everything you have done today. Don't discard it all as impulsive rubbish, for some of what you observe and think today will be very valuable. It is just that today is for being creative, and tomorow will be for working it out critically and in detail.

If you have difficulty keeping up with the pace of your mind or the pace of events in the world today, your thinking may become very nervous and scattered. In that case avoid any kind of work that requires concentration, because you would probably have to go over it all tomorrow. Also be very careful not to make rash, impulsive judgments or hasty statements to others that you might regret later on. You are inclined to base your views on half-thought-out ideas, especially if you are feeling rather nervous under this transit. When driving, be careful not to make sudden impulsive moves that could lead to an accident.

Mercury Trine Uranus

This is a very stimulating transit that will make you feel more alive and awake mentally than at any other time. Everything you encounter now has an exciting quality, and you can stay active enough to avoid boredom. Although your thinking may be somewhat lacking in care and discipline, you will make up for this in the scope of your intuition. This is an excellent day to tackle some problem that you have been unable to solve with tried and true solutions. New ideas will come more rapidly than usual. Solutions that have eluded you will be obvious, and your vision will have considerable breadth and scope.

Any new phenomenon will interest you, and the idea of traveling to foreign places will be especially appealing. If at all possible, break with your usual routine and go off somewhere, at least for the day. If you do, you will be glad for the freshness that such a break introduces into your life.

For the same reasons it will be profitable to take up the study of a new subject today. Fields that are particularly appropriate to the symbolism of this transit are astrology, the occult, science, math and technology. In fact any subject will interest you that reveals some entirely new aspect of the universe.

Conversations and other communications with people will have the same electric quality that your mind has today. You will quickly become bored with anyone or anything that reflects the daily routine. Seek out stimulating people and listen to their insights, for you are open to opinions and ideas that would normally surprise or even shock you. You may not accept such ideas, but at least you will be much more tolerant of deviant views. You may even hold them yourself.

In general this influence gives you fine intuition and perception. You will gain the most from this transit by being open to everything that comes your way. The more experiences you allow yourself to have, the better the day will be.

Mercury Opposition Uranus

You may need to put the brakes on in your mind today, for you tend to think and speak hastily. Others may seem too slow for you today, and in your haste you may overlook something significant. At its worst this transit will make you feel scattered, undisciplined and nervous. But on the positive side, it acts like a stimulant upon the brain. You seem to understand ideas faster, perceive what is happening very quickly and have intuitive insights that are usually unattainable. However, you should subject all these results to the test of time. In most cases they will be quite accurate, but they will need some firming up and correcting of the errors that always occur when your mind works too fast.

You are interested in new kinds of experiences and very impatient with the usual routine. Do something different or meet new people who will challenge your thinking. Even your long-time associates can show you aspects of themselves that you never knew existed. Some of this newness may be upsetting, but don't take it too seriously. It is a sign that you need to develop greater flexibility of thinking.

Do not attempt tasks that require great discipline or care today, because you probably won't be able to maintain the discipline. You will become impatient and restless and start making mistakes. In the work you must do today, develop a systematic approach and keep strictly to your system in order to minimize errors. Even so, some errors will probably creep in, so do your work in such a way that you can check it over tomorrow.

In conversation with others, you are inclined to be blunt. Just be careful not to overdo it, and avoid saying things simply to shock people. Be prepared to back up your words later.

Assuming that you can control your tendency toward sloppiness, this is a good aspect for studying mathematics, astrology or technical and scientific disciplines. Although you will not have the discipline to do the necessary drill work to master these subjects today, you will be so fascinated that you will really be able to get into them.

Mercury Conjunct Neptune

Like many other transits involving Neptune, this one has two distinct potentials, one useful and one difficult. The positive side of this transit is that it enables you to think and express yourself with great subtlety, allowing you to express ideas and feelings that you usually cannot. Therefore this transit is very favorable for all forms of artistic expression. Even at best, however, don't expect everyone to comprehend what you are trying to communicate, because it will be very difficult for most people to understand.

This transit also inclines you to study mysterious subjects, the occult and spiritual philosophy. It arouses your imagination in all areas, and the more mysterious a phenomenon is, the more it will fascinate you. And this is fortunate, because the great power of your imagination will enable you to understand ideas that are otherwise beyond you.

On the other hand, this "imaginative" power can get so out of hand that it changes from imagination to illusion. Be sure to subject all the ideas that come to you now to the test of time to find out whether they are of lasting value or just a fantasy of a moment. This transit can indicate unclear and confused thinking. Be particularly careful in your personal communications, because others may misunderstand you even though you think you have been completely clear.

Another difficulty with this transit is that in a direct verbal confrontation with someone you may lack confidence and be tempted to take a dishonest way out. If you find it difficult to be honest with people at this time, you would be better off saying nothing. At least that cannot be thrown back at you later. With the projected form of this transit, you may encounter someone who tries to mislead you, so this is not a very good time to enter into legal negotiations, contracts or sales agreements. Avoid any situation that depends for success on the complete honesty and clarity of each participant.

Mercury Sextile Neptune

This transit stimulates the imagination in a very positive way. Your sensitivity to and awareness of the subtler aspects of the world around you is greatly increased, and your intuition is much stronger than usual. Sometimes this transit accompanies a period of dreaminess, in which you spend much time fantasizing. Because you would like the world to be a more beautiful place than it is, you will probably be attracted to fantasy novels, extremely romantic stories or any distraction that helps you escape from your daily concerns. But this withdrawal from reality is not all that bad. For we each have a world within us that provides the inspiration that makes life worth living. And we can get to that world only at times like this. This intangible reality is as important as the solid material reality of our daily world.

In your contacts with people, you have a much clearer sense of what is going on in others' minds. If you can keep your perceptions straight in your head, you will be astonished by the insights about people that this transit can bring. However, even with this relatively mild Mercury-Neptune transit, it is often difficult to keep your intuitions sorted out. Clear thinking is not one of your strong points today, and in fact you should try not to use your rational mind very much. Rely more on your inner senses and feelings.

This is not a very good day for performing any task that requires great clarity and attention to precise detail. You will not feel like doing it, and if you do, it will not turn out very well.

On a higher level, this transit can signify turning your attention to spiritual or religious matters. This is a very suitable time to study the occult, mysticism or spiritual metaphysics.

Mercury Square Neptune

This could be a day of considerable confusion, when your communications are hopelessly misunderstood or perhaps not even delivered. Be careful to formulate very precisely everything you say to others. If there is any possibility of misunderstanding, it will probably happen.

Be wary of idealizing persons or situations. Longing for "pie in the sky," you may have great difficulty relating to the world as it really is today. Daydreaming is one manifestation of this transit — a relatively mild one, of course — but make some effort to keep track of the world around you.

You may feel inclined to keep a secret or hold back information in order to avoid a confrontation with someone. It is not good to do this, because it will only contribute to the fog of confusion and unclarity that surrounds you today. For the same reasons, avoid any form of misrepresentation or distortion of the truth, even if you think it might be politic to mislead someone. In every way you should strive to keep all your communication and thinking clear, lucid, factual and rooted in the real world today. Any tendency to the opposite could get you into unpleasant situations. If you try to avoid confrontations by acting evasively under this transit, you will run up against even more demoralizing confrontations later.

Also be careful in any kind of negotiations or business dealings today, because you could be the victim of misrepresentation, even if you are not the perpetrator. Or because of a misunderstanding you might become involved in a situation that you would rather not have anything to do with.

If you are studying any kind of religious, spiritual or mystical subjects now, this transit can further your efforts. But even in this case you must remain in touch with the real world; if you don't, you may become very confused. This is a very deluding transit. You are quite likely to get caught up in truly wild ideas today, especially if they appeal to the idealistic side of your personality. But if you can maintain control over your fantasies, you will experience a greater sensitivity and awareness of the subtler aspects of the world than is usually possible.

Mercury Trine Neptune

This transit stimulates your creative imagination and makes you much more sensitive than usual to aspects of the world around you. While you may be tempted to spend the day daydreaming, you will probably be more satisfied if you read romantic literature and poetry or listen to music. This is a good day for leaving the humdrum, everyday world and traveling in your mind to a fanciful and pleasantly unreal world. Don't worry about wasting time. Everyone needs to fantasize like this from time to time, and you are not likely to get so caught up in it that you cannot return to reality.

Conversations with others today will not revolve around practical matters, if you can help it. You will want to talk about fancies, dreams, ideals or just getting away from it all. You might as well, because under this transit you are more than unwilling to deal with hard, cold, practical reality. Probably you lack the necessary discipline today.

On the other hand, you are much more sensitive to subtleties and can catch other people's moods effortlessly. Your attitude is very sympathetic, and you genuinely want to aid anyone who needs your help today. The advice you give, no matter how flawed, is motivated by a sincere desire to help, with no interest in gain for yourself.

Mystical and spiritual subjects will fascinate you under this transit. This is a very favorable influence for studying art, religion, poetry, music and spiritual and occult subjects. You are able to transcend the limits of your rational intellect at this time and understand directly by intuition ideas that would usually seem senseless or be beyond your comprehension. Nevertheless, your thinking lacks discipline to some extent. Tomorrow you should study very carefully any ideas that you come up with today.

Mercury Opposition Neptune

This transit can indicate a day of mental confusion and unclearness. It may seem that so much material is coming into your mind at once that you can't possibly make any sense out of it. Your confusion results from the heightened sensitivity conferred by this transit, and there is the challenge of it. You are able to perceive things, mostly subconsciously, that you usually would filter out. However, to some people on certain occasions this transit gives a great spiritual awareness and concern with the true nature of the world that lies beneath our usual level of perception. The tricky part is to tell when you are perceiving deep truths and when you are simply being confused by so much coming at you. The best practical solution to this problem is to avoid making permanent commitments or decisions on the basis of what you learn today. Wait a couple of days for this transit to pass and allow your mind to sort out what has happened.

This is a very poor day for doing any work that requires disciplined thinking and precision. The world looks like an impressionist painting today, slightly out of focus and emphasizing large patterns of color and shadow. Work with numbers or strict logic will be especially affected. If you do this kind of work today, check it over for errors in a couple of days. Almost certainly there will be some mistakes.

Communications today will be especially difficult. Even when you and another person are trying to be very clear, you may have misunderstandings. This is a poor transit for any important discussions about business or personal matters. Even if you are sure that you are speaking clearly and honestly, make sure that others are treating you the same way. This is a classic transit for being taken, swindled or lied to.

On the physical level you may feel somewhat anxious, confused and unable to stand very much stress today. Nervous weakness is a common symptom of this transit.

Mercury Conjunct Pluto

This transit signifies a time of very intense mental activity. Your thinking and your communications with others have an intense, penetrating quality. You have a strong desire to get to the bottom of every question, and you will not be satisfied with superficial answers. This is a good time for any kind of research, investigative work or other mental activity that involves solving a mystery or answering a question.

You also have the capacity to influence others, if you need to. Any combination of Mercury and Pluto confers the ability to speak with persuasive force and vigor. You make it clear that what you say is the answer, not merely your opinion. The only danger here is that others will believe that you are right even when you do not know the answer. You must take the responsibility of not misusing this energy and not misrepresenting yourself.

However, you may encounter some opposition from others, especially if you phrase your statements in a way that indicates no regard for other people's feelings and sensitivities. If people feel threatened by your words, they will resist you with just as much energy as you put into your statement. Be particularly careful in talking about people. Under this transit you have the ability to make penetrating analyses of human nature, but be careful whom you discuss these with and what you say. These talents are useful, but you do have to be extra careful in handling them.

You may also encounter this problem in a projected form; that is, you may have to contend with someone who acts toward you in any of the ways described above. This transit can indicate a mental power struggle in which you may be either the victim or the perpetrator.

One side of this transit is not so useful. Sometimes it indicates a day when you tend to become totally preoccupied with an idea or a point of view. It is as if the idea, instead of you, were running your life for the moment. This transit is usually too short and light for this to be a serious problem, but it can mean a wasted day. For example, if you have lost something, you might spend the whole day looking for it, whether or not it is important to find it. And you won't hear of letting the matter go until another day. Or an idea may run through your head all day, leaving no room for other thoughts.

Mercury Sextile Pluto

This transit arouses your love of mystery and gives you a desire to solve difficult puzzles. This is a reflection of the deeper purpose of this transit, which is to penetrate below the surface layer of reality to the core of truth where all real knowledge is to be found. Therefore this is a good time to study subjects pertaining to deeper knowledge, such as psychology, astrology, the occult in general or even healing aimed at regeneration of the self.

In your everyday world you will use this energy to examine, scrutinize and probe everything that comes your way. It is not that you are suspicious but that you want to get at the total truth. If someone makes a proposal, you will investigate and ask searching questions until you know exactly what the proposal entails. Under this transit it would be very difficult for someone to swindle or mislead you.

When you find the answer to a question, you work very hard to let others know it, too. If you are sure you are right, it is virtually impossible for someone else to change your mind. In fact you will try to make others change their views. You have a strong urge to persuade, propagandize and change people's thinking about any matters you are interested in. At its best, this transit enables you to teach others valuable truths you have learned, but at its worst it makes you stubborn and concerned only with being correct.

Usually this transit works out favorably, helping to ensure that what you learn is more than an intellectual abstraction. What you learn today will affect you deeply and become a part of you, changing your life for the better.

Mercury Square Pluto

Under this transit it is very important to keep an open mind on all issues and not become obsessed with one idea or thought. All day you may be preoccupied, even with a thought that you don't especially care about or that is unimportant to you. In itself, this effect is harmless, but if you do consider the idea important, it may crowd out your other thoughts to the point that nothing else can make any impression.

In discussions and conversations, do not try to force your point of view upon other people, as you may be inclined to do. It may seem to be the most important thing in the world to make everyone come around to your views, and your efforts may provoke arguments over matters that you have no real stake in. It is also quite possible that you will encounter someone else who acts this way to you.

The main problems with this transit are compulsive thinking and trying to coerce others by your statements. These characteristics can produce great unpleasantness and even give you a profound feeling of frustration, because you will probably not get your way with others.

On the other hand, if you turn this energy inward into yourself, you may achieve something of real value. This transit can bring to light hidden forces, psychological energies within you that could change your life. If you use this introspection positively, you can get in touch with the inner dimensions of your being and gain greater awareness of and control over them.

This is also a good time to begin or continue studying subjects that deal with the hidden or covert aspects of people or the world, such as psychology, magic or other occult studies, as well as human potential studies and mental development studies such as yoga. Unwilling to accept events at face value at this time, you want to know what goes on under the surface as well.

Mercury Trine Pluto

This transit signifies a concern with the very deep issues in life. Today you are interested in what goes on underneath the surface of events and phenomena, and you are willing to dig until you find out. Because you are attracted to mysteries of all sorts, you could spend the day reading a mystery or horror story. Or you might search out a deep problem or look for something you have lost.

This energy can also turn inward, which is often very profitable. Pluto helps to overcome Mercury's tendency to make you think of yourself solely in intellectual terms. With Pluto you want to feel what is going on inside yourself at a very deep level. Therefore this is an excellent time to look at your inner self and try to understand it better. It may be beneficial to be alone so that others cannot distract you from your inward search. For this reason you are likely to be attracted to subjects that reveal the inner dimensions of the psyche, such as psychology or astrology. If by chance you are consulting a therapist, a session today would be very fruitful, although you might not be comfortable with all of the material that comes up.

You may encounter someone today whose ideas have a great effect upon your mind. This is a good time for learning something new, because you can allow your beliefs to be transformed by what you learn. Also you will tend to have a strong effect on other people's thinking today. Communications with others, therefore, will be rather serious and profound.

All Mercury-Pluto contacts have an obsessive quality, meaning that you tend to be possessed by an idea that crowds every other thought out of your mind. However, under the relatively mild influence of the trine, this becomes more of an ability to concentrate and force irrelevant thoughts out of your mind. You will not feel the negative, obsessive side of the combination so strongly.

Mercury Opposition Pluto

This is a good transit for getting to the bottom of any problem, either in a relationship or in some other encounter between you and another person. Or you may become involved in an intellectual conflict of wills with another person. Someone may try very hard today to convince you of some truth that you would rather not accept, or you may do this to someone else. It can go either way. Be very careful about these attempts to persuade, because they can become the basis of a very subversive, smoldering conflict between you and another person. It may be hard to bring such a confrontation out into the open where the two of you can air your grievances. And it may be that there aren't any real grievances at all, but that one of you is trying to pull off a naked power play.

This combination rules all kinds of propaganda and indoctrination, any communication that is designed to change your thinking. Be careful not to get talked into doing something you don't really believe in.

However, this transit is also good for getting at hidden and secret things, especially elements of yourself. One form of encounter that you might have is a consultation with a counselor or psychologist who helps you get in touch with your unconscious mind. This is also a good transit for doing research, because you are in a puzzle-solving frame of mind.

You should also be careful if you feel compulsive or obsessed by an idea today. Under this transit your mind can be totally taken up with a single thought that prevents anything else from entering your mind. Obviously this can be useful in certain circumstances, but most of the time it is not particularly helpful. If you become completely wrapped up in a difficult task that you are trying to finish, this transit is helpful. But you may be possessed by an idea that has no relevance to anything, except that it has great subconscious power over your mind.

Mercury Conjunct Midheaven

Today your attention will be focused on your work, profession or an important social duty that you must exercise. You have an opportunity to plan for the future in these areas of your life, and you will discuss with others your proper course of action. You are likely to announce your plans to others today and let people know exactly where you stand on some issue. You may do this in person or by means of letters, telephone calls or some other form of communication. Occasionally this transit means that you are discussed publicly in a newspaper or on television or radio.

You may also receive an important communication about your professional or public life today. Because the Midheaven does not relate so much to personal life, your private affairs are less likely to be affected.

On the psychological level, this is a good time for being alone to reflect upon your long-range plans and how well you are fulfilling them. The Midheaven is strongly connected with the ego structure, and Mercury transiting it may indicate that you are dwelling upon your basic ego needs. This is especially important if by nature you are a meditative person, who wants to plan everything out before acting. A more extroverted person will go right out and talk to the world, even though that may mean going off half-cocked.

Your work and mental processes are definitely emphasized today. Use this time to clarify your thought and actions to yourself and others.

Mercury Sextile Midheaven

This is a good time for communicating with people, writing letters or planning a course of action in your career or your home and personal life. You are inclined to spend a lot of time thinking under this transit, and others may see you as being all thought and no action. However, this is the time for plans, not for action. Your mind should be very clear today, and you should be in touch with your feelings and emotions to an unusual extent, even about aspects of yourself that you normally keep hidden because you cannot express them clearly. Therefore, the plans you make today are more in keeping with your real inner desires than usual.

This is a good time for making deals and negotiating. It may not be the best time to actually conclude a transaction, but it is not bad. At least you will know exactly what you are doing, although you cannot be sure that the other persons know what they are doing.

In your job this is a good time to clear away paperwork and handle the more trivial aspects of your work. You can pay close attention to details, and any such work you do today will be reasonably well done.

Mentally you are alive and very active. You enjoy mental games and putting your mind to various tasks, such as solving crossword puzzles. But you also enjoy intellectual challenges from others, and you may even be in a mood for playing pranks. Certainly you will want to keep your mind busy, and if you do not you will feel quite bored.

Mercury Square Midheaven

This is a good day for carrying out plans that you have been making, for making decisions and for communicating with others about important matters. It is a day when your mind will be busy with job and career concerns. You are very clear about your objectives, and you are willing to let others know exactly what you are doing. But you are willing to hear other points of view, just to give your mind something to chew over, if for no other reason.

However, there is one danger with this transit. Although you will hear other people's ideas, you may not heed them adequately. It is not enough to play around in your mind with new ideas; you must also allow them to affect your own thinking. Do not be so caught up in your own cleverness that you cannot see it in others. While you can very effectively communicate your position to others at this time, let them communicate to you as well, and really listen to what they say. Otherwise this transit will be characterized by verbal disagreements and disputes.

This is one time when you really do have to keep your mind occupied with ideas that are significant and meaningful to you. If you don't, you will fasten your attention upon some insignificant matter until you have analyzed it to death and blown it up out of all proportion. And this can also lead to problems with others, because they do not attribute as much importance to the matter that you are focusing on.

But if you keep the dangers in mind, you can do extremely good work under this transit and make it come out well. As long as your frame of reference is objective and you see the needs of others as clearly as your own, your thinking will be very effective.

Mercury Trine Midheaven

This is a good time for mental work. You plan very effectively, with a clear objective perception of the facts, and you think very carefully, paying close attention to detail. Your mind easily resolves a difficult and complex issue into its component parts so that you can handle each part separately and come to a valid conclusion.

This is a good time to make plans concerning your career, even if you aren't going to execute them right away. Your clarity of thinking enables you to see the whole situation clearly and put everything into the proper perspective. If you make up a detailed course of action now and follow this plan, it will almost certainly work out. Figure out exactly what you will need and how to go about each step without overlooking a single detail, although it is unlikely that you will overlook anything with this transit.

This is a good time for talking with others, even about matters that you usually find difficult to discuss. Your objectivity will impress other people, and they will not worry that you might try to force them into a position that they do not want to take. You will establish an environment in which any subject can be brought up and discussed. Therefore this is also a good time for business negotiations. You know what you want, and you will listen to what others want and arrive at a satisfactory compromise.

On a more external level, this is also a good time to make plans concerning your household and family or the physical dwelling that you live in. It is a good day to organize your personal affairs, pay bills, schedule the coming week and such.

You may find that there is a danger in letting your thinking become too subjective at this time. Do not let your personal perspective completely cancel out your ability to see another's point of view. Because of this tendency this is not an especially favorable time to get involved in heavy negotiations with someone, either in your personal life or in business. A notable exception to this is that buying or looking for real estate is favored. The lower meridian and the fourth house are traditionally connected with real estate, and this seems to bear up in practice.

Mercury Opposition Midheaven

This is a time for making plans about your personal life and for thinking about your goals and objectives, not in terms of your career but in terms of your inner feelings and personal desires. Often the demands of the outside world become so great that we lose track of what we really want in life and spend our time trying to live up to someone else's expectations. Even worse, we internalize those expectations and convince ourselves that they are our own. Now is a good time to cut through all of those ideas within yourself and to think about what you want and about yourself as you really are.

On a more external level, this is also a good time to make plans concerning your household and family or the physical dwelling that you live in. It is a good day to organize your personal affairs, pay bills, schedule the coming week and so on.

You may find that there is a danger in letting your thinking become too subjective at this time. Do not let your personal perspective completely cancel out your ability to see another's point of view. Because of this tendency this is not an especially favorable time to get involved in heavy negotiations with someone, either in your personal life or in business. A notable exception to this is that buying or looking for real estate is favored. The lower meridian and the fourth house are traditionally connected with real estate, and this seems to bear up in practice.

Mercury Conjunct Ascendant

Under this influence you are likely to have a rather busy day communicating and engaging in exchanges with others. It is a favorable time for all negotiations and business dealings, because your communication is likely to be clear and concise. Your mind is sharper than usual today, and you are receptive to what others have to say. You express your thoughts in a way that is easily understood.

It is not an especially good day to relax, however, because the tempo of your life is likely to be rather brisk. You may use the telephone quite a lot, both calling others and being called. Or you will be busy writing letters or engaging in some other type of communication.

You may travel more than usual today, but it is likely to be in the world that is familiar to you rather than in a new and different environment. Under this influence you might have to run around town doing errands or taking care of routine business.

This is not likely to be an extraordinary day, so you might not notice this influence unless you are looking for it. It is a good idea to use a day like this for routine business that requires a clear mind and considerable attention. Such matters will go much more smoothly than usual.

Sometimes this transit can signify a day of activity with younger people, for Mercury in general indicates youth. Whatever you do will engage your mind. And if nothing else comes up, it is an appropriate day for working on puzzles or other mental games.

Mercury Sextile Ascendant

This transit has the effect of quickening your mind and increasing your exchanges with other people — mentally, verbally, through traveling and even commercially. You feel mentally more alert than usual and eager to see and talk to people, even if it is just small talk. But it would be pointless to waste this transit on small talk, because it favors more serious kinds of communication between you, your friends and neighbors. In anyone's life there is always a need for some serious communication. This transit assists you and others in reaching agreements, even about matters that have been points of dispute.

This is a good day to get rid of paperwork and to write letters. The more energy you put into staying in touch with others, the better you will feel. However, you needn't feel that the initiative is all yours, for you will receive communications from others as well. Sometimes the phone never stops ringing on a day like this.

In the course of your routine business today, you will probably move about considerably more than usual, taking many short trips around town or even a longer drive to another community. Although this transit seldom indicates anything more than day trips, it is a good time to start a longer trip.

This is a good day for any type of commercial transaction, contract negotiation or buying and selling, either for personal reasons or for business. Communication is flowing so smoothly now that you can easily get all the information you need in order to make the best deal.

Mercury Square Ascendant

Normally this transit is quite favorable for all forms of communication, for getting around and getting in touch with people. Your mind moves quite quickly and cannot stand being idle. This transit makes you eager to exchange ideas with others, and you may feel like sitting and chatting with someone all day, if he or she is interesting enough. But the drive of this energy is such that you may waste a good deal of time chattering to yourself and not really accomplishing much of anything.

While it is quite easy to express yourself under this transit, do not expect everyone to agree with you necessarily, especially if you talk so much that others feel they will never get a chance to say anything. They may disagree with you just to make you pause and listen to them. Or there may be a real difference of opinion between you. The trick is to slow your mind down somewhat so that these negative energies don't emerge and so you can be detached enough from your own point of view to hear others.

Sometimes with this transit there is a tendency to analyze people endlessly and tear them apart intellectually. If you do this openly, you obviously won't endear yourself to anyone. You can use this ability to great effect in making your own plans with regard to others, but it is often best to keep this process to yourself, unless asked. Also this transit often signifies a desire to joust verbally and intellectually rather than to communicate legitimately.

Mercury Trine Ascendant

This transit is generally good for the flow of ideas and communication between you and others. You are intellectually alive, curious and willing to learn. This is a good day to attend a lecture or a class in some subject. You are willing to have people challenge your ideas and thereby broaden your thinking. At the same time you are happy to share your insights on any subject. Thus all interchange with others today should be fruitful and expansive, both for yourself and for the people you meet.

Travel is sometimes indicated by this transit, although usually not over long distances. In the course of daily business you may cover a lot more ground than usual.

This is a good day for conferences and negotiations in which it is important to make yourself clear to others. You are willing to communicate your thoughts without reserve, and you should not have much difficulty in getting agreement from others, because this transit gives you a clear, detached and objective viewpoint that others will appreciate. Also you make it clear that you will make intelligent compromises. You are tolerant of opinions other than your own, and you may even welcome them because they expand your perspective.

Letter writing, telephone calls and all other forms of routine communication are favored by this transit. You should be able to get a lot of paperwork done.

Mercury Opposition Ascendant

At this time you will seek increased mental stimulation through contacts with others, probably through either conversation or debate. As long as it doesn't get too acrimonious, you will enjoy repartee. Also you may seek out other people to learn their views on some matter. This is a good transit for consulting any kind of expert for advice, such as a lawyer, doctor, psychologist or an expert in some branch of business. It is also a good time to negotiate with others for contract settlements or business deals. Your mind is reasonably clear, and you are attracted to people who are similarly inclined. This makes it possible for you and another person to make things very clear between you without leaving a lot of matters unsettled and unspoken.

Communications are good between you and your spouse or any other close partner. It is a good time to get something off your chest that you have had trouble expressing recently. And others may do the same with you, so you may be on either the giving or the receiving end of important communications at this time.

Occasionally, if other transits concur in the symbolism, this transit can denote some legal contest or legal negotiation. By itself, this transit does not signify either success or failure in such matters.

This transit can also mean that a younger person will play some kind of prominent role in your life today. A Mercury transit such as this one often indicates that the younger person is playing a role that you would not normally expect of a younger person in your life.

Chapter Seven

Venus

Significance of Transiting Venus

The transits of Venus are usually rather brief in their effects, because Venus is a fast-moving planet. Although its effects may be felt for no more than a day, they are quite pleasant and easy to deal with. There are some things that you should understand, however, to get maximum benefit from the transits of Venus.

Venus is a Yin planet, that is, a planet of negative polarity, as opposed to Yang, or positive polarity; the word negative does not imply difficulty or evil. The influence of Venus seldom results in positive action. Usually, it draws things to you, a process in which you play rather a passive part. Venus rules the spontaneous power of attraction between two entities that differ in such a way that together they form a higher and more complex whole than would otherwise be possible.

In its highest manifestation Venus is love, the emotion that brings people together without force or compulsion. Venus is also the power behind creativity, which stems from the recognition that components in the outer world may be combined to create a beautiful whole. When working properly, Venus always creates something spiritually higher than the original entity. But it always has to work with the power of Mars, the ego drive, the drive of an entity to be itself. Only a fully realized entity can experience the power of Venus. Only a human being who has become as perfect a manifestation as possible of what he or she is can experience love. The balance between Mars and Venus is rather delicate and easily upset. Egotism and the desire to control may become confused with love, and love may be used to manipulate.

At times Venus causes entities to be brought together in a passive manner, resulting in the creation not of a higher entity, but of a useless conglomeration, a pointless accretion. In human terms this is manifested in the tendency of Venus to produce a mood of self-indulgent slothfulness in which one simply sits and waits for nice things to roll in without contributing any effort. This side is also seen in Venus' indulgence of softness and luxury, which can result in the inability to maintain oneself in times of adversity.

Venus is a social planet, and one of its most pleasant effects is to bring about happy social occasions. Parties and entertaining are best done with Venus transits. At least you will have fun!

The classic manifestation of Venus is the love affair. Although Venus transits are usually too short to bring about a major love relationship by themselves, they do signify good times within existing relationships and can indicate an evening's dalliance. Friendships are also made more enjoyable by Venus transits.

There are few difficult transits of Venus, except to Saturn, which of all the planets is the most inimical to Venus's energies. Transits to Neptune, although pleasant, often produce dangerous delusions in love relationships.

Venus transits are often considered to be good for financial matters, because of Venus's tendency to attract material things. This author, however, does not agree with the prevalent opinion that Venus "rules" money.

Venus in the First House

This transit marks a period of several days in which Venus influences your whole manner of expressing yourself to others. You have a great desire to relate to others, and you are willing to make whatever personal compromises are necessary. Venus in the first makes you feel rather unaggressive. In fact, you may not even defend your own personal rights. Instead you may try to work out a compromise or evade any contest. Because your personality is filled with warmth, you project a feeling of social agreeableness, making a favorable impression and avoiding controversy.

During this transit you may be able to make peace among others. Since you do not feel like fighting, you are willing to act as a go-between to help others smooth over their differences.

This is a good time to have a good time with friends, take a vacation or do whatever you enjoy. Venus ranks pleasure above work. If you can get away to have fun at this time, you ought to do so.

During this period you may attract other people, not necessarily potential lovers, because the Yin action of Venus makes people come to you. If you are clever, this can be to your advantage. Do not attempt to use this energy to manipulate people, because this is not a long-term influence.

Venus in the Second House

This transit can be financially either good or difficult, depending upon how you handle it. The good side of this transit stems from the power of Venus to attract material possessions and money, as well as people. Financial opportunities may come up, but difficulties may arise from your tendency to be extravagant. Not that spending is wrong, but be careful, for Venus's influence is not practical. Often your tastes will be more lavish than your budget can afford. You are especially susceptible to beautiful clothes, jewelry and art objects to beautify your home or entertainment to make your life more pleasant and enjoyable. Care in spending is advisable.

This transit can be quite favorable to financial negotiations. You will be able to handle the relationships involved in any transactions, to your benefit, for Venus always grants the ability to handle people. Borrowing money should not be very difficult.

Investments made under this influence are usually quite advantageous, especially investments in art or objects of beauty. Again, be careful not to invest money that you need for everyday living.

Venus in the Third House

This transit has the effect of making your everyday surroundings and activities more pleasant and agreeable. Your social life often picks up at this time as you get together with friends and neighbors to have fun or simply socialize and talk. All your dealings with people in the everyday world will be pleasant and light. You will not want to discuss serious matters, because Venus makes one interested only in the pleasures of life.

On a somewhat deeper level, this transit can provide an opportunity to discover that there is a considerable amount of love in your everyday life. You do not have to search for true affection. Many of us go through life without ever acknowledging the love that we encounter every day. This is a good time to let people know how much you love them. Do not leave it to the imagination. The third house is a house of communication, either directly through speech or through an exchange of letters.

You will also want to encounter beauty in your everyday surroundings. You may beautify your neighborhood or introduce art and artistic activities into your environment. Even if you only go for a short drive to enjoy the scenery, you are much more sensitive than usual to the beauty around you and can appreciate it tremendously.

Venus in the Fourth House

This is usually a peaceful time, when you will enjoy quiet hours at home, either alone or entertaining guests and feeling at ease. Barring a contrary indication from another transit, this is usually a time when you feel neither self-assertive and outgoing, nor shy and withdrawn. You feel amiable in a quiet way and are fond of having congenial people around you.

Relations with your parents, if they are near you, are good under this transit. In general, this is a good time to experience the closeness and warmth of family living.

Redecorating is often undertaken under this influence. You want your home to be elegant or gay and light while Venus is transiting the fourth house. Fortunately, you are usually quite sensitive and in tune with your inner feelings, so that your home decorating efforts should be satisfactory. Try to avoid the usual Venusian tendency to do things lavishly or expensively, and keep practical considerations in mind.

About the only real problem that you might encounter with this transit is that the fourth house influences your digestive tract. Unless you are careful you may overindulge in food and drink with no regard for your digestion or your weight.

Venus in the Fifth House

More than any other position of Venus, this transit signifies an appropriate time for fun, entertainment, having a good time. The fifth house is the house of amusement and creative self-expression, as well as love affairs and children. Activities pertaining to any of these are favored strongly during this transit. Your self-discipline may be at an all-time low during this period, but everyone needs a break from time to time, so enjoy yourself. Just make sure not to overdo it.

You can relate well with children now, and this is a good time for games and fun. It is not conducive to serious work or discussion with them, however, because you may not want to be serious, yourself.

Creative activities are also favored; in fact, you need to express yourself through some creative activity. Try to find the medium most appropriate for you. If you are not especially creative, enjoy the creative works of others at concerts, museums or wherever good art is to be found.

Love relationships in general are favored during this transit. You will get along smoothly with loved ones without feeling that you are surrendering your identity. Venus in the fifth house has the happy faculty of making it possible for others to enjoy *you* being exactly yourself. There is no need to pretend to be what you are not.

Venus in the Sixth House

The sixth house is intrinsically incompatible with the nature of Venus. You will find it necessary to subordinate your desire for amusement to the needs of the present. In your relationships it may be necessary to confront difficulties that you have not handled earlier. Sometimes problems in relationships arise when tacit agreements are not clear to both partners. This is a good time to discuss those agreements openly. Until each of you accepts the real duties and obligations of the relationship, and properly meets them, the relationship will not go smoothly.

This transit is good for all matters relating to your work or profession. During this time you should enjoy good relationships with both superiors and employees. You understand how good interrelationships make it all work well. You are willing to work with others to resolve any difficulties that may arise. You may gain financial or other favors, quite unexpectedly, from your employer.

This transit is also good for health in general, although fattening or sweet foods may cause problems. Avoid any overindulgence at this time.

Practical matters are important in all your relationships now. This is perhaps the least romantic position for the transiting Venus. You need to deal with the real world, not with the fantasies in your mind.

Venus in the Seventh House

This is one of the best positions for all relationships: love affairs, relationships with partners, with coworkers, even with enemies. Ego forces are so in tune at this time that you can create a proper balance between yourself and everyone you meet, which makes all your encounters with others work out smoothly.

In your marriage or other love relationship, you will be able to express affection easily and make your feelings clear to your partner. If other indications concur, a wholly new love may enter your life under this transit.

In other partnerships, including professional ones, you are able to understand the needs of your partner so that you can arrive at maximum understanding and work together harmoniously. Be careful not to let your amiability prevent you from standing up for your own rights. You need not worry about alienating your partner, because you will be able to make it clear that you are working for your mutual benefit.

If you are in conflict with someone in your life and would like to make peace, this is the best of all transits for doing so. Even persons who are openly hostile to you will be receptive to your overtures. This extends even to legal confrontations, where strong potential exists for settling lawsuits out of court.

Venus in the Eighth House

Venus in this house can have several effects, often quite subtle. It can stimulate the sexual side of existing relationships and give love relationships a greater intensity. This is because sex goes beyond the physical act and becomes a vehicle for self-transformation and inward change. A love relationship that begins with Venus transiting this house in your horoscope will be intense throughout its duration and will have a greater impact, for better or worse, on your life than other relationships.

This transit may attract money to you through your spouse, your business partner or through a bank or other public financial institution, without any special effort on your part. Obviously, this is a good time to seek a loan or other financial support.

During this time, in your most intimate personal relationship, factors that you may not have been aware of but that have been instrumental in determining the course of the relationship may come to the surface, where you can recognize and learn to deal with them. The eighth house has a strong connection with psychological evolution and confrontation. Love relationships may be instrumental in bringing these about at this time. You will learn much about how you relate to people and events.

Venus in the Ninth House

This transit provides that through a Venus encounter — love or the experience of beauty in art — you will have a consciousness-expanding experience that will broaden you and bring about personal growth. The form that this experience takes can be quite varied.

This would be a good time to see an art exhibit that challenges your preconceived views about what is beautiful. Probably this will be entertaining rather than unsettling, and you will experience something new. Or you might go to a concert that features music entirely different from anything you have ever heard.

This transit can signify a long and enjoyable pleasure trip. You will derive the most benefit from a trip to a place you have never seen before, where you can encounter something totally new. This is a fine time for a vacation.

Your experience may be broadened through a loved one who shows you new things. Or something may happen that will teach you more about your relationship, not to disturb you but to increase your insight.

You will be attracted at this time to new persons who are strange and different in terms of your past experience. It will be this very difference that attracts you to them. Such persons may be foreigners or people who have gone to strange places or simply persons whom you regard as better educated or more experienced than yourself.

Whichever of these effects you experience, this is usually an easy and rewarding transit.

Venus in the Tenth House

This transit can be useful in many ways. It creates favorable circumstances in your business and professional life, attracting persons and circumstances that facilitate your work. People in authority are favorably inclined toward you, and most relationships in your professional life will run smoothly. It is apparent to everyone that you are primarily interested in working harmoniously with others, and they respond by being agreeable. Ultimately, Venus attracts only because you exude favorable energies.

Regardless of what you do for a living, this transit may involve you temporarily in artistic matters, such as design, layout work, office redecorating, even public relations for the purpose of making the company look more attractive. All such activities should go smoothly at this time.

Any new love relationship at this time would be with someone older or someone who acts as a "guide figure," who can help you learn more about getting ahead in life. On a mundane level, this can take the form of falling in love with a boss or employer. The fact that this person's station is higher than your own, normally a barrier, becomes a source of attraction under this influence. Be careful of mercenary motives, which could ruin the relationship.

Venus in the Eleventh House

This is one of the best of all transits for group activities or activities with friends. You will feel friendly toward almost everyone, and they will be friendly in return, of course assuming that there is no contradicting major transit. It is a good time to have friends in for a party or to go out with a group of friends for a good time. You will enjoy each other's company immensely and be much more loving and affectionate with each other.

This benefit is not limited to activities with friends. Any situation in which you deal with many people in a group setting, for example a business conference or organizational meeting, is favored by this transit. Your ego energies are low enough so that you can deal agreeably with others, making whatever compromises are necessary without feeling that you are losing something personal that you should defend. You feel secure in yourself and willing to help the group achieve its objective. You may even identify your own objectives with that of the group.

All love relationships at this time in your life, both preexisting and new ones, possess a friendly quality. At other times loved ones may not be the best company for ordinary social occasions, especially if there is discord between you. But this will not be a problem under this influence, because friendship brings love, and love brings friendship.

Venus in the Twelfth House

The transit of Venus is one of the best planetary transits through the often difficult twelfth house. At its highest, it indicates an unusual degree of selflessness in love. You may be called upon to take care of a loved one who is in need of help, or you may become involved in some charitable activity, such as working for the underprivileged or in a hospital or similar institution.

In personal relationships, the need to care for someone else may mean that you will not get immediate gratification other than the pleasure of helping someone you love. If your relationship is basically sound, this transit will assure greater rewards of love and satisfaction later. There are, however, certain pitfalls to avoid.

Although this is a time for self-denial in love relationships, do not fall into the negative trap of playing martyr. Do not inflict on others, especially the ones you are helping, a constant awareness that you are "unselfishly" devoting yourself to them. This will undo your efforts and create trouble. If you cannot serve with a true spirit of selfless devotion, do nothing. It will be less harmful. This applies to group social work as well as to individual relationships.

It may be necessary to endure some difficult psychological energies as unresolved problems within your relationships come to the surface. Your forbearance and grace in handling these tensions as they arise will eventually work to your advantage.

The normal effects of this transit should be quite good. What may be lacking in pleasure will be made up for in spiritual rewards and real satisfaction that you have done all that you can.

Venus Conjunct Sun

This is the day for creativity or love. You will want to express yourself in as many ways as possible, but principally with someone else. You feel very affectionate and sociable, as well as just plain good. Your physical health is excellent, although you feel more like sitting around and luxuriating than like doing something vigorous. This is a good day to please yourself.

Like many Venus transits, this one is good for entertaining or going out for amusement. The harsh realities of the everyday world do not appeal to you today, and you would enjoy escaping to a brighter and prettier world, which would do no harm. You may be quite popular today, as the magnetism of Venus attracts other people to you. You may not have to go looking for fun at all, for it is likely to come looking for you. Your relationships with men are likely to be better than those with women today, but both will be good. If you are male, you will find that your own attractiveness is inexplicably enhanced by this transit. If you are female, you will attract men more easily than usual.

This transit favors creative activities, and whatever artistic ability you have will be useful today. You create much more easily than usual, and even if you are not especially artistic, you will have a strong drive to express yourself in an artistic way. Seek beautiful surroundings, for you will enjoy them more than ever.

Venus Sextile Sun

This is an excellent transit for all kinds of group activity and for being with friends. You feel unusually sociable, and people will enjoy your company. Friends may be of considerable benefit to you today. You should certainly seek out other people, and if you need a favor from someone, this would be a good time to ask. This applies not only to personal favors, but to any situation in which you have to depend upon someone's good will, for example, applying for a loan or financial support. Incidentally, this transit will work most favorably if you are being personally interviewed, rather than filling out a form. This transit is extremely good for any interview in which you must make a good impression.

You will get along very well today with persons in your immediate environment. By chance, you may make a new friend in the course of your everyday activities. The familiar setting in which you meet will set the tone of the entire relationship, a tone of easy familiarity and friendliness.

Because the Sun relates to persons in authority, this transit is also likely to provide opportunities for personal advancement as a result of the favorable impression that you have made on a boss, employer, or other person in authority.

Today is a good day for working with others. Your concern is only that the group achieve its objective, and to that end you bend your efforts. You are also good at helping others resolve differences that arise in the course of the day.

Venus Square Sun

Normally this is a very pleasant transit with little difficulty. You seek out good times and pleasurable forms of recreation, and you may not feel much like working. In fact, the only real flaw in the transit is that it is not conducive to self-discipline or labor. You will be more interested in your own well-being and in indulging yourself than in accomplishing great works. Obviously, this can be either bad or good according to the circumstances.

This transit is usually good for all social interaction and for getting along with people. Love relationships are favorably affected. The old texts often describe this transit as leading to scandalous affairs, but that assumes both a Victorian sense of morality and the presence of other heavier transits that produce compulsive behavior.

You will not be very self-assertive today. If you find yourself in conflict with someone, you will compromise rather than fight. Only be careful not to give up something that is important to you. There are situations in which peace-making is not the best resolution. Also, it may arise from your desire to avoid conflict rather than from your belief in peace.

Avoid the temptation to overindulge in rich and fattening foods, for your body is sensitive to these now. At the least you are likely to gain weight, and at the worst you could have physical problems such as indigestion.

Venus Trine Sun

This is one of the most pleasant of all transits. It does not signify anything earth-shaking, but it is a good day for all kinds of enjoyable activity.

Although this is not an especially energetic transit, it is good for any work you have to do with others, because you create a spirit of camaraderie and togetherness, which makes the work go faster and more smoothly. If you need to make a good impression on others, this transit will assist you.

But it is for recreation and pleasure that this transit is really at its best. You feel like having a good time, and almost anything you do will work out that way. It is especially good for amusing yourself with friends and is an excellent transit for a party.

Personal and love relationships are favored by this influence. You will enjoy your loved ones with complete relaxation and ease. Just being yourself works fine. You will probably feel affectionate and will have little difficulty showing it to the people who are important to you, and they will no doubt respond in kind.

This is also a good day for creative and craft projects. Not only do you have the physical energy for the work, you also have the creative ideas.

Venus Opposition Sun

Like most transits of Venus, this one is not especially troublesome. It can introduce much pleasantness into your life through good times, agreeable relationships, sexual attraction and friendship. The problems that you will confront during this transit are: overindulgence, lack of self-discipline, and unwillingness to work.

This transit of Venus does not fit you for demanding work or trying situations, for you are likely to be lazy and unwilling to rouse yourself. If you don't have to accomplish anything, there is nothing wrong with this mood. In fact it is a good time to take it easy. But be careful not to overindulge in food or drink; today's good feelings may be tomorrow's headache!

You may be in a rather amorous mood, which can be extremely good in an existing relationship or in one that begins under this transit. But you are not likely to be discreet about your actions at this time, so it would be a good idea to avoid any involvement that requires discretion. Be careful of any new relationship that is formed today, because you may be lacking in discrimination. Such a relationship may be all right, but make it withstand the test of time before you decide to commit yourself.

Your creative energies are stimulated by this transit, but you may lack the creative self-discipline that can turn a random outpouring of feelings into an artistic medium and disciplined art. Today's work may have to be corrected tomorrow.

Venus Conjunct Moon

This combination rules feelings of love and affection. You are loving and affectionate to people around you today, unless there is an extremely difficult transit at the same time. You are likely to be in a dreamy and romantic mood, and you will seek a quiet place to spend time with someone you love. This is not a wildly erotic Venus transit, and although good for sex, it is mainly a time for two people to quietly express their affection. You want to be with someone whom you have a lot in common with or someone who has shared your experiences. With friends, you will want to talk about old times and things that happened in the past. More than anything else, you base your relationships today upon experiences that you and others have shared.

This is a good day to spend pleasantly at home. Domestic surroundings appeal to you and it is easy for you to express your affection. You will have strong feelings of love for your family and relatives under this transit.

Relations with women are especially fortunate today, and you may gain some benefit through such an association. This is a good day to see your mother.

The only thing to be careful of is a tendency toward overindulgence, which could affect your digestion. Enjoy sweets and alcoholic beverages in moderation to avoid digestive upsets.

Venus Sextile Moon

Your emotions are softened by this transit. You will find it difficult to feel anger or resentment against anyone, particularly the people who are close to you emotionally or those whom you encounter in the course of everyday life. Toward friends you feel protective and nurturing, and you want to help them in any way you can. If you have to work with others, you are able to keep things running smoothly because of your sympathetic understanding of their feelings.

Relations with women are very good today, especially with female relatives and with your mother. Whatever tensions there might be between you are not evident just now. Female friends may provide unexpected opportunities.

If you have a choice, you should have people visit you today instead of going out, because the benevolent nature of this transit is best expressed at home. This is one of the finest transits under which to relax and take it easy, and probably you will not feel like working anyway.

If you must deal with the general public today, you will be effective. Your audience will be aware that you are communicating with your emotions as well as with your words, and they will appreciate it. The warmth that you project will impress them favorably. But even though your charm is more potent than usual, do not use it to take advantage of others. Eventually people see through that phoney, plastic warmth and you will lose your effectiveness.

Venus Square Moon

Not a difficult square, this transit usually creates an amorous mood, making you want to relate to the opposite sex. But there are some problems with this transit. If you are jealous and possessive of your partner, it may produce feelings of love that are suffocating to him or her. Recognize that even the closest relationship needs room to breathe, and avoid being overprotective and smothering. Your partner needs a lover, not a mother! However, you will encounter this problem only if you already tend to be possessive in love.

Discordant transits accompanying this one can indicate conflicts with women, regardless of your own sex. Your mother may present a problem because of the possessive smothering emotion that is characteristic of this transit.

This type of emotion has a positive side also, for it can be transmuted into a very warm, protective kind of love that nourishes and supports a lover. In itself the emotion is neither good nor bad; it just has to find an appropriate outlet. However, the one who feels protective seems to think that this is always good, leading to misunderstandings and hurt feelings in a relationship. You should certainly be aware of any tendency at this time to confuse loving with "parenting."

Any kind of glandular disturbance will probably be adversely affected by this transit, and women may experience menstrual irregularities.

Venus Trine Moon

This is an excellent transit for all matters concerned with your domestic, personal and emotional life. Relationships work out far better than on other days, because you are imbued with a strong desire to be warm and friendly to everyone you meet. Others can sense the sincerity of your feelings and will respond in kind. Relations with women should be especially favorable under this influence.

Sexual relationships are strongly supported by this transit, not by directly increasing the sex drive, but by indirectly increasing the strength of love within the relationship. The emotions are quiet, not turbulent, and this is a good transit for you and a loved one to be alone together quietly.

If you must deal with groups of people, this is the day to do it. Beneficial aspects to the natal Moon, such as this one, favor confronting groups in organizations or in business. This transit would help you sell a product or an idea to a group of people, not because you are unusually convincing, but simply because people like you better than usual.

This is also a favorable transit for all types of recreation or amusements at home, for example a party for a small group of friends. A small group would work better than a large group, by the way, although either would probably be successful.

This is also a good time to look about for ways to beautify and decorate your home. You are fond of beauty and pleasant surroundings, and you want your immediate physical environment to reflect your emotions.

This transit is not usually spectacular in its effects, but the days on which it occurs are pleasant.

Venus Opposition Moon

Like most transits by opposition from Venus, this one is not troublesome; any problems are likely to come from doing something to excess. On the positive side, this transit does arouse your affections and makes you willing to give and receive love. Relationships with women will be especially meaningful. Between you and your loved ones there is a real desire to protect and nurture. Moon-Venus brings out the maternal side of love, the desire to "take care of."

On the negative side, this transit leads to rather indiscriminate affection, because your desire to love someone overrules your normal sense of discretion. This is not especially dangerous, although Victorian astrologers believed that this transit was likely to produce scandalous relationships. We are not so easily scandalized now, but a certain amount of discretion is still desirable. It would be unwise to make a permanent commitment to a love affair that begins under this influence until you have had time to think about it.

This transit might produce such extreme emotionalism between you and a loved one that you would not be able to handle your problems objectively. If you have been having problems with each other before this transit, don't try to have a calm, rational discussion just now, for it would lead only to an emotional confrontation with little communication.

If all else is well, this transit should be a time of warm and friendly feelings between you and your loved ones.

Venus Conjunct Mercury

Today your thoughts are on light topics, and you find it difficult to take things seriously. Your good mood will affect every encounter today, making conversations agreeable, sociable and friendly, punctuated with humor. You are not likely to have any patience with serious or heavy topics, although you are willing to discuss relationships and matters pertaining to love and affection.

This transit stimulates your creative intellect. You may want to write poetry or take up some other literary art form, even if you have no talent. You will certainly appreciate poetry, music and other intellectual arts.

This is a good day to take pleasure trips, to visit people, to see the countryside. Pleasant scenery will greatly appeal to you.

You will find it very easy to express love and affection for others today, even if you are usually tongue-tied. If you want to say something to make a favorable impression on someone, you will succeed today. You can win people over by what you say and how you say it.

This transit also favors commercial transactions and negotiations for favorable financial terms, particularly in the entertainment field or an industry supplying women's products.

Venus Sextile Mercury

This day is good for arranging and participating in social get-togethers. Spend time with friends and enjoy yourself. You probably won't want to talk about anything serious, because this is a light-hearted transit. Nevertheless, it is a good time for talking to loved ones and making it clear how you feel about them. Even if there are tensions within your relationships, the influence of this transit should enable you to discuss them, straighten them out and leave nothing behind but good feelings.

Your daily surroundings will seem more pleasant than usual, because somehow you can see the good in everything around you. Interactions with friends and neighbors will often prove fruitful under this transit, and one may even present you with a pleasant surprise.

This transit favors all forms of commercial transactions, including buying and selling for yourself as well as dealings in your professional life. You have a better than usual understanding of the interrelationships in business and concerning money, and you should take advantage of it. This transit is also good if you have to make a presentation to a group. Not only will it be clear and concise, but you will project your own personality effectively and make a good impression.

If you do not have any work that has to be done, this is a good transit for attending a concert, art exhibit or other intellectually stimulating activity. Or you might take a trip and spend the day in pleasant surroundings away from home. Whatever you do, this should be a light, pleasant day.

Venus Square Mercury

Like the other squares of the transiting Venus, this one is normally quite easy, indicating a day of light and pleasant thoughts and social interaction. You will avoid serious topics of conversation or any that might produce conflicts. This is not a good day to negotiate any difficult or contentious matters, because during a Venus transit you are more concerned with keeping peace than with making a favorable arrangement. Real problems that you might sweep under the carpet now can emerge and cause trouble later. This transit is bad for dealing with difficult or unpleasant problems, so you would do well to avoid such things today. Favorable Mars transits (certain conjunctions, most sextiles and trines) are better for this purpose.

In relationships you will look for interesting activities that are mentally and intellectually stimulating rather than physically or emotionally exciting. You want to be amused and entertained today, either by or with your partner. This is a good transit for going to an art exhibit, a show or a concert to engage your mind with something beautiful, pleasant and mentally stimulating.

If difficult transits coincide with this one, it can indicate disputes and arguments with loved ones, but that is not a normal effect of this transit by itself.

Be aware that you lack mental discipline during this transit, if you are engaged in any activity that requires it.

Venus Trine Mercury

This is a day of pleasant thoughts and communication, of easy intellectual exchanges with other people, general light-heartedness and good times. This is a good day to tell someone that you love him or her. It is also a good day to discuss any aspect of a relationship. If something has been bothering you today, you can discuss it and clear the air in such a way that there will be no negative feelings. Today it will be easy to let the other person know that you are fond of him or her and that you are only trying to make the relationship better.

Go out for a drive today, or better, begin a long vacation. A trip started under this transit will give you great pleasure, stimulate your mind and expand your consciousness. You may meet new friends who will stay with you for a long time.

A business meeting in which you are trying to get everyone to work together on a project should work out well, if you control the proceedings. You are able now to see how all the different personalities interact, and you can manage them accordingly. Contract negotiations held today should proceed smoothly and work out to your advantage.

But if there is nothing particular that you have to do, this is a good day to relax, sit back and let your thoughts wander. If you have been feeling nervous about something, this is a particularly good day to relax and unwind.

Venus Opposition Mercury

This is a favorable time for communication about love and relationships. It will not make the communication either good or bad, but it will help to ensure that communication happens. You will think about and want to discuss your relationships, not only love affairs but also friendships and other kinds of relationships.

This is a good time to confront your partner with any problems in your relationship. You may be able to reduce the tension between you because you are calm, rational and detached. If other transits at the same time signify heavy emotional confrontations, this transit will not prevent them, but it will guarantee that a confrontation will occur and that the air will be cleared.

The Mercurial side of your personality does not take emotional matters seriously. It likes talk and intellectual exchanges, without giving thought to any emotional consequences. Be careful of what you say about friends and loved ones under this transit. Someone may take your casual remarks seriously, and you could inadvertently hurt someone. Be careful of this tendency in any discussions with loved ones. This is one of the most unemotional of all Venus transits.

Venus Conjunct Venus

This is a time to take the initiative in all kinds of relationships, especially love relationships. All transits by conjunction favor new beginnings. If you reveal your love for someone at this time, it may turn the relationship in a new direction. Even if you believe that your loved one knows how you feel, don't leave it to his or her imagination. This is also a favorable transit for a new relationship, although it would require another sign along with this one to indicate anything more than a casual encounter.

The desire for beautiful things is strong under this transit, influencing you to buy things of beauty, such as clothes, cosmetics, objects of art, things to beautify the home, or works of literature and musical recordings. Surround yourself with beauty and take advantage of the lighter and more pleasant aspects of life.

Under this transit you are affectionate and want to be with friends. Like many other Venus transits, this is a good time for parties or entertaining at home or on the town or for a casual get-together with friends. You will be in a good mood and able to enjoy almost anything that comes along.

Venus on Venus will help in a situation in which you need the cooperation of others, particularly if there is some problem or if you need to make a good impression.

Venus Sextile Venus

This transit just makes you feel contented and at ease. Today all your dealings with family, loved ones, friends or business contacts will go very well, because you project warmth and concern for others. New connections made today may be beneficial in the future. This transit would be a good sign of success for a new romantic interest in your life.

You will be occupied with love and beauty today, and you will want to be in pleasant surroundings. Probably you would like to escape from work and practical matters into fun and amusement, but if you must work today, you will be more efficient and cheerful than usual.

This is a good day for a short recreational trip to indulge your desire for beautiful surroundings.

Financial transactions are favored by this transit, and you should be able to negotiate in business to your advantage. Anything that you buy today should prove to be a worthwhile investment.

In general under this influence you will feel that life is going more easily than usual, that with little effort everything is going as it should.

Venus Square Venus

Although this is normally a pleasant transit, producing good times and pleasant leisure, under some circumstances it can be a period of testing to see if relationships are on a sound footing. The test may consist of situations that will determine your ability to maintain your individuality within your important relationships. This is one of the Venus transits that produce a tendency to compromise rather than to stand up for your beliefs and rights. Someone may take advantage of your good nature at this time, which is not a tremendous danger, but something to keep in mind when dealing with people today.

At this time your energies are rather low, not so that you feel sick, as with Neptune transits, but so that you feel like doing nothing. Your work may not be done carefully because your heart is not really in it. You may be deluding yourself that whatever you do will work out, no matter how little energy you put into it. If you do put out the effort, however, this transit may actually produce positive results and satisfaction.

Be careful of self-indulgence and extravagance, which are not in your long-term interest today. This is not the best day to go shopping if you must stay within a budget.

Venus Trine Venus

This is a pleasant transit that is good for all relationships, but you may not feel especially active. Both Venus and the trine aspect tend to attract circumstances, persons or objects, including money, that can be useful later on. This is a spontaneously "lucky" transit. The quotation marks around "lucky" mean that it is not so much luck that helps you as your attitude of relaxation and willingness to let your life flow without the tension of resistance. Many things are prevented from entering people's lives because they are too tense to let them in. At other times you might unconsciously alienate a potentially helpful person, or you might be too cautious or overlook an opportunity because of tension. This transit helps to prevent such negative states of consciousness.

Relationships work very smoothly under this double Venus influence. You have a special attraction to and for beautiful people, but be careful not to let superficial considerations dictate your tastes. Love relationships are unusually romantic under this influence.

You are also attracted strongly to beauty in the creative arts. Attend a concert or art exhibit, or go to a garden or other spot where you can surround yourself with beauty. If you are creative yourself, use these energies that are so favorable for creative activity.

In many respects this transit is a time of rest from other transits that require more effort.

Venus Opposition Venus

This can be a very pleasant transit. You feel at ease with yourself, benign and rather self-indulgent, which is fine as long as you don't have work that must be done. As with many other Venus transits, you feel that there is nothing you do not deserve, and you are likely to buy some expensive frivolity on a whim or indulge in an expensive pastime only to regret the cost later. The sexual self-indulgence that may accompany this transit is not likely to do you any real harm, in spite of the warnings of thousands of Victorian manuals!

This transit is not a good time for getting work done. In fact, you will do anything to avoid working. Unless it is absolutely necessary, do not schedule heavy work projects for a day with this transit.

Love relationships will normally be smooth during this transit, although a problem may arise if you have a disagreement with a loved one or friend. Instead of defending your own position when you have a perfect right to, you may compromise on issues that really should not be compromised. If you have a difficult negotiation to transact, avoid doing it under this transit. The negotiation will succeed, but the results will not be to your advantage.

Venus Conjunct Mars

This transit arouses a strong attraction to and desire for the opposite sex. You will be much more aggressive than usual in going out and finding a partner. This transit is often a sign of physical passion, and because Venus is acting upon Mars, rather than

Mars upon Venus, the effect is to soften the nature of Mars and make you more willing to meet your partner's needs. Under this influence a sexual relationship is very satisfying to both of you.

Even without sex, you will be very happy with other people. You feel more vivacious and attractive than usual and may well be the life of the party. You will work hard to gain the approval of others under this transit, so strong is your need for affection.

Artistic activity is also indicated, for the general significance of this transit is self-expression through creativity and love. Your ego drives are most readily satisfied by successfully relating to another, so you may seek out an entirely new person to begin a relationship with. But for the relationship to be significant in the long run, there should be more indications than are provided by this one transit.

Venus Sextile Mars

This transit favors love relationships and the formation of friendships. As with other Venus-Mars contacts, this one indicates a balance in your life between self-assertion and the need to relate to others. In a sexual relationship this balance is manifested by your ability to give and receive equally. In friendships you can be yourself without difficulty, and by being yourself you can get along better with your friends.

Creative activities are also favored by this transit. If you are not artistic, you may spend the day working to beautify your immediate surroundings.

Try to become involved in some kind of activity with others — a party, a night out on the town, or some such. This will give the energy of this transit an adequate outlet. The energy and liveliness that you have now will attract the people you want to attract, especially the opposite sex. You are likely to be in a fun-loving mood, and you will need company to make the most of it.

This transit may bring about financial opportunities, particularly for investment in a new and unique venture. Your own individuality is best expressed by getting involved, financially or emotionally, in projects that are different and innovative.

Venus Square Mars

This transit usually arouses your interest in the opposite sex and contributes to the physical side of a sexual relationship. But its energy may cause discord, especially if there are hidden tensions in the relationship. A reasonably healthy relationship will have little difficulty during this transit.

One function of this transit can be to test a relationship to discover what ego tensions have been built into it. In the best relationships there will be a lot of love energy, to be released in whatever style pleases you and your lover. But if your relationship is in trouble, you will probably have arguments and other forms of discord, all arising from unexpressed sexuality.

The main difficulty of this transit is that the desire for a nice, easy relationship, as indicated by Venus, is sometimes hard to balance with the self-assertive drive of

Mars. Mars demands that it be satisfied in precisely the way that it wants, and this can be hard on a relationship. Obviously a spirit of compromise would help out immensely at this time, but the needs and desires of Mars can be urgent.

If you are not currently involved in a sexual relationship, you will probably be inordinately attracted to someone of the opposite sex, without being very discriminating. Therefore this is not the best transit under which to start a relationship, since it may be based only on physical attraction.

Venus Trine Mars

The effects of this transit can vary considerably, but it is generally favorable for most kinds of activity. You are able to assert yourself today so as to get what you want without offending anybody. People will appreciate that you have been direct without being abrasive or pugnacious. You want everyone to have the same freedom you have to go after their own objectives, and you are willing to help them as long as they will return the favor. There is an almost perfect balance now between your need to be an individual with individual wants and desires and your need to relate to others.

Of course, like all other Venus-Mars contacts, this transit is likely to arouse your sex drive, but in a somewhat gentler way than many of the other transits. You can charm the opposite sex by being genuinely friendly and agreeable, and you are concerned that your partner enjoy the relationship as much as you do, thereby fulfilling important requirements of a successful sexual relationship. A relationship begun under this transit has a good chance of lasting, but even a casual liaison will be satisfying and leave no bitterness when you separate. The action of this transit in your life assures that no one will be exploited now.

Venus Opposition Mars

The normal effect of this transit is to stimulate sexual and creative energies. It can be good for a sexual relationship if things are generally going well and you both are able to release sexual energy and achieve ample gratification.

If this is not the case, there may be difficulties associated with this transit. On one hand, if serious problems are preventing ample sexual self-expression in this relationship, or if it is a nonsexual relationship with the opposite sex, there is likely to be conflict between you. When the ego energy of Mars is not allowed to express itself sexually via Venus, it transmutes into conflict energy.

If one of you is not fulfilled in this relationship, again the Mars energy becomes transmuted into conflict energy, or sexual expression is overwhelmed by the selfishness of one person.

If you have no ongoing sexual relationship, you can expect to be attracted sexually to almost anyone you encounter. Be careful of a new relationship that starts under this transit, because you may be seeking a sexual outlet with little regard for other areas of compatibility. Do not make a commitment until the relationship has proved itself.

For persons involved in creative arts or crafts, this is a good transit for completing work that gives you plenty of room for self-expression.

Venus Conjunct Jupiter

This is probably the most agreeable transit of all in its effect upon your mood and in the way it makes your life work. The only drawback is that the effects last only one day. This transit is extremely good for all types of relationships, whether professional, personal, social or intimate. You feel optimistic, eager and outgoing, warm and friendly to everyone you meet, and you have no desire to engage in disputes.

This transit is also lucky financially. You may have a sudden windfall, although this is not the usual manifestation. You are inclined to indulge yourself and to spend money, especially on lavish or beautiful objects. In many respects, self-discipline is at an all-time low at this time, but it usually is not needed. Celebrations held at this time are unusually successful, for you at least, as is any kind of entertaining or social occasion. This will be due partly to your infectious good mood. People will like to be with you.

This is a good time for love relationships. The same warm feelings will have a good effect on these relationships, and sometimes a totally new relationship will begin under this transit. Certainly this is an excellent transit for a wedding.

Venus Sextile Jupiter

You feel contented and benevolent under this influence. You are at peace with the world and want to share your feelings with everyone whom you meet. Friends, in particular, may be the beneficiaries of your generosity, as you may benefit from theirs. In either case you both will benefit, because everything done under this transit becomes a fair exchange in the long run.

This transit is favorable for all financial enterprises, especially those involving foreign investments, medicine or the law. Any legal matters decided under this transit will also work out to your benefit.

A new friendship or love relationship that begins under this transit will be beneficial. Such a relationship will bring out your best qualities and can truly be described as a growth relationship. You are attracted to high-minded and upright people.

Like many Venus transits, this one is good for getting together with friends for fun. It is usually a rather lighthearted transit, and you are not attracted to serious matters or to hard work. A general lack of discipline and unwillingness to work are the only negative influences of this transit. This is a time for rest and recreation, not for attending to the routine business of the day.

Venus Square Jupiter

This is usually an agreeable transit, in that you feel well and enjoy the company of others. It is good for doing anything that you really enjoy, as long as there is nothing that you *have* to do. You are likely to have very little self-discipline. In fact, you are likely to indulge yourself in many ways that may not be good for you. Be careful of eating or drinking too much, especially of sweet or rich foods. This is usually a very bad day for dieters.

Also be careful if you go shopping. Do not buy anything unnecessary, unless you have some surplus cash. There is a tendency to buy expensive things, especially jewelry, fine clothes and art objects.

On the other hand, if you proceed with some discipline and know what you are doing, you can make some excellent investments at this time. Avoid doing anything on impulse, because although your mind is capable of making good decisions, your emotions are likely to lead you to excess.

Personal relationships are favored by this transit. Your good feelings rub off onto those around you, and everyone enjoys being with you. The one exception to this is if you succumb to a state of mind in which you assume arrogantly that everything you touch will turn to gold. Even if it is true, you will irritate people to the point that they will have nothing to do with you. Only certain personalities will have this problem. Otherwise this is a good transit.

Venus Trine Jupiter

Classically this is one of the best transits, except that it has a rather short duration. It brings grace, ease and pleasant social interaction into your life. Like any Venus-Jupiter energy, it can also bring laziness and self-indulgence, but only if you are likely to be that way anyway. For most people this transit will be a pleasant respite from the daily grind.

You just feel content with this transit, and your contentment affects others favorably, so that everyone around you today will be in good spirits. This is an excellent transit for all social occasions, amusements and entertainments. You may meet someone who will be of great service to you later. There may be a romantic interest in the course of the day as well, although like other Venus transits, this one is usually not strong enough by itself to bring about a major relationship.

This influence often benefits financial interests. It is a good day to make a major investment, particularly in entertainment, leisure activities or the arts.

This is also a good time to begin a vacation trip. The influence of this transit will ensure that your trip will be rewarding, enlightening and fun. It is generally a good time to reap the rewards of past activities. It is not a good time to start new enterprises that require a lot of energy, because the energy may not be there, and you may find it difficult to take the enterprise seriously enough!

However, if other planetary influences are giving you energy, this transit will certainly provide a favorable influence. You may be inclined to sit around and do nothing, rather than get involved in any daring enterprise.

Venus Opposition Jupiter

Of all the transits, this one is the most inclined to promote excessive indulgence, but it also indicates great pleasure, joy and satisfaction, if you have the sense not to overdo.

You are certainly not going to feel driven by ambition and the desire to conquer the world. You will want to sit around and take it easy or go out and buy some expensive, luxurious toy. This is certainly not the day to go shopping if saving money is your object, because you will want to buy every nice, pretty or luxurious thing that you see. And probably you will buy them, even against your practical common sense.

Perhaps your worst trouble will result from overeating. Venus and Jupiter together signify heavy, rich, sweet foods. A bad day for diets! You also may drink to excess, leaving tomorrow for recovery. This much must be said: you will enjoy doing it, and that is not all bad.

On the plus side, this transit can bring a very pleasant relationship, if other testimonies coincide. However, you must beware of being influenced solely by beauty, money or qualities that are ultimately short-lived.

If you can handle the energies of this transit with reasonable discipline, you will find it quite enjoyable and good for you.

Venus Conjunct Saturn

Under this transit, love and affection are strongly tempered by practical considerations. It is not as difficult for love relationships as other Venus-Saturn contacts are, but it is more sober concerning love. You will be restrained in expressing affection, but the affection is still there. Sometimes under this transit you will ask an older person's advice about relationships, for you are reflecting about the state of your life and what the relationship means to it. On occasion, this transit will signify saying goodbye to a loved one, either because of a temporary separation or because of the breakup of the relationship.

Unlike other Venus transits, there is little tendency toward self-indulgence with this one. Your actions are characterized by restraint, which is usually good if you have to economize or recognize the limitations of your pocketbook.

Under some conditions, this transit can indicate difficulties with your love relationships. You may not feel warm or affectionate, and you may alienate loved ones by seeming to be indifferent. The real problem is that you are lonesome and unable to bridge the gap between you and others. Fortunately this is not a long-lasting transit.

A relationship that comes about under this transit may be a long-lived but not flamboyant one, characterized by loyalty and soberness.

Venus Sextile Saturn

This transit will show you in a positive way the duties and obligations that you have to live up to in your relationships. This will not be especially difficult for you, because you get considerable gratification from being of service to your loved ones. Group standards and ideals will be more important to you today than your own, and you will work to further those ideals, even at the cost of much self-denial if necessary.

The reality of your emotional relationships is extremely important to you. Because you want relationships that are real, this transit is a good time to sit down with a loved one and arrive at a conscious understanding of what you expect from each other. A relationship can be ruined by not knowing what each party demands and needs from the other. Today you can make this clear to both lovers and friends and minimize a possible source of trouble in your relationships.

This transit is fortunate for most business affairs, because of your positive concern with practical reality. It especially favors commerce with art objects or other things of beauty.

If you are creative, this transit favors any creative activity demanding close attention to details. Your work will be carried out with great discipline and thoroughness under this influence.

In friendships, you may be attracted to older people or people who you feel can guide you. Seek their counsel, because they could be a great help to you at this time. A love relationship under this transit may also be with an older person, or you may be the older person.

Venus Square Saturn

On this day you will probably have difficulty relating to others, feeling cool and reserved even toward those you love. The problem is that you will have to spend today reevaluating what you are getting out of your relationships and what you are putting into them. You will have a strong awareness of yourself as an independent, even isolated human being, realizing that no one can really get inside of you and feel what you feel. Obviously, this can lead to loneliness and depression, but it can also lead to a radical reappraisal of your life and to a sober consideration of yourself as a human being relating to other human beings. It is necessary to separate yourself from the illusions that run through even the best relationship and to look at what is really there. While you are doing this, it may be rather difficult to fulfill the demands that your loved ones make upon you, leading to dissension within your relationships.

Be wary of falling victim to fears about your relationships, thinking that they are worse than they are. Saturn often indicates acute dissatisfaction with people who do not live up to a rigorous and rigid standard. You and your loved ones are only human, and there is a limit to what you can expect of them and yourself. You may feel guilty about your imagined inadequacies with regard to your loved ones. Do not take these feelings too seriously, for it is only Saturn overdoing itself.

Perhaps this is a good day to be by yourself, no matter how lonely you feel, for if you sought company, you would still feel lonely. This time is best for self-reflection and introspection. What you learn may improve your relationships when this transit is over.

Venus Trine Saturn

This is perhaps the least flamboyant of all Venus transits, much easier to handle than the other Venus-Saturn contacts. You are satisfied with reliable, stable relationships and do not make unrealistic demands on others. You recognize that your loved ones are human, and you ask only that they live up to their obligations and you will do the same in return.

This is a good time to discuss any problems that may have arisen within a relationship, because your sense of reality is strong and you can be objective. You are not carried away by foolish ideals.

In financial affairs you are rather conservative and concerned about protecting limited resources. Business affairs are governed by the same concerns, and this can be quite a good transit for business matters and relationships. You are able to deal with associates in the detached manner that is often necessary in business relationships, yet you are fair in your dealings.

Relationships that begin under this influence are characterized by sobriety and stability. They may not be demonstrative, but there is a steadiness of feeling that enables them to survive when others fail. There may be a large difference between you and your partner or a radical difference in class or educational background. Often such a relationship occurs because of practical rather than romantic considerations, but this does not weaken it.

Venus Opposition Saturn

This transit does not usually produce feelings of warmth and tenderness. It is one of the least favorable transits of Venus, although by no means dangerous or destructive. You will experience today a great conflict between your sense of duty and discipline on one hand and your desire to enjoy yourself or relate to others on the other hand. If you feel emotionally cold today despite the overtures of a loved one, it is best to do nothing. Remember that this is a short-term transit. You should not pretend to have emotions that you do not feel, because of a misguided sense of duty; the other person will sense this and it will only increase the hurt.

It may be that duties and responsibilities will prevent you from engaging in a pleasant activity, and you may feel somewhat resentful. The best thing to do is grin and bear it, because even if you neglect your work for fun, something would prevent you from enjoying yourself. Such is the way of Saturn.

Loneliness and self-pity sometimes come with this transit. You feel surrounded by bright, positive energies that you simply cannot relate to. You may feel like a gray presence among colorful people. Do not take such feelings seriously, unless you have them frequently. Even if you do, such feelings probably don't represent anything real, but feeling sorry for yourself can be a symptom of a serious problem. You should examine yourself and the kinds of energies that you demonstrate to other people. You may have built a wall between yourself and others out of fear.

In general today, relationships will force you to encounter aspects of yourself that you would prefer not to face. However, like all oppositions, this one could heighten your self-perception and give you knowledge that will help you.

Venus Conjunct Uranus

This transit can produce some rather unexpected events, for it influences you to seek excitement and new experiences through love and creativity. The effects can vary considerably, because Uranus in a transit always produces unexpected consequences.

This transit can produce an unexpected disruption in an existing love relationship, caused by your feeling that things have become dull and routine. You seek excitement, and if it is not forthcoming, you may become quite irritable. Or something unexpected but not necessarily unfavorable may happen.

Sometimes this transit suddenly produces a new relationship from a totally unexpected quarter or with a person who is radically different from anyone you know. A relationship that begins under this transit is usually exciting but unstable.

There may also be sudden financial gains under this transit or, if you are not careful, unexpected losses. But if you spend or invest your money wisely on this day, it should work out quite well.

Whatever you do to amuse yourself today must be stimulating and different. You will not tolerate anything stale or routine, but you are willing to experiment, and you are not afraid of something new.

Venus Sextile Uranus

As with all combinations of Venus and Uranus, under this transit you will seek an exciting break from your daily routine. You will seek out stimulating friends, avoiding anyone who might bore you.

You also attract new friends, because under this influence you show a fascinating, different side of your personality in a way that is winning and attractive. You will find the people you meet today instantly agreeable, but the relationship may not be long-lasting, whether they are lovers or friends. You are not likely to seek a permanent attachment at this time.

This is a good transit for a fling with friends or a party. You will be able to make yourself interesting to everyone you meet, and you will also find them interesting. The air around you today is charged with pleasant electricity.

If a relationship that starts today does last more than a short time, it may revolutionize your life in some way. You will have to give your friend or lover great freedom, because there is no room for possessiveness or jealousy in a Venus-Uranus relationship. But if you can live in such an unstructured relationship, your understanding of life and of yourself will be greatly broadened. In most relationships people do not need to make as many demands upon each other as they do, mostly out of mutual insecurity. You are able to understand this at this time.

Venus Square Uranus

This is not usually a profound transit, but when it operates it can produce some interesting results.

Today you seek excitement and stimulation through your love relationships, even to the point of provoking a fight. The existing patterns of your relationships will become difficult to deal with even if you know that they are basically constructive. Be careful of being impatient with loved ones, demanding that they gratify your need for excitement, unless, of course, you want to have an argument. On the other hand, this is a good day for getting things out into the open, where the two of you may reach an understanding. If you and your loved one are under no constraints, then you can enjoy many new experiences with each other. In fact, this transit can be a test of the flexibility of your relationship. The less flexible it is, the more disruptive this transit will be.

There is a tendency to flirt under this influence, which need not be harmful, if you don't take it seriously. Do not make anything more out of an encounter than it really signifies.

This is definitely a day to look for new experiences. You are attracted to any novel artistic expressions, and modern art may interest you more than ever. Be careful about spending money, however, because you are likely to be impulsive.

Venus Trine Uranus

This is a good day for doing something different. You are probably bored with the daily routine and would like to do something that provides a stimulating, unusual change of pace. You seek this not only in diversions, but also in your relationships. The people you meet today are likely to be quite different from your usual friends. A love relationship that starts under this transit is apt to be electric, exciting, unstable and short. You are not looking for a steady relationship under this transit; as a rule you desire the unusual. You may make some unconventional arrangement with your lover, such as agreeing to have other lovers. This transit also causes relationships to begin suddenly and then quickly go through all the stages of a love affair.

You will seek different forms of entertainment today. If you usually prefer popular music, you might attend a concert of experimental modern music. Perhaps you might enjoy the more dangerous rides at an amusement park.

This transit will bring a little excitement into your life, something unexpected and stimulating that will help to make the ordinary days more easily borne.

Venus Opposition Uranus

This can signify various events or reactions: on one level, a sudden unexpected occurrence in a love relationship, which may or may not be upsetting, or the onset of an unusual, stimulating, but rarely stable, relationship. However, this requires some concurrence from other transits. This transit may only influence you to spend the day seeking unusual entertainment or recreation.

For the duration of the day you may be driven to look for exciting and stimulating activities and experiences. The ordinary experiences within relationships will not satisfy you. Unresolved tensions in a love relationship may cause sudden upsets as one of you seeks freedom from the restrictions and tensions. Another person may provide the occasion for a flirtation that unsettles your relationship. However, unless the tensions are severe, it is unlikely that you will suffer any permanent damage.

A new relationship at this time is intended by your subconscious mind to provide an escape from your everyday routine, not to lead to anything permanent. Some people, however, need the sort of offbeat relationship that Uranus provides with Venus. For them, this transit may bring about a valid, long-term relationship. But you won't know if you are one of these people until the relationship endures for awhile.

Whatever you do today for fun will be intended to provide a break from the norm. Therefore, look for something exciting, meet new people and have new adventures. These will be upsetting only if you are afraid of and resistant to new experiences. The power of Uranus is difficult only to the extent that you are wedded to your habits and the rigid structures in your life.

Venus Conjunct Neptune

At its highest, this transit denotes a refined spirituality in love, with a total lack of selfishness and a feeling of complete soul-union with a loved one. At its worst, you might be disappointed in a loved one who did not live up to your expectations, which were probably unrealistic in the first place.

Daydreaming, probably the most common effect of this transit, is usually harmless and pleasant as long as you are aware of reality. You will experience a refined sense of beauty and a desire to have your surroundings be as lovely as possible. However, you are not in a practical frame of mind and should postpone anything that requires good judgment in relationships or finances.

If you are creative or artistic, this transit indicates a day when your creativity can be truly inspired. The combination of Venus and Neptune gives you the ability to visualize ideas in your mind and to translate what you see into physical reality. This combination is useful in art, but less useful in relationships, where it tends to confuse the ideal with the real. An artist's goal may be to create the real out of the ideal.

A positive effect of this transit upon relationships is that you feel a selfless kind of love, and you want to do everything for the benefit of your loved one.

Venus Sextile Neptune

This transit arouses the creative and romantic imagination, either giving you a greater appreciation for and sensitivity to beauty, with a strong desire to be surrounded by it, or sending you off into a pleasant daydream.

If you experience the first response, make an effort to expose yourself to art, music or poetry today, because they will have a marvelous effect upon your consciousness. Aspects of reality and perception that you are normally not aware of are yours under this influence. Even placing yourself in beautiful surroundings, such as a pleasant country spot, a beautiful garden or a striking landscape, will have a very powerful effect upon you.

In relationships the double potential of Neptune is strongly evident. At its best this transit gives you an acute sensitivity to the needs and feelings of your loved ones. You are willing to put your own needs second to theirs and will derive satisfaction from their happiness, without sacrificing your own. You can experience a real feeling of "soul-union" with someone under this transit.

If this transit puts you into a pleasant dreamy fog, in which your mental illusions and fantasies are preferable to the demands of reality, it must be said that everyone needs this occasionally, and it is beneficial if kept within reason. Perhaps this is the way that you should indulge yourself today.

Venus Square Neptune

This transit stimulates your romantic imagination to a considerable degree, making you somewhat unrealistic in your dealings with loved ones. Usually this is not serious; this transit may bring pleasant times of soft lights and romantic reveries. Daydreaming is also a characteristic of this transit, which is fine unless it interferes with necessity. In fact, this daydreaming tendency can manifest itself as artistic inspiration. If you are an artist, creativity of a high order can result.

In relationships you must be most careful. You may expect your loved one to live up to an impossible romantic ideal that no one could or should try to attain. Relationships must operate in the real world, but today you do not want to deal with reality. You may feel that real mortals are disappointing, and prefer your fantasies. In most cases this transit has a short effect, constituting a passing mood and not a source of real problems. But fantasy could become a permanent part of a relationship started today, and that is something you should avoid. Any relationship that begins now should be experienced over a long period of time before making commitments.

At its worst this transit can signify a breakdown of a relationship, which could be damaging to your ego. But do not take your disappointment too hard. Relationships that are damaged by this transit do not usually have a basis in reality to begin with.

Venus Trine Neptune

This can be a very pleasant transit, although it is not very good for getting things done. You are more likely to spend time in fantasy and daydreams than in working in the everyday world. But if you are involved in any creative activity that has to develop completely inside your mind before taking physical form, this is an extremely useful transit.

At its highest, this transit enables you to deal with people with great compassion and tenderness. You can understand what they feel and think. In your close relationships you act for the benefit for all concerned, not only to satisfy your own needs and desires. This transit induces unselfish and spiritual love. However, the dreamy quality of this transit may delude you into thinking that you exhibit these spiritual characteristics, when you are really just wandering about in a fog. You have to make this transit work out positively and usefully, in the real world, although at the worst it is unlikely to do any harm.

A relationship that begins under this transit has the double potential of being very spiritual or insubstantial and illusory. Time will show you whether it is a real spiritual relationship between "soul-mates" or just a delusion to that effect. Even at its worst this transit only brings a romantic interlude into your life, quite pleasant, with no permanent consequences.

Venus Opposition Neptune

Under this transit you should be careful of your relationships. It has many possibilities, some good, some difficult. Your unrealistic ideals may lead to acute disappointment with loved ones, unless you make an effort to understand and accept the reality of your relationships. This is not a good time to daydream about loved ones or about anything else.

A typical Neptunian illusion to beware of is picturing yourself in a love relationship as the unselfish, giving one who sacrifices everything for the other. This is a blatant ego game in which the ultimate purpose may be to gain control over the other by manipulating feelings of obligation. Even if you were that unselfish, it would not do anything positive to build up the relationship. You have real needs that must be met by any relationship, and if they are not met, the relationship will not work out. Dismiss your illusions of unselfishness from your mind. You may discover that your loved one is not as grateful as you think he or she ought to be.

Under this transit there is the real danger that you might be deceived about a relationship. This is certainly not a good transit under which to begin a new one unless you can view it with a careful eye and great discretion. It is possible that this transit signifies the romantic beginning of a relationship that will later be firmly based upon reality.

Although this transit is capable of producing a beautiful romantic experience, you cannot depend upon it continuing forever. Enjoy it for itself and do not make demands upon it. Beauty does not need to be justified.

If you are really concerned for others, this transit can also bring about circumstances in which you can act unselfishly, particularly in an institutional setting. However, examine your own motives carefully lest they trip you up.

Venus Conjunct Pluto

This transit makes you seek unusual and intense love experiences. You hope to find escape from everyday life through love, but this can create problems if you are not careful. You may create a disturbance in a normal, happy relationship because you are not willing to accept things as they are. Another troublesome effect of this transit is that you may feel insecure about your loved one and suddenly become excessively jealous or possessive. This is a passing effect, since Venus transits quickly, but it can create misunderstandings. However, if your loved one is able to respond to your mood, this can be an extremely rewarding time because of the greatly intensifed level of feelings between you.

Under this transit, you may be completely fascinated and infatuated with a new lover, but be careful. You may be under the influence of powerful subconscious drives triggered by the encounter that have nothing to do with the real potential of the relationship.

In an existing relationship, do not use love to manipulate your partner. There is a strong tendency to use jealousy, guilt or other negative emotions to control your partner's actions. This can lead only to negative reactions that may eventually weaken the relationship.

Venus Sextile Pluto

This transit deepens the emotions, like other Venus-Pluto contacts, and creates a greater need to belong to an individual or to a group. Friendships are extremely important to you today, and they may change your life. Love relationships are more intense, and physical sexuality is experienced as something transcendental.

This is a good time to try to understand your emotions and how they affect your relationships. Today you can enrich and enhance a relationship as you realize the strength of your feelings, in a moment when you experience the full force of your emotion.

Certainly any emotion that you feel today will have extraordinary force and vigor. No experience under this influence is superficial, nor would you be satisfied with any that was. If you are with someone who is trying to avoid a deeper confrontation on a transit such as this, you will penetrate and dig until you have reached the truth.

This Venus-Pluto transit can denote the beginning of an unusually intense relationship. Such a relationship often has a peculiarly "fated" quality that is possibly an illusion, but powerful in its effects.

Venus Square Pluto

At its best this transit can signify intense emotional experiences within a relationship. Pluto and Venus together create powerful love experiences that draw you in and change your consciousness for a time. But there is also a difficult side to this transit.

You may become aware of changes occurring in a relationship to which you will be forced to accommodate. They cannot be ignored, because a real breakdown in your relationship would result. In itself change is not a bad thing. But we crave stability above all else in our relationships, and stability is not available at this time.

The natural tendency is to hang on to the other person out of insecurity and try to exert greater control over the relationship. This is ultimately destructive because your partner will soon regard the relationship as smothering and restrictive. You must examine your relationship and see what needs to be changed or accept the changes that have already occurred. It will do no good to pretend that change is not happening. Every relationship needs to grow in order to remain healthy and alive. Resist the desire to use subversive tactics to control your loved one, such as manipulating feelings of guilt or responsibility, for that will create bitterness, which could finally destroy whatever goodwill exists between you.

Venus Trine Pluto

This transit intensifies your emotional expression throughout the day and makes your relationships more intense. You will feel your love for someone quite strongly today, and you will be able to express it meaningfully to your loved one. Sexual desire is also stimulated by this transit, but only as part of the overall emotional intensification. Under Venus-Pluto combinations, love is not an intellectual abstraction. It is something felt and expressed through the mind, emotions and body.

Your experiences today will reveal the inner workings of your relationships and your approach to them. This transit is capable of producing profound and useful psychological insights, but don't be afraid of them, for they will make your relationships better.

A new relationship that starts under this influence is likely to be quite intense. You feel drawn to another as if by magical power, because the other person represents something inside you that needs expression through a love relationship. It is really the power of your own psyche that you feel. Such a relationship can be quite good, although it is desirable that the compulsive quality wear off before you settle down to a long-term relationship.

Artistic work done now will also exhibit the emotional intensity characteristic of this transit. Such work will reveal the inner depths of your soul, and that alone will make it impressive.

Venus Opposition Pluto

This transit may have the effect of intensifying experiences in your love life. Through love you will seek feelings and emotions that transport you out of the ordinary. This same energy may lead to indiscretions in love relationships, which could cause problems later on. If you bear this in mind, however, you will find little difficulty associated with this transit.

A new relationship that begins under this transit may be compulsive in nature. A peculiar fascination may prevent you from accurately evaluating the potential of this relationship. And if one of you tries to exert power over the other by manipulating jealousy, guilt or some other negative emotion, there may be real problems. You may even be irresistibly attracted to someone who you know is not good for you. Caution is advisable until you know what the relationship will bring.

Existing relationships may suffer difficulties at this time because of obscure conflicts arising between you and your loved ones. Subconscious impulses may cause you to behave irrationally. On days like this you must be aware of yourself at all times. Do not let hidden resentments and tensions flare up to ruin an otherwise sound relationship. Air your tensions, but be careful not to express them destructively. Be careful also of manipulative power conflicts in which the tactics are subtle but powerful.

There are powerful energies at work in your love life today and they can work to bring about constructive changes in your relationships. These energy patterns are dangerous to your relationships only if you are unconscious of their processes or if you are unwilling to deal with their root causes. You may have to handle quite a bit of energy to make this transit work out, but it could be a powerful force for good.

Venus Conjunct Midheaven

Matters of love and affection are uppermost in your mind today. You are conscious of your loved ones and your feelings for them. If other testimonies agree, you might fall in love with someone new. In any case, you are more concerned with love and your relationships than with your own ego. One manifestation of this transit is a pleasant daydreamy mood in which you are not disposed to work, other than creative activity.

If you are in any Venus-ruled profession, such as the entertainment industry, art, relationship counseling, crafts, or even agriculture to a certain degree, this transit is favorable. In other professions, you will be able to create relationships conducive to business negotiations.

This is a good time for any kind of social activity. You feel warm and friendly to everyone and are really in the mood for company. Do not waste the day by yourself, because the effect of Venus would be to make you feel lonely.

All personal relationships are favored by this transit. Unless an extremely unfavorable transit intervenes, you should experience no disputes of any kind today, only good times and agreeable companionship.

This is a favorable day to announce your love to someone, and an excellent transit for getting married. Venus on the Midheaven has the effect of making you proclaim your love to the world at large.

Venus Sextile Midheaven

This transit makes you think a great deal about your relationships to others, not in unhappy terms, but quite positively. In a relationship you are much more willing to give up what you normally consider your inalienable rights for the sake of maintaining peace and harmony. You are in a compromising mood and feel that few problems are important enough to warrant fighting over. Obviously this has its bad and good side, but for most people this transit has a very cheering and positive effect.

In your relationships you are much more willing to give. You do not feel that you have to defend yourself, and you are much more tolerant of others' faults. In fact, you may not even notice them. You want to do what you can to help anyone who is having problems, even if it is just a kind word. You are also willing to listen to people's problems. Unfortunately, if you are alone now you will want very much to be with someone. Therefore this transit can actually signify a time of loneliness, if for some reason you have to remain alone.

If you are a creative person, this transit will stimulate your creativity. You will at least want to be involved in an artistic project, which you can express by going to an art museum or attending a concert, poetry reading or other art event.

Venus Square Midheaven

For most people this is a good transit, a time when you will feel like being with another person and expressing your love. For lovers this can be quite an amorous transit. You will have a strong feeling that by yourself you are not quite complete and that you need someone else to make you whole. This feeling is not born out of personal insecurity; it is a real need and desire to give and receive love.

However, for some persons at some times, this transit can have a negative effect, almost the reverse of the above. It can make you overly self-involved, so wrapped up in yourself that you do not relate very successfully to others. Or you may demand more love than you are willing to give. But for this to occur there must be a predisposition to it in your nature.

Another, more difficult effect of this transit may be that a relationship will be blown up out of all proportion in your consciousness, so that you cannot see it for what it is. The result may be overpossessiveness, jealousy and unwillingness to see a loved one happy in the presence of someone else. Here again, you must have a tendency in this direction already.

Venus Trine Midheaven

This is a good time for any kind of creative activity. If you are employed in a creative field, you should be unusually productive today. Under any circumstances this is a good time to get involved with the arts or any other activity concerning beauty. It is also an excellent time to redecorate your home and make your personal surroundings more attractive. Your taste for beauty is aroused, and you are much more sensitive to the aesthetic nature of your surroundings.

This is also a time when you feel very affectionate and have a great need to express your affection for others. You want to give and receive love. Usually this is a very pleasant transit, because you are pleasant to be around. Others can sense how you feel about them, which makes them feel good in return.

As with the sextile, the trine transit usually makes you feel very peaceable and anxious to avoid conflicts. Thus you are ready to play the role of peacemaker and anxious to make any necessary concessions in order to keep relationships smooth. Just be sure that you don't compromise something that is essential to you, although that is not likely to be a problem for most people. You have an opportunity now to smooth out any difficulties that have arisen recently in your close relationships. You can make it clear to others that your real objective is to improve relations, not merely to win an argument. Also, since others feel the energy of your love, they are less likely to stir up trouble. For this reason you can deal with some very critical relationship problems under this transit, if you have to.

Venus Opposition Midheaven

This is a good time to enjoy yourself at home. Your most intimate and personal surroundings will give you the greatest pleasure and you will want to be with those who are closest and most important to you. This is a favorable transit for entertaining at home, because today you have more ability than usual to make your house a friendly place where people will be happy. Entertaining at home will definitely prove more rewarding than going out, because the point opposite the Midheaven draws you inward into your personal world.

You feel content with this transit, not like conquering the world. It is a time to enjoy what is around you every day. You feel affectionate, and, under certain circumstances, you may meet a new lover under this transit, probably in your home surroundings.

Although this is usually a good transit, you should avoid overindulgence, especially in rich and sweet foods. You may have an appetite for these today, and if you do indulge it you might regret it later. You feel lazy, which is only bad if there is work that must be done.

Venus Conjunct Ascendant

This is one of the most favorable transits for personal relationships. You can readily express your love and affection, and others are likely to show their affection for you. Seek the company of others, because you are in a sociable frame of mind today. Like many other Venus transits, this is a good time for entertaining.

Today is also a good time to resolve any problems in your personal relationships. You will be able to discuss any tensions that exist without difficulty, assuring your loved one that your love is sincere.

This is a day when you may meet a new lover or friend. It is a good time for any necessary new encounters because the environment favors pleasant first impressions.

You can expect to feel content today. The world looks good to you, and you are in harmony with the world. You will attract people and things that are favorable to you, for this is the kind of action that Venus generates; you may even be presented with a favorable financial opportunity.

Venus Sextile Ascendant

This is a very lighthearted time, when you should be able to relax and enjoy yourself with friends and loved ones. You will enjoy being with groups of people, and you will wish to express your feelings of affection. Your favor will extend even to the people you encounter every day whom you have no special feelings for. You feel so good that you want to share it with everyone, as long as there are no heavy long-term transits that indicate the opposite. But even if there are, this transit will help to lighten your mood for awhile.

Needless to say, this transit helps to improve your relationships with everyone, especially those closest to you. A love relationship may start under this such a transit, especially if there is a long-range indication of this at the same time.

This is also a good time to go out and meet people. You will not have the fear and shyness that may sometimes make it difficult for you to encounter new people, nor will you need to worry about making a bad impression on the people you meet. This transit helps to ensure that you will make a favorable impression upon everyone. If you usually enjoy being the life of the party, you will certainly have the chance to play this role now.

Venus Square Ascendant

This square is far from difficult. In fact, it usually denotes an extremely pleasant time when you reach out to others to give and receive affection. It is usually good for relationships and may indicate the start of significant new ones. One of the few problems that can come with this transit is a reluctance to voice your real complaints for fear of being unpleasant. You will try to smooth over ruffled feelings wherever you go.

You will enjoy being with people and going out to have a good time, but this may cause you to avoid work that must be done and to be self-indulgent. Be careful of doing anything to excess and avoid wasting money on items that appeal to your fancy now but do not have any lasting merit or appeal. Self-discipline is not one of the strong points of this transit.

In a related area, you should be careful about financial affairs in general. This transit does not signify any kind of bad luck, but it does indicate the danger of carelessness and sloppy management, unless you make a special effort to the contrary. And if you are careful, this transit will not be a problem in this way at all.

Aside from these few areas where you must be careful, you should enjoy yourself as well as other people during this transit. It will be a period of unusually harmonious relationships, especially if you make an effort to give as much as you receive.

Venus Trine Ascendant

This is an excellent transit for good times, entertaining and just having fun. Before you plan any hard work for this period, keep in mind that you are likely to put self-gratification and pleasure before work. You may find it difficult to put off something that you want to do in order to fulfill some duty.

But this is not selfishness on your part, for you are quite capable of being generous and giving to others. You are more openly affectionate than usual and feel real love for the people around you. It is just that this aspect of your life — love, affection and pleasure — is more important to you now than work. This is a good time to give or attend a party. It is also a good time to be with loved ones, not only a lover or spouse but also children, from whom you will derive much pleasure now.

During this period you may be rather lucky in doing what you want, especially if you do not often give in to self-indulgence. For you this transit can provide a welcome release, which could have very good consequences. If you are usually rather disciplined about investing and spending money, this is a good time for these activities. And if you are not very thrifty by nature or are rather more self-indulgent, this transit will increase these tendencies. Also be careful not to overindulge in food or drink.

This is a good time to spend money on beautifying your home or other surroundings.

Venus Opposition Ascendant

This is an extremely favorable transit for close relationships and one-to-one encounters of any sort. A marriage or love relationship should go smoothly today, with both of you showing a great deal of affection. If there are any difficulties between you, smooth them out today, because neither of you will want to argue. You will both be much more interested in making peace. If possible, avoid arguing a position today. Your mood is too agreeable to successfully present an aggressive case!

On the other hand, this is an excellent time to make an agreeable impression on someone new. If you have to work within a partnership, where keeping the peace is an important factor in your success, this is an excellent day. Any persons who are normally difficult to deal with will be easy to handle today.

If other transits agree with this indication, this might mark the beginning of a new love relationship. With this transit you will attract people who will be good for you, not only emotionally but in other ways as well.

This is not a good time to be alone. You are in the mood for relating, and the day will not be complete in any way unless you share it. This is a time to be aware of how much your completeness depends upon others.

Chapter Eight

Mars

Significance of Transiting Mars

Mars has traditionally been considered a malefic planet in astrology, that is, more likely to produce evil than good. But this is not so, although as is the case with any planet, if the energies of Mars are allowed to operate to excess, its effects can be quite difficult. But usually there is nothing to fear from its transits, and in fact its energies are a vital part of life.

Mars is an energy planet. Specifically it rules the energy that an individual uses to maintain himself in the face of pressures from his environment. The Mars energy says, "This is what I am and I can be no other way!" and prepares the individual to fight, if necessary, to maintain his position. Obviously one can have no individuality without this energy. It is a fundamental part of the ego drive, and anyone in whom this energy is weak is not much of a personality. Persons with a weak Mars often do the things that are attributed to a strong Mars, such as acting extremely pugnacious, irritable or argumentative. These people have to constantly reassure themselves that they are strong, which would be unnecessary if they really were strong. It is true, however, that a person with a strong Mars is likely to be rather domineering.

Mars is also connected with work and physical energy, and often its transits signify a day when you feel very energetic and vigorous. In fact one way to ensure that a Mars transit will not cause disputes or arguments with others, which is a sign of malfunctioning Mars energy, is to have plenty of hard work to do. The negative side of Mars most often manifests itself when there is no other outlet for its energies.

As Mars transits each planet in your horoscope, the areas of life related to that planet will become energized. When Mars transits Venus, you seek out physical love. When Mars transits Mercury, you look for mental activity. But there is more to it than that. When Mars transits a planet, your ego drives are likely to incorporate that planet's energies. You will try to establish your individuality toward others through the issues related to that planet. This can result in conflicts with others if the energy gets too strong or encounters serious resistance from others. And of course, there is nothing wrong with a good fight, if it serves some purpose. Fighting is one way to learn about your own strength in an interpersonal sense.

As Mars transits each house, the affairs of that house become energized, just as with the transited planets. Also you will be most active or seek to assert yourself through the affairs of the house occupied by transiting Mars. Here again you are most likely to have conflicts with others in these areas of your life.

The only real danger with Mars is that its energies, when sublimated to the physical level, can signify accidents, specifically from burns or fire, and illnesses involving fever and infection. This is often the result of frustrated ego energies, although you may have to dig around in your psyche to realize this. You must learn to express your resentments and anger, for they are a legitimate part of your being.

Mars in the First House

This should be a time of great activity in your life, when you work very hard to further your own interests and assert yourself among others. You have the chance to show the world what you can do now. You come on to others with much more vigor than usual, and you are likely to make a great impression upon them at this time.

If you are insensitive to other people, however, this can be quite a difficult time for all your relationships. Every relationship requires that you bend a bit to the needs and demands of the other person, but you are not especially inclined to do that now. In fact you will be much better off if you can work independently without worrying about how your actions affect others. With Mars in this house, your personality is is much more dominant than usual, but you aren't interested in having great power over others, as long as they don't try to dominate you. You are perfectly happy as long as you are completely free to do whatever you want and to have your individuality acknowledged by others in whatever you do.

During this time you are much more of a fighter for your own rights than usual. You will not let anyone take anything away from you, although you will not be especially irritable or touchy. You will fight if somebody attacks you first.

Your physical energy level is quite high, and you should be able to do a lot of work during this transit. If there are badly aspected planets in this house, however, you should be careful of illnesses or accidents as these planets are transited. This should be a period of upbeat independent activity, when you can work out a lot of problems and accomplish a great deal. This should be a positive time in your life.

Mars in the Second House

At this time you are inclined to identify your ego with what you own and what you value. This can have many different effects, some negative, some positive.

To deal with the negative effects first, you may consider your financial position to be a sign of your personal worth. If you have money, you feel that you are a good person. If you don't, you feel bad and discouraged, quite aside from anything you have accomplished. You act as if you are what you have. But it should be obvious that you are not your bankroll, your car, your furniture or other property and possessions. Your reactions in this case are completely inappropriate. You may become overly touchy about your beliefs, opinions and desires in some area and get into arguments about their merit or worth. This transit·can also lead to disputes with others over the ownership or use of property — other than real estate — which can lead to estrangement from others.

Your desire to have possessions is rather strong at this time, and you may be inclined to make unwise and impulsive purchases, because you feel that you must have the item. You do this to gratify your ego, not to get something you need. This transit is often a sign of wasteful spending.

On the psychological level, you may get into disputes about values in the abstract, that is, whether some value is important or not. Here again you are falsely identifying your ego with what you value, just as if it were a material object.

On the positive side, you are willing to use your possessions to get work done. If you have something that can help you accomplish a task, you will use it. The things you own are not likely to sit around uselessly and gather dust. Once you have gotten over petty ego problems with your possessions, you will allow others to use what you have, so long as they acknowledge your willingness to share.

Again on the abstract psychological level, you are willing to work to establish and defend your values and make others understand them. Just be sure that you don't try to shove your beliefs down people's throats.

Mars in the Third House

The tempo of your everyday life will pick up considerably during this transit. Your energies will be high, and there is considerable danger of conflicts with immediate neighbors, relatives or other persons whom you encounter daily. However, you may be able to get together with these people and collectively accomplish something. That would represent a positive working out of the energies of this transit.

You identify very strongly with your ideas and opinons at this time, and you are rather inclined to be argumentative. If someone disagrees with you, it seems like a personal affront. Instead of identifying with your possessions, as in the second-house transit, you identify with your beliefs. Of course there are times when you have to defend your ideas on any subject, and you ought to do so then. The problem here is identifying whether or not there is a real issue at stake. You may get into pointless arguments by defending a position that doesn't need to be defended.

Beware of trying to coerce others into believing as you do. You put forth your ideas with considerable vigor at this time, which may provoke others. Even your routine communications — letters, conversations, etc. — may take on a defiant tone, especially if you feel that others have had the upper hand at other times. Remember that an overly aggressive Mars energy is a sign of deficiency, of someone who does not really feel secure. On the other hand, if you have to "sell" an idea of yours to someone in your job or anywhere else, this is a good time to do it. As long as you refrain from giving people the impression that you are attacking them, you will impress them by the power with which you state your ideas.

This transit is also good for any kind of vigorous mental work. Your mental level is high, and you can work longer than usual at intellectual tasks.

Mars in the Fourth House

This transit tends to stir up energies from the deepest unconscious level of your mind and activate unconscious attitudes and behavior patterns from the past. This can result in your behaving compulsively and acting inappropriately in various situations. Also you may find yourself fighting about something that you don't even understand. It is very important to be quite conscious of what you are doing now. Otherwise you will behave in petty and irritable ways that no one around you will be able to understand, let alone deal with.

This transit is also a sign of great activity where you live. Positive activity might be working hard around your home and getting a great deal accomplished. You are very strong on having your surroundings exactly the way you want, and you should make an effort to have them that way if possible. Of course, if someone else in the home has a different point of view about this, you may have problems in coming to an agreement. Domestic strife is another side of this transit that you may have to contend with, if you don't make an effort to agree with the people you live with. If you identify so strongly and uncompromisingly with the way you want your home to be, you will force them to resist you. At times like this it is best not to live with other people. Living with your parents can be particularly difficult now. This transit can also signify disputes with others over land ownership and use.

Your professional activities may be somewhat difficult at this time, for others may oppose you whenever you make a proposal, and they may be able to block your efforts completely. For this reason, it might be best to keep a low profile during this transit. It usually lasts only a couple of months and is followed by a more favorable time.

Mars in the Fifth House

Above all else, this is a time when you will demand to be yourself and to express to others what and who you are. You are filled with energies that want to cry to the world, "I am!" You will not be especially inclined to self-denial, discipline, postponing self-gratification, or taking a back seat to another. However, this is not a conflict-laden transit unless your self-assertive energies are totally denied by circumstances or you give them no expression.

It is much more likely that these energies will be expressed in a playful and sportive way, for this is the house of amusement as well as self-expression. In fact, any athletic activity, if you are so inclined, is an excellent outlet for this transit. You are more competitive than usual, so you might as well make good use of this spirit; although you could use it in some other area of your life also. Your aggressiveness is relatively benign at this time because the fifth house is not a house of cutthroat ego drives.

In love relationships, this transit signifies that your desire nature is rather strong, that you know what you want and will try to get it. Physical lovemaking will be more important than staring fondly at your loved one over a candlelit dinner at an elegant restaurant. Sex as a form of self-expression is energized by this transit, although by itself this transit is not usually strong enough to bring about a new sexual relationship.

If you have children, you may have real but not serious conflicts with them. About all that will happen is that your children may be somewhat harder to handle than usual. As with other Mars transits, it is just that the energies that are aroused must be used. In other words, keep them and yourself busy. Be careful, however, about situations in which there is any danger of accident, because in rare instances this transit can signify an accident to the children in your life.

Perhaps the only real flaw in this transit is that you lack discipline in doing things that you really don't want to do. You find it hard to get down to a task that is unappealing. Perhaps you should let your energies roam wherever they choose now and wait until Mars enters the next house before trying to work with any real discipline.

Mars in the Sixth House

At this time you will throw your ego energies into working hard and getting things done. In contrast to the transit of Mars through the fifth house, now you are much more able to defer tomorrow's pleasure for today's work. In fact you are likely to take considerable pride in how much work you can do during this transit. So the best way to handle this energy is to find plenty of work and do it.

But there are some inherent problems with this transit. The sixth house is a house of service, by which astrologers mean that you should place the needs of others above your own ego-gratification. The classic notion of the sixth house is work done for the sake of someone else, usually an employer or other such person. But this kind of work does not square very well with the ego-oriented energy of Mars. You may not want to work for someone else; instead, you want the credit for your accomplishments yourself, so that you are identified with what you do. This can lead to conflicts with your superiors and general difficulty in your work situation. Even if you are the employer, there may be difficulty if the people who work for you feel that you are not giving them enough credit. The best solution is to maneuver yourself into a position where you don't have to work with or for others any more than necessary. If you are not self-employed, that is a problem, but you may be able to get some work that requires working alone and depends largely upon your individual initiative. This is not a time to be a team player.

The sixth is also a house of health, and the transit of Mars through it can signify health problems such as infections, fevers or accidents. But these are probably the result of frustrated ego energies, which are characteristic of this transit. Keep up a program of rigorous physical activity and avoid any situation that is not good for your health. Above all, do not keep your frustrations bottled up in silent patience, for you are likely to become ill if you do.

Mars in the Seventh House

While Mars transits this house, there is tension in your life, but it can be used creatively if you are conscious of what you are doing. If you are not, this transit can signify a time of conflicts, especially with those closest to you, such as your spouse and others whom you must cooperate with — partners, fellow workers and such.

The spirit of the seventh house is the intimate one-to-one cooperation of two people in a partnership. However, it is also the house of open enemies and people with whom you are in conflict, because being someone's enemy or opponent is also a form of one-to-one confrontation. Because the nature of Mars is self-assertive, it is very likely that you will experience the seventh house as the house of open enemies. Even your intimate, positive relationships may suffer at this time. The problem is that you will find it difficult to give in and compromise as necessary for proper cooperation, either in marriage or in a business partnership.

There is a positive side to this transit, however. In any close relationship, there is often too much compromise, so that the real complaints and grievances are not aired, which in the long run tends to weaken even a fine relationship. Now is the time when these repressed grievances can be brought out into the open, which should result in a real clearing of the air between you.

This transit can be put to another positive purpose also. If there is really a great deal of harmony in the relationship between you and your partner, this can be a time when you put a great deal of energy into working through and with each other. Despite the inherent contradiction between the nature of Mars and that of the seventh house, the real meaning of this transit is that you will use your energies most efficiently by working through a partnership. As soon as you realize this and make the required adjustments, your affairs will begin to work smoothly.

Be careful of the primitive manifestation of this transit, however, and try to avoid unnecessary conflicts with others. Be sure that any conflict that occurs is over something worth fighting about. Sometimes this transit can signify legal conflicts and lawsuits. Try to compromise if you can, in order to avoid a needless controversy.

Mars in the Eighth House

The effects of Mars' transit through this house can be either very subtle or very blatant. It is hard to tell in advance which it will be. Basically your ego drives will create a confrontation with something, which will force a transformation of some kind in your life. For example, you may encounter someone who has a powerful effect upon you and causes you to change. This may happen through a conflict with this person, or he or she may gain influence over you and thereby affect you strongly. Because the eighth house is the house of values that you share with others, there may be a conflict concerning values or objects that are valued, such as property and possessions. The conflict might force you to reexamine and modify your position.

In a marriage or partnership relationship, the two of you may disagree strongly on the management of jointly held resources—how to spend a limited amount of money, for example. It is also quite likely that the two of you will use your joint resources, particularly money, rather foolishly and wastefully. Be careful of this, because it can lead to conflict at this time.

Because of the problems with resources held by or jointly with others, this is usually not a good time to try to obtain a loan. Ego conflicts, either subtle or obvious, are likely to foul up negotiations.

This transit stimulates sex as an expression of your ego, which it is for most people much more than they are willing to admit. You are more likely now to seek through sexual relationships an intense and transforming quality that will take you out of the ordinary into a transcendent realm. Just keep in mind that this is a rather large demand to place upon a frail human relationship.

The sum total of all of your experiences at this time will lead in either great or small ways to transforming the ways in which you assert yourself in the world. Both literally and figuratively, there will be the death of an old order and the birth of a new one.

Mars in the Ninth House

This transit can be a time when you do more creative intellectual work than usual and attempt to convey your experience and view of the world to others. The beliefs and ideas that you consider true and important you will assert and defend wherever necessary. Obviously this is valuable if you have to influence other people and make an impression on them, but it can also be a danger if you try to beat people over the head with your opinions and ideas. The problem is to avoid identifying your ego with what you believe. When you identify your ego with your ideas, you really believe you are that idea, and you will defend it as if it were literally your own body. Even the physiological reactions are the same.

But you are not what you think or believe, and proceeding as if you were can only lead to problems. It is perfectly all right to defend your beliefs, but other people do not have to feel and believe exactly as you do on every issue. Do not try to force your religious and philosophical views or your overall view of the world on others.

What you can do now is put all of your energy into expanding your mind. Look for experiences that will open up new dimensions of reality instead of wasting your energy on defending your ideas. Expand and enlarge your present beliefs. Travel can be quite gratifying now, if you don't have serious afflictions in this house by transit or natally. If you do, any travel would be frustrating or unrewarding. It could even mean an accident while traveling, although that is not likely unless you have a number of accident indications coming in at once.

The ninth house is also the house of law and the courts. Under certain circumstances this transit can indicate legal difficulties. If there are serious afflictions in your ninth house, this could work out quite badly for you.

Mars in the Tenth House

Mars, the planet of ego drives, is very much at home in this, the house of highest ego expression. This transit indicates many positive energies and, as usual, certain problems if you are not careful and do not recognize the needs of others.

More than any other, this transit arouses your ambition ·to achieve. If you can identify with a project, you will work extremely hard at it until it is done. It is especially important now that you find an independent project that requires your individual initiative and effort. You should try to gain independent authority in your work at this time because you are not likely to be very tolerant of other people's authority over yourself. You prefer to be your own boss. But your energy will make an impression upon people who are in a position to help you, as long as you do not challenge them unduly.

One of the problems of this transit is that you are much more likely to be in conflict with authority figures than at any other time. Parents, employers or bosses, or even government officials may feel it necessary to stop your efforts in various areas. But this will happen only if you insist on being a threat to them. If you can align your interests with theirs, these people can help you.

Conflicts with coworkers may arise if they feel threatened by your efforts to get ahead. You should try to play down such conflicts unless something real is at stake, for they will only block your efforts and make advancement more difficult. If you can remain reasonably conscious of other people's interests and not come into conflict with them more than absolutely necessary, this transit can help you make great progress toward the objectives you have set for yourself. But if you feel that you must defeat every challenge from others at all costs, it will probably cost you all the progress you might have made.

Mars in the Eleventh House

This is a time to formulate your goals and actively pursue them. You identify your basic ego energies very much with the future now, and you want to work today for the sake of what you can bring about tomorrow. This is also a house of group relationships, which means that you will be able to achieve your goals most ·fectively by working cooperatively with others. This is not a good time to be a loner, nor should you allow your own ego drives to conflict with everyone else's. Team action is the watchword with Mars in this house.

But this presents a problem, since the Mars energies within you, as in everyone, are expressed through totally individual action rather than for or with others. The trick with this transit is to create a balance between your own self-interests and other people's interests. But you should not deny your ego or subordinate yourself to the needs of others. Rather, you have to *coordinate* your needs with others'. Part of the problem may lie in finding people with whom you can work, but when you have found them, this should be a productive time.

Needless to say, if you do not succeed in finding such a group, there will be difficulties between you and your friends, for your own ego needs will be in conflict with everyone else's. Likewise, you will be more than usually resentful of group pressures, and you will find it difficult to work with another person on any project. But remember that this kind of problem represents a poorly handled use of the Mars energy. If you handle the energy correctly, this should not happen.

Physical activity with friends, such as athletics, is especially good for you now, as are projects in which you work with a number of other people. Mars always demands that you get some strong personal gratification from what you do, so do not put yourself in a back-seat position with others. That will only lead to negative manifestations of this energy, as discussed above.

Mars in the Twelfth House

This can be a difficult transit if it is not handled properly, especially if your natal chart shows affliction to planets in this house. It can be a time of frustration and self-denial, when you don't seem to get credit for anything you do and always have to stay in the background.

For this reason, you will often feel vaguely irritable and uneasy during this transit. This is simply the psychological expression of repressed energies within you that are often so subtle that you are not even aware of them.

Usually when you set forth to make an impression upon others or assert yourself during this transit, you find that somehow you have created the wrong impression and thereby undermined your position rather than helped it. This is because of the largely unconscious nature of twelfth-house energies. Past behavior patterns that have become completely unconscious now become active and come into play without your knowing it. Your efforts at self-assertion are undermined by these behavior patterns that you are not even aware of. And unfortunately the people who are alienated by these actions probably will not come out and say so, but will work behind the scenes to block your efforts. This is the origin of the "secret enemies" label so often attached to this house.

The only way you can counter this effect is to become completely conscious of yourself and these little self-defeating acts. If you feel emotionally upset, as you often will during this transit, refrain from any kind of significant confrontation with others. Instead, confront yourself.

It is best at this time to work alone as much as possible. Or you can work in a social-service field where helping others is the primary requisite. The main task is to get your ego out of the way so that the counterproductive energies in your personality will not become activated. Hospital or prison work, social work, or any kind of charitable activity is suitable. If you don't feel inclined in this direction, however, don't force yourself, for that will benefit no one. In this case, work by yourself, as mentioned above, or prepare for a project to be done when Mars has left your twelfth house. Or do research by yourself in a laboratory or library or some such secluded place.

Mars Conjunct Sun

This transit has tremendous potentials and definite risks. You will have to be careful in everything you do, because the high energy level of this transit can have explosive consequences.

Your ego energies are high, which means that you can stand up for yourself against almost anyone today. You have great confidence and will not easily allow someone to take advantage of you. Unfortunately this may also mean that you will get into fights and arguments. Try to remember that other people have egos too. You don't have to defeat others in order to maintain yourself. You should be especially careful in your dealings with supervisors. They will not expect you to be as assertive toward them as you are likely to be today.

You have a great deal of physical energy also, which means you can work hard and long. You prefer physical work to mental work, because it uses your energy more completely. After extensive mental work you may still feel very restless and in turn irritable. Here again there is the danger of getting carried away with your energy and taking unnecessary risks or overstraining yourself. If you are not careful, you could have an accident or injury, but only if you have been accident-prone in the past. Otherwise you needn't worry about it. Certainly fear of an accident should not make you avoid activity. In fact if you suppress this energy it is most likely to come out negatively in arguments, fights, accidents or injuries.

However, if you use these energies intelligently, you should be able to accomplish far more worthwhile work than on other days.

Mars Sextile Sun

This transit stimulates your physical vitality, giving you the chance to work hard and accomplish much. Your health is good under this transit, and you are able to approach everything you do with vigor and self-confidence. And this carries over to the psychological level as well, as an ability to assert yourself toward others and stand up for your views in any controversy.

New opportunities to be personally effective often open up under this transit. For example, in your job you might get a chance to take on an important responsibility, which will lead later to a promotion or increased salary. This is a good time to demonstrate that you can work on your own and do it well. But you can also work with groups now, because your energies complement the group's energies, and you are able to work together for individual ends. The group work you do now will also show you off as a person who can be effective.

During this time you work with great consciousness of your objectives. You know what you want and how to get it without forcing people to resist you. You simply take advantage of every chance that you get and use it to the utmost.

In your everyday exchanges with others, you will project your ideas with more power and energy than usual. Thus you will be able to get your point of view and objectives across in any group that you deal with. Others will recognize your achievements.

If you have to debate or argue with anyone, your self-confidence will put you in a good position. Business and commercial negotiations are similarly favored. If you need to bargain a price down or get more favorable terms, you can do it because you are clear about what you want.

Mars Square Sun

This is a very energetic time for you, when you can assert yourself effectively and accomplish a great deal of work. The problem is that you will be tested all along the line and forced to demonstrate the validity of what you are doing. You may be challenged either by circumstances or by other persons. Your success depends largely upon how well you express yourself in a situation. If you act unconsciously and follow your own ego drives blindly, you are likely to fail.

Even at best your high energies now will probably lead to disputes and disagreements. Being quite unwilling to back down on any issue, you are not moved to make compromises with others. But that is precisely what you should do, especially if you can manage to compromise without giving ground on essential points. Be careful that you don't become so wrapped up in your own beliefs that you cannot see which parts are essential and which are not.

Anger and irritability are frequent with this transit. Here again it is your responsibility to stand up for yourself on important matters but give way on little ones. Nevertheless, you may have to have a knockdown, drag-out battle with someone in order to clear the air of tension that has been building up.

However, if you make a successful stand in any confrontation at this time, your efforts will bear real fruit at the next conjunction or opposition of Mars to your natal Sun, which will probably occur in about six months. If you do not make creative compromises now, or if you manage to create more opposition, in that same period you will experience significant failures, as the opposition becomes too strong for you to handle.

Mars Trine Sun

During this transit your energies are high, and you feel vigorous and willing to work. At the same time, your self-confidence is unusually strong. You feel no need to struggle against others, because you know your normal energies will carry you through any situation. And since you are able to work from such a calm position, your work is more effective and more competent than usual.

This period is favorable for initiating all kinds of activity, especially physical activity, but it is much more likely that you will work on projects that you have started earlier.

You do not feel violently competitive, but if someone offers a challenge, you won't back down. Therefore this is a good time for all types of athletics. You will enjoy the contest, but you will not feel driven to win at all costs. The game will seem satisfactory by itself. And you will carry this viewpoint over into all the activities you become involved in at this time.

This is a favorable transit for situations that require decisive action. Your mind is operating with great energy while maintaining equilibrium. Consequently you are very clear about your intentions, and you know what course to follow at every turn.

No matter what you do under this influence, others will see you as someone with a definite personality. Your vigor and enthusiasm will make a favorable impression, so you will be in a good position to deal with bosses or other persons in power. In general this is a favorable time for dealing with men, regardless of your own sex.

If you are involved in a love relationship, this is a favorable transit for that. The present balance between your needs and your loved one's needs for self-gratification enables both of you to give and gain from each other.

Mars Opposition Sun

This transit can have two completely different effects, depending upon how you have handled your affairs in the recent past.

On the negative side, this can be a time of furious conflict with others. Recent actions by you or by other people may have created energies that lead to anger, rage and general disagreement between you and others. If you have not been careful to enlist people to your side in any work that required your individual initiative and if you have alienated them thereby, you may find now that the forces of opposition have become too great to control. Thus this transit of Mars can represent your defeat in some matter.

If you yourself have not taken the initiative and have remained largely inactive, this transit will stir up all manner of subconscious energies that will make you irritable and difficult to get along with. Because of the nature of the opposition, you will feel this most strongly in intimate one-to-one relationships such as partnerships and marriage.

The other side of this transit is quite different and much more positive, because an opposition can also mean a time when some activity of yours is brought to a triumphal climax. Quite often this activity was started during the last transit of Mars conjunct your natal Sun. However, at the last transit of Mars by square you had to face a challenge either from other persons or from circumstances that tested the validity of what you were doing. If you survived that challenge successfully, you will now enjoy the fruition of that effort.

But even though you have completed a great achievement, you must be able now to achieve a creative working relationship with others, because your present actions will create consequences for the future. What you do now will largely determine how the whole project will work out in the long run. In other words, you can still ruin everything, even though it may seem that you are "home free."

Mars Conjunct Moon

During this transit you may be much more irritable than usual and snappish with others, even though you cannot consciously recognize what you are angry about. Perhaps the most puzzling effect of this transit is that your irritability and anger seem completely irrational. They may not actually be irrational, but your anger may be about something that happened a while ago. Mars transiting the Moon may create events that remind you of past anger that you didn't show at the time. Now it is revived with such force that you have to show it. In this kind of situation a trivial incident makes you mad simply because it is the "last straw."

You are likely to be more angry with close friends or members of the family than with people you don't know so well, immediate family being the most likely targets of your anger.

But this transit brings more than useless anger. It can also make you stand up for yourself and fight for your rights with complete confidence. Your whole emotional being is suffused with a feeling of strength and unwillingness to let others pull anything on you. Just be careful that your confidence doesn't become a kind of arrogance in which you refuse to accept any challenge. There is a strong tendency to project your ego into situations and make every issue that arises a test of your personal validity.

Mars Sextile Moon

This is a time of strong emotions when, much like the transit by trine, you seek out experiences that involve both your mind and feelings. You will have a strong desire to experience with all of your faculties as a whole person, not just with your mind. Also you will defend your beliefs and opinions with emotional and passionate fervor. It is not that you are looking for a fight, but you will not run from one either. You won't allow anyone to walk all over you so long as this transit lasts. Nevertheless, you are not irritable or pugnacious, merely high-spirited and unwilling to lose.

You seek out relationships and friends who will arouse your emotions as well as your intellect, and you may be on the lookout for someone with whom you can have a passionate sexual relationship. This transit also makes existing sexual relationships more intense.

You will have the energy to work very hard, but only on projects that affect you personally. This may take the form of working in your home or doing some kind of work for your immediate community. But unless the project appeals to you emotionally, it is unlikely to arouse your interest at this time.

There is some impulsiveness with this transit and a tendency to leap to conclusions. Also your thinking is not very objective, because you identify too strongly with your personal interests and attitudes, which colors your perception of the world. Even if you recognize that something is objectively true, that does not carry as much weight as your feelings on the subject. Obviously this is not a good time to make a decision that must be unbiased and objective. Nor is it a good time to make decisions concerning matters that will affect you long after the present, because your current subjective orientation will change, and what is appropriate now will be inappropriate in the future.

Mars Square Moon

Be extremely careful of your tendency toward moody irritability at this time. You are very subject to outbreaks of irrational and compulsive behavior that will not serve your best interests. You may find yourself snapping at someone for almost no reason. Or an insignificant action by someone else may trigger a response that makes no rational sense whatsoever. Close domestic relationships are the most likely theater for your fireworks. It will be harder to deal with your loved ones because of the ferment in your own mind at this time.

On the other hand, long-buried tensions may surface now and demand to be handled. The problem is that they may surface in such a way that you cannot readily figure out where they have come from. Frustrated energies in disguised form mean that you should not take emotional upheaval at face value during this transit. The tensions are significant, but not what they seem.

Be careful about falling into childish behavior patterns. You will feel like behaving childishly, but you don't have to act out these feelings. You must be very conscious of what you are doing at this time.

Your general rashness under this transit can lead to an accident if you are not careful. The problem is that you will tend to act from an unconscious impulse, suddenly and without thinking. Accidents are most likely at home or in some other domestic situation, for that is where you act with the least consciousness and forethought, simply because you are most used to it.

Be particularly careful of injuries to your eyes. This is not a normal manifestation of this transit, but you should be careful anyway.

Mars Trine Moon

During this transit you will experience life with greater emotional intensity than usual. You will feel everything more strongly and deeply. You will want every experience that you encounter to touch your feelings, and they probably will. Your relationships will be more intense, and you will seek out those that allow you to experience yourself very vividly.

Whatever you do will be done with complete unity of emotion and conscious intention, which gives an unusually strong intensity to your way of doing things and your manner toward others. Consequently you are much more likely to take events rather seriously, but this is not a problem, because your intensity makes it possible to deal with others in a frank and straightforward manner. You are not willing to play games with people's feelings, which makes them respect yours as well.

As with other Mars-Moon transits, there is a tendency to act according to the dictates of emotion, but this tendency is not so strong that you cannot control it. Besides, it is very good to have your actions in touch with your emotional self as long as you maintain some balance, as you are doing now.

This transit often indicates a strong emotional involvement with the opposite sex. It is hard for you to react neutrally to someone who comes into your life now. You either love the person or hate him with all your soul, and this intensity comes over into all your love relationships, whether they are new or old.

Although this transit does not make you feel violently aggressive, you will not allow anyone to step on your toes. You make very clear to others exactly where their limits are in dealing with you, and you will not let them transgress those limits. You are in a fighting spirit in the positive sense, in that you will stand up for what you believe but still be reasonably tolerant of other people's ideas.

Mars Opposition Moon

Emotionally based relationships may be somewhat difficult at this time. If you are not very self-aware, your actions will be dictated largely by irrational drives and compulsions and by behavior patterns carried over from childhood. Yet like every other opposition, this one can mean a time of culmination and climax, in this case in your close personal relationships. This is a period of testing and of confrontation, which will point out the pressures and tensions in those relationships, as well as the positive and strong parts.

Also, because of the nature of the opposition, you may find your own inward unconscious drives mirrored in someone else's actions. Usually this occurs as a conflict in which the other person acts very irrationally and compulsively in ways that are detrimental to your goals. Look at this person very carefully. Although it may seem quite magical, he or she is really reflecting your own inward ego problems. The other person is yourself! This is because you tend to project your inner attitudes onto the other person, rather than experiencing the other person directly as he or she really is. Unpleasant as it may be to deal with someone who is being difficult, you may learn a great deal about yourself in the process.

Women may be especially hard to deal with at this time. You may have difficulty with women who know exactly how to set you off and make you experience your own emotions. This brings us to a central theme of this transit, which is that it creates emotional confrontations, some of which may be quite bitter, forcing you to encounter aspects of yourself that you are not usually aware of. You may see yourself directly through your own actions, or you may see yourself reflected in another, as described previously. These confrontations will be most powerful in your closest personal relationships, at home with loved ones, spouse, children or parents. Conflicts at this time all serve to creatively release tensions that have been buried within you and to increase your self-knowledge, if you will allow it.

Mars Conjunct Mercury

Today your ego is unusually involved in communications with others. Consequently you are unusually touchy and irritable and likely to get involved in disputes with others. Your anger may be touched off at the drop of a hat. Or you may unconsciously provoke opposition by making remarks to others that cause them to feel threatened.

On the other hand, you are also capable of great mental effort today. You have very high energies for doing any kind of work you want to do, but it is best to do work that keeps your mind occupied, so that the energies don't leak out in disputes as described above. If you have to convince someone of a point of view or sell them something, you should be very effective, as long as you can avoid high-pressuring them. Assuming this, you will make a positive impression upon others with your enthusiasm, vigor and strength of purpose. But if you antagonize them, you will drive them away from your point of view.

These same high energies affect the way you move from place to place. If you drive anywhere in a car, be careful not to speed. You may be inclined to recklessness and risk-taking while you travel, which can lead to accidents.

Mars Sextile Mercury

This is an excellent transit for all kinds of mental work, especially if you have to plan a future course of action with decisiveness and firmness. This is also a good time to negotiate with others or arrange any kind of deal. You will be in a positive mood and have great confidence in your position, which will enable you to make a positive impression and probably convince people of your point of view.

This transit also favors working with others in a cooperative planning venture. You can make plans together or hash out differences of opinion in such a way that you make your point without anyone else feeling threatened. It should be possible for everyone to feel that they have contributed to the transit.

This is a good time for traveling in connection with your work. Because your energy level is high, you are restless to get things done. This is not a bad time for recreational traveling, but it is more favorable for travel that gives you some outlet for your energy.

During this couple of days you will feel confident of yourself, your ideas and the effect you make when talking with people. It should be a successful time in a very general sense.

Mars Square Mercury

Be careful how you talk to others today. Your energy level is very high, and you tend to identify your ego very closely with your ideas and opinions, so that you are quick to take offense. You have great capacity for mental effort today, but if any obstacle gets in the way of your energies, you will quickly become angry and irritable. And you are not likely to keep your irritation to yourself. There is considerable danger of arguments and disputes, particularly at home or at work. When you look back at this later, you may realize that there was nothing to argue about except egos; no real issues were at stake. But it is better if you have a real issue to argue about, for if you have to fight for your beliefs, today is the day to do it. You are sufficiently strong to carry your point of view. But it would be a pity to waste this energy on a matter of no importance and create hard feelings over nothing.

Others may seem to be picking fights with you even though you offer no provocation. Make sure that you aren't provoking them subtly by an attitude or an implicit point of view.

You should be careful under this transit, because you are likely to be accident prone. Be careful while traveling, drive cautiously and avoid cuts and injuries to your legs or hands. Be very cautious if you handle any cutting machinery. If you have any irritation or anger in you now, avoid using any kind of machinery or sharp instruments.

Mars Trine Mercury

This is an excellent time for all kinds of mental work and for negotiations and dealings with others. You should feel mentally alert now and able to put forth your point of view on any matter so that others understand it. Whether they agree with you or not, they will at least respect your opinions.

In negotiations with others, you will be able to assert your position and make it carry, if that is your intention. This is because you can explain your position clearly and unambiguously so that there is no question in others' minds.

This is an excellent transit for studying and broadening your understanding, either through academic methods, such as taking classes and reading books, or through conversation with others. You feel sufficiently confident of yourself so that you can listen to others without feeling threatened by their views.

This is a good time for planning, writing or any other predominantly mental work. You have a good grasp of how situations relate to you personally, and you can make plans accordingly.

This is a favorable time for traveling, because you have lots of energy and want to be on the go. It is most favorable for travel that involves physical effort, such as walking or bicycle riding. Your mind may be too active for sitting on a bus or train, unless you have plenty of work to occupy your mind with.

Mars Opposition Mercury

Whether or not you yourself feel irritable, and you very likely will, today may be full of disputes and arguments, unless you try to understand other people's points of view. This is not a good day for trying to settle arguments, because both you and your opponent will become so firmly entrenched in your own position that neither of you will budge an inch.

What you must recognize today is that your ego is thoroughly bound up with your opinions and that you are acting as if a challenge to your ideas were literally a challenge to your physical self. On rare occasions this may be the case, but usually it isn't. If you do have a real position to defend in any confrontation now, by all means work hard to defend it. Your energies will be equal to the occasion. But make sure that there is a real issue at stake.

This is an excellent day for any kind of mental work as long as you don't have to work with others. The only difficulty is that you may tend to scatter your thoughts or be too hasty, because your energy is so high. But some self-discipline and care should overcome that.

Be careful of any situation that has a potential for accidents, especially traveling. Drive carefully and avoid speeding. Also watch carefully at intersections for other people driving in a dangerous manner. Legal troubles would certainly ensue from an accident today. Also be careful of situations involving risk to arms and feet.

Mars Conjunct Venus

This transit is most likely to arouse your interest in the opposite sex, because it represents the union of the two planets that most strongly affect the sex drive. Sexual energy is strong and you will have a strong desire for physical love-making. These energies are high and demand some kind of gratification, and with Mars involved, there is considerable ego-drive here. You may want to make love with someone even though you do not care for him or her emotionally. And if there is no outlet for this energy, it may cause arguments and discord between you and your lover.

The effects of this transit are not limited to physical love, however. In a larger sense it arouses all creative energies. This is a good time to be involved in any creative work that requires you to be physically active. Abstract or intellectual creation, such as writing poetry or music, would not satisfy the Mars side of the combination. But performing music, especially some of the current popular forms, would be excellent, as would vigorous work in sculpture or another art form that demands physical energy, such as dance.

If Mars crosses your Venus slowly, it can signify the beginning of a new love relationship, which will almost certainly be physical. It is very certain that if such a relationship is not consummated, it will not be very happy or long-lasting. You are kidding yourself if you think you can be "just friends" with someone of the opposite sex whom you meet under this transit.

Mars Sextile Venus

Like all Venus-Mars contacts, this one arouses your sexual drives and makes you seek a physical relationship with someone of the opposite sex, if you do not already have one. This transit favors an existing relationship, for both of you will be able to give and receive from each other and thereby gain gratification through the relationship.

Entertainment and fun are two key themes of this transit, which favors get-togethers and parties. You will get the greatest personal satisfaction from associating with others and having a good time. You will enjoy any activity much more if you can share it with others, for this is a very gregarious transit.

This is a good time for artistic activity, as well as for getting together with others for artistic purposes. You feel a strong need to express yourself through beauty, and even if you are not artistic, you may want to beautify your immediate surroundings. This is a good time to repaint, clean and redecorate your home.

Whatever you do will be guided by your need to express and receive affection from others and your need to experience and create beauty. This transit should present you with ample opportunities to fulfill both needs. Financial activities are also favored now.

Mars Square Venus

During this transit you may try to assert your individuality in a relationship. Sometimes this occurs when you feel that you are giving too much in a relationship and getting too little. You are driven to wanting more self-gratification from it. Or the situation can be the exact opposite; that is, you have been giving too little, and your partner is resentful. Any successful relationship, especially a sexual one, is a delicate balance between the needs and desires of each person as an individual ego and their desire to achieve meaning through a relationship. This equilibrium is very delicate and easily upset now.

At this time the two of you have to define what you want from each other and what you are willing to give. Then you must try to reach a balance between them. It is sometimes necessary to be quite explicit about what you want, because whatever is left unsaid may very well be the main source of conflict between you.

However, this transit does not inevitably lead to conflict by any means. If the two of you are generally harmonious, your relationship will allow for ample self-gratification and expression, which you both will seek and receive at the same time. Sexuality is very strongly aroused by this transit, and especially if you are not presently involved with someone, you will very much want physical sex. But sex under this transit is demanding and vigorous rather than soft and loving. Above all, it will be very bad for your relationship if one of you is uninterested in sex, for that can create the kind of frustration that leads to disputes. For this reason, two people who want to have a relationship should have favorable Mars-Venus contacts between their horoscopes, so that both horoscopes will be transited at the same time.

Your creative and artistic energies will be stimulated now, and if you have any artistic inclinations, this will be a very productive time.

Mars Trine Venus

This transit is favorable for sexual relationships and for all kinds of creative activity. The trine between Venus and Mars symbolizes the perfect balance between your need to be yourself and your need to relate to another. Thus you will be able to express yourself very well in a relationship, deriving complete gratification and allowing your partner to do the same.

But like all Mars-Venus combinations, this transit is strongly physical rather than psychological in its effects. A purely romantic relationship with no physical sex would not be very satisfactory, but such a relationship is not likely to occur under this influence.

If you are not currently involved in a sexual relationship, this transit by itself is not quite strong enough to bring one. That would require the assistance of other similar transits. However, your erotic fantasies will certainly be stimulated, and persons of the opposite sex whom you would not usually look at twice seem much more attractive now. In fact you need to have a certain amount of discretion, lest you get involved in a totally inappropriate relationship. But again this transit is not usually that compulsive.

Artists and creative people will find this transit extremely stimulating, although it does not provide creative inspiration. That must come from other sources. But it does provide the energy to actually do the creative work, which will be unusually expressive of who and what you are.

Mars Opposition Venus

Almost more than any other transit, this one stimulates sexual desire, but it can also produce problems within a sexual relationship. Mars and Venus are complementary principles that both strongly determine the nature of sexual attraction. Venus rules the mutual attraction between two people and the desire for a relationship, while Mars rules the ego's need for gratification. Psychologists are aware that sexual relationships in all animal species show characteristics both of a "loving relationship" and of combat. This dichotomy is true in humans as well and is particularly strong during this transit.

Sexual relations at this time may lack real tenderness. You seem to be using sex as a way to dominate your partner, and you may find it difficult to give as much to your partner as you want to get. This can create a situation in which one of you feels that the other has stolen love rather than allowed it to be freely given. Consequently this transit can lead to conflict between the two of you. Sex tends to have no real emotional commitment now, and to be nothing more than the desire for release from physical tension that is part of the sex drive.

However, all that is really necessary is to make sure that your partner is in a similar frame of mind as yourself. Then there is very little likelihood that either of you will exploit the other.

If you suppress your sexuality in platonic relationships with the opposite sex at this time, you may become irritable and feisty. This effect may be so subtle that you are not even aware of what is happening at the time. If you cannot fulfill your secret desire to make love to someone, you may become angry and harsh with that person.

There is nothing to be done about this except to be aware of it and not take your feelings too seriously. But if there is any possibility of a sexual relationship with the person in question, feel free to initiate it.

Persons in creative activities such as arts or crafts can also express the energy of this transit through their work. If you have any ability along these lines you will be able to express yourself through your art more effectively than usual, and your work will have a unique and special quality about it.

Mars Conjunct Mars

Ego energies and physical energies run very high during this transit. You will feel positively loaded with energy, for which you must find an adequate outlet, or you will have problems. The best way to handle this transit is to do some necessary heavy physical work. But that will work out only if you derive satisfaction from doing it. Otherwise you will feel resentful, which brings out the negative side of this transit. Sports, if you are at all athletic, is an excellent outlet. If you just sit around, you will begin to feel itchy and restless for no apparent reason and then become quite irritable. In this mood you will snap at anyone who comes along for no reason at all. Or you may be spoiling for a fight, even if there is no justification for one.

If you feel none of these effects, look deep inside yourself. You will probably find that you are doing a good job of repressing your feelings. And this is the most dangerous response of all, because the energy will out, either physically through an accident or by projection; that is, you will experience the energy through another. This means that you may have to endure another person's aggressive acts, which may bring you harm.

On the other hand, this transit is quite good for initiating any new project on your own. It is a transit of beginnings, and you should use it for that purpose, particularly for projects that you will be identified with and be given great credit for. Don't expect such projects to go along without opposition, however. Watch for strong resistance from others when Mars squares your natal Mars in about six months, although the precise time may vary. About one year from now, when Mars is in opposition to your natal Mars, you will know whether or not your project is successful.

Mars Sextile Mars

You will feel energetic and vigorous under this transit. Your physical health will be quite good, and you should seek activities that will give this energy an outlet. Sitting around will not have any particular bad effects, but you would be wasting a valuable opportunity. Athletic activities are an excellent way of expressing this energy. You will want to work with friends and neighbors, so this is an excellent time for a group project such as a neighborhood clean-up campaign. You will probably enjoy whatever work you do because it makes you feel so alive.

If you have to be personally effective in an activity, such as business or negotiations with others, you will be able to achieve the desired results now. Like other Mars-Mars contacts, this transit gives you the necessary self-confidence to influence others and make a positive impression. If you have to debate with someone on any matter, you should be able to carry the day. However, do not be tempted to rest on your laurels, for this transit does not signify energies that will force you to act. You may simply wake up with a feeling of smug self-satisfaction and do nothing at all. But that would be a waste, because you can work very effectively now.

This transit is favorable for traveling and expressing yourself through new experiences and new encounters. You are intellectually restless, and you want to do something different. You should — it will be good for you.

Your energies are in very good balance now, so take this chance to do whatever has to be done.

Mars Square Mars

Under this transit you should avoid rash and impulsive actions, for they will alienate others, create enemies and in the long run undermine your own interests. Your ego energies run rather high now, but in such a way that you are likely to assert yourself inappropriately. You may feel that you can conquer the world and issue completely unnecessary challenges to the people around you. Most frequently you express this feeling as irritability, excessive impatience with others' actions, argumentativeness and general touchiness.

On the other hand, you may have to contend with someone else who is acting this way. In this case there is nothing to do but be patient as long as possible, fighting back only if there is a serious issue at stake. Remember that with this transit you will have a strong tendency to regard all issues as serious if they involve your pride. Be very careful in your evaluations.

This is a good transit for getting work done, if you can control your impulsive behavior. Any task that requires sheer physical energy with little finesse or attention to detail is excellent, because it allows you to work off energy without totally suppressing the natural impulsiveness and exuberance of this transit. Work requiring very carefully controlled energy is not very likely to be successful, because you tend to work in little explosive bursts. Frustration of any kind, even self-imposed, is almost unendurable under this transit.

In the final analysis, the way you express this transit is a good index to what shape your ego is in, that is, your pride and sense of worth and personal effectiveness. If you are off in any of these areas, you are likely to experience the disruptive and difficult side of this transit.

Under some conditions this transit can affect you physically through illness or accident. Don't take unnecessary risks, and avoid situations that might weaken your body and make you more susceptible to illness.

Mars Trine Mars

This is a time of vigorous self-assertion. Without being excessively aggressive, you can make it clear to people that you are willing to work for what you want. Your energy level is high, and you can accomplish a lot of physical or mental work in a short time, although physical labor releases the energy somewhat more effectively.

This is a good time to take the initiative and start a new project. It will go very well, because you will have the insight as well as the energy to follow it through to the conclusion. Although you can work very effectively with others under this transit, it might be better to work alone, unless the others can keep up with your pace and don't need to be constantly told what to do. Mars is an ego-oriented planet, and you will be most strongly motivated toward tasks that bring credit to you and express you as an individual.

If you are already working on a project, but it has become bogged down, now you will be able to resume your work with greater effectiveness than before. If you have been trying to do something, but have lacked the right opportunity, this transit should get it moving. Your work won't seem to resist your energies, as so often happens at other times.

Greater self-confidence usually accompanies this transit, so if you have to present a project to someone, you will be able to do it much more effectively. Also, pushing your own interests will be much more successful than usual. Everything you do now will give you greater self-assurance and the extra drive and confidence that you will need in the future, when things may not run as smoothly. Probably the worst way to handle this transit is to do nothing, for you will lose an opportunity to prove your own worth to yourself.

Mars Opposition Mars

During this transit you have a very strong need to assert yourself, but you may do it in a way that provokes conflict with others. And if you try to suppress this need for ego-expression, you may have to contend with someone else's attempts to be overbearing. On the other hand, this could possibly be a time of very vigorous and successful work, in which you succeed by asserting your own individuality toward others in some way. The lesson that you must learn is that your own success does not have to be at someone else's expense. But under this transit you may feel that it does, and so you respond either by trying to dominate others unnecessarily or by reacting negatively to anyone else's successful self-assertion. Be very careful about feeling jealous and resentful of someone else's success. You may feel that their success was stolen from you, but that is not necessarily true. Work for your own interests, but not against someone else's.

Even under the best circumstances you may encounter serious opposition from others. The best way to deal with this is to get the encounter out in the open and get it over with. Otherwise you will have to deal with your own or the other person's sullen irritability. If you feel a vague undefined anger at the world in general during this transit, it is because you have tried to ignore the anger or hurt within yourself. Now it is bubbling up in a form so disguised that you cannot readily diagnose its source.

But your energy level in general is very high now. If you can work with others without getting entirely wrapped up in your own ego, you can accomplish a great deal of work and bring many affairs to a successful conclusion. The effects of this transit depend on your ability to handle one-to-one relationships.

Mars Conjunct Jupiter

This is an excellent transit for almost any kind of physical activity. Your energy is high, and you feel very strong and vigorous. If you have physical labor to do, such as working in the yard, housework or athletics, this transit will give you the energy you need.

The only problem to watch out for is that your feelings of exuberance may lead you to take unnecessary risks, especially in athletics or in work that has any inherent danger. If you are foolishly overconfident, you can have accidents with this transit.

You may also be inclined to indulge in other risks, such as gambling or speculative financial ventures. But if these ventures are at all valid or have any potential for success, you should succeed. This is basically a "lucky" transit, or so it seems. Actually it is not so much luck as the fact that you have such total confidence now that your activities are much more likely to succeed. Mars-Jupiter has the general connotation of "fortunate action" and is favorable for launching any new enterprise.

Mars-Jupiter has a strong effect upon muscle action, which is why this transit is so good for physical exercise. In fact, Mars transiting Jupiter or vice versa is an extremely good childbirth transit, helping to make labor easy and short and guaranteeing a successful delivery. A mother and child often have the Mars of one aspecting the Jupiter of the other.

Mars Sextile Jupiter

This is a very positive transit, opening up opportunities for just about any kind of activity that you wish to engage in. Enterprises begun at this time are likely to do quite well, unless some very powerful negative transit coincides with this one.

This transit is especially favorable for all business and commercial ventures and is excellent for negotiating personally advantageous deals. Your objectives and goals in the matter will be much clearer to you than usual, which enables you to deal very intelligently with others and thus get the best possible deal for yourself. Also everything you do has a kind of buoyant optimism that is also favorable to success. But you aren't so wildly optimistic that you overlook the details that are necessary to the success of any endeavor.

This is an extremely favorable time for dealing with authorities, for they will be open to your ideas and easily persuaded to your point of view. Legal interests are also favored now.

Your physical energy is high, and you should enjoy good health and good spirits. This is an excellent transit for any kind of athletics, because this combination of planets relates to muscle tone, and physical exercise will improve your health even further.

Your activities under this transit should bring opportunities for personal growth by expanding your range of activities as well as your experience.

Mars Square Jupiter

This can be a time of very successful and energetic activity, if you proceed with caution, don't act recklessly, and keep close track of what you are doing. You will be tempted, however, to run off quickly, without taking all factors into consideration and reaching a balanced judgment. You may be infected with an unjustified optimism that anything you do today will "turn to gold." It may, but it won't happen by luck. It will happen through intelligent planning and foresight, which are available to you under this transit if you make a conscious effort to take advantage of them.

You act for the future under this transit, because you are more concerned with what can be than with what is. Therefore this is a good time for furthering new projects. But do not overextend yourself and go beyond your resources, which is another temptation now.

As you extend your own sphere of influence and experience, don't overtax your own strength, psychologically or physically. On both fronts you feel so strong and vigorous that you may go beyond your normal energy limitations, but the time will come when you have to pay for this, and it may not be very pleasant. Also your fondness for taking risks can lead to accidents at this time, so be careful. You are not unlucky, you are just somewhat impulsive.

Jupiter rules your desire to include more of the universe in your own experience. This can mean being more conscious of the universe and experiencing more of it, or it can mean trying to dominate the universe for the greater "glory" of your own ego. The latter tendency is especially strong now, and it can lead to trouble later on. In a very real way this transit tests your efforts to grow as an individual. The more flaws you have and the more mistakes you make, the more likely you are to do something foolish that will lead to trouble. But those energies that are working satisfactorily will do extremely well at this time.

Mars Trine Jupiter

This is one of the best transits for almost any kind of activity, for your energies are high, you feel good, and you believe that you can do twice as much work as usual, which you probably can. Your muscles have unusually good tone and vigor, so this transit is extremely favorable for any physical activity, especially athletics.

This transit is often characterized as lucky, but it it not really luck that is operating here. Rather you are able to act with a complete picture in mind of what you are doing. You can plan with greater foresight and thereby avoid pitfalls that others might characterize as "bad luck" if they encounter them. You will not encounter them, so you will be regarded as lucky.

This is a particularly favorable time for any work that can advance your own interests. Because you want to grow in as many ways as possible, this is a good time to do whatever will help growth take place in your life. One warning, however. Self-aggrandizement is also compatible with this transit, but if you take this course you may be in a more difficult position later, during more difficult transits. Instead use this transit to bring about a growth of consciousness and knowledge.

This transit is also favorable for most business activity, for your actions are blessed with insight that helps you succeed in business where others might fail. For the same reason, this is a good time for making decisions. You have a very clear sense of yourself and your needs, so that you can make decisions according to your best interests, in the largest and most enlightened sense of the phrase.

If you must take chances or do something that you can't foresee the outcome of, this is as good a time as any. Your optimism now creates a positive energy that will attract favorable results from your gamble. Besides, you have the sense at this time to avoid any real risky ventures.

Mars Opposition Jupiter

This can be one of the so-called "lucky" transits, or it can be a time fraught with conflict and foolish actions.

This transit represents the culmination of your efforts to expand the domain of your activities. There is more and more that you want to do, and you resent anything that narrows your freedom and limits your scope of action. The challenge of this transit is to be conscious enough of yourself and of what you are doing so that you can plan intelligently and work effectively with enlightened self-interest as opposed to pure selfishness.

The negative side of this transit is manifested when you are not conscious of what you are doing. In that case you may act toward others in a domineering, overbearing manner, which will cause them to desert you later when you may need their help. You may try to come on to others as more than an ordinary human being, which will tempt them to test your strength.

Foolishly overestimating your own abilities may cause you to bite off more than you can chew in a number of areas of your life. It may happen on the physical level if you overexert yourself and exhaust your body or take foolish risks that lead to an accident. Or it may happen in business if you overextend yourself so far that when resources become more limited in the future you won't be able to meet all your commitments.

With self-awareness, however, this whole picture changes. As long as you stay within your own limitations — that is, your inherent limitations as a human being and the limitations of your situation or circumstances — you should be extremely successful under this transit. The sense of timing of your actions may leave others amazed and sure that you are lucky. But really you have succeeded because you have a complete understanding of the situation.

242

As long as you don't suddenly overexert yourself, your physical health is improved under this transit, and your muscles work better than at any other time. Pregnant women often give birth during this transit, for it favors the contraction of the smooth muscles that are involved in childbirth.

Mars Conjunct Saturn

This may be a somewhat difficult day, full of frustrations and irritating occurrences. Do not plan to launch any daring or risky activity, because the chance are that you will not succeed. Your energies do not have the necessary vigor or power. It is better to concentrate upon routine activities that require you to follow a well-established pattern.

Other people may seem unusually irritating to you today. They may seem to be trying to "get your goat," or worse, to be taking actions that are quite destructive to you and your interests. You feel angry, but this transit does not often give you the opportunity to express your anger. You may be forced to seethe in silence, although it is not a good idea to let the energy just sit inside you. It can become physically destructive. If you feel angry under this transit, find some hard work to do and really get into it. Then the energy will dissipate, and you will be able to face the problem without also having to deal with your anger.

In fact, this transit is especially good for work that requires concentrated energy and great discipline or very careful technique. Working with metals, especially steel and iron, or with cutting instruments is favored. But avoid working with cutting tools if you are experiencing the angry side of this transit. You could hurt yourself.

Mars Sextile Saturn

This is an excellent transit for carefully planning and executing projects that require great diligence and patience. But this is not a high-energy Mars transit, so do not expect to have great flamboyant energy. You will not feel like going out and moving mountains, but you will be capable of sustained effort.

This is a good time to undertake intricate work that requires attention to detail, such as working with hard materials like metal or stone. These materials represent the kind of energy that this transit puts out.

You can work patiently now toward goals that will be fulfilled in the future, for this transit often means deferred results. You are working more for tomorrow than today. But your concerns are very practical, and if you know that your present activities will be of benefit in the future, you will be content with modest results now.

The immediate demands of the ego are subordinated to your knowledge of what can be done. Reality and practicality are more important to you than self-gratification. In fact you are capable of considerable self-denial if necessary. This transit can be very useful in times of scarcity or need, because you are willing to get along with considerably less. Even in times of plenty you will have a sense of discipline and will avoid wasting valuable resources that may be only temporarily abundant.

If you feel anger or resentment, you will hold it back because immediate expression will not seem to be the most practical way to deal with the situation. Just be sure that it doesn't become part of a hidden reservoir of anger that will break out uncontrollably later on. Even though you have tremendous self-discipline and restraint now, you do have valid needs that have to be met eventually. Don't defer this gratification indefinitely, or there could be problems later on.

Mars Square Saturn

Under this transit it is necessary to proceed slowly and cautiously. The more thoroughly and carefully you perform any task, the more chance there is that it will succeed. If you are careless it has very little hope of success. Usually this transit is a very frustrating and irritating time, when all your efforts to assert yourself are blocked in some way, more by a sense of internal inadequacy than by circumstances or other people. You may feel that your inner energies are struggling to assert themselves against your inhibitions and to get you moving in some way.

Fear is often an important factor preventing you from being as effective as you would like to be now. You think that you will fail because of your inadequacies as a person. The challenge is to recognize what you really are and what you can do without being overwhelmed by imaginary inner fears.

Authority figures, such as parents, employers or even persons whom you respect, may discourage you at this time. Somehow their remarks embody the very essence of your own worst suspicions about yourself. But you cannot derive your ultimate feelings about yourself from others, no matter how much you respect them. The purpose of this transit is to learn whether in your daily life you can act with true knowledge of who you are.

However, you are not likely to take negative reinforcement lying down, even if it comes from within yourself. The part of you that is struggling to break free from inhibitions will feel very angry at being held back. Consequently you are likely to be irritable and easily angered, although your inner doubts make you reluctant to show your anger openly. But no matter how you try to cover it up, everyone will be quite aware that you are seething inside.

The ambiguity that you feel during this transit makes it difficult to act successfully, for one part is holding on and the other part is trying to be free. The best way to handle this transit is to confront yourself and not try to initiate anything very grand in the outer world.

Mars Trine Saturn

This transit confers patience and willingness to do difficult and exacting work. In many other combinations, the energies of Mars are too difficult to control for work that requires concentration and skill. The bursts of energy that come with these transits are often too erratic and impulsive. But with this transit, the Mars energy is given off at a very controlled and regular pace, so you can direct it to any task that you must do and keep it concentrated there.

Therefore, this is a good time to do any work that you have to keep on plugging at, even though it isn't rewarding. Saturn does not demand that work be glamorous or instantly rewarding. It is satisfied simply to meet the demands of the day.

If this transit comes during a period that is otherwise difficult, it guarantees that for the moment at least you will be able to cope with your situation, no matter how difficult it becomes.

Intellectual or physical work that requires great attention to detail is favored by this influence. Intricate work with mathematics requiring perseverance rather than skill, fine detailed art work, and working with metals or stone are all examples of this kind of labor.

You will do any task very carefully. You never have to do the same job twice, and you will win at least modest credit for your careful work. Under the best circumstances you will win great credit from your superiors and may even get a promotion. And others will feel that you deserve the promotion because you have worked so diligently to get it.

As you work, your goals will be rather modest and very carefully defined. Because you know exactly what you want, you will be able to get it. Your concerns are extremely practical now, and your first question about any matter is, "How useful is it?" or "What good is it?"

Nevertheless, this transit will help you to get to know yourself better. The close attention to detail that characterizes your way of seeing now will help you see yourself and your own reactions very clearly.

Mars Opposition Saturn

For many people, this is an extremely irritating transit, requiring great patience and forbearance as well as willingness to keep yourself in the background for a while. Also your relationships with others may not be as satisfying as usual during this time.

The problems that you are likely to encounter with this transit include the following: irritability, often justified by others' actions; a tendency toward a "slow burn" rather than explosive anger; annoying ego conflicts; and a general sense of inadequacy about yourself vis-a-vis others.

One particularly serious psychological problem that you may have to contend with now is that others will hit you in your psychological weak spots. Usually when someone does something that makes you mad, you simply get angry and say or do something about it. However, under this transit, the attack is made in such a way that you feel incapable of really hitting back, so you internalize the hurt and suffer accordingly, or at least that is what you want to do. But the proper response is to recognize that the other person's act has hurt you in some way and then to air your grievance. Holding in your anger will only make you feel more angry as well as inadequate.

Another characteristic of this transit is feeling lonely and cut off from others, as if you couldn't get through to them or make an impression. You feel inhibited when you are with others, especially if some decisive action is called for.

However, this transit is not entirely useless or negative, although most people find it difficult to handle. At this time you can do work that requires great concentration of energy and meticulous care. Also, if you have been working on a project of this sort, it is now approaching completion and reaching a critical culmination. Since the last conjunction transit of Mars to your natal Saturn, you have been building up something slowly and carefully that is now ready to be finished. But if at the last square transit (roughly six months ago), you experienced a major defeat connected with this project, its total collapse will become apparent now. Usually this happens because other people's aggressive actions have blocked your success, but also you did not prepare adequately for the challenges that any personal initiative must face.

At times this transit can signify illness, so it is not a good idea to strain your body unnecessarily. Try to relax and avoid situations that produce needless tension. Physical tension at this time can be quite debilitating and harmful to your health.

Mars Conjunct Uranus

No other transit is more conducive than this one to sudden upsets, rash behavior and surprising incidents. Energy seems to burst out all over the place and in surprising forms. It is very often difficult to make plans during this transit precisely because so much happens without any warning.

In its direct psychological expression, that is, when it is not sublimated or converted into a different form of energy, this transit indicates a sudden desire to assert your freedom, to kick away all limitations and break free. It is a transit of rebellion and often indicates difficulties with others who may try to limit you in some way. Your relationships with authority figures are not likely to be very good, unless they are willing to give you a lot of room to do what you want.

You tend to act rashly and impulsively now, and in so doing you may set yourself up for an accident. You move so fast that you may overlook a critical danger that can affect your movements. This is not an immutable fate, however; if you have an accident under this transit, it is the direct result of your own carelessness. Usually this transit passes without a serious accident, but you should especially avoid working with dangerous tools, sharp instruments and iron or steel for these few days, particularly if you are feeling at all angry and resentful toward someone. If you are, take it out on them verbally, not on yourself by accident.

Under certain conditions, for instance, other horoscope indications of health problems, this transit can signify the need for an operation, but that is not a routine manifestation of it.

A positive use of this energy would be to begin a totally new and innovative project that consumes a great deal of energy and that will be largely identified with you when it is completed. You need to assert your individuality at this time, and this is a constructive way of doing it.

Mars Sextile Uranus

This transit will make you feel rather restless and impatient with your daily routine and inclined to seek out new experiences and activities. This impulse is ·not so uncontrollable that it will seriously disrupt your life, but you will be driven to make a number of changes in your daily routine that introduce some excitement.

Your thinking is much more impulsive and changeable than usual under this influence. On the one hand, this makes you rather unpredictable and even unreliable, as far as the people around you are concerned. But it also gives you the capacity to break out of the rut, both psychologically and in your activities. You are able to see fresh new viewpoints and to think originally. More to the point, you are able to make practical use of your new insights in everyday life.

In your drive for new experiences, you may also seek out new friendships or associate with your more exciting and stimulating friends, persons you don't normally associate with because they are too unsettling or unpredictable. Now you are in just the mood for that kind of personality.

You are not particularly patient with restrictions, nor are you very disciplined about your work. In fact you tend to be erratic, valuing your own independence over discipline and order. Again, however, this is not likely to create serious problems, and indeed you should do things that are completely different from your usual routine at this time.

Mars Square Uranus

This transit represents a time of great restlessness and impulsiveness. Like all the Mars-Uranus transits, this one means that you want to be free of all restraints, and you may rebel quite actively against restrictions. It is also a time when you are challenged as to whether you can be yourself and whether you can periodically renew your life so that it doesn't become completely stale.

Your goal now should be to create a situation of ongoing creative change in your life so that you don't have to create either a sudden and total revolution or live with a situation that doesn't change at all. Don't wait until circumstances have become totally intolerable before you try to reform them. If you do, you will exhibit the worst attributes of this transit — impulsiveness, rashness and complete disregard for your obligations.

Authority figures and close relationships, especially old ones from the past, are most likely to be the objects of your revolt, if you feel it necessary to rebel. You will be much more easily angered than usual, because you quickly interpret everything as a threat to your ego. Above all else, you feel that you must assert your ego in your own highly individual way. And if you have been unconscious of the need for creative change in your life, you are likely to be quite explosive. Sometimes, however, the "explosions" happen *to* you, which is a sign from your environment that you need to break away from something, although what that is may not be at all obvious. An accident can be the sign of frustrated ego energies transmuted into destructive powers.

Some persons, however, are always aware of the need to make changes in their lives to prevent it from becoming dead and lifeless. If you are one of these, this transit will be a time of unexpected disruptions that test your new way of living. But you can quite easily survive this test, if you are aware of what you have been doing and why. In fact you may even find a new opportunity to become more free and less structured, but only if you are capable of seeing the possibilities behind the mask of apparent disruption. Certainly you should not deal with new situations in old ways. New challenges require new solutions, which you will have to keep in mind during this transit.

Mars Trine Uranus

This will be a time of new activities and new encounters, some quite unexpected, that will generate both excitement and personal growth. You are not satisfied with your daily routine under this influence, which signifies a time when you can break away from the routine and introduce into your life fresh elements that will keep you alive psychologically.

Personal inhibitions often keep people from doing many things that they would like to do. With this transit you will find the courage to break free of these inhibitions, at least for a while, and thereby gain new freedom. Also at this time you may be liberated from many of the duties and obligations that have prevented you from doing what you want.

If others try to discourage you or keep you from having an experience that you want, you will pay little attention to them. Although you are aware that there may be unpleasant consequences if things don't go just right, you are willing to take the risk. In fact, taking risks gives you a greater feeling of being alive than you usually have.

As a consequence of all this, you can do some quite extraordinary things under this transit. Yet the energies are modulated enough that they are not difficult to control. You can break down barriers in your life without having to destroy everything impulsively. Nor do you feel the need to lash out blindly against restrictions and authority figures, as is the case with other Mars-Uranus transits.

In whatever you do, you will have the chance to show off aspects of yourself that others may not have known you had. You may not have known about them yourself. Consequently this is a transit of personal growth and self-discovery that can be quite significant in your psychological development, as well as being positively exciting and interesting.

Mars Opposition Uranus

Like most opposition transits, this one has two sides. Most commonly it makes you strike out rashly against people who seem to have held you back in some way or who have angered you consistently in the past. Or you may suddenly act impulsively to escape duties and obligations that circumstances have imposed upon you.

Most frequently this transit signifies the explosive release of tension through sudden anger against someone, especially persons close to you. These people will make you feel restless and irritable, and you will blow up at them easily. Expect to have feelings of great impatience.

You may also experience this transit in projected form; that is, you may have to contend with someone who makes a sudden move against you. An enemy or some person who frequently acts against your interests may disrupt your life at this time. Unexpected ego conflicts are common with this transit, as are sudden disruptive events that force you to alter your plans completely. If you are not the agent of creative change in your life, this transit will bring change in the form of disruptive circumstances.

On the other hand, this transit can represent a time when your efforts to liberate yourself from unnecessary and inhibiting restrictions start to succeed. Now you can really feel that you are becoming free of these bonds. Your life may take a new tack that represents a radically new direction for you. If you are prepared and have consciously tried to bring about this situation, this will be a very good time, for you will be able to act with more freedom and self-determination. But you can expect considerable resistance from others, and it will not be easy. The actions you take in response to other people's resistance will force you to face very important challenges about six months from now, at the next square transit of Mars to Uranus. Keep working, for your efforts to expand and liberate your life are not finished. The process will continue for some time, but this period is one of the most important.

Unfortunately most of us are too attached to our life restrictions to take full advantage of the positive side of this transit, and some will suppress its energy completely. This can result in physical disturbances that could require surgery. Other people will act impulsively and unconsciously, thereby creating the likelihood of an accident.

Mars Conjunct Neptune

This is a very peculiar transit and is usually accompanied by strange feelings. You are likely to feel extremely irritable and itchy without quite knowing why. And at the same time you may feel discouraged and incapable of doing anything useful. Feelings of weakness and inferiority are quite common with this transit, the result of Neptune's ego-denying quality in conflict with the essentially egoistic nature of Mars. It is best not to take these feelings too seriously.

You should be careful to avoid any kind of Neptune-dominated activity during this period, including actions that are ill-thought-out or based on personal delusions rather than on the facts. Make sure that you know what you are doing under this transit. Better yet, don't start anything new, except for the kinds of activities mentioned below. Also you should be careful of people who appeal to you through your favorite ideals or delusions and then take you for a ride. Your delusions may be the basis of someone else's success.

This transit is good for any activity that is totally selfless and involves serving others, such as charity work, working in a hospital or institution or in the context of a religious or spiritual group, or even working wholly and consciously for someone else's interests (as opposed to being taken advantage of). These activities are the exception to the rule that you shouldn't begin anything now. However, you must be certain that you are not working for secret and selfish advantage through these activities. If you are, it will come to naught. Neptune is quite rigorous about denying one's ego.

On the physical level, you should be careful not to abuse your body during this period. Your energy level will probably be rather low anyway, and if you push yourself too hard, you will physically exhaust yourself and possibly bring on an illness. You may be subject to infections, ranging from pimples or other small infections to full-scale fevers, but this problem can be minimized quite easily by simply taking good care of yourself.

Mars Sextile Neptune

Under this transit the demands of the ego are not very great, and you are able to see the world around you with greater sensitivity. Also you are more perceptive to the needs of your friends and neighbors and more inclined to help them. Your greatest fulfillment will come through activities that benefit others. You will enjoy being involved in group activities for charity or working in hospitals or institutions for sick or disadvantaged people. Working with a religious or spiritual group is also likely.

This is a good time to retire by yourself and think about your life or meditate. You don't feel an urgent need to do any particular thing right now, so you can be free to reflect quietly upon the quality of your life. Indeed, your physical energy is likely to be rather low during this transit, although not so low that you are in danger of illness or extreme fatigue. This is a good time to relax.

You may find it gratifying to study psychic or occult literature and see what these subjects have to offer you. Because demanding ego drives are detrimental in these disciplines, this is a good time to study them.

The insights you gain under this transit may very well alter your goals. You may learn that a course of action that you have been following has served no real purpose at all, even in terms of ego-gratification. With this insight you can adopt a more enlightened course of action that may also be spiritually superior.

Mars Square Neptune

During this time most people have to deal with feelings of doubt, discouragement and inadequacy. Also you may find yourself unpleasantly confronted by the consequences of past actions that you hoped would simply go away. The challenge is to confront them without caving in and feeling hopeless. Whenever this transit occurs, about every six months, you will question whether you are doing what you should with your life. The temptation is to decide that you are not, and to give up. Others may try to convince you that you are on the wrong course and give you very demoralizing advice. Of course, you may in fact be wrong in some area, and there you should change course. But you must avoid the tendency to cave in. Evaluate what you are doing in your own terms, not someone else's, and decide whether you are acting properly in various matters. Make the decision either way without self-recrimination and give yourself the credit you deserve for handling it yourself.

At a time like this you may be tempted to take a devious course of action in the face of adversity. Mars-Neptune can mean "deceitful actions." But taking the easy way out will not reinforce your position at all, because you will have to face even more discouraging consequences as a result.

Your physical energies are so low at this time that you may not feel like getting out of bed in the morning. You won't want to do as much as you should under this transit, but it is hard to relax now, and you don't feel good about resting either. Don't try to force yourself into doing something you don't really have the energy to do. Also try to avoid confrontations with others, because they will probably be demoralizing, and you are not likely to settle the problem.

Excessive physical strain should be avoided, because your body is more subject than usual to minor infections, chills and fever. Allergies can often be a problem under this transit, if you have a tendency toward them.

If you conserve your energies and confront your own fears, you will have accomplished the most useful tasks possible under this transit.

Mars Trine Neptune

Under this Mars transit your energy is best expressed by useful activities whose principal goal is helping others rather than yourself. This is also a time when you may become involved in a spiritual search to learn how you and all other people relate to each other and to the universe.

This is one of the few Mars transits that does not create high physical energies. In fact you may feel like doing very little, and certainly you will not be very self-assertive. But you are able to work with a spirit of true self-sacrifice and a desire to help others. Although your own ego drives are relatively weak at this time, you won't feel weak and inferior, as you may during other Mars-Neptune transits. Instead, you are more conscious of other people's needs and wants, because your own ego needs aren't very great now.

You are also capable of getting along with relatively little, because your desire nature is not very strong and you view life with considerably more detachment than usual. For this reason, this is a good time to look at your life and world objectively to see what it really is without judging or condemning. You may become involved in work with religious or spiritual groups at this time or in charitable or social-service work in hospitals or with poor and disadvantaged persons. The only problem to watch out for is the temptation to view yourself as a kind of "savior" helping those who are lower or worse off than yourself. Neptune can always create illusions, and you may think you are being totally unselfish when you are really on one of the strongest but subtlest ego trips of all.

Nevertheless, you can work with less real concern for yourself and your own needs now than under any other transit, and it is always good to do this kind of charitable work (in the highest sense of the term) at some time.

Mars Opposition Neptune

Like the transit of Neptune by conjunction, the opposition transit is usually rather debilitating. You are likely to feel discouraged and inadequate in the face of life's daily demands. Your physical energies are low, and you may set yourself up for illness if you are not careful. Avoid any situation that will place undue stress upon your body, because you don't have the resistance that you usually have. Infections and fevers are a possibility if you let your body get run down.

Encounters with others may be especially discouraging. Be careful that people whom you have to deal with at this time represent themselves truthfully. Others will probably try to deceive you and if they do, the results could be even more discouraging. Don't let your desire to have things your way cloud your ability to see what is really happening, especially with people.

At the same time don't become involved in any devious action yourself. You are not likely to be especially lucky at such schemes, and you may not want to face the consequences in the future.

In situations involving a close partner, such as your spouse or business partner, there may be extremely poor communications, resulting in misunderstandings and feelings of anger and mistrust.

During this time you may have to face the unpleasant consequences of past actions that you would rather avoid. You will be greatly tempted to turn your back and pretend that they didn't happen. You may even be tempted to take refuge in drugs or alcohol, but this is not the proper course. You have to bury your ego for awhile and take a good look at your past actions. Face them and take whatever action is necessary. You may not feel good about this now, but the situation will improve later on.

Avoid using drugs except on a doctor's prescription. Your body is negatively sensitive to drugs at this time, and you may have unpleasant side effects. Allergies also tend to kick up under this transit.

Working alone and in seclusion on some projects is favored by this transit, and you may even be able to bring such a project to a successful conclusion. However, this is not the right time to announce your results to the world. For some reason you probably would not get the credit you deserve. This transit also favors social work and other activites in the interests of other people.

Mars Conjunct Pluto

With this transit you will be tempted to take over and run whatever is happening around you. This transit is a strong stimulus to any kind of ambition, but the danger is that its energy can be rather violent and disruptive. It represents a ruthless burst of ego energy that does not take kindly to limitation. And it is not only that you will try to have power over others, but that you may also be the vicitim of someone else's power play. In cases of violent assault, this or a similar transit usually occurs in both the victim's and the assailant's chart. But that is not a typical occurrence with this transit. One indication is not enough to account for an incident of violence, and you needn't anticipate it. However, it gives you some idea of the strength of these energies. You should be warned, though, to avoid dangerous neighborhoods during the few days that this transit is in effect.

Positively speaking, this transit is excellent for doing any kind of heavy work, particularly if it involves making major changes of any kind whatever. Even if you think you are totally uninterested in power, you will get a great deal of satisfaction out of having and using power. There is no reason why you shouldn't be able to use this power creatively. Just don't try to kid yourself that you aren't thinking of your own interests during this transit. You are, and there is nothing wrong in that unless your interests conflict with everyone else's.

There is danger now of severe ego conflicts, of which violent assault is an extreme example. Your strong energies attract people who have similar energies, and before you know it, you may have quite a power struggle on your hands. As forcefully but benignly as possible, you must convince others that your interests and their interests are interdependent.

Whatever task you take on, you will be able to work long and hard to accomplish it. You have the opportunity either to accomplish a great deal or to wreak havoc, if you are not conscious of your own energies under this transit.

Mars Sextile Pluto

This is a good time to make moves toward realizing important goals in your life. But you will have to make some changes in the course of action that you originally planned. Don't worry, your new plans will undoubtedly be an improvement over the old ones. You work zealously toward your goals now, and you should have enough energy to carry you through against any opposition that you might encounter.

This is also a good time to work with others for group goals and objectives, because Mars-Pluto energies are much more effective when used cooperatively than when they are used for purely personal ends.

You may have to strive very hard to get anywhere now, but if so, your goals when you do reach them will be more permanent and far reaching. If you are unclear about what you are doing in some area, this is a good time to look inside yourself to find out what you really want to do. You should not and probably cannot move until you are clear about your objectives. In examining yourself, you may discover hitherto unknown psychological forces that you can use to gain your ends. A considerable change in self-understanding may be one consequence of this transit.

If you are at all clear about your purpose and if you understand yourself at all, this transit should assure you of success in any undertaking that you become involved in now. Proceed full steam ahead and do not worry. Just avoid stepping upon other people's toes unnecessarily, because that can have dangerous consequences later on.

Mars Square Pluto

This can be a time for creatively transforming the world around you, or it can be a time of fierce power struggles and disagreements. These are the two poles that this transit swings between. Like all aspects of Mars in transit to Pluto, this one arouses your ambitions and makes you want to get ahead. Your energy level is very high, and you can use it to get a lot of work done. But unfortunately you will have a tendency to go about your work in such a way that you arouse great opposition from the people you confront. Or you may have to confront someone else's energies. In any case you will have to deal with serious challenges to your ego energies, which may result in your taking a different course of action from what you originally intended.

Be sure that you haven't left any loose ends in what you have been doing up till now. If you have, they will trip you up and cause you to suffer defeat. Avoid the temptation to act ruthlessly or underhandedly toward others no matter how angry you are or how much you feel that they deserve to be beaten. Transit cycles involving Pluto have a strange way of producing total destruction of your own ends if you take illegitimate shortcuts. However, the consequences of your deceptive actions will not be apparent until the next time transiting Mars either conjoins or opposes your natal Pluto.

This transit can also signify a serious conflict between individual energies and the energies of a group. In this case you may be a member of the group or you may be the individual. In either situation, this confrontation will be a significant test of the strength of your intentions. Depending upon how badly you may want to do something, you will either fight for it harder or give up altogether. As you strive to get ahead, be careful that those in power over you do not oppose you. They are stronger now, and you would probably lose in a confrontation.

As with other Mars-Pluto combinations, the energies of this transit can lead to being the victim of someone else's ruthlessness, even to the point of violent assault in rare cases. Therefore you should avoid dangerous places and violent people. It isn't likely, but it isn't worth the risk either.

Mars Trine Pluto

This is a good time to make reforms in your life and to become more effective in changing the world around you. This transit is often a great stimulus to your ambitions, but it is subtle enough so that you don't make others feel threatened, as so often occurs with other Mars-Pluto transits.

You should formulate objectives for long-range efforts at this time. Find out what you want to change about yourself and your world and get to work on those changes. The energy you have now will allow you to keep up a sustained effort for a long time. At work you may be given an opportunity to wield more power and thereby be more effective personally. However, Plutonian energies are not readily subordinated to the demands of the ego. If you work solely for your own benefit under this transit, you will sow the seeds of your own undoing when Mars and Pluto form more stressful combinations in your horoscope. You should work for your own good and for the social good by identifying your own needs with those of society. If you do this, you will be given considerable credit for what you do.

Sometimes this transit brings an opportunity to understand your motivations and to operate from this new understanding. This can lay the framework for a creative transformation of the self, in other words, the birth of a new you. Transits to Pluto often signify major changes in your life that lead to growth and maturity.

As long as you keep in mind the greater needs of society as you proceed under this transit, you have an opportunity for many gains and successes. Use it as creatively as possible.

Mars Opposition Pluto

At this time your efforts to affect others and to transform conditions around you may meet with considerable resistance. Nevertheless you strive to get ahead and are prepared to work hard. This transit can represent the culmination of successful effort, or it can be a time when the opposition becomes so fierce that you have to give up.

This transit is a powerful sign of severe interpersonal power struggles. The chief danger is that either you or your opponent in a struggle will act with absolutely no regard for ethics or for the other person's feelings and situation. This combination acts ruthlessly and relentlessly. You can, of course, do something about your own actions, but it is hard to control the other person's. The best course to take is to make your position as secure as possible and enlist the aid of as many people as you can. Resist the temptation to go it alone, because that will bring out the negative side of this transit.

If you are tempted to try to gain control over others, be very careful. Eventually you might find yourself opposed by everyone whom you have ever tried to rule.

Nevertheless, your energies are high under this transit, and you should express them by making creative and positive changes in your life. If you try to suppress these energies completely, it is more likely that you will have to contend with someone else.

Under extreme circumstances this transit can signify acts of violence. While you should not necessarily expect this, you could encounter some kind of physical assault. For this reason, avoid situations that involve real danger, bad neighborhoods and the like. Also avoid making others so angry that they will try to strike out against you. This is a greater possibility now than at other times.

Mars Conjunct Midheaven

This transit stimulates the ego drives, both positively and negatively, more than any other transit, so be a bit careful. At this time you are very certain who you are, and you are not about to let anyone tell you otherwise. You may express this energy as a strong desire to work, and indeed this is an excellent transit for work, especially if you get the credit for it. This is not a good time to work behind the scenes for someone else. You are likely to have serious conflicts with anyone who tries to take credit for what you have done. If your employers do not give you adequate scope, you may very well feel very angry toward them.

Beware of acting impulsively or from purely egotistical motives. While it is necessary to assert yourself, don't overdo it. You will provoke opposition from people who try to cut you down, and you will not further your own interests at all. Carefully planned activity, however, can bring you great success. Instead of aiming your ego energy at everyone else, aim it at tasks that have to be done.

Unless you are given charge of a group of coworkers, it is probably best to work alone, because you are not inclined to think in group terms now. You can work much better by yourself, and you don't want to waste time trying to relate to others.

Whatever you do, you will know what you want to get out of it, and you will drive toward that end with great vigor. If anyone or anything gets in the way, you will probably become angry. Make sure that you have plenty of freedom to move.

The traditional symbolism of Mars indicates that this transit is favorable for the following activities; athletic competition; working with metals, especially steel and iron; hard physical labor; daring work that requires independent thought and action; work that requires you to be original and innovative; or any other work that depends upon your independent energies.

Mars Sextile Midheaven

This is a time of considerable self-confidence and courage. You pursue your objectives with greater assurance than usual and in a way that does not alienate other people. You are able to reconcile your personal interests with those of the people around you, so this is a good time to take initiatives in your work and to get others to work with you.

Although you can work effectively with people, you do not feel dependent upon them. You present yourself as an independent, self-reliant person who is willing to help others and to serve the larger society. As a result you are able to obtain material backing from others, as well as moral support. You could never do this as easily when you feel that you *must* have the assistance of others in order to succeed. Your confidence in yourself makes people feel confident in you.

In general, the clarity with which you see your objectives enables you to plan very thoroughly and decisively. You plan a course of action and follow through on it directly. There is no need to act covertly or deviously. Direct and forthright action will always be the most successful way to attain your goals. When it is necessary, you do not shrink from a confrontation with someone, but if it is not necessary, you do not seek it out.

This transit is a sign of a healthy ego. You are not afflicted with the kinds of problems that arise when you feel doubtful, insecure or inadequate.

Mars Square Midheaven

This transit usually makes you feel quite aggressive and self-assertive. While this is hardly bad in itself, there is the possibility that you will overdo it and get into needless conflicts with others. Also you may think only of your own objectives and completely forget that it is important to get along with others. It is often best to work very hard by yourself now, without anyone to get in your way — at least that is how it will seem to you.

Conflicts are especially likely in your professional and domestic life or any area in which your ego is intimately involved. There will be less tension in areas that you are more detached about, where you are not so concerned with getting your way or achieving a particular objective. Disputes with superiors, persons in power or parents are quite likely, if you feel that they won't let you have your way.

The energy of this transit is impulsive. It comes rather explosively and may take on a life of its own. Its basic intent is to help you achieve a certain objective or make an impression on the world. But if you feel frustrated for any reason, the energy may be expressed in such a way as to work against your interests, as you would realize if you were in a calmer frame of mind. But in acting impulsively you just want to release the energy, and you do not care about the consequences. Thus you may start out with a clear goal and end up completely frustrating it.

If you can control yourself during this transit, it will help you accomplish a great deal of work and initiate projects that you might otherwise be reluctant to tackle, usually because you lack self-confidence. With this transit, self-confidence is usually high, although if your normal level of confidence is low, it may come out as irritability and peevishness instead of positive assertive energy. This may also happen if for some reason you can't release this energy and have to hold it in. This transit is particularly likely to cause trouble in your home if you hold in your anger at work but allow it to explode at home.

Mars Trine Midheaven

At this time you feel very self-assured and confident, and you will have the necessary material and physical resources to carry out whatever objectives you have in mind. If necessary, you work very hard to gather people who will work with you and to assure whatever backing you need.

You undertake every task with great zeal and energy. And you don't stand about waiting for someone to give you directions. You take the initiative yourself and finish the task swiftly. Also you will contribute everything you have to the effort. You are sufficiently confident of success that you are willing to take risks, and such risks are reasonably likely to turn out well. This process takes place in such a way that you learn more about yourself, and at the same time you are able to let others know clearly where you stand.

Under this transit, others will look to you for direction because you exude the energy of authority. People who lack your present confidence and energy will want you to supply what they lack.

Your physical energy is unusually high at this time. It is a good idea to incorporate some vigorous physical activity into your usual routine, for you may need to work off some of that energy. Sports or athletics may attract you more than usual.

Mars Opposition Midheaven

During this period your "light is hidden under a bushel" more than at other times. Your efforts to get ahead in business or professional life may meet with opposition that is very difficult to handle, and others may work against your personal advancement. This would also apply to activities that you work on with a group. You may feel very self-assertive, but somehow it just does not work out as you plan. The problem is that your energies are not turned toward the outer world. Instead they are turned inward toward yourself, your personal and home life. Here you can accomplish much more, if you apply yourself.

First of all, be aware of any tendency toward anger or irritability. This signifies tension in your personal life that you should attend to. However, you may find that the source of the tension is not something that is currently at work in your life. A current situation may have reactivated a memory or perhaps a psychological pattern from the past, which is causing you to feel defensive and argumentative. It is best to do whatever you can to bring this tension source to the surface. Don't merely repress the energies, for they will only surface on another Mars transit.

Ego energies are running rather high on the home front during this transit, and you may run into conflicts at home. Be careful not to step on the toes of the people you live with, but don't let them step on you either. You may have an argument or disagreement with one of your parents under this transit. The only problem to watch for is that arguments triggered by this transit tend to be rather unconscious; that is, each person argues as if programmed, not like a real, thinking person. Old patterns are activitated, and no one really addresses the current problem as a new and unique situation with its own special solution.

Many tensions and pressures in your personal life can be released at this time if you avoid the kind of trap described above. Try to get at the root of what is really wrong and deal with the truth.

Sometimes this transit can signify domestic accidents, so don't be careless.

Mars Conjunct Ascendant

The symbolism of this transit is self-assertion with regard to others. It is not enough that you are yourself and able to do your thing. With this transit, you have to show other people that you are someone to be reckoned with. Or you may have to defend yourself against an attack from someone, whether or not you have provoked it. This transit is most likely to produce conflicts, anger and resentment. The best thing to do, if a conflict situation arises, is to have it out immediately. If you try to keep things cool for the sake of propriety, you may only create a fund of resentment in yourself or the other person that will boil over at an even less convenient time. But if you deal with it now, the air will clear.

On the other hand, you also have the chance to show the world what you can do. You may have the opportunity to direct others in some kind of joint project. And as long as you pay attention to the feelings of the people you work with and try to win them over to your group aims, you will be very successful at such endeavors. But if you merely try to dominate the other people in such a situation, which is a danger with this transit, you will foul it up completely and create anger and disputes.

If you do not find a satisfactory outlet for your energies at this time, you will be easily angered, resentful, irritable and quick to take offense. If you must blow up at somebody, make sure that you understand the real source of the conflict, so that it can be aired. All too often, conflicts occur over phony issues that are only symbols of a much more profound problem.

Rarely, this transit will signify an illness or accident, especially if you do not have an adequate outlet for your energies. You should indulge in vigorous physical activity and avoid physically debilitating situations. Avoid overstraining yourself, either now or especially before this transit. If you are in good physical condition as you come into this transit, your health will be all right during it.

It is a good idea to avoid sharp instruments and cutting tools now, because Mars signifies steel and cutting in general.

Mars Sextile Ascendant

This is an excellent transit for working with others in a team effort, as long as you are a leader within the team or are given a lot of independent initiative. It is also important that the people you work with are energetic and can do their share of the work. You would be very impatient with anyone who is slower or less energetic than yourself. Your physical energy level is likely to be high with this transit, and you are a bit impulsive, so you want things done quickly. Fortunately, with this transit you are likely to attract the kind of people you need. And if you do not, try to work alone.

With respect to your immediate environment, the surroundings that you encounter every day, you are likely to feel more self-assertive than usual. This can be a good time for telling people how you feel about anything, for you are not willing to let others get away with intruding on your rights. Usually the energy of this transit is mellow enough that you can make yourself clear without causing a fight. In fact, people will probably respect you for your honesty.

Although you are not looking for a fight with this transit, you will stand up for your rights. If you have to present a controversial point of view to a group of people, you should be able to present it forcefully enough to win their approval, if it has merit.

Obviously this transit is good for any kind of work that depends upon your personal effectiveness.

If you are with friends now, you will be happiest doing hard physical work or being very physically active. With the energy of this transit, you are not likely to be very happy just sitting around.

Mars Square Ascendant

This transit is likely to coincide with a stormy period in your personal relationships. There will probably be a difference between you and your partner about some personal objective that you both are very closely involved in. Or a difference in your background and conditioning will cause you and your partner to see a situation very differently. Associated with these problems is the problem of identifying so closely with your own point of view that you feel your personal honor depends on having your views triumph. You are not likely to be in a compromising mood with this transit. Also it is possible that you will draw to yourself a person who behaves uncompromisingly, making agreement unlikely or difficult. Under this transit any kind of team effort that you become involved in is not likely to work. If you can possibly arrange it, try to work by yourself on a project in which you have the total initiative.

In personal relationships, especially in marriage, this transit can coincide with disputes. The only way to handle this is for each of you to make your position clear to the other, but don't try to resolve it now. If you feel you must blow up at each other, it is probably best to do so and release the tensions. This can often help out when a marriage becomes difficult. In fact, if you blow up more often, the conflicts become less acute, unless the two of you are really incompatible. Repressing the anger you feel now will only lead to a more violent outbreak later, with disastrous consequences and even physical violence.

On the other hand, if you can work out your aggressions by yourself, you will be able to get a great deal of work done. But even here there is a danger. This is not a good time to do dangerous work or work with dangerous machinery. There is the real possibility that you will act impulsively and injure yourself, unless you take every precaution and make sure that you are really calm.

If you do not express the energy of this transit consciously, you may experience a period of illness, especially minor infections and irritations.

Mars Trine Ascendant

This is a time of self-assurance and confidence in dealing with others. Without being overly aggressive or pugnacious, you get your point across to people in such a way that they respect you. Also you have a great deal of physical energy, so that you feel like taking part in some kind of vigorous activity. If you are at all athletically inclined, this is an excellent transit.

In most areas of your life, you are able to act much more decisively than usual, especially in dealing with others. You know where you stand, and you ask others to let you know where they stand. And despite your self-assertiveness, you are able to create a balance in a group so that everyone benefits from working together and no one feels dissatisfied.

Under this transit you will want to enlarge the scope of your activities somewhat. It will not be enough to express your energies as you have in the past. At this time you want to find new expressions, and you will look for people to share in this. For this reason you want to be with active people who have enough energy to go along with your plans.

On the physical level, this is usually a period of good health, but it is important to remember that using your energy will have a very positive effect on your body. Also, if you don't use this energy now, it can build up within you and be expressed as irritation. This can lead either to disputes in relationships or to health problems the next time that Mars makes a more difficult transit to your Ascendant.

Mars Opposition Ascendant

This is the most conflict-prone of all transits! The point opposite the Ascendant, also called the Descendant, signifies open enemies and conflicts, among other things. Anything you try to do now is likely to encounter stiff opposition from anyone who has any reason to oppose you. You will have to fight for what you want, unless you are very clever at wheeling and dealing behind the scenes. Ego energies run very high in all your direct confrontations with others, and in many cases all you can do is to be prepared for the confrontations and to release whatever tensions there might be. There is a serious conflict between your need to assert yourself and your need for relationships.

Even partnerships that usually run quite smoothly can be a problem. You may have to contend with a partner or spouse who is trying to dominate you, or you may be the one who wants to dominate. This results in the most intense ego struggle. You will have to be somewhat conciliatory when dealing with a partner, as opposed to an "open enemy" as described above. It is possible to transmute the energy of this transit into an extremely energetic cooperative effort, but only if both of you are certain that your best interests are being served. Neither of you will want to play second fiddle to the other.

Physical activity with others is an extremely creative way of handling the energies involved in this transit. Team sports are particularly recommended because they encourage cooperation and use the self-assertive and the aggressive energies of this transit.

As with the transit by conjunction, there is some danger now of accident or illness, so be careful, especially if you are feeling generally frustrated. Avoid sports that are unusually dangerous and be careful of sharp instruments and cutting tools.

Chapter Nine

Jupiter

Significance of Transiting Jupiter

Jupiter is traditionally known as the "greater Benefic" and in old astrology was thought to produce nothing but good. And indeed a Jupiter transit is usually quite pleasant and often very beneficial. Life seems to flow more easily during a Jupiter transit, and whatever you set out to do usually succeeds just as you intended.

At the most fundamental level Jupiter signifies the individual reaching out to include more and more of the universe and its experience within himself or herself. It is a planet of growth and enlargement. In fact, at a trivial level Jupiter will sometimes just enlarge something or make an action grandiose or overdone. The effect of Jupiter's energy on your life can range from making you gain weight to enlarging your mind and consciousness.

Jupiter has a strong social dimension as well. It is concerned with the social "glue" that holds everything together. Thus it rules the law and the legal system, as well as persons in power and government officials, a function it shares with the Sun. One negative manifestation of certain Jupiter transits can be problems with the law. Of course, under other transits, Jupiter can confer legal power upon you.

The house that the transiting Jupiter is in indicates the area of life in which you are trying to grow and the means by which you are doing this. The process may be necessary growth that makes you a wiser and more successful person (in a philosophical sense), or it may be pathological growth — in other words, you are trying to get too much or go too far in this area. Wherever Jupiter transits, you should not take the matters ruled by that house at face value. The chances are that everything will work out very well, but you should always make sure that you aren't overdoing or going too far. Also it is important to avoid taking more than your share.

Planets in your natal chart that are transited by Jupiter represent energies in your personality that are working smoothly and attaining your objectives. But the warnings given above in connection with the houses apply here too. Do not overdo. One problem with Jupiter is that you should be careful about what you want, because you are likely to get it.

Nevertheless, most Jupiter transits are quite beneficial for the areas of your life that they relate to. Most people have an adequate dose of Saturn in them, which keeps them from going overboard with Jupiter. Even the square and opposition transit aspects, which are difficult with most planets, are fairly easy with Jupiter. However, those are the times when you must be careful not to do things in excess.

And Jupiter also signifies some of the highest aspects of your life — your overall life view, your attitudes toward religion, and your sense of idealism. Jupiter can be a very consciousness-expanding influence.

So enjoy your Jupiter transits while exercising a little care. They could be the doorways to your objectives in life.

Jupiter in the First House

This transit is the beginning of a major cycle of growth in your life. While Jupiter is in this house, you should try to discover what you really are as an individual. You should get to know yourself and what you can really accomplish, because under this influence you feel more secure about yourself and the impression that you make upon others. You feel less need to withdraw from people or hide your talents. But you should not react to this transit by exaggerating your own importance either. Look at the truth of who you are; that should be entirely adequate.

This is also a time for learning and gaining new experience. All this is part of your present need for growth, which affects not only yourself, but also the way you deal with the world as a whole. At this time it is very important to outgrow childish attitudes or prejudices that may have hung over from your childhood, parochial concerns that are not adequate to understanding the world that you face now.

Persons and resources are likely to be drawn to you now, and you should take constructive advantage of them. In other words, anyone whom you become involved with at this time should benefit from the association as much as you do. Only through mutual help will you really achieve growth.

The spiritual dimension of your life should be greater now. The concrete and tangible aspects of the world are not enough; you have to know the deeper dimensions of life as well; otherwise the rest becomes meaningless.

This year should be quite fortunate for you in personal terms. Your relationships and encounters with others should work to your advantage consistently, assuming that some more powerful influence isn't upsetting this one. Your increased self-confidence and poise should serve you well and enable you to increase the scope of your activities. But try not to be overbearing. Even if you score significant successes, don't delude yourself into thinking you have all the answers. You are still learning under this transit.

Jupiter in the Second House

This transit has traditionally been associated with making money or gaining wealth, and there is something to that, for you will attempt to grow in the sphere of material possessions and resources now. But in a larger sense, what you are doing at this time is actualizing in your life whatever it is that you value. If it is money or physical possessions that you value, that is the area you will try to increase in and through. Or if your values are more spiritual — involving ideas, a standard of justice, or whatever — you will attempt to increase this dimension of your life.

Obviously then it is very important at this time to understand how you use resources, because the chances are that you will indeed get more of whatever you want, within reason. Unfortunately there is great potential for mismanaging resources with this transit, if you are not clear about what you need and want. It is very easy to get so much of something that it runs your life instead of making your life more pleasant and fulfilling. This is particularly true of efforts to gain more money.

What you must do at this time in your life is to look at your overall goals honestly and see what you really must have in order to achieve them. It will be relatively easy to make the necessary changes in your resources to help attain your goals, so plan these changes wisely.

This is not a call for total asceticism. If you want to buy something that is very expensive, perhaps a bit self-indulgent, there is no reason why you should not go after it. Just make sure that you really want it, that it is not merely a symbol of something you think you want. Many people acquire possessions simply because they think they are expected to in order to show social status. To acquire for reasons of this sort would truly be a waste. Nevertheless, during this time material resources can be a great comfort, and you can derive a real and honest pleasure from them.

In a larger sense you will learn more about yourself at this time through encountering possessions and having to handle them. Managing the material world will be of great value in promoting self-understanding. For this reason, this is a good period in your life to invest money with a little self-restraint or to buy possessions either for enjoyment or for investment.

Jupiter in the Third House

The effect of this transit is to increase your contacts through and within your immediate surroundings. You will not have to go very far from your everyday world to find experiences that expand your perception of the world and increase your level of consciousness. This may manifest itself in several ways.

First of all, it is quite likely that through your everyday life you will receive an opportunity for advanced training in a field of study that could be useful to you. Your concern with communication will increase, and you may do some writing, even if that is not one of your usual activities. During this period, extended travel may be necessary for some reason, but you will come out of it understanding a lot more about your world.

Your relationships with relatives — brothers, sisters, cousins etc. — will be very good. It is quite possible that you may receive some kind of financial benefit from one of them, but that is not the only way they could benefit you.

Perhaps more important in the long run is the possible effect of this transit upon your mind and consciousness. Old thought patterns, attitudes that you have adopted more or less unconsciously or that you don't think very much about consciously, will be broadened and expanded. Your thinking will be less subject to the limitations imposed by these attitudes. Consequently your attitude toward the world around you will be much more generous, understanding and tolerant of other people's differences. You are less likely to be influenced by prejudices. Instead, you will want to know everything on the basis of your own experience.

Your plans for the future will be larger and more expansive. You will realize that many of the limitations that you thought were imposed from without are actually self-imposed. Also, in looking at the world, you take more factors into consideration and plan more effectively than you might at other times. Just be careful not to go to the opposite extreme and overdo it. Don't commit yourself to projects that you cannot possibly fulfill.

As a general rule, communication with others is better than usual now. You are able to say what is on your mind, and you are less subject to failures of communication. At the same time you are frank and willing to talk about every aspect of a given problem, whether it relates to your emotional life or to some situation in the outer world.

Jupiter in the Fourth House

This is a time when you will seek inner peace and security. The fourth house is the house of all aspects of your innermost life — your home, your personal life, your family, your past and your innermost sense of self. Jupiter here will help you improve all of these areas of your life.

On an external level, you may express this transit by purchasing real estate or a new home. Land and houses are an external symbol of the desire for a stable inner world. Or you may expand, redecorate or otherwise improve your present home, thereby increasing its value. This is quite a good time to invest in real estate, even if you are not planning to live there.

This transit supports your domestic life, and during this period one or another domestic problem should be cleared up, usually because something new comes to light that helps you straighten things out. You feel generous and open to your family, and they respond to you in the same way. If you have any problems at all during this time, your family is where you should turn for solace. They will be able to help you. Your relationship with your parents is also good, and they may be a source of benefit to you in some way.

There are times in your life when you have no choice but to go out into the world and forge ahead. At this time, however, you have a choice. If you wish to go out into the world, your personal life will not cause problems that distract you from your quest. But it might be even better to concentrate your energies on your personal life rather than making a great effort to get ahead in the world. Now is a time when you can make your home, family and personal life more secure than ever and guarantee that it will always be a source of support and comfort. This is the time to put down roots, if you are ever going to. You will find that having a real sense of belonging to a place, a community and family will help prevent many psychological crises when circumstances get rough in the future. If you handle this transit properly, you are not likely to ever feel alone, lost or alienated. Security in life is a real need, and now is a time when you can do a great deal to gain it.

At the most psychological level, this transit helps to increase your sense of inner confidence. You are more in touch with your inner self now than at most times, and you are able to handle truths about yourself that you are normally reluctant to face, thereby preventing them from becoming a problem in the future. What you know you are is seldom a problem. The difficulties stem from what you are afraid that you are.

Jupiter in the Fifth House

At this time your creative self-expression grows as never before. You find the courage to be yourself and to express yourself to others without fear or apology but without selfishness or egotism. This has the immediate effect of improving your relationships with others tremendously. This transit by itself is not usually enough to bring about a sexual relationship, but it certainly helps one that begins at this time. Because you don't feel that you must hold yourself back from another person, it is possible to have a truly authentic relationship with someone, in which each of you knows who the other is.

If you have children, this transit will improve your relationship with them, and there will probably be many occasions when you feel proud of them. And you are able to give them whatever they need for their own development without feeling in any way diminished.

Your creative potential is also increased. If you have any artistic aptitude at all, this transit may very well bring it into play. You will produce more work, and it will be completely expressive of yourself. Also if you are working in a creative or artistic field, you may possibly make more money than usual with your art or craft.

Love relationships will also expand the range of experience in your life. You may encounter persons from a radically different background or from a different country. But no matter what their origin, any relationship at this time will teach you more about the world than you ever dreamed possible.

But the most important point about this transit is that it brings you the opportunity for personal growth and increased wisdom, along with greater freedom of self-expression. You do not feel it necessary to hide from the world anymore, even if you did before. In fact there may even be a danger that you will act in an overbearing manner. This depends largely upon your attitude prior to this transit. Most people will respond only with a healthy increase in self-assurance and self-expression.

Jupiter in the Sixth House

This is a very good time for any kind of work and for fulfilling duties that contribute to your personal growth. This transit indicates good health, with one exception as noted below.

Very often the demands of this house come into conflict with one's personal growth and, especially, freedom, for this is the house of fulfillment of duty, responsibility and service. One's ego needs are gratified here only at a level that most people cannot readily understand. But with Jupiter in this house you are able to make progress in the world precisely because of these matters, and you realize this. Work is very fulfilling and enjoyable to you now, giving you a sense of purpose and a structure for your life. Quite often this comes about through an improved job situation, better working conditions, or even a new job with better pay or opportunities for self-fulfillment. But you are not likely to advance to a position of greater power or standing at this time. This is a period of work, and you will achieve the most satisfaction simply by doing the work as well as you can and to the highest possible standards. You are quite ready to take on even more work if you can, and even though you probably won't be promoted, you will certainly gain the esteem of your superiors and of those under you, which will ultimately put you in a good position.

This is usually an excellent period for health, because Jupiter gives your body physical strength and vitality. However, you do have to be careful about gaining weight. In both the fortunate and less fortunate meanings of the term, this is a growth transit on the physical level. If for some reason your body has to heal or recover from an illness, this transit will assist the process. But you should be careful of fat or sweet foods, for they will not only cause you to gain weight, but they are not very good for your pancreas. Avoid any kind of overindulgence.

Jupiter in the Seventh House

During this period your intimate one-to-one encounters with other people can show you aspects of yourself and of the world around you. By and large this transit favors the formation and maintenance of all kinds of partnerships, including marriage. Although this transit by itself does not especially indicate marriage, it does make a marriage work very well at this time.

During this transit you will encounter people who can help you out in various ways. You approach all relationships with the idea that you and the other person should help each other. You are not inclined to go it alone now, and you would be well advised not to. You very much need another person's assistance, not because you are a weak individual, but because the other person fulfills your individuality.

This is also a good time to call in a professional for any kind of assistance, especially a lawyer, but also a doctor or other consultant, as well as personal counselors. If you have to go to court at this time, especially in a civil suit, the outcome should be favorable, although it is important to make sure that you have every angle covered. Don't take this transit for granted, for you might overlook some detail that could trip you up. Also don't try to get more than your due, nor overestimate what you are to get. That could get you into trouble. As with every other Jupiter transit, this one requires a certain amount of moderation in order to get the most out of it.

Since Jupiter refers to foreign places and persons, this transit could indicate a partnership or close relationship with a foreigner. Or it could indicate a relationship with someone whose background is sufficiently different from yours that you have to expand your views and your understanding of the world simply to deal with him or her. Any intimate relationship at this time will certainly have a consciousness-expanding effect upon you. In other words, the relationship won't permit you to continue in a narrow frame of reference.

If you marry under this influence, your partner is likely to be a slightly older person who has established himself or herself in the world. Your respect for this person is one of the main factors that attracts you. This is a sign of a person more experienced than yourself.

Jupiter in the Eighth House

Traditionally this transit indicates an inheritance. However, this transit occurs several times in the course of everyone's life, whether or not you get an inheritance. But even though that old delineation is not usually applicable, it is based on correct principles, because with Jupiter in this house, you are likely to benefit from other people's resources. Consequently this is a good time to enter a relationship in which you and another person have to pool your resources, such as a business partnership. This is also a good time to request a loan from a bank, unless there is another transit at the same time that negates this reading. In general, other people are more than usually willing to help you out in some way.

On another level, there will be many powerful but fortunate changes in your life at this time. It may not always be obvious, but any sweeping change that happens now will be for the best and will make your life richer and more rewarding in the long run. It will also give you a much greater understanding of the psychological patterns that operate in your life. If you have recently been through a time of psychological stress or are encountering one now, this transit will help the healing process within you.

Sometimes this transit can indicate a time of religious and spiritual regeneration, what used to be called a "conversion experience." Certainly you would derive great benefit from studying occult and mystical literature at this time in your life, especially if you feel very troubled or distraught.

Jupiter in the Ninth House

This house is a very good position for Jupiter. At this time the perspective of your life can be expanded tremendously. You may have opportunities for extensive travel, for learning and also for teaching others in either a formal or an informal setting. Your desire to learn, however, is very great, and you will probably do much more reading than usual and about more abstract and profound subjects. Philosophy, metaphysics and religion are typical studies associated with this transit. And you will encounter these not only as books, but as real issues in your life. Your need is for real and useful knowledge about your world.

This is a good time to become involved in a human-potential effort or some other consciousness-raising group. There are many such groups around now, and you should pick the one that seems most suitable for you.

If you are a writer or have any desire to be one, this is an excellent time for it, because the ninth house is the house of publishing and other communications media that reach the world at large.

As you are exposed to a broader world, your views on life will change. This transit is a very powerful maturing influence in the most positive sense; in other words, you become wiser now than at any other time in your life. But you have to be fundamentally open to this process. If you think you know all the answers already, this transit may only make you smug or self-righteous, which would be a terrible waste of this energy.

Along with the possibility of travel to foreign countries, there is also the likelihood that you will become increasingly involved with foreign persons or lands either in your business or in your personal life.

The main effect of this transit is to make your consciousness grow so much that you can no longer live with your old prejudices and beliefs. You must *know* rather than just believe, and the more you can replace belief with knowledge, the better off you will be.

Jupiter in the Tenth House

During this transit your attention will turn toward your profession, career, social status and reputation. It is a time when you will try very hard to move ahead in any or all of these areas, and any reasonable effort should result in considerable progress. For most people this is a time of getting ahead, but you should observe several cautions.

First of all, it is very important to avoid being overbearing, domineering and arrogant. Some people have trouble with superiors at this time, because this transit can indicate an inflated ego, that is, thinking you are much more than you are without anything to back it up. If you start thinking that you are truly significant or special, sit down and review your real accomplishments to see if they justify your feeling. But even if they do, be careful not to behave in a way that will cause others to resent you and even work against you when this transit is over.

However, this is not a general problem, for most people have been taught to underrate their achievements. In that case this transit is likely to signify recognition for what you have accomplished. You can expect a promotion at work, public recognition, or the esteem of your contemporaries during this time, as long as you don't fall into the trap described above. You will also feel more confident about yourself, and this may be one of the few times in your life when you are really in touch with what you can do.

You may also experience other effects of this transit. For example, you may have to travel in connection with your work, or you may have increased dealings with foreign persons. It is also possible that you may change to a field of work that pertains to the nature of Jupiter. These fields include medicine and healing, the law, higher education and travel. In this case you should not expect the same recognition that you would if you stayed in your established line of work.

Jupiter in the Eleventh House

At this time your hopes, ideals and wishes for the future play an important role in your life. Your friends may be of considerable benefit to you now, and you will become more involved in group activities, for you understand the importance of group goals and values to you as an individual. This is not a time when you should try to go it alone, nor should you limit yourself to working with one other person. You need to be with many people, for through working and dealing with them you will learn a great deal about yourself. Friends will be more than usually supportive, and you may make many new friends who will prove to be extremely valuable as time goes on. But this will not be a one-way street, for you will help them also.

At this time in your life you will be more than usually idealistic and will want to improve the world around you in every possible way. If your perspective is relatively broad, you will want to translate this desire into broad social reform or at least make changes that will affect both you and your friends. Lacking such a perspective, you may work only to improve your personal situation in accordance with what you have always wanted. However, this is not a time to be selfish. The nature of this house is such that if the improvements in your life do not affect others, the changes will not be as meaningful or long-lasting. Whatever you put out will come back in an even greater quantity.

Jupiter in the Twelfth House

This is one twelfth-house transit that is likely to be quite beneficial, although the benefits won't be as obvious as they are in other houses. At this time you have the capacity to learn a great deal about the spiritual and religious dimensions of life. You also can learn a great deal about yourself without encountering the fear or resistance that you often experience when you come face-to-face with the aspects of yourself that you consider less desirable.

This is a time when the demands of your ego are less exacting than usual. You can look dispassionately and even compassionately at yourself, the world and other people. You feel more direct empathy for the suffering you see, and you genuinely want to help. You seem to have a new understanding of the fact that we are all in the same boat and that what is done to help one person is done for all.

During this time you may find a person who acts as a spiritual teacher for you, but remember that such a person can come in any guise. He or she need not be someone who is publicly recognized as a teacher. Even an old friend may suddenly assume this role. You may feel that something in you needs to be healed now, and this person will come forward to help you.

It is also possible that you will play this role for someone else. You are very concerned about spiritual truth and wisdom now, and you may pass on what you learn during this transit to others.

In a general way this transit may incline you to the study of metaphysics or the occult. In the hidden aspects of existence you seek knowledge that will give you support and comfort, as well as meaning for your life. This transit may even signify a greater involvement with orthodox religion and the church.

Jupiter Conjunct Sun

Traditionally this is considered one of the most marvelous transits, and indeed it is quite good. However, its influence may be masked by other transits that are longer-lasting and more powerful. If your chart is severely afflicted by other transits at this time, this one will serve largely to give you a break.

At the very least, you will feel good at this time. Your health is good, and you feel very optimistic. For a while it may seem that everything is working out perfectly, and if you make an effort, it will. But if you simply sit back and enjoy this transit, its beneficent influence will pass away with little to show for it afterward.

This is the beginning of a new twelve-year cycle of growth in your life. It is a time to initiate new projects and expand your activities so that you can experience life from a broader perspective. You may find that you can escape from some narrowing and inhibiting circumstance that has prevented you from realizing your full potential as a human being. Sometimes people travel under this configuration, but usually the traveling is more in the mind.

This is a good time to study a subject that raises your consciousness or expands your view of the world, and it is an excellent transit for going back to school. You may also meet new people who expose you to aspects of life that you have never known before. Your freedom will certainly increase.

Even with this transit there are some pitfalls. First of all, your exuberant optimism can cause you to overdo or overreach yourself, so that when this transit is over, you find yourself out on the proverbial limb. Exercise a certain amount of restraint and build upon what you have rather than trying to increase your holdings beyond your ability to handle them. Be careful of extravagance, and if you invest money, remember that today's luck is not permanent.

Otherwise, you can have a good time under this transit. Remember, the feeling of well-being that you experience now is really closer to the truth of what you are than the gloomier or more depressed feelings that you have at other times.

Jupiter Sextile Sun

This is a time when life seems to flow very easily. With little effort, you are able to move in the direction that you intend, and even your ideals seem to be within reach of fulfillment. It is a period of growth, optimism and taking it easy. In many respects this is a good time to sit back and take a long look at how well your life is working out.

Your relations with people in power or those who can help you out in some way are good. Because you project the image of someone who can accomplish, you attract persons who are similarly inclined. If you feel vigorous and energetic, this is an excellent time to advance your interests in almost any area, although that impetus may be lacking.

Relationships with others are usually quite good now, and you enjoy being with friends. This transit often indicates good times, as your enthusiasm for life bubbles over and affects everyone around you.

This is also a good transit for making plans, for you are inclined to "think big," which is a general function of your optimism. While you can overdo this tendency, you will probably be alert to opportunities that you would normally overlook or be afraid to take.

You feel generous and tolerant and not easily bothered when something goes wrong in your world. You recognize that there is plenty of time to correct the problem, so you don't get upset. You aren't annoyed by persons who usually irritate you, and you may even feel like patching up relationships that have gone bad or become difficult. You just cannot bear to be angry at anyone or have them angry at you now. But in the process of making peace you won't compromise yourself; instead you will do it in such a way that you both truly benefit from the exchange.

Sometimes this transit can bring about unexpected income, and this is certainly a favorable time for most financial transactions.

Jupiter Square Sun

This can be an excellent transit, but you must watch out for some pitfalls that could undo all the benefits. Basically this transit is a test of your discipline and self-restraint. If you are not a restrained person, you will react to this influence by going overboard in some way, overextending yourself or living in a fool's paradise where you think nothing can go wrong. Or you might squander a valuable resource, only to find on another day that you do not have enough of what you need. Sometimes there is a feeling that luck will provide everything that you need without any effort on your part, but this, too, is a false notion.

On the other hand, this transit can provide a chance for real growth and expanded opportunities. It is a matter of how much control you have over yourself. You have to know precisely where you are and what your real needs are in order to take the most advantage of this transit. You also have to know when you can't handle more. Knowing when to stop is the real trick.

Sometimes this transit encourages ego inflation and excessive pride. There is an arrogant streak to the negative expression of Jupiter. Be careful not to act in an overbearing manner, for you will set people in motion who will try to knock you down a peg or two. Here too, you must know where to stop. This transit gives you feelings of great confidence, which allows you either to go ahead, knowing precisely what you are doing and what your limitations are, or to act arrogantly and overstep your bounds. At any rate, this transit tests your self-knowledge, and the more accurately you know yourself the better it will work out for you.

Under certain conditions this transit can trigger conflict with the law or with someone else in a court of law. You may or may not lose, but don't act the role of outraged honor and dignity. Try to find out exactly what the problem is and arrive at a solution that is satisfactory to all. Above all, show a spirit of compromise.

Jupiter Trine Sun

This is another very pleasant Sun-Jupiter contact. In fact it is so pleasant that you may be inclined to sit back, enjoy it and do nothing. However, this is really a very important time in your life because you can reach out into new areas of life and have new and rewarding experiences. Your creative potential is enormous at this time, and you can very easily accomplish a great deal that would be difficult at other times. Your inner energies are strong, and you are full of self-confidence and the feeling that you can do anything.

This transit usually indicates good health and a feeling of well-being, although you may be inclined to put on weight if you are not careful. You may not feel inclined toward physical activity, but it would be a good idea to get some exercise. Make a particular effort to be outdoors. Hiking is very beneficial at this time.

If you are inclined to physical activity, especially athletics, don't take foolish risks through overconfidence. This is not an accident-prone transit, in fact it is rather "lucky" for most people. But it does tend to make you overestimate your energies, and if another influence is operating that makes you accident-prone, this transit could have a bad effect.

This is an excellent time for all financial matters. You will feel like making your surroundings appear more elegant, and you may spend quite a lot of money doing so. This is perfectly fine, and you should think positively in all ways, but don't let this concern with material acquisition blind you to some very real possibilities for inner growth.

Travel, either physically or mentally, often accompanies this transit. Take this time to broaden your understanding of the world around you. You have a strong interest in ideas that are different from what you normally know and encounter, and you are much more tolerant of different ways of living. Even people's usually irritating traits do not bother you at this time. Also your sense of humor is much greater than usual, and you can appreciate the dance of life in all its glory.

Jupiter Opposition Sun

This can be and usually is a very positive transit. But you can make more or less out of it, depending upon how you handle it. In most ways it represents a period of culmination in your life, and you will be tempted to expand beyond any reasonable limit. There is no question that you have a good chance for success in any one of a number of endeavors at this time and, within reason, you should pursue them. However, you should not restrict yourself solely to material and physical growth now. Even if you don't have all the material goods that you want, you should turn your attention to spiritual and inner needs. Ultimately, nothing satisfies like satisfaction. Objects that you acquire, possessions, money and even social prestige are merely devices to make you feel that you have satisfaction. They are not the state of satisfaction itself. It is your inner difficulties that make your life less than it could be, even if you have corresponding problems in the material world. You must look for the solutions within yourself, and this transit represents a turning point, where you should begin to look for the answers.

Under this influence, the tendency is to go after everything that you want in the material world without caring especially about whoever is in your way, to gather as much stuff as you can and indulge yourself in what you want. Then, as the transit subsides, you will feel that this effort has failed, leaving your life as empty as it was before. In the first half of this cycle, your growth has been material. Now it should be inward.

Do not be arrogant toward others or assume that you have everything right. Through meaningful encounters with others, especially intimate one-to-one encounters, you can find out which way you should go at this time. Work with another person and think in terms of mutual growth. By trying to achieve goals set by both of you and by trying to be a twosome, you each will become more conscious of what you are as an individual.

On a more mundane level, this transit can signify difficulties with authorities, if you overstep your bounds or are out of place. Your tendency to think that you have all the answers can only get you into trouble.

On the other hand, if you recognize the real meaning of this transit in terms of your own life, this can be an extremely productive and growth-oriented time, a period that will always have meaning for you.

Jupiter Conjunct Moon

This is an extremely positive transit. You feel emotionally secure and in touch with your feelings, which you can express clearly and honestly, both to yourself and to others. At the same time you have an enormous feeling of generosity, which enables you to give to others much more freely than usual without feeling diminished in any way. This combination of influences relates to the nurturing function within you, the desire to protect and care for as well as the desire to be supported. You can nurture another at this time, or if you need help yourself, you will get it.

Your home and personal life are very important to you under this transit, and you will work to make this area as positive as possible. You may simply make your home more comfortable and elegant, or on a more psychological level you may bring friends and neighbors to your home in order to make them feel good, as well as yourself. This is an excellent time to invest in a new home or real estate.

At this time you will realize how your past has positively contributed to your present situation, and you will want to be surrounded by things that remind you of your past. This is a good time to go home and see old friends and loved ones.

Regardless of your own sex, you may receive some benefit from a woman who offers to help or care for you in some way. Often her function in your life will be to reveal to you what is within and to make you more self-sufficient. This person could even be a man, but he would affect you in a maternal way.

About the only negative side of this transit comes from its symbolic connection with nutrition and digestion. Psychologically you are in a period of incorporation and assimilation, of taking into yourself whatever can nourish and support you. Obviously the physical correlate of this is gaining weight, which can happen if you are not careful. Fatty foods are especially difficult, so try to avoid them.

Jupiter Sextile Moon

This transit makes you feel quite good, optimistic and positive about life in general. You have strong feelings of warmth and generosity toward others, particularly friends and those whom you encounter on a day-to-day basis. You feel that you would like to protect and care for everyone you meet.

The effects of this transit are not usually spectacular, and they may be quite subtle. You should use this time for getting in touch with your feelings and learning how you relate to the everyday world. You will derive uncommonly deep experiences from what appear to be ordinary, routine interactions with others. Your everyday surroundings, your family and relatives will provide satisfactions that may be missing at other times. And these encounters will provide opportunities to grow and to enlarge your life. The usually confined limits of daily routine can actually become the vehicle for new chances and opportunities.

Cultivate your friendships, for there is a good chance that a friend will be able to perform a valuable service for you at this time. And it is just as likely that you will do the same for a friend. In either case you will come out ahead.

This transit may stimulate your interest in spiritual or religious matters, usually in the form of a renewed interest in the religious or spiritual beliefs that you learned as a child. Such experiences from your past can be very valuable to you now. Reliving them does not mean you are backsliding to attitudes that you have outgrown. There is still something there for you to realize and learn from.

Friendships or other relationships with women quite often prove rewarding at this time, with various benefits. You could have an emotional experience that enriches you, or a business opportunity, or she could act as a guide to aspects of yourself that you do not normally experience, but which help you come to complete self-understanding.

On occasion this transit signifies that you are in the public eye or that you have to deal with large groups of people in some way. In either case, you should be successful.

Jupiter Square Moon

This is usually a very favorable square. It gives your emotions a great deal of power, so that you feel them much more emphatically and are more in touch with them. At the same time you want to establish empathic relationships with others, to hear their problems, to help out and play a protective role toward them if possible. This transit may make you feel very sentimental about and attached to your surroundings and to familiar objects. Your past is very important to you now, and if there are events in your past that you find uncomfortable, they are likely to come up. There is often a need to confront the unconscious areas of the psyche under this transit, but you should regard this as an opportunity to be healed of the wounds made by these energies from the past.

In emotional relationships, this transit can create a tension between your desire to be close to someone and the desire to free. Be careful to give your loved ones the same freedom that you want, and do not try to be unfairly possessive of them. Also, confrontations with the unconscious aspects of yourself mentioned above can affect relationships adversely during this time. In such cases it is necessary to cultivate a sense of detachment and not become so wrapped up in your emotions that you cannot see beyond them.

This transit gives an enormous concern with social and individual justice. You are easily outraged when you see someone getting the short end of the stick, but your emotionalism may make it difficult to see a good solution to the problem. Try to avoid feeling self-righteous and intolerant. You will need to have a very open and generous point of view in order to clear up any conflicts that occur at this time, and emotionalism masquerading as righteousness will not accomplish anything useful. Instead, take advantage of the ample positive side of this energy by helping those who need it. Protect the people you can protect and succor those who have been hurt. Magnanimity is just as much in accordance with the meaning of this transit as are extreme emotionalism and self-righteousness.

Jupiter Trine Moon

This is a very pleasant transit, but it does not usually produce much energy. Unless it is energized by another transit occurring at the same time, it probably will not signify very much. Usually, however, you will feel very good with this transit, quite optimistic and generous. You will be concerned about the welfare of those around you and will want to protect the people you love.

This is a good time to be at home or in familiar surroundings. You will derive maximum support from being with your family and loved ones, for they will recharge your spirits, even if this transit does not coincide with any particularly significant event.

At this time you will attract favorable circumstances and resources with little effort, which will seem very pleasant now. But you should not expect this to keep on happening indefinitely. In particular, people may come after you to meet you for some reason, and these people could be quite beneficial to you in business or personal affairs. Regardless of your own sex, you may very well benefit from women during this transit.

In some people this transit may stimulate an interest in religious and spiritual thought, but your views would be more strongly concerned with ethics and morality than with a more mystical approach to religion.

At the very least you can expect to feel quite good at this time, and even if nothing tremendous comes out of this transit, you will have a feeling of satisfaction and of being at peace with yourself.

Jupiter Opposition Moon

This is a time when feelings and emotions play an important part in your life, and relationships based on feelings and emotions become very important. This transit is usually experienced positively as warm feelings within yourself and from others. You feel emotionally very generous and giving. Relationships are usually quite good and rewarding now, and those that you have been building up for years may begin to produce results. You can now decide clearly which ones are worthwhile and which are not.

But there is a negative side to this transit also. It can make you feel very self-indulgent and undisciplined. You may feel that the world "owes me a living," whether or not you really deserve it. It may also make you feel that others ought to be breaking their back to help you. In personal relationships, you may become very demanding without really offering anything to your partner in return. Instead of reaching out to make things happen in your life, you wait for others to make the first move and become quite angry when people insist that you take some initiative. The Moon is basically passive, and the opposition transit of Jupiter only serves to make it more demanding, if the negative side of the transit is expressed.

The self-indulgent side of this transit can also be expressed physically as overeating or drinking. At the risk of seeming old-fashioned, remember there is a danger in doing anything to excess, and with this transit, moderation is extremely important, even more than with other Jupiter transits.

Your love relationships and relations with women can be either very good or very bad, probably not anywhere in the middle. It all depends upon your general reaction to this transit. If you are demanding in the manner described above, then your relationships will be bad. But if this transit arouses your feelings of warmth and generosity, they will be quite good. And this is a good way of gauging where you are with this transit, because encounters with others, especially women, will bring out its effects.

Jupiter Conjunct Mercury

At this time you are able to combine breadth of vision with sharp perception and intellect, knowledge of the particular with knowledge of the general, and thereby see the whole scope of anything you are involved in. This reveals itself as foresight and long-range planning ability. This is a good time to map out your future, because you can understand and interrelate all the elements that will affect your life.

At the same time, you feel optimistic and proceed with the belief that everything will come out exactly as you want it to. And it probably will, because you don't get completely carried away with grandiose thinking. This transit usually indicates a good balance between details and generality in your thinking, but there is also a tendency to deemphasize the details and not pay adequate attention to them. If you are not careful, this can result in sloppy or hasty thinking. Be sure to slow down somewhat and do not get carried away with your plans. Otherwise, this is an excellent time to make decisions or to conclude any kind of transaction. It is a superb time to buy or sell, because you will almost certainly be satisfied with the deal.

As your mind tries to expand, you will want to learn more and more. This is a good transit for returning to school, but even on a less formal level you will be anxious to learn. You may even travel long distances with this aim in mind.

Any dealings with the law should prove to be quite fortunate for you now. You will prepare for such a confrontation skillfully, leaving no loose ends to trip you up.

Often this transit arouses an interest in religious, spiritual or philosophical matters. The ordinary perception of reality no longer seems to be enough; you want to expose yourself to its higher-level manifestations as well.

Communications with others are exceedingly fortunate under this influence. Your optimism and positive state of mind bring you good news from others concerning matters of importance. At the same time, everything that you say to others is very positive and reinforcing, which leaves good feelings behind you wherever you go.

As with all major Jupiter contacts, the only warning is to make sure that you don't overextend yourself. Be sure that the plans you make can be realized without committing you to more than you can handle. Aside from this warning, this is an excellent transit.

Jupiter Sextile Mercury

This is a good time for planning and making decisions. Your powers of perception are quite sharp, and you are able to take a good overall view of any matter that you must make a judgment about. It is also a good time for communicating with others on important matters. You are able to get in touch with group sentiments and opinions more effectively than usual and to come to conclusions that are acceptable to everyone in the group. This is an excellent time for negotiations, business transactions and contract discussions, as well as buying or selling. All of these activities should work out very favorably for you financially.

This is also a good time to resolve differences that may have arisen between yourself and others. You have the diplomatic and persuasive ability to smooth over hard feelings, and everyone you deal with in this way will feel that you have arrived at a fair and adequate compromise.

Friends may well bring you good news at this time. They may be able to point out opportunities that you would have overlooked otherwise. Also you may hear from someone whom you have not heard from in some time. This is a good time for writing letters or for any other form of communication with others. You may be able to do some serious writing, particularly if Jupiter makes a station somewhere near Mercury, causing the transit to stay close for a long period of time. Interest in ideas and the literary arts is high at this time also.

Everything that you do now will be characterized by foresight, planning and an excellent grasp of the important essentials that make any project a success. But as with other sextiles and trines, this transit represents an opportunity that you must take advantage of. If you don't take the initiative, the energy of this transit is not powerful enough by itself to drive you forward. By taking no action, you could experience this transit simply as a time of optimism and positive thinking, but you will have little to show for it.

Jupiter Square Mercury

This transit signifies increased mental activity and a desire to communicate to others something that you consider important. Whether or not your message is important, you probably think it is, so you should take the time to see if that is true. There is no point in loading people up with your ideas and opinions unless they are worth something. And when you speak to others at this time, it is vital that you listen to their response. For although you have big ideas and plans, with Jupiter there is a tendency to overlook details. You may be unwilling to listen to criticism, but if you listen and heed what you are told, this can be an excellent time for making decisions, planning, negotiating and concluding deals or agreements. But this will happen only if you listen to others' opinions.

This is usually a time of optimism and positive feelings. You have confidence in your ideas and are able to get them across. Communications of all kinds are important to you; for example, you may conceivably do some writing at this time. But always keep in mind the advice given above about letting others be heard. They can do you a lot of good.

It is also important not to overextend yourself. Make sure that your plans are no larger than your ability to cope with them. Sometimes with this transit the pace can get pretty hectic, because you have to handle many different affairs at once. This is when sloppy thinking can become especially dangerous.

During this period you may encounter resistance to your ideas and opinions from a number of sources. It is a good time to examine your ideas and see how well they really hold up in an argument. It is a good time to change any views that do not hold up because you can easily enlarge your viewpoint under this transit. You feel no need to be petty or quarrelsome, but you do feel compelled to defend the ideas that are important to you. Any truly important beliefs will hold up during this confrontation and become more a part of your basic mental pattern than ever.

Jupiter Trine Mercury

This is not a time when you should wait for things to come to you. But you can do quite well with it if you communicate with people, look for opportunities, especially in business, and look for good items to buy or sell. This transit confers the ability to see events clearly and to make plans intelligently, which will serve you well in any of these matters.

This is also a good time for talking to others about your opinions or a point of view. You are able to put yourself across with confidence and warmth, which will make other people believe you. They will also respect your sincerity and the clarity with which you communicate your ideas. Even if you tell someone something he or she doesn't want to hear, you can do it so that the other person will feel good about you for saying it.

This is an excellent time to take up the study of a new subject, and the more abstract the better. But you also have the ability now to translate abstract ideas into practical reality, which can be very useful in organizing and planning your activities in any sphere of life.

As with most Jupiter transits, on the psychological level you can expect a period of optimism and positive thinking, fortunately based on reality. You have big ideas, but you have the basic sense to understand what can and cannot be done. This contributes greatly to your effectiveness at this time.

Jupiter Opposition Mercury

This is a time of very big plans and the culmination of many ideas that you have had in the past. It is possible now to make your ideas become reality, as long as you avoid certain pitfalls. In this case the primary problem is to avoid thinking too big or attempting something that is totally grandiose and impractical.

If you can keep track of all of the details that go into a well-thought-out business deal, this is an excellent time to sign contracts or to conclude any kind of commercial transaction, but it is very important not to overlook any details that might affect the outcome. More than any other Jupiter-Mercury contact, this one enables you to see the overall patterns in anything and to plan with foresight and wisdom. But if you are not careful, it can also lead to sloppy thinking or planning. It is best to work with someone else who can check over your work or plans and call your attention to anything that you have overlooked. A lawyer would be especially good for this, because lawyers are ruled by Jupiter.

Projects or plans that began up to six years ago may come to fruition now, but only if you have been careful about details as described above. At any rate, events now will make it clear whether these ideas were based on reality or on pipe dreams. Work out everything in detail and leave as little as possible to chance; this will help you immensely.

Although recognizing the truth of any matter is important to you now, you must deal with others tactfully. There is a danger of alienating people by being self-righteous or arrogant in telling them about your ideas. It is extremely important that the breadth of vision conferred by this transit be accompanied by tolerance and generosity. Usually it is, but sometimes people react in the negative way just described.

The pace of events may become rather fast moving for you at this time, and that is another reason why you must plan everything very thoroughly. You could get confused, not because the situation is undefined or vague but because the scale of events is too large for you to grasp. But this shouldn't happen if you have worked everything out in advance.

Jupiter Conjunct Venus

This transit helps to smooth over all difficulties in your relationships, as well as promote friendship and give you a strong desire for happy and peaceful times. You enjoy being with and talking with friends and will probably attend or hold several social gatherings during this time. You may also be the center of attention for some reason, and you will enjoy basking in the limelight.

This transit occasionally will bring a new love interest into your life. If it does, and other factors are equal, the relationship should prove to be an unusually successful one in which you both grow a great deal and in which there is an excellent balance between love and freedom. Such a relationship will be devoid of jealousy or pettiness to an unusual extent.

The same energy affects existing relationships, so that you are able to relate to loved ones with great ease. Because you are concerned with the larger issues in your relationship, you are not about to cause trouble over any problem that is not extremely important. And such a problem is not likely to surface under this transit.

At this time also your taste is likely to become more elegant, and you may be tempted to buy something that is very expensive or fancy. At the worst it might even be gaudy or tasteless. In fact one of the few real dangers to watch out for under this transit is the tendency to waste or squander money or other resources. Depending upon your own state of mind, however, this transit can also bring in money and increase your resources. Whichever way it goes, it should be well under your control.

Another, less severe danger to watch for is related to the foregoing. There is the danger of self-indulgence at all levels, but particularly with food and drink. It is even possible to make yourself quite unwell this way, so proceed with caution.

You have a strong desire to surround yourself with beauty. Sordid or ugly surroundings are much harder than usual for you to bear, so make an effort to avoid them. You are concerned with the beautiful side of life at this time, and you should do everything to expose yourself to it.

Jupiter Sextile Venus

This is a very pleasant transit, although you may not feel it very strongly. But if you know it is coming, you can act in certain advantageous ways during this period. However, you will have to take the initiative, which you may not want to do, because one effect of this transit is to make you feel very pleasantly unambitious. It may be difficult to rouse yourself to action. Therefore this is a good transit for a relaxing vacation or any other kind of good time that doesn't require much energy.

This transit favors relationships, romantic and otherwise, because you are able to project warmth and friendliness more easily than at other times. You are attracted to other people, and they are attracted to you. Sometimes this transit can signify the beginning of a major love relationship. At the very least you feel like flirting and drawing in people who are similarly inclined.

If you have to make a good impression on someone, this is the time. You are much more able to feel the subtle nuances of relationships, which helps you make the right moves. On top of that, your feelings for other people are sincere, which they recognize and respect. In general with this transit, you act honorably in relationships and attract others who do also, aside from the flirtatiousness that has been described. However, this is very unlikely to put you in a compromising situation.

With some persons, this transit brings out a taste for the gaudy and the flashy. If your tastes usually run this way, you will be quite ready and willing to spend a considerable amount of money on some flashy bauble.

You will be attracted to pleasant and beautiful surroundings at this time and more than usually repulsed by ugly and sordid conditions. You may very well feel compelled to do something about such conditions if you encounter them now, although this is not usually a very socially conscious transit.

Financial affairs usually run quite well at this time. Money may come your way unexpectedly and if so, you will probably be tempted to spend it on something frivolous. Follow your own conscience!

Jupiter Square Venus

This transit can create within you genuine warmth of feeling and the desire to give and express love to others. Unfortunately it can also make you feel very unenterprising and passive, so that you wait for things to come to you when you ought to go out after them. It is very hard to tell which of these two broad classes of response to expect, but generally speaking, the first is more common.

On occasions this transit may mean that you will attract someone with whom you could have a significant relationship, but it may not be an easy relationship. It is likely to be quite constructive, however, and whether or not you realize it immediately, you will gain from it in wisdom and maturity.

The principal difficulty with this transit is that it inspires rather compulsive feelings, which do not leave you enough room to maneuver and handle the new relationship properly. Because you act compulsively, your feelings may overwhelm the other person. And it is very important to realize that in all Venus-Jupiter combinations there is tension between the closeness of Venus and the love of freedom of Jupiter. It is quite possible to combine these into a very creative relationship that will be pleasant and constructive for both of you, but you will have to calm yourself down a bit and proceed with less excitement. If you can do this easily, this transit should be very good for you.

Because this transit combines the two most pleasure-loving planets, you will find it difficult to get much work done. You feel much more like having a good time and socializing, which is perfectly all right in itself, but don't put yourself in a position where you have to assume much responsibility. This is a good transit for taking a trip for purely recreational reasons.

As with other Venus-Jupiter transits, this one stimulates your love of beauty. Make every effort to surround yourself with beauty, such as pleasant surroundings, art objects or beautiful scenery. With some people, this feeling becomes perverted into a love of gaudy, showy things that have no real worth. To each his or her own, of course, but do not get seduced into wasting money on some trifle that you will regret in soberer moments.

Jupiter Trine Venus

This is one of the most pleasant transits of all, in a light and passing way. You feel very light-hearted and sociable now and want to spend as much time as possible with others. This is a good transit for taking a vacation, attending social gatherings, or participating in other forms of amusement and fun. It is not conducive to any kind of serious effort, because you are inclined to feel pleasantly lazy and unenterprising. There is also a very strong self-indulgent streak to this transit. Be very careful not to eat or drink too much. Even with the pleasantness of this transit, you may feel bad afterward.

Fortunately you have the ability to make others feel good if they are unhappy or depressed, and as a result, people enjoy being around you at this time. You may have the chance to do favors for others that will eventually be returned. And since you feel generous and giving, you will not mind doing them.

Sometimes this transit can signify the beginning of a new love interest, but it is much more likely to mean a passing, flirtatious encounter with the opposite sex. A relationship that does begin under this transit will probably be quite good for you.

In some instances this transit has a way of drawing money or other material resources to you. But don't sit around planning how to spend a sudden windfall from heaven, as many people do with this transit. It is a possibility, but only one among many and not the most likely.

Actually it is more likely that you will spend money on objects that you consider beautiful. Others may not appreciate your taste at this time, however, because it tends toward the flashy or gaudy. Be careful that you don't get stuck with something that will offend your own taste in a soberer moment.

You have a great desire for beauty, however, and if your taste is sound you will surround yourself with objects that you can enjoy for years and that will also gain in value.

Jupiter Opposition Venus

This is usually a very pleasant transit, indicating harmony in relationships and perhaps even a new relationship that will be of great significance in your life. You want love very much, and you are able to give it to those around you. You feel that you can fulfill yourself better through being with others than through being alone.

This transit encourages a taste for the lavish and beautiful, and you are not likely to let much stand in the way of what you want. Therefore you must be careful not to waste valuable resources and squander money. If you are cautious, it is possible to make excellent investments at this time, but only if you examine all of the possibilities very carefully. Like all Jupiter transits, this one has the negative attribute of carelessness, so you must concentrate on being careful.

On occasion, especially if other, more negative transits occur at the same time, this transit can signify a period of emotional turmoil in your relationships. This is because of a struggle either within yourself or between you and a loved one about how free you should be with each other. Venus demands close emotional involvement, while Jupiter demands room to move. The opposition brings out this polarity very strongly, so that in a love relationship one of you may want more freedom, while the other wants a more possessive relationship. Ultimately the issue boils down to respect and trust, and only by bringing everything out into the open can the two of you resolve this controversy.

On the physical level, this is another Jupiter transit that signifies the danger of gaining weight, because it stimulates your desire for rich, sweet and otherwise fattening foods. It may be necessary to avoid such food for awhile.

Jupiter Conjunct Mars

This is a very exuberant transit, with high energies. You feel physically strong and fit, and you are more willing to be active and take chances than at other times. Vigorous physical activity is one of the best ways to use this energy, which strengthens your body and allows you to accomplish more than usual. This is quite a common transit when women give birth, for that is a kind of physical action that it seems to favor especially. However, in itself this transit does not indicate pregnancy.

A keyword phrase for this transit in one book is "fortunate action," which sums up its strength quite adequately. Almost anything that you direct your energies to, especially an activity that requires a lot of energy, will seem to flow and happen as if you were not making any effort at all. It is important to realize, however, that you are in fact working quite hard; after this transit is over, and even during it to some extent, you will need to stop a while and rest. One of the problems at this time is that because you don't realize how hard your body and mind are working, there is a real danger that you will overwork yourself. Certainly, if you are not in excellent physical condition you should not take up heavy physical work without preparing for it, but that is just what you might do with this transit.

The same tendency can also mean that you will be accident-prone under this influence. It is not that the transit is accident-prone, but that you are inclined to take foolish risks on the assumption that nothing can go wrong.

This is a good time to begin a new project, as long as you don't overextend yourself. You have much more initiative than usual, and you can accomplish a great deal by yourself. Working with others may be frustrating, because it is hard for you to put up with their slower pace.

Often this transit is expressed through doing something that requires a magnificent sense of timing or planning. Or you will do something that works out very well for you in the long run. Even if it doesn't require great energy, it will pay great dividends in the future.

Jupiter Sextile Mars

This is a time of high energy and independent initiative. You feel very self-confident and capable of tackling almost anything within reason. It is a good time to start a project, and most activities that you take up now should have a successful outcome. However, as with other sextiles, you must take some positive action in order to get the most out of this transit. It brings you opportunities, but you have to pick them up. However, this should not be much of a problem because this transit usually makes you feel like taking action.

You are unusually clear now about what you intend to do in any situation. Your will is strong, and you aim at achieving certain very definite goals. You can act decisively and with conviction. Under a transit like this you can convince other people of your point of view and get them to follow your lead. In fact, unlike other Mars-Jupiter combinations, this one is unusually good for working with other people because you can get others to identify their interests with yours.

Everything you do is aimed at enlarging your sphere of interests. You do not act out of petty motives, always having high-minded and high-level goals in mind. Others will respect your obvious integrity, which will make them more willing to help you.

If you have to go to a court of law at this time, the proceedings should turn out to your benefit. In fact, the chances are that you will be able to work out a compromise that will be advantageous to both parties.

Professional success is likely at this time, because of your excellent sense of timing and your ability to take advantage of every opportunity that comes along. You should be able to advance yourself without alienating others. They will recognize that your success is well deserved.

This transit is usually good for physical health, and for pregnant women it is a good sign of a successful pregnancy with no complications.

Jupiter Square Mars

This can be a very constructive and useful transit, as long as you make some effort to control its exuberance, especially in certain forms that are often very obnoxious to others.

This transit gives you a great deal of confidence and makes you feel very self-assertive. Usually this is all right, but some people will express this energy by becoming arrogant and domineering. Also be wary of overconfidence, resulting in attempts to do things that are simply beyond you. As with other Mars-Jupiter contacts, in any physical activity you should be very careful not to take foolish risks that could lead to an accident.

Intemperance in almost any activity could completely undo the basically positive nature of this transit's energies. Avoid exaggeration and try to maintain some sense of proportion. If you can do all of this, you will be able to get more work done than usual, and you will do it well. You will be able to accomplish things that you are usually afraid to tackle because you feel inadequate, and you can take the initiative when you would otherwise wait for others to take the lead.

With care and planning and adequate restraint, this transit is a general sign of fortunately timed action that takes advantage of the proper moment and makes the most of it. And that is not luck on your part, but insight and skill. All of this requires preparation, however, because impulsive actions at this time are not likely to be very effective.

It may be particularly important to placate persons in authority over you. If you act precipitately, they may become alarmed and think of you as a threat, whether or not you intend to be. Of course, if you do consciously intend to be a threat, this transit could be a help, assuming again that you have planned carefully. But if you are not conscious of your intentions, you may experience opposition from your superiors without ever quite understanding why.

Jupiter Trine Mars

Unlike the harder Mars-Jupiter transits — the conjunctions, squares and oppositions — this one does not create the irrepressible energy that can be hard to control. It does create an easy flow of energy that enables you to act much more effectively than usual and to take initiatives that demand foresight, careful planning and considerable self-confidence. Almost any initiative that you take now will work out as you want it to. It is a good time to start any enterprise.

Your actions are governed by a strong sense of integrity. You may be ambitious with this transit, but you feel that it is very important to achieve your goals correctly and in accordance with ethical standards. Others will recognize your integrity, which will increase their confidence in you.

Under this transit you have a strong desire to make something of yourself in the broadest sense of the term. For example, there is the drive to succeed, particularly in some project that you have started yourself. There is also a strong need to create, even extending to the biological realm, where this transit can signify a desire to have children. Often this transit coincides with a particularly easy childbirth.

As usual with Jupiter, this transit signifies actions aimed at enlarging your scope of action, giving you more freedom of movement and creating opportunities for new experience.

This is a good time to approach a person with whom you do not usually get along or someone you have had a temporary dispute with and make an effort to settle it. You will find it easy to convince the other person of the integrity of your motives because it is true, and they will respect that. If you are involved in a legal controversy, this transit is a good time to settle that dispute on terms favorable to yourself.

Jupiter Opposition Mars

This is an extremely exuberant transit, which inclines you to do everything in a big way. Your energy level is high, and you are ambitious in everything that you do. You have a great need to expend physical energy, but be careful not to act recklessly. Discipline and restraint are necessary, no matter what you do.

Do not overestimate your abilities, either to yourself or to others. You are capable of doing quite a bit under this transit, so you don't have to exaggerate. It is especially important not to kid yourself about your abilities, however, because you will genuinely try to do the impossible and quite possibly exhaust yourself in the process.

For the same reason, don't take unnecessary chances. The feeling of omnipotence that this transit confers is not real, at least not to the extent that you feel it.

Sometimes this transit can signify a conflict with another in which you try to break away from the other's restrictions. It is difficult to say in general whether your estimate of the facts is accurate, that is, whether the other person is really demanding too much or restricting you too much. Therefore you must examine the issue very carefully before you act. You have a great need to be self-assertive at this time, but be sure to reserve it for a situation in which it can be constructive. Avoid acting upon impulse. It could get you into needless trouble.

On the other hand, this transit also confers real courage. The difference between courage and foolhardiness is simple self-knowledge, which you must have in order to make this transit work out positively. If you are cool and collected in what you do, this can be a time of considerable triumph as you overcome obstacles and accomplish deeds that you usually would feel incapable of. If you have to stand up for yourself, you can, and in a way that makes further dealings with your opponents constructive rather than destructive. But this will happen only if you keep your head.

Jupiter Conjunct Jupiter

This transit occurs at eleven- or twelve-year intervals, when you are eleven, twenty-three, thirty-five and so on. It indicates the beginning of a new cycle of growth and progress. However, for people who are not very skilled in astrology, this transit is often the focus of exaggerated expectations. They expect sudden windfalls, great wealth or luck, and all kinds of wonderful opportunities. And these things do happen sometimes with this transit, but most people should expect more subtle, but equally useful effects.

Events now, such as meetings with persons or even changes in your psyche, open the way for you to become wiser and more mature and to have a broader understanding of the world. At this time you will reach out consciously and unconsciously and ask more of the world, but at the same time you are willing to give more to the world. This transit can make you feel either more demanding or more giving toward others, but you are not likely to get much out of it if you think only of what you can get. The law of conservation of energy in the universe says that you can transform the energies in your life from one form to another, but you cannot create them out of nothing. This is why you must put as much into the world as you expect to get from it. This transit represents a time when you should see whether you are doing that in your life.

Concretely, you can expect persons who are good for you to come into your life. Or circumstances will arise that give you increased freedom or an opportunity to do something that you have never done before. Educational opportunities may come to you at this time, or a chance to travel. Sometimes this transit does in fact bring about financial advantage, but you should not sit around passively waiting for it to happen. This is an excellent time to invest or expand in business as long as you are very careful not to overdo it or overextend yourself.

Jupiter Sextile Jupiter

This is a time of balance and equilibrium in your life, when all your affairs seem to run smoothly and without much effort on your part. It is a time when you can relax and take it easy for a while, knowing that your life is in good working order. This is also a time when growth seems to occur without much effort — growth in consciousness, in your profession, in your social life or wherever you feel that personal growth is important.

But this is not really a time when you should just enjoy yourself. You should do that, to be sure, but you should also be examining your life to see what needs to be done. You probably will not take much action at present, but if you become conscious of these matters now, you will be able to take the appropriate steps later on. It is important to think this way now because the equilibrium that is characteristic of this transit enables you to look about yourself with reasonable calm and detachment. It is much harder to achieve a perspective when you are in the middle of some major and possibly chaotic change.

This is a good time to achieve perspective in all possible senses of the word. It is a good time for education, either formal or informal, for getting in touch with yourself through self-awareness studies, or for seeing the larger world through travel.

Business and professional matters usually run quite smoothly at this time. Your relationships with people in positions above you are likely to be quite good, and you may receive some kind of recognition for your achievements. Business transactions or negotiations are also favored now, and this is a good time to expand your business, as long as it is within reason. Legal affairs also usually run quite smoothly.

Jupiter Square Jupiter

With this transit it is very important that you keep your affairs from getting out of hand. There is a strong tendency to excess, which may make it impossible to keep up with whatever you are involved in, simply because it is more than you can handle. Be particularly careful concerning financial matters, for you are likely to spend without thinking, confident that there is an abundance of money or other resources to back you up. You may not notice the pinch immediately, but shortly after this transit you may experience shortages that will be severely exacerbated if you spend money foolishly now.

But money is not the only area of concern. You may be overcommitted to projects that demand more time than you really have. So in every area of your life, make sure that you really have the time or resources to do what you have set out to do. Do not overestimate the resources at your disposal.

If you avoid that pitfall, this can be a very fruitful transit, because it gives you more confidence and optimism and allows you to undertake projects that you would ordinarily be reluctant to take on. Also your basically positive attitude helps to ensure that your affairs will turn out the way you want.

Under this transit some persons experience a kind of ego inflation in which they have delusions of grandeur or overestimate their self-importance. This can lead to arrogant behavior and inflated pride with little or no real substance behind it.

What this transit does is test your sense of proportion. You have to know what you really can and cannot do and who you really are. Insofar as you fulfill those conditions, this transit will give you apparent luck and greater power to achieve. Insofar as you do not know about yourself, you will experience the negative effects of the transit.

Jupiter Trine Jupiter

This transit usually represents a time of optimism and positive thinking in your life. You seem to be at a quiet point of balance that enables you to look over the affairs of your life and get a good perspective on them. Therefore, it is a good time to make long-range plans and to reorganize. You should use this transit to gain new perspectives through education or travel or by participating in one of the consciousness-raising activities or groups that exist now.

This is a time of psychological and physical equilibrium. If you have recently been ill in either body or mind, this transit will help tremendously with the healing process. It is very unlikely that you would contract any kind of illness under this influence.

This is also a good time to examine your ideas and your goals, for it may be possible to actualize them in various ways now. At other times there is too much tension in your life or too much resistance from others. If you are involved in any movement for reform, now is a good time to take some positive action. Or you might become more involved in religion or philosophy, because you need to know much that is beyond the apparent order of things.

It is quite possible that you will do nothing with this transit, because it gives you a feeling of balance but no drive to do anything in particular. You have an unusual sense of ease and relaxation now. This is also a good time to travel, both for relaxation and for educational reasons.

The important point to remember with this transit is that it is fundamentally an opportunity. You will not feel driven by any energies, nor will you feel any resistance to your efforts to do something. You can make great use of this time, but you have to take the initiative.

Jupiter Opposition Jupiter

Under this transit you are likely to feel quite good, with enough confidence to handle just about anything. It is a period in your life when you feel optimistic and as though you can do whatever you want. As with other Jupiter transits, however, you may be somewhat overconfident, so be careful not to take on more than you can handle.

At this point, several time-consuming projects may be coming to a head at once. This could be either quite advantageous or quite difficult, depending upon how well you have estimated your capacities in the past. What is happening now may be more than you can deal with, so you may have to cut back a bit.

This can also be a time of restlessness, for you feel that your everyday world is simply not "big" enough or does not provide enough experience for you. If you feel this way, you need to enlarge your scope of activity somewhat, but again be careful not to overreach.

Conflicts with authorities are possible, even if you have been careful to follow the rules. You may have given others the impression that you are overambitious or that you want too much (in their terms, at least), and they may try to prevent you from getting any further. If this happens, all you can do is confront them directly and try to reassure them that you are not after their position (unless, of course, you are). Because of this possibility, you must be somewhat compromising. The nature of Jupiter in this transit is such that if you do stir up opposition, the other person is likely to have considerable power or pull and could cause you a lot of trouble.

However, none of this is necessary. With a little care and restraint, you can convert this into an excellent transit that will produce considerable good, especially in financial matters. This transit can make you either extremely extravagant or extremely successful in such matters, depending upon your natural bent.

Jupiter Conjunct Saturn

During this transit you will confront your own inhibitions and self-restrictions, as well as the restrictions placed upon you by circumstances. You may wish to break free of them in order to enlarge your scope of activity, so you can go places and do things that you have never been able to do before. On the other hand, you may choose to grow within the structure of restriction in your life, using that very structure to enlarge your life. It can go either way, depending very much upon your temperament. And neither way is better as a general rule. It depends entirely on what is appropriate in terms of your own life.

If you respond by trying to break free, you will begin to feel very restless. Events and circumstances will make it clear that you have neglected much that must be done, and the structures of your life that have held you back will seem intolerable. You can no longer accept barriers such as responsibilities that you have put up with for years, onerous duties or perhaps a built-in fear of breaking away from the established order. Consequently, if you react in this way, this is often a time of breaking away and leaping out into a new freedom. This is often accompanied by a change of job or residence or the breakup of relationships. And however catastrophic these changes seem to others, they are usually quite fortunate and allow everything to work out for the best.

If you respond in the second manner, you will also seek to expand your life and find new freedom, but for a variety of reasons you will not overthrow the structures of your life in order to do so. Instead you will seize every opportunity to build new structures and expand the already existing order. For example, if you are in business, you might use this time to expand in a careful and cautious way. You will not overextend yourself, and whatever you build up now, either in yourself or in the outer world, will be lasting. The other reaction is characterized by impatience and restlessness, but this one is very patient and careful.

Finally, your reaction to this transit will be determined by your life situation as you go into it. If there are many tensions in your life and you are unable to express yourself adequately, you are likely to respond in the first manner. On the other hand, if your life is working out reasonably well, you will be more likely to respond in the second way.

Jupiter Sextile Saturn

During this transit you approach expansion and growth from a very careful and pragmatic point of view. Everything you do, every plan you make is characterized by prudence and caution. You are interested in what could be, but this concern is well balanced by your concern for what is already. You are neither idealistic nor excessively conservative.

You do not see duties and obligations as limitations upon your life but as routes to achieving wisdom and maturity. This is a fundamentally correct view, but you must balance your need for freedom with your need to get work done in order to see it that way. That is what you are doing now. You are oriented to work and duty, but you can also see that certain apparent responsibilities are really not validly yours. And you are not willing to take on someone else's share of the work unless you can see real benefit from doing so.

In financial terms, you are very thrifty at this time. You can see what the best investments are, and you proceed very carefully while putting your money into them. Therefore these investments are more likely than most to work out well.

During this period you will discover how to turn your ideals into reality, partly because you can see which goals and ideals are realistic and which are not. You discard whatever is not realistic, and you work for your goals very patiently, laying a solid groundwork for success.

In business this is usually a good time, because your prudence and thrift enable you to separate the real opportunities from the illusory ones and thereby make real gains. You will be inclined to expand your business, but you will do so very cautiously rather than incautiously.

Jupiter Square Saturn

Under this transit you will make many adjustments in your life, separating yourself from persons or circumstances that are doing you no good. You will change many standards of behavior and morality that you realize are inappropriate and generally realign your conception of duty and responsibility more in accordance with reality. In the process you may experience a considerable amount of tension, and for a time you may be confused, not quite knowing whether to go backward or forward, to expand or cut back. Probably you would be well advised to go off by yourself for a while, because other people's advice will be of little value, unless you select your advisors with great care. The challenge here is to increase and go forward in some areas but to cut back in others. You will not be able to keep everything going, no matter how much you want to. Unfortunately there is no way of telling in advance which areas of your life will be affected.

As with other Jupiter-Saturn contacts, there is often a strong feeling of restlessness and uncertainty. You know clearly that something is wrong, but you are not sure what it is. The best way to deal with this is not to be in a hurry. Usually you will have all the time you need to make a decision based on careful observation of the facts, so don't rush.

In business and professional matters, this is a critical time, but not necessarily a bad one. It simply means that whatever you do now will have a more important effect than usual on the future. Therefore you should be patient while you find the right solution to any problem in this area also. Be especially careful with your finances, because you will have a strong tendency to resent the limitations that they impose on your freedom of movement, and you may act impulsively, as if there were no real limitations at all.

It is possible that you will change jobs under this transit, because a new offer gives you more opportunities to get ahead than your old job. In that case, take it, because such changes are often beneficial with this influence. In general you should take any opportunity that comes along now to broaden your scope and release yourself from limitations that have held you back. The trick is to do this in a way that is not destructively disruptive.

Jupiter Trine Saturn

With this transit you can work patiently and slowly to build something up. There is little of the tension and ambiguity that one experiences with the conjunction, square and opposition transits of Jupiter to Saturn. Under this influence you are able to keep in mind your long-range goals while dealing with all the everyday concerns that arise. Consequently the work that you undertake now is usually very well done. You have an unusual understanding of the relationship between parts and the whole.

This is an appropriate time to handle all manner of practical concerns. Your mind is earthbound, but you don't lack vision and foresight. Therefore this is an excellent time to expand an existing business, start a new one, or branch out into a new area of business. After you find the most practical solution to any problem, you move immediately in that direction. Clarity of intention is one of the strongest points of this transit.

Unlike most transits of Jupiter, with this one you will not want to be with other people especially. It is a good time to go off by yourself and think things over so that you can arrive at the clearest idea of what you want to do. But don't worry about feeling lonely. The seclusion will be good for you and not at all unpleasant.

All your actions are governed by a strong sense of duty. You recognize the many responsibilities that you have in the world, and you are willing to live up to them as best you can.

You may take a rather paternal attitude toward the people around you, wanting to protect them and take on their troubles as your own. Be careful not to overdo this, however, because even though you have good intentions, beyond a point you have no right to take over people's lives. They must deal with their own problems.

Even if you encounter setbacks during this time, they are not likely to affect you seriously. You will take them philosophically, cut your losses and move on to the next phase. You will keep in mind where you want to go, and you will not be easily dissuaded from following your objective.

In general, Saturn rules the material world, while Jupiter rules growth. About the only real caution with this combination is not to allow material expansion, through property, possessions or whatever, to reach the point of limiting your freedom of action and giving you more responsibilities than you want. You can handle them now, but you might have trouble later on. At this time in your personal Jupiter-Saturn cycle, you should work only on what you need and go where you have to go.

Jupiter Opposition Saturn

This can be one of the more difficult transits of Jupiter, because Saturn is so different in nature from Jupiter. Often you will feel psychologically that you are shrinking and expanding at the same time. With this transit it is very difficult to know exactly which direction the trends in your life are taking. Thus you must be extremely careful in your guesses, because of the danger of misjudgment.

Decisions in general are difficult with this transit because you are caught in a conflict between caution and optimism. Whenever one attitude gets the upper hand in your mind, the other comes along and undermines it. Often it seems very difficult to know whether to expand or retrench. This problem will be especially bad if you have overextended yourself in the past and had to cut back. This creates a lack of self-confidence, which may surface now.

You may also experience a conflict at this time between the desire for greater freedom and opportunity and the desire to hold on to the safe and predictable circumstances that you are used to. Often the temptation is to break away from everything and start over without the weight of the past holding you back, so you think. The restlessness resulting from this conflict can cause you to make many significant changes in your life, especially about your career. Relationships are also frequently difficult, especially those that involve much responsibility. Casual relationships and friendships are less likely to suffer.

However, if you are basically satisfied with your life and you don't feel that your duties and obligations are onerous, you should experience the positive side of this transit, which is actually quite considerable. This is a time when you can expand the structures in your life to include much more than ever before. For example, you could safely expand a business, because the cautiousness of your natal Saturn will probably prevent you from overextending yourself. Or you could take on more responsibilities, which would make your work more satisfying. If you can strike a balance between the two opposing forces of Jupiter and Saturn, this can be a time of considerable achievement and prosperity.

Jupiter Conjunct Uranus

This is a transit of surprises and sudden opportunities. And you will strive now for a kind of freedom you have never known before. You may throw over all kinds of responsibilities and try to recapture your lost youth or, if you are young, you will seek in every way to express what it means to be young and free.

The most negative aspect of this transit is reluctance to live up to your responsibilities. Be careful that in your desire for freedom you do not let people down who are really counting on you. On the other hand, you have to strike a balance between the demands that others make on you and your need to be yourself.

At the same time, this transit arouses your idealism. You find it very hard to accept sordid or unjust conditions, either in your personal surroundings or in the outer world. For this reason you may become involved in a reform movement or group that works to change social conditions.

But this transit can work out in an entirely different manner. It may mean a sudden break or opportunity from an entirely unexpected quarter — a sudden promotion, for example, a sudden windfall or a sudden encounter with someone who proves to be beneficial to you. These are just a few of the possibilities. It is difficult to say exactly which of these might occur, because Uranus is an erratic influence, whether it is transiting or natal.

Another effect of this transit is that it can open your eyes to new possibilities. The consciousness-expanding nature of the transiting Jupiter can help you see situations from a totally different angle, and you may think of solutions to the problems that you have had to face. Often these will be radical solutions that you would usually be afraid of, but the transiting Jupiter gives you the confidence to try them.

Sometimes this transit can produce a sudden opportunity for travel, quite often to a foreign part of the world. At the very least, you could expect to be exposed to completely new aspects of life.

Whatever the effects of this transit, you can expect a sudden broadening of the scope of your life and the opportunity to encounter life from a new, richer and broader perspective. This may come about through a major transforming event or through a series of minor ones that collectively have a large impact.

Jupiter Sextile Uranus

At this time you desire to make positive changes in your life that will lead to greater knowledge and experience. While the energy of this transit is not usually disruptive, it does make you impatient with the routine limitations under which you normally live. You will probably try to make changes in your immediate environment in order to deal with this impatience. It is also quite possible that the changes will occur more or less spontaneously, with little effort on your part.

This transit can be mentally very exciting. You are attracted to new ideas that are challenging in a positive way. Not only are you receptive to them, but you can grasp them more easily than usual. Often under this influence you are able to solve difficult problems in your life because you can approach them from a fresh perspective. You may develop an interest in science or other technical disciplines.

Social reform is another area that you might be attracted to, feeling that the old solutions are not adequate. However, this transit does not usually express itself with the compulsive revolutionary spirit of some of the other Jupiter-Uranus combinations.

Sudden opportunities may arise, such as a sudden financial gain or a sudden job promotion that will allow you to do much more than you have done before. This transit may also tempt you to take chances with finances by speculating or gambling.

In a larger sense, it is difficult to say precisely what you can expect with this transit because the nature of Uranus is so unpredictable, either natally or in transit. But you can expect some occurrence that will materially alter your plans for the immediate future, and you can expect that it will be a favorable change. Your immediate future is likely to have many more possibilities than are apparent now.

Jupiter Square Uranus

The effects of this transit can vary considerably. On the one hand, it can indicate a "bolt out of the blue" lucky chance or change in fortune, a sudden opportunity that significantly changes your life. But on the other hand, it can indicate such restlessness and impatience with restrictions that you create a major disturbance in your life in your efforts to become free.

Under any circumstances you are likely, rightly or wrongly, to see change as the only way to get ahead, and to a certain extent this is always true. But the danger here is that you will seek change for its own sake and not take the time to examine carefully which changes will be most effective. There is a strong tendency to be negatively suggestible, that is, to always go in the opposite direction from any pressure.

Freedom in general is very important to you at this time, and you will work very hard to get it in some area. In relationships, this can be disruptive because you are likely to be hostile toward anything that keeps you "in line." Also this transit can signify a time of constant change, when you cannot tell from one day to the next what you are going to do.

But opportunity will probably come, if you can maintain a certain degree of restraint without putting yourself into such a straitjacket that you cannot move when the opportunity presents itself. You do in fact need freedom from something at this time, and you will probably get exactly what and how much you need, as long as you avoid moving so quickly and impulsively that you ruin your chances for creative change. If you remain calm, you will suddenly see and be able to take an opportunity to get ahead or to become free from restriction Be patient, and you will discover that not much more patience is required.

Jupiter Trine Uranus

This transit gives you a strong need to express yourself by doing something that is different from your normal routine. You need to experience a new kind of freedom in your life and to discover dimensions of living that you have not known before. This may take the form of a search for inner truth on the metaphysical or philosophical level, or it may take the more external form of a new activity in your life.

You are much more receptive to new ideas with this transit, and you should be a bit careful about getting into something solely because it is a novelty. However, for the most part this desire for the new is constructive and will probably be quite good for you. This is one of the transits that prevent you in a positive way from getting into a rut.

Sometimes this transit can denote a sudden opportunity or a piece of good luck that seems to come completely out of the blue and take you by surprise. Often it is a sudden change or an event that gives you a new chance in some way. It could be a sudden windfall or promotion or even a sudden chance encounter that works out to your benefit. If such an event occurs, take advantage of it. This is one of the few times when you shouldn't stop to ponder carefully before acting. Such a decision often requires split-second action.

This is also one of the few transits that can be very lucky in gambling. But remember that this transit will have this effect only if you are reasonably fortunate in such matters anyway. If you are usually unlucky at gambling, this transit will probably not affect you positively.

This transit also enables you to grasp new ideas quickly. You can learn subjects faster under this influence than at other times, and you see very quickly the patterns in anything. On occasion this transit can signify a fortunate discovery or invention.

Jupiter Opposition Uranus

This transit signifies a desire to release yourself from restrictions and obligations that you feel have limited your life unnecessarily. Often the point of the exact transit coincides with a sudden break from some limiting circumstance, such as a person, a job or simply a way of life. This need for newness in your life and for something different from the daily routine is a powerful force, and it will be very difficult to continue as you have.

You will feel the breaking away itself as an enormous relief, a lessening of tension. One writer has described this transit as "Thank the Lord!" For this reason you must review your life very carefully to find out what needs to be overthrown and what does not. The danger is that you will overthrow worthwhile things along with the useless. Be careful of this, because it could substantially vitiate any advantage you gain from your new freedom.

Relationships are especially affected by this transit, particularly those that obligate you in some way. A partnership, either marital or business, may be quite difficult to maintain during this time. And to add to the confusion, it is sometimes your partner who wants out. This is an example of a transit experienced in projected form; instead of putting out the energy yourself, you encounter someone who is apparently doing it for you. In this case, do not attempt to hold on to the other person, for that is the surest way to drive him or her away. Give your partner all the freedom he or she needs, for you need it, too, although you are not as aware of it.

A related expression of this transit is encountering a person who seeks in some way to liberate you from yourself or from some duty that you have voluntarily taken on. You may find such a person irritating, but he or she is performing a valuable function in your life. Again, the roles may be reversed, and you may set out to change someone else's life. This transit can arouse your desire to reform and improve, even using disruptive measures if necessary.

The point is that this is a valuable transit, even though it may be somewhat disruptive. It can prevent your life from becoming so static and stabilized that you cease to be truly alive.

Jupiter Conjunct Neptune

During this transit your ideals will be aroused as they seldom are at other times, and you will approach life with a greater sense of compassion. People who cannot help themselves will win your sympathy especially, whether you encounter them personally or through working with others in a charitable enterprise. Your primary concern is to help individuals by giving them a hand. You may be less concerned with transforming the social order that has given rise to the conditions that oppress the people you are dealing with.

Your interest in spiritual, religious and mystical philosophy is likely to grow at this time, and you may become involved in a group that is studying these subjects. This world no longer seems to meet your needs adequately, so you have to turn inward to find a world that can give you what you really need. Here, too, you will discover that the ego's drives for self-gratification and self-assertion may be the major factors in preventing you from getting what you want out of life. At this time the demands of the ego must be quieted at least a little, so you can hear what the inner self is really saying.

Unfortunately there is another side to this transit, which you should watch for. Some people develop a feeling of false happiness, like living in the dream world of an opium smoker, with no basis in reality. You may feel that everything is all right when it is not, or you may feel that you can do anything you want and get away with it.

That is why this transit is often associated with gambling or taking risks with limited resources, often with disastrous results. This is not a very good transit for investments, not because you will necessarily lose out, but because you just won't know for sure, and you will be tempted to gamble even when it is a poor risk. For the same reason, in business deals be sure you are not the victim of a massive misrepresentation.

With this transit it is best to avoid purely selfish concerns, for when your actions are thus motivated you are most likely to encounter the negative side of the transit.

Jupiter Sextile Neptune

This is a time when you are particularly concerned with fulfilling your ideals in life, and you will formulate your eventual goals in very idealistic terms. Also you are less concerned with the negative aspects of life at this time and better able to appreciate its positive aspects. Just be sure that you don't adopt a "Pollyanna" attitude toward the real problems of your life.

You don't feel that satisfying your own needs is as urgent as usual now. In general you want to help others who are less fortunate than yourself. Helping others gives you a great sense of personal fulfillment that outweighs any personal sacrifice you may have to make. For this reason you may become involved in working with charities or other institutions that aid the less fortunate.

With this transit, your religious, philosophical and spiritual concerns are often great. You have a strong drive to experience the higher aspects of existence, but this need may not be satisfied by orthodox religions, so you may become involved in one of the mystical or spiritual groups that flourish now. Or you may encounter an individual who can reveal something of this aspect of the universe to you. In fact, the nature of this transit is such that you will probably gain spiritual insight from those parts of your everyday world that you take for granted.

On another level entirely, this transit can often signify a desire to gamble. Money that you receive under this transit can best be described as "easy come, easy go." But the danger here is that you may invest or gamble on the basis of inflated expectations or a false belief that nothing can go wrong for you. Unfortunately this is not true, so be as careful as you usually are.

Jupiter Square Neptune

At this time you will work very hard to actualize your ideals and find a concrete way to put your spiritual views into practice in the real world. But you can expect the real world to put up some resistance to your ideas. Among other things, you will be challenged to demonstrate that your ideals are not just irrelevant, impractical abstractions. You will also have to demonstrate that your views are based on realism rather than some dream world, which is where you may very well be now. At any rate, this transit will give you the opportunity to find out.

You will give readily when called upon now, because this transit signifies great generosity to people who are less fortunate than yourself. But you may not be very discreet in choosing the people on whom you lavish your charity. Some people can be helped, and it would be worthwhile to spend your time on them. But others are not worth wasting time on, although with this transit you may not be able to tell the difference.

On another level, this transit, like the other Neptune-Jupiter transits, can signify the kind of false optimism that makes you take foolish risks, especially with limited resources. In any financial dealings be very careful that everything is exactly as represented to you by others. Otherwise you could be taken for a ride.

This transit is a test of your grasp of reality and your ability to translate ideals into practice. There is no reason to assume that you will not pass the test, but you do have to be careful.

Religious or spiritual delusions are another danger of this transit. You may be tempted to run after false messiahs or teachers whose ability to dazzle with spiritual phrases exceeds their ability to teach you how to cope with your life.

Jupiter Trine Neptune

This transit stimulates the idealistic and possibly the spiritual side of your personality. You seek out the more subtle manifestations of truth and are unusually inclined to inquire directly into the secrets of life. Religious, spiritual and mystical subjects attract you, and studying them could indeed bring much needed insight into your life. It is quite possible that this transit will signify someone coming into your life who will act as a teacher or guide in your quest for meaning. It is also possible that you will play this role for someone else. The only recommendation is to be careful not to overidealize such a person and not to allow yourself to be overidealized, for this could lead to disappointment later on. In spite of this problem, the chances are that everything will work out very favorably in the long run.

In a related way, this transit arouses the humanitarian side of your personality. You have great compassion for the sufferings of others and want very much to do something about them. You may become involved in charitable work for others, either on the personal or on the institutional level. And if you need help from someone, you will probably get it.

About the only negative side of this transit is that you may get into such a pleasant dreamy state that you have little ambition or desire to achieve anything of significance. Neptune, either natally or in transit, is not inclined to fulfill ego drives, and you may notice a slackening of this drive in your own life. By the same token this transit can lure you into feeling that everything is just fine, even when you really have to do certain things or face serious problems.

The desire to gamble or speculate is another aspect of this transit. As long as you realize that it is possible to lose and that you must use some planning and foresight, it should be all right. But don't let a feeling of overconfidence and the desire to take unnecessary risks get you into a losing situation.

Jupiter Opposition Neptune

During this transit it is often difficult to keep the real and the ideal sorted out. It is an extremely spiritual transit, which may make the real world seem inadequate to you, causing you to seek an escape into a more ideal and perfect "reality." Normally this escape is not through drugs or alcohol, but if you have a predisposition toward them, it could work out that way. Usually, this transit indicates a mental state in which you become wrapped up in all manner of abstract speculations or high ideals that are difficult to actualize.

On another level, this transit may tempt you to become involved in unrealistic schemes that you could only believe if blinded by extreme optimism. You want to gamble and take risks with your resources, and if you are not careful, wild speculations and gambling could leave you bankrupt. Oddly enough, some people are are so geared that they can handle the gambling aspect of this transit very well and make seemingly wild investments pan out. Usually these people have a talent for calculating the risks, however. Remember that there is a difference between amateur and professional gamblers. The main point here is that if you are tempted to get into some investment scheme, make sure that it is within your area of personal expertise.

Under certain circumstances this transit can signify the beginning of a very idealistic kind of relationship, one in which you look to your partner as a kind of god or spiritual guide. This may or may not be an accurate picture. You must be careful here also, because you could idealize a person beyond all reason, even when he or she does not want you to do so. And of course, you too could be the victim of an outright deception. Be careful to deal with people as they really are, by accepting them as they are and not demanding that they conform to an ideal in your mind.

Jupiter Conjunct Pluto

This transit brings the urge to achieve to the forefront of your life. You will make great, even extraordinary, efforts to gain success as you personally define it. You work harder and strive to gain your objective with every ounce of energy at your disposal. Consequently, this transit often occurs just at the moment when some tremendous effort in your life bears fruit.

Sometimes there is a tremendous drive to gain power, and this transit can bring you power even when you are not trying especially hard to get it. Remember that each person has opportunities for a different kind of power. It may be great or relatively humble in terms of the larger society, but it will be meaningful to you.

Unfortunately, this power drive is sufficiently strong that it is difficult to deny, even if it has absolutely no outlet. In that case you are likely to get into some kind of conflict with authorities, even to the extent of arrest. If your ambition becomes the irresistible force against an immoveable society, you will probably be the loser.

Therefore you must scan your life to find areas where you can let the energy of this transit manifest itself. Surely in some area of your life you can better yourself and achieve something that would bring you recognition and respect. This is true no matter how depressed you think you are or how downtrodden your circumstances. If you put all your energy into working on that, it is quite likely that you will accomplish what you want.

The dominant drive of this transit is self-betterment, but each individual has to define that term for himself or herself. You can work in that direction now, and how well you succeed depends largely on what you mean by betterment. Unfortunately, for some people it means simply money or power. If you are one of them, throughout this transit you will act as if obsessed, and indeed, power can become a fanatical preoccupation. Other people may become obsessed by an idea, usually concerning righteousness or morality. This also carries the danger that you will lose track of all normal human values and try to live with a distorted set of standards or concerns.

This transit clearly has a double potential. Either you can create something great in your life with it, or you can distort your life. It all depends on what you are as a human being now.

Jupiter Sextile Pluto

This is a time for making creative changes in your life, for reforming and remolding your immediate surroundings so that they can better express your inner essence. It is a time when you will exert considerable energy in order to gain greater freedom of movement in all your activities. You may have the opportunity to gain power over others, but if so, you should use this power to achieve what you and those around you collectively need. Do not use it for purely selfish purposes, for this is not so likely to work to your advantage. Pluto is oriented more toward group expression than toward individual expression.

If you gain power to lead others in any capacity, you must have the highest ideals in mind. This combination symbolizes regeneration to a higher plane of existence, and although it may express itself on several different levels, you should always keep this basic idea in mind.

Changes may occur spontaneously in the world around you with little or no effort on your part. Take advantage of them, for they will work toward your ends even though you did not originally intend that. You may come into favor with someone in power at this time.

Sometimes a "regeneration" theme is expressed through religious or spiritual rebirth, through understanding the deeper significance of your life and having it transform your being. And you will do what you can to share your learning with others. Sharing everything that comes to you at this time is very important to you. Either this transit will transform you by transforming your surroundings, or you will become the vehicle through which your world is transformed. Either way, you are transformed along with your friends, neighbors and your everyday environment.

Jupiter Square Pluto

This transit can have the effect of arousing your ambition to achieve great things. You feel as if your energies could carry you higher and farther than usual, and you are willing to strive for power and success. But your efforts may run into considerable resistance from others, especially if you are not completely scrupulous about your methods. This transit can bring you success and social standing, but it also can deprive you of these. Instead of gaining power, you may simply provoke conflict with those who are in power, sometimes quite innocently. You may have no intention of challenging anyone, yet you find yourself in a tight spot with the authorities.

Another manifestation of this energy is that you may become involved with a project to repair, restore or rebuild something. It might be physical property, a neighborhood or a more abstract matter, such as reorganizing or reforming a government, business or other institution. Your aim is to improve, but here again you may encounter opposition from people who do not agree with your ideas or who feel threatened by your actions.

You must avoid becoming obsessed with any plan or course of action, and be particularly ready to reexamine your ideas of right or wrong in any matter. Stand up for what you believe is right, but first make sure that you are right. This transit sometimes may make you feel convinced of a point of view that is actually shaky. You should look at religious, philosophical or metaphysical views very closely. If you wish to lead others to enlightenment, first make very certain of the quality of your own.

In some cases this transit can lead to legal conflicts, and you should be very sure that any legal matter you are involved in is strictly legitimate. Avoid underworld or shady persons in any matter.

Jupiter Trine Pluto

Under this influence you will move to make positive changes in your personal and your social world. But the most important question you can ask is, "In whose name do I want to change things?" You should realize that under this transit it is quite easy to exert power and make changes. The energies seem to flow in the direction you want, presenting you with opportunities for taking control in some way. However, you should be motivated by something more than your own personal ambition, even though that will be favored along with any ambition in your life now. But if this power is selfish and personally oriented, you will have trouble later on, and the results will not be lasting. You have to strike a balance and adopt a philosophy of "enlightened self-interest." You must recognize that you benefit most when you can couple your own interests with those of the people you live and work with. In some way you must embody collective interests truly, not merely in your rationalizations.

You have a strong desire to reform and remake at this time, and you should be striving to improve conditions all around you, to renew and to serve as a vehicle for regeneration in your world. If you attain personal power in any way at all, use it to clear up and clean out. You may have the chance to lead or influence others, so use that influence to help everyone concerned to grow with you.

On the mundane level, this transit can coincide with professional success, political power or tremendous gains in personal wealth or resources. On a more humble level, this transit can give you the chance to straighten out situations in your life that have been sources of trouble for you.

Jupiter Opposition Pluto

This transit can represent the culmination of a long drive for success or power. However, it is very important that you proceed with caution, because the forces opposing you are likely to be strong, unless you make a special effort to placate them. This can be a time when you get a promotion in your work or gain power in some other way to change and affect the lives of those around you. But it can also be a time when all your efforts come to nothing, and you find yourself losing out in a perpetual war with people in power.

Sometimes this transit can stimulate a rather ruthless desire to get ahead. Most of us are tempted to cut corners, but that can have very unfortunate consequences, for this transit can indicate trouble with the law or even arrest. In fact you should do as little as possible to arouse the authorities against you, because this transit is so likely to create just that problem.

Another problem can be obsessive or fanatical behavior, feeling that you alone are right about some matter to the point that you are unwilling to hear any other point of view. Avoid becoming totally convinced of your own righteousness, and do not try to force your own views upon others. Your ideas may in fact be quite good, but your problem comes from the style you would be likely to use. You must try to be open to other points of view and be able to compromise.

It is also possible that you may try to coerce someone into doing something that he or she doesn't want to do, or someone may try to coerce you. As with most transits, it can go either way. In this instance it may be a naked power play, with little or no pretense of righteousness. If you are the perpetrator, heed the warnings given above. If you are the victim, all you can do is resist with all your strength.

You can avoid the negative side of this transit if you have built up your affairs carefully and enlisted the aid of others in your efforts, making them understand that you are also working for their interest. And even if you are encountering the negative effects, it is not too late to enlist other people's aid. You may have to enlarge your personal goals to encompass a group's goals, but it can be done.

Jupiter Conjunct Midheaven

This transit represents a period of culmination in which you make a greater effort to get where you want to be, either in your profession or in some other area. And your efforts appear to produce results more easily than at just about any other time. Therefore you feel better about yourself and your life than at other times, and you feel confident that you can handle anything that comes your way.

Professionally, this is often a period of great progress. If you are in business for yourself, your business will expand greatly. If you are employed or a professional person, you will be recognized within your field for the quality of your work. A promotion is quite likely with Jupiter in this position. But this transit does not usually represent the peak of your professional achievement, which will come when Saturn is in this position. You are on the way up, however. Jupiter here means a period of rapid expansion and personal progress.

If you are in business for yourself,, you should be careful not to expand too rapidly or overextend yourself. You will be tempted to expand in order to take advantage of your prosperity, but you might leave yourself vulnerable to the more difficult times that will eventually come. Make sure that all expansion is carefully planned and that you have safeguards against future times of difficulty.

Another negative side of this transit will come up if you do not get the recognition that you feel you deserve. If others do not acknowledge you openly, you may feel cheated and go on to assume the station and privilege that you think you deserve. Even if you are recognized, you may act arrogant and smug. Be careful of this, because it creates a negative energy that could lead to your total downfall when Jupiter is out of this area of your chart. Metaphorically speaking, Jupiter can represent either real growth or the growth of fat. Make sure that for you this is a period of real growth.

In general the sphere of your activities will broaden at this time, and you will probably meet new people from unfamiliar parts of the country and even from other parts of the world. They may come into your expanding sphere of action, or you may travel to their worlds. All of this is most likely to happen through your work rather than your personal life.

Jupiter Sextile Midheaven

This is a time of confidence and benevolence. You are secure in your knowledge of yourself and in the direction your life is taking. Even so, you are willing to learn more, and you will have many opportunities to do so. Your career and home life should be going quite smoothly at this time, and you may receive opportunities for personal advancement. This transit sometimes indicates an important position of leadership. Certainly your relationship with the people in power over you should be good, which will be important in your quest for personal advancement.

Your present attitude of confidence and security is not likely to degenerate into selfish pride or arrogance, unless this is part of your basic character. You are much more likely to appreciate this chance to grow in wisdom and maturity. This is a good time to pursue an education if you desire, because you are open to new ideas and will be receptive to your studies. Law, philosophy and medicine are particularly appropriate subjects to the symbolism of this transit, but you are not limited to these.

This is also a good time to get in touch with your inner feelings. You are much more willing than usual to face the inner hidden aspects of yourself that you have been afraid to face in the past. Now you see a confrontation with your inner self as another opportunity to learn, and in truth it is. Also you will be able to understand how your past has affected the present, and you will learn to gain control over parts of yourself that used to control you. This increase in self-knowledge may be accompanied by or may come to you through an increased religious or spiritual self-awareness.

Jupiter Square Midheaven

During this period you will try to achieve something of significance in your work or career. You will not find it sufficient to continue as you have, and your ambition will become more powerful than usual. This can be either good or bad in the long run, depending upon how you go about getting ahead. On the positive side, this transit helps you overcome your previous limitations, which were caused largely by fear and lack of confidence. Now you feel capable of greater achievements and willing to work for them. This transit usually creates great optimism and self-confidence, but you must be careful that it does not become overconfidence. Your life will not take care of itself if you neglect the important details of daily existence. Do not let your seemingly more important present concerns cause you to neglect these other aspects of your life.

But this transit can also signify an inflated ego, a state of mind in which you attribute to yourself powers and talents far beyond your actual abilities. In rare and extreme cases, a person may think of himself as godlike. But for most people this is expressed simply as overestimation of one's talents. Be careful not to take on more than you can handle. There is so much positive energy in this transit that it would be unfortunate to waste it with pride, foolish arrogance and overestimation of your capabilities.

You want to be important now, and it is quite possible to attain that goal, but only if you know yourself adequately. Dare to do more than you have ever done before, but balance your daring with reason and care.

Jupiter Trine Midheaven

This is a time of increased optimism and self-confidence. You feel capable of doing much more than you have ever done, and you are willing to make the effort. This transit quite often signifies professional success, and you may receive a promotion of some kind. Others will look to you for leadership, for they recognize your self-confidence and see that you deserve it.

You have a good idea about where you want to go at this time, and you have probably mastered the techniques and skills needed to get there and have acquired the material resources as well. Under this influence you may gain financially, but you are not likely to squander your money. You will use it to get ahead.

If you are in business for yourself, you may want to expand your business under this transit, and you may have an opportunity to do so. Since Jupiter is also favorably aspecting your fourth-house cusp, you may want to make improvements in your home or move to a larger and more spacious one.

Even if nothing very obvious happens on the material plane, as may be the case, this transit is usually a time of inner peace and contentment. You feel good about yourself, with none of the torments and insecurities that may afflict you at other times. Your confidence comes over to other people, and they feel good being with you. As a result you may be able to support or cheer up someone who is not feeling very well.

As with other Jupiter transits, you should be careful not to overextend yourself or become overcommitted in your boundless enthusiasm. Keep in mind that even now your energies are finite.

Jupiter Opposition Midheaven

This is a time for expansion and growth in your innermost personal life, a time when you will seek security at home and with your immediate family. It may be necessary to reexamine your past life to find out what it can teach you about yourself. But this should not be a source of anxiety. In fact, you should feel quite good about what you learn at this time. Your parents may be able to assist you considerably in this process.

The symbolism of this transit is that you incorporate more and more of the outer world into your innermost life. On the material level, you may buy a larger, more elegant or more spacious home. Or you may buy land as an investment. But be careful of that, because the nature of this transit is such that you may not want to sell it again. Certainly it would be a good expression of this symbolism to improve your existing home and make it more comfortable.

At this time you should do everything to ensure that your personal life is as comfortable and secure as possible. You need to have a feeling of inner peace and security in order to continue to move out in the world. In fact you should not think so much about outward success now as about the more personal and inward needs that we have discussed here. And you should realize that your real need now is not land or a larger home, but a feeling of strength and inner growth.

This is the time to tie up any loose ends in your personal life, straighten out any relationships that are not working well, any leftovers from your past life that are still affecting the present adversely. To do this you may have to speak to others very openly about yourself and your innermost thoughts.

So this is a good time to settle and put down roots. The feeling of belonging to a place and a group of people is very important to you now. You don't have to do this in a way that limits your freedom of movement, and with Jupiter here it is very unlikely that you will do so. But everyone needs a solid home base so that they can feel at peace in their other activities. If you don't make an effort to construct such a base now, you will have difficulty later when your principal concerns are turning elsewhere.

Jupiter Conjunct Ascendant

During this period you feel good and project warm positive energies out into the world. This in turn affects your relationships very positively and enables you to encounter people who can be good for you precisely because you are good for them. In all personal and professional transactions with others you will give and receive in equal measure.

For psychological and physical health, this transit is excellent. You feel very optimistic and positive, and your body is unusually resistant to disease and infection. The only physical problem with this transit is that it sometimes signifies a gain in weight, so be very careful if you are at all inclined to gain.

Personal relationships expand under this influence. If you have been living in a relatively small circle of friends and acquaintances, you will expand your circle and meet people whom you wouldn't ordinarily, possibly including the rich and famous or people in power. Just be careful that you don't become involved with these people for superficial reasons; make sure that you can grow through them. The fact that a person is socially significant may not have any relevance to your relationship.

The basis for all this is that in a very real sense you are growing and taking more and more of the outer world into your personal sphere. You are trying to include more of the world in your experience. Properly handled, this process can make you a much wiser and more mature individual. Your view of life should expand, and you should become increasingly tolerant of the wide differences among people in the world. You have the opportunity to become a man or woman of the world to a much greater extent.

As with other Jupiter transits, you should be careful not to assume arrogant airs or to think that you are better than you are. You are probably a fine person, but that does not mean that you are necessarily better than everyone else. Think in terms of your personal growth, not in terms of your status with respect to others.

Travel and professional success are sometimes associated with this transit, but you should realize that these are just outward manifestations of your inner personal growth. If you travel, you should do so to learn about the world. If your business or career expands, apply your gains to your personal life and do not make a distinction between your personal and your professional life now. This transit represents the beginning of a new cycle of development in your life as Jupiter begins another twelve-year cycle of the houses. Make sure that this cycle will help you become a better human being.

Jupiter Sextile Ascendant

This is usually an extremely fortunate transit for all kinds of social contacts. You will benefit through others, and they will probably benefit through you. If you choose to go it alone at this time, you will waste a valuable opportunity, for you will profit tremendously from team efforts with friends. Also you will have opportunities to work on projects that may be to your personal advantage; these will come from persons you encounter every day at work or around your neighborhood, people from whom you do not expect much beyond the usual social exchanges.

At this time you will have the opportunity to expand your contacts with the larger world. Sometimes this transit is a sign of travel, but certainly you will encounter people whose backgrounds are quite different from yours and whose experience will increase your understanding of the world. Several of these people may become permanent friends whom you will benefit from knowing.

You may also benefit from old friends. You may be offered a chance to go into business with a friend, or a friend may tell you about a good chance to get ahead in some way.

At the same time, you feel benevolent and well disposed to your friends and acquaintances. You are willing and able to help those who need it, and generally you display an attitude of supportive kindness to the people around you, for you don't want to see people in trouble.

This basic willingness to give and to help others enables you to receive much from others as well. People sense that you will conduct all transactions fairly, so they are willing to be fair to you. Actually this is always true, but you are more able to see it at this time.

Jupiter Square Ascendant

This is usually an excellent transit for most kinds of relationships, but there are some pitfalls. Basically this transit signifies a desire to grow and advance through contacts with others. Probably you are willing to give as much as you get, although in some people this transit triggers a desire for advantages through others without giving anything in return. In fact as they get ahead, such people act arrogantly toward everyone, even those who helped them. This causes others to reject them, and when they hit hard times there is no one to help them out.

But this result is totally unnecessary, and all you have to do to avoid it is to keep a sense of humility and recognize what others have done for you. With this transit you have the potential to become a truly better person, but only if you keep these warnings in mind.

Quite frequently this transit brings a seemingly "lucky" chance through a friend or associate. But it is not luck so much as the fact that you are very sharply on the lookout for opportunities that can benefit you. Your sense of timing is very acute, and your sensitivity to others and their needs is greater than usual. That is one reason why it is so bad to ignore others' needs, because you don't even have the excuse of ignorance.

Benefits can come to you in either your personal and domestic life or in your work. There may be an opportunity to make money or to make improvements in your home that will make it much more pleasant. Or you may meet people who will help you learn more about the world and expand your view of it in various ways. You have to be willing to let this happen, however, which means you must be receptive. This is another area in which being arrogant brings the risk that you will get nothing of lasting value out of this transit.

One other point. In all negotiations and transactions with others, you have a pronounced tendency to overlook details and to assume that everything will work out. But it won't if you don't pay attention to the details. The little matters of human relationships, either professional or personal, are not beneath you. Attend to them properly.

Jupiter Trine Ascendant

This transit signifies your willingness to grow in consciousness and experience through your contacts with others and to be more magnanimous and willing to help others. In this you are helped by the fact that your relations with others are very good at this time, and you experience people at their best. This makes you more optimistic, and you rightly believe that whatever you give to others will be returned with interest. A person may enter your life now who really helps you out in various ways, especially by teaching you something about the universe and your role in it. This learning will be on whatever level you are ready for, perhaps simply learning to be more tolerant and open to new ideas or even encountering deep spiritual and religious truths through this relationship. Certainly you are ready for a greater spiritual understanding of the world now. You need to experience more than the superficial banality of life that many people become mired in. Although you are inclined to idealize the world in general and certain persons in particular, in the long run you will find that this is not a delusion but a period of truly expanding knowledge.

Your learning at this time is not limited to spiritual truths, for you are in general more intellectually eager and willing to learn. This is an excellent time to go to school or take a course in a subject that will give you greater insight into the questions that interest you.

On occasion this transit will signify the beginning of a relationship that can bring you great emotional happiness. It could be a new love, although that is much more likely if indicated more specifically by another transit at about this time. Any new love that comes now will be very beneficial to your personal growth, whether or not it lasts.

Jupiter Opposition Ascendant

During this period you seek to grow in various ways through your closest contacts with other people. You try to create relationships that will further your life, not in a spirit of selfishness, but in a desire for mutual growth. Often at this time a person will come into your life who offers to help you out in some way, usually through a partnership. In business, for example, this is an extremely good time to enter into a partnership or a contact with someone. In your personal life, you will work more closely than usual with someone, which will work out very well for you both. If other indications are compatible, you may meet someone who will be important to you romantically, but that is not the usual result of this transit.

This is also an excellent time to seek out someone for counseling, especially a lawyer, but also any other kind of counselor. Related to this, incidentally, is that if you have a case in court at this time, it will work out as you want it to.

If you are married, your marriage should work better than usual now. You and your partner will be anxious to help each other grow and to further each other's interests in all possible ways. You do not want to restrict your spouse or be restricted by him or her in any possible way. Because you understand the need for freedom of individual self-expression within your relationship, you will try to find ways to bring that about. If your marriage is not working out very well in general, this transit can have either of two effects. It can either bring a time of healing in the relationship so that it ceases to be such a problem, or it can make your desire for freedom so strong that you break off the relationship altogether. At any rate, the problems themselves will cease. And a marriage that does break up under this transit (this only applies to one that is on the rocks) will do so relatively amicably.

Chapter Ten

Saturn

Significance of Transiting Saturn

Saturn is one of the most important planets to examine in your transits, for it represents the way you see and experience the universe as you have structured it. The location of transiting Saturn in your chart indicates the part of your life that is being examined and tested at that time. The house that Saturn is in represents the areas of greatest tension in your life, to which you must direct your closest attention. The planets that Saturn transits in your natal chart represent energies in your life that are being challenged and behavior patterns that require examination.

Most people experience Saturn transits as if Saturn were an external force that was utterly out of control. Frequently a Saturn transit seems like the product of fate, usually an unpleasant fate. But you must understand that Saturn represents the way *you* program your universe at the deepest, most fundamental level. Consequently, the energy of a Saturn transit is never truly external. But your conscious mind avoids responsibility for what is happening, so the unconscious mind takes over by programming the event unconsciously. You do not experience its effects until the outer world reacts and a "fated" event occurs, which is nothing more than the universe responding to your own actions.

No matter how unpleasant a Saturn transit seems at the time, it represents what you really want in life and is helping you get it. Most people are out of touch with what they truly want. If you thoroughly understand your needs and wants, you will find that Saturn simply brings about their manifestation. The "losses" that Saturn brings are of things that you do not want or need. No matter how much you think you want them, let them go, especially relationships that Saturn may end.

When Saturn transits a house, you should pay great attention to the affairs of that house. It is not a sign that everything in that house is going wrong, but you should direct your consciousness there and find out how you should relate to those affairs. If you are in a good position, that is, one that is appropriate at this time in your life, the transit will firm up and structure that house for you. If you are not in a good position, Saturn will bring great changes that will be unpleasant insofar as you resist them.

Depression, sadness, physical and emotional loss are all signs that you are not well adjusted to the issues of the houses and signs ruled by Saturn. Do not be dismayed, however, if you have these feelings. They are normal responses. Very few people are so in touch with themselves that they can react to Saturn positively. In a very real sense Saturn is the teacher, but it is each of us teaching ourselves about what we really are.

Saturn in the First House

This transit represents a new beginning of internal growth. The period when Saturn crossed your Ascendant was a time of shearing away those aspects of your life that no longer had a valid role, a time when projects were completed. As Saturn continues to transit your first house, your responsibilities will continue to be heavy, but your accomplishments may also be great. During this transit it is not a good idea to start any new, long-range projects that will take years to complete. Obviously you should proceed with anything that has to be done in a shorter time span. Don't use this transit as an excuse for sitting around and waiting for a more favorable time.

Now is the time to turn your attention inward. You have just completed a fourteen-year period in which your attention was focused primarily on interactions with others, your social life. While you have built up a very elaborate external world, you may be quite unaware of what is going on inside yourself. Now is the time to turn inward and restructure yourself wherever necessary. This restructuring will take several years, so don't be in a hurry. You have learned a great deal about the world, now learn about yourself. What do you really want and need? What have you learned about yourself over the last several years? You have to understand what you are in your own terms, not in other people's terms.

Regardless of what type of person you are, this is a time of introversion and introspection. The more you get in touch with yourself during the next few years, the more successful you will be in the future.

Saturn has a way of forcing you to deal with the appropriate issues. Since this is a time for looking inward, it will obviously present difficulties if you have elaborate commitments in the outer world. If those commitments get in the way of investing energy within yourself, you will begin to have trouble with them. You may feel that you just don't have the energy to cope; you may feel withdrawn and tired. If you are naturally introspective, you may become more so. Often people experience significant failures in their work at this time, because the work is distracting them from an encounter with themselves.

This is an excellent time for any kind of psychotherapy, human potential work or consciousness-raising. You need to unlearn all of the incorrect and inaccurate ways of thinking about yourself that you have learned from others. You need to know who you are. Then you can properly lay the foundation for restructuring your inner life. This must precede the restructuring of your outer life, which will happen about fourteen years from now.

Saturn in the Second House

When Saturn transited your first house, you had to learn who you really were in your own terms. Now, as Saturn enters your second house, you have to learn what is really important to you, what you value. This does not mean just material things, but also psychological, spiritual and moral values. In fact these may take precedence over material values, if that is where you need to work on self-understanding.

Many of the old texts discuss this transit as a time of financial loss and poverty. This is not necessarily true, although it can be. If material wealth is keeping you from discovering your true values, then you are likely to experience financial losses. Otherwise, your circumstances will probably be all right. Even so, however, you may feel financially insecure at this time. Control over your material possessions may seem to be slipping from your hands. So you work very hard to keep everything going as you want it to. But try to avoid letting fear and financial insecurity run your life now, for this takes attention away from the task of restructuring your value-system on the inner psychological level. The best course is to organize your finances as well as possible so you don't have to pay much attention to them. If you get wrapped up in money matters, they will be a source of trouble.

Your material possessions reflect what you value on the psychological plane. If you are not conscious of your inner values, your possessions will reflect that unconsciousness; that is, they will not accurately reflect who you are. They will require much more involvement, because they are not really natural to you. And above all, your experience of material possessions will seem to be out of your control! When you discover your real needs in this area, they may be quite different from what you thought, which is usually what you were taught to think. Most unhappiness about possessions comes because there is some disparity between what you think you should want and what you do want.

Be careful with your finances, and be economical. Above all, do not become concerned with them any more than you have to in order to function in your everyday world.

Saturn in the Third House

Saturn's transit of this house completes the phase of inward preparation and self-encounter that began several years ago with Saturn's transit of the first house. The main issue that you will confront at this time is the actual structuring of your mind and how it operates on a day-to-day level, in other words, your everyday mental patterns, attitudes, habits, styles of speaking and ways of listening to others. Normally you take these issues for granted and don't think about them very much. But they are very important in structuring your world.

The third house is the house of immediate environment as well as of the everyday aspects of your mind. Your immediate environment is the part of your world that is most affected by your unconscious mental patterns, attitudes and habits. And of course it is strongly influenced by your way of communicating with others. Therefore you need to understand these areas completely so you can gain greater control over your daily life.

As you encounter this aspect of yourself, you may find it necessary to make extensive changes. Even if you do not realize this, the changes will occur automatically. In either case, as these changes occur you may experience difficulty with people who are so used to your old ways that they cannot handle the new ones. You may have trouble with people in your immediate environment, especially relatives and close neighbors. These changes may also cause you to become discouraged and to be unable to communicate as readily as you used to. That is understandable, but it is not a very good way to handle the situation; it only makes things worse.

When you learn what is happening in your mind, it may be quite difficult to accept yourself. This leads to depression, withdrawal and a general sense of discouragement. You must learn to see what is happening dispassionately, without making value judgments. You should be concerned with what is, not with what you think should be. This is especially true now, because you should be restructuring your notions of what should be to reflect your potentialities more accurately. Saturn's energies can make you live according to ideals that have no relevance to yours or anyone else's reality, if you start by making value judgments. When you live for such Saturnine abstractions, you live for no one and nothing!

As Saturn completes this transit, your attention will move away from concern with inner truths. Once again you will begin to deal with how your inner world relates to the outside world. If you are a person who defines success in purely external terms, you may feel that a period of frustration is ending. However, it hasn't been failure, but rather learning.

Saturn in the Fourth House

This is an extremely important transit of Saturn. At this time you will focus on your innermost personal and domestic life, for this is the area that requires work now. Any problems in your domestic life will become more critical at this time, and anything you have been "putting up with" but not really handling will have to be dealt with. Consequently the effects of this transit range from a simple reorganization of your domestic environment to a total reshuffling of the personal relationships and contacts that affect your domestic life. Your home itself may become a tremendous burden because of payments, repairs or other such responsibilities.

Elements that used to be important in your life often come back into prominence now, especially if they were never resolved in the past. Therefore this is an especially good time to get in touch with your innermost self through psychotherapy or other consciousness-raising and consciousness-expanding techniques.

During this time you may have to take on a parental responsibility for someone, not necessarily your own child, or you may seek out someone who will play a parental role for you. If you do find a "parent," however, make sure that this situation will ultimately lead to independence on your part. Be certain that it is a growth relationship for you and not the beginning of a long-term dependency, which would prove detrimental in the years to come.

At this time a period of several years' preparation is coming to an end. You are ready to emerge from comparative dormancy, at least in terms of outward success, and begin to move upward and forward to achieve your ambitions. But you must start modestly. The fourth house acts as the foundation of your horoscope, and you must pay attention to securing and building up this foundation. This is what lies behind your outward concern with your physical home. It is really the inner "house" that you are attending to, which is the reason that this is such a good time to be involved in psychotherapy. Inner problems that you do not clear up now will be the source of most of the problems along your personal road during the next fourteen years. The fourth house is opposite the tenth house of career and social status. Any negative factors at work here will oppose your successful achievements later. This is a time of new beginnings, so get off to a good start.

Saturn in the Fifth House

During this time you will learn more about yourself and how to express yourself in the best possible way. But you will have to work for this result; it will not happen by itself. You should proceed in a careful, organized manner. Although the fifth is usually considered the house of recreation and amusement, Saturn's transit through it is not likely to be very amusing. It is as if everything in your life has to have some teaching or learning purpose. During Saturn's transit through the earlier houses, you redefined and restructured your inner self. Now you will begin to give that self new form through interaction with others.

Areas traditionally associated with the fifth house may become a burden at this time. You will have to attend to these matters, for they will not take care of themselves. For example, children may become a heavy responsibility for some reason. Love affairs may become quite difficult, especially if they do not permit your newly restructured self to be expressed. A love affair may involve an older person who acts almost as a parent to you. Or you may play that role for someone younger. You may first become aware of certain aspects of yourself through an intense emotional encounter with another person. Even if it is an unpleasant encounter, it can be a positive growth experience.

During this transit you may also simply withdraw from encounters with others. This is understandable because every encounter poses challenges, but you should not avoid them anyway. In so doing you are avoiding the experience of what you have become, which is so necessary for your proper development at this time. If you feel that you want a relationship, but your opportunities seem to be frustrated, examine your real feelings. Usually you will find that you are subconsciously avoiding the people who would be right for you in order to avoid the confrontation you fear.

The fifth house is also the house of gambling, speculation and other such risks. Needless to say, these activities are not at all in accord with the methodical and work-demanding nature of Saturn. Do not take such risks at this time, for they are not likely to work out.

Anything you produce during this time will be the result of hard work. You will have a much more disciplined approach to creative activity than you have had in the past. This is as it should be, because again the aim is to understand yourself through careful, disciplined action. In this case the activity means giving form to something through your own efforts. This principle applies whether or not you are artistic. All of us are creative in some way.

Saturn in the Sixth House

This is a critical time in your development. When Saturn leaves this house and crosses the seventh-house cusp, your efforts to attain your goals and ambitions will begin to bear definite fruit if you have handled this house properly. Even if you have not received much recognition for your efforts in the past few years, you will begin to receive it then.

The transit of Saturn through the sixth house can be compared to preparing for a debut. You have to put everything in order so that you will make the maximum impact. Consequently this is a time of very heavy responsibility and hard work. At times your responsibilities may seem overwhelming, and you may not feel equal to the challenge. If you are employed, you may find it difficult to live up to your employers' demands, which can lead to difficulties on the job. This situation is made worse by your feeling that even if you did better, you would not be adequately recognized or compensated for your efforts. And you would probably be right, at least in the short run. But in the long run, if you can keep with it, the work will be beneficial.

Your effectiveness as a human being will be tested during this time. Therefore, you should try to get your performance into shape in many areas, especially work and professional matters. Later you will be in a more public position, where it will be harder to make necessary changes.

Conserve your energies now in order to devote yourself more efficiently to whatever must be done. If you scatter or waste your energies, you will not have enough. And if you try to compensate with an extra burst of energy, your health may suffer. The sixth is also the house of health, and this Saturn transit means that you must attend to your health. Treat your body as a tool that has to be well cared for in order to achieve its desired purpose. If your health breaks down during this transit, you should examine the way you handle your physical energies as a whole. Make whatever changes are necessary so that your lifestyle more accurately reflects your intrinsic reality. Both your body and mind must be in shape for the impending emergence of your energies into the outer world, where everyone can see them more clearly. That will happen shortly.

Saturn in the Seventh House

The transit of Saturn through this house represents the culmination of the process that began about fourteen years ago when Saturn entered your first house. The need then was to redefine yourself in your own terms. Now you need to experience yourself through one-to-one encounters with others, through partnerships and intimate associations. Close relationships are the area of attention.

During this transit you will discover that your close associations with others test you out and make increasing demands. Often these will be sources of difficulty in your life, and dealing with them will require great effort on your part. Some relationships will end, because they demand more than they are worth. This transit often coincides with a marital breakup. Even a good marriage will have to confront its flaws when one of the partners has Saturn transiting the seventh house.

Coworkers will make greater demands upon you than in the past because they see you as someone who can accomplish things, and they want you to prove it. This brings us to the other major point about Saturn's transit through this house.

On entering this house, Saturn has once again come above the horizon of your natal chart. This means that your attention is again focused primarily away from your inner world, out into the social world. If you have been preparing yourself properly during the last fourteen years, getting to know who and what you really are, what you can do and cannot do, then you will begin to get recognition during this time. But this house also calls forth tests of your ability through confrontations with others. This may be particularly obvious in your profession, but it applies equally to your personal life. This is another factor in the marital tensions that accompany this transit. The better you handle such confrontations, the better your relationship will be in the immediate future. Basically the situation is quite simple. You must do the best you can at any particular task, and you must understand the nature of your relationships with others. Exactly what are your expectations of them and their expectations of you? In other words, what agreements have you made with others? Once you know, live up to them. It is not terribly important what the agreements are, but it is important that you fulfill them. This is the fundamental test of this transit.

Saturn in the Eighth House

This transit brings into focus finances and possessions that you hold with others. In a larger way it brings into question the greater transformations that you have been going through.

It is not enough simply to know who you are and how you relate to others. You must also come to terms with other people's values. You must learn to live with those values and to incorporate them constructively into your life without destroying your own individuality. With Saturn transiting this house, you will become aware of this issue, often through conflict with others' values. Other people's resources may be cut off from you and be unavailable when you think you need them. A concrete example of this would be not getting a bank loan because you have not met the bank's criteria. Or in a marriage, your partner may encounter financial hard times that cut you off from an accustomed source of income. During this transit you cannot count upon others for any kind of material backing. They may not have the money, or they may not want to share it with you now. It would be a good idea to get into a position where you don't have to depend on anyone else's resources.

The eighth house is also the house of major transformations in life, including death. However, it must be said immediately that your own death is an extremely unlikely result of an eighth-house Saturn transit. If death enters your life at all at this time, it is likely to be someone else's. Or you may suddenly become psychologically concerned about your own mortality. You may think about death more often.

You have just finished a phase of intense encounter with others, which has enabled you to define yourself by becoming aware of how you deal with people. This phase is more or less finished, and now the question arises of what all this is for. During this time you are likely to review the changes you have gone through in the years since Saturn crossed your Ascendant and to look for a pattern in it. Through this analysis you hope to arrive at an understanding of where you are going. This process and learning to understand other people's resources and values will prepare you for the transit of Saturn conjunct the Midheaven, which will happen in a few years. Also you will learn the limitations of your own resources and the degree to which you have to cooperate with and depend upon others.

Saturn in the Ninth House

At this time you are approaching a life peak, when all your ambitions and efforts should bear their greatest fruit. That peak will occur during the transit of Saturn through the tenth house. Now, while Saturn transits the ninth house, your views about life are becoming stabilized. You understand the rules of the games you are playing in, and you are concentrating on how to play more skillfully. In this phase of the cycle of Saturn, your understanding of yourself and how you live has reached a climax. If you do not know who you are now, you will probably have to wait until the next cycle to find out — about seven to nine years from now.

There is a danger here, however. It is tempting to assume that you have reached the point of complete understanding, so that you may become narrow unless you remain open to new discoveries about yourself and the world. Let your philosophy of life be a guideline, not a straitjacket. If you assume that you know everything, you may suddenly find yourself losing the "game." Strangely enough, legal difficulties can be a manifestation of this problem, for the ninth is also the house of law.

Older authorities have claimed that this transit is dangerous for long journeys; but it is not, unless the planetary combinations in your natal ninth house suggest that you are violently accident-prone. But it does mean you may take long journeys for learning or to fulfill obligations rather than for fun.

You will be attracted to all subjects relating to higher consciousness, such as religion, metaphysics or philosophy, as well as the law in its highest sense. But you are also concerned with practical results. You are coming to a stage that will test your ultimate effectiveness as a human being, so this is not the right time for abstractions, unless they really help you get a firmer grasp on the real world. Your approach to learning is very pragmatic at this time. The understanding you gain in this house will be of enormous benefit to you when you encounter the transit of Saturn through the tenth house.

Saturn in the Tenth House

In many ways, Saturn's transit of this house represents the harvest. During this time you will experience the consequences of the preparations you have been making for the last twenty to twenty-four years. If you have prepared well, the results will be excellent, but whatever is not so well prepared will be the basis of the difficulties you will encounter.

In your professional life, you will gain many responsibilities. If you are ever to be a leader, it will be now. If you are ambitious for leadership, this will be a period of great achievement. If you prefer not to have such responsibility, this may be an onerous time for you, but still productive, if you let it be.

In your personal development you will function with the most complete sense of who and what you are in all areas. The tenth house governs those aspects of your life that really represent your individuality as it is expressed by your unique accomplishments. At this time you have the greatest opportunity to make an impression upon the world as an individual.

But this can also be a time of disaster. Negative energies that you have unleashed in the past may have negative consequences now. President Nixon resigned from office during this transit. In the past he had created great opposition, a large body of people who were anxious to see him fall. He also brought about his fall through his own unethical conduct. Saturn's transit through this house is especially dangerous if there are difficult aspects to planets in the tenth house in your natal chart. Even so, you can control the results of this transit by preparing carefully and not taking any shortcuts as you rise to the top.

Another danger that can occur during this transit is that you may become so focused on external affairs — your job, social prestige, status, etc. — that you overlook what is happening in your personal life. This is why it was so very important fourteen years ago, when Saturn was transiting your fourth house, to lay a strong foundation in your personal life. Anything that was done badly in that area then may be a source of problems now and may vitiate whatever success you are enjoying now.

Nevertheless, if you have prepared well in the last several years, this can be one of the most rewarding times in your life, because you have earned every bit of it.

Saturn in the Eleventh House

At this time your principal task is to integrate your individual self with some kind of group expression. Whatever group you belong to will demand that you become integrated. During Saturn's transit of your tenth house, you had the opportunity to shine and achieve as an individual. Now others require that you join them and be less of a star on your own. In general, however, this transit is a continuation of the high period in your life that should have begun when Saturn transited your tenth house, especially if you answer the challenges presented by this house.

If you find it difficult to work with others, to cooperate in team efforts, you may feel that coworkers and friends are getting in your way. They may give you responsibilities that you don't want. But as with the transit through the tenth, you should try to come to terms with these demands rather than avoid them, because this is how you will be rewarded.

The eleventh is also the house of your hopes and wishes, your ideals and objectives in life. During this transit you will find out whether or not you have worked effectively to attain these ideals. Saturn in your eleventh house should bring about the results you have been trying to attain, if you have prepared well. If not, your expectations will be disappointed, and it will be clear that you are not going to get what you want.

In this case, Saturn's transit of the twelfth house will be a time of breakdown and clearing out, so that in the next Saturn cycle you can try again. Most people have at least two Saturn cycles in their life. Frequently the first transit through the eleventh house is not as successful as the second, because it comes too early in life for you to take full advantage of it. At least two transits of Saturn through the chart are usually required for you to gain enough experience and maturity to make events work out in the best possible way.

Saturn in the Twelfth House

At this time the decks are cleared for new action. Now you should be finishing up anything that was not done completely during the last several years. This is not a good time for starting new projects, for the energy just isn't there even if you think that you want to start anew.

Even if you don't want to take some project through this final finishing-up phase, circumstances will compel you to. Important elements of your life may begin to pass away, and activities that used to work well no longer do. Your ways of handling people and situations no longer achieve the desired response. You get the impression that in order to succeed you will have to change everything, yet you don't know how to make the changes. People tend to "withdraw" into themselves during this time so that they can get more in tune with what is happening. It is very important that you use this time to understand what you have accomplished and what you have failed to accomplish. Do not judge or evaluate; simply observe and recognize.

If your life has not succeeded according to your expectations during the last several years when Saturn transited your natal tenth and eleventh houses, now you have an opportunity to clear away the barriers that prevented you from achieving what you wanted. But this effort will not bear fruit immediately. This is the end of a cycle, not yet the beginning of a new one.

It is tempting to fall into despair over the "failures" that seem to haunt you now. During this time you are more likely to feel guilty and to brood about your inadequacies. But these feelings are neither productive nor therapeutic. Recognize that this is the time to clear away leftovers from the past and to make ready for a new start. You will feel pressures for tremendous changes both in the direction of your life and in the manner of proceeding in that direction. Heed these pressures, for they are the first signs of the new order that is about to begin in your life. You will go through a new cycle of defining your individuality within yourself and with respect to others and of experiencing its effectiveness before the world. Cut your losses, if any, and look forward rather than backward.

Saturn Conjunct Sun

This transit can bring both fulfillment and difficulty. Roughly fourteen years ago, when transiting Saturn opposed your Sun, you went through a period of adversity and low vitality. But at the same time you made new beginnings, which are having results now. These efforts will either reach a climax and be successful, or you will realize that they have failed. In any case this is a time of tremendous responsibility and hard work, either to guarantee the successful conclusion of your old projects and endeavors or to salvage the best from the failures.

In those areas of your life that you have handled successfully — your job, your domestic life or whatever — the responsibility of bringing your activities to a successful climax will limit your freedom of movement. Even if you know that events are turning out as you want, you may feel restless under the burdens. Try to be patient and concentrate wholly upon the tasks at hand.

Do not take on any new projects at this time that are not directly connected to what you are already doing. The additional responsibility could be too much for you and could cause health problems, especially with your heart and circulatory system. When you have successfully completed all your current projects, you may start new ones. This is a time of perseverance, hard work and heavy responsibility, and there is great potential for reward.

Those areas of your life that have not worked out as expected should not be regarded as complete failures. Several years ago when you embarked on these projects, you may not have understood as much as you understand now. This transit will make you aware of this fact. Don't start out on a new course until you have cleared up whatever has not worked out. Otherwise you will only work hard to no avail and cause possible damage to your health. This can be a time of personal and professional defeats.

The energy of Saturn holds back the energy of the Sun, which is your basic life energy. Saturn confines and restricts it so that you can do only certain things. As a result, you may feel cut off from others and lonely, but do not be too concerned about this. Even if this transit coincides with the breaking up of a relationship, which it may, it means that the relationship itself is distracting you from matters that you must attend to now. This is a time for concentrating energy, not scattering it.

Saturn Sextile Sun

This transit will present many opportunities for achievement. At this time you will be able to strengthen many areas of your life so that they can withstand adversity later. But you have to take control of this moment. Nothing will be given to you without some effort on your part. You will have to exercise considerable care and responsibility and pay attention to what others require of you and the commitments you have made to them. This is not a "lucky" transit in the ordinary sense of the word, but it can be exceedingly fortunate for you, if you work hard to make it so.

This transit is very strongly related to one of two other periods in your life — either the last opposition of Saturn to your natal Sun, nine or ten years ago, or the last conjunction, four or five years ago. In either case, the activities that you began at that time have overcome their initial crises and now are running very smoothly. You are in a position to achieve many of the goals that you set for yourself then, if you work at it.

Recognition by others, particularly persons in authority over you, may come now. Do everything in your power to be worthy of that recognition, for it will help you later on. At this time you have more patience and perseverance than usual. You are able to work in a disciplined and careful manner and make your work enduring. This is an excellent time to tackle difficult and demanding projects.

Even your health is better than usual, but that does not mean that you should abuse it. Instead, you should be building up your strength. In the not-too-distant future you will need your good health, so don't waste it now. In general this is a time of successful preparation for climaxes and periods of crisis to come. How well you are able to deal with the future depends largely upon what you do now.

Saturn Square Sun

This transit represents a time of critical developments. Various factors in the outside world will challenge you strongly, and it may seem difficult to maintain your freedom of action in whatever you are trying to do.

You may feel unusually discouraged at this time, because your vitality is at a low point. It may be best not to struggle too hard against any adversity that comes into your life now. Patience and perseverance will carry you through until your energy level is up again.

Authority figures, such as employers, government officials or parents, may prove difficult to deal with. You may find that they are not receptive to your plans or suggestions, that they resist your efforts. It is advisable to work patiently to bring them around to your point of view. Don't withdraw from the confrontation, but don't fight blindly. That would guarantee defeat.

This period of your life is directly linked to a time seven years ago, a time of new beginnings for you. The projects you began then are encountering their first major crises now. This transit is made especially difficult by the fact that many of these projects have been going quite well, and the current difficulties seem totally unexpected.

However, this is a period of trial, which will demonstrate whether or not those new beginnings were valid. Anything invalid is likely to fall by the wayside. You will probably regard it as a failure. But you may not be aware right away that this is happening, especially if you are not paying close attention. If you try to save something that isn't worth saving, you may be able to fool yourself into thinking that it is working out, but only until Saturn opposes your Sun, seven years from now. Then the consequences will become devastatingly clear. You would be well advised to cut the losses you are experiencing now as soon as you realize that they *are* losses. Concentrate on the successful areas of your life so that you can bring them to a successful climax at the end of that same seven-year period.

Your ambitions may be thwarted now, but be patient and make sure you are on the right course. If you are, this transit will be a trial rather than a defeat. Even if it is a defeat, you can still accomplish a great deal by transferring your energies to more productive areas.

One final comment. This transit can be very important to your health. One sign of inappropriate activity is bad health. Even at best, you are not at your most vigorous under this transit. If you are not careful, you could undergo a serious health breakdown, particularly in the cardiovascular system. Try to make changes in your life that will help your health.

Saturn Trine Sun

At this time the circumstances of your life and your own inner energies are working quite well together. But this transit will not seem especially lucky; rather, your life as a whole will run smoothly, and whatever you do will come out well. Without any special sense of effort, you are actually able to make significant progress and get a great deal done. Take advantage of this and accomplish as much as possible. If an opportunity arises for further training to expand the range of your experience, take it, because you will build up a bulwark against possible adversity later on. The more you accomplish at this time, the easier it will be to live up to demands that will be made upon you a few years from now.

Like the sextile transit of Saturn to your Sun, the trine is a time of preparation for the climaxes that come at the opposition and conjunction transits. Therefore you should use this period to make your world strong and secure against difficulties. Either you are laying the framework for success that will come in nine to ten years, or you are capitalizing on some earlier success. That phase of activity will end about four or five years from now. Either way, you shouldn't waste this time. Saturn, even with the trine aspect, always demands that you live up to obligations and responsibilities and very seldom gives you something for nothing, as the other planets often do.

Like the sextile transit, the trine is a good time for building up your physical strength rather than wasting it. If you waste your energy now, it won't mean immediate trouble, but in a few years, when you need strength and energy, you may not have it.

This is a good time to win recognition from others for your achievements. Employers or others with whom you work will be impressed with your diligence. And you should strive to impress them, because in a few years your goals will be challenged, but if you have convinced others that you are worthwhile, you will overcome those obstacles more easily.

Saturn Opposition Sun

This may be a very discouraging time. Your vital energies are at a twenty-nine-year low, and you may feel quite incapable of dealing with the adversities that often accompany this transit.

These adversities may come from a number of sources. First of all, other people — particularly employers and other persons in authority — may oppose your plans in several areas. This is not usually a good time for successfully attaining your goals.

You may feel physically tired, as if the burdens of your life are too much for you. Quite commonly during this transit people feel old, even if they are in fact young, and there is a profound sense of world-weariness. Avoid excessive strains on your health, because that can lead to a major health breakdown, particularly if you *are* older. Be careful of your health and conserve your energies. You will have plenty of opportunities to use them later, despite your feelings at the moment.

Your ambitions may also be thwarted by circumstances or by other people. Even though you and your associates have the best intentions for your future, something seems to block you.

It is possible that you may be caught in some kind of relationship, for example, a bad marriage or love affair that limits your self-expression. Quite frequently this transit brings such relationships to an end.

This transit is best dealt with by understanding that it is part of a natural cycle in your life. Nothing is gained by fighting it; instead you must learn to flow with it. This transit is the end of a twenty-nine-year cycle in which you have put energy out into the world and built up important structures in your life. From them will come the foundation of a new cycle. This transit represents a period of endings, which will be followed by new beginnings. The problem is to avoid being discouraged and frustrated by the endings. Soon you will have the opportunity to begin new projects that will build up to new peaks of achievement in about fourteen years, when Saturn conjoins your Sun. There will be a time of significant trial in about seven years when Saturn squares your Sun, as your new projects are tested to see if they are of real value in your life.

If you hang on and are patient, opportunities will soon return for success and achievement. But don't try to strike out right now, for you would not be likely to succeed, and you would only have to start over again. Your life is changing very rapidly, and it will be difficult to anticipate exactly what course it will take from here on.

Saturn Conjunct Moon

During this transit you will need to engage in deep introspection, self-examination and self-criticism. Quite possibly you will feel lonely and depressed. The way in which you handle this transit will have important consequences later for your physical and psychological well-being.

Saturn represents your notion of reality and how you fit into it. It strongly affects your sense of who you are as distinct from other people. It also represents an ideal of perfect orderliness, righteousness and sternness. When you compare yourself to your Saturnine ideal, you become extremely self-critical and self-demanding. If you do not live up to the demands of your ideals, your confidence will suffer and you will feel a sense of weakness, defeat and inferiority.

The Moon, on the other hand, represents your need for emotional nurturing, for belonging to a larger whole and for compassion and understanding, as well as your ability to give these to others. The strict justice of Saturn does not blend well with the need to be human, as signified by the Moon. This is the great danger of this transit.

You may very well weigh yourself in the balance and find that you are wanting. You become too self-critical and even self-destructive. Feelings of guilt are characteristic of this transit. Often you have the feeling that your emotions have completely dried up.

Do not let self-questioning lead to self-doubt, and don't let your human feelings and emotions become subordinated to the too-exacting demands of Saturn. If you do, you will be creating distance between yourself and others, which may lead to further self-questioning and doubt, a vicious circle.

This is a good time for self-searching, so long as you are not judgmental. It doesn't matter whether you are good or bad according to the Saturnine ideal. The real question is what you are. This transit can help you find out. If you proceed from this point of view, it can be a very constructive time, even though it is commonly experienced as painful.

During this transit you may withdraw from others, have difficulty in relationships — especially with women — experience depression and feel quite inferior to life's demands. The best way to deal with this is not to take it all so seriously. Your perspective is warped, so that small matters seem too important. Do not make final decisions about your emotional life now. Wait until you can see more clearly what you have learned from this transit.

If you have recently broken off a relationship, it may be best to leave it that way. Do not make a real effort to put it back together until this time is over.

Saturn Sextile Moon

This transit gives you a sense of discipline and self-control, which will make it easier to deal with the emotionally complicated issues in your life that you normally avoid. At this time you can deal with difficult relationships that you could not handle in the past with proper detachment and objectivity. You can reflect upon your feelings and examine them without letting them control you. Make whatever changes should be made in your personal life with confidence that you are seeing the truth clearly.

The Moon rules your past and what you have gotten from it, while Saturn rules the patterns that you are building into your life now. Consequently this transit enables you to build constructively upon your past and to embody its best teachings into your current life. Anything you do at this time must have a strong connection with your past life. This is not the time to make a radical break with tradition.

A related effect is that during this time family matters may become very important to you, especially matters concerning one or both of your parents. Here again the self-control that this transit confers will ensure that your family interactions are constructive. You are in better control than usual of your unconscious attitudes and the behavior generated by them, especially as regards family and loved ones.

However, along with all of this is the need to be aware of what you are doing, which is relatively easy with this transit. But if you take a passive attitude and simply let things slide by you with no effort on your part, the old patterns in your life will take over, and little progress will be made. This transit is an opportunity to take conscious control in your life. Nothing will force you to do so if you don't want to, but you would lose an excellent opportunity.

Saturn Square Moon

This transit can be quite a difficult time for your personal and domestic life. On the psychological level you may feel lonely and isolated from others. You may feel depressed and undeserving of love. Sometimes remembered past actions make you feel guilty that you have not lived up to your own expectations.

Externally this transit can create difficulties in personal relationships, especially with women, because your emotional communication seems to be cut off. Your job may make demands that conflict with your domestic responsibilities, so that you are forced to neglect one or the other. Your parents may also be a source of concern at this time.

Saturn represents the structure and formation of your ego, your sense of individuality and uniqueness, while the Moon represents your need for connections and roots. The conflict at this time is between aspects of these two principles. Somehow it is difficult to be yourself and do what you must, to maintain your relationships and get much-needed emotional support and reinforcement from your loved ones.

These elements of your life are not truly in conflict, for they are complementary principles that need to be properly balanced with each other. The problem is that one element has gotten out of control at the expense of the other, so a time of readjustment is at hand. Usually it is the Saturnine element that has gotten out of control and the Lunar principle that has suffered. This situation is the underlying cause of the loneliness and depression that often accompany this transit.

You may have to make important changes in your life priorities. You may have to deemphasize your work in favor of your emotional and personal life, or you may have to break off a relationship that has interfered unnecessarily with your work. In either case, you must restore the balance between these two aspects of your life so that your life will run smoothly again.

Saturn Trine Moon

This transit indicates a time of equilibrium in your life, when the demands of the world are in balance with your emotional needs. Emotional maturity and past experiences have prepared you for this, and now you can put your understanding to work to make your life run more smoothly. Tensions that in the past have seemed to pull you in opposite directions are now working in balance and harmony.

At this time your emotional attitude is sober. Your mental state is relatively quiet, and you can see objectively what is true for you, what your needs are and how much you can give and get from others. Your domestic life and your work reinforce each other, and you are able to attend to both without sacrificing either.

Now is a good time to take care of any business matters concerning your home and personal life, such as buying or selling real estate, making home repairs, reorganizing your finances and making provisions for the future. On both the psychological and material levels you are unusually well organized, and your plans should work out successfully.

Older people, especially women, may give you great insight and understanding. Your own emotional attitudes are "older" at this time, and you are in a better position to take advantage of the insights of age, both your own and other people's. The counsel of such people will benefit you tremendously.

Now is a good time to plan for the future in all areas of your life, because you are neither foolishly optimistic nor excessively conservative. You can adopt a very careful and pragmatic attitude and see what needs to be done. Your plans will be built upon reality without neglecting your real needs.

Saturn Opposition Moon

This is one of the most emotionally trying transits. It is frequently associated with domestic or professional problems, emotional depression, loneliness, difficulties with women and difficulties with personal relationships, often leading to breakups.

This transit represents an "alienation crisis," that is, a crisis brought about by the discovery that you have been neglecting your emotional and psychological needs. As a result you feel alone and disconnected from others, like an alien in the world whom no one else can ever adequately understand.

To a greater or lesser extent, everyone's life revolves around an overall task or purpose that makes one's life unique. The purpose may be a job, motherhood, fatherhood, some movement that you believe in or anything else that gives you a sense of purpose. This aspect of your life is strongly connected with Saturn. The Moon represents your emotional needs, which you have to fulfill in pursuing your life purpose.

Often an alienation crisis occurs when you discover that you have gone too far too fast in pursuit of your life purpose and have neglected your psychological and emotional needs. Perhaps you have neglected your relationships or your domestic life, or you have repressed your feelings. In this way you build up a wall between yourself and others, which makes you feel alone and alienated.

This problem has arisen because you think of the Saturnine and Lunar aspects of your life as being in conflict. Consequently you neglect the one that you consider less important. Then, when unexpected new demands come from the other element, your whole sense of order is upset and disoriented.

You have to learn that these two aspects of your life are necessary to each other. You must make your personal life and your profession or other central purpose work together. That will require changing your lifestyle so that you can pay equal attention to both.

Saturn Conjunct Mercury

This transit is a time of serious, heavy, even pessimistic thinking. Communication with others becomes more significant, but also more difficult. In fact this transit often means saying goodbye. You take life more seriously than usual and look at things more seriously, but you run the risk of losing your sense of perspective.

Your mental and intellectual viewpoint is narrowed by this transit. You are likely to concern yourself with a smaller range of ideas, but you are more likely to think about them thoroughly. You are beginning a major new cycle of ideas and opinions, of communicating in new ways. This consumes your mental energy and limits your ability to range over a large number of topics. Also you root out old ideas and notions that have outlived their usefulness in your life. Your mind is very disciplined, but with this discipline and narrowing of focus there is the danger of thinking too narrowly. You may overlook important alternatives because of your tendency to concentrate single-mindedly at this time. Also, with your tendency toward depressed thoughts you may overlook possibilities that seem too idealistic or risky; probably they are not at all — it is just that you are thinking "small."

Nevertheless this is an excellent time for working a single idea through completely, planning very carefully and realizing ideas that can have important consequences many years from now.

Mercury also rules the nervous system, speech and hearing. Occasionally this transit signifies problems in one of these areas — nervous ailments, speech or hearing problems and the like, although these are not the most common results of this transit. More commonly this is a period of depression because of a natural tendency to be excessively concerned with serious and difficult subjects.

When dealing with yourself and others, be careful that you do not become too concerned with an unattainable perfection. One effect of the Saturn-Mercury combination can be to make you too exacting and critical, with the result that you alienate others.

Saturn Sextile Mercury

At this time your thinking has settled into stable patterns, and not very much is changing in your mind. But you have discipline and concentration, which enable you to get a great deal of work done. You have a clear idea of what you want to achieve intellectually, and you are willing to work for it. This is an excellent time for any long-range planning that requires great attention to details. It is not so good for the kind of planning that requires you to see the larger scope all at once and handle it as a single system. This transit favors any kind of work involving organization and restructuring. It is excellent for most business transactions, especially those requiring carefully thought-out plans for development. It is not so good for risky or speculative investments, because your level of intuition is lower than normal. It is also a good time for serious study and difficult mental work.

You have a very serious cast of mind now; that is, you approach everything seriously. You want to get your work done, and you aren't interested in playing games with people.

Your views about the world have reached a point of stability, so you act from a consistent position. You believe that you understand what the world is about and you operate on that basis. Obviously this can create some problems. If your mental patterns become too fixed, you close out viewpoints and opinions that will help you grow. Narrow-mindedness is a danger with all the transits of Saturn to Mercury. Saturn can either organize your knowledge into its most useful form, or it can cut you off from knowledge through intellectual rigidity.

This transit sharpens your critical faculties. Your standards are very exacting, and you are likely to judge everything by them. Consequently you are very quick to see exactly what is wrong in any situation. But here again there is the danger that critical thinking may become an excuse for nit-picking and narrow-mindedness. You can too easily learn to see the flaws in everything before you see the strengths, which makes your world seem a great deal more imperfect than it is.

Another point you should keep in mind is that there is a very small difference between stable patterns of thinking and being in a rut. In a few years Saturn will either square your natal Mercury or conjoin it, depending upon whether this is a waxing or a waning sextile. If you allow yourself to become rigid now, your problem will be greater when either of those transits occurs. On the other hand, if you use this time to stabilize your thinking without becoming rigid, you will be better able to withstand future challenges.

Saturn Square Mercury

This can be a time of difficulties in communicating with others and of problems arising from a serious conflict of viewpoints. During this transit your ideas and opinions, as well as your ways of communicating with people, will be seriously challenged by others. Disagreements may lead you to sever relationships or at least to consider doing so. You may feel gloomy, depressed and worried because people do not seem to share your ideas. This makes you feel alone, and at the same time you may withdraw from communicating with others. Therefore this is usually a poor time to make any decisions unless you have to. In your present frame of mind you are incapable of seeing the whole picture upon which any decision must be based. Also your tendency toward pessimism makes you underestimate the real possibilities.

Instead of withdrawing from intellectual conflict with others, you should try to recognize the sources of conflict and help everyone clarify the problems. The differences between you and others are real. Your ideas are fixed and clear enough that others may feel called upon to challenge them. You are in the position of having to defend and justify to others what you believe and think.

It may be that your thinking has become too rigid over the last several years. Challenges by other people can force you to examine your ideas and opinions to see whether they are broad enough to encompass your experience. If you discover that they are not, this should be a time of radical mental reconstruction. If you do not succeed in incorporating other people's challenges into your idea-structure and instead just ignore them, you will undergo a much more serious period of mental confusion and readjustment in about seven years, when Saturn opposes or conjoins your Mercury.

Since Mercury rules the lungs and speech organs, this transit sometimes coincides with illnesses and afflictions of these organs, usually meaning that your communication is interfered with. Laryngitis is such an illness.

Saturn Trine Mercury

At this point in the Saturn-Mercury cycle, your mind, point of view and style of thinking and communicating have reached a point of stability. You are quite secure in them, for you know how and what you think about most things. This is not a time of change but of preparing to use your mind. Consequently it is an excellent time for any task requiring mental discipline and hard work, such as study, schooling or learning any new mental discipline. It is not a very good time for work requiring great inspiration, intuitive insight and creativity. You will get results through hard work and scholarly methods, not through "divinely" inspired insight.

This transit favors planning and organization of various aspects of your life. You have a definite sense of order in mind, which you can make manifest in your life. This is a good time to put your ideas into practice on the material level and to carry out long-standing plans. If you have planned a project, such as building up a new business or starting a new organization, this is a good time to do it. Saturn represents material reality, while Mercury represents the thought behind it.

Of all the Saturn-Mercury transits, whether by hard or soft angles, this one puts you in the most danger of letting your ideas and opinions become too rigid. It is important that your ideas acquire definite form and stability at this time, because in the future they will be challenged very strongly. You must be reasonably definite and sure of yourself in order to withstand the challenges. But rigidity will only make those times worse, because your thinking will have to be flexible, no matter how certain you are now that you are right.

At this time you have an unusual ability to see every intricate piece of a whole, and your position on most matters is very clear. Consequently your critical ability is greater than usual, and you can see instantly what is wrong in any situation. Just don't let this degenerate into nit-picking.

Saturn Opposition Mercury

At this time your ideas and plans may be defeated, or they may have their greatest concrete realization. In either case, you will run into considerable resistance from others to what you say. This may result in severing relationships with those who disagree with you because there is no longer any communication between you. Or it may result simply in the breakdown of communication that was once quite good.

Other people's resistance to your thinking is not intended solely to defeat you, although you may think so. You may be tempted to give up if you are not secure in your thinking and plans. But the resistance of others also forces you to give your plans clearer form and to take definite steps to implement them. This takes hard work and much heavy thinking, but the results can be quite good.

If your ideas cannot withstand the challenge or you do not have enough confidence to defend them, this is likely to be a time of self-doubt and questioning. You will seek to find out what is wrong with your ideas, and if you can be sufficiently detached, you may indeed find out what is wrong. But if you just wallow in guilt, doubt and "being wrong," you will accomplish little except to become depressed.

Although this is not an especially easy time, you shouldn't take a negative or pessimistic view of matters. There are concrete challenges to be met, and you should use your energy to recognize and meet them. Negative thinking is a form of self-indulgence that you cannot afford at this time.

One factor in this transit may be causing you problems. If you have already allowed your thinking to become too rigid and fixed, you will find it difficult to make occasional necessary compromises when you are challenged. Even with the best ideas, a certain amount of mental flexibility is necessary. Rigidity is almost certain to spell defeat, because the forces that oppose you will become equally unbending and rigid.

Sometimes this transit can signify illnesses involving the speech organs and lungs. For instance, during one such transit the author experienced a severe case of laryngitis.

Saturn Conjunct Venus

This transit will have a strong effect on your relationships with others. Relationships that are solidly based will go through a period of testing and examination during which you and your loved ones and friends will become increasingly concerned about what is valid between you. A weak and unstable relationship will go through the same process, but you are more likely to conclude that it is not worth preserving. Consequently, at this time the relationships that have no purpose or that have outlived their purpose in your life will be cut off. Often you will be reluctant to let go of them.

Even in the best of circumstances you are likely to withdraw from others. During this time you have to evaluate who you are, what your individuality consists of and how all of these fit into your relationships with other people, particularly loved ones. You may come to some harsh realizations about your relationships, and even those that you thought were quite good may have to be given up. But you can be sure that any relationship that comes through this period in good shape is very real and important to you.

New relationships with a strongly "fated" quality may also come into your life now, which will have very profound significance for you in about fourteen years.

On a very different level, this transit can also mean a period of austerity, in which either voluntarily or otherwise you will give up many of the little indulgences and luxuries that have filled your life previously. This situation should be viewed as an opportunity for self-examination, for seeing your relationship to the appurtenances with which you have saddled your life.

This is definitely a time to be conservative in financial matters and not take on any new financial obligations, for you may have trouble meeting your existing ones. On the other hand, this is an excellent time for firming up and organizing the financial structure of your life.

In general you should look upon this transit as a time for withdrawing into yourself with respect to others and to material possessions. This withdrawal will enable you to get a clearer idea of what and who you are, so that your future relationships with people and possessions will be more solidly based on reality and therefore more reliable and useful.

Saturn Sextile Venus

At this time your relationships will work for you in very practical ways. You understand how you need to have others work with you, and you are willing to meet the other person's needs within a relationship as long as he or she does the same for you. At this point in your life, you are not particularly idealistic.

Professional and business relationships fulfill the symbolism of this transit perfectly. Both parties are concerned about what each expects of the other, and both are willing to live up to the agreements that are made. If there are real differences, you will work to smooth them out. You will not just sit back and assume that it will all work out by itself.

Romantic relationships are neither aided or hindered by this transit, except that you are less likely to enter into a purely "starry-eyed" relationship. You ask yourself what the relationship can do for each of you. If a sexual relationship begins during this time there may be a considerable age difference between the two of you. The older partner may act as a kind of teacher-parent toward the younger. You may be either the younger or the older partner. Even if there is no age difference, the teacher-parent aspect will probably still exist. Basically you are too serious now to let Venus's nature express itself fully. Love, romance and affection are subordinated to what you consider real and practical needs.

Venus in your natal chart also rules creativity. This transit gives you the ability to work on particularly exacting and detailed creative projects, especially involving media that require very involved techniques. Any craft work you do now is probably aimed at producing useful objects.

On the whole, all your relationships will achieve a degree of stability at this time. Ultimately relationships survive only if they are able to satisfy the real needs of the people involved. You are particularly conscious of this now, so you examine your relationships accordingly. The more real your relationships are now, the better they will survive the crises that come when Saturn squares or conjoins your natal Venus.

Saturn Square Venus

This is a time of considerable tension and difficulty in your relationships. Love relationships often cool off and may even break up altogether during this transit. You may discover that a love affair wasn't what you thought it was, a rude awakening after a period of lovely illusions. Or you may suddenly lose interest in a relationship that had seemed perfectly viable up until now. Of course, the other person may be the one who leaves you.

Aside from love relationships, there is a sense of tension and a feeling that it is somehow more difficult to relate to people. You may feel that any sort of relationship exists at the cost of your freedom and sense of individuality. Relationships seem to be more trouble than they are worth.

Another effect of this transit may be that "circumstances beyond your control" seem to get in the way of an existing relationship and force it to break up, even though neither of you wants this to happen. But this is almost never what is really happening. Usually one of you has a conscious or unconscious need to withdraw from the relationship, and you subtly maneuver circumstances to make it break up. Or you may be testing the relationship to see how much it can take. A good one will survive and be stronger.

This is a time of unloading and clearing out. Every relationship must be an honest expression of yourself. But we often get into relationships that have little to do with our true selves, usually because of fear, a need for security, or a sense of personal inadequacy. Relationships sometimes simply outlive their time, and these are the ones that will suffer and perhaps die now. They are at cross purposes to your pursuit of life and self-expression.

Loneliness is a problem at this time, because your need for relationships and your need to be yourself are equally great. Instead of working harmoniously, as they should, they are in conflict. But consciously or unconsciously, the need to be yourself is the greater at this time.

Creativity in arts or crafts may be at a low point now for similar reasons. Your work may not be expressing your individuality, so you must make adjustments where necessary.

Saturn Trine Venus

This is an excellent time for you to achieve real stability in your relationships. Your individual personal needs will not conflict with the demands of the relationship, and you can base them on a realistic understanding of who you are and what others need from you. Your vision is clear, and you are not likely to enter a relationship under the spell of romantic illusions. If you are romantically inclined, in fact, your relationships may seem rather practical and dull now. However, you can use this kind of experience. A relationship should be an encounter between yourself and another individual that helps you define and understand yourself more clearly. That can happen now.

Sometime in the last few years, when Saturn squared or opposed your natal Venus, many relationships that were inappropriate for your life were weeded out. That process may have been quite painful, but it was necessary at the time. Now, however, the only relationships left are those that have real value in your life. You should be working on them to improve your understanding of yourself and how you relate to others. This is a time for growth relationships that expand your awareness. For this reason, as with the sextile transit, you may have a relationship in which there is a considerable age difference between you and your partner. The one who is "older and wiser" may act as a guide, exposing the other, through the dynamics of the relationship, to a larger and more realistic view of the world.

Also like the sextile, this transit favors most business and professional relationships, because you now are able to negotiate on the basis of your real needs and self-understanding while appreciating the other person's real needs. And since you understand the need for realism in relationships, whatever you decide on at this time will be mutually profitable.

Creativity under this transit is not stimulated or checked, but it does have greater discipline and rigor. You may be attracted to difficult and exacting techniques or involved in particularly painstaking craft forms. Anything that you make now is likely to be practical or useful.

Saturn Opposition Venus

This transit often signifies a crisis in your personal relationships. Love seems harder to come by, and you may cool off toward those who used to be dear to you. Or they may cool off. This is a period of testing old relationships to find out whether they can survive and make a contribution to your life. It is rather difficult to establish new relationships, for this is a time for culminating the old, not beginning anew.

As with the other strong transits of Saturn to Venus — conjunction and square — the opposition indicates that your need for relationships is in strong conflict with your need to feel like a distinct, separate and definite individual. Either you are such an individualist in your relationships that others find it difficult to relate to you, or the relationships smother your sense of individuality. You may feel very lonely even in the presence of your loved ones, because a wall has been built up between you and them.

It is absolutely essential to reexamine your relationships at this time to determine exactly your rights, duties and obligations and those of your partner. Probably you have been trespassing upon each other's prerogatives, and the tension that this causes has led to your current difficulties.

One common manifestation of this transit is becoming involved in a relationship that makes very heavy demands on you. Although you would rather not be involved in it, you find it difficult to break out of. These relationships can be called "karmic" in that they balance out your past actions and are the direct or indirect consequence of those actions. All you can do in this case is to persist and do whatever you have to do. At a certain point you will realize that the karma has been completed; that is, the relationship has fulfilled its purpose. If you simply abandon it, you will almost immediately encounter another relationship like it, and another and another until you live one of them through. Saturn has this relentless quality.

Venus also rules artistic creativity, but this may not be an especially creative period for you. This is because you are redefining what you are trying to do with your creativity. Like all oppositions, this one signifies a reorientation of consciousness. Don't worry that you have lost a gift — it will return in new forms.

This may also be a time of material and financial adversity. Here again you will have to examine your past attitudes toward material resources and perhaps change your whole orientation toward them. Try getting along with less; you may find that you need less than you had thought.

Saturn Conjunct Mars

This is often a time of enormous frustration, when you really feel as if you are beating your head against a wall. It can also be a time when you accomplish a great deal of hard work. Which it will be depends on how you handle the energy of this transit. Its basic meaning is "inhibited energy," but it can also be "disciplined energy" if you don't try to do too many things over too broad a spectrum.

On the negative side, the energy of this transit can produce feelings of intense irritability. The least little thing seems to set you off, and unfortunately you are often confronted with considerably more than "little things." People or circumstances seem to get in the way of whatever you try to do. At work your boss or employer may oppose your ideas without giving any real reasons. Or he may saddle you with so much work that you don't have time to do anything else.

Sometimes you will get involved in the most acrimonious ego disputes with others. It may be tempting to chalk this up to some kind of plot against you, but that is probably not the case. It is more likely that — even with the best of intentions — you put out some energy that is threatening to others. They respond by trying to stop you. Even if you don't mean to be threatening, you must try very hard not to make people feel threatened. Also you may be the victim of other people's aggressive intentions without any obvious stimulus on your part.

This transit can affect your health. It seems to coincide with accidents, especially bone injuries, and illnesses such as arthritis and rheumatism. If you are subject to such illnesses, take good care of yourself during this transit.

The problem with this period is that your energies are being curbed. The energy of Mars wants to assert itself in every direction, but transiting Saturn signifies limitations imposed from without. You should take on only projects that are limited in scope but that require great exertion and concentrated effort within that scope. If you concentrate your efforts on relatively narrow objectives, you can make constructive use of this energy. But if you proceed with grandiose and far-reaching plans, you will probably encounter the worst effects of this transit.

One other danger should be mentioned. The combination of Mars and Saturn can signify a kind of cold, cruel anger, which you should avoid projecting. If you get angry, bring it out into the open. Don't act sullen and bitter, even covertly, for that can bring about an equally angry and bitter response from others. If you don't deal with these feelings within yourself, you may become the victim of cruelty.

Saturn Sextile Mars

At this time, controlled activity in any aspect of your life can do a great deal for you. You are able to direct your effort toward building a project slowly and thoroughly, so that whatever you build at this time will probably last. Your attitude toward your objectives is reasonable and practical, which helps greatly in attaining what you want. This is not a time for big ideas, but rather for very thorough accomplishments in limited areas. Often it will help enormously to subordinate your own ego drives in order to work in groups with other people now.

Your physical efforts are more disciplined at this time. You are able to work long and hard on a task, whether it is physical or mental, and not give up until it is done. Superiors and coworkers will admire you for this, and you may get much more credit than people who work in a grandiose style but less thoroughly.

You find it relatively easy to accept limitations that are imposed upon you and to work within any framework that is presented to you. This makes it easier to work with other people.

Others may think of you as a "grind" at this time. In fact, your disciplined attitude toward work makes you a very formidable person, because you will accomplish whatever you set out to do, not by luck, but by hard, unstinting labor.

This transit favors hard work for relatively modest objectives, all forms of careful, precise work — polishing, metal work, working with stones — and work that requires very careful measurements.

Saturn Square Mars

This can be a time of intense ego conflicts with others, and you are very likely to be the loser if you are not careful. Your ambitions in various areas may provoke others to try to stop you because they feel threatened. Or it may be that you come across people whose goals are intrinsically opposed to yours. This may happen in any area of your life; most commonly it will affect your work and social life, but it can also affect your personal and domestic life.

During your first run-ins with others, you will probably be very bitter and antagonistic, but you will also become cautious about venting your anger. The result is that you will constantly be in a state of suppressed rage. Then someone who has nothing to do with your mood may be the victim of a sudden unexpected burst of anger. Needless to say, that is not the way to win anyone over.

You must not get discouraged by the failures you experience at this time. This period will not last, and you can consider it a testing time for yourself and your ambitions. There is no need to assume that your present setbacks are permanent.

There are dangers associated with this transit. It can signify accidents and injuries, especially broken bones. You are not particularly lucky under this transit, so you should not take unnecessary risks. You could get hurt, although you should not go about expecting that. If you are older, have regular checkups for your blood pressure and other cardiovascular signs. Many astrologers associate this combination of planetary influences with hardening of the arteries, as well as arthritis and rheumatism. Good medical attention is always a good idea.

Saturn Trine Mars

At this time you are capable of hard work undertaken from a very broad perspective. You can put great effort into tasks that are rather narrow in immediate scope but that fit into a larger plan. You are able to organize many small details into an overall pattern in order to accomplish larger tasks.

You express your energies in a careful and controlled manner, which will win you the respect of others for your diligence and perseverance. If there is hard exacting work to be done, you can do it better now than at other times.

This is a favorable transit for any kind of work that requires precision and concentrated effort. It is good for metal or stone work, drawing up exact plans, building, grinding, polishing and cutting, especially with metal tools.

This is a time when you are content to be patient and to work slowly toward your objectives. Your expectations are modest, and you are willing to do whatever is necessary to attain them. Others will find you a formidable opponent, simply because you look at all the alternatives and choose your course of action carefully and methodically. One could describe your manner as "relentless."

This is not a glamorous time in your life, but your actions can lead to real and lasting accomplishments.

Saturn Opposition Mars

This can be an extremely difficult transit, because you feel that everything you try to do is blocked by circumstances or opposed by others. You may feel angry, but you have no obvious outlet for your anger, so you are left boiling over inside and seething with frustration. And there is no doubt that your actions are very closely circumscribed at this time. People who are important in directing your life — parents, employers, officials — may be a serious source of trouble at this time.

One possible reason for this is that you are experiencing the consequences of actions that you initiated many years ago, which have built up a structure around you that limits your ability to act freely. To find the roots of this problem, look to the period about fourteen years ago when Saturn last conjoined your natal Mars.

You may feel tempted to lash out against the forces that seem to be conspiring against you, but this is probably not a good idea. They will probably prove too strong for you. Instead of rebelling and fighting, it would be better to wait and in the meantime find some outlet for your pent-up energy. Hard work, physical activity, and concentrated effort will help dispel the energy build-up that may accompany this transit. However, take reasonable precautions in whatever you do along these lines. Accidents can occur now, because the pent-up energy is hard to control, and if it comes out in a sudden uncontrolled burst it can cause an accident. Be especially careful with sharp objects and anything made of metal.

It is not a good idea simply to hold in your feelings, even though it seems futile to let them out. The stored-up energy within you provokes responses from others and from your environment in very subtle ways, which can lead to even greater problems. You can conceivably become the victim of your own violent feelings, and this can happen in very subtle, unconscious ways. So you have to find the middle road between lashing out violently and holding all your anger in.

Health problems that may occur during this transit include diseases of the body's hardening processes, such as bone formation. Arthritis, arteriosclerosis and high blood pressure are all examples of Mars-Saturn illnesses. It would be a good idea to have a careful physical examination during this period.

Saturn Conjunct Jupiter

This transit can represent different things to different people. It can be an opportunity for very careful sustained growth through patient endeavor. Or it can be a period of extreme restlessness and impatience.

The structured nature of Saturn, which demands that conditions be met and obligations be fulfilled, is not very compatible with the unrestrained exuberance of Jupiter. Yet together they can play a valuable role in your life. Saturn gives you the discipline to make a solid structure of your life. Without Saturn's influence, Jupiter can symbolize wild unrestrained growth and gross overextension of your energy. Jupiter is often characterized by waste and inefficiency, because you feel there is always enough of everything, even when there isn't.

But at the same time, Saturn can be the ultimate wet blanket for Jupiter, turning optimism to pessimism, bold risk-taking to overcautious conservatism. Your Jupiter energy can make this a restless time. And it is very difficult to tell which reaction you will have to this transit.

With a Saturn-Jupiter transit you may expect any of the following: a change of job or residence; a change in financial status, often for the worse; withdrawal from others in order to work; fondness for solitude; industry and perseverance.

Two attributes probably determine which kind of effect you will experience. First of all, if you are disciplined and persevering you will react with patience to the energies of this transit. But even more important is your attitude toward the areas of your life that the transit may affect. You will persevere with the areas of your life that you are contented with, and you will work even harder on them than otherwise. In those areas of your life that seem oppressive, you will experience tension and the desire to rebel against limitations.

It is difficult to say whether you are justified in being impatient with the areas of restriction in your life. Certainly you are more than justified in trying to improve your life. You will have to decide whether to cut off some element or build it up to a higher level. Either response may be appropriate.

Saturn Sextile Jupiter

During this time you should work very hard to take advantage of every opportunity for growth and expansion that presents itself. This transit gives you the ability to work very hard and patiently in building up your life. It is not a period of flamboyant expansion, but what you build will have an enduring quality that will help you withstand any heavy crises that may arise in the future. This transit requires that you work for these results, but it does not provide the drive to work. It merely gives you opportunities to work effectively. Its effects are so subtle that the transit could pass without making much of an impact. But if you allow this to happen, you may experience difficult times when Saturn comes to either conjunction or square of your natal Jupiter.

This transit favors most business and professional activities. You have the ability to handle the broad, general planning of projects as well as the details. You can work on projects that you might be too impatient to work on at other times. This will impress your employers and other superiors, and their good will will be useful as you advance in your work.

This is also a favorable period for intellectual and spiritual growth, because now you can see the restrictions in your life as elements that provide form and structure, not as just obstacles to total freedom. In a very real way, your life derives its form and individuality as much from what you cannot do as from what you can do. This transit gives you the ability to see the structure of your life in such a way that you can gain more control over it. Whatever your long-range goals are, you will be able to build a foundation for success at this time. Don't waste this opportunity.

Saturn Square Jupiter

During this transit your opportunities may be curtailed and your freedom of action may be quite limited. Restrictions seem to come from nowhere, and you may have to work very hard just to maintain your accustomed level, let alone improve it. This transit can be quite unfavorable financially, especially if you have not been very careful in recent years. It tests how well you have put your life together in almost every area, but especially in matters related to finances, business and your profession.

You may discover that many aspects of your life cannot withstand real adversity. They begin to crumble away at the slightest challenge.

Approximately seven years ago, many new activities began in your life. Now they are being tested to see whether they have any real importance in your life. Anything that does not withstand this test should be abandoned or substantially changed. It will be possible to hold on to something that clearly does not work, in spite of opposition from others and restrictions from your surroundings. And if you do that, after this transit it may appear to be working out all right. But that is only because the current challenge is over. However, in about seven years anything you have clung to will be tested again and will cause far more trouble than it does now. In other words, if something isn't working now, let it go!

Typically this transit produces extreme restlessness. Jupiter's drive for freedom is relentlessly curbed by the restrictions of Saturn, and you feel very strongly that you must break out of these restrictions. You may experience job or residence changes and the breakup of personal relationships that seem to interfere unduly with your freedom. However these changes are usually just hasty reactions to this transit. You would be much better off to calmly evaluate what is and isn't working in your life and to consciously eliminate the elements that do not work. Don't just react blindly because of frustration. That will only make matters worse when Saturn comes to the opposition or conjunction of your natal Jupiter.

You may experience great frustration in your work. First determine whether you are just being impatient, or whether your work really doesn't allow you the necessary scope for development. Either way it would be better not to make up your mind until after this transit is over.

Saturn Trine Jupiter

This is a time of balance and order in your life. You may have to work hard for financial gain, but at least your affairs are in order. Your business or professional life is well organized, and you should be making steady progress toward your goals. The gains you make at this time are not strokes of luck, they are the solid results of good organization. Work hard to make them even more solid.

Your greatest asset at this time is that you can see clearly how various parts of your life are working out. You understand the rules, and you are willing to play by them. Your attitude toward life is pragmatic and practical. You are more than usually willing to accept a situation as it is while working patiently to improve it. You are now in a position to make important choices that will greatly affect your future.

Your employers, bosses and other authority figures can help you out now. At other times these people may have seemed to be obstacles to your advancement, but now they are extremely willing to help. This is in part because you make it clear that they will gain by helping you. You are much more capable now of real give-and-take than you have been at other times. When others see this, they are more willing to work on your team.

Older persons may provide opportunities for real insight into your life. From the perspective of their age, you can see how to improve your own life and help it grow.

This is a time to consolidate and buttress various aspects of your life. Put aside money for the future, invest or buy life insurance. Make peace with the difficult aspects of your life or with those people who are potential sources of trouble. In the not-too-distant future, when Saturn squares or opposes your natal Jupiter, it will be difficult to deal with the loose ends you leave now. You have enough foresight now to see this and make the necessary adjustments.

Saturn Opposition Jupiter

During this time, your opportunities for growth and expansion in life are limited. You may feel that you are moving sideways, if not actually going in reverse. There may be financial problems, especially if you have overextended yourself in the recent past. Another effect of this transit is restlessness and impatience with restrictions imposed upon you. This period requires patience, but unfortunately yours seems to be almost exhausted.

This is a period of readjustment after a period of possibly too-rapid expansion. Certainly it is necessary to examine your recent past to make sure that you have acted according to what you really want to do and really ought to do. This transit can have the effect of getting you back into a path that you have wandered away from. Do not be discouraged by any recent setbacks. Quite likely they were for the best, as you will probably see in a little while.

Other people may inhibit you at this time. For example, in your work you may propose new ideas, only to have them put down by more conservative coworkers or employers. You must build up a better case for your ideas so it will be more difficult for others to challenge them. You can be sure that you will not be allowed to get away with sloppy thinking and planning at this time. Someone will always point out your errors.

Make things more secure and more stable, but do not start any new projects now. If your expectations are overly optimistic, you may be disappointed, but at least the reasons will become clear. You will see what aspect of reality has interfered with your ideals, and in the future you will be able to take this into account.

Also at this time personal relationships may go through a period of trial. You often feel as if your personal freedom is unduly limited by others. Separations sometimes come about because you feel that that is the only way to achieve freedom. And, in fact, you are usually better off after a separation that occurs under this transit.

Like so many other transits of Saturn, this one represents a time of cutting back and finding a more stable form for your life. It is not a time of growth and expansion. In fact, too much expansion in the past may be the reason for what is happening now. In the future you will have to make plans on a more solid basis so that changes in your life and pressure from circumstances and people cannot interfere so much. This transit is a useful, if not always pleasant, encounter with reality.

Saturn Conjunct Saturn

This is one of the most important times in your life. A major cycle of experience is closing, and great changes are about to take place. How great these changes are depends largely on what you have been doing with your life over the past several years. Have you been living as you feel you should or as you think others want you to? If you have been doing the latter, Saturn will have a greater impact.

The transit of Saturn conjunct natal Saturn occurs about every twenty-nine years. The first such transit occurs when you are about twenty-nine, and the second between the ages of fifty-eight and sixty.

In the year before this transit, many aspects of your life have begun to change. Relationships have changed or ended, and you may have changed your residence or your job; you have been dominated by an urgent feeling that if you don't do everything you have always wanted to do or felt that you should, you will never have another chance. Whether you are twenty-nine or fifty-eight, you will feel that a substantial portion of your life has passed and that you had better get on with making it all work. If your marriage is unsatisfactory but you have been making the best of it, you will examine that relationship even more thoroughly now and may decide to end it. Certainly you will have to change it substantially. The same is true of any other aspect of your life that you have tolerated but not found very rewarding.

Consciously or unconsciously, you are pruning your life of everything that is not relevant to what you really are as a human being. If this process is not happening consciously, you may experience a sense of loss for the elements of your life that are coming to an end now. However, do not dwell upon these losses, for they are necessary in order to clear the decks for the major period of action in your life. If this is your first return of Saturn, particularly, you should roll with the punch and voluntarily let go of these elements. If you try to hold on, you may be somewhat successful, but twenty-nine years from now the second Saturn return will be much more difficult. Then you will be more firmly established on paths that are inappropriate for you. If this is your second return, you are faced with the need to make radical changes. However difficult this may be, make the changes. Your later years will be much better if you do.

This is a time of endings and new beginnings. If you have built your life up to now around activities that are inappropriate for you, it will be a period of crisis. If you have been doing what you should in previous years, this transit will simply mark a time of solidification and the beginning of new phases of activity. It is this transit that makes people over thirty different from those under thirty because the Saturn return is one of the most maturing of all transits.

Saturn Sextile Saturn

This is a time of equilibrium and balance in your life, because now you have a pretty good idea of how to handle your own world. Events will run along more or less easily during this transit. But it is important to note that it will not necessarily be an especially happy or peaceful time. Our lives are directed by our own demands much more than we realize, but very often those demands are unconscious. We would often be horrified if we knew what we are really trying to do. We try to protect ourselves and what we feel belongs to us from "threats" that often are not real threats according to adult criteria. Yet we structure our world according to them. The sextile transit only guarantees that you will be successful in patterning your world. If you are very unhappy at this time, you had best get in touch with what you are really doing.

This transit can be a time when you are successfully approaching your main conscious goals in life. Or it can be a time when you are being run largely by unconscious "programs," as if you were a computer. Usually you will experience a little of both of these effects. However, in the long run the positive possibilities are more useful to know about. Concerning the negative side of this transit, suffice it to say that the difficult and unsatisfactory aspects of your life that you are experiencing now require you to look into yourself more closely.

The sextile of Saturn to Saturn represents a time of moving forward to achieve goals, whether they are material or spiritual. This transit will relate to one or the other at different times in your life. Certain changes that occurred in your professional life several years ago, when Saturn either last squared or conjoined Saturn, have now reached the point of becoming part of your new self. You can use these new aspects of yourself effectively.

At this time you are particularly good at working with other people. You are able to see your individuality and differentness in a way that makes it possible for you to work with others in a complementary way so that neither you nor they feel competitive. You can work just as well with people who are above you and with those at your own level.

You approach your own goals methodically and practically, for you are not particularly idealistic at this point. You are much more concerned about how to achieve what you want in concrete practical terms. Use this time well, for like all sextile transits, it gives you the opportunity to lay a foundation that will protect you in the future.

Saturn Square Saturn

This transit is a critical period in which several aspects of your life and experience will be tested, especially those that began to be important about seven years ago. Most often this transit is experienced as a sort of identity crisis in which you begin to question what you are doing. You may suffer a crisis of confidence at this time, fearing that you have made the wrong moves in life or committed yourself to some course of action that will not be good in the long run. During this period you will think about and question all the long-term trends in your life. You will not be thinking about trivial matters.

Sometimes a particular event triggers off this period of soul-searching. Others may create difficulties for you, especially in your business or professional area. Perhaps they detect the first signs of insecurity that will afflict you during this period. If they are people who naturallly compete with you, they may try to take advantage of your apparent weakness. Employers and other superiors may also sense your feelings of insecurity and wonder whether you are the right person for the job you are doing.

You must recognize that some aspects of your life need to be questioned at this time. But don't stand in one spot quivering about your life. Examine it and make whatever changes are possible and seem appropriate. Any project you started seven years ago or any new aspect of yourself that first surfaced then that is truly worth continuing will still be worthwhile after this transit. This is a time of testing, and anything that withstands the test will be better for it. Things that do not pass the test are well gotten rid of. Shortly you will enter a period of stability and fruitfulness that will justify the events that take place now. In fact, if you are truly conscious of your life and your objectives, you will not undergo a real crisis at all. You will only go through a period of examining what is working and what is not. Your difficulties with the outer world at this time are signals about what you *should* be doing.

Because Saturn has so much to do with your sense of yourself and how you are different from other people, this transit is very likely to affect relationships. Saturn transits generally make one feel like separating from others, so some relationships may end at this time. Here again examine, appraise and make adjustments where necessary. Do not condemn yourself and feel guilty about your shortcomings. Action speaks louder than suffering!

Saturn Trine Saturn

At this time you can reach a stable understanding of what you are, and you can take control of your world and prepare to achieve your goals in life. This is primarily a time of preparation; you will not necessarily reach your goals now. But the base you lay down now will be very important.

At this time you can incorporate into yourself the fruits of previous successes, look them over and appreciate them for what they were. The key idea is that you are in a position to understand your life and therefore better able to be in conscious control of it. This is not merely an intellectual understanding, it is born of experience. You have lived through certain things, and now you can proceed on the basis of that understanding.

Your business or professional life will run smoothly at this time. Employers and superiors appreciate your calm, controlled way of handling your work, and they can see the results of your past experience. Relationships, which reflect what you are, are also more stable at this time because of your own inner stability.

Your outlook on life has also reached a point of equilibrium. You have a good understanding of how you look at life, and it works well enough that you may not question it very much. But the problem is that this is not a time of testing, so you don't know how well your ideas will stand up to future crises. You only know how well they withstood past tests. But the future is always different, and what happens in the future depends upon what is true at that time. Therefore you must keep your mind open and flexible. You only know what you know, and that is not everything. Continue to examine yourself and see what could be improved. Even if your life is satisfactory now, it may not always be. It helps to have a contingency plan for those times when Saturn either squares or opposes its own position.

Saturn Opposition Saturn

Your reaction to this transit depends a great deal upon how you have handled your life during the past several years. Fourteen years ago, when Saturn last conjoined your natal Saturn, you made a series of new beginnings and entered a new phase of awareness about life. You may have changed jobs or even entered an entirely new field of work. Old relationships may have broken up and new ones begun. If things went well for you, you probably had a feeling that now you were on the right path.

Seven years ago, those new beginnings encountered their first period of trial, which, whether or not you were aware of it, tested the strength and validity of what you had been doing. This took place during the last square of Saturn to your natal Saturn. If you did not clear away the structures and patterns in your life that were working badly then, this transit will be quite difficult. The old failures that you have not handled properly in the last several years will make your life exceedingly difficult now. However, everything that you have handled well will reach a culmination and prove more fruitful than ever before. This is the high-water mark of the Saturn-Saturn cycle.

In your work you may reach a peak of success, which will be accompanied by increased responsibility. In that case you will work extremely hard but very successfully. On the other hand, you may receive abundant evidence that you are working in the wrong area altogether. This would be manifested by extreme difficulties in your work situation, such as finding your efforts blocked by coworkers or superiors. If your superiors disapprove of your performance, you should completely reevaluate your work. Even if you are doing good work, this may be a signal that the job is inadequate from your point of view. This should not be an occasion for self-doubt and despair. Rest assured that you are supposed to be doing something else. Invest your energy in finding what that is, for the situation is not hopeless.

In a similar way, relationships that were not straightened out several years ago during the last square will also prove very difficult at this time and may very well break up completely.

If your affairs are working out positively, this transit represents a material peak in your life. The structures you were going to build in this Saturn cycle have been built. By this time you have made the impact upon others that you were supposed to make. It is as if you have said to the world, "Here is what I am." Now, during the next fourteen years, the world will reply, "And here are the consequences of what you are."

If your experience of this transit has not been so successful, during the next fourteen years you will gather your resources for the next try, beginning at the next conjunction of Saturn with your natal Saturn. However, there can be productive periods during that time if you can clear out whatever isn't working now.

Saturn Conjunct Uranus

This is an extremely powerful transit, for it represents powerful internal forces for change colliding with powerful resistance from the external world. It is a time of tension and sudden release. You will be likely to take sudden actions that the people around you have not anticipated. These actions are the products of gradually building tension within you.

You are trying to escape the routine, dull and ordinary aspects of your life. You try to find new things that will make your life more exciting and stimulating. But with every effort of this kind, circumstances, duties and obligations seem to hold you back and keep you stuck in an oppressive situation. Uranus is the planet of rebellion, especially if its action is blocked for a long period of time, as it is now.

You may get to a point where the pressure is unbearable, and then you will make a sudden break for freedom. You may suddenly leave a relationship, an oppressive job or your place of residence, without warning anyone.

On the other hand, it may be possible to create a balance between the force of Saturn and the force of Uranus. If so, you will be able to sustain a great deal of tension over a long period of time and accomplish a great many changes in a highly structured way. Tasks of considerable difficulty are often accomplished under this transit, and people make Herculean efforts that would otherwise be impossible for them. Serious study and long-range projects requiring great concentration and effort can be undertaken.

Even though this manifestation of the energy of Saturn on Uranus may seem more productive, it really depends upon your situation. Very often a sudden break with what feels like an oppressive situation will clear the air and allow you to make a new and better beginning. On the other hand, it can cost you more than you are willing to pay. But the patient, hard-working manifestation of this transit's energy may create severe mental and physical tensions, even to the point of physical illness. You have to decide what you can handle realistically and determine for yourself the proper course of action.

One thing is clear. At this time in your life you must make changes at the most fundamental levels. If you do not, in approximately fourteen years the consequences of not making these changes will become very obvious, and you will be confronted with the same issues again under more difficult circumstances. That time will be signified by the transit of Saturn opposition Uranus.

Saturn Sextile Uranus

At this time there is a balance between the old and the new in your life, between conservatism and the desire to experiment. You are able to take a new experience, see its potential and give it a concrete form in your life. You approach life with patience, willing to give everything a chance to prove itself. Consequently this is an excellent time for studying any kind of demanding new material. You can also teach the techniques you have learned to others.

You may find it desirable to work with other people in the projects that you undertake now. Their insights will help you transcend your own limitations.

The changes you made in your life several years ago, when Saturn last conjoined or squared your natal Uranus, have taken a concrete form now. You may have moved, changed the structure of your relationships or changed your job at that time. Under this transit, these matters are stable, for you realize that your life is different now and perhaps more appropriate to what you are.

You may feel that you can encompass anything new that comes along now, and it is quite likely that you are more able to do so than usual. And it is good for you to try new approaches — don't reject challenges to the status quo. Incorporate them into yourself if they reveal valid flaws in your life as it is. In a few years Saturn will either conjoin or square your natal Uranus. Then it will be much harder to make these challenges a part of your life, and you may be forced to make changes under less desirable conditions. Your sense of internal pressure will be much greater then, and you are more likely to act in a disordered or disruptive way.

Saturn Square Uranus

This can be an extremely upsetting and tense period, particularly if you have allowed your life to crystallize into rigid patterns that cannot easily be changed. This is a time of great tension, because your desire for change and new experiences seems to be thwarted by circumstances or other people. If you have been putting up with unpleasant conditions in any area of your life, these will become much more difficult to withstand now. The tensions may become so great that you will unexpectedly take very radical actions that you would not have anticipated a short while ago.

Everyone's life needs both structure and change, but most people structure their lives in such a way that it is very difficult to change. Although they need change, they are afraid of it. Consequently changes can take place only by totally overthrowing the structure. A person who is sufficiently afraid will endure the greatest tensions and frustrations just to keep from upsetting the apple cart.

During this transit you face the challenge of creative change without destructive revolution. If you try to endure the pressure of a situation crying for changes in the face of profound obstacles, you subject your body to extreme tensions, which is not good for your health, especially your nerves.

Some people are utterly unconscious of the need for change in their lives. When this transit hits them, changes start to happen suddenly, which can be quite upsetting and unpleasant. The changes may even take the form of accidents, which are often an unconscious and inadvertent release of subconscious tension.

You will have problems with any relationships that seem to be holding you down too much. Relationships may break up during this transit, but not usually those in which both people are open to new and challenging experiences. This transit is most threatening to structures that have become routine and rigid.

Your work situation may also become oppressive if you are given new responsibilities without any new stimulation or opportunity for a different experience. Here also there is the danger of a sudden break, such as quitting suddenly or even being fired, unless you can learn to incorporate change into your daily routine. Authority figures in general seem oppressive and become the focus of negative energy on your part.

Like all squares by transit, this one is an opportunity to clear out elements of your life that are not working. Any changes that you fail to make now will cause greater trouble in about seven years, when Saturn next opposes or conjoins your natal Uranus.

Saturn Trine Uranus

This is a time of stability and creative balance between the old and the new in your life. You are able to live within a structure and also engage in new and stimulating experiences, which keep you from becoming stale. Any changes you have made or any structures that have been changed in the last several years, since Saturn last squared or opposed your natal Uranus, can become a permanent part of your life now. These changes are no longer challenges, but interesting aspects of your life.

You have a feeling of patience about what is happening. You can see the need for change, but you do not feel like rushing out and overthrowing everything. You can make the change in an orderly manner. You can present ideas to others in a very careful, logical way that still manages to impress them with the originality of your thinking. Your employers and superiors will especially appreciate your disciplined approach to new and original ideas.

Any task that requires long and disciplined application — learning a new skill, studying a new body of knowledge or simply working patiently at a long task — is favored by this transit, as long as it is leading up to some kind of creative change. Tedious tasks that leave no room for new experiences will not be so useful to you at this time. You should be working for change, even if slowly and patiently.

In fact you must not allow yourself to fall into a rut. Otherwise the next square or opposition in this cycle could prove to be very difficult Even change can become routine, if you go around in circles with the same changes. That is not the proper function of the Saturn-Uranus energies. The critical aspects of this cycle — the conjunction, square and opposition — are made most unpleasant by such an approach. During the trines and sextiles of this cycle you can make changes in a disciplined manner without having to make chaos.

Saturn Opposition Uranus

This transit can have two different effects. Either you will succeed in making your life an original statement of your uniqueness, or you will be in a state of extreme tension because of forces that are constantly obstructing your self-expression. Most people experience the latter effect, at least in part. Very few have a strong enough belief in themselves to fulfill the Saturn-Uranus energy in the best way. Uranus represent life's constant challenge to keep your perception free, fluid and always open to new views and experiences. From time to time almost everyone settles into patterns that are quite rigid and inappropriate to themselves. During the "hard" transits (conjunction, square and opposition) of Saturn to Uranus, the energy builds up to create crises in these rigid patterns, which are represented by Saturn.

All around you are persons whom you are involved with and structures that you created, representing your efforts to build order and predictability into your life. But you are not a static organism, and you need creative change to keep you alive. At this time you are likely to feel that your life structures are oppressive and maybe even killing you. This may be literally true in a physical sense, for a Saturn-Uranus conflict is very hard on the heart and nervous system.

The most structured aspects of your life, such as your job, your marriage and relationships and your daily routine, are all potential sources of trouble, insofar as they have become dull routines.

You are irritated by people who try to tell you what to do. You feel that you have had enough, and you may be tempted to throw everything away and leave. This transit very often breaks up marriages and other relationships that have become dull, oppressive and routine. However, even the best relationships may have to be substantially redefined at this time. Don't try to sit back, grin and bear it. Some steps obviously have to be taken, but the trick is to take them calmly and not fly off the handle. It is necessary only to make changes, not to wreck everything.

The readjustments you make now can go a long way toward making your life more interesting. Achieving a balance between the Saturn energy of order, discipline and predictability and the Uranus energy of change and original experience is one of the greatest challenges in life.

Saturn Conjunct Neptune

During this transit you may have to contend with negative moods that can be quite upsetting. This transit often results in confusion, self-doubt, uncertainty and a general tendency to look at life from the worst possible point of view. At its worst, it can make you completely uncertain about what is real in your life, resulting in a sense of fear and free-floating anxiety. This is because Saturn rules what we normally think of as reality, while Neptune rules the ideal, the illusory and the apparently unreal. It is *apparently* unreal because what Neptune rules is actually another order of reality. When the two planets are combined, the two categories of reality blend and become difficult to separate. It is important to remember that this transit usually makes things appear worse than they actually are.

Your confidence and sense of well-being are at a low at this time, and you should not take your own gloomy evaluations too seriously. You seem to be aware of only those facets of life that you are afraid of and totally unaware of those things that can comfort and reinforce you.

You should particularly watch your health at this time. Saturn-Neptune combinations are sometimes connected with chronic illnesses that become visible only when it is almost too late to do anything about them. If you feel that any part of your body is not quite as it should be, have it checked by a physician. Even with this transit, the chances are that it is nothing, but don't take the chance!

Strange as it may seem, there is a constructive side to this transit, although most people usually experience the negative side. But if you are very well attuned to your inner needs and secure enough not to be led astray by illusions, even fearful ones, then this transit can give you the ability to make extraordinary self-sacrifices. One effect of this transit is to detach you from the material universe. In that case you may become disoriented and afraid, as described already, or you may find that the demands of the material universe no longer concern you particularly, and you can sacrifice your material needs to spiritual needs.

Either way, your perception of reality at this time is quite different from what it normally is, which you should take into consideration when making any plans for the future.

Saturn Sextile Neptune

During this transit you are able to achieve a most unusual balance between your material and your spiritual needs, and you see the relationship between them so that you can build your life upon both of them equally. This transit helps you bring your spiritual ideals into focus in the material world so that you can see precisely what role they play in your life. Consequently this is a time of sober reflection and deep understanding about your life on several planes.

Like all combinations of Saturn and Neptune, this is a time of serious thought. Your mood will not be especially light-hearted, but you will be in a position to make great breakthroughs in understanding. You will be able to deny yourself rewards that you have wanted in the past, because now you can see that if you wait a bit, your daily life will come closer to your ideals. You are in the right frame of mind for disciplined self-denial and sacrifice without being a martyr. In other words, you are realistic about what you are doing.

Now you can work to further your ideals, such as working for religious or charitable organizations, spiritual groups or whatever. In general you will be attracted to groups of people who share your views, and you will be able to express your philosophy better in a group than by yourself. Neptune has the effect of making your ego subservient to higher needs, so that if you believe strongly in what you are doing, you will be able to work hard even if given very little credit or positive reinforcement.

With this transit there is the danger of taking your own actions too seriously. This can be a very covert form of egotism in the name of spiritual awareness and devotion, and no form of egotism, even if it goes by another name, is compatible with Neptune. If you do not heed this warning, a few years hence when Saturn is in conjunction, opposition or square to Neptune, you will probably experience an extreme crisis of confidence.

Saturn Square Neptune

This transit signifies a time of great uncertainty and possible confusion. Your objectives are unclear, and you may feel incapable of coping with even the ordinary details of your everyday life. One of the best ways to cope with this transit is to make your everyday life as simple as possible, because you are so easily overwhelmed at this time.

This is not a time of robust confidence. You are questioning almost every aspect of your life, particularly your goals and ambitions, your ability to attain them and even whether you are worthy of attaining them.

At the same time you may feel that your universe is constructed in such a way that you cannot ever live up to your ideals. Saturn rules the way you view reality, while Neptune rules your ideals. Disappointment, discouragement and pessimism are all likely effects of this transit. The danger is that this kind of negative thinking may actually undermine your effectiveness in your work or other important activities. Feeling insecure often creates circumstances in which you really are insecure. Do not take things so seriously! Your negative state of mind is probably not justified by the facts of your life. This is just one of those times when your spirits seem to sag.

You should try to hang on without making any permanent decisions or commitments on the basis of your current pessimistic views. In a short time, you will understand that right now your view of reality is changing in a way that ultimately should be very constructive, although it does not seem so now. Later, when Saturn trines or sextiles your natal Neptune, you will be able to make constructive changes in your life based upon your new understanding. This is probably not the best time to make changes.

Hard aspects between Saturn and Neptune, such as this one, can bring physical and health problems in the form of diseases that are difficult to notice and diagnose. Take good care of your body and have a thorough physical examination, especially if you are over forty. In that way these diseases can be spotted and taken care of before they get too far.

Saturn Trine Neptune

At this time you will reach a new understanding of your own being and the world around you. In recent years you have probably been through periods of great doubt, uncertainty and confusion. Although those periods were painful they have contributed to your new view of the world. Now is the time to deepen and take advantage of your new understanding. This is an excellent time for studies that can raise your consciousness, such as yoga, occult metaphysics, spiritualism and mysticism. Now you are able to study these subjects and put them into practice in your everyday life. They will not be purely intellectual or mental activities — you can make them real and useful!

At this time your own ego involvement in your activities is low. You are more likely than at other times to act for altruistic reasons. You can devote yourself selflessly to movements and activities that help you bring your ideas to reality. Yet you do not feel that you are denying yourself, for everything you do seems to be a logical expression of what you are.

Your ideals are not in conflict with the realities in your life at this time. They are in creative balance, with the ideal giving form and the real giving life. Your approach is one of calm sober reflection. This is not a transit of lightness and gaiety; instead it produces an almost monastic consciousness that contemplates the world with detachment.

You have learned much in the last several years, and now you will be able to put into practice what you have learned.

Saturn Opposition Neptune

This is a time of extreme inner conflict, which can severely undermine your effectiveness with others. You will become extremely self-critical and uncertain about the ideals by which you structure your life, as well as about the structure itself. You make very great demands upon yourself, and you feel you must live up to them. But they are very far removed from what you should realistically expect. You will almost certainly fail to live up to these ideals, so you will be acutely disappointed in yourself. Your self-condemnation is unjustified but very convincing at this time.

Guilt, remorse for alleged "past sins," feelings of unfulfilled responsibilities, depression and self-doubt are all characteristic of this transit. But you must remember that everything seems worse than it really is. Sometimes you have an irrational sense of fear or apprehension, when your world seems to be populated by ghosts that haunt you. Illusion is indistinguishable from reality. Clearly this can be one of the most difficult of all transits.

Actually your ideas about the world are being changed, and the first step is a process of disintegration that leaves you feeling extremely disoriented.

If you can, it would be a good idea to go into some kind of retreat or at least try to minimize the demands of the everyday world for awhile. And as you simplify your life in this way, concentrate on the very concrete aspects of reality. Don't involve yourself in abstractions, for you can become lost in them. Deal with everything on a very mundane, practical level, until your sense of equilibrium begins to return. This is not a particularly good time to study the occult or psychic disciplines unless past study has given you a strong sense of proportion in these matters. If you study such subjects for the first time now, your sense of disorientation will only increase, with possibly devastating results.

When your life begins to settle down again, you will find that you have a new understanding of your world. You will begin to put it to good use in four to five years, when Saturn trines your natal Neptune.

Saturn Conjunct Pluto

During this transit you may have fewer resources available for doing what you want, and you may have to focus the available resources on more restricted and concentrated objectives. Pluto is the power of transformation, while Saturn narrows and focuses. The effects of the combination are several. First, structure in your life will change significantly, but not suddenly or without warning. The changes brought about by Pluto are inherent in what is being changed, if you look carefully. It is rather like an inevitable conclusion of a situation. During this transit some things will come to an end or an old order of life will cease. On a metaphysical level, this transit means that factors are now being incorporated into the structure of your life that will later bring about evolution and growth. This process involves getting rid of old structures. What happens now will have great consequences in fourteen years.

On a material level, this transit often causes financial problems or other kinds of shortages. Sometimes government or other officials will impose heavy burdens that greatly restrict your freedom of movement. It is also possible that some incident or accident may affect your health and thereby restrict your freedom of movement.

All of these effects confine your energies so that later they can be focused upon matters that will require your full attention. If your energy is spread too thin, later crises will be much more difficult to bear. Then you will have to go through a most unpleasant house-cleaning of everything in your life that interferes with your natural pattern of evolution.

One danger of this transit is that Pluto can signify tremendous evolutionary energies, which Saturn restricts. This can lead to an apparent suppression of the Pluto force. When the suppressed force erupts, it may be dangerous, explosive and quite violent. As you are more and more restricted by circumstances and the need to use your resources conservatively, do not simply hold in your energies. Build new structures to correct the problems you face now, and concentrate all your energy on bringing about necessary evolution in your life. Saturn can give form to Pluto as well as repress it, and then it is much more fruitful.

Saturn Sextile Pluto

During this transit you will be able to withstand great tests of strength if you have to. Your own power and internal strength form a structure that can withstand considerable difficulty. You can work hard and focus tremendous energy on the tasks before you.

Within yourself you have some understanding of the forces that make you an individual. You know exactly what you can demand of yourself, and you push yourself to the limit, but not beyond. Consequently this can be a time of great achievements.

At the same time you will voluntarily restrict the focus of your energies, which makes them even more effective. You understand what area to work on, so your focused energy hits exactly the right target. Fortunately this principle applies to work that you do within yourself as well as in the external world.

In the outer world the manifestations of this transit are many and varied. First, you will probably work harder than you have in many years, and the work will be extremely productive. People will see that your achievements have grown directly out of your inner being, that they are a product of your own growth. In your work, your employers will see that you apply yourself with unusual diligence to the tasks at hand, and they will be favorably impressed. They will recognize that you are someone to be reckoned with. This may well be a time of professional advancement.

Saturn Square Pluto

This transit can be a difficult time in your life. Because of circumstances and other people, you find it very difficult to make the changes you would like to make in the world around you. For example, your ambitions for your work may be frustrated. Bosses or coworkers may try to prevent you from accomplishing what you want. Financially, you will probably have to curb expenses because you simply do not have the resources. Sometimes the experience of this transit is much like struggling against chains that hold you down. The temptation is to resist and struggle with all your might.

However, resisting is not the best way to handle this energy, because that would set in motion destructive powers beyond your control. This transit is sometimes associated with violent incidents, so take care. The best way to handle it is with some degree of detachment. Understandably you will be quite upset with some of the obstacles that crop up now, but regard them as a way of finding out which areas of your life are working and which are not. A square from transiting Saturn usually represents a call to eliminate the unnecessary and superfluous elements in your life. Of all the Saturn squares, this one most requires that you get rid of the dead and useless structures. Pluto rules breakdown and rebuilding, and that is exactly what you are forced to do. If you do it voluntarily, it will be easier.

When this transit is over, you will emerge from the crisis considerably tougher than you were. Conserve your resources, and if you are in financial difficulty, reorganize your life so that you can get along with less.

Saturn Trine Pluto

This transit gives you the ability to see deeply into yourself and find out what creative forces are at work. At the same time it lets you take advantage of that understanding and make use of it in your daily life. You are able to move forward in your work and other areas of life to fulfill your ambitions. You can work harder now than at almost any other time in your life, because your energies operate in a controlled and almost relentless manner.

You will be greatly concerned with your innermost self at this time. Therefore it is a good time to undergo psychotherapy or some other consciousness-raising technique, if you feel that it would benefit you. Disciplines involving self-understanding and regeneration, such as yoga or meditation, are particularly effective under this transit.

Professionally you will be able to advance in your field because you can work harder and more effectively and because others are impressed by your effectiveness. You assert yourself in such a way that others realize that you are not to be trifled with. They take you and your efforts seriously. Nevertheless the energies of the trine transit are not likely to arouse great opposition, as can happen with the square and opposition transits of Saturn to your natal Pluto. With the trine, others are willing to work with you, because they feel that you can get the job done.

The effects of most transits to Pluto are subtle but not weak. Do not look for specific events with this transit. The strongest effects are on the psychological level. You will simply notice that you are more effective and can make a greater impact. This can be an extremely useful transit.

Saturn Opposition Pluto

Like all opposition transits, this one can have two opposite effects. You will experience one or the other or a combination. This transit represents the culmination of efforts begun fourteen years ago, when Saturn last conjoined your natal Pluto. This can be the peak of their effectiveness in your material universe. But it can also be the time when it becomes clear that those efforts did not succeed. Most commonly you will experience a mixture of these two effects.

On one hand, the conjunction of transiting Saturn with your natal Pluto was the beginning of certain efforts to build structures that would allow you to fulfill your ambitions and give you control over your life. At that time you excluded certain areas of activity so you could focus more effectively on the areas you wanted to influence strongly. Now the consequences of those decisions and actions are manifest. You have succeeded in making your energies felt in your world, both personally and pro-fessionally, and you have the control you want and need.

But you have to work extremely hard, and you have tremendous responsibilities that you cannot let down. For this reason, even at its best, this transit is a time of great physical strain. Take great care not to damage your health through overwork. No matter how well you have prepared for this time, you may have taken on more than your physical vitality can handle. Unfortunately this is not a good time for letting up or taking a vacation.

In struggling to get to your present position, you may have triggered off opposing forces, possibly enemies, which are waiting to move in when you show signs of slackening. The best thing to do is hold on, maintain your efforts and do everything in your power to conciliate these forces. Make it clear that they have nothing to gain by your defeat and everything to win by your victory. Make yourself indispensable to them.

If this is a time when your expectations are disappointed — that is, if the other side of this transit is manifest — you will feel that something in your surroundings gets in your way every time you try to make a move. As described above, you have aroused opposition from others. But if you have not been successful in reaching your goals, the forces of opposition will be stronger than you are. The best thing to do in this case is to stop resisting, find out what you can salvage from the current crisis, and start moving in new directions.

However, remember that you are most likely to experience a combination of these effects. Work to maintain the areas of life that are working, conciliate the forces that oppose you and cut your losses. If you try to win losing battles under this transit, you will only succeed in losing the winning ones as well.

Saturn Conjunct Midheaven

This is the time when all your past preparations for the future will have their most important consequences. This transit represents an important life pinnacle for you, but it also entails very important duties and responsibilities.

About fourteen years ago, you began a new cycle of personal development. During this entire period you have laid the framework for what will happen now. If you are relatively young, that is, under forty, during this transit, this is the first of two or three such cycles in your life; the later ones will be more significant. If you are older, this is one of the most important times in your life. It is almost as if you have been climbing a mountain for many years, and now the peak is in sight.

As you approach this culmination of years of effort and ambition, it is very important to review just what you have been trying to achieve and how you have been going about it. The more solidly you have laid the foundations for your success, the greater your capability for achievement at this time.

But if you have taken shortcuts anywhere or broken the rules of the game you are playing, you will have trouble in those areas of your life. President Nixon fell from power as a result of actions taken at this time and in the years previous. The Watergate break-in occurred within days of Saturn's transit over his Midheaven.

The areas of your life that you have prepared carefully will become tremendously productive now. Your opportunities are at a peak for achievement and for additional responsibility and power in your work and in your personal life. This period will continue for several years. People will look to you for leadership, whether you want it or not.

The period of the immediate transit may seem rather difficult, because the responsibilities it signifies may come on rather suddenly, and you will need some time to adjust to them. Do not try to avoid responsibility, however, because that could bring about serious problems over the next several years and could lead to a time of defeat and self-doubt in both your personal and professional life.

If your preparation for this period of your life has been sloppy or full of shortcuts, or if you try to avoid its increased responsibilities, you run the risk of losing everything, even in the areas where you have prepared well and have taken responsibility.

Your task now is to take responsibility for your past and your present and, no matter how difficult it may seem, to persist at your tasks and keep moving forward. You will get used to the responsibility and enjoy one of the most productive times of your life.

Saturn Sextile Midheaven

During this transit you will work to establish yourself more solidly in the eyes of the world, your community and your friends. It is often a time of professional advancement, frequently aided by the favor of people in positions above you.

Inwardly you are able to arrive at a clearer idea of who you are now and how you measure up to your own expectations and those of the community. Your goals and expectations may be set rather high at this time, so you should be careful not to set yourself a task that is beyond you, or worse, one that you don't really want to undertake. Under this transit you are powerfully influenced by your early conditioning about duty, responsibility and obligation toward others, and therefore you are quite likely to pursue a course of action to fulfill what you think others expect of you, rather than one that is appropriate to you.

This time is usually marked by cautious action. You are just getting the feel of managing your life, and you do not want to upset everything now. You are anxious for material achievements that others can recognize and that you can point to as if to say, "This is what I have accomplished."

During this transit you work best by yourself, but you are conscious of how your work fits into a larger scheme involving other people. It is just that you prefer not to manage others as well as yourself at this time.

Nevertheless, you pursue your objectives with unflagging zeal and energy. It is not likely that you will make any significant changes in your goals now. This should be a time of accomplishment, if you put enough energy into the task, and if you are like most people, you will. But you should realize that this transit will not drive the unwilling person to work. You have to choose to do so or waste a valuable opportunity.

Saturn Square Midheaven

This is a challenging time in your life. You will have to make many choices about what areas of your life to emphasize. Will you work to build up a new career or continue to build upon a current one? Will you work to make your personal life as satisfying as possible? Will you work collectively with many other people or by yourself?

Often there is an "alienation crisis" with this transit, a sudden feeling of being cut off from everyone else, as if you had spent too much energy pursuing purely personal goals. This in turn generates loneliness and a feeling of being distant from others, even loved ones. Or you may suddenly feel that you no longer have the strength to go on in the direction you have chosen. Fears of your own inadequacies may distort your perspective.

All of this is most likely to happen if you have neglected personal relationships in your life. You cannot go on forever without supportive emotional relationships, and you may have been trying to do so.

Sometimes this transit can have the opposite result, and you discover that various personal entanglements have been interfering with the pursuit of your valid goals. In this case you will break off relationships and gain the freedom to go your own way. The issue here is the balance between personal relationships and advancement in life.

On another tack, this transit can test your choice of goals. You may encounter opposition from others that forces you to examine whether your goals are really valid for you. If they are, the conflict with other persons or against trying circumstances will be useful. But if you find that your heart is not really in the path you have chosen, you may have to make adjustments and change your course of action. It is far better to do this now than several years from now, when you may be overcommitted to an inappropriate course and discover that you are trapped. Now is the time to change. It may not be pleasant, but it is possible.

Saturn Trine Midheaven

This transit is usually characterized by self-confidence and assurance. You are able to see where you are going now and to obtain help in getting there. At the same time you are very concerned with knowing yourself on a deep inward level, usually to facilitate achieving your ambition.

This is a time when you try to rely primarily on yourself. You will not refuse help from others, but it is more desirable to go it alone or at least on your own. You need to prove yourself to yourself and, to a lesser extent, to others. It is also necessary to establish patterns in your life now that will lead to accomplishment later on. You must develop disciplined work habits and learn specific ways to deal with situations that arise. Here too you must rely on yourself, because you will be able to judge your effectiveness only if you know that what you are doing is entirely your own.

Most people are rather conservative in their ways of doing things at this time. You may be rather reluctant to experiment with new ways, but that is a pitfall. This should be a time for making careful and considered changes. Such changes can be made voluntarily and without much difficulty now, but later they will be forced upon you in a manner that may be quite unpleasant. Getting into a rut now will ensure the survival of inappropriate behavior patterns, which will create trouble later on.

You should specifically examine your attitudes toward authority figures, work and achievement, responsibility, change and most important, although somewhat abstract, your attitude toward Reality. Is the real world a forbidding place to you, cold, unrewarding and merciless? Or is it a stage where you can comfortably play the drama of your life? To all of these questions there is no one answer that is correct for everyone. You must consider how you feel about your own attitudes. It is possible to hold certain attitudes just because you feel you ought to, not because they really reflect your position. If you are trying to live by attitudes that you have been told to have that are not really yours, you will feel tense and uneasy when you think about them. Normally you suppress these feelings because you consider it important to maintain the attitudes. But these are the attitudes that have to be changed, because they signify that your thinking is divided about that issue and that you cannot really put energy into making that part of your life work. Failure is usually the result, usually about the time when Saturn conjoins the Midheaven.

Saturn Opposition Midheaven

In this extremely important period of your life, you must pay very close attention to what you are doing, because you are beginning a new phase of activity that will have important consequences in the years to come. The difficult aspect of this time is that the process is very subtle, and it may not be obvious that what you do now is important. But you will realize that it is when Saturn comes to your Descendant (opposition to your Ascendant) several years from now.

You have just gone through a period of preparation that probably seemed like treading water, getting nowhere and accomplishing nothing. Some people may experience the time just before this transit as exceedingly difficult, with one defeat after another. Others will find it less difficult, but it will not seem terribly significant.*

This is the end of a relatively low period in your life, and from now on you will gradually climb to the most significant time in your life. That will happen in about fourteen years, when Saturn conjoins your Midheaven.

You should be looking to your personal and domestic life, for this is an area of great responsibility for you now. Do not neglect it in a misguided attempt to get ahead in your professional life. Make whatever changes are necessary so that this aspect of your life is secure. Personal relationships may have broken up just before this transit. Now you may have the opportunity to make new ones that will fit your new lifestyle better.

You are on your way up again. The future depends upon the foundation that you lay now.

Saturn Conjunct Ascendant

This is one of the most significant transits of your life. During this time your responsibilities will increase considerably, and you will try to eliminate everything in your life that is not necessary to fulfilling them. Therefore your life will become more complex and simpler at the same time. You are finishing up certain tasks in your life and going into a five- to eight-year period of relatively quiet preparation for a new beginning. You will be cutting some elements out of your life and working hard to complete others.

During this transit you may have less freedom of movement than usual because of the pressure of circumstances and the need to get things done. Old tasks that have never been completed must be finished now. At work you may have to exert more effort in order to get the job done. Your superiors may give you even more responsibility than you would choose to have. This may not be a very light-hearted time, but it should be quite productive. But do not start out on a completely new project, because in a few years you may find that you do not have the material or psychological resources to complete it. Finish what is unfinished and simplify your life.

---

*Persons with the Sun in the third or fourth house of their natal horoscope seem to be an exception to this. Since the Saturn conjunct Sun is a cyclical peak and the Saturn transit of the fourth-house cusp is a cyclical low, the two cancel each other out. Witness President Ford with a third-house Sun coming into the White House near to Saturn opposition MC.

ррект2

Good relationships will not suffer appreciably during this time, but bad ones will break up completely. You are withdrawing from everything in your life that is unnecessary or in the way of your development during the next few years. Bad or difficult relationships may be among the elements that are discarded.

Try to avoid building a wall between yourself and others, for this is a great danger now. Duty, responsibility and obligations do not preclude personally satisfying relationships, even though you may feel that they do. If you cut yourself off from others unnecessarily, you will become lonely and depressed. The people who belong in your everyday life are very important for you now, especially since you are excluding those who do not belong. Often it is good to seek out the company and advice of older people, for they have the insight and understanding you need.

Despite the difficulties that will arise, this is a productive time. Follow through on the tasks that need to be done, and get your life in shape for the next phase of preparation.

Saturn Sextile Ascendant

At this time your avenues of communication with others are stabilized and solidified. Also you will probably create a set of fully formulated goals and expectations for the next several years. Therefore it is very important to take this transit very seriously and be very aware of what you are doing, because the patterns that you establish now will be very hard to alter and will determine the success or failure of your relationships over the next several years.

It is very important to learn other people's views of you as a human being and as a member of society. But this does not mean you should take everyone's words at face value and deny all your own beliefs. People operating under Saturn have an unfortunate tendency to do this, even with a relatively easy transit. You may have an exaggerated respect for someone else's views and give them more credence than they are worth.

You should simply talk to the people whom you personally respect and use what they say to help you come to conclusions about yourself. Older people may be especially helpful in this process.

Because of the weighty concerns that are occupying your mind at this point in your life, you will prefer serious work and the company of serious people. Of course, at times you will want to relax and enjoy yourself, but generally this is a period when discipline, organization and growth are your paramount concerns.

If you don't handle this transit well, you will have considerable difficulty with your relationships at the next square or conjunction of transiting Saturn with your Ascendant. And these difficulties will be the result of unfortunate patterns established now. The border between discipline and habit is often hard to distinguish, but that is precisely the difference that you have to keep in mind at this time. Habit is mindless and unconscious, whereas discipline is self-imposed and suited to achieving your goals.

Saturn Square Ascendant

This transit signifies a time of severe testing in your relationships with others. The demands of your work or the demands of your personal life will force you to reevaluate which relationships in your life are worth keeping and which are not. If you do not face this challenge consciously, the pressure of events will force you to do so, because people who have been with you for a long time will leave against your wishes.

There is often a strong tendency to build a wall between you and others without even realizing it. The only way you will know is that suddenly you will feel alone and out of touch with everybody. You may feel that you have no support from others, even loved ones whom you have counted on in the past for love and support. This may represent a temporary state of affairs or a passing mood. Or it may represent a serious breakdown in your relationships because of misplaced priorities in the past or because of associating with people who were wrong for you in terms of your personal goals and needs.

In the case of misplaced priorities, perhaps you have paid more attention to getting ahead in life than to giving and receiving love. Or perhaps in the past, fear of your own inadequacies or fear that you are unlovable has made you withdraw from others. Now the consequences of these problems are emerging, causing you to feel alone.

In the second case, the problem is that in terms of your direction in life, the people you associate with are a distraction or are actually opposed to your interests. In this case, no matter how much you love them, walls will form between you and them, and you will have to begin a new life without them.

With this transit several significant relationships will inevitably end. But if you have a clear idea of where you are going, this will not be a great disadvantage. Whatever remorse you feel will be quickly displaced by a new sense of freedom, because you are no longer wasting energy in trying to maintain inappropriate relationships.

Saturn Trine Ascendant

During this period of time you will establish yourself with respect to the rest of the world. People will come to know who you are and what you are doing. At the same time this transit indicates that you have reached a point of equilibrium at which your actions and behavior toward others are reliable and consistent. You will not feel like surprising people with sudden or unpredictable actions, nor will you want others to surprise you. Your whole objective is to reach the point where all your affairs are running smoothly and on schedule. Your approach is disciplined, well ordered and mature. In fact it could be said that you probably act older than your years, unless you are already advanced in age.

About the only problem with this transit is that you find it difficult to make changes when necessary. You think in terms of old solutions to new problems and act conservatively. And if that response is inappropriate to the situation, you will have difficulty. You are not very flexible, but that is not usually a great problem.

At this time in your life, you are very concerned with gaining experience, particularly in your profession. You are likely to be ambitious and will work hard to get ahead and improve yourself. You will seek out people who can help you, and probably you will make very sure that you give as much as you get from anyone who does help you out. Not only do you want to be fair and just, you don't want to be in debt to anyone. This is a time when self-sufficiency is very important to you.

This is reflected in your relationships also. You are somewhat more reserved than usual and cautious about forming new relationships. Usually this is to the good, although if you are too cautious you may overlook persons who could assist you. Older, more experienced people attract you especially, because you know you can learn from them. A person who will play a very important role as your teacher may come into your life at this time. But don't expect him or her to necessarily conform to your preconceived image of a teacher. He or she may come from any area of your life, and you may not recognize what has happened until later.

Saturn Opposition Ascendant

This transit has two quite different meanings. First of all, it can indicate a period in which intimate one-to-one relationships become an area of great responsibility. Chief among these is your marriage, if you are married, but it also refers to close partnerships of any sort. You must pay close attention to these relationships. Strains and tensions that have been developing in the recent past are likely to surface now and must be dealt with immediately! Sometimes the only way to handle these problems is to end the relationship, so this can be a time of great trial for a marriage. Even under the best of circumstances you will have to work harder on partnerships and try to solve as many problems as possible.

Related to this is another possible area of concern: namely, problems with people who oppose your interests in various matters. Such people can range from outright enemies to those who simply want to keep you in check for some reason. If this kind of problem arises, all you can do is try to understand the person's motivation and do what you can to eliminate their reasons for opposing you.

But aside from these two kinds of problems involving others, this Saturn transit means that at this time you are making a significant breakthrough in your life.

For several years now you have been working quietly to get ahead and make new beginnings, particularly in your professional life. Now the work you have been doing is beginning to bear fruit and you will be acknowledged. In fact, one of the reasons you are having conflict with enemies is that now you are really beginning to get somewhere in life, which is likely to be threatening to others.

At any rate, now you are ready for the upward climb to attain your goals in life. This is a very critical time, when you must work very carefully to get ahead. Do not take any shortcuts to success that violate what you believe to be right. Every time you do, you plant a seed that will create severe problems several years from now, when Saturn conjoins your Midheaven.

Chapter Eleven

Uranus

Significance of Transiting Uranus

During the transits of Uranus to your natal chart, you will experience phenomena that are out of accord with your everyday life. The events that occur will be unusual, upsetting, sudden and unexpected. For this reason astrologers are often circumspect about giving precise delineations concerning Uranus. Almost all that can be said for sure is to expect the unexpected.

But the transits of Uranus are not malefic in the traditional sense, *except* to the extent that you are unwilling to accept newness and change in your life. Uranus challenges the rigid structures in life that most people work so hard to build. Many people value regularity and predictability so much that they will even sacrifice personal happiness to get it. Think of all the unhappy marriages that continue only because both persons are afraid of the insecurity that breaking up would bring.

But this kind of rigidity is ultimately destructive to life in its highest sense. Life is or should be a constant, ongoing confrontation between yourself and the world, with an energy that keeps everything fresh and lively. The problem with this confrontation, however, is that there is always the danger of losing, so most people avoid the confrontation if they can. To survive half-dead, they reason, is better than to lose. But those are not the only alternatives; it is only fear that makes it seem that way.

Uranus in the First House

This is approximately a seven-year period, depending on the exact length of your first house. During this time you will radically redefine your relationship to the outside world. Old patterns will be broken down, which will force people to look upon you differently. They may be upset by the changes simply because they, like yourself, are afraid of change. And during this period you may act in ways that are quite unexpected and upsetting, particularly when Uranus transits planets from the first house.

The old limitations you have placed upon yourself or accepted from others are no longer acceptable now, and you feel the need to change them even if you have to break away from many things that have been important in the past. A marriage or other close relationship that has become stultifying may end during this transit. However, any relationship that really allows you to be yourself will be changed but not destroyed. This is also true of your work and any other area of obligation in your life.

The transit of Uranus through the first house is predominantly a drive for freedom. To others it may seem to be a period of pointless rebellion. And indeed, in terms of your old life, you may be acting quite irresponsibly, but if you feel very strongly the need to break free, it is a sign that the change is overdue.

As you change your way of handling the world, you will become open to experiences that you would never have allowed before, and your life may take on a whole new outlook. Certainly this is a good time to explore new kinds of awareness or to encounter astrology, yoga, human potential studies and other consciousness-expanding techniques. The avenues to new perception are open, and if you allow yourself to receive it, you will gain new tools for your future life.

It must be said that some people find this transit upsetting rather than revivifying. If this is the case, you should ask yourself what you are trying to hold onto that is keeping you away from new experiences. If your life is filled with upsetting incidents and accidents, you may be unconsciously setting the stage for them. Your conscious mind is afraid of change, but your unconscious knows that the time has come, so its energy leaks out to bring about these accidents. See what aspects of your life are truly limiting your scope of action and experience. Even if you feel that these limitations are necessary, and that it would be irresponsible to overthrow them, these are precisely the areas that must be changed.

Uranus in the Second House

For the next several years you will experience great changes in your economic and material situation. You should be certain that your finances can withstand some sudden changes. If you are in a rigid position, completely geared to the situation remaining exactly as it is, you will be very vulnerable to the effects of this transit. It requires you to be extremely flexible in all matters having to do with money and possessions.

On the inner level, this transit signifies that your values are changing. The values you are beginning to consider important are different from your old values, and this is reflected in the material objects that you value, that is, your possessions. But these changes may not be obvious to you on the surface. Your inner needs for further psychological growth may make your current relationship to material possessions inappropriate. Therefore you will have to make radical changes in order to give yourself room to grow.

On the other hand, this inner change may be conscious, in which case you will be aware of the need to be free from the responsibilities and encumbrances that accompany material possessions. If you are consciously aware of the need for change, this transit will not be upsetting. If you are not aware of it, your unconscious mind will create change anyway. But the changes will come in the form of events that are upsetting to your conscious personality.

If you feel encumbered and limited by your material possessions, this transit will take them away, until you are as free as you need to be. But by the same token, if you need a certain resource in order to grow further, Uranus may very well bring it. The only fact you can count on is that the changes in your material resources will be revolutionary ones.

This transit can be the signal for sudden windfalls or sudden losses. You may suddenly gain or lose property, or you may radically change your means of earning a living, which also is ruled by the second house.

If your means of earning a living has become deadening, events may change that completely. The nature of your work may change, or you may get a different job, but the end result will be that your way of making a living will become a source of excitement and challenge in your life. This transit may also signify that you will make your living through a profession ruled by Uranus, such as one of the sciences, some branch of technology, astrology or the occult.

Under any circumstances, you can be sure that over the next several years your material resources will change significantly, and your relationship to them will be altered so that you can continue to grow as an individual. The ultimate effects of this transit are positive, although you may initially be upset by the changes. Keep yourself open to the new opportunities that appear as the changes occur.

Uranus in the Third House

For the next several years the focus of change will be on a part of your life that you normally count on for reliability and predictability, namely your everyday encounters with neighbors, relatives and friends, your everyday business dealings and all other routine day-to-day activities. Your everyday mental attitudes will change, and you will be forced to look at life in a new way, to see things that you have never seen before and to communicate with others in new ways. Even your habits will change.

If you are involved in intellectual pursuits, this will be an exciting time, because you will see and understand facets of life that were never apparent before. Under the influence of Uranus your old habits of thinking and seeing will fall away. Your new flexibility of thought will become apparent as you turn to new interests, particularly those that are Uranian in nature, such as the sciences and technology, yoga, astrology and the occult. Many persons who have become well known in these fields began their studies while Uranus was transiting this house.

Expect the tempo of events in your daily life to increase. Routine, everyday communications will suddenly be important as they never were before. You won't be able to take much for granted, because you will have to give little everyday details the same attention that you previously reserved for exceptionally significant matters. This happens because these "little" details contain the germ of changes that will revolutionize your consciousness if you are willing to let them. If you are not willing and are consciously or unconsciously afraid of change, everything that happens will be upsetting. You will feel that you can't rely on anything, and you will look desperately for security where there is none. But if you can be flexible, you will see that none of this is terrible, it is only new and somewhat unexpected.

The signs of change will come through normal daily communication, letters, phone calls and conversations. Short trips and routine travels, such as commuting, may produce totally unexpected events. However, you will not necessarily have accidents, as many older writers say. This transit can lead to accidents on short trips or in your everyday life, but that is an exceptional manifestation, which is not likely to be encountered unless you try to prevent any changes from occurring in some area. An accident is almost always a sign of energy escaping in an improper place because it was not allowed to be used elsewhere.

The transit of Uranus through the third house is the beginning of a fundamental reorientation of your inner self that will continue as Uranus transits your natal fourth house. If you allow necessary changes to surface during this time, Uranus's transit of the fourth house will be easier. Also your everyday world will become a new source of wonder and excitement. But you must be flexible about your world and yourself to gain this benefit.

Uranus in the Fourth House

Over the next several years the focus of change will be in the most personal and intimate aspects of your life, including your home and your relationships with parents and other family members. There may be upsets that will show where your life needs change and reform, but at the same time you will acquire a new sense of freedom and release from the influence of the past.

A common effect of this transit is a sudden change in your home environment or even a complete change of residence. A settled family life may be threatened by divorce, accident or even, on occasion, someone's death. The deepest, most internal and personal aspects of your life are no longer reliable and unchanging.

The fourth house rules the ultimate basis of your being. It is the one aspect of reality that you assume will not change and the base from which you experience life. So changes in this area are extremely upsetting. To benefit from this transit you must be willing to become more flexible and to encounter new ideas in your most personal world. The structures being challenged are those that are rigid, not ones that are still alive and vital.

Old ties with the past may be broken, which can give you a feeling that you have lost your roots. But ultimately this break may free you from old patterns and habits that have enslaved you. Later you may be able to reestablish the old roots, but you will never again be so dominated by them.

Problems and tensions that you haven't been dealing with in your personal life will probably surface now, and you will be forced to handle them. The problems can range from powerful psychological encounters with the people to whom you are most intimately connected, to repairs that are needed in your home. If your living conditions have been unsatisfactory in any way, you will probably change them now. After this change it may take a few years for your living conditions to settle down again. But when they do, you will be a lot freer than you ever were in the old situation.

At the deepest level, the transit of Uranus through your fourth house signifies deep changes in your unconscious mind. And since the unconscious mind has a powerful effect on your view of reality, your whole experience of the world will be quite different after this transit.

Uranus in the Fifth House

This should be quite an exciting period in your life. The preceding transit of Uranus through your natal fourth house should have revolutionized your basic approach toward life, so that now you can seek out new forms of self-expression and creative self-release.

Concretely this energy should take the form of new recreations and amusements. You will be attracted to new experiences, which will expand your consciousness and make you more willing to experiment with life. Possibly you will have rather unusual relationships with the opposite sex. In a typically Uranian manner such relationships will revolutionize your life and break down your old rigid patterns of approach to relationships. However, do not expect such relationships to be very durable. They *may* last, but at first you should not expect them to.

Characteristic of Uranus in the fifth house are relationships in which the two of you are very different in age but nevertheless act as equals. This is in contrast to Saturn-ruled relationships in which one partner acts as a parent to the other. Other likely possibilities are a sudden infatuation that breaks up an existing relationship, on-and-off relationships or one with someone whom you would not normally expect to be with. A relationship that begins during this time will not easily settle down into the daily routine that most other relationships do. When faced with such a routine, it will tend to become unstable, because the excitement that characterized its early stages is one of the reasons for its existence. It has to remain in a state of continual flux to keep going.

Children are another fifth-house matter that can change or even become upset during this time. If you have children, you will not be able to take them for granted. Their development or activities will require that you pay attention and be very conscious of what is happening with them. They may be going through stages of growth that continually challenge you to adapt, or they may be unusually rebellious or difficult. Upsetting incidents may happen to them, such as illnesses or accidents, especially if any aspects in your natal chart indicate difficulties with children. On the other hand, this transit may mean that through your children you will encounter very positive, new and stimulating experiences.

If you are involved in a creative enterprise, such as arts, crafts or any type of design work, you will be better than usual at innovating and taking new approaches to your work. New media and techniques will attract you, as will fresh, new approaches to the plan and design of your work.

Like the other Uranus transits but more strongly, this transit is an opportunity to redefine yourself and to approach life with a new kind of understanding.

Uranus in the Sixth House

This transit indicates that you will take a new attitude toward work and form a new relationship with it. You will also seek out opportunities to become free from the excessive demands of others. Among the common manifestations of this transit are a change of job, although not usually of profession, changes within the job that give you more freedom, or a general revolt against duties and obligations in your life that you regard as oppressive. You are not especially happy with what you feel you have to do now.

The proper, that is, the most creative, response to this transit would be to make changes in the areas of your life that seem too binding and obligating. You are probably too caught up in certain patterns, so you must break free and find new kinds of work and service roles that allow you greater freedom for new experiences. Your job may have degenerated into a dull routine, or you may feel overly involved in taking care of others, with no time to be yourself.

The wildly rebellious response that Uranus often calls up is probably too destructive in the long run to be profitable. In your job the best thing to do is to look for new responsibilities that offer different challenges. If that is impossible, seek a new job. Sometimes this transit may signify that you have to learn new techniques in connection with your work. You may encounter an increasing amount of work with computers, for example, or other kinds of data processing and electronic apparatus. And if you have never worked with these machines before, that may be quite a challenge.

Whatever the challenge is, deal with it in as conscious and controlled a manner as possible. Do not simply try to repress the tension that is often associated with this transit. Sometimes people feel that there is no way to escape their duties, or they are afraid to try. So they attempt to go on as if nothing were happening. Then the Uranian energy is repressed at the conscious level and is expressed physically as a health problem, which forces the person to alter his or her work pattern and lessen or change responsibilities. The sixth house is the house of the body's physical efficiency as well as your mental efficiency at work. If you do not make changes consciously, your body will force you to make them. Heart trouble, accidents, nerve problems or the need for an operation are typical manifestations of the Uranian energy through your body. These can be avoided by allowing the transit to revolutionize your work and your attitudes toward duty.

Uranus in the Seventh House

The transit of Uranus through this house can be extremely difficult if you are involved in any close one-to-one relationships that are not working out very well. It is possible to go along with an unsatisfactory relationship for years and keep it together somehow. For example, you might be keeping a marriage going for the sake of the children or because of finances or emotional dependency. But when Uranus comes to your seventh house, it becomes extremely difficult to contend with the tensions in your relationship. Consequently this transit often coincides with a marital breakup or the end of some other partnership, such as a shaky business partnership. However, a partnership that is reasonably secure will usually weather the storm.

Even in the best relationship, this transit signifies a time to make needed changes. You may see a new relationship at this time as a way to escape from the daily routine of your old ones. That is why one manifestation of this transit can be a wild, highly improbable and usually very unstable love affair. New love is seen as an escape and a source of excitement.

Another type of problem may occur during this transit. The seventh house is also the house of open enemies, and open conflicts with others may occur much more frequently than usual. This manifestation requires that you change your strategy toward whatever has involved you in the conflict. You may become involved in disruptive legal encounters at this time.

During this period the energy of Uranus, which keeps you from falling into patterns that are ultimately destructive to life, is experienced largely through intimate encounters. If your relationships are being disrupted seemingly against your will, you are probably sending out unconscious signals that you are growing restive and need to break free. Other people, also unconsciously, respond to those signals, and the trouble begins.

If you see this happening and can determine what kinds of changes need to be made in your life in order to make it more alive, you will not suffer especially from the effects of this transit. Indeed, the new experience that you gain will give you a greater mastery of life. If you resist change and regard it as a threat, you will only increase the violence of the Uranian energies, and you will lose a great deal. Uranus, like the other planetary energies, is not difficult if it is expressed freely. But if it is suppressed, it is likely to explode. Your relationships are trying to teach you something about life — let them.

Uranus in the Eighth House

During the next several years you will gradually become aware that powerful subconscious forces are operating to bring about great changes in your life. However, the changes themselves do not come about gradually but rather through sudden unexpected events of a peculiarly intense and fateful quality. Suddenly an old order in your life is passing away, and a new one is coming to be. In extreme cases, someone may die who was close to you and very much connected with your past life. This is a signal that it is time to begin a new era of your life. Restrictions that you have imposed upon yourself or allowed others to impose upon you will become intolerable now, and you may be forced to take steps to break away from them. Because your life is changing, you don't need these restrictions anymore. What has been gradual evolution now must become a revolution.

The eighth is also the house of joint finances and resources that you share with someone else, such as a spouse or business partner. There may be unexpected events connected with these matters, such as a sudden change — either up or down — in your partner's income. If your own financial situation is dependent upon your partner's, it will not be very stable now. However, sometimes the effects are more subtle, such as a sudden change in your partner's *sources* of income. Because this house is associated with death and with other people's money, this transit can indicate that you will receive an inheritance.

With Uranus transiting this house, it is wise to avoid becoming dependent upon anyone else's money, even through a bank. The obligations involved could become very disruptive in your life.

On the other hand, this transit can mean that you are becoming impatient with the duties and obligations involved in sharing property with someone or being in debt to someone. You may try to break away from such obligations or even avoid paying the debt. This would probably lead to considerable trouble, however, as it could bring about the most disruptive manifestations of this transit.

Many authorities look to the eighth house for matters concerned with sex. This transit can indicate a new sexual relationship quite different from any that you have ever been involved in before. However, you should not count on such a relationship to last, because the psychological changes you are going through now mean that your needs a few years from now will be quite different. Avoid new long-range commitments. Even relationships you are already involved in will have to change at this time.

Uranus in the Ninth House

During this time you will have the opportunity to greatly expand your awareness of the world and gain insights that you never could have had before. But in order for this to happen you must be willing to keep an open mind. Otherwise, you will only be upset by what Uranus reveals, because Uranus is the enemy of rigid views of the world. If you can remain flexible, this transit will simply point out new ways of seeing the world, frequently through circumstances that do not fit in with your old views. If, like most people, you have identified yourself with a particular point of view, you will feel threatened by this change and try to resist this new understanding and insight. That is the response of the social reactionary who views anything new with horror, which makes more devastating the triumph of the realizations he fears.

Many events that take place now will notify you that some aspect of your thinking is wrong. This does not mean that you are invalidated, but that you have to adjust your thinking. At other times your views are not challenged by others, even though you are equally in error. At least now you are finding out what is wrong so that you can change. And if you do not resist this process, it will not be terribly difficult.

If you are in a flexible frame of mind, you will be attracted to new and stimulating ways of thinking. You may begin to study science and technology or new techniques in your work. Many people who study astrology begin under this transit. Also you may be more than usually attracted to radical and innovative solutions to social problems.

Older books often mention this as a dangerous time for traveling because sudden unexpected events, such as accidents, may result in injury. But that is not very likely. It is more likely that travel or a change of residence will revolutionize your life in some way. You may have to travel so much that it is unsettling, especially if you are normally a homebody. Accidents usually happen because some violent energy within you is inhibited and not allowed expression through your conscious personality. For example, you may have a strong feeling of rage at someone or at people in general, but you repress it, feeling that you must exhibit a meek, quiet exterior. The negative energy, deprived of its normal outlet, turns on you and causes an accident. It takes much more than Uranus in the ninth or third house to cause an accident.

Because the ninth house has a connection with law, try to avoid legal encounters now. They may not turn out the way you want.

If you are open to new experiences, perceptions and ways of looking at the world and willing to change your views, this can be an extremely constructive transit.

Uranus in the Tenth House

A radical change in your professional life, a change of profession or conflict with authority figures are all possible under this transit. The way you express your identity in the world, as well as your social status, reputation and profession, will be challenged. And if any of these aspects of your life has become stale and no longer offers opportunities for new experience, there will be great changes.

One manifestation of this transit is that people over you — bosses, employers, parents or government authorities — seem particularly repressive, and you experience a strong desire to lash out and break free from their restrictions. If indeed you are being held down unreasonably by some authority figure, you should make changes that will enable you to act more freely. However, some caution is needed, because if you act too hastily, you will encounter very repressive forces, which could cause you to lose a great deal, especially if you are reacting against some part of the government.

Very often this transit operates quite benevolently and provides you with sudden new opportunities in your work — a chance to work with new techniques or to begin a revolutionary new enterprise and take off on unbeaten paths. You may change your field of work altogether at this time. In any case your work environment must provide you with stimulation, or it will become oppressive and boring. Remember that when you choose not to be consciously aware of Uranian energy, in your subconscious mind it takes the form of events that happen to you.

If you are in a highly responsible position, it may be very hard to discharge that responsibility. You may be tempted to throw the whole job over, to quit and start off in a new direction. That may in fact be the best response, although it is clearly not the safest. However, since it is so dangerous to repress Uranian energies, starting over may be safer than trying to ride out this transit without making needed changes. If you try to hold on to a situation when you really don't want to, because you feel a responsibility to do so, events may drive you from the position you find so difficult. This transit can signify a drastic fall from power and authority. But if this happens, it is a reflection of your inner, unexpressed reluctance to have power and authority. This transit may also affect your social status. People sometimes experience a sudden fall from social grace, usually because of some action that their peer group considers socially unacceptable. Uranus is quite often socially unacceptable.

Examine who you are and what you are doing in the world. Make whatever changes are necessary in order to experience new life. Don't wait for lightning to strike!

Uranus in the Eleventh House

This transit of Uranus through the natal eleventh house signifies a potential revolution in your hopes and expectations in life over the next several years. You begin to see that new and different lifestyles are possible and that you can achieve goals you didn't even dream of when you were thinking more conservatively. Consequently you will not settle for as little as you would have earlier.

However, the eleventh house is also the house of friends and your identification with group activities. During this transit you will be attracted to new kinds of friends, people who challenge your old ways. Even people who have been your friends for years may challenge you by involving you in new experiences, some of which may be quite upsetting at the time. Also it is possible that your friends will get into situations that you find upsetting.

Another frequent manifestation of this transit is the need to rebel against the group pressures you are subject to. You feel that others in your group are trying to make you into something that you are not. You feel the need to establish yourself as an individual against their pressure. If your friends are conservative, the situation is likely to be worse. As a consequence you may look for new friends who fit in better with what you want in life now.

Each of us identifies with certain groups, and our expectations are usually heavily conditioned by the groups we belong to. During this transit you will either seek new freedom through the groups you identify with, or you will rebel against their standards. Uranus has a natural affiliation with the eleventh house, because it is associated with Aquarius, the sign ruled by Uranus. Thus this is one of the more favorable transits of Uranus, if you are willing to be as flexible as Uranus demands.

Uranus in the Twelfth House

The effects of this transit can be quite subtle, but they are nevertheless important. Possible manifestations include sudden events that are clearly the result of past actions; unconscious compulsions and compulsive behavior; upsets and difficulties involving institutions; sudden disclosure of secrets and hidden things; and sudden acts by persons who had not seemed to be working against you.

All of these effects are manifestations at various levels of one basic principle — upsets, surprises and instability generated by factors that you are unaware of. Typically it is your own unconscious mind that is most involved here. All of these effects listed above are directly or indirectly involved with your unconscious mind. For example, it may seem that someone who works against you secretly is part of fate, which your unconscious mind cannot be responsible for, but that is not the case. Such hidden enemies, to use the traditional term, are provoked by signals that you have sent out unconsciously and by your own actions that you have not thought out.

The twelfth house rules that part of the unconscious mind that suppresses experiences the conscious mind finds difficult to deal with. The energy associated with suppressed experiences does not simply disappear, it operates subversively in every action, triggering off consequences that you find difficult to understand.

With Uranus transiting this house, these repressed elements of the mind become a source of upsets and sudden events, which can be understood only through some technique such as psychotherapy. Matters that you are consciously aware of but have hidden from others may also become a source of problems, because Uranus can cause them to be revealed at the most inopportune moments. Anything you have hidden from others or from yourself may emerge at this time and demand to be dealt with. This is a good time for clearing up old problems that have been floating around in your unconscious mind. Now they can be handled once and for all.

Symbolically related to the hidden aspects of the twelfth house are institutions such as prisons, hospitals and asylums, where society hides those elements that people do not like to face. Just as you may have to confront some personal "skeleton" at this time, you may also encounter one of these social skeletons. With this transit you are unlikely to be in a prison, hospital or asylum, but they may suddenly enter your life in some connection.

This transit helps you prepare for the transit of Uranus over the Ascendant. If you take this opportunity to confront your hidden self, you will be able to free your whole self and to express it more completely and honestly when Uranus crosses your Ascendant.

Uranus Conjunct Sun

This is an extremely significant transit in many ways, for it is a time when you will try to achieve new means of self-expression and to become more free than you have ever been. This is one of the most revolutionary periods in your life.

At its most productive, this transit can clear away limitations that have made your life less meaningful and fruitful, whether those limitations have been imposed by yourself or by others. Your life can become more real. However, at its worst, this transit can signify a time of wild instability and chaos, when events seem to happen unpredictably and disruptively.

No matter how you feel about change in your life, you will be forced now to break up old patterns and embark on a new course. Whether this process is completed depends largely on whether your life has degenerated into a dull and safe routine. It also depends upon how much energy you put into resisting change.

The Sun represents your heart, physically and psychologically, your vital core. Uranus calls the energy of your vital center to break free and express itself. If you live according to the rules you have been taught and not as an honest expression of yourself, these energies will make you change. You have obligations to the people around you, but you also have obligations to yourself. For the present, your own needs will take precedence, until you feel free enough to be yourself.

If you do not succeed in this effort, or if you are afraid to try, this energy may turn inward and cause physical damage to your body through accidents, or even damage to your heart. If a competent physician has determined that you have any tendency toward cardiovascular disease, you should be extremely careful at this time.

You will be attracted to anything new and exciting, as well as new techniques in your work and in personal development. You may develop a new interest in science and technology. Younger persons will experience this as a time of rebellion, particularly against authorities, such as parents, officials and employers. You will not be very patient with restrictions at this time.

However, this transit need not be destructive. It is a call to examine your life and see what changes you must make to keep from becoming too rigid. You may make tremendous changes in many aspects of your life in order to feel freer and more completely yourself.

Uranus Sextile Sun

The effects of this transit are not always spectacular, but if you watch carefully, you will notice that there are all kinds of new and stimulating happenings in your life. It is not running along in the usual manner. But the changes and the unexpected events are not especially disturbing to you. Instead they open up new understandings and opportunities and give you a feeling that life still has some excitement and potential for growth.

Specifically, you can expect sudden opportunities to arise in connection with any activity that is important to you through which you really express yourself. These opportunities may come about through friends, or they may simply pop up in some other area of your everyday environment. You may become involved with a new group of people who live in a way that you hadn't thought possible before. You may be attracted to new philosophies and new techniques for managing your life. This is one of the transits under which people begin to study astrology.

All of these events are expressing your desire for greater freedom of self-expression. During this transit you have the opportunity to gain greater control over your life and to make it a better vehicle for what you want to do. Any relationship that begins under this transit will be an expression of this fact, and even old relationships will be changed so that they further your objectives. Opportunities for advancement in your work will come suddenly through relationships with your superiors.

All of this sounds like luck, but this transit actually is showing you that your life can be much more free and that your potentials are greater than you have realized. We all have a natural tendency to settle into comfortable ruts, which can be severely limiting. But the energy of Uranus acts suddenly, so that you are forced to sit up and take notice. The purpose of this transit is to tell you who you are. It is not giving you anything you haven't earned.

Uranus Square Sun

During this transit sudden, unexpected events will test your ability to withstand change and to stay on the path you have chosen. Each of us sets forth certain objectives that we must accomplish in order to successfully maintain our sense of being a unique and strong individual. This transit seems to ask the question, "Do you really believe in what you are doing? Can you perform your tasks in the face of upsets and challenges from the outside world and even from psychological forces within yourself?" How well you withstand this challenge will determine how well your life will go during the next several years.

On one hand you may suddenly realize that because of circumstances that have developed over the last several years you can no longer do what you want without making a lot of changes. It may be necessary to struggle and break free from circumstances that you encounter in your work or with authorities, such as employers or government agencies. There may even be limiting circumstances in your personal life, such as a bad marriage or parental domination. At any rate some obstacle is preventing you from doing what you have to do, and you want to rebel against it.

On the other hand, you may be doing perfectly well in all of these matters. Your job may be perfectly satisfactory, and your personal life may be fulfilling, a real expression of who you are. But something comes along, some unexpected incident that forces you to reevaluate what you are doing. For example, at work someone may throw you a "curve ball," such as an employer suddenly questioning your effectiveness in work or a similar disruption. You may have to reevaluate your relationships to the various groups you belong to. Are they smothering your individuality? If so, you may have to break free of this influence.

If you are doing what you should in terms of your life and experience, these disruptive events will only be a test that you will withstand successfully. But if you find the energies of this transit destructive beyond your control, you should consider what changes must be made either to minimize these effects or to turn them into positive ones. For instance, one unemployed person wanted a particular job but was holding out because she was unwilling to make certain compromises that would have made the job less worthwhile. Under this transit she suddenly got the job without having to make any compromises. The transit tested her willingness to do things her own way.

Like the conjunction and opposition transits of Uranus to the Sun, the square may be dangerous to your health if you are not careful. Health problems usually arise from a conscious or unconscious suppression of the Uranian energies that are operating in your life now. These suppressed energies often emerge physically as accident-proneness or a heart illness. Don't suppress the energy of Uranus, deal with it.

Uranus Trine Sun

Sometimes it is very upsetting to make fundamental changes in your life. But at other times you feel that change is creative and exciting, and this is one of those times. You are eager for change and hope it will lead you to a life that is more exciting, interesting and alive. You look to new ideas and new experiences for insights that will make your life more real. Consequently this is an excellent time to begin studying disciplines that will allow you to develop and grow as a human being. Such disciplines can include encounter or group therapy, yoga or other spiritual disciplines, astrology or any other subject that allows you to see yourself in a new light and to grow in consciousness.

At the same time events may occur that allow you to experience yourself and thereby let you express yourself more effectively than ever. You may encounter new relationships, new friends or even a new love that will allow you to be yourself more than ever before. Your everyday being is compatible with change now, and you are hungry for it in every possible way.

This is a good time to adopt a new physical regimen—a new exercise program, new health habits or a different kind of nutrition—that will allow your body to grow and develop. Break out of old physical habits that have been damaging your body. You might conceivably be able to quit smoking or drop some other physically debilitating habit at this time.

You will be successful in every way that you reach out to encounter new experience. Do not allow conservatism or insecurity to deprive you of this great opportunity. Now you can make changes that will make your life better later on. If you don't make these changes, many years from now when Uranus squares or opposes your Sun, you may be forced to make them in a way that is less pleasant and much more disruptive.

Uranus Opposition Sun

During this transit you should look for sudden changes in your environment that challenge your expression as an individual and force you to take a stand about what you really are. The conjunction of transiting Uranus to your natal Sun signifies that you are likely to break away from restrictions that you encounter, but with the opposition it is more likely that a sudden challenge in the outer world forces you to take more responsibility for your life. Typical effects of this transit would include sudden events concerning men or your superiors or employers; unexpected circumstances that force you to change your course of action; sudden changes in a relationship, especially if you have not allowed self-expression for yourself or your partner; and sudden changes in health, involving your heart and circulatory system especially.

By this time you have built up a lifestyle that you consider valid and practically realizable. Most adults by now have given up certain ideals and goals as impossible. You have probably surrendered large parts of yourself as an accommodation with reality. The suppressed energies from this source lie behind the manifestation of this transit. Uranus demands that hidden pressures be released, but with the opposition transit you will probably feel that these events are happening *to* you rather than that you are doing them. What is happening is the passing away of something that has prevented you from being free. The trouble is that most people come to value security and predictability over freedom of self-expression. Consequently this transit is frequently upsetting.

Even if the manifestation of this transit is as extreme as a loved one's death, which is not very likely, it is a sign that the relationship must end because it has served its purpose. Continuing the relationship would have made it a limitation on both of you. Remember that whether a relationship is severed by death or by departure, it is time for it to be over. Uranus seldom destroys something you really need, even though you think so.

The health aspect of this transit is especially critical. Health problems result primarily from your resistance to the changes that Urnanus calls for. Your suppressed vital energies break forth as a "broken heart," which a coronary literally is, or as an accident. Especially if you are a middle-aged man, you should try to be as free in your self-expression as possible and also to take whatever precautions your physician recommends to prevent heart disease. Also avoid extremely dangerous places, where accidents could occur.

Uranus Conjunct Moon

This transit signifies a time of enormous psychological change and possibly emotional turmoil. Among its manifestations are the following: sudden incidents involving women; emotional upsets; emotional rashness and impulsiveness; sudden changes of mood; changes in your most intimate domestic and personal life, especially at home; and possibly sudden incidents concerning your mother or another female relative.

The effects of this transit are not so much bad as sudden and surprising. The most disturbing effect is the sense of upset, but you may also feel very excited. You can count on this transit to change your daily routine. Sudden infatuations with the opposite sex, especially if you are a man, are one of its consequences.

The Moon signifies your innermost emotional nature, your habits, your emotional responses, and your belief that you are supported and nurtured in life. These aspects of yourself as well as the possessions that you identify with them, such as your home and land, are most subject now to the surprising effects of Uranus.

What is most difficult to do but most important is to maintain your sense of equilibrium. Like the other aspects of your life, your usual emotional expression can become rigid and routine to the point that you are not really experiencing your life anymore. Viewed positively and constructively, this transit can get you in touch with life again, although it may do this through some event that you consider unfortunate. No matter what occurs, if you have the courage to look, you will discover that you are feeling alive again. The feeling may be sadness if you have lost someone or something. But the aliveness that comes when you are truly in touch with your feelings is worth as much as anything this transit takes away.

Uranus Sextile Moon

This transit stimulates your emotional life. You will experience your own feelings and allow yourself to look at the world subjectively. Your own inner feelings and your attitudes toward the world will seem as important as whatever you consider to be true or real in the external world. At this time you are able to glory in yourself and feel what you want to feel.

This effect manifests itself in a variety of ways. First of all, you will demand more emotional satisfaction in your relationships. It will not be enough for a relationship simply to go on as it has. If your existing friendships and love relationships do not meet your needs, you will find new ones that do. Your goal is freedom of emotional self-expression and experience.

Another manifestation of this transit is that you are likely to make changes in your home environment, demanding that it too be more emotionally satisfying. At this time it is not enough that your house is adequate to keep out the rain. You want it to be as interesting and stimulating as any other aspect of your life.

As your ability to experience your inner life is stimulated, your imagination will also be stimulated. You will see how you can make your life more interesting in areas that you had never considered before. Also the intellectual and emotional functions of your mind are more unified now. This is an extremely good transit for creative work, not because it directly stimulates creativity, but because it makes you see and feel from new perspectives, which gives your creative work a new freshness and innovative quality.

Uranus Square Moon

This transit will create tensions and sudden changes in your personal and emotional life. Every little tension that you have suppressed over the last several years will suddenly seem to surface and demand to be released in some way. In your close relationships, such as to parents and spouse, problems that you have been ignoring may reach the point that you have to deal with them. In a marriage, this transit can have the effect of either you or your partner suddenly breaking away and seeking a relationship elsewhere. But that would happen only if the tension between you has been very severe and neither of you has been doing anything about it. In any case, you may have to make some changes in the demands you have been making upon each other.

Your domestic life may be the source of considerable upsets now. There may be accidents in the home, a sudden need for house repairs, or other sudden problems on this front. Certainly this is not a good transit under which to buy a home, because what you look for now will not reflect your usual needs. If you are forced to buy a new home or to change residence at this time, go ahead, but be very careful. The energy of the transit has already worked itself out by disrupting your previous home and forcing you to move.

In general, you are seeking more emotional freedom at this time. If you can, change your existing relationships so that they embody what you are looking for. Otherwise, if you seek out new relationships, your persona l life may be more disrupted than you want. Men in particular should be wary of this transit, because their attitudes toward women may be rather unstable now, which can result in upsetting relationships.

Whatever you do, you will probably find that your emotional wants and needs are not consistent with those of the people around you. Others may think you are "crazy" (not clinically insane, of course), because of your actions at this time. But this is only a temporary period of instability, during which you will come to a new understanding of your emotional needs.

Uranus Trine Moon

This transit represents an excellent opportunity for you to make changes in your emotional life and personal surroundings, such as your home. And you can make these changes without causing great problems and upsets, as might be the case at other times. For example, you could remodel your home or change your personal habits. Either of these changes would be appropriate to the energy of this transit.

Events may present you with opportunities to experience your emotions in a new way. You may begin a new relationship that will bring feelings you have never had before. A love relationship that begins under this transit will have a wonderful excitement that may be missing at other times. Existing relationships may also change so that they, too, allow your new emotional experiences.

A situation may occur that brings up an event from the past so that you can examine it in a new light and change your attitudes toward it. By understanding the past differently, you will be able to change its effect upon you. For example, this may be an encounter with your mother or other female relative that clarifies and allows you to change your attitude toward something that happened in your childhood.

You may have gotten into certain routines with friends and other people whom you see every day, with the result that you have not been experiencing them as they really are. Unconsciously adopted attitudes may have gotten in the way of seeing them clearly. This transit gives you the chance to recognize these attitudes and to change them. Consequently you may experience your friends as new individuals.

Take advantage of this opportunity to make graceful changes in your personal life. Now it will be easy to get rid of unconscious attitudes, habits and routines that will be much harder to get rid of later on. If you can do this now, in several years, when Uranus comes to the next square or opposition to your natal Moon, you will be able to use that transit for more creative change and growth. If you do not change the things that you could easily clear away now, during the later transit they will be cleared away anyhow, but with upsets and difficulties.

Uranus Opposition Moon

This transit can signify sudden events in your personal and emotional life and sudden changes in your home. The pressure of circumstances will reveal your unconscious emotional patterns, and you will learn to handle your life with fewer habits and inappropriate unconscious behavior patterns. You may be upset by these changes, but you should recognize that this transit can free you from characteristics that you don't need.

The Moon has to do with patterns of behavior that were created in infancy, which may have been appropriate then but are not now. For example, it was once appropriate for you to seek nurturing and protection from your mother, and you did what you had to in order to get that. But as an adult your life should no longer follow that pattern. Uranus raises the need for you to be an independent, self-sufficient adult, to relate to others as an equal, even though you may not feel ready. But most people retain some infantile behavior patterns, which create patterns in adult life, particularly in relations with others, that make further growth difficult. You may still seek out relationships in which you have the same emotional dependency you had toward your mother. Your emotional reactions to people are only habits that interfere with communication. Or you may play a parental role toward someone else who really needs to be independent. Uranus breaks up such relationships and makes it impossible for you to behave according to old patterns, which you will be forced to reexamine. Intimate personal relationships may be disturbed, because this is the area where infantile and childish behavior patterns usually surface. Also, women in general may be a source of difficulty at this time, regardless of your own sex. This is because all your relationships with women are patterned on the relationship with your mother, and any holdovers from that period will affect relationships with other women.

Once you accept the fact that the old patterns are no longer appropriate, and you are willing to either make changes or accept the ones that have occurred, you will begin to feel liberated. You are freed from chains you have forged for yourself. You will approach life with a greater sense of freedom and a heightened ability to experience it as it is now, not as it was when you were a child.

Uranus Conjunct Mercury

This is one of the most completely positive transits of Uranus, a time when your mind will be stimulated as never before. New ideas, new techniques and new approaches to life will continually come to you. Radical ideas that you would never have entertained before seem perfectly all right now, and you are able to use them positively.

Communication will take on a more important role in your life at this time. You need to share with everyone the new insights that are coming into your life. Consequently you are likely to become a proselytizer for new ideas, trying to break others out of their rigid patterns of thinking. Astrology and the occult in general will attract you now, if they haven't in the past. You will also be interested in scientific and technological disciplines. This is an excellent time to begin studying science and mathematics.

However, if you want to take advantage of these opportunities, you must be quite flexible in your own thinking. If your thinking is very rigid, this will be an extremely upsetting period in which your ideas are challenged and found wanting. Under these circumstances you may become more tense, nervous and threatened. Even if you go along with the insights that Uranus can bring, this transit may be upsetting, because the pace is too fast to keep up. Nervous ailments and anxieties can be a part of this transit if the pace becomes too hectic.

A related problem is this transit's tendency to scatter your thoughts so that you don't think things through very carefully. There is the danger of making decisions impulsively without adequate forethought. In general, this is not a good time to make decisions, but rather a time to learn. Make sure you are in a position where you are free to change your mind, for you may do it frequently. If you try to make a permanent commitment to some new course of action, you are likely to embarrass yourself by seeming inconsistent. The problem is really that you are so constantly exposed to new data that your conclusions have to change as your understanding changes.

Traveling may be difficult under this transit. Accidents, delays or other unanticipated events may make travel upsetting. If you do have to travel, it may be because you must deal with a suddenly urgent situation.

Radical mental and intellectual change enters your life during this transit. Allow the insights that come now to become part of your thinking. Make the necessary changes in your immediate world and do not resist the new ideas that you are being exposed to.

Uranus Sextile Mercury

This transit stimulates your thinking and your communication with others, giving your life an excitement and interest that it may normally lack. You also feel that you cannot stand boredom, so you aid the natural energy of the transit in every way possible. During this time you may seek out new contacts and friendships that reflect your desire for new experiences.

This same restlessness of spirit may also make you want to travel, at least to see more of the countryside around you, if not for long distances. You desire to know your immediate environment as completely as possible and let nothing escape you. If there is anything happening, you want to know about it.

Your natural curiosity is stimulated now, which makes this an extremely good transit for beginning to study a new subject. However, you will not be particularly disciplined, so your interest must be very strong in order to keep your motivation up. If the subject becomes dull, you are likely to drop it. The study of science, mathematics, technological studies — especially electronics and computer work — as well as astrology or other occult techniques is favored by this transit.

One strong point of this transit is that it helps you make constructive changes in your thinking. You are not rigid at this time, and because you are so receptive to new ideas it is easier for you to change your mind. Even when you discover that you have been wrong about something, you are not very upset. You are only too happy to find it out and add this to your understanding.

Uranus and Mercury are jokers, which results in a tendency that you should try to resist, at least a little bit. Their combined influence may put you into a rather prankish frame of mind, especially when you are with someone who seems pompous and overbearing. You will want to prick that person's balloon and bring him down to earth. Also, because you are so open to new ideas and experience, you feel that everyone else should be too. You may have difficulty in leaving people alone, but do try it. They have a right to their own narrowness, just as you have a right to your beliefs.

Uranus Square Mercury

This can be an extremely confusing transit, because new information and data may come at you very rapidly. It may be very difficult to make intelligent decisions on most matters. If you have to make a decision, but your attitude toward the matter is not calm and cool, try to put it aside until your feelings are sorted out. This may be more difficult than it looks, because often under this transit people are tempted to make rash, impulsive decisions. Business transactions are also difficult now because of this tendency. However it is possible to handle transactions in scientific or technological fields, especially electronics. These fit the symbolism of the transit and may not be so difficult. But even under the best of circumstances, be careful!

A negative effect of this transit can be that you feel extremely nervous and tense, because of the fast tempo of events. This transit may signify nervous ailments, if you have a natural tendency in that direction.

Traveling under this transit may be quite disruptive. No matter how carefully you make your plans, your trip will not work out as planned, and you may be forced to travel at the most inconvenient times. Unfortunately there is also the danger of accidents, so traveling should be kept to a minimum. Drive carefully.

One important psychological manifestation of this transit is that your ideas and opinions are likely to be strongly challenged by others. Your beliefs may very well be right, but the universe will force you to examine them so that you know for certain whether they are. You may be attracted to radically different ways of thinking, which can also provoke opposition from others at this time. This will affect your professional life in particular. If you express your opinions strongly in any area, be sure that you are in a position to defend them. But even if you are right, avoid stating your position dogmatically. Try to understand others' points of view, for you may learn from them. Even though Uranus generates radical, new ideas, it can be dogmatic in its expression of them.

Uranus Trine Mercury

This transit often produces excitement and interest in everyday life, without pushing the tempo to the point that you can no longer enjoy it. Your everyday activities bring new and interesting encounters that open up aspects of life that you may not have encountered before.

This transit particularly stimulates mental activity. Your mind is sharpened, and your interest in the world about you is increased. You feel ready for anything, as long as it is exciting and different. Your conversations with other people, even those whom you meet every day, become more interesting. When new topics are discussed, you are ready for the new ideas that you are exposed to. This is an excellent time to encounter people and ideas that help you elevate your mental habits and build up better patterns of thinking.

This is also an excellent time for learning new skills, particularly of a scientific or technological nature, and new techniques for expanding your mind and experience. It is also favorable for studying astrology, yoga and other occult techniques. Because of Mercury's association with travel, this is also a good transit for traveling, but not if your objective is to "get away from it all" on a lazy relaxing trip. This transit will make travel exciting and interesting in a positive way.

If you have been faced with problems in research or a situation in which you have to come up with a new and creative solution, this transit will help. At other times your mind often gets into a rut in which it runs through the same solutions over and over. This transit allows you to escape from the rut and to think along different lines.

This is a favorable time for introducing new elements into your life. Communications from others may bring an unexpected surprise. Or you may say something that surprises others. This is a favorable time to announce anything new or innovative to the world. For example, this is a good time for a manufacturer to introduce a new product or to begin a new and innovative advertising or administration policy within a company.

Uranus Opposition Mercury

This transit may bring considerable excitement into your life from several different quarters. Its general effect is to stimulate and quicken the tempo of your everyday communication and thinking. You will not be able to sit back and take it easy, for you will constantly be exposed to news, conversations, letters and other communications that will challenge you to make a quick response and which can be quite upsetting. You will have to face life with more flexibility than usual and be prepared to change your thinking on a number of issues.

At its best, this transit gives you an opportunity to become involved with new and stimulating ways of thinking and looking at the world. You will be attracted to challenging systems of thought that let you discover new facets of life. You may begin to study astrology, other occult disciplines or a scientific or technical field. Any subject that allows you to experiment and try out new ideas will appeal to you.

However, this transit also has a problem side. Be careful not to let the tempo of your life become too rapid, for it can accelerate to the point that you cannot keep track of what is happening. There is a danger that you can become mentally exhausted and suffer from nerves and anxiety, particularly if you are used to a rather quiet routine. Try not to be too bothered by upsetting news. Deal with events as calmly and carefully as possible, and if you begin to feel harried, don't take on any more responsibilities than you have to.

Traveling at this time is not a very good idea. A pleasure trip would bring too many unexpected surprises to be enjoyable, and it would not be at all relaxing. If you travel for business, so many things may go wrong unexpectedly that you would be better off not making the trip. This transit may also scatter your thinking so much that you should not make important decisions. This is an excellent time for new discoveries and new experiences, but it is not good for making commitments that will bind you in the future. In general this period is not good for business negotiations.

Uranus Conjunct Venus

The effects of this transit are often quite spectacular. You are likely to seek new freedom and excitement through your relationships, especially those with the opposite sex. You may even decide to break away from an old, steady marriage or other relationship and seek a second youth through a new affair. But this is an extreme response which is by no means inevitable, especially if your current relationship is basically sound. It is more likely that you will change your existing relationships, sexual and otherwise, so that they are more interesting and less routine. Every relationship, no matter how good, settles into behavior patterns that kill spontaneity and make you both feel that you have little to offer each other. In other words, you get bored. You can count on this transit to change the situation.

The means by which you revive and renew a relationship will vary according to your temperament. If a relationship is quite unsatisfactory and you are naturally impulsive, you may respond in the "classic" manner by seeking a new love affair. If you are more conservative and also happier in an existing relationship, you will go through a period of tension that will lead you to reexamine the relationship and make necessary changes. If you are married and having problems now, a marriage counselor might be helpful. You need new ideas to enliven your marriage, which an outsider might be able to provide. Some married couples create new arrangements under this transit, such as an open marriage, in which they allow relationships outside of their own. In this regard you must do what is appropriate for the two of you.

If you are not married, you may become involved in a relationship that is completely different from anything you have experienced before. However, in this case, you should be aware that the excitement and newness of such a relationship may be a large factor in making it work, and when it becomes older and more routine it might not last. But it could, for you cannot tell with Uranus on Venus! Make no permanent plans in such a relationship until after this transit is over.

Venus also rules creative art. If you are involved in an artistic activity, you will brim over with new ideas. This can be a very creative transit, although you may have to wait until it is over to integrate what you have learned into your regular techniques.

Uranus Sextile Venus

This transit will considerably enliven your social life and relationships. You will have opportunities for different kinds of encounters with others, and you will form new friendships and perhaps a new love interest. All of these new relationships will be different from your old ones, and all, even the love relationships, will give you and your partners more freedom. You are not inclined to be jealous and emotionally possessive under this transit, and you demand that others be equally free with you. You are seeking new kinds of experience with people, and you need to be free to have them. Your new relationships may have an unusual quality that makes them departures from the past. You may be attracted to people from a very different social background or to people who are older or younger than you; or a relationship may begin under unusual conditions.

A relationship formed at this time can be long lasting, but only if it continues to have the freedom, spontaneity and interest that attracted you in the first place. If it becomes stale and routinized, it may not hold up too well.

During this time you may also become involved in unusual social activities, doing things for entertainment that you don't normally do. And that is precisely why you want to do them. If your life is like most people's, you are seeking to break out of the routine that has dominated it, and you are trying to do this through your relationships, an area where most people quickly fall into habits. If you are willing to see it, this transit can show you the whole range of potential for experience with other people. You will have the chance to find out exactly what kind of social contacts you need, and you will be able to choose all your relationships more intelligently.

Uranus Square Venus

Your love life and relationships in general will be unpredictable and difficult during this transit. You may suddenly become involved in relationships that are quite different from what you would normally expect. If your relationships usually go along from day to day without much excitement, you may suddenly want one that is more exciting. You may be attracted to people who are quite different from yourself in age, class background or personality. Differences are themselves an escape from everyday relationships. At the same time the relationships you seek will be ones that are not binding, that allow you more freedom to come and go. This desire is not always conscious, so you may think you are looking for a stable and peaceful relationship, but instead you become involved in something unpredictable and unreliable. It is actually your own desire not to be committed that is making the relationship unstable.

A stable marriage may go through a period of readjustment now. This is a good time for releasing all the hidden tensions that have built up between you and starting afresh. An unstable marriage may break up at this time, especially if you or your partner is attracted to someone new. Domestic boredom can be very destructive under this transit.

A new relationship that comes along at this time may not prove very lasting or reliable. As long as it introduces excitement into your life, it is fine, but as soon as it becomes routine one of you will probably want out. Very often a relationship that begins under this transit represents a rebellion against your peer group standards. Pressure from your friends may be so great that maintaining the relationship is not worth putting up with the disapproval of others.

A milder manifestation of this transit is that you may begin collecting unusual and beautiful objects for your home. Or you may seek out new and different kinds of amusement. But be careful not to saddle yourself with anything that cannot stand on its own merits later on. Your tastes are not following their usual pattern at this time, and what you like now you may dislike later.

Uranus Trine Venus

During this period your relationships will have a new feeling of freedom and excitement. If you are not currently involved in a love relationship, this transit may very well mark the beginning of one. And it is likely to be quite different and unusual in terms of your past experience. You may find someone who is quite different from you in social background, ethnic group, age or interests, and it will be this very difference that attracts you. You are seeking to escape from the everyday rut through this new love, and you probably will. However, unlike the "hard" transits of Uranus to Venus (conjunction, square and opposition), with this transit the relationship should last, because the two of you will be able to build interest and excitement directly into your relationship so that it won't become stale and dull. Also you will be able to give each other enough room that you can avoid smothering each other with excessive closeness and possessiveness.

If you are already involved in a relationship, this is a good time to make changes so that it becomes renewed and fresh. You will learn that neither of you needs to fear the other's desire for independence and individual self-expression.

This transit also brings about friendships that possess the Uranian quality of being exciting and challenging as well as constructive. Every kind of social contact, even those that are usually routine and unexciting, may provide fascinating new experiences now. Life will not be dull during this transit.

Uranus Opposition Venus

Your love life and relationships will be the sources of change in your life at this time. A loved one may become restless and begin to question the basis of your relationship. He or she may demand more freedom and ask that the relationship be changed considerably. This is not the time for you to become rigid and possessive, however. If you try to hold on now, you are likely to lose everything. A good relationship probably will not break up, but all kinds of tension will surface that you and your partner may not have dealt with before. You should allow this to happen and not try to smooth over feelings that should be expressed.

It is also possible that you may be the one who becomes restless and demands a change in the relationship. You may begin to feel that it has become boring, so you seek out a new relationship that will provide the excitement that you feel is lacking. Under the influence of this transit, people often form relationships that would seem highly improbable to themselves and others under other circumstances. You may form a relationship with someone who is very different in age, background or culture or with someone who is already committed to another. Often a relationship begins between two people who cannot really get together, as exemplified by a young woman falling in love with a married man who has no real intention of leaving his wife.

The problem is that there is a real ambiguity in your mind about yourself and your relationships. You want to be close to people and to be free at the same time. Consequently you will be attracted to relationships that either express your desire for freedom or that are impossible to consummate, as described above. For this reason you should not expect any relationship formed under this transit to last very long. It could last, but you should not expect it. This is a good time to enjoy the present. Don't live in the future!

It would be much better to use the energy of this transit to redefine and change your existing relationships, if they have anything at all to offer, so that they are a more complete expression of yourself and your loved ones. The best relationships are those in which the compromises that you make do not require you to become a different person.

If you are working in a creative art form, this will be a tremendously stimulating period. You may not get much actual work done, but you will be exposed to new ideas and techniques, which later you will be able to integrate into your overall technique.

Uranus Conjunct Mars

This transit calls forth very potent energies that can be quite disruptive, but they must be handled. Any effort to sidestep the issues that this transit raises could be disastrous.

Uranus and Mars together represent explosive forces that may break out in any area of your life, but especially in areas ruled by the house in which this transit occurs.

On the psychological level, you may be much more irritable than usual and prone to outbursts of anger. Conditions in your life that you have put up with for years, even though they are wrong, now become intolerable. You simply will not allow them to continue. Even limitations imposed from without that always seemed quite reasonable now seem completely impossible to bear.

What you are feeling is the need to assert your individuality against all the forces that have been blocking its expression in the past. You want to be yourself and have your individuality recognized for what it is, not for what others expect it to be. You want to do things immediately that you have never done before. With some degree of care and moderation, this energy can be used quite creatively. It is imperative that you release the tensions you are feeling now. Suppressing this energy will only lead to worse problems.

If you try to suppress this energy, it will usually surface as a sudden urgent physical illness that requires an operation. It is as if your body suffers from the effects of the explosive energies that your mind has refused to deal with.

The energy can also leak out and generate usually unconscious actions on your part that set you up for an accident. An example of this is an insignificant action when driving, such as pulling out of a side street when an oncoming car is a bit too close. If you are at all psychologically accident-prone at other times, then take special care during this transit. It must be said, however, that contrary to the older texts, accidents are not the most common manifestation of this transit, because most people encounter its energies at a more conscious level. Even so, you should be careful in dealing with any sort of machinery, firearms or explosives. These are Mars-Uranus objects, and you may find that they are not under your control when you have to use them. Avoid them as much as possible during this transit.

Uranus Sextile Mars

This transit will give you opportunities to assert yourself and your individuality and do things that you have never done before. The keynote of this transit is "freedom to be myself!"

Your physical energy level will be stimulated, so that you will be able to work quite hard at any task you want to do. You will not be in the mood for disciplined, self-sacrificing kinds of work. It is not that you are feeling selfish or self-indulgent but that you really understand your personal needs and are unwilling to compromise.

You may be suddenly released from restrictions that have been holding you back from many activities you would like to engage in that would truly help your personal development, and this will give you a new freedom to act. At other times you may have felt the need to lash out and rebel against obstacles in your life, but now that is not necessary. The opportunities to get rid of the obstacles arise of their own accord. However, the opportunities carry an obligation to take advantage of them in order to understand more completely what you are capable of doing. This transit will enlarge your idea of your capabilities, which has probably been too limited in the past. You will enjoy taking chances and risks even if you have always acted conservatively, and you will probably discover that you have been too careful before.

Freedom is important to you now in every way. You will probably be attracted to others who have experienced similar restrictions in life, and you will work with them. If you have ever been attracted to movements for social reform and change, it is especially likely that you will do this now. Having found out more about your capabilities by getting rid of restrictions, you will enjoy stirring up others so that they can find that out for themselves, too. However, you must recognize that the limitations you have encountered in life were not put there solely by powers beyond your control. You at least acquiesced to them, either out of fear, a sense of personal inadequacy or a desire to be careful.

Uranus Square Mars

Watch out for impulsive actions, rash decisions and other actions that may have sudden, unexpected consequences and undesirable results in the future. You may feel that your ego is at stake in some way and that you have to assert yourself now regardless of the risk of getting involved in an accident.

There may be considerable tension with others who seem to be in your way all the time. It may be difficult to avoid disputes and "blowing up" at others. This transit challenges your sense of security and just how much you believe you can assert yourself. The more insecure you are, the more likely you are to do something rash as a way of saying to the world that you are a person to be reckoned with. Authority figures who limit your freedom of movement and self-expression are very likely targets for your rebellion, which may be through petty acts or through larger actions that could get you into difficulties. It is not that you are wrong in wanting to assert yourself, but that the ways you choose to do this are not very well considered or effective. Do what you must, but act with a little discretion.

Quite often the effects of this transit are more unconscious; that is, you will not be aware of the feeling described above. This can lead to unconscious eruptions of the energy that can be quite disruptive. Accidents that you have not apparently caused but have somehow made more likely are one outcome of this. An illness that requires an operation may be another, especially if you have really been trying to repress the energy created by this transit.

The only real answer to this transit is to try to achieve some security about who you are and what you are doing. Then you will not feel such a great need to break free and take rash and ill-considered actions. You may still feel obliged to do something that is a significant break from your normal routine, but it will not be so destructive.

Uranus Trine Mars

This transit represents an opportunity for vigorous activity and self-assertion. Even if you are naturally a somewhat shy and retiring person, this transit will enable you to make your mark on the world around you. Others will stand up and take notice when they see that you are able to break out of your old habits and ways of acting around others. You will show new sides of yourself and attempt to do things that you wouldn't usually try. Quite likely you will succeed. It is not that you couldn't have done these things before but that you didn't believe you could.

Mars represents the principle of individual self-assertion, and Uranus enables you to find new ways of doing things. Together they enable you to express your individuality as never before and to acquire new confidence in yourself.

You may choose to work at new activities with others, but only if they allow you to be yourself. You are not in the mood to compromise, because you do not see any need to, and you are probably right. At the same time you don't feel any particular need to make other people go along with you either. You are quite content to go your own way and work by yourself. You will set out to accomplish tasks and begin new projects on your own that are expressions of who and what you are.

Under the influence of this transit you may become interested in other people's freedom, because you understand from your own efforts that it may be difficult for them to gain their freedom. For this reason you may become involved in organizations that work for the rights of others and help them to become liberated in some way. You will help those who are engaged in the same kinds of fights that you have had to wage in your life.

If you feel that you have never had the opportunity to show everyone who you are and that you have been limited by other people or by circumstances beyond your control, this transit gives you the opportunity to take control of your own life and make it what you want.

Uranus Opposition Mars

With this transit you can expect rebellious and explosive energies to enter your life. You may begin to chafe at the restrictions on your life and break free of them, or others may rebel against restrictions that you have placed on them. Mars represents the urge to assert your own individuality, and Uranus is the urge to become free and unstructured. The combination is very dynamic.

You are likely to be in a fighting mood toward anyone who says that you cannot do something. You will act more impulsively and fly off the handle at the slightest provocation, especially if you usually tend to hold everything in. You want to assert yourself, and you are not terribly concerned about the obstacles you come up against.

One manifestation of this transit can be a new fondness for taking risks. You take chances and do things that don't have much chance of working out. Subconsciously you may be trying to prove yourself by pulling off a "long shot" or making a big splash if you fail. But this can also lead to accidents and injuries, if you are too rash.

Sometimes you can suppress this feeling of rebellious self-assertion and make your life go on as if nothing were happening. But this is not a good idea, because the energy does not go away. If you suppress it, the result is some kind of physical illness that does not seem to be your fault. This transit signifies that you need to make changes in your life that will allow you to be more self-assertive than you have been.

This transit may also affect your relations with other people. If others feel the need to be more assertive with you, let them state their case and then try to come to some accommodation with them. If you allow others to be themselves with you, it will be easier to be yourself with them. Trying to live according to your old plan is not likely to work out very well at this time. Psychological explosions are expressions of unresolved tensions that should have been handled before when there was less energy behind them. Even now it is not too late to handle them, if you are willing to be flexible. You may have to make truly revolutionary changes in your life, but you will benefit in the long run.

Uranus Conjunct Jupiter

It is very hard to predict the exact effects of this transit. It is best described as a sudden change in fortune, but which way the change will go is not easy to say. More often than not it is a positive change in fortune, beginning with a sudden unexpected event that opens new possibilities for free action. This may be a sudden windfall, an unexpected job promotion or success in gambling, which is related to this combination. But with this transit there is a danger that your good fortune can be "easy come, easy go."

Often this transit signifies a new restlessness, a desire for freedom and new activities that will broaden your horizons. It does not have the explosiveness of other Uranus transits, but it can signify that you are ready to make sweeping changes in your life.

You are likely to be attracted to new philosophies and new ways of looking at the universe. You may feel that your old viewpoint was too narrow, so you seek new experiences that will give you greater understanding. These experiences will be quite different from anything you have done before. You are inclined to take chances and break down barriers with a tremendous feeling of optimism. However, you should recognize that with this transit the situation can change very quickly. Take any opportunity that comes, but do not count on anything that comes into your life now to last a long time. Make sure you have an alternate plan in case of changed circumstances.

You may have sudden opportunities for travel, which will expose you to new aspects of life. You will see new worlds altogether rather than the world that you have always known. You can expect that whatever happens will be quite challenging and stimulating.

Because you value your own freedom at this time, you respect the fact that it depends upon other people's ability to be free. This realization makes you more tolerant of others' lifestyles as long as they do not interfere with yours. And you may become quite a fighter for other people's rights as well as your own.

Uranus Sextile Jupiter

Under this transit you will have several opportunities to expand your horizons and broaden the range of your experience. These may arrive from several directions, but they all will make you understand more about your life and let you see how it fits into the overall pattern of the universe.

One manifestation of this is a sudden educational opportunity, although not necessarily a regular school or college situation. This transit can encompass many different types of educational experience. For example, you might take up the study of astrology or other occult techniques of mind expansion and self-understanding.

This transit can also present an opportunity for travel, but as with all Uranus transits that signify travel, you should expect an exciting rather than a relaxing trip. In the course of your travels some of your cherished ideas about life may be upset, but that should not be too disturbing. One effect of this transit is to make you want to change your views in order to experience life in a new and richer manner.

This transit can produce sudden runs of good luck. Taking chances at this time may pay off, and long shots may come through. But don't take your luck for granted, for eventually this transit will pass, and you may not be so lucky in the future. Also, if you sit back and let this transit bring you results without much effort on your part, this is a misuse of the transit's creative capabilities. Indeed, you should examine every "lucky" break to see what it can teach you about how the universe works and how you can take advantage of it. Each piece of luck can show you how you have needlessly accepted the limitations that were imposed on you in the past.

Personal growth and increased freedom of action are the two major consequences of this transit, if you take the opportunity to make this a learning experience. Most people recognize that hard times can be a learning experience, but it is more difficult to recognize that you can learn from the good times also.

Uranus Square Jupiter

This transit brings a great feeling of exuberance and optimism, which is fine, but it can lead you to be foolishly overconfident and to take unwarranted financial and material risks. This combination brings out the gambler in almost anyone. However, like all Uranus transits, it is hard to know exactly what to expect from this one, and you may find yourself in trouble if you don't restrain your optimism a bit. Nothing at all may happen, but you just don't know. So proceed with caution, especially in financial matters, and be careful not to leave any loose ends.

Even if you don't take risks, this transit can sometimes cause unexpected expenses or financial shortages. But that happens because you have failed to take into account some factor that could cause trouble for you at this time.

Jupiter symbolizes your ability to go along with the social and economic system in which you live and to make it work for you. The square from Uranus provides a series of unexpected events that test your ability to handle your relationship with the system.

If you have a realistic attitude toward the way the world works, what you can and cannot do effectively, especially in financial matters, this transit will not do any particular damage. It may even bring a sudden chance to take advantage of a situation. Just make sure that it's a real opportunity. If you are not clear about your limitations, this transit could bring some unpleasant surprises.

At the same time, this transit may symbolize striking out against the system. You may adopt a different set of values from the prevailing culture and pursue a lifestyle that is quite different from the way you have lived. If you do, you may experience considerable disapproval from your friends and others around you at this time. But this is not the violent rebellion that comes with other Uranus transits, it is just that you have begun to experience the world differently from those around you. As a result your point of view is different. You wish to be free of the narrowness that you see in others.

Uranus Trine Jupiter

This is one of the few transits that can be truly characterized as lucky. That is, it brings about unexpected breaks and good fortune, as well as a feeling of being free and able to take on any new experience that life has to offer. You feel more daring than usual and willing to experiment with life.

Everyone's life is hedged about with certain restrictions — your job, your family responsibilities, your finances — that sometimes seem to unduly limit your freedom and prevent you from growing. You cannot really afford to throw over these limitations completely, but you would like a break from them once in a while, and this transit provides that break. It may happen through a sudden windfall, a sudden opportunity for personal advancement or the sudden lifting of an onerous burden. But it may also happen in more subtle ways.

For example, you may become increasingly interested in new areas of thought that open up new vistas of understanding. In this way you escape from the killing routines of your life, not by a sudden overthrow, but by a gradual change in your understanding. This transit can bring about new involvement with spiritual teachings, astrology or other revolutionary techniques of mind expansion. You will revolt against narrow ways of thinking and be on the lookout for new approaches to the truth. Yet it will not be enough to understand these truths yourself; you will want to teach others what you have learned. You may become involved in groups or organizations that teach new ideas or are involved in the occult. Under this transit you are extremely conscious of the larger social order, and you always have it in mind, whatever you are doing.

You are also inclined to be less materialistic than usual. It is not that you don't value material resources, but you don't fear that you will have any shortage of them. "Cast thy bread upon the waters" is your motto while this transit is in effect.

Overall, this transit represents an enormous opportunity to broaden yourself and encounter tremendous new experiences that will make your life much more interesting and rewarding.

Uranus Opposition Jupiter

During this transit you should watch the affairs of your life very carefully. Situations will arise suddenly that can be extremely productive and beneficial if you recognize them in advance or extremely difficult if you do not. Events happen so fast that you will not have the usual time to figure them out before you act. If you act too quickly, you may find yourself out on a very unpleasant limb, but if you don't act quickly enough, the chance is lost. Consequently this transit can produce both sudden losses and sudden gains. As a general rule, however, you would be well advised to be cautious. The opportunities you miss by acting slowly may not be worth the risk. This is a gambler's transit, and many people respond to it by taking very long-shot risks. It makes you want to gamble, but it does not make you especially lucky.

In your relationships the theme of freedom will be emphasized. You may become restless and want to be free of an excessively restrictive relationship. You are inclined at this time to break away from secure situations and leap out into the unknown simply for the sake of the challenge. However, it may be that someone else will struggle to break free from your influence. Someone who has been with you a long time and has seemingly been satisfied may suddenly want out. But this is not likely to happen unless you both have been feeling a strain in your relationship, although you may not have chosen to recognize it until now.

If you have been putting up with a tense and strained situation but not getting any benefit from it, you will break free of the tension now and probably experience an enormous sense of release. Even if you don't want to let go of the situation, you will probably be happier once it has gone.

Uranus Conjunct Saturn

At this time in your life, structures you thought were dependable and permanent will be threatened by sudden events. It is often a time of great tension and sudden releases of tension. This is a powerful combination because the nature of Saturn is radically different from that of Uranus, and the two together almost always represent a serious conflict of principles.

Saturn represents your reality structure, those aspects of existence that you believe to be truly real, unchanging, material and definite. It represents the inevitable circumstances of life that must be accepted by anyone who claims to be realistic. Uranus contradicts this structure by causing sudden change in areas that you don't expect to change. And the more definite you think your situation is, the more rigid and inflexible your idea of reality, the more shocking your experience of this transit is likely to be.

Usually tension has been building up for many years in several areas of your life. These tensions are most commonly the result of the little compromises that we all make between what we want out of life and what we feel we can get. But some of these compromises may violate your inner integrity even though you don't realize it. Subconsciously you are aware of it, however, and a force for change begins to operate that eventually will try to overthrow the limiting aspects of your life. It begins to surface as an unbearable tension between your desire to be free of restrictions and your fear of insecurity and change.

Eventually you get to the point that something has to give, which happens suddenly. People usually respond to this transit with sudden actions that surprise others because they happen without warning and are apparently unpremeditated. You may break off an unsatisfactory relationship, marriage or business partnership, leave a job that has become oppressive or suddenly break away from something else that has become a burden.

Ultimately, no matter how disruptive this transit seems, it is a force for good, because it clears away those built-up structures that had been holding you back. You must be willing to let go of those aspects of your life that Uranus has disrupted and not suppress this energy for change. Suppressing it can lead to tension-related diseases, such as colitis, ulcers or even heart and cardiovascular problems. At the very least you will be subject to extreme and uncomfortable tension.

Uranus Sextile Saturn

During this transit you have the opportunity to make creative changes through a system. It can be any kind of system, such as your work, the government or other aspects of the social system, or it can be the "systems" you have created in your personal world with your friends, family and loved ones. At other times you may feel that the system you are involved with gets in the way of your individual freedom and self-expression. But now the rules of the game afford you the chance to make whatever changes are necessary for your own personal growth.

In your work, this is an extremely favorable transit because your superiors will be impressed by your innovative ideas. You may be rewarded with a higher position in that particular system. Both at work and in your life generally you are unusually willing to learn new techniques, and you have the discipline to master them.

You will work for change in the organizations you deal with, but you will not be satisfied with airy schemes that have little practical value. Instead you will try to achieve a carefully thought-out, rigorously planned course of action. Others will have no doubt about how your plans are to work. Consequently there is potential for much solid achievement under this transit.

All structures in your life serve two purposes. First, they eliminate chaos from your perception of the world so that you can deal with it more easily. But these structures also present a constant challenge to grow and change within them. If you do not accept the challenge, the structures in your life can become extremely limiting and deadening. Eventually this results in a crisis situation in which you must either strike out or die psychologically, if not literally. These crisis situations are symbolized by the hard-angle transits of Uranus to Saturn (square conjunction or opposition). But the sextile transit gives you the chance to make creative changes under relatively favorable conditions so that structures in your life do not become stifling. You should use this opportunity to ensure that you can always work within the structures of your life.

Uranus Square Saturn

This is a time of considerable testing. Events will challenge your sense of order, discipline and duty, as well as your notions about the world. You may encounter disruptions that make you wonder whether you really understand what is going on around you. You may be forced to revise some of your ideas, although any valid beliefs will survive this transit without difficulty.

Restrictions that you have accepted but that have no real purpose in your overall individual growth may become unbearable at this time. For example, if you are putting up with a bad relationship for the sake of emotional or financial security, you may find that the tensions have become too great. You will experience a sudden desire to break free at all costs, even if it means violating your own standards of behavior. Your actions will surprise others who have believed the outward appearance that everything was all right. They will not expect your actions.

In your professional situation you may have greater difficulty than usual in getting along with your employers. If the tension becomes too great, you may want to change jobs. But you should make such a change only after carefully considering what your present job has to do with your real purpose in life. You should think just as carefully before deciding whether or not to leave a relationship.

The purpose of this transit is not to overthrow everything that you consider important in life, but it does force you to examine the factors that are causing you to fall short of your potentials. In accepting these limitations you have settled for less than you deserve or need.

As the conflict builds up between your desire to break free and the normal desire for order in your life, the physical tension may become quite intense. It is very important that you be able to communicate with someone in order to help release the tension, because it can be quite damaging to your body. This transit does not usually cause but it will worsen such conditions as heart disease, ulcers and other diseases related to tension.

Uranus Trine Saturn

At this time in your life, discipline, order and responsibility can lead you to understanding and freedom. You will learn to understand and respect your limitations and work with them so that they are no longer so limiting. Everyone has limitations, but they can be used in a positive way and actually become tools for managing your life.

Your approach to life is very methodical and thorough, but you are not satisfied with the status quo. At this time you will seek out ways to constructively create changes, taking a very definite course of action to achieve what you want. Not satisfied with abstract formulations of principles, you want to know exactly how to do something, so that you can immediately get to the task. Therefore this is an excellent transit for studying any difficult but practical technique.

This is a good time for learning new ways to advance in your profession. You may appear ambitious, but you are really working carefully to expand your world and avoid undue limitations on your life. Whatever your motivation, you will win favor from your superiors, because they can see that you have balanced hard work and discipline on one hand with innovation and originality on the other. For this reason you may get a promotion of some kind now, which will bring you greater power and authority. But even if you achieve a new position, you are not likely to cease working for change within the system that you are part of. You will continue for some time, and perhaps always, to work for reform and new ways of doing things, but always in the practical manner that got you there in the first place.

Uranus Opposition Saturn

During this transit the structures that you have built up in your life will more than ever be challenged by circumstances. Areas of your life that you think are reliable and dependable may cease to be, and you will be forced to make a lot of changes. It is likely that you will feel a strong sense of uneasiness, because you don't know quite what to expect next.

What is happening is that all the hidden tensions in your world are being released. They may be released in a relationship, even to the point that one of you suddenly breaks it off, or in business, where a problem suddenly surfaces between you and your employer, or even in your body, where tensions that have long been hidden and ignored cause serious nervous problems.

Saturn in your horoscope tells a great deal about the way you experience reality. Although you may not like everything about your life, the Saturn element of your consciousness says that basically you understand what it is all about. But when a Uranus transit such as this one comes along, you discover that you don't know what you thought you knew. Uranus reveals aspects of life that you haven't considered at all, usually by creating a sudden event that does not fit into the pattern of your life. This is happening now, largely through encounters with others in close relationships or with enemies.

The physical tension that this transit can give rise to is one of its more difficult manifestations. The tension can become so great that you develop a psychosomatic illness such as colitis or ulcers or simply a bad case of nerves. To avoid this, try to get in touch with the problem that is causing the tension and release it. You are much better off in many respects if the manifestations of this transit are not in your body but in the outer world, because there you can deal with the source of the tensions. Bodily tension is only a response to the tensions you feel in dealing with the outer world.

But you are not being "hurt" pointlessly. Like all Uranus transits, this one is letting you know that you don't have all the answers about reality and that there is still room to grow. Look at the situation that way and assimilate what you are shown. The more you resist and try to deny what happens now, the more difficult this transit will be.

Uranus Conjunct Uranus

In some cases this transit occurs very soon after you are born and then not again until you are eighty-four. It can occur immediately after birth, if at birth or soon after, Uranus becomes retrograde and transits the position it held at birth once or twice more. At that time it signifies conditions that occur very early in life that tend to disrupt the normally tranquil environment of childhood. If this happened in your case, it could have one of two effects. You might have a continuing sense of unease, not quite knowing where the next upset or surprise will come from, even when everything is moving smoothly. Or it can instill a lifelong urge to be free and to do things in your own way.

When this transit occurs when you are eighty-four, it signifies the closing of an entire life cycle, with very positive results. The effect of this transit is to free you from being so involved in the kinds of mundane concerns that have dominated your life thus far — paying bills and taxes, making appointments and such. This transit signifies changes that allow you to put your entire life in perspective and to relate it to eternity in some way.

Your perspective is vastly increased, and you know now that this world is not all there is, which in turn causes you to alter your sense of what is really important. Life is sweet, but you also understand that there is something beyond. You can enjoy life for what it is and yet not be so attached to it that you fall prey to its little illusions and snares. This transit confers the highest degree of wisdom and serves to prepare you for the next step in your evolution.

Uranus Sextile Uranus

This transit occurs twice in your life, once at the age of fourteen and once at about seventy.

The transit that occurs when you are fourteen has a great deal to do with adolescence. This is when you begin to encounter the world as something larger than your immediate home and family. You look at yourself and wonder exactly how you fit into the society around you. You will have to change many of your old ideas about the world as you learn more about what the world demands through sudden encounters with others.

During this time you will be inclined to question what others tell you. You are no longer willing to take everything for granted and believe what you are told. You are very interested in new learning, so when you recognize that something is true, you find it very exciting and want to know more. Friends will become more important to you at this time, and you may discover many new things about the world through them. In fact, they may be more influential than your parents and teachers.

The second sextile transit of Uranus to Uranus, which occurs when you are seventy, is also a time when you can gain great insights into your relationship with the larger world, but the emphasis is different. Instead of learning about the outside world and your place in it, you are likely to focus on what you have gotten from your life. You will reflect on your encounter with the outside world and what your personal values mean in it. Throughout much of your life you may have been so concerned with making your business, professional and social life work out as you wanted that you haven't paid enough attention to your inner life and needs. Insights gained at this time will cause you to reevaluate your goals and give your personal needs a higher priority. You are no longer bound by the obligations that prevented you from doing this before. Now you are free to explore your own inner world and come to a better understanding of who you are and how your life has fitted your needs.

Uranus Square Uranus

This transit occurs twice during your life, once when you are in your early twenties and again when you are in your early sixties. Each time it signifies major changes in your life that require significant reorientation.

The first time this transit occurs it signifies that you are no longer an adolescent and must take your position as an adult. Uranus is the planet of rebellion against established standards, which is the reason so many young people go through a period of rejecting everything that they have been taught. It is necessary for you to experience your own individuality by asserting it against someone else's. There is nothing wrong in this, and the constant challenges of youth help keep society alive. It also helps you, because you need to be on your own and find your own ways of doing things, unhampered by the ways of the past, which may no longer be appropriate.

Even if you do not go through an especially rebellious phase, this will still be a time of intense and rapid change, when you go out into the world and pursue your own goals without the comfort and security of doing what your elders tell you. Doing what you are told may not always have been pleasant, but it did allow you to avoid responsibility, which you will have to take on now.

The second Uranus-Uranus square signifies the changes that take place as you approach old age. There is often a crisis associated with this transit, when you suddenly realize that you are getting old. Roughly twenty-one years ago when Uranus opposed your natal Uranus, you confronted a crisis of reorientation. At that time you should have turned your attention toward your inner values, those that were important to you alone. If you handled that time properly, this transit will not be especially upsetting. Your life as an individual will have enough richness that you will know how to handle the years ahead.

A common problem for people approaching retirement is that they have no idea what to do with their coming leisure time. All they know is their work, and when that ends, their life effectively ends. This is the crisis presented by this transit. You must realize that the richness of your life does not come only from your achievements in the outer world of business and society, but also from what you know and understand about life.

Many people ignored the challenge that was presented during their early forties and continued to rely totally on the outer world of their careers and social life. Now those people may be asking, "Why did I do all that anyway?" You must ask the question, "Did I do what was appropriate for me, or did I live according to totally external standards that had nothing to do with me?" If the answer is the latter, you should spend the rest of your life getting in touch with yourself and learning to derive your values from your inner self.

Uranus Trine Uranus

This transit will occur twice in your life, and the effects will be slightly different each time. The first time is when you are about twenty-eight, and the second is when you are fifty-six. The first transit comes rather close before Saturn's return to its natal place in the horoscope, so the first Uranus-Uranus trine is part of that important cycle of change in your life.

During the first trine transit at twenty-eight, you become conscious that you have grown up. Any structures in your life that have held over from childhood and adolescence appear inappropriate now. You recognize your adulthood and want to take your place among adults and no longer be regarded as a child. You are seeking independence from the factors that limited you as a child, and you are trying to establish your own way of thinking about the world. If during your early adult years prior to this transit you were part of a group that tended to think alike, you may no longer want to think that way. That was fine when you were a young adult, relatively insecure in your independence and needing assurance from others. Now you want your own way of thinking.

At this time you are likely to make rather significant changes in your life in order to achieve more perfect self-expression. You may be inclined to throw over an existing personal relationship in order to liberate yourself from the restrictions it imposed and to look for new relationships that will better fit your needs.

The transit that occurs when you are fifty-six represents a point when you look back over what you have accomplished in life. You try to evaluate and understand exactly what you have learned and what it means for you personally. It is no longer enough to have the approval of others; you need the approval of yourself as well.

If your life does not stand up to your analysis, you may decide to make certain changes. You may choose a very early retirement from your profession so that you can go off in a completely new direction, one that will give you more personal satisfaction. You will be interested in new ways of dealing with your life that help you succeed purely in your own terms.

No matter what you are doing now and after this transit, allow yourself these experiences so you can learn what you need to make your life really fulfilling. In a few years Uranus will come to its own square, and if you have not taken this opportunity to really live in the way that is appropriate for you, the tensions then will be very severe. You may have to make much more radical changes then in order to improve your life, if you can make them at all.

Uranus Opposition Uranus

This is one of the most important transits of your life. Like the Saturn return that occurred when you were twenty-nine, the Uranus-Uranus opposition when you are forty or forty-one marks a period of major transition in your life. This is the crisis of middle age when you have to come to terms with a number of realizations that may not all be pleasant. For example, even though you are not very old, you are no longer young. Have you accomplished or begun to accomplish what you wanted when you were younger? If you have, was it an appropriate accomplishment for you? Are you happy with your close relationships, your marriage, your work?

Many people encountering this transit discover that the answer to several of these questions is no. If this is your situation, you may become seized with a feeling of urgency that you have only a short time to correct the problem. Consequently you may begin to act rather disruptively and quickly. You may leave a marriage or an old job and take up a lifestyle quite different from your earlier one. Your friends are likely to be rather shocked at the change. You may spend more time with younger people, for their youth is a symbol of the opportunities you feel you have almost wasted. This seems to be your last chance to take advantage of those opportunities.

It is also quite possible that you may make none of these drastic changes. If you have taken advantage of opportunities right along and have not allowed your life to become prematurely old and rigid, this transit will not be so upsetting or disturbing. You will experience the real meaning of this transit — a climax of the direction your life has taken since childhood and a shifting of direction toward the issues you must confront in old age.

Each period of life has particular functions. Roughly speaking, during the first half of your life, prior to the Uranus-Uranus opposition, you encounter the outer world, make an impact upon it and learn all you can about it. During the second half of your life you will turn your focus inward and begin to reap the consequences of what you have done and encountered in the first half. From now on you will turn your experiences inward and recreate — make something new of — yourself. You will deal with issues of ultimate concern: the meaning of your life, your relationship to the universe and so forth. This is why some people begin to get a "last chance" feeling, because the main thrust of their life is turning away from issues that they haven't dealt with fully.

If you have been successful in your dealings with the outside world, you will continue to be, but now it will have to mean something in terms of your own life and perception. You will not be able to live for some external purpose, the purpose must come from within. If you don't reorient yourself, your life will become hollow and meaningless, regardless of what you accomplish from here on.

Uranus Conjunct Neptune

This can be one of the strangest of all transits. You will be exposed to new kinds of ideas, radically different from any you have encountered before; strange new influences, very subtle in effect but quite powerful; and new kinds of consciousness, some very high, others very low. This transit can be quite dangerous if you are not aware of its negative side, but it can also represent some of the greatest advances in consciousness that you may ever experience.

On the negative side, this transit can involve people with various mind-altering drugs, ranging from psychedelics such as LSD to depressants and narcotics. Drugs that you take during this transit can give you tremendous insights into your life, but you are likely to become dependent on them if you are not careful. Even drugs taken for conventional medical reasons at this time can have consciousness-altering side effects. Be very careful what you take.

At this time you may be attracted to ideals that are quite revolutionary. You may be willing to completely throw over parts of your life that have been important to you in order to realize the ideals that you want to follow now.

During this transit you will be interested in mystical and occult approaches to reality, but you are inclined to be indiscriminate. Anything that lets your mind escape from the dull everyday world will seem attractive. You could get involved in anything from the lowest forms of magic to the most elevated forms of mystical philosophy. Or if you are not usually attracted to the occult, mysticism or magic, you may come under the influence of some other philosophy or belief system. Anything that provides an escape! There is nothing wrong with escaping if it enables you to get to a better place, but there is no guarantee that this will happen with this transit. Consequently you need to be very careful.

Illnesses that cause you to fall asleep or be fatigued and drowsy are characteristic of this transit. If you notice any such tendency, have a checkup immediately to get at the causes. Illnesses that begin under this transit are often very subtle and difficult to diagnose. Most of them, however, are more dangerous to your mental state than to your physical health. In older people the condition known as senility may come on under this influence.

Uranus-Neptune rules all non-normal states of consciousness, both positive and negative, and there are many positive forms of non-normal consciousness. Your psychic sensitivity is heightened under this transit, and you may discover that you have psychic powers. This transit may also signify an enlightenment experience. It is not an especially fearful transit unless your psychological health is not good to begin with. If you are psychologically healthy, you will experience the most positive effects of this transit.

Uranus Sextile Neptune

This transit stimulates your interest in spiritual ideals and occult concerns. You will discover that your usual way of viewing the universe does not provide satisfactory explanations, so you will turn toward concepts that provide better explanations, even though they are not consistent with what you have been taught. Ideas that you have always regarded as impossibly idealistic become more important, and you work harder to make them part of real life.

Many people under this transit become very much concerned with occult philosophy, metaphysics, spiritualism and mysticism. You have a great need to see the universe as a whole and to understand your relationship to it. However, orthodox religions and philosophies will not fulfill your needs at this time, so you turn to less orthodox studies.

The overall effect of this transit is to open your mind to entirely new levels of consciousness. But this happens through sudden insights in your experience of the everyday world. It is not necessary to travel to some exotic foreign place in order to experience this. Some people go through a kind of enlightenment during this transit, whether through a positive drug experience or through a spontaneous event in their own consciousness.

As your consciousness evolves, you will begin to associate with others whose views are similar, so that you can reinforce and strengthen each others' insights. In this way you may get involved with organized groups that work to further occult and metaphysical studies.

Whatever else happens now, your ideals will be transformed, as will your aims and objectives. After this transit you will not be content to follow the same goals; the old ones simply won't have any meaning for you any longer.

Uranus Square Neptune

This transit can be a severe test of your grip on reality. It can be very confusing and cause you to be misled in a variety of ways. You may suddenly find yourself in the grip of a total delusion that you believe to be the most real thing you have ever encountered. It is very important that you consider very carefully any new idea or philosophy before allowing it to take control of your life. One danger of this transit is that you may allow some idea to control you.

At best, ideas and philosophies are devices that help you understand and make sense of the confusion of everyday experience. But under this transit ideas may become a substitute for experience, so that you begin to believe in things that you have never experienced. You will be particularly attracted to ideas that help you avoid confrontations with the everyday world.

Sometimes this transit may cause you to turn to drugs, usually psychedelics or amphetamines, which provide mystical-seeming experiences, rather than alcohol, barbiturates or opiates. But this manifestation is likely only if you have a tendency in this direction anyway.

You may turn to the study of mystical disciplines in an effort to understand what is happening to you. In itself this is not bad, but you will have to be very careful that such studies do not totally alter your sense of proportion. It is best to expose yourself to these new ideas gradually, so that you can integrate new understandings with old and thereby prevent this energy from being disruptive.

You may also be attracted to very abstract revolutionary ideals that call for total change in the name of a highly elevated ideal. But here again you may only be withdrawing from an unpleasant confrontation with everyday reality instead of dealing with it effectively.

With older people, this transit may signify the onset of an illness that makes the conscious mind less acute or an illness such as senility that causes the mind to withdraw from the world. Follow the recommendations of a competent physician in order to minimize the chances of such an illness.

If you live consistently and are willing to deal with the real world and handle its challenges, this transit can open up aspects of reality that you have never dreamed of. It can signify an enlightenment experience at some level. But if you try to avoid reality altogether, this transit may bring about the state of unconsciousness you desire, but with undesirable consequences.

Uranus Trine Neptune

This transit will bring idealistic, spiritual and philosophical issues to the fore in your life. You will become concerned with the meaning of the world, and you will find new ways of investigating it.

If you are at all interested in mystical and spiritual ideas, you will be more involved in these studies than ever, and it will be very profitable. You will take up ideas that you had considered too abstract to be of any use, and you will see clearly how you can apply them in your life. This is an excellent time for the study of any metaphysical, occult or spiritual doctrine.

Even if you have never been concerned with these subjects, you will suddenly be interested in aspects of life that you may have considered too idealistic. You may work very hard with others to actualize your beliefs about how the world ought to be. Under this transit you are not likely to sit back and let the world go along as it has. But at the same time you are not doctrinaire; you have great compassion for different points of view and are willing to try to reach an understanding when disagreements with others arise.

You may take a new interest in working with the poor, the sick and the downtrodden to improve their lot in life. You find it difficult to allow suffering in the world about you, even if you have been relatively unconcerned about this in the past.

Usually loved ones are the last to receive the benefits of your own growth, because your behavior with them is most governed by habits, but you will be more compassionate toward your loved ones and will try to help them grow.

In general this transit makes you feel that you have experienced some new aspect of truth and that the universe is much more complex and varied than you had previously thought. You want to share these realizations with everyone who comes into your life.

Uranus Opposition Neptune

For the rest of this century, this transit will occur very late in the lives of people living now, because of the present angular relationship between Uranus and Neptune.

How you will react to this transit will depend upon how well you have learned certain of life's lessons. If you are extremely materialistic and so caught up in the mundane concerns of daily life that you cannot see or conceive of anything higher — whether it be a religion, a system of ideals or whatever — you will experience this transit as extremely confusing. Events will occur that simply do not fit into your scheme, and you will become confused and perhaps act in ways that you consider very unwise. You may suddenly start chasing after wild and impractical dreams, become involved with persons who are very out of touch with reality and generally get your goals thoroughly scrambled.

All of this arises because this transit exposes you to higher dimensions of existence, to a world that doesn't work like the one you have been taught to see. Nevertheless this higher world is real and important, in that it gives life meaning even though seemingly far removed from it. If you have always frowned on idealistic notions of higher metaphysical dimensions, this transit will confuse and upset you, because it reveals these dimensions to you. But if you have learned that the universe does not stop with what you can see and feel with your senses, this transit will allow you to experience profound revelations and understanding. Your degree of enlightenment or confusion depends entirely upon how well prepared you are.

Uranus Conjunct Pluto

[Note: This transit has already occurred for those who are now adults and will not occur for those who are young in the 1970s until they are quite advanced in years. This is because of the current relationship between the orbits of Uranus and Pluto. This delineation is included for those who want to check back for purposes of understanding the past.]

This transit is an indication of revolutionary changes in your life. Forces that have been gathering slowly in your environment or within yourself have reached such a critical point that changes begin to occur now in a swift and sometimes rather devastating manner. Many aspects of your life that you have been putting up with quite successfully for some time are now likely to become a source of intolerable mental pressure, forcing you to change them as quickly as possible.

You are likely to confront new and radically different circumstances in many areas of your life. You may be attracted to persons who are quite different from those you have known in the past, and your relationships may become quite different. Do not expect many of these new contacts to be permanent ones, although some may be. Your life is in such a state of flux now that you cannot count on anything lasting for very long, except for those elements that have always been with you and are not affected by this transit. The unchanging elements vary from person to person and cannot be described on the basis of this transit alone.

The best way to approach this transit is to maintain the maximum degree of flexibility and not try to hold back change in those aspects of your life that are being transformed. The aspects of your life that are really valid for you in the long run will not be adversely affected. They may even be improved, because you will not be wasting energy in trying to maintain the structures that are no longer appropriate.

The main difficulty is that the tempo of change may accelerate to the point that you become fearful of losing everything, and you try to hold on. This fear, if you experience it, is actually the worst danger, because it provokes such resistance to change that the transit becomes far more difficult and even dangerous. But if you can go along with the energies of change as much as possible, this transit will be much more constructive and will serve to clear out the refuse of your past life that is holding you back from growth.

Uranus Sextile Pluto

This transit will bring about many far-reaching but constructive changes in your life. You will encounter the deepest elements of your own consciousness, and you will have an unprecedented opportunity to understand your innermost workings Therefore this is an excellent transit for beginning psychotherapy or becoming involved in any of the various human potential movements.

Your concerns at this time are not superficial ones. You will be concerned with the issues that make your life what it is. Under this transit you have opportunities to make the most fundamental and far-reaching changes in your life. Your values will change, as will your objectives in life. At its deepest manifestation, this transit can signify a period of new birth, especially if the last few years have been difficult.

You may become involved in occult studies, astrology and metaphysics at this time, and even if you do not pursue these issues systematically, you will pay more attention to issues that they relate to.

Friendships may take on added significance now. A friend, possibly a new one, will be instrumental in making you see what aspects of your life need to change and will help you make those changes.

Uranus Square Pluto

Pluto is in approximately the same part of the zodiac for everyone who was born about when you were. Therefore you and others within a couple of years of your age will experience this transit at about the same time. As changes induced by this transit begin to affect your life, you may notice parallels in the lives of your friends.

The effect of this transit is to sweep away all the old and outworn structures that you have built up in your life. Pluto is the principle of death and regeneration, which is now combined with the Uranian principle of sudden change. The effect of the combination can be to create a total revolution in your life.

Your life is probably circumscribed by many elements from the past that no longer serve any useful purpose in your life. You have not gotten rid of them because they represent a certain security, but they are getting in the way of your continued growth and therefore must be cleared away from your life. The events that occur now will force this change upon you, if you have not already begun to change voluntarily.

Pluto's forces do not operate suddenly. They are deep psychological forces that operate very slowly over a long period of time. They keep you moving and growing, make you throw off the old and enter new ways of living. This transit represents a time when these forces have built up to a critical point and must be released. Uranus provides the trigger.

It is not possible to say exactly what will pass away from your life at this time, because it will be different for everyone. But you will have a sense that a powerful force is emerging in your life that you have been dimly aware of for some time. If you look into yourself, you will realize that what is happening now is not really a surprise. You were hoping that this new force would go away if you ignored it, but it didn't, and now you have to deal with it.

Because this transit affects a whole generation, the drastic changes you encounter now may be partly the result of social and economic forces beyond your control. You may even feel like an unfortunate puppet moved by historical events. But these forces, even though they appear to be impersonal, play a vital role in your individual development. Accept this as a challenge to you as an individual, and allow the old order and old ideas to pass away. This will pave the way for your rebirth into a new way of life, where you will have the opportunity to be more alive.

Uranus Trine Pluto

This is a time of positive evolution in your life that can lead you to a new and greater understanding of your inner being and how you relate to other people. Uranus and Pluto are both planets of transcendent consciousness and are usually difficult for everyone to handle except those whose consciousness is most advanced. However, the trine of these planets gives you the opportunity to experience the higher levels of their manifestation.

Under the influence of this transit you will be able to see what is wrong with your life and to make corrective changes without great upset and pain. Your insight is enormously heightened, aided by your willingness to learn. If you have ever felt that psychotherapy would be helpful, this is the time to consider it, for you will benefit from it now. You might also consider other techniques of consciousness expansion, such as are found in occult studies, astrology, yoga and the various human potential movements.

You will be involved with what one theologian called matters of "ultimate concern," that is, your life, its total meaning and how you fit into the universe as a whole. Therefore you will also be attracted to systems of thought that deal with these concerns — religious and spiritual movements or more unusual kinds of activity such as ceremonial magic. But in any case you will not be satisfied to live at the superficial level that most people live at.

This transit will deepen your philosophical concerns, enrich your understanding of life and give you the chance to make constructive changes that will make your life more worthwhile later on. Take advantage of this opportunity.

Uranus Opposition Pluto

Because of the current angular relationship between these two planets, most persons will not experience this transit until quite late in life.

The wisdom gained through the experience of your life will serve you in good stead now, as long as you are willing to be flexible. You may discover that events and deeds from your own distant past are now beginning to produce consequences that may revolutionize your life. You certainly can't expect everything to go on as it has in the past. Now is the time to make sweeping changes, not only in your consciousness, but also in the circumstances in which you live. Conditions that have been developing slowly will force major changes upon you now. If you are flexible, you will be able to start a whole new phase of life, even though you may have thought that the time for new starts in your life is past. You will have a new birth of awareness, and you will be able to deal with your life unhampered by old patterns of thought that have limited you.

But if you cannot adapt and be flexible, this will be a period of great turmoil and stress as you try desperately to hold on to circumstances, possessions and relationships that no longer have any real function in your life. What you are trying to save is not something real, it is only an illusion.

The impetus for change may come through persons who present you with many upsetting surprises, all of which show that your life is no longer what it was. The key point to recognize is that this process is not bad for you, it is just upsetting at first until you get into the flow of events. It can be quite exciting and will certainly inject an element of youth into your life again, with the advantage that now you will have the wisdom to handle it properly.

Uranus Conjunct Midheaven

With this transit you can look for sudden changes in the way you define your individuality before the world. This will be reflected in your profession, your social position and your reputation in the eyes of others. These changes can allow you to break free and encounter life with new freedom and readiness for fresh experience. But they can also be profoundly upsetting, depending on your orientation toward your public life. If your public and professional life is a source of achievement and satisfaction, it is unlikely to be damaged by this transit, only broadened and made more challenging. But if there is tension in your public life and you feel that you have had to surrender your individuality for your achievements, this transit may be more upsetting. So much has to be cleared away in order to release you from the limitations that are blocking a fuller and more profound experience of life.

If you are working in an area that is generally good for your overall development, this transit may present sudden opportunities for advancement, especially if you work in a Uranian field, such as science, technology, astrology or the occult. You will have the opportunity to do new kinds of work, to work with new techniques, and to have new experiences. There may be a sudden promotion to a position with new responsibilities. Whatever happens will make it possible for you to stay alive and feel fulfilled in your profession.

Even if you experience the negative side of this transit, its purpose is the same. However, you are probably resisting the effects of this transit through fear that you will lose security or from a misguided sense of responsibility, a feeling that you should stick with something even if it is totally unrewarding and stultifying. Events may force you to change your line of work altogether or to change your position in the kind of work you do.

Possibly you are aware that your work is not very rewarding, in which case you will suddenly begin to feel that it is oppressive and will want to break free of it. This transit can signify a revolt against authority figures of all sorts, but especially employers.

The Midheaven also relates to your parents. This may be a period of sudden changes in their lives that affect you in some way. Whatever happens to them will force you to change your direction in life somewhat and to take more responsibility for getting what you need out of life.

Uranus Sextile Midheaven

Under this transit you will make creative changes in your life direction. For example, you may change jobs if this will improve your chances of getting where you want to go. You will not change simply for the sake of change. You may get a sudden promotion, but only if you show that you can take a completely different approach to the demands of the new job.

It is possible that you will change your life direction altogether at this point toward something that gives you more freedom to reach your desired goals.

But the changes during this transit are not limited to the professional sphere. At this time you will also make changes in your personal life so that your domestic situation, your family and other intimate relationships do not prevent you from accomplishing your life's task. In both professional and domestic spheres you will take risks and try things that you would never try at other times. You want to experience all that life has to offer and not be limited solely by the inadequacies of past experience.

In any kind of creative work this transit signifies that you will work with great innovativeness and originality. You may create an invention or make a new discovery, but remember that it is just as likely to be a discovery about yourself as about the world.

One of the greatest benefits of this transit is that you can be in control if you want to be. You can neglect this opportunity for creative change in your life, but if you do, life may seem so stultifying that you feel you have to change everything, violently and compulsively and without forethought. Changes made under those conditions are not likely to be as creative and positive as ones made now. Now you can exercise caution, restraint and care and still make many positive changes to release mounting tensions that will otherwise explode within you later.

Uranus Square Midheaven

This transit can be either quite disruptive or quite liberating, depending largely upon how you have handled your life prior to this time. It usually indicates a sudden rebellion against restriction and old patterns of behavior that have unnecessarily limited you. The problem is that with this influence many people act compulsively and blindly, without forethought or consideration. If you have toed the mark and lived up to everyone else's expectations for years, under this transit you might suddenly kick away the traces. Without any apparent thought for anyone else, you might break away, throwing over all thought of duty or responsibility.

This is admittedly an extreme manifestation of this transit. For you it will probably be milder than this, unless you have consistently denied your own needs and priorities over the last several years. The more you have lived up to others' expectations, the more compulsively you will act under this influence. If you are relatively young at this time, you may have intense disagreements with your parents. Actually, for persons of any age, this transit can cause a sudden disruption through or concerning your parents, quite apart from any other effect it has on you.

If you are not conscious of any effect, but the hidden tensions are still present in your life, you will experience this transit as disruptions in your work or at home. These will force you to reconsider your chosen life direction and to make changes that will allow you greater freedom of self-expression. At the time you may not think of this process in these terms, but that is what is happening.

If your life has been running smoothly and you have been able to pursue your valid life goals, this transit will not be severely disruptive. Some adjustments will occur, but mainly you will discover sudden new opportunities for increased freedom. You will be able to do what you want more easily and with less resistance from yourself and from others. For example, you may get the chance to work without supervision along lines that you have chosen yourself. Or various restrictions and limitations in your life may suddenly pass away, leaving you free to live in ways that were never possible before. Potentially that is how this transit could affect everyone, but most people fight change so hard that they create the more difficult circumstances described above. The choice is really in your own hands, although you may not be aware of it at first.

Uranus Trine Midheaven

This transit represents a period in your life when you can make creative changes in both your professional and your personal life. In your career, sudden opportunities may come about that enable you to move in radically new and different directions. Often this transit signifies a change in career to a field that is strongly Uranian, such as scientific or technical professions, including electronics, computers and engineering. This transit can also signify an interest in the occult, especially astrology.

But this transit has a larger significance. At this time you are able to change your life direction and do something that more truly expresses your individuality. The problem for most people is that this new field may be quite different from what you were taught was a "proper" profession. Most people's focus in this regard is too narrow. It is very important now to let yourself explore any field of endeavor that attracts you, regardless of how well it fits your preconceptions of a career. Please note that your new direction may not be a career in the usual sense but a field to which you devote your life, although it is unrelated to making a living. One's avocation may well be one's true calling.

The only restriction is that your new direction should be ethical and legal, simply because Uranus can create serious problems with the law if you are not careful about legality. Our society has a significant mistrust of persons who are excessively Uranian.

This is also a time in your life when you will be innovative in whatever you do. Your thinking is fresh and original, and you do not try to solve new problems with old solutions, either in your profession or in your personal life. Thus you will be attracted to new techniques and new ideas, especially for your own personal development.

Uranus Opposition Midheaven

At this time there will be many changes within yourself, which will be reflected in your immediate personal environment — your home — and in your most intimate personal relationships within the home, as with parents or spouse. This transit can signify disruptive events in this area of your life and energies that require you to drop everything else to deal with.

On the most mundane level this transit can signify a sudden event in your home or real estate — damage to the buildings, a sudden need for repairs or the like. But this is only an outward sign of the need for change within. Something that has been hidden away for years and years struggles to break free. But if you suppress it, the energy transfers to your environment and causes disruptions. You may have to deal with aspects of yourself you never even knew existed in order to come to a new understanding of yourself. People may not be very aware of this happening, but you will be, and so will those closest to you. You may find it necessary to make tremendous changes in your home and in those relationships that most affect your home to reflect this new encounter with yourself.

This transit can also signify sudden events that affect your family, especially your parents, such as accidents, sudden illnesses and the like. In this connection, you should make sure that there aren't any safety hazards around your house, because accidents in the home are very possible at this time.

Since the Midheaven signifies your profession and social status, you may also expect changes in these areas. You may encounter opposition from others in your profession, people who do not want you to get ahead or achieve your purposes. Try to find out what the problem is and come to terms with these people. If you ride roughshod over them, they will try to hurt you as much as possible. This is also true in any aspect of your social life, if your actions seem to threaten someone else. There is a danger of a sudden fall in social position with this transit, usually because you have acted without considering others. They then feel that there is no recourse but to bring you down.

Take this time to discover new truths about yourself, deal with them as honestly as possible and make these insights part of a new way of being. Then you will not have to contend with the worst effects of this transit.

Uranus Conjunct Ascendant

During this period your relationships will alter tremendously, and you will try to break free of the restrictions and obligations that have held you back. You begin to feel very impatient and rebellious toward limitations of any kind. Others will find it very difficult to predict what you will do and may be quite upset by your actions. The people you draw into your immediate environment now may be radically different from those whom you used to associate with. You may attract to yourself or be attracted to aspects of the counter-culture, which as a whole embodies the Uranus-Ascendant energy.

This transit has its most difficult effects on marriage and other intimate relationships. You may find it difficult to continue living up to the rules of marriage and may begin to look for other relationships. You can anticipate the effects of this transit on your marriage or other intimate union simply by examining your inner feelings about the relationship. If it really feels good, you will not have much of a problem. A husband during this transit may become impatient with the standard masculine role of bread-winner with all its accoutrements, as defined by our culture. Similarly, a wife may suddenly become impatient with being merely a housewife and begin to demand a more active role in the world. This transit gives both sexes a desire for liberation.

If you are well prepared, this transit can also bring about the only meaningful liberation, that is, the mind being free of its illusions. Many people begin to study astrology or the occult at this time, seeking this very liberation. While these studies may be a useful step on the path, you will ultimately learn that all structures for interpreting the world have the same limitations as your old ones, if you allow them to become rigid. True liberation involves coming to a point where all structure is taken on by choice and your life is self-created.

Uranus Sextile Ascendant

At this time you will seek greater flexibility and freedom in your friendships, as well as with your neighbors and the people you associate with daily. And opportunities for favorable change in your life may come through any of these people. Often this transit has an electric quality, so that everyone you meet seems to give off an energy charge that makes you move faster and more suddenly. The people you meet now will be quite different from those you usually associate with, and if your attitudes are rigid you may be mildly upset by them. But this is a sign that you should enlarge the range of people whom you will accept and associate with. Do not limit your circle of associates too much; these new persons can show you a lot about life.

It is quite likely that the tempo of change in your life will increase to the point that others will think of you as unstable and unreliable, but this is a reflection of their conservatism. It is their problem, not yours. You may suddenly discover that your friends of many years seem limited and narrow and no longer interesting. Instead, you may become involved with some group that is considered by the rest of society, particularly your old friends, to be offbeat and eccentric, if not completely crazy.

If you have not been asserting your own individuality in relationships, you will do so now, and it is important that you do. If you try to suppress these drives, they will burst forth later on in a manner that is difficult to control.

Often this transit signifies an interest in new and different studies. Technical and scientific disciplines are suitable to this symbolism, as are the various branches of the occult. Under this influence people often get into astrology.

But the main point to keep in mind is that this transit represents a creative stirring up of your personality and your relationships to the people around you. Let it happen!

Uranus Square Ascendant

This transit is likely to have a very disruptive effect on your relationships. Influences may enter your life, either through your home or your profession, that will challenge the foundations upon which your life is built. This challenge will be reflected in surprising encounters with others that upset your way of living or in sudden separations from persons who you thought would remain in your life for some time. Or it may be that you yourself are the catalyst of all these changes as you seek to become free of circumstances that have become oppressive.

During this period it is quite likely that you will do things and go places you never would have thought of in the past. The old patterns of your life simply can no longer encompass what your life is becoming now.

From all of the above it should be obvious that this is not an "evil" transit, although anyone who is wedded to the status quo in life or to their own past will find this period difficult to contend with. Old patterns that have acquired a stranglehold over your life will break up. You may not have been aware of these patterns, because many people find their "strangleholds" quite comfortable, at least until much later on.

The people who enter your life at this time may be quite different from anyone you have known before. Some of these relationships may be quite brief. You may encounter someone for a specific purpose, which you may not be aware of at the time, and once that purpose is accomplished, the relationship ends.

Marriage is one intimate relationship that is often affected by this transit; in fact, a marriage may break up under this influence. If your marriage is good, you have nothing to worry about. It will simply go through a phase of readjustment and reorientation in which you and your spouse seek to eliminate those aspects of your life together that have limited freedom of self-expression for one or the other of you. But a difficult marriage, in which there are a number of repressed tensions, may very well not survive this transit. If it does, it will be much better off after releasing the tensions.

If a new love interest enters your life at this point, it is likely to be exciting, free and totally unpredictable. Do not make a permanent commitment to it until well after the end of this transit, for such a relationship is likely to be very unstable and brief.

Uranus Trine Ascendant

This is a time of increased freedom in and through your personal relationships. You are able to express yourself to others in ways that have never before been possible for you. This may take the form of a new interest or hobby or a new field of study. You may be attracted to technical and scientific subjects, as well as to occult studies such as astrology. Under this transit some people begin the study of astrology.

You respond much more quickly to people around you now and generally give the impression of being more alive and willing to challenge life, and you are. You may also seem somewhat impulsive and perhaps a bit nervous, but most people will not find you upsetting.

Sudden new contacts with others may provide opportunities to branch out and do things that you have never done before. You may have a chance to travel, for example, or to take up some completely new activity. Your old way of life no longer interests you, and if someone tries to convince you to keep to your old ways, you just get bored.

New relationships may begin now that challenge you creatively, but they may not last longer than this transit, so it is well not to make any permanent commitment until later. Even though the relationships may be transient, they will have a liberating effect upon you and increase your capacity to experience life. Often the other person will act as a "guru," that is, he or she will open up spiritual dimensions that you have never experienced before. However, do not expect this person to come in standard guru clothing. It could be anyone, and very often he or she will not look at all like the conventional notion of a spiritual teacher. Enlightenment takes as many forms as there are teachers and students.

The worst thing you could do with the changes coming into your life now is to resist them. Because this transit is a trine, which is not a compelling aspect, you can prevent the changes from happening if you try. But in preventing them, you would not only waste an opportunity, you would also postpone needed changes until the time when they become so urgent as to be irresistible. Then they will happen with much more disruptive force.

Uranus Opposition Ascendant

This transit brings about disturbing close encounters with others. Relationships in general will be a significant challenge, and you won't even be able to take the old reliable ones for granted. Other people seem to be trying to disrupt your life and make you uneasy.

Marriage is the most intimate one-to-one encounter, and any hidden tensions, any problems that either of you has been holding back will come out now. Consequently your marriage may go through some rather startling changes. If it has not been working out but you have been holding it together anyway, this transit may very well signify its breakup. Even in a good marriage you may have more arguments and disagreements than usual. This applies as well to two people living together. A business partnership may also be affected in a similar way. Clearly this is a time when you will have to do a lot of straightening out.

Other types of confrontations may also be quite disturbing at this time. For example, you may become involved in very disruptive legal disputes. Settle these as quickly as possible, because you will not be able to count on the outcome of any legal confrontation at this time, no matter how good it looks. Be careful of acting in a way that stirs people up against you, for they could become extremely disruptive, if you give them any excuse.

This transit indicates a general reworking of your relationships with others, and you may not always be happy about the outcome. In general, others are resisting your efforts to control the relationship, which you may be doing in spite of your best intentions. But your partner will not ask that the relationship be totally destroyed unless you are so rigid and unwilling to change that there seems no other way out. All your partner wants is to redefine the relationship so that he or she has a greater say and more room to move. It is possible that these effects may work the other way, that you are the one who is struggling to gain control in a relationship. In either case, the relationship has to express each of you more appropriately than in the past.

Chapter Twelve

Neptune

Significance of Transiting Neptune

Neptune is usually one of the most difficult planetary influences to handle. It causes life to become confusing and unclear, and under its influence people often believe what is not true. At the same time, Neptune often has an ego-denying influence, which may make you feel discouraged, futile, undeserving and unworthy. Or it can lead you to perform great acts of selflessness and self-martyrdom. Neptune can also expose you to some extremely beautiful and ideal influences, which may not always be real but are worthwhile because of their beauty. Everything that man dreams of making come true as well as everything that man thinks is true, even though it isn't, comes under the influence of Neptune.

The difficulty of the planet's influence arises from the fact that Neptune dissolves whatever Saturn builds, such as your ego, your sense of duty and responsibility, your sense of a definite reality and everything else about the world that is definite, clear and predictable. Neptune works against all these structures. It dissolves or threatens to dissolve your ego, so that initially you feel lost, confused or defeated. But this effect can also make you feel exhilarated and at one with the entire universe. It depends on your level of consciousness. It is safe to say that most people experience the first effect more than the second.

Neptune dissolves your sense of reality, leaving you prey to confusion and doubt. Vague unreasoning fears can result from a Neptune transit, especially if Saturn is involved. Neptune can destroy your sense of responsibility and make you feel that others should take care of you. Yet at the same time, because of its ego-denying effect, you can feel responsible for all the "sins" of the world. This energy makes some people spend their lives in social service, trying to make the world better without any thought of personal advancement.

As Neptune transits each house, watch the affairs ruled by that house. In those areas of your life, you will have to be careful not to fall prey to mistaken illusions. Anything connected with the matters ruled by that house may dissolve and pass out of existence in the subtlest, most imperceptible manner.

As Neptune transits each of the planets, you can expect matters ruled by that planet's energies to become confused or idealized. The planets pertaining to the ego drives — Mars, the Sun, and Saturn — may produce fear, insecurity and anxiety when transited by Neptune by conjunction, square or opposition. Neptune transits in general are not good times to make permanent commitments concerning matters ruled by the transited planet or house, because you are rarely in possession of the pertinent facts. You may be right about a belief that you hold under a Neptune transit, but you will not know for sure until it is over.

Neptune in the First House

For the next several years you will be changing your ways of interacting with other people. During this period, self-knowledge is difficult but essential. It is difficult because you will constantly be presented with new aspects of yourself as others see you, and you will try to incorporate what they see into your view of yourself. This is nearly impossible, however, because you are going through a chameleon phase in which you quite unintentionally present a wide variety of faces to people.

It is essential that you know yourself during this transit, precisely because others will not know you clearly. You have to learn who you are in your own terms and to recognize that the way you project your personality to others is not the true inner you. It is only the aspect of yourself by which you relate to people.

The changes you are undergoing at this time may confuse you and certainly will confuse others. Consequently your relationships may become quite difficult, because the people you attract relate only to the currently projected image of yourself, not to your real needs. And just as you may confuse and delude others, perhaps inadvertently, they may do the same to you. Be wary of getting caught up in weird schemes and projects that others propose. Your sense of reality is not at its best during these years.

You may also operate very idealistically during this period, acting on the basis of what you want to be true rather than what is true. You may get involved with very idealistic projects that have little basis in reality, with unfortunate results.

Another effect of this transit may be to stimulate your compassion for others. You may take care of someone you love who needs help, or you may work in groups with others for people who need help. There is a tendency to want to save others under this transit. But avoid having people become improperly dependent on you, for that may prevent them from fully realizing themselves.

You may also want to seek out someone who can help you during these years. If in your confusion you become demoralized and feel that you are a totally unworthy individual, you may look to someone who seems stronger in order to be sustained by his or her strength. The chief problem with this is that you may become permanently dependent upon that person.

Neptune in the Second House

During the next several years you will have to undergo a fundamental change of attitude toward your material possessions, which will coincide with and be reflected in a change in your sense of values. The more you are attached to what you own, letting considerations of their value determine what you can and cannot do, the more likely you are to lose whatever you consider important. Neptune works against the ego and the objects it is attached to by muddying and confusing your ideas about them prior to bringing about a complete reorientation of your views.

This does not mean that you are going to lose everything. Probably you will experience considerable confusion about property matters, and you may be deluded into making some very costly mistakes, but there is no reason to expect that all your possessions will be lost. You will experience the worst trouble only if you totally identify yourself with your material possessions, giving them an inordinate importance in your life. Neptune rules the mystical principle of detachment, of not being excessively involved with the things of this world, giving them no more importance than they deserve. Wherever Neptune transits, it is ultimately teaching this principle.

You may be tempted to gamble with your possessions or to become involved in risky speculative ventures in an effort to increase your holdings. If you are able to do this in a playful spirit, you might do rather well. But if you are very serious, determined and care a great deal about the outcome, you will probably lose. You cannot gamble if you worry about losing.

Another effect of this transit is that your sense of values may become spiritualized and idealized. This is the positive side of Neptune's second-house transit. You learn that material possessions are not so important, and that what you need will be provided to the extent that you are detached from it. Needless to say, most of us have been educated to believe that we must struggle to attain possessions, which makes it very difficult to learn this principle.

Whatever your orientation to this issue, during this transit you should be careful about managing your money and possessions, and you should avoid gambling unless you are truly detached. Also, avoid becoming involved in risky schemes proposed by others. You could be swindled under this transit.

Neptune in the Third House

Your dealings and communication with your everyday world and the attitudes by which you function in it are seriously affected by this transit. Be very careful how you communicate with others. Be as clear as possible, because at this time it will be difficult to make yourself clear to others. Serious misunderstandings may occur that disturb your personal life. This is particularly true in communicating with immediate neighbors and relatives. Enter into any kind of negotiation with extreme care. Misunderstanding or deliberate misrepresentation could get you involved in projects you otherwise wouldn't have anything to do with, and this can lead to losses.

Aside from these manifestations in your relations with the outer world, this transit will also have a powerful effect within you. It will alter your ways of dealing with the world and cause your thinking to be very profoundly transformed. Most positively, this can happen through an increased concern with metaphysical and spiritual truth. You may begin the serious study of a metaphysical discipline during this transit. You may become very interested in such ideas as karma and reincarnation, and you will learn as much as you can about how these ideas apply to your personal life. Your imaginative creativity will also be greatly increased. Only make sure that imagination doesn't interfere with your ability to see the truth!

However, if your thinking has been excessively structured and inflexible, this period will bring a number of upsets, as you discover that what you thought was true is not. This can lead to confusion, self-doubt and uncertainty. If you encounter this problem, try to put off making any rapid decisions for a while. If you can afford to wait, your view will eventually clear, and you will be able to develop a completely new view that will better conform with the truth.

Also, if your mind is basically flexible, Neptune's effect may be the reverse of the above description. Neptune can confuse, but it can also give you very subtle insights. You may find that you immediately understand ideas that your rational mind could not usually comprehend, because Neptune transiting this house can stimulate latent psychic abilities. In fact it is this attribute that makes Neptune so confusing, because if you are not ready to receive psychic input, the input will simply seem confusing.

Neptune in the Fourth House

While Neptune is in your fourth house, your domestic and personal life will undergo many strange and subtle changes, reflecting psychological changes that are going on within you. During this period psychological forces will be changing your inner self quite noticeably. You may become attracted to spiritual and occult subjects as a direct result of your own experiences.

If you have not had much of a home life over the last several years, during this transit you may begin to create in your mind an ideal of what your home should be. And you will work very hard to make a home that represents what you want. However, if your mental picture is too ideal, it may be difficult for anything in the real world to live up to it. Certainly, with Neptune in this house you will seek to make your home a very beautiful place.

Unfortunately there is another side to this transit. Your home life may become a source of confusion and difficulty because someone in your home is working against your best interests in some way. It may be difficult to find out exactly what is being done, but it often has the effect of demoralizing you and making you feel less confident and secure. In fact you may experience these emotions without any problems at all in your personal life. In either case, these feelings are a sign of the tremendous inner changes that are taking place, which are reflected in your personal life.

During this time communications with your parents may become difficult for some reason, or one of your parents may begin to have difficulties that affect your own sense of well-being and security. Sometimes this transit coincides with the illness and hospitalization of a parent, but that is not likely unless there is a difficult transit involving the fourth house.

Neptune in the Fifth House

During the next several years this transit may have various different effects on you. First, you will be inclined to seek out relationships with the opposite sex that fit a very romantic image. You will not want any relationship that does not meet your highest expectations. Curiously enough, sexual satisfaction may not be your highest priority in a relationship at this time. Because of Neptune's antimaterialistic nature, you are concerned with creating a spiritual union rather than a purely physical one. And it is possible that you will find such a spiritual relationship, if you don't confuse what you are actually seeing with your ideal.

One rather difficult pattern that often arises when Neptune is in the fifth house is that you may tend to idealize a lover as someone who can save you from yourself, a person so far above you that he or she almost seems to be a god. Needless to say, this is a most Neptunian illusion and should not be taken seriously. It is highly unlikely that anyone could really live up to such expectations.

On the other hand, the pattern may be reversed, so that you become involved with someone who regards you as a savior. Under such an influence you could have an alcoholic lover, to cite an extreme example, and spend all your energy trying to reform him or her. This is an exercise in futility, because it is very unlikely to succeed. Try to relate to people as equals during this transit, however difficult it may be.

Avoid getting involved in risky financial ventures now, since the fifth is the house of gambling and speculation. Under this transit you may enjoy the illusion that you cannot lose, but you can lose and probably will as long as Neptune is here.

Children may be a source of difficulty during this transit. They may have illnesses, or you may simply have difficulty in understanding and getting along with them. Above all, avoid a tendency to idealize your children, for they are only human beings like yourself. You may idealize them as being innocents, but in truth they operate from the same crazy motives as adults, only a little less skillfully.

This transit stimulates artistic creativity. If you have artistic ability, your imagination will be very much improved, and you will be able to come up with new ideas for your art work in any field or medium.

Neptune in the Sixth House

This transit will affect two areas of your life — your health and your work — very strongly. Be especially careful of your health now, for you may be more subject to illnesses and passing infections than at other times. This is not to say that you will be constantly sick, but you should be careful. Usually you will not have health problems unless there are difficult transits to planets in your natal chart at the same time. Be especially careful of diseases caused by poisons and toxins in the body from drugs or alcohol.

People often get rather strange ideas about nutrition and hygiene while Neptune is transiting this house. Because of Neptune's nature, this usually takes the form of a dietary regimen in which you abstain totally from a particular kind of food. Vegetarian, fruit and low mucus diets all fit this description. These diets are not bad in themselves, but you should observe their effects upon your body carefully and not follow them blindly. Also you may be inclined for religious or spiritual reasons to follow a diet that has nothing to do with your bodily needs.

In the area of work, this transit is best handled by working in a field of social service, perhaps with sick people in hospitals or asylums or with the poor. This is not an especially good time for advancing your career for purely egotistical reasons. The ego-denying effect of Neptune often means that the harder you work for your own benefit, the less you get out of it. You can make great achievements while Neptune is in this house, but only if you are working in a spirit of service to others.

With this transit you may encounter serious misunderstanding with employers or employees and general difficulties in dealing with them. Your path to advancement may be mysteriously blocked by someone who will not confront you directly or state the reasons for opposing you. You may not even be aware that this person is acting against you. It is possible at this time to become involved in work that is actually dishonest or subversive, although you may not be aware of it at the time. But these effects are minimized if you regard your work as a service to others without worrying about what you will get out of it personally. If you enjoy your work and do it creatively, this transit will not interfere, because that is ultimately the best way to make your work a service to others.

Neptune in the Seventh House

This transit can have several effects, but in general it affects all the one-to-one relationships in your life. These include your marriage or living with someone, other partnerships (including business), conflicts with others and relations with people whom you consult, such as lawyers, physicians and other counselors. In any or all of these relationships there is the danger of poor communications, misunderstandings and misrepresentation.

In a marital relationship you may have problems because resentments are not brought out into the open where they can be handled. Instead, one or both of you keeps your feelings hidden and acts surreptitiously, making it difficult for the other to help solve the problem. There is also the danger of overidealizing your relations, which can be a problem even if you aren't married. You may simply idealize your relationship out of all proportion to the reality and think everything is just fine when it isn't. This is the old Neptunian problem of thinking that what you want to be true is true already. If you are attentive to what is really happening in the relationship, you will be able to see the truth.

Also during this transit you may have to take care of someone close to you who is sick or has some other problem that requires care. This person is most likely to be your living partner, but it could be someone else who is close to you.

If you are in business, be very careful about forming any new partnership at this time. It is not very likely to work out as you want it to, and your partner may be more of a problem than a help. In extreme cases this transit can even indicate being swindled or otherwise taken by a partner. An established partnership that has worked out well in the past will probably continue to do so, but be careful to communicate clearly with each other, because misunderstandings are a standard consequence of a seventh-house Neptune.

This transit is normally not a good one for dealings with lawyers and lawsuits, because the seventh house rules people whom you consult, as well as lawsuits. You probably won't get a good deal if you hire a lawyer to represent you. Also the factors that will determine the outcome of your case would be difficult to discover, let alone deal with. This same advice applies to other people whom you hire for consultation.

Neptune in the Eighth House

During this transit your attention will turn to the hidden areas of your life and the deepest aspects of your subconscious mind. Your interest in psychic and occult sciences will increase as you try to find out more about the hidden underpinnings of the universe. By the same token you will want to learn more about yourself and make changes that will help you work with your unconscious drives more successfully. This is a good time to begin psychotherapy, if you feel that it would be of benefit to you.

During this period an old order of your life is passing away and a new one is coming into existence. But the process is very subtle, and you may not notice the effects until several years have passed. Someone close to you may die, which may change your life considerably.

One area that this transit may affect adversely, however, is that of joint finances. The eighth house rules finances and resources that you hold with someone else or another person's resources that you have access to. Neptune in this house may cause misunderstanding with others concerning money or other property. There is the danger of misrepresentation and fraud. Hidden forces may be at work behind the scenes that prevent you from knowing what is happening. Because of these energies, this is not a good time to borrow money. You may have trouble getting a bank to lend to you anyway. Certainly you should not under any circumstances borrow more than a little money from friends. The strict business relationship of a bank loan mitigates the fogginess of Neptune considerably, but the more casual nature of private borrowing from friends leaves the situation wide open for the worst type of Neptunian misunderstandings.

Neptune in the Ninth House

For the next several years this transit will stimulate your interest in higher consciousness and spiritual truth. But if you are not careful, it may totally misguide you and confuse your outlook upon the world. The effects of this transit are rather abstract, so the discussion of them must also be a bit abstract.

You live in the world as an ego, that is, as a self that is consciously aware of being distinct from other beings and of having its own life course. One way in which you are distinguished from others is in your point of view and general outlook upon the world, which are symbolized by the ninth house. Neptune rules an energy that comes from a deeper realm of being where there is no ego and no differentiated being. All is one under this planet. Consequently Neptune blurs the distinctions between yourself and others, and even blurs distinctions in the world itself. For most people the effect of Neptune in the ninth is to expose them to ideas and influences that blur their usual viewpoint and make it harder for them to make distinctions. You may become less confident about your way of dealing with your universe, or you may be confused and disoriented. But these are not inevitable consequences of the transit.

The problems that this transit creates arise because you are desperately trying to replace the ideas that the transit has invalidated with new ideas. But because of the influence of Neptune, each new idea appears as invalid as the old ones.

The way to handle this dilemma is to wait and allow yourself not to know, to give yourself permission to be ignorant. In time, new mystical and spiritual ways of handling the universe will crystallize out of the Neptunian fog. You will begin to understand your relationship to the universe, and you will see that everything really is one, as Neptune shows. It is only the frantic survival efforts of your ego that confuse everything.

However, there is still a pitfall with this transit, even when you deal with it as just described. Unfortunately, once you accept the spiritual lesson of Neptune in the ninth house, you begin to use it as a way of being superior to others, which puts you back into the ego game again. You begin to wander off alone into your own little intellectual world, becoming more and more removed from the feelings of others and less compassionate toward those who think differently from you. Eventually you will come out of this phase, but you may not gain much from it. Neptune transiting the ninth house is not a good time for playing any ego games with others. It is a time to learn and be grateful for what you have learned.

Neptune in the Tenth House

This can be a very confusing and disorienting time, but it can teach you basic truths about life, if you are able to get over the fear and confusion that sometimes accompany this transit. The problem is that this transit makes you feel unsure of where you are going in life and why.

The effects of this transit depend upon your attitude toward what you do for a living (in the broadest sense). If you regard your work as a justification for your existence, something that gives your life a purpose it would not otherwise have, then this will be a very difficult time. Neptune will make you wonder whether there is any purpose in what you are doing and whether there is any particular reason to go on. Your disillusionment may come about through personal defeats with others or through some incident that shows that your work was not what you thought it was. Perhaps another person may misrepresent something or deceive you. No matter what you do during these years, be careful about deceiving others or being deceived by them, for such actions could have very negative consequences. You may also feel discouraged, because people oppose your efforts to get ahead for no apparent reason.

You may decide that your present calling is not adequate, that you should change to an area that will have more meaning for you. However, you really need to change your whole attitude toward what you are doing. You should not be doing something just because it justifies your life or gives you a sense of purpose. It should be an appropriate form of self-expression that allows you to be yourself most successfully. At the same time you should try to be less attached to what you are doing. You are not what you do, even though people often respond to the question, "What are you?" by giving their profession. Probably it is the fact that your ego is wrapped up in your work that is causing problems with others.

This transit favors certain types of work, for example social-service work with poor or disadvantaged people or with those who have emotional, drug or alcohol problems. This transit will not be destructive, if you work in a spirit of helping others.

This transit can also bring you a great interest in psychic, spiritual and occult matters, and you may even become involved with these subjects in your profession.

Neptune in the Eleventh House

During the next several years your ideals will become more important to you, and you will work very hard to actualize them in everyday life. You will be attracted in friendship to others who share your feelings. However, because of the idealistic nature of Neptune, you will have to be sure that you are dealing with reality even as you attempt to actualize your dreams.

Be careful particularly with the people you choose as friends. You may be relating to what you would like them to be rather than to them as real people, which lays you wide open to disillusionment and deception. Also be careful not to become a martyr to your friends by letting them take undue advantage of you. Even though this transit arouses your compassion, make sure that the people you help with your time and energy are worth helping, that both you and they will get something out of your effort.

New friends may enter your life who do not need this kind of "help." But they will share the ideals that you are coming to hold at this time. You can give each other moral support and pool your energies to work together. Only make sure that you aren't helping each other foster an illusion that keeps each of you from achieving real growth.

If you are at all interested in psychic and spiritual matters, you will probably be attracted to movements that work for these causes. These efforts can be very useful and helpful, but again make sure that you don't join a mutual self-delusion society.

Neptune in the Twelfth House

The next several years will be a time of reflection and deep inner concerns. You will no longer consider it adequate to be successful on the external or material plane of your life. Now you must question and evaluate what your life has meant in spiritual terms. Have you been inwardly fulfilled? Or has your life been a shallow masquerade, with little meaning for you as a spiritual being? Whether or not we like it and whatever our feelings about the existence of an "immortal soul," we all have to deal with this dimension of life.

At this time you may want to withdraw from the rapid pace of normal everyday existence in order to find peace to examine yourself and see what you have accomplished. It is very hard to meditate upon your life in noisy surroundings. If you have been working hard on your career, for example, you may want to slack off now. You will be more concerned with meaning in life, and it will be necessary to find that meaning.

For all of these reasons, the transit of Neptune through the twelfth may stimulate a concern with religion and faith. You will very likely discover the inadequacies of your rational intellect and decide that other aspects of your mind, such as your capability for belief, intuition and sensitivity, are more important now. If you have any psychic inclinations, you may discover that your psychic abilities are aroused by this influence. Probably you will take a great interest in the psychic sciences at this time. You will be concerned with any means for getting in touch with the deeper dimensions of existence.

You will encounter the most difficult effects of this transit if you examine your past life and find that you have not served your spiritual needs very well. You may become subject to depression and periods when your whole life seems meaningless and empty. If this does happen, make changes that will facilitate encountering the spiritual dimension of life. It is never too late to begin this effort, and it will help you. One of the greatest diseases of the modern age is alienation, the feeling that life is meaningless and that we have no connection with anyone or anything else. Neptune in the twelfth is your opportunity to discover that this is not true for you and that you share an essential oneness with all being.

Neptune Conjunct Sun

Like many transits, this one has both positive and negative points. On the positive side, it can greatly increase your sensitivity and compassion for the people around you and allow you to help others in new ways. Like many other Neptune transits, this one greatly elevates your concern with religion and metaphysics and makes you much more concerned about the ultimate meaning of life. You are inclined to subordinate your own ego drives to the needs of others, to feel that what benefits them is as important as what benefits you.

But the Sun is the will, which is usually harnessed to the ego drives. The energy of the Sun in your horoscope signifies your ability to express yourself as an individual. The Sun is the basic energy system of the body and mind. It is not the ego, the sense that you are a particular person with your own identity and needs, but the ego draws heavily upon the Sun for its energy.

Neptune represents a state of consciousness beyond the ego for which most people are not prepared. If you are prepared, you will experience this transit in the positive ways described above, but if you are not prepared you will experience the less positive effects. When Neptune transits the Sun, it rechannels the normal energy that your ego requires, but it is not always apparent where this energy is going. A very common reaction to this transit is fatigue, the feeling that your body just doesn't have any more energy. Or you may feel psychologically fatigued, futile and ineffectual. You may tend to be disappointed in or even sorry for yourself. Often this sense of weakness surfaces as confusion, aimlessness and purposeless actions. This is an extremely difficult transit for people who have problems with drinking or drugs. In fact, even medication that a doctor prescribes may cause problems. It is best to avoid ingesting any chemical that is foreign to the body's normal experience at this time. Your body is extremely sensitive to external influences and less able to resist strain. Be very careful about making excessive demands on your physical energy, for you could become ill.

Another result of this transit is that you may be inclined to deceive others, as if your ego energy is trying to make you appear as something other than what you really are. Whether or not you choose to deceive others will be decided by your own morality, but if you do, you had better be good at it. Neptune has an embarrassing way of letting the truth come to light at inconvenient moments.

You are likely to be unusually idealistic under this transit. Just be sure that your ideals are rooted in reality and are not merely a device for escaping it. If they are an escape device, disappointment is almost certain.

Neptune Sextile Sun

Under this transit, concern for others in your immediate circle will become a much more important part of your life. You will begin to realize the significance of friends and how important they are to you, and you will be less interested in getting your own way with them. Concerned about their welfare, you are willing to work for them if necessary. This belief may extend beyond your personal friends to groups you are associated with. Group ideas and values may be more important to you than your own.

Spiritual concerns are also more important to you at this time than they have been before. This may mean that you will become involved in an organized religion or one of the other cults that have sprung up in recent times. Or you may travel on an individual spiritual path by yourself, depending upon what is the most appropriate approach for you. At this time you are able to devote your basic energies to transcending the limitations you have always accepted in life. If you work toward this goal, you can achieve great understanding.

Under the influence of this transit you may work to assist people who are less fortunate than yourself or for causes you believe in. If so, you may work very selflessly, without thought for your own personal gain. It is not that you don't care about yourself but that you identify with the goals of the people you are helping. You perceive that you are much more than the self within your body, as you had thought in the past.

During this time you will be much more sensitive to the world around you, so it might be a good idea to retire temporarily to a place where you can meditate upon your life in peace, unless your everyday environment provides this opportunity. You won't suffer terribly if you cannot retire in this way, but you will not get the most benefit from this transit.

Neptune Square Sun

This can be a period of confusion and uncertainty in which your life direction becomes unclear. Even if you have previously felt that you knew what you were doing and why, now you may encounter circumstances that force you to question your assumptions. Your will may seem to be temporarily paralyzed, and you won't have your usual energy. In fact this transit can coincide with times of low physical vitality and low psychological energy. For this reason you should avoid any unnecessary physical stress and follow good health habits to maintain strong overall resistance to illness.

But it is much more likely that this transit will result in disorientation, as alluded to above. You may experience disappointments in your work, career or even in your home life that make you feel defeated and dispirited. But you must not sit back and allow this reaction. Certainly you may suffer defeats during this transit, but these defeats occur only when you do something that is not a true reflection of yourself. Because your total energy as a human being is not behind your actions, you don't push through with the vigor that would guarantee success: hence your failure. Also you may suffer a disappointment during this period, if you allow someone to talk you into a project you do not really believe in. Above all else, you must be true to yourself under this transit. In fact its main function in your life may be to point out that you do not really know who you are. While this is not a very happy discovery, it is important to make it so you can proceed to find out who you are.

You should avoid several types of activity during this transit, because your insecurity about yourself will make them turn out badly. First this is not a particularly good time to become involved in spiritual or mystical sects. Your sense of self needs nourishment and growth, not denial. You are not yet ready for that, and the teachings of such groups are likely to confuse you and retard your development as a human being. Similar warnings apply to the study of the occult in general.

Second, avoid risky or speculative ventures, because your sense of reality is too weak to appraise the risks accurately. Besides, you are likely to be swindled. If you are having trouble in your work, avoid the temptation to change jobs now. Later, when you understand your needs better, you may be able to make the change. Any new job you start now would not be an improvement over the present one.

Remain active, and do not withdraw from people to ponder your problems. That will only inflate them out of all proportion and make them harder to deal with.

Neptune Trine Sun

This transit will alter your attitude toward the world tremendously. If you have always been a materialist, you will find that spiritual concerns, perhaps disguised in some way, will become important to you for the first time. This does not necessarily mean that you will be attracted to an organized religion, for your expression of spirituality is likely to be more unorthodox. You will be concerned with a direct experience of the divine or nonmaterial aspects of being. You will recognize that purely material considerations do not give ultimate meaning to your life.

This transit stimulates your compassion for others. You may express this by working for charities or in institutions for people who are physically, mentally or economically disadvantaged; or you may become more concerned with helping people in your immediate environment. One peculiar characteristic of this transit is that you will not be terribly concerned about gratifying your own ego through such work; you only want to be of assistance to others.

In general, this is a rather idealistic time in your life, and you will want very much to actualize your ideals. But nothing will be handed to you now. You will have to work to achieve what you want.

Your creative imagination is also stimulated by this transit. This is a good time for any kind of creative effort, particularly if it involves rather abstract notions. Neptune operates in a rather immaterial way and is at its best when dealing with the abstract. Artistic creativity, especially in music and poetry, is favored by this influence.

A related effect of this transit is that it greatly increases your sensitivity. You are able to perceive very subtle ideas and thoughts and to understand them at the "gut" level. This perception can be useful in all your relationships with others. You will be able to perceive their needs and to help fulfill them. Just as this transit minimizes your ego drives so that you can work for others without feeling resentful, it also enables you to get out of the way and give others what they need once you have perceived it.

The most negative side of this transit is that you may be tempted to sit around and daydream. Reality may not seem as interesting as your dreams, but this is a time when you can work successfully to realize your dreams, so it would be a tremendous waste of very creative energy to just sit! Any course of action as described above would help you become a more creative and happy individual. There is much potential in this transit.

Neptune Opposition Sun

You should be very careful under this transit. First, your physical vitality will not be as great as it could be. You may become weakened by a variety of ailments, if you are not careful. Avoid exposure to illness, and if possible don't use any type of drugs, prescription or otherwise. Be sure to eat the proper foods and stay away from dietary regimens that involve giving up a particular kind of food for philosophical reasons. Unfortunately your body does not live on philosophy! Iron deficiency or similar debilitating conditions are a great danger at this time.

In your relationships, make absolutely certain that you present yourself to others as clearly and as straightforwardly as you can. Do not leave people in any doubt about your intentions or your position on any matter. If others have any reason to misunderstand you, they will, and they are likely to work against you because misunderstanding easily turns to fear or mistrust. For the same reason, avoid any involvement in underhanded or devious schemes, for they probably will work to your detriment.

Work only with people whom you can trust and communicate with, so that if there are any accidental misunderstandings, you and they can straighten them out without becoming suspicious of each other. Give anyone who enters your life now plenty of time to prove that he or she is honest before you place a great deal of trust in that person.

The problem at this time is that defeats in connection with others can be unusually debilitating. Feelings of discouragement and futility are a great danger and can make you want to give up, thus creating even worse results. If you are not careful, you may come out of this transit feeling very badly about yourself.

Be careful about new elements in your life, such as becoming totally involved with some new movement or organization or adopting uncritically a new approach to life or a new philosophy. You are unusually subject to self-delusion at this time. Let every idea or movement prove its worth before you commit yourself to it.

If you follow these precautions, this transit can show you a very spiritual dimension to life. You can become aware of a deeper meaning in life than you have ever been aware of before. The problem is that the road to this understanding is full of snares and delusions that you must carefully find your way through.

Neptune Conjunct Moon

This transit will cause many changes in your emotional and personal life. These changes may be quite hard to handle initially, but they can be constructive if you take the trouble to master the energies involved.

The basic effect of this transit is to greatly increase your sensitivity to the world around you. This is one of the psychic transits, in that it stimulates your latent psychic abilities and makes them the vehicle for much input from the outer world. The problem, however, is that at first your conscious mind does not know what to do with this material, so you become confused or misinterpret the information from the unconscious. This happens especially when the conscious mind receives feelings that cannot be easily reduced to rational considerations.

This transit may produce the following kinds of problems. First there is the danger of being confused by your emotions, believing that you feel one way when your real feelings are quite different. This is particularly difficult in a love relationship in which you are romantically fascinated by someone who is completely inappropriate for you. The "spell" that lovers work upon each other is a classic Neptunian state.

There is a great danger also of being so fascinated by an idea or an ideal that you can no longer clearly see the world around you. You should be very cautious about taking up any idea or belief that seems strangely obsessive and fascinating now. Such ideas are significant and important, but they do not mean what you think they mean. Your unconscious mind speaks very loudly during a Neptune transit, but to understand what it is saying you must learn its peculiar symbolism and not take its words literally.

On the physical level, this transit can lead to ailments related to fluid disturbances in the body, such as excessive cellular fluids. Also it can signify the flare-up of a drug or alcohol problem, if there is a predisposition to this in your birth chart. Also if you have any tendency to contract eye diseases, have your eyes checked. Usually there will be no problems, but don't take the chance.

Sometimes you will be very reluctant to deal with the real world under a Neptune-Moon transit, because the Neptunian illusion is rather alluring. The challenge of the transit is to relate what you get from it to the real world and not try to separate the two. If you can learn the language of the unconscious mind and discover what it is saying, you will gain great insight and wisdom through this transit.

Neptune Sextile Moon

This transit increases your emotional sensitivity so that you are much more aware of the moods and feelings of others. When you encounter people, you are intuitively aware of what they are feeling at the moment. But because you have this empathic understanding of others, you should try to avoid people who have negative thoughts and feelings, because in your state of increased sensitivity, you will be constantly aware of and influenced by them.

In general, even though it may still be difficult to put your perceptions into words, you will know clearly that your emotional understanding at the gut level is high. If you are at all artistic, this will make your imagination much more active and creative, which will aid your work immeasurably. Even if you are not artistic, you will be much more imaginative. Just be careful that this does not lead to endless daydreaming.

It is very likely that whatever your usual attitudes about the mind and feelings, during this time you will be much more concerned with emotions than with intellect. Purely intellectual considerations seem too dull and colorless. Nevertheless, a certain amount of intellectual discipline can be very useful at this time in gaining great emotional understanding of life.

In your relationships, it is quite possible that you will idealize a woman who somehow signifies all of the interesting and fascinating developments that are taking place inside your own mind. If you are a man, this could lead to a very highly romanticized relationship.

This transit stimulates your interest in psychic and mystical phenomena, and you may very well have some sort of psychic experiences. You may not recognize them as such, however, unless you are consciously on the alert for them.

Neptune Square Moon

Under this influence you may have to contend with rather strange moods and feelings. You may feel that your hunches are extremely accurate, but be careful — the language of your unconscious mind, which is speaking rather strongly to you now, is very different from the language of the conscious mind. Your hunches may mislead you badly.

At the same time, you are more subject to outside influences now. If you are around an angry person or someone under the influence of any other intense feeling, you will feel their energy strongly. For this reason, you should avoid people who are under the influence of strong negative emotions. Your empathy is so great that you will easily become subject to their feelings. And avoid anyone who tries to control your thinking through subtle suggestions and hints, which is very likely to happen, because the thoughts they instill will seem to come from within you — another good reason for avoiding negative people.

There may be other problems in your home or personal life or with emotional relationships. It is extremely important that you try to communicate with those around you as clearly as possible. Misunderstandings are rife under this transit. You may begin a love relationship that is hopelessly unrealistic and yet very fascinating.

Moods and emotions may appear and disappear with great speed. Do not take them too seriously or get too wrapped up in contemplating them, for you will only make mountains out of molehills. Even when you are disappointed about something, do not dwell on it. Your own negative emotions can be very destructive.

Avoid using any type of drug unless it is absolutely necessary and you are under a physician's guidance. Your body is much more sensitive than usual and can quickly build up a dependency pattern, even on drugs that don't usually carry that danger. Digestive problems may also occur under this transit, which is another reason for not confusing your system with unusual substances such as drugs.

Neptune Trine Moon

The main effect of this transit is to increase your sensitivity to everything that happens around you, especially to the feelings and moods of others, and even their thoughts to some extent. This is a strongly intuitive transit. The "feelings" you get about a situation will be remarkably accurate. At the same time you will be eager for experiences in which you can go past surface appearances right to the very heart of the matter. And your increased sensitivity makes it easy to do this.

This transit especially arouses your compassion for other people's condition. You feel so exquisitely and empathize so completely with people's problems that you want very much to get involved in their lives and help them. This is a good thing to do, but first make sure that they really want to be helped. Neptune trine your Moon makes you aware of the intrinsic oneness of all beings, an awareness you will want to demonstrate in your own life. This combination also arouses a kind of idealized mother function within you, regardless of your sex, so that you want to protect and nurture those in need. Again, be sure that they want to be nurtured. And don't get so carried away with your idealistic feelings that you cannot relate to the actual conditions you will have to deal with in helping others. If that happens you will accomplish little.

It is possible that this transit will bring you a very idealized and spiritualized love relationship, even to the point that the two of you will not have a physical relationship. You may prefer to remain platonic because it seems more pure and ideal. And although you are idealizing, in the long run a relationship such as this is likely to be very helpful to your development. Unlike many other Neptunian relationships, in this instance you should be able to make the change from illusions to reality without too much trouble, and you may discover that your illusions about the other person were not so far removed from the truth after all.

Under any circumstances this transit will greatly stimulate your imagination and give it a much more poetic cast. If you have any latent psychic ability, this transit will bring it out. You are also likely to be much more interested in the occult, psychic studies and spiritualism. This is all part of your increased sensitivity to the world, as mentioned earlier.

Neptune Opposition Moon

This transit produces strange moods and obsessions that can make your life quite difficult if you take them at face value or too seriously. Your perception of the world is not terribly acute at this time, and you tend to see things as you want to see them rather than as they are. Psychic and spiritual studies and teachings, which usually are quite valuable, should be taken up with extreme care at this time because you may misunderstand or misuse them. Often this transit denotes that you are weary of the world as it is and want to escape from it. Spiritual teachings can be used as an excuse for escape, but that is not their most constructive use by any means. The world is here so you can learn to handle it, not so you can avoid it. You can only disguise it, which makes it much more damaging to you.

You can be deceived by your feelings under this influence. For example, you may idealize someone out of all proportion to the truth and insist that what you see in that person is really so because your intuition tells you it is. But you are likely to be disappointed if you do this. Be especially careful in love affairs, which are often subject to overidealizing anyway. Also watch out for a tendency to saddle yourself with "stray dogs," that is, forlorn and woebegone people who appeal to your compassion. If you can really be of assistance to them, fine. But first make sure you can. Your efforts may be wasted on people who do not really want to change at all.

At the physical level, be very careful of what you eat or drink. Your body is unusually sensitive to poisons and chemicals at this time and may react badly to some substances. Even if you are careful, you may have some kind of digestive difficulty or other problem in assimilating foods.

Events in your personal and domestic life may become very unclear at this time. Keep your home life as neat and orderly as possible, for any serious problems there could undermine your self-confidence and make you more fearful in dealing with the world. You may have a problem with female relatives or friends during this transit.

Neptune Conjunct Mercury

This can be an extremely difficult transit to handle, because Neptune and Mercury are so different in their functions. But as with many other Neptune transits, this one has a positive side that you should seek to bring out.

The logical and rational faculties of your mind are likely to be scrambled by the influence of Neptune, so that you are no longer quite sure what you think about anything. Or you may come under the influence of ideas that you would not have held previously. You are likely to make the worst mess of this transit if you try to organize and restructure your life now. The ordering function of Mercury is so much at odds with Neptune's lack of orderliness that any arrangements you make will not make sense later to yourself or anyone else. Consequently this is a bad time for making important decisions that will affect the direction of your life. It is also a bad time for most business decisions, because there is a danger that you are poorly informed about what is going on.

Neptune and Mercury combined always raise the issue of self-deceit, being deceived by others or your deceit toward others. Be extremely careful of these hazards in any kind of negotiations. Deceit may be inadvertent. For example, you may find that you are unable to clearly express what is on your mind because the thoughts seem so complex and disorganized, and when you do say something, others misunderstand you completely. Be very sure that people really understand your meaning when they say they do.

On the plus side of this transit, you will be much more receptive to subtle influences around you. Your rational mind may be confused, but your intuition is likely to be very sharp. The only difficulty you might have is in making others understand the basis of your understandings.

You may become interested in psychic matters and in mysticism under this transit. You will arrive at a profound and direct knowledge of the inadequacies of unaided logic, and you may seek to expand your understanding of the more hidden aspects of the mind. You may even encounter hidden psychic abilities in your own mind.

Neptune Sextile Mercury

This transit stimulates your imagination in a creative way, giving you greater inspiration and an immediate grasp of ideas that are usually too subtle for the intellect. And you are better able to communicate these subtle ideas to others and give people some understanding of what you are seeing now. This can be a very creative time if you are interested in art, music or poetry.

If you have any latent psychic ability, this transit is quite capable of activating a kind of extrasensory perception within you. Certainly it increases the level of your sensitivity, and you are much more able to understand what others are trying to communicate to you. Previously these ideas have been too difficult to comprehend, requiring too much intuition and subconscious understanding. Now, however, you get an immediate idea of what they are feeling.

With your imagination so aroused, the everyday world may not seem very interesting, and you may begin to dream of strange regions in your mind where you can escape. But if you can tie yourself down to earth long enough, you will discover that the world of your normal life can be fascinating in its own right. This is such a great opportunity to understand aspects of the world that you could not usually comprehend; you shouldn't waste it by wandering off into a private world that has no relevance to anything else.

Because of your increased ability to communicate the spiritual or psychic experiences in your own life, this is a good time to teach others what you have learned. At other times it may have been difficult to convey to people anything more than the outer shell of your experience. Now, because of the vividness of your imagination, you are able to make them feel your experiences. It may be useful to associate with other people who are having similar experiences so that as a group you can teach others what you know.

In general, faith and reason are in a state of balance at this time. You do not believe anything simply because a guru has told you so, but at the same time you recognize the limits of rational intellect. You do not try to make either intellect or faith serve the functions of the other.

Neptune Square Mercury

The principal challenge of this transit is to keep your thinking and communications straight within yourself and with regard to others. The quality of your mind is being tested now, and any loose ends in your thinking or attitudes will become a serious source of trouble. Any unclear ideas will become a source of confusion to you in many aspects of your life.

Avoid making important decisions under this transit, especially about your career and overall life objectives. You probably are not seeing clearly enough to make intelligent decisions that take into account all of the relevant factors.

Similarly avoid business decisions if possible, for buying and selling are not favored by this transit. You may be operating under a misconception about the transactions, or your buying and selling may be influenced by unconscious compulsions. It is also possible that the person you are dealing with is dishonest.

The main problem with this transit is that it stimulates your imagination to the point that you may spend too much time fantasizing. You may find it difficult to keep your attention fixed on the real world, or you may become obsessed with strange ideas and fanciful beliefs, especially religious and mystical notions.

This transit may also bring on nervous problems, such as worrying about problems that don't amount to anything. Don't let yourself become overwhelmed by imaginary fears or anxieties — they are almost certainly not real. In rare cases this transit can also coincide with some type of paralysis or other motor nerve problem, but this is not very likely unless there is a predisposition in your birth chart. Avoid drugs that affect the mind at this time, for your mind already has enough unreality to contend with.

Communications may be difficult at this time. Others may deceive you, and you may deceive others, either intentionally or inadvertently. Certainly you should not misrepresent yourself or anything else, because the deception may not succeed, which will undermine people's confidence in you.

Neptune Trine Mercury

This is one of the most imaginative periods of your life in a positive way. Your mind will be able to create with unusual facility, but you will still be able to distinguish between reality and the products of your imagination, which is not the case with some other combinations of Neptune and Mercury. If you have ever wanted to write prose or poetry, this is the time to try, although success in this area requires some indication of writing ability in the birth chart. Transits can only stimulate the potential that exists in the birth chart; they can't create a talent out of nothing.

This combination of Neptune and Mercury signifies one of the few times in life when the rational intellect and the intuitive and feeling functions are able to work as a team. For most people these two areas of the mind usually operate at cross-purposes. But now they can cooperate, which is what makes this such a fertile time.

Fortunately, the intuitive sensitivity stimulated by this transit extends to your relationships with others. You understand what people are thinking with much less verbal communication than usual, almost as if you can look into their minds and see what is happening there. Consequently your efforts to communicate with others will be much more effective now. Others will understand and appreciate the fact that you understand them.

You are likely to take an intellectual interest in metaphysical and spiritual subjects at this time, and your innate psychic abilities may be manifested. But your approach to these subjects is a bit different from most people's. You demand that spiritual matters make sense to you intellectually as well as intuitively. You want to know, not merely to believe. But your newly intuitive sensibility tells you that there are limits to understanding through rational intellect. Your understanding of almost any subject is greatly heightened by this transit.

If you are involved in any kind of teaching, this transit will be an invaluable aid. You will be able to communicate what you know in such a way that others really understand the subject and also your experience of it.

Neptune Opposition Mercury

Thinking and communication will be problem areas in your life for the duration of this transit. You are more subject to confusion at this time than at any other, and it is a very dangerous time to make important decisions. Either you misunderstand the circumstances that affect your decision, or you do not have all the facts. It is also possible that someone has deceived you about the facts.

In communicating with others, be very careful that what you say is clear, and if you don't understand what someone else says to you, clarify it to yourself. Misunderstanding others is a great danger at this time and can lead to most unpleasant situations.

You are more than usually subject to strange ideas now. Be careful not to become obsessed by delusions, for you will find it very difficult to tell what is a delusion and what is not. The tried and true principles that have guided your life are more reliable than newer ones.

In business deals or any other buying or selling negotiation, be extremely careful, for you can easily be deceived. In difficult combinations such as this one, both Mercury and Neptune rule thievery, and you could be the victim. Make sure that what you buy is exactly as it is represented, and always be sure to get a guarantee when you make a purchase. If you are selling, be sure to make some kind of contractual arrangement with the buyer.

Avoid getting involved in any scheme that you know to be dishonest. When it comes to deceiving others, luck is not with you; the one who gets hurt will be you.

You may have to contend with strange nervous ailments at this time. These can be either physical or psychological illnesses. Psychological ailments are likely to take the form of peculiar anxieties and nervousness. Taking vitamins may be helpful in dealing with your nerves, but consult your physician first. You must realize that any fears you have under this transit are probably groundless and have arisen from your overactive imagination.

On the other hand, you could have a real physical problem. This transit can signify nervous weakness or a condition in which the nerves do not transmit impulses as they should. If you are having severe psychological problems, they may have an organic basis. Consult a doctor to find out.

Neptune Conjunct Venus

This can be a fascinating transit. It will stimulate the idealistic side of your nature in a most beautiful way, and you will see beauty in everything. For artistic and creative people this is one of the most powerful of all transits. Your imagination will be more active than ever before, presenting you with innumerable beautiful images to create from. Even if you are not especially artistic, this transit will bring poetry, music and art into your life.

Although this transit brings the "beautiful illusion," the "beautiful image," it does not bring the reality of beauty. You have an ideal of beauty in your mind that you project onto reality or onto a loved one, but otherwise it is not real. You have to create the fact as an artist would create his work. If you delude yourself that the ideal is already here, you will have problems. You may be so oriented toward seeing only the beautiful images in your mind that you overlook and refuse to deal with the very real and possibly difficult aspects of your life.

Relationships can be particularly difficult if you do not keep a clear head. Neptune conjunct Venus is the romance transit par excellence. You may fall madly in love with someone because he or she seems so perfect and ideal, although the truth may be quite different. Neptune does not automatically mean a bad love relationship, and the object of your love may or may not be worthwhile. That is not the point. Even if your loved one is worthwhile from a clear-headed point of view, that is not what is attracting you. If you are lucky, when the fog lifts you will find you have picked someone who is quite good for you. But you may have difficulty accepting his or her faults, because you were so wrapped up in your ideal of perfection that you did not notice them before. Disappointment in love is a frequent consequence of a Neptune-Venus relationship. And the disappointment will be more acute if you fall for someone who is not at all worthwhile.

One other theme that occurs in Neptune-Venus relationships is selflessness in love. This is the illusion that your only need in a relationship is to make the other person happy. Sometimes people will carry this theme to the extent of seeking out someone who is truly a loser in order to "save" him or her. A relationship with a sick person, alcoholic or drug addict is a manifestation of this pattern. Be very careful to avoid this tendency; when the transit is over you may find that you have committed yourself to a very ungratifying situation.

Another situation may arise that is related in reverse, if you feel that you are the unworthy person who needs to be saved. In this case you would seek out someone who could "save" you, rather like falling in love with a guru figure. The problem with both of these Neptune-Venus manifestations is that you are not relating to the other person as an independent equal.

Neptune Sextile Venus

This transit stimulates your creative imagination and is likely to put you into a very pleasant and dreamy frame of mind, in which you will be capable of great creativity. You may not act very practically, however. If you have any creative or artistic talent, this will be a good time for using it. Your sense of color will be heightened, and your sense of form and design will be improved. Even if you are not especially artistic, you should surround yourself with various forms of beauty in order to better appreciate it.

On the emotional front, you are inclined to idealize your partner in a love relationship and not deal very well with his or her less ideal aspects, the "warts," so to speak. This transit may in fact bring a very romantic new love. But even though you won't have a very realistic attitude toward it, you are unlikely to do yourself any harm. The effects of this transit are mild enough so that afterward you can make the necessary adjustment to reality. If the relationship turns out to have no real merit, you will simply drop it with little regret.

While this aspect affects love relationships most strongly, it will affect friendships also. In the name of love for your friend or lover you will be able to act much less selfishly than at other times. Love is more important than getting your own way at this time, and you want to do whatever you can for the person you love. Just make sure that the person you are devoting yourself to is worth the effort. But even if he or she is not worthwhile, the energy you put forth will help you greatly in the long run, because you have been able to act selflessly and give for the sake of giving.

If all other factors are right, this transit can bring a most spiritual love, a true "soul-union." You may feel that you have met the person who has always been destined for you. And this may in fact be true; with other transits this feeling is often simply an illusion, but with this transit it can be real.

Neptune Square Venus

Unrealistic attitudes in personal relationships may cause problems during this transit, and you may experience disappointments that will seriously affect your domestic life. You tend to avoid the truth about yourself and about your relationships at this time, and your reluctance to deal with reality could set you up for a very severe fall. This will undermine your self-confidence as well as the relationships. Your sense of reality in relationships and your ability to accept others as they are is being tested by this transit.

If a new potential lover comes along, you may be swept off your feet. You are not excited by the reality of the person but by something within yourself that you are projecting upon the other. When you finally learn the truth about the other person, you may have difficulty accepting it, even though the truth is perfectly all right in itself.

A danger you should watch for especially with this transit is that of being attracted to an unattainable person. You may be setting yourself up for a situation in which you cannot win. The other person appears as an unrealizable dream, someone who is too far above you to be attained. You have to recognize that your real objective here is avoiding an actual encounter. If you play this as a dreamy kind of game, you are unlikely to do anyone, including yourself, much harm. But if you take your "suffering" seriously, the resulting sense of defeat may be quite harmful to you. Also, others may find your martyred role in love very difficult to be around.

It is also possible that the person you choose to love can only be described as a loser who dreams that you can save him or her. Here again you play the martyr, suffering from the hurts and outrages perpetrated by your loved one. Again your objective is to avoid having to deal with the real person.

Neptunian relationships like these are often born of your feeling of inadequacy. By avoiding confrontations with real people, you also avoid a confrontation with yourself, in which you fear that you will be the loser. Yet a real confrontation is just what you need. If you persist in one of these relationships after this transit, you will have to confront both yourself and your partner as real individuals. Whatever the outcome, this could be the most valuable part of the relationship.

Neptune Trine Venus

This transit will stimulate your romantic imagination considerably. This may lead you to an unusually romantic relationship with someone of the opposite sex, or it may arouse creative talents that you were not even aware of. The symbol of this transit is the beautiful dream or illusion. Even though it is an illusion, you have the ability now to make it real if you recognize that you must work to make any dream real.

If this transit does bring about a love relationship, it will probably be more romantic and idealized than any you have ever experienced. It will seem like a perfect soul union between the two of you, the realization of your most perfect ideal. However, even with the Venus-Neptune trine there is the danger of overidealization.

You will eventually learn to see your partner's flaws, but this relationship should broaden your understanding of people to the point that you can accept the inevitable flaws. This transit is not as likely to produce great disappointment in relationships as the other Venus-Neptune combinations. In fact, under this influence you will be more compassionate and understanding of your lover, almost as if you and your love were one, and his or her problems are yours too. This sense of oneness is based on a deep spiritual truth that you can recognize more easily now, that we are all one. Under this transit you are much more sensitive to the mystical aspects of love.

Only remember that a trine transit does not create anything. It will require effort on your part to make this relationship real and lasting.

You may not encounter an ideal love under this transit, of course, but even so you will display much more sensitivity in your relationships and understanding of other people. Any sort of love will help you gain understanding, which is the most positive result of this transit.

If you have any intrinsic creative abilities, this transit will stimulate them tremendously. This is an excellent time to begin the study of an art or craft. But this influence is most favorable to the pure arts, those whose sole objective is the creation of beautiful images as opposed to useful art objects. Even if you are not artistic, your ability to perceive beauty in the world around you will be enormously heightened, and you will be much more sensitive to the spirit of life that animates everything in the world.

Neptune Opposition Venus

During this transit, love relationships, especially, may cause problems because either you or your partner has an unrealistic attitude about the relationship. Disillusionment and disappointment are the likely result when the romantic cloud lifts and the truth about the relationship becomes clear. All of us idealize a new lover to a certain extent, for that is part of the normal process of falling in love. But this transit indicates that the problem can be much more severe because of your unwillingness to accept reality as it is. You are inclined to look for partners and relationships that can help you escape from the humdrum, everyday world into a magical world of fantasy and beautiful illusions. But unfortunately you must pick your partner from the human race, and the people who can truly fulfill a Venus-Neptune dream are extremely rare. So you create a beautiful image in your imagination and pretend that a specific person fits the image. And you are likely to persist, even though everyone can see, even you if you open your eyes, that your loved one is not what you fantasize. This is the most extreme manifestation of the Venus-Neptune transit, and it is not an uncommon reaction.

This transit can create other kinds of relationship difficulties as well, such as obscure problems within an existing relationship. For example, you may find it difficult to communicate with your partner, or one of you may do something behind the other's back, thus undermining your mutual confidence. It is important to play as straight as possible with your partners, because Neptune can leave long-lasting scars in a relationship, if you do not work to minimize its effects from the very beginning.

The most useful effect of this transit is that it stimulates the creative imagination. In fact, every illusion or delusion is really only a misuse of creative imagination or a confusion of imagination with truth. If you can keep truth and imagination separate, you will derive great benefit from this transit, especially if you are intrinsically creative. Artistic creativity is heightened by this influence, and even your relationships can be more interesting, if you don't lose sight of their real nature.

A new relationship that begins under this transit should be forced to withstand the test of time. Make sure that it can take the transition from dreamy ideal romance to hard reality. Perhaps it can, but it will have to undergo fundamental changes. You cannot assume that such a relationship will be able to survive the changes.

Neptune Conjunct Mars

This is not a good time to strike out to further your own self-interest in life. Your energy level is low, and you are subject to fits of discouragement and malaise. This is one of the more difficult transits of Neptune, because the nature of Mars and that of Neptune are very much opposed to each other. Mars in your horoscope stands for your ego drives, but Neptune manages to pull the rug out from under them. Mars makes you assert your individuality and take the necessary actions to establish your place in the world among other people. Whatever you do along these lines — working to get ahead in your job, beginning a new enterprise or embarking on a program of vigorous mental or physical activity — Neptune will make it difficult for you to succeed. It is not that you are unlucky exactly but that you don't have enough push to follow through. Under this transit your efforts are likely to be half-hearted. Even if you want to do something, you may just feel too tired.

Another side of this transit is that you may get involved in an activity or project that is dishonest, misrepresented or simply subversive, although not necessarily politically. You may not be aware that it is dishonest, but if you are and choose to be involved anyway, you are running an enormous risk. Avoid any scheme that you know to be dishonest, because with this transit you simply cannot count on it coming out favorably for you.

This is not a good time to advance yourself, but try not to get discouraged, for that will not help you. Instead, cut your losses and disengage yourself if possible from any activity that could create difficulties. Get into a position where you can afford to be unconcerned about results. Detaching yourself from your own energies is the best way to deal with this transit. Act because you enjoy the action, not because you are trying to win. If you can take this course of detached consciousness, you may learn something about how your life works; in fact, you may learn that your own efforts have fouled you up. In your eagerness to succeed, you may have aroused opposition that was not expressed openly, but waited subversively in the wings to trip you up.

On the physical level, this transit can give rise to infections that severely debilitate the body. It is a good idea to adopt a rigorous physical regimen and avoid situations that tax your physical strength or expose you to disease. Also avoid using drugs during this transit unless absolutely necessary, whether medically prescribed or not. Your body is unusually sensitive to poisons now.

Neptune Sextile Mars

At this time success and getting your own way will not seem so important to you. You are much more concerned with whether your life serves higher goals and principles than with your own needs. It is very important to you that your own individuality be expressed as part of the larger scheme.

Consequently you are likely to work with others toward shared spiritual or metaphysical goals, and you may actively participate in a religious or spiritual movement. But you will probably stay out of the limelight for the most part, because you are in a rather retiring mood. It is as if the effort of pushing yourself into the forefront would disturb your attempt to find peace, which is more important to you now. This is a time for reflection rather than vigorous action.

As you succeed in quieting the demands of your ego, you will discover the smaller, quieter voices that exist within us all. You may discover that the furious activity that has dominated your life hasn't really meant much to you, that you did it for others in order to feel better about yourself. You may discover a psychic side to your consciousness that you haven't noticed before because you have been so busy rushing around.

One of Neptune's more benevolent effects is that it gives you empathy for others and the ability to intuitively understand their positions. With this transit you realize that you have been where they are, and you know from first-hand experience the tricks that people play on themselves and the foolish mistakes they make. So along with your increased understanding of spiritual truth comes the ability to understand others and to accept their shortcomings. You know that you are in the same place they are.

Neptune Square Mars

There are a number of dangers with this transit. It affects your sense of who you are and challenges the validity of the life course you have set for yourself, as well as your image of yourself as an effective person.

The chief danger of this transit is that it sets you up for situations in which you will emerge as a loser, especially in your work and at home. Or someone else may set you up in such a way that you are forced to act without knowing what is really going on, and therefore you act ineffectively. Since you are not likely to get much reinforcement from others at this time, you will be forced to rely on your own inner resources and self-confidence. Do not expect others to provide you with backbone; you need to provide your own.

Be careful not to get involved with any dubious schemes, and make sure that any project you do get into is real. Certainly avoid anything you know to be corrupt or dishonest, for you will probably lose out and lose face as well.

Defeats may make you feel discouraged, but don't take them too seriously. Like all transits, this one will pass. And there is a lesson to be learned here. The more you identify with what you do rather than what you are, the more difficulties this transit will cause. You are not what you do. This transit may force you to confront that issue, and if it does, you will learn to handle your life much more successfully because you will not always have to protect yourself.

Another danger with this transit is that you may become wrapped up in fighting for some terribly idealistic cause that has little chance of succeeding or of giving you any real satisfaction. All that you can count on is that you will be required to surrender your individuality for a "higher purpose," which usually turns out to be someone else's ego!

This may be a period of low physical energy. You may even feel like sleeping all the time, and within reason it is probably best to take it easy. Don't subject your body to unusual stresses or strains, and avoid exposure to illness, for your body is unusually subject to infection now.

Neptune Trine Mars

As with most Mars-Neptune transits, this is not a good time to strike out boldly into the world to further your own interests. However, this transit does provide the opportunity to learn certain very valuable lessons without the discouraging defeats that most Mars-Neptune transits engender.

During this time you will not feel inclined to assert yourself at other people's expense. Instead you may wish to work to help others without any concern for your own advancement. This is a good time for any kind of charitable work or for working with poor or otherwise disadvantaged people. Similarly you may become involved with others in an organization concerned with mystical or spiritual teaching. Whatever your area of work, the main consideration is that you work for knowledge and insight and to help others, not for your own advancement.

Do not be afraid that your life will lack fulfillment. You will find that ultimately all your activities for and with others for a common purpose will be fulfilling. We often have an idea that our own interests are somehow not consistent with those of others. But at this time you will discover that your needs and desires are identical with other people's. In order to learn this, you must get away from working solely for yourself. This transit will help you do that.

Related to the above effect is a greater concern with metaphysical and spiritual truth. You will become increasingly able to understand how you as an individual fit into the entire universe. Your idea of who you are and what your individuality consists of will expand greatly. You will not be so isolated by the notions you have had about what you are.

Neptune Opposition Mars

For the duration of this transit you will have to be very careful in a number of areas, and in others it would be a good idea to keep your expectations rather low.

First, be careful not to get yourself involved, wittingly or unwittingly, in any kind of bogus enterprise. Mars-Neptune can mean "deceitful actions," and this transit may involve you in such acts either as the victim or as the perpetrator of some swindle. To avoid becoming a victim, you should scrutinize with great care all seeming "opportunities" that come up now and stay away altogether from any speculative or high-risk ventures. With regard to the second danger, you should avoid perpetrating any kind of swindle, not only because it is unethical, but because you're not likely to succeed. Schemes do not usually work out as anticipated under this transit.

At this time you should also be careful of your health. This combination can produce illnesses such as anemia, which weaken you, making you feel tired all the time. It can also make you subject to infections that are hard to diagnose and cure. Even at best, you are not likely to feel as vigorous as usual. Be particularly careful about taking any kind of drug, prescribed or otherwise, under this transit.

You should not plan to launch new activities during this period. Because your energy level is low, you can't put the necessary energy into a new project to make it work out as you want. This transit can produce a crisis of self-confidence, resulting either from personal defeats by others or from a totally unpredictable and irrational spell of depression. Consequently you will find it hard to continue with projects that require great exertion. It would be best to avoid starting any new projects at this time, and you should try to maneuver yourself into a position in which you don't have to do anything critical. But above all, don't take these feelings of defeat too seriously; you are just going through a period of low energy. There is no reason to contemplate giving up, because very soon you will be back to your old level of competence. The only permanent effect of this transit is that you may learn to have a more realistic understanding of your limitations and to be more conservative with your energies.

Neptune Conjunct Jupiter

This is one of the most idealistic times in your life. This transit arouses your natural sympathies for others and makes you want to help them. You may help some person close to you who needs assistance, or you may work with sick and disadvantaged persons in an institutional setting or with charities that aid such people.

This transit may also motivate you to work in some other way to actualize your ideals. Now it is not enough to simply believe in something, you want to make your beliefs come true as well. But you may tend to believe that what you want to be true *is* true, even when it isn't. Do not get carried away by your idealism.

Under this transit you may also begin to take an interest in philosophy and religion. You are very concerned now about how you fit into the universal order, and you are more inclined to deal with abstract issues and how they relate to your life. In fact you may not want to bother with the everyday aspects of life, feeling that they are beneath your concern. Needless to say, that attitude can get you into trouble. Nevertheless, if you can keep track of life's daily requirements, you will also be able to gain insights into your life that will make it much more meaningful.

There is another side to this transit also. It can give you a foolish confidence that anything you will do will work out all right. As a result you may take risks and gambles or actually indulge in gambling. This is not an especially lucky or unlucky transit. All it does is make you confuse your wishes with reality and make you act according to your wishes. It is not a good time to make long-term investments, because you are seeing the world through rose-colored glasses and are unwilling to look at business affairs in the cold, hard manner that is required. In fact you can easily be swindled by anyone who appeals to your innermost wishes and desires.

Use this transit to gain insights into your life, but do not try to advance your material interests, for you are not likely to be successful.

Neptune Sextile Jupiter

This transit creates a strong desire for a very special kind of knowledge. You are interested in what the rational mind can tell you, but you also want very much to understand the subtler spiritual truths that give your life dimension and meaning. You may want to learn more about metaphysics and spiritual teachings through studying the occult. Or you may become involved with a religious group that gives you greater insights into the meaning of your life. You may emphasize the Neptune side of this transit and throw over all human knowledge for the way of pure faith. In any case you will eventually discover that all these paths have precisely the same goal.

On a slightly more mundane level, this transit may stimulate your interest in faraway places that seem completely different from your everyday world. You may want to travel, and this is a good time to do so because your sense of awe about the unknown makes your discoveries through traveling all the more fascinating.

This is usually a very optimistic time when you feel that nothing can go wrong, which may be so, but it would be foolish to tempt fate with wild and ill-considered actions. The effects of this transit are not so strong that you can get away with living dangerously. But on the other hand, your optimistic and positive frame of mind can help to ensure that your plans work out as you want them to.

You enjoy the company of friends at this time, and you feel sufficiently secure and magnanimous that you don't need to bother with the silly ego games that people often play with their friends. In fact you are much more inclined to take a back seat to other people's ego games and let them have their way. Conflicts with others aren't worth it to you now. You are very giving and generous during this transit, because you genuinely want to help others, and you make it quite evident.

Neptune Square Jupiter

During this period you will be impatient with the restrictions imposed by everyday existence, and you will be preoccupied with fantasies or ideas that help you escape the ordinary. Your grasp of what you can and cannot do with your life is being tested now, and it is very important that you try to accept the actual limitations on your life. If you can, this transit will expand your life by helping you perceive the tremendous possibilities that are inherent in your situation, even though it isn't ideal.

Your fantasies may take the form of an overdeveloped belief in your own strength and power. You may feel that you cannot lose, but if you succumb to this belief, the day will come when you lose very badly, and then your foolish overconfidence will be replaced with defeat and discouragement. Be particularly careful to avoid wild speculations and risks, for you will almost certainly lose out; you aren't paying enough attention to the reality of the situation, and you are seeing only what you want to see. You are more than usually gullible at this time, especially if someone flatters your sense of importance.

You may take a somewhat more exalted but equally futile path by becoming involved in a religious or spiritual movement that makes you lose all touch with reality. Either you do not see the world as it is and think that it is something altogether more beautiful, or you are disgusted with the world and reject it as unworthy of your attention. No matter how high your vision, you will benefit from your existence only insofar as you recognize what it is. Do not allow spirituality to become an illusion and an excuse for not dealing with the world.

On the plus side, this transit stimulates your desire to help others, and you can be of great benefit if you deal with situations as they really are. Starry-eyed idealists are not very useful when there is much hard work to be done.

Neptune Trine Jupiter

This transit can affect you in several ways, but in any case it will make you feel optimistic and hopeful about the future. You will feel that everything is going to be all right, and that is not a delusion, because under this transit you will gain insights that can make your life much better.

You will feel very idealistic but also very concerned about understanding, so your idealism will not get in the way of perceiving the truth. In fact truth is very important in your life now — not so much facts, but understanding how the universe works. Just be careful not to make truth into such an abstract consideration that you cannot experience it in everyday life. However, given that warning, you do have the opportunity to gain great insights through the study of philosophy, metaphysics and the occult. And you want to understand what you study rather than being told what is so with no explanation of why.

At another level, this transit works to increase your optimism and self-confidence to the point that you are willing to take risks you would not ordinarily take. This may happen through gambling or speculation, or it may happen through getting rid of the elements of your life that you have always depended on for security. You now recognize that they have also limited the expansion of your consciousness, and you want to be free to experience the world. You realize that some material considerations you have thought necessary in the past are now clearly expendable.

You may decide to travel, particularly by sea or by air. However, the main purpose of this travel will be learning, not recreation. It would be best to take a long trip and get to know the land and people without the structure of a guided tour. You need and want direct experience.

Your desire to help underdog elements of society is great at this time. You have a strong feeling of social justice, and you do not want people to get the short end of the stick. Justice, you feel, should be tempered with mercy and compassion.

Neptune Opposition Jupiter

Inflated expectations, excessive and impractical idealism and sudden disappointments are among the dangers of this transit, if you do not make a concerted effort to keep your feet on the ground. Neptune opposing your Jupiter makes you feel that nothing can defeat you. You feel tremendously lucky and are inclined to take foolish risks that you wouldn't normally take, especially financial risks. But any form of speculation or gambling is extremely risky under this influence and should be avoided altogether. By the same token you should be careful that this foolish overconfidence does not make you overlook factors in your job or home life, for example, that could trip you up and cause serious problems. But be particularly careful not to overextend yourself financially.

This combination of planetary factors arouses your intrinsic idealism. The limitations of the real world may seem very difficult to bear, because you so badly want the world to be better. This feeling may lead you into involvements with some extreme religious, spiritual or mystical sect. Although it may be a perfectly constructive group, it is not very good for you now, because you are not approaching it with a realistic idea of what you can get from it. You have to deal with this universe before you can leave it. Study religion or mysticism if you want, but don't make any commitments that will prove to be a trap when this transit is over.

Like all combinations of Neptune and Jupiter, this one stimulates and arouses your compassion for others. You want to help people out and share whatever good fortune you have. But with this transit, make sure that the people you are assisting will get some real benefit from your efforts. You are very likely to be preyed on by "leeches," people who take advantage of your generosity but who gain nothing from the experience.

Neptune Conjunct Saturn

This is a difficult transit of Neptune, because it can be very confusing as well as rather depressing and desperate. But it also has a brighter side, which you should work to bring out.

Under this transit you will discover that in many ways your view of the world isn't at all correct. This may occur through a series of obvious disappointments, or it may take place more subtly through an increasing sense of anxiety that has no obvious cause. Fear and loss of self-confidence are two of the most difficult effects of this transit. You may suddenly become afraid for almost no reason at all, and you may fear things that are not at all threatening to others. It is as if you were becoming disoriented.

Saturn rules the structure we give to our universe, the way we see and experience the world. Neptune reveals higher aspects of the universe, including the fact that it has many possible realities, of which ours is only one. When Neptune shows you this, reality becomes very confusing, and you become lost in a sea of infinite possibilities in which everything is true but nothing is true. This is the "dark night of the soul" referred to by mystics, the period of confusion that precedes the understanding that you can live with a reality that is different from what you had thought. At the highest level this transit can be a prelude to enlightenment, understanding the true nature of the "illusion" we call reality.

In most cases, however, this transit simply means that your concept of reality is changing, which begins with the dissolution of your old concepts, leaving you temporarily disoriented. The best way to handle this period is to get into comfortable surroundings and reduce the stress level in your life as much as possible. Stress will only prolong the confusion. Try to avoid making any decisions, because you are not in a very good frame of mind for seeing things clearly. Avoid people who seem difficult or demoralizing. You need to be in a calm position so that you can see what new truths emerge from the fog and confusion. And they will emerge.

With some persons the psychological effect of this transit surfaces physically as a slowly developing illness that is very hard to diagnose. If you have not had a physical checkup recently, have one now. You may feel fine, but the illnesses that sometimes come with this transit do not show up right away.

Neptune Sextile Saturn

At this time the ideal and the real are well balanced in your life, and you are in an excellent position to reflect upon their relationship to each other. Ask yourself what is true for you and then ask what you would like to be. In this way you can see which is which without the confusion that so often marks our efforts to separate the ideal from the real. At the same time you can see what actions you can take to help bring about the ideal in place of what is presently real and to make it a solid and useful part of your own life and of the lives of those around you.

But you are not impatient now, and you are much more willing to accept what is real than at other times. You see no real contest between the real and the ideal. Also you are not so concerned about getting your own way that you insist on the kind of ego battle with the real world in which either you or it wins. (And reality usually wins in these cases.)

You are patient now because a Saturn-Neptune combination such as this one enables you to live on very little. You are inclined to be abstemious and opposed to self-indulgence, and you may subject yourself to a rather stern regimen of alternating work and introspection. At this time you are most concerned with higher truths and how you can actualize them in your own life.

This is a good time to withdraw somewhat from your usual activities, to stand back and see what you have accomplished and what remains to be done. You are capable of adopting a very calm and meditative attitude so that you can choose intelligently and take the proper course of action.

This is also a good time to do work that helps others. It would satisfy your need to act selflessly and to be a part of the larger scheme.

Neptune Square Saturn

During this transit you will have problems with insecurity and anxiety that seem to have no apparent cause. Your grasp of reality seems to be slipping away, and you feel very disoriented and confused. Regardless of your material circumstances at this time, this is ultimately a psychological transit; that is, it affects you by causing your moods and your views of the world to change. Any problems you have now will probably have their origins in your own mind. That is the first principle to grasp with this transit. If you can handle its effect on your consciousness, you can handle anything.

The chief problem is that you will begin to have doubts and fears that you are not adequate to handle your life, and you may feel like withdrawing from everything. That is not a good idea, however, because you need others' points of view to balance your overly pessimistic views. However, if someone is contributing to the shakiness of your self-confidence, you should cut that person out of your life, at least for the present.

Insecurity and lack of belief in yourself have the greatest effect on your job and your domestic life. Remember that you have the same rights and privileges to be yourself as anyone else has, and don't allow others to walk over you. But don't become so committed to a position on any matter that you cannot let go of it without further damaging your belief in yourself. One important effect of this transit is that it takes away elements of your life that you have identified with — property, possessions, opinions or whatever. It shows you that your existence does not depend upon being able to hold on to these elements.

In fact one manifestation of a Saturn-Neptune combination may be that you will voluntarily give up your material possessions for a self-denying, ascetic way of life like a monk's, although probably not so extreme. The best way to deal with this transit is to see just how much you can do without. You may be surprised at how little you need, and your burdens may be much lighter as a result. The influence of Saturn can cause you to be preoccupied with the material, but Neptune's square is a challenge to this aspect of Saturn. At the time you may not be very happy with the results, but it can be a positive experience, once you get over the initial fright.

This transit can also signify the onset of a slowly developing illness that debilitates the body. Have a thorough physical examination at this time·to make certain that everything is all right. It probably is, but do not take the chance.

Neptune Trine Saturn

During this period there is a balance between idealism and reality in your life, which enables you to work very hard in the most thorough and practical manner to actualize your ideals. You understand exactly what is true for you, and you are able to work within that structure to make changes. Your attitude toward the world is not pessimistic.

Because of your vast experience, you have come to know what you need and what you don't need. You are reluctant to saddle yourself with possessions that may be pleasant to own but that complicate your life. Others may think of you as rather abstemious and self-denying, but you don't deny yourself anything you really need; it is just that now you have a clearer idea of your future necessities.

This is an extremely good time to become involved in psychic, spiritual and occult studies. Your sense of reality is strong enough now to withstand the disorienting shock that many people receive when they begin to study these subjects, and it won't get in the way of your understanding. Under this transit your spiritual development is measured and disciplined. You may feel that work is the best path toward understanding.

No matter what your situation demands, you can make the necessary sacrifices now. You can work very hard in the pursuit of an ideal or be very self-denying in order to accomplish a task. But again, you are not really denying yourself — you simply have a very well-developed sense of priorities, which you follow carefully.

Others will feel that they can depend on you, because you do not seem to get upset by problems that make most people feel lost and disoriented. No matter how confused the situation, you can see and work with the underlying pattern. Because of this ability, you have a capacity for creative organization now that you may have lacked at other times.

Neptune Opposition Saturn

This is an extremely significant transit, but it is not usually very pleasant. During this period some aspect of your reality will be severely challenged in such a way that you will not know for a time what is real and what is not. Your sense of proportion will be distorted so that you place too much importance upon matters that do not deserve such emphasis and perhaps ignore the matters that really are important. And the matters that you are overemphasizing are those that make you afraid and fearful. In fact the chief problem with this transit is that it produces fear and anxiety for no apparent reason. With this transit you should always keep in mind the fact that things are almost certainly not as bad as they look.

However, in spite of the fear and depression that often accompany this transit, a very valuable change is taking place, and that is causing you to feel disoriented. Your perception of reality is being radically altered so that you can experience a vaster, more unlimited universe than you have ever known before. Exposure to this new perception triggers off your subconscious fear reactions. If you discover that what you have believed no longer applies, consider this an opportunity to find a larger truth. Don't wallow in fear — you will only lose this opportunity for growth. However, we are structured to react with great anxiety when this kind of influence enters our lives. You will feel that you literally cannot live without the structure that Saturn provides, even though it is often oppressive and incredibly limiting. When Neptune dissolves this structure, you are likely to react as if your life were being threatened.

This is an extremely good time to begin psychotherapy or to explore one of the varieties of human potential work. However, even in these areas you have to remain very flexible. Do not simply accept a rigid new reality in place of the old one, for then it will work out just as badly. Make whatever you encounter part of your new way of perceiving and experiencing the universe.

Relationships that develop now may greatly challenge your concept of reality. You may encounter someone who forces you to examine your world view and to defend it in a confrontation with his or her view. This may not be a pleasant encounter, but it is valuable to see how well you have thought out your position in life.

In some cases this transit may signify the onset of a long-term chronic illness. If you start treatment now, you can arrest it. Just to be safe, have a thorough physical if you have not had one recently.

Neptune Conjunct Uranus

Because Uranus moves faster than Neptune, this transit will happen later and later in people's lives as the twentieth century goes on. At this writing, in 1976, it is happening to people who are in their middle seventies. By 1984, it will be occurring for those who are eighty. Because I have not had the opportunity to observe its effects first hand, I cannot delineate it. However, I would expect its effects to be similar to those of Uranus conjunct Neptune.

Neptune Sextile Uranus

This transit awakens your interest in unusual, out-of-the ordinary states of being and consciousness. You suddenly become aware that life has a deeper dimension than you have previously known, and you want to learn everything you can about it. This transit can expand your consciousness greatly.

People react to these energies in various ways. If you are very much rooted in the material universe, regarding nothing as real unless you can touch it, you will become much more concerned about abstractions, principles that previously seemed too disconnected from the material world to be important. You may be surprised to discover that you actually do have ideals that you are willing to stand up for, even though you have always considered yourself a hard-headed pragmatist.

If you are among those who are less interested in purely material concerns, you will find your interests becoming even more spiritual. This transit can awaken an interest in the occult or in mysticism, and it is one of the transits under which people begin studying astrology and related subjects. Any technique that helps open up a new aspect of the universe will attract you at this time.

A related but somewhat different manifestation is that you may become involved in movements of social reform. You see that the world does not work as it should, and you want to work very hard to improve the lot of people who are less fortunate. While your views at this time are inclined to be idealistic, your idealism is not totally removed from reality. You can work with a situation as it really is in order to bring about the changes you want. Your activities along these lines could range from the relatively conservative approach of working with the poor, ill or disadvantaged in hospitals or other such institutions, to working with groups that have much more revolutionary aims.

Neptune Square Uranus

During this transit you will be subject to sudden changes of mood, and your opinions on many matters will change suddenly as well. You will be constantly exposed to other dimensions of reality that you may have long suspected were important in your life but were reluctant to acknowledge. This effect can manifest itself at many different levels. On the lowest level, it may simply indicate that something you have been trying to keep secret from others will be revealed suddenly. If this happens, it is just as well, because the secret was in some way limiting you and preventing you from growing. Or a secret that someone else has kept from you may be revealed with the same consequence. In either case your initial reaction is likely to be upset, not pleasure, because you really don't want to deal with what is revealed. However, if you do deal with it, your life will be greatly improved.

At another level, this transit will expose you to truths that you have never been willing to recognize about the world in general. You may discover that some point of view you have held is totally wrong. A person whom you had a definite opinion of, either positive or negative, may be quite different from what you thought. In any case the revelation will startle you and make you feel confused and disoriented. You may try to escape the truth of what you see. Some people may even resort to the use of drugs or alcohol.

At yet another level, this transit can expose you to profound psychic and mystical experiences, which also will upset you because they challenge your way of looking at the world. However, you should be careful about getting really involved in the occult or other spiritual-mystical fields. During this transit you are likely to be too upset to handle the knowledge you gain in any reasonable way. Do not attempt to place the insights you encounter into any kind of system. Allow yourself time to assimilate the material spontaneously and make it part of you. Then, after the effects of this transit have passed, you can begin to study these matters systematically if you still want to.

Neptune Trine Uranus

This transit will expose you to ways of looking at the world that are quite different from any you have known before. Uranus-Neptune rules alternate states of consciousness. However, the alternate states designated by this transit are not terrifying or confusing, as can be the case with some Neptune transits. Problems with drugs or peculiar mental conditions are not likely. Instead you are much more likely to experience a widening interest in the greater depths of the universe and an increased ability to perceive them. Your intuition will be enormously heightened at this time, and if you have any innate psychic talents, they will appear now. You will be increasingly interested in the occult and astrology, and these disciplines will give you understandings that you have never had before. It is quite likely that you will have an enlightenment experience — a perception of your true place in the universe — on some level that is meaningful to you.

Idealism is also part of your life now, but its nature is very abstract. You are much more interested in philosophical truth and absolutes than in practical reforms in the world around you. The exception to this is that you could become directly and practically involved with the plight of the underprivileged. You might work to reform conditions in a hospital or other such institution. Neptune always relates to the condition of the downtrodden, and Uranus rules reform in general.

Another consequence of this combination of symbols is that you may become involved with a religious or spiritual movement that works for social reform — a movement motivated not by political doctrines, such as Marxism, but by religious views, for example, the American Friends Service Committee.

Neptune Opposition Uranus

This transit represents an enormous revolution in your consciousness, as you are exposed to aspects of life that you never dreamed possible. And when you come to understand these aspects, your views about reality will have to change. In fact this revelation may come with such force that you will become involved in philosophies or movements whose purpose is to transform the world according to your new understanding. These philosophies might include any of the following: the occult or metaphysics; astrology; magic; altered states of consciousness, perhaps through drugs or meditation; or groups whose ideas are extremely idealistic and radical.

What is actually happening is that tremendous new understandings are asserting themselves in your life with such force that they seem to upset all your past ways of thinking. However, this is only a problem of perspective. At this time you are in the middle of these changes and cannot see the relationship between your new consciousness and your old. But they are related, which you will come to understand as the immediate impact of this transit begins to pass. Only then will you be able to take the necessary steps to incorporate your new insights into everyday life.

This is a period of tremendous psychological insight and change, but not much stability. Therefore keep your situation fluid enough that you can make changes as necessary. Do not try to build permanent structures at this time, because you will have to change them again and again. It should be noted, however, that the primary effects of this transit occur at the psychological level Your material universe will be affected only as it reflects your old psychological state of mind, which is being revolutionized.

Possibly you will respond to this transit with confusion, doubt and uncertainty. Let it be, and wait for the situation to settle down. Try to minimize the elements of your life that require you to make long-range commitments, because your changing consciousness will make it difficult to continue such a commitment. If old goals lose their meaning, that is what must be. Be patient, and new goals will enter your life that will better fit your new state of mind.

Others may think you have gone out of your mind because of what you do and see at this time, but do not be concerned. This revolution in ideas and consciousness is a fundamental part of your life, and it must be allowed to pursue its own course.

Neptune Conjunct Neptune

This transit does not happen to anyone except possibly right after birth.

Neptune Sextile Neptune

This transit occurs at about the same time as your first Saturn return (Saturn transiting conjunct your natal Saturn), and their effects are closely linked. This is a time of new awakening to a sense of what your life is about. Before this time you have been working to establish your sense of who you are in the community of adults, and by now you probably have a pretty clear idea about that. But you may also have discovered that what you are doing with your life is not entirely appropriate. You may conclude that in the past you were motivated by too narrow a conception of what you are, by a need for security, or simply by petty ego-drives.

Now, since this Neptune transit roughly coincides with the Saturn return and because Saturn is the principle of material reality, you will begin to see your life in terms of a larger perspective. You should do whatever is necessary to make sure that you can live according to this new understanding. This transit does not arouse your sense of idealism particularly, but it does make you see that the universe is a very large place, and you are a much larger part of it than you have realized.

You may be attracted to rather mystical ideas, but they will have meaning only according to how they affect your everyday world. At this time you don't need more abstractions to chase around — you need to make positive reforms in your life. And you will do so!

The combination of this transit and the return of Saturn will cause you to cut away your past and reorient your life in accordance with the larger vision you have now. The many changes that occur may seem somewhat scary (more because of the Saturn return than because of this transit), but they are ultimately for the best. You will find new freedom in a new consciousness.

Neptune Square Neptune

This transit is often a part of the "crisis of middle age," since it occurs when you are about forty-two. During this period you are likely to intensely question your life, your goals and how far you have fulfilled your ideals. Depending upon the results of that evaluation, you may begin to make certain changes. The problem is that Neptunian vibrations are not the best influence for making well-thought-out changes in your life. There is a great danger that you will go off half cocked in pursuit of some dream that is unrealizable and not even worth realizing. It is very important to use this period for self-scrutiny, but it is not a good idea to act yet.

If you act too quickly, you will only create severe disturbances in your emotional and domestic life or in your work. You are likely to operate on the basis of partially formed ideas about yourself and your needs. Unfortunately, since you are in your forties, you have probably convinced yourself that you know who and what you are. And perhaps you have known, but the function of this transit is to make you reevaluate who you are, which at this moment you do *not* know. The best solution is to recognize this situation and simply allow yourself to see the truth, whatever it may be. Give yourself plenty of latitude and have whatever experiences seem necessary. Just don't make any permanent commitments during this transit. You don't want to spend the rest of your life with the consequences of ill-considered actions taken under the influence of a passing delusion.

Many of the insights you receive during this period will be real, and many will not be real. Only the passage of time will allow you to determine which are which.

Neptune Trine Neptune

This transit occurs when you are fifty-five. It is a chance to examine your life and to see within it the seeds for something greater than you have imagined. This greatness is not in the material realm, nor will it give you power over others. Instead your opportunity is to see your life in a spiritual dimension that you have never before perceived. This can manifest itself in a number of ways.

First of all you may discover an increased empathy for the people in your everyday life. You can put yourself into another's place in a way that you have never been able to do before; you can see and, more importantly, feel what someone else feels. Consequently you will have more sympathy and compassion for other people's problems.

Your compassion springs from a realization of the essential unity of yourself and all being. For most people, this is not an entirely conscious realization. You may feel an increased involvement with others, but you don't quite know where it has come from. On the other hand, this can be a conscious feeling, in which case you may become more attracted to mystical philosophies and metaphysics, which try to verbalize what you are beginning to experience. You may experience a reawakened interest in religion, even if this has long been dormant in your life. Possibly you may even have a profound psychic or mystical experience.

Even if by temperament you are not inclined to mysticism, you will experience its effects as increased idealism and an increased willingness to work for the kind of world you want to see.

Whatever else may happen, you will feel more capable of selfless actions in your relationships with others. You will be willing to help, seeking little or nothing in return because your own ego seems less important to you now.

Neptune Opposition Neptune

This transit will not occur to anyone before they are in their mid-eighties. It comes at about the same time as the transit of Uranus conjunct Uranus and has much the same significance. It is a time in your life when the old categories of living and experience cease to have any real meaning for you. Your consciousness will be heightened, although your initial feeling is likely to be one of confusion. But you will be able to learn the lessons of this transit only if you are willing to be patient and allow the universe to reveal what it has to show you.

The general effect will be a blurring of categories, an ability to see relationships among things that you were never aware of before. You will have a better understanding of the inherent unity of all existence, which will be reflected in a greater empathy between you and others, an ability to put yourself in another person's place. You will learn many things, even after a full life of learning everything that you thought you could. And you will be in a position to teach others as well.

But these developments will come about only if you are willing to let go of old ideas. Otherwise this will be a time of confusion and defeat, when you feel that you must withdraw into yourself. This inner drive to withdraw is likely to be manifested as a need for some sort of hospitalization. Or you may choose to withdraw as a sign of completion rather than defeat, in which case this transit signifies that you will begin to find peace and respite. At your age, Neptune should not hold the horrors that it sometimes holds for younger people, unless you have become fearfully rigid.

Neptune Conjunct Pluto

This transit has not happened to anyone since the 1890s.

Neptune Sextile Pluto

During this time many aspects of the life you have known will pass out of existence, leaving you in a position to make a new start at a new level. This transit is not likely to be very troublesome under any circumstances, but it will be least difficult and most profitable if you don't try to hold on to whatever is leaving you right now. It is a natural part of life that everything must die and decay, to be reborn again at another level. This is the cycle you must go through now.

To a large extent, what happens to you now will be caused by larger forces for social change around you rather than by your individual actions. But make no mistake — you must respond to the energies of this transit in terms of your own everyday life.

Experiences may prove that beliefs and opinions you have held all your life are invalid, but this will not happen in such a shattering way that you lose all sense of direction. Instead you should feel that this is an opportunity to clear away the deadwood in your brain and start over again. Therefore this is an excellent time to undergo psycho-therapy, if you feel so inclined, or to explore any other mind-expanding philosophy of human potential. You will be in closer touch with your innermost psychological drives than at almost any other time of your life. This is not an opportunity to be wasted, especially since these energies may be operating much more benevolently than usual. Now you can do voluntarily what you would be forced to do at some other period in your life.

Neptune Square Pluto

This is a period of subtle psychological changes in your life that may have very dramatic consequences or that may not be at all obvious to others. It is hard to tell in advance which result is likely to occur.

In any case, you are changing inwardly very much, which will be reflected in your changing values. Matters that were once important to you are not any longer. But during this process you may have to deal with considerable tension, because you will feel pressures and compulsions surging inside of you that you have never felt before, which is rather disconcerting. You will find these new desires particularly upsetting if you have always stood in the background and let others get their own way at your expense, denying your own impulses. The changes might be a simple desire for more control over your life, eliminating elements that have bothered you. Or you could have a strong desire to destroy everything that has ever frustrated you or stood in your way. Most people will not react to this transit by acting destructively, but you are likely to feel some destructive impulses. These are the results of frustrated drives within you that you have never expressed adequately. Energies that you feel but don't express do not merely vanish; they go into a permanent reservoir within you from which they can later reemerge. This is the time when they will emerge.

It is especially important now that you get in touch with these internal compulsions. Therefore this is an excellent time to consider psychotherapy. Your repressed energies can be used positively to do a lot of creative work within your own psyche. They can also be very destructive, if you either try to suppress them further or simply allow them to explode.

These energies may be negatively expressed as subtly destructive or undermining actions either by you alone or with other people. Even if you have no conscious awareness of these energies, you are unconsciously programming your environment so that events work out in a negative way. If you find that people are working powerfully behind the scenes to do you damage, it is probably an inevitable reflection of the negative energy within you. Often you acquire enemies who try to harm you secretly because your methods leave them no room to oppose you openly. A secret enemy is often someone whom you have frustrated completely, who feels that he or she has nothing to gain by direct confrontation. This is a reflection of those aspects of yourself that you will not confront directly, so the only solution is to confront them!

Neptune Trine Pluto

This transit quickens your interest in the hidden psychological forces that are operating in your life. This can happen in several ways.

First, you may become involved in a group or movement whose purpose is to expand consciousness — for example, one of the various human-potential groups that are thriving today. You may not feel satisfied with the way you have managed your life up till now, and you want to understand and gain greater control of the strange compulsions that everyone experiences from time to time, often with disastrous results. These compulsions are emotionally based drives that seem to operate without any bidding from the conscious mind. They often make you behave in ways that are not appropriate to the situation. Under this transit you will want to change this aspect of your mind, so this is a good time to begin psychotherapy, if you feel that is the best course to take.

Another effect of this transit is to create interest in mystical and occult subjects, again with the aim of increasing your understanding of the universe and of yourself. You are not interested in power over others, which attracts some people to these subjects, or in mystery for its own sake. You are interested in learning what the deepest aspects of the universe can teach you about self-mastery.

If you have already embarked on such a path, you may very well make a significant breakthrough in your search now. Your soul-life may reach an intensity that you have never felt before, increasing your understanding with totally unprecedented insights. But this knowledge will not be abstract — it will transform your life and your ability to experience it.

Neptune Opposition Pluto

This transit will occur to most persons now living when they are in their early sixties or later. It signifies encounters that cause various aspects of your life to be transformed. Most commonly, this transformation will take the form of disappearances of persons, circumstances or even possessions that you have become used to. You will also encounter forces that try to reveal aspects of your life that you have long kept hidden from yourself. Initially you will probably resist these revelations, believing that they cannot teach you anything very constructive. A transit like this often reveals aspects of ourselves that we have been taught to consider evil or at least negative. These aspects are often a source of positive energy, but because we refuse to acknowledge them, that energy is wasted and is usually out of our control. There will be much psychological compulsiveness at this time, but the less you resist facing yourself, the less difficulty you will have.

On another level you will be shown a spiritual dimension of your existence that can immensely broaden your life and experience, if you are willing to look at it. This dimension may seem so far beyond your ordinary life that you will consider it impossible to accept, but this knowledge is necessary for your growth.

On a practical level, avoid taking at face value any new encounters with persons or circumstances. Even when persons are not trying to deceive you, they may do so unintentionally, because you won't immediately understand what they are really showing you. Until you have arrived at this level of understanding, simply adopt a waiting attitude and commit yourself to as little as possible.

Neptune Conjunct Midheaven

This transit can have a very powerful effect on your life direction from this point on, as well as a very powerful effect on your view of yourself.

Very commonly this transit brings sudden confusion to people who have had a pretty clear idea of what they want to do with their lives. You may feel as if you have suddenly become lost, although the way had seemed very clear. If possible, do not make any permanent decisions about your career or long-term direction during this transit.

Among the problems you may encounter is a feeling that what you have been doing is inadequate. You may feel that your work is too restrictive, that you have to be too concerned with ordinary mundane reality. You may suddenly be attracted to a wildly romantic, idealized way of life that seems very plausible to you now, although later it will seem ridiculous. You may be attracted to working with people in hospitals, charities or other social-service institutions. This is a perfectly positive direction, but you should examine your motives for doing this work. Are you doing it because you feel personally unworthy and think that working with the downtrodden will make you feel better by comparison? Or are you somehow going to bring them the "truth"? If either of these is in any way true, forget this kind of work, or at least wait until the transit is over.

During this period you may also be attracted to mystical and spiritual subjects, especially philosophies of ego-denial and abandonment such as are taught in many Eastern sects. You may be particularly attracted to a movement led by a charismatic guru-father figure. In general Neptune on the MC is a sign of idealized father figures. Little harm is likely to come of this, and there may be great benefits, but again do not make a permanent commitment until the transit is over.

Above all, this is a transit of ego-transcendence, that is, of climbing to a state of consciousness in which your ego needs are no longer the determining factor in your life. However, your ego must be fully matured and completely developed before this can happen. Otherwise you will simply find yourself confused and deluded. Some of the greatest and fattest egos in history have been people who thought they were giving themselves up for their God, when they were really identifying themselves with God. This is a negative Neptune manifestation.

If feelings of defeat and weariness arise during this transit, do not allow yourself to succumb to them. You are no worse than what you have always been. You may discover that you have been excessively concerned about yourself and made yourself too important, but you shouldn't berate yourself for that. Everyone does it at some time. Meanwhile open yourself up to the very splendid influences that can come into your life now and teach you much about the nature of the cosmos. Much of what you learn now will later prove to be of permanent value.

Neptune Sextile Midheaven

At this time in your life you are likely to change your objectives in a way that your friends may see as hopelessly idealistic and impractical, but to you it seems the only way to give your life real meaning. The chances are that both you and your friends are right to some extent, so your task now is to strike a balance between your spiritual and your material goals. No way of life will be good for you unless you can make it work in the real world somehow, although right now you may not be very concerned with the real world.

Often this transit signifies a new interest in spiritual, metaphysical and occult subjects. You have a great need for deep spiritual understanding, and you may turn to religion, probably a mystical sect that emphasizes direct experience of the divine, rather than an orthodox church.

The most positive effect of this transit is that it teaches you that you must get your ego out of the way before you can do anything good with it. That is, you have to learn to act without selfishness, to flow along with events as they happen without having a stake in a particular outcome. If you can do this, you will gain a great deal of wisdom from this transit without losing anything.

Some persons experience psychic ability under this transit, and there is evidence that most people have some psychic ability. However, you should not expect to necessarily experience anything more than heightened intuition, which can easily be destroyed by too much reliance on your rational intellect. In fact, one positive truth that you may learn under this transit is that even at best the rational intellect is limited and cannot deal with every aspect of life. You will learn this through your own intuitive faculties telling you, if you let them, things that you could never possibly know through the rational mind.

This transit is likely to be somewhat disturbing if you insist that all knowledge must come in neat, packaged categories, as happens with the Saturnian intellect. Neptunian truth comes in its own ways.

Neptune Square Midheaven

This time in your life is likely to be confusing and full of doubt and fear, if you are not very secure about your life direction. You will ask fundamental questions about what you are trying to do with your life as a whole. And if you, like many people, are not living for yourself and your own objectives, you will probably conclude that what you are doing is worthless and pointless. Even at best you will question your planned course.

In dealing with others, you may find it difficult to stand up for your own position because you are questioning it so much yourself. You may allow yourself to become the victim of other people, simply because you lack the confidence to fight back. But a far worse effect of this transit is that you might get into a routine of making yourself seem to be a victim in order to gain others' sympathy. This kind of negative aggression is characteristic of Neptune, because it enables you to avoid taking responsibility for your own actions. It is difficult to take responsibility when you are feeling insecure.

For this same reason there is a strong temptation to avoid direct confrontations with others for fear that you cannot stand up to them. Therefore you may try to get what you want from people in covert or subversive ways, usually involving some kind of dishonesty. Needless to say, this will only worsen your insecurity, not give you more confidence.

But all of the above concerns the worst side of this transit, which does have something positive to teach you. Even as you suffer apparent defeats, you may discover that what you are losing is not really anything significant. You may learn that the needs of your ego are not your real needs at all. Under this transit some persons find a capacity for selfless action and spiritual self-denial that makes it impossible for them ever to lose in a way that hurts them. In that case you will learn that there is really nothing to lose. This transit can be the gateway to a very highly evolved spiritual understanding, and it is quite likely that you will become increasingly involved with spiritual teachings and disciplines. However, it is possible to go off the deep end spiritually, and this transit may very well delude you into doing so. But in the long run this is one of the less dangerous traps of Neptune.

Neptune Trine Midheaven

Under the influence of this transit you are likely to deemphasize practical and material concerns in favor of spiritual understanding and truth. And this can be a very positive thing, so long as you do not completely ignore the affairs of the material world. You must remain connected with the practical world but keep it from overwhelming your consciousness.

Under this transit you become more involved in service to others, perhaps on a personal level by taking care of someone who is close to you or perhaps through an institution, where you help take care of the poor or disadvantaged. You may have to take care of a sick friend or loved one.

On the other hand, you may change to a field of work in which social service is the goal. Welfare or social work and nursing — particularly psychiatric nursing — are appropriate to this transit. What happens is that you identify your personal gratification with service to the larger social order. Personal reward or personal recognition for your efforts are not important to you now, and you may be quite content to work behind the scenes.

On the negative side, your own ego drives are usually not very strong under this transit, which is why you are able to engage in the kinds of work described above. But this means that you may not stand up for your own valid interests or take adequate care of your own world. Sometimes personal relationships suffer at times like this because you don't consider them important enough. You think that they are only gratifying to you personally and are therefore not significant. If that is the case, you are forgetting that you must take care of your personal needs, not merely to gratify your ego, but also to make you a healthy and happy human being. Only if you are happy and healthy can you be really effective. One cannot live on self-sacrifice forever, and if you try, you are likely to become a depressing and joyless person. Those who are most effective in helping society are also able to enjoy themselves.

Neptune Opposition Midheaven

The danger of this transit is that it is likely to kick your props out from under you. In your job or any other activity that is important to you, something may happen that will make it very difficult to continue in your present direction. This event is probably not something that can easily be foreseen, and it will be difficult to describe even as it is happening. It can take the form of a psychological crisis that results in your feeling that you cannot go on. You may feel suddenly weak and ineffectual, even though others may not be able to see any reason for this. It is also possible that events in your most personal life will make it difficult to continue in your profession with the self-confidence and assurance that you need to be at your best. There may be domestic problems or difficulties with members of your immediate family. Someone very close to you may be doing or saying things to you that are very discouraging.

But this transit can also have another effect. You may no longer feel like advancing in your external social roles now, because you feel they have become meaningless and empty. You may want to withdraw a bit and look at your life in terms of your own criteria instead of others' and ask whether you are accomplishing what you yourself want to, rather than what others want. Sometimes in life we go ahead too fast and lose track of our original purposes. This is an excellent time to sit back and look at whether this has happened to you.

Many important elements of your life may come to an end and pass out of existence now. Let them go, for it is the right time for this to happen, and it will ultimately be good. This is a time to renounce those things, for you will soon discover that you do not really need them anyway. As the old saying goes, we are naked when we come into this world and when we leave it. Therefore what we have inside is important. Now is the time for you to find the strength of what you have inside.

Neptune Conjunct Ascendant

This transit will alter your relationships with others and change the kind of impression you make on people. The greatest single danger is that you are susceptible to deception by others, because you are in an unusually idealistic frame of mind, and you believe in the merit of proposals that you are invited to join, even when they are useless. In fact, with your excessive idealism, you are likely to get involved in many situations that you would usually avoid. Relationships, in particular, should be watched, for you are inclined to idealize people, especially a lover, and be blind to their real faults. Those faults may not be all that bad, but in your present frame of mind you probably would not be able to accept the truth. And when you finally do accept it, you will be disappointed. Do not expect more of others now than you could reasonably expect at other times. People are people, although you may lose sight of that fact while Neptune is transiting your Ascendant.

At the same time, there is a danger that you might lose sight of who you are and what your limitations are. You may expect too much of yourself, or you may think that you impress others in certain ways that are not at all true. If you feel that others like you, it may be that you are utterly unaware of certain complaints they have about you. And they may not be bothered at all by habits you think they really dislike, which you try to repress.

There is one constructive aspect of the idealism that this transit may engender. You may become attracted to social-service work with poor, sick or disadvantaged people. Under this influence you are inclined to put your own needs second to the needs of others and to take upon yourself a ministering role. Just be sure that you have the strength to do this, for idealism alone can't carry you through. You should be prepared to put up with the very real obstacles that will arise. If you have an idealized image of yourself as a selfless savior, you are almost certainly kidding yourself, and you won't be effective at all.

In relationships with others you may be inclined to play a martyr role. Stand up to people for what you believe to be your personal rights and do not pretend that things don't bother you if they do. If you play the martyr, someone else will surely be willing to play the role of persecutor. This applies especially in love relationships.

You may also become more interested in psychic, spiritual and religious matters during this time, but since you are searching for direct experience of the divine, you are unwilling to put up with movements that are excessively formal, ritualized or intellectual. Consequently you will probably not be attracted to an orthodox church.

Neptune Sextile Ascendant

This transit will change your relationships with people, usually in a positive way, although there are some pitfalls to be observed.

The principal effect of this transit is to greatly heighten your sensitivity to the feelings of other people. You become aware, at least on a subliminal level, of the deeper and more complex attributes of friends, neighbors and those whom you contact on a day-to-day level. Persons whom you have taken for granted now assume a very different look as you go below their surface appearance and look into their hearts. Thus you are able to be much more compassionate and giving to those around you. You may also become more interested in the plight of disadvantaged groups, which may lead to working with a charitable organization or an informal group to help these people. But even in your everyday contacts you act more selflessly and with greater understanding.

Someone may enter your life in very casual guise who will show you deep spiritual truths. And you may become involved in spiritual or religious groups in which you can share the new understanding of this transit. You may study mystical philosophy and metaphysics for the first time in your life.

But no matter how you react to this influence, the central issue is that in your immediate environment you learn to act toward others with much less ego involvement. You are less selfish and not so concerned with getting your own way.

The danger of this transit is that you may overidealize people, especially acquaintances who have made a profound impression upon you. You may regard them as spiritually and morally superior to any of your old friends, whom you may neglect as a result. The important point here is that these new people in your life are human also, and they may still have something to teach you. Most of us have a strong tendency to think that only a very spiritually elevated person can teach us about higher truth. With this transit you will learn about higher truth through everyday contacts. Do not invalidate what you learn from these people simply because you discover that they are only human.

Neptune Square Ascendant

At this time in your life your relationships with others are likely to become confused and difficult. You may encounter persons who try to dissuade you from a course of action that you have been committed to for years, with the result that you become confused about the direction of your life. The other person's intentions in this may be either good or bad.

This is not a good time to become involved in any kind of contractual or business negotiations. Even if the people whom you are dealing with are completely honest — and with this transit they may very well be dishonest — you will find it difficult to think clearly about your own goals and objectives in the negotiations. As a result you will not get what you want from the procedure.

Neptune is an ego-denying planet. That is, it has the inherent effect of making you feel unsure of yourself or unworthy and undeserving. Thus in your transactions with others, you tend to be not very assertive about protecting your interests, and you may attract people who will take advantage of your vulnerability.

On the metaphysical plane there is a lesson to be learned from this transit. Neptune is related to detachment, so that the less involved your ego is in a situation, the more freedom you will have to do what you want. By bringing about a loss, Neptune often shows us that our attachment to material objects or to certain personal relationships has prevented us from being free. So it is not usually Neptune that causes losses or confusion, but your ego's relentless drive to maintain the game it is playing. And this may be happening at your expense, when viewed from a higher perspective. When your ego takes over in this way, you set your priorities incorrectly, and you are not likely to be successful.

The strategy with this transit, as with other transits of Neptune that are commonly considered difficult, is to flow through it without any particular set plan of action nor any special objective. Simply treat this transit as a learning experience. If a relationship doesn't work out, ask yourself why you got into it in the first place. If you attract dishonest people or if your dishonesty has brought you trouble, ask yourself what purpose this served in your life. Often you will discover that you were trying to protect something that really wasn't worth protecting.

Neptune Trine Ascendant

Under this transit your relationships take on a spiritual cast, and you are much more inclined to idealize the people you meet. If a lover comes into your life at this time, the relationship will be so romanticized that it will be in great danger when you discover that the other person is not as perfect as you thought. Overidealization in any relationship is a danger to be watched for with this transit.

There is also a strong tendency to get caught up in an ideal philosophy, a spiritualized world view that is so abstract and removed from the real world that you are neither able nor willing to function here. You may have a strong desire to escape and withdraw from the world, which can be useful in some cases. If you are aware of this tendency and know that it is temporary, you can make positive use of it. There are times when it is important to go off by yourself and meditate upon the meaning of your life and what you are doing with it. The only problem is that you probably cannot go off for the whole duration of this transit, because it usually lasts more than a year. But for part of the time this might be a desirable plan of action.

A spiritual teacher or guide figure may enter your life at this time, and regardless of his or her personal merits you are likely to learn something valuable from the encounter. That does not mean that you should take everything you are told at face value. After this influence has passed, you will be able to reevaluate what you have learned in the light of your own intelligence and experience. At this time your ego drives are rather low, which makes you less interested in questioning what someone tells you. You reflect very strongly on your own failures and inadequacies, not destructively, but with the aim of improving yourself. Nevertheless, you judge everyone and everything but yourself uncritically. Eventually you will learn that you, too, are a source of spiritual truth, and that it is all right to question what another tells you, although that might be your own ego at work.

As with the sextile transit, your relationships are characterized by increased empathy and spiritual understanding of other people's situations and needs.

Neptune Opposition Ascendant

At this time your close, intimate relationships will be difficult and confused. Also you should be very careful about consulting others for advice now, even professionals such as lawyers, marriage counselors or doctors. Of course, not all of these people will give you erroneous information even under this transit, but you would be well advised not to suspend your own critical faculties just because someone else seems to be an "expert."

A marriage or other partnership will be difficult because communications are unclear now. Perhaps either you or your partner is trying to conceal something from the other. If so, you should stop concealing it as soon as possible, for it can only undermine the confidence you must have in each other. Even if you are concealing something for the other's "own good," your partner will not see it that way, and his or her confidence will still be undermined.

However, you may not be hiding anything. It may just be that communications between you are getting worse. Make sure that you really understand each other, and do not assume that you understand or that anything you say or do is understood automatically. Spontaneous and immediate understanding is not a feature of this transit.

Avoid legal confrontations at this time, if at all possible. Completely unexpected events are likely to happen, which you won't be prepared for. And your opponent may use underhanded tactics that could hurt your position badly. In general your enemies, if you have any, will be very deceptive during this transit. It will be very hard to understand their tactics, let alone deal with them. They may even make false overtures of friendliness to you. Do not treat everyone with suspicion, but don't take everything at face value either.

At this time you may be tempted to take on a relationship with someone who badly needs help. This is perfectly appropriate, so long as your objective is to help that person, not to bolster your own image of yourself. Sometimes, if you are surrounded by people who are worse off, you can deceive yourself into thinking that your situation is all right even when it isn't. Also it is best to avoid a close, personal relationship with someone who really needs help, because it could become a very sick dependency relationship that would be very hard to break. This is especially true in relationships with the opposite sex.

Chapter Thirteen

Pluto

Significance of Transiting Pluto

The nature of Pluto is similar to that of the Hindu god Shiva, the creator and destroyer. Pluto usually begins by breaking down a structure; then it creates a new one in its place. This entire cycle of death, destruction and renovation is accompanied by tremendous powers, for Pluto is not a mild or even very subtle planetary influence. You can always see its effects very clearly — ranging from machines breaking down and needing repair to full-scale destruction or death. Decay at one level or another, followed by new life from the old is the typical Plutonian process.

Characteristically Plutonian people are those who seek to change, transform and take control of everything around them. Often a Pluto transit will signify the arrival of a person who transforms your life, either for good or evil. Or it can symbolize an event or circumstance that has the same effect.

Pluto also rules those energies inside you that lead inexorably to change. It rules the death and regeneration of the self, as old aspects of your life pass away and are replaced by new ones that could not otherwise have come into being. Pluto does not signify death in the literal sense; instead it refers to a metaphorical death, something that ceases to be.

The energies of the planet that Pluto is transiting become a source of change and transformation in your life. You may get involved in serious power struggles with others about changes in the areas of your life associated with that planet.

As Pluto transits your houses, it signifies the areas of your life that are due for radical transformation. In the area ruled by the transited house, structures in your life have built up to the point that it is no longer possible to patch up whatever is wrong. It is time for a full-scale reconstruction, preceded if necessary by destruction of the old change-resistant patterns.

It is extremely important that you recognize the inevitability of Plutonian change, which is built into the very structure of things and cannot be prevented. And you should not try to prevent it, because it is a necessary stage in your evolution. All that you will do is force the energies to build up until they are explosive. Then the inevitable changes come about disastrously.

Not only should you go along with the Plutonian energy of destruction by letting go of whatever must depart, you should also assist the rebuilding process that follows, for this is the equally inevitable consequence of the Plutonian breakdown.

For reasons that are not entirely understood, Pluto also has to do with secretive and subversive elements of society — revolutionary groups, organized crime and the like. A Pluto transit may bring such elements into your life, although it is often quite dangerous to allow this during a Pluto transit.

Pluto in the First House

At this time you will gradually reshape many aspects of your personality, and you will have the opportunity to get in touch with the forces that have shaped you and made you what you are. Getting in touch with yourself in this manner is especially helpful because it gives you greater control over the unconscious drives that in the past have surfaced in subconsciously directed urges, compulsions and irrational impulses. You will also gain greater control over the ways in which you project your personality to others, which will make your relationships more rewarding.

However, en route to this desirable goal of self-improvement, you will have to meet certain challenges in order to make anything good come out of this period.

First, you will find energies rising within you that want to control everything and everyone around, which could make relationships with others exceedingly difficult, if you are not careful. Now you have the chance to be either a positive or a negative force for change in the world around you, but you will almost certainly be a negative force if you don't make the effort to understand yourself. You will be the vehicle for blind and irrational ego forces, the result of infantile and primitive urges that you haven't dealt with as an adult. These forces are not directed toward what is best for you. But if you understand yourself well, you will be able to bring about a complete rebirth of energy and effectiveness in your life.

Fortunately, under the influence of this transit you will be more and more driven to seek out the inner dimensions of life. You will be attracted to the mysteries and hidden aspects of life, which will make you very interested in your own and other people's inner workings. This same interest may lead into the study of astrology, yoga and other occult or spiritual doctrines whose purpose is the total regeneration of the self.

Pluto in the Second House

During the next several years your values will undergo a complete metamorphosis, which will affect both your personal possessions on the material plane and your sense of values on the psychological level.

The process may include major changes in your financial picture over the next several years. The most upsetting aspect of this change is that quite frequently it begins with a breakdown phase, in which you may have to get along with much less in the way of resources. In a business, for example, circumstances beyond your control might lessen your volume of business, or you might have difficulty borrowing money. You might have to change the source of your income, resulting in less income during the changeover. If you own property, you might have to invest considerable money in repairs or modernization. Your material base, no matter what it is now, will change enough that it will be hard to count upon your accustomed income.

You are by no means doomed to poverty, however. This is a temporary phase that will pass as soon as the breakdown phase of this transit is finished. If you try to hold on to the possessions or sources of income you are used to, you will only slow down the process and delay the beginning of the new phase.

At another level, your whole attitude toward property may change completely. You may come around to the view that physical property is not so important to you. Metaphysical and moral values may become more important, so that you no longer seek to acquire material possessions. Considering how little control we have over the material universe, it is a little ridiculous that we put so much stock in it, thereby putting a large part of our lives at the mercy of fate, so to speak. Only our inner values are within our total control.

Pluto in the Third House

Everyday contacts, everyday communications and conversations take on a much heavier tone while Pluto transits this house. Elements of your everyday life that you normally take for granted — neighbors, immediate relatives, daily business and other such routine matters — now become fraught with significance. You may be forced to examine your day-to-day actions as you have never done before. Great changes are taking place in you, triggered by circumstances in your immediate environment. Situations that you have been contending with for years and have come to regard as a permanent part of your life may now reach the crisis point. You will be forced to do something about them now, and indeed you should. This is the beginning of a period of deep psychological change and inner regeneration that will continue for many years and reach another phase when Pluto enters your fourth house.

It will be necessary to examine your everyday beliefs, for the ideas that you have held to be true without question may be undermining your life in some subtle way that will now come out into the open. It is not a good idea to take anything for granted during this time, because repressed psychological tensions will inevitably surface. You will find it very difficult to keep problems buried, and it will become even more difficult as time goes on. Expect a period of acute self-questioning for the next several years. However, you should not assume that you are wrong about everything. Not taking things for granted does not mean that you have been wrong about them. It only means that you have become so used to them that they no longer register in your life, and it is time to become aware of them again. To be aware is to experience, which makes life much more interesting in the long run, although it may be rather upsetting at first.

Do not settle for superficial explanations, although it is unlikely that you will. You should try to get as close as possible to the inner workings of elements in your life. You may become interested in psychology, yoga and occult studies, although in this phase you will probably study them as intellectual disciplines rather than apply them to yourself as living experiences. That will come when Pluto enters the fourth house.

Changes of scene and traveling over short distances may trigger off important changes that will have far-reaching effects. Wherever you go, strive to gain a new perspective that will enable you to understand your everyday world a little more deeply.

Pluto in the Fourth House

The tremendous psychological changes of the last several years with Pluto transiting your natal third house continue now as Pluto enters the fourth house. But now the effects become much deeper, more internal and personal. Your inner psyche, your home, your family and the other most personal areas of your life will be affected.

On the psychological level, you may have to deal at last with certain problems that you have been living with since childhood. In fact, many issues from childhood will reemerge now, as you begin to understand their consequences to you as an adult. You will no longer be satisfied to just live with them. You want change, and you will be able to change at the most fundamental levels now. The irrational compulsions and inappropriate childish behavior that most of us indulge in under certain conditions will be called into the light and examined. This is generally an excellent period to undergo psychotherapy or a similar process if you feel that it might be useful. However, this is not to say that it will be necessary. Even without psychotherapy you will undergo tremendous inward changes.

On a more exterior level your home life may change tremendously. There can be a number of possible causes for this, including a change of residence; changes within the house, such as extensive repair or remodeling; changes within your family, such as divorce, death or other separations; or a tremendous change in the nature of your family relationships.

Your relationships with your parents are likely to change a great deal. If you have been overly dependent upon them for any reason, you may find it necessary to break away from them. You may have a rather serious power struggle with your parents under this transit, if they try to hold on to you as if you were still a child. But the changes within your family or between you and your parents need not be negative by any means. All that can be said for sure is that they will certainly be significant and that when this transit is over a new order will begin.

Pluto in the Fifth House

The impact of this transit can have many consequences, because the fifth house rules several areas of your life. It relates on one hand to recreation and amusement in the literal sense of the word, and on the other hand to children, who are a re-creation of the self in another sense.

If you have children, this is likely to be a fateful period in your life with them. The precise nature of this fatefulness is not easy to pin down, but it isn't necessarily bad.

But your relationships with your children are now entering a phase in which everything you do with them will have a powerful effect on them later. So it is important to be careful and to use common sense when dealing with your children.

Specifically, this transit can relate to periods of tension between you and your children as you attempt to apply too much pressure upon them — or vice versa — to change in some way: in other words, a power struggle with your children. If there are severe afflictions to planets in this house and if other transits warrant it, this can also be a dangerous period for your children. Suffice to say that during this time it would not be a good idea to take unnecessary risks with your children's health.

The fifth is also the house of love affairs, that is, the early phase of a relationship between two people who enjoy being together, as opposed to a serious commitment (a seventh-house relationship). With Pluto in the fifth house, a love affair is likely to be very heavy, very emotionally involved and intense. You are likely to regard your relationships as fated, which is not bad in itself, but it could distort your sense of proportion. Also be wary of a relationship in which you feel totally fascinated by someone whom you know is not good for you as a partner. Your subconscious may be playing tricks and getting you into something that you don't need. An existing love relationship will be very intense during this period and will go through a complete change. It is unlikely that a relationship in severe trouble will survive this period, but if it does it will last forever.

The fifth house also relates to creative self-expression, art and other forms of recreation in the more usual sense of the word. During this time you will be attracted to activities that are very powerful and involving, that may even carry a risk of life, because you want to experience everything you do very intensely. Superficial experiences do not attract you at all.

Pluto in the Sixth House

First, be very careful of your health under this transit. During these years you are likely to overstrain yourself physically and pay inadequate attention to your body's needs. Also, for years you may have had a physical condition that you haven't considered worth attending to, but now it may reach a critical point so that you have to do something about it. At its most severe, this transit can produce a complete physical breakdown. But this is likely only if you completely ignore your health needs as mentioned above, so this problem can easily be avoided.

In fact this transit can also indicate complete physical regeneration. If you adopt a careful physical regimen now you can rebuild your body even if you have neglected it in previous years. It is a good time to take up yoga or a similar physical-spiritual body culture. This is also a good time to examine your diet and how your body reacts to it. If necessary, change your diet for one that is more suitable to your individual needs. Be careful of fad diets that assume everyone's needs to be identical or that are based solely on religious principles with little scientific backup. A poor diet can lead to physical breakdown at this time.

481

The sixth house also concerns your work, either at a job or wherever you perform duties on a day-to-day basis. Pluto's transit through this house is as likely to affect this part of your life as it is to affect your health. You can expect great changes in your work, possibly a complete change of job or even career. There may be a difficult period of tension, because Pluto creates tension with people in your job, particularly bosses. You may be compelled to look elsewhere for work even if you don't want to. If this kind of tension arises, it is probably best to get another job. You may change jobs frequently as you cast about for the proper situation. It may take several years to find it, but when Pluto gets near the end of this house, you probably will.

It is quite possible that you will get into a line of work that is Plutonian in nature, a job that involves tearing something down in order to build anew, such as wrecking. Work that involves regenerative therapies, either physical or psychological, is Plutonian. Or your work may deal with secret or subversive elements of society or with secret projects.

Pluto in the Seventh House

At this time either all of your relationships and partnerships will go through profound and significant transformations, or your life will be transformed through a close encounter with another person. The relationships affected include your marriage or other close love relationship, partnerships in business, encounters with enemies or with people whom you consult (lawyers, doctors, psychiatrists and the like) and any other one-to-one relationships.

In a marriage or love affair, this transit signifies a profound change through or within the relationship. The two of you may reach a crisis that requires you to redefine the entire nature of your relationship. You may discover that long-hidden tensions within your relationship cannot remain that way and must be released now. A business partnership may go through a similar transformation. A marriage or business partnership that is not basically sound will probably not survive this transit.

Obviously, for most persons this is not a particularly good time to start a business partnership or marriage. The energies present in such a relationship may make it difficult for you to settle down into any kind of comfortable routine. In a marriage, particularly, you may be operating under unconscious compulsions that make it difficult to create a structure that is in your interests in the long run. Some people, however, need the emotional intensity in a relationship that this transit indicates. For such persons marriage at this time is quite all right.

Encounters with others, including professional consultants as listed above, may bring about significant changes in your life. Pluto transiting this house often signifies that you are looking for someone to aid you in transforming your life. This transit often coincides with psychotherapy. Just don't expect the therapist to do all the work for you.

It is important to avoid power struggles with enemies during this time, for they are likely to be extremely nasty and destructive, with no bar on dirty tactics. If you do become involved in such a conflict, expect your opponent to use every sneaky device in the book to thwart you. But I don't recommend that you reciprocate in kind. Aside from ethical considerations, you would not be very successful. This transit is much more likely to mean receiving underhanded treatment than giving it.

The people you encounter during these years who will affect your life so strongly are only mirrors of your inner psychic impulses. Stop attributing everything that happens to you — good or bad — to other people and begin to recognize that you trigger off these encounters by subtle unconscious cues. When you learn this you will receive the real understanding of your life that this transit can convey.

Pluto in the Eighth House

In many ways Pluto is "at home" with this transit, since its symbolism is very closely related to that of the eighth house. Both relate to death and resurrection symbolically as well as literally.

During this transit the issues of major transformation — even death, rebirth and regeneration — will become more significant in your life than ever before. Although your own life is not in any great danger, there may be deaths of people around you that will have a very important effect upon you. Such a death may radically change your life circumstances in some way or force a confrontation within you about the nature and meaning of your life. In general your concerns will become quite deep during this transit.

You may become involved in the occult or other teachings that relate to the issue of life and death. You will find it difficult to accept explanations that do not get to the very bottom of the matter and explore its innermost parts. This will be true for every question you ask, not only questions of your own life and death. You are seeking the answers to mysteries.

On an entirely different level, this transit can affect possessions and resources held jointly with others — a spouse's finances, for example, or corporate finances. A major change may occur in your life through one of these sources. This is not a good time to go into debt, because indebtedness will put you very much under someone else's control.

One possibility that combines both principal themes of this transit is that of an inheritance. However, for this to happen there should be other transits that reinforce this possibility, as well as indications in your natal chart.

Pluto in the Ninth House

During the next several years your overall view of the world around you will change considerably, often because of crises in your life that demonstrate the invalidity of your former views. At the same time, however, it will be obvious that your ability to see and understand the world in depth and your wisdom in handling it will grow and deepen. There is no reason to fear this transit. At worst it is a maturing experience, but at best it will transform you into a far better human being. You should strive to learn everything you can from the experiences you have in this period, because the knowledge you gain will be extremely useful during the transit of Pluto through your tenth house, which follows this one. You needn't be in a hurry, however, because this transit will take several years.

Whatever your interests and concerns prior to this transit, you will turn now to more profound subjects, such as your relationship to the people around you and to the universe, as well as your role in the general scheme. You may turn to religion if it can give you the deep and intimate experience that you need at this time. Pluto brings knowledge, not through the mind but through the viscera. The mind cannot comprehend this knowledge, it must be an experience. Mystical and occult philosophies may attract you because of their direct appeal to the inner being.

But remember that your knowledge-bringing experiences now are extremely powerful, and you will take everything that comes as profound and powerful. You must avoid the danger of becoming fanatically obsessed by these experiences. Pluto always tends to produce obsessions, and during this time you may be inclined to cram everything you have learned down other people's throats. Your conviction will help you persuade others of what you have learned, but give them the chance to keep their own views as well.

Since the ninth house is concerned with your relationship to the larger social order, this transit can cause you to become involved in a group or movement that wants to transform society, but probably not in a revolutionary way. Pluto operates more slowly and effectively.

If you have difficult aspects in this house, Pluto may cause difficulties with the law if you are not careful. This would be likely to happen if, convinced of your own righteousness, you operate without considering the ideas of others. If you keep in mind the context of your actions and their appropriateness as far as society is concerned, you should have no trouble.

Pluto in the Tenth House

This is a most important time in your life, for you will strive to achieve more now than you ever have before. You aim to make the greatest possible mark upon the world, and now is the time to do it, but only if you have truly found out who you are and what your life is about. If you haven't found out, now is the time to do so. Pluto gives you either the power to achieve your life goals or the insight to find out what they truly are. Consequently, if you are secure and knowing about yourself, you have the opportunity for great success, as long as you heed certain warnings. If you do not know your goals, you will probably change your path. You may change jobs rather often and spend several years apparently quite lost, while you find out what you are supposed to be doing.

However, let us return to your striving for success and self-realization. Pluto arouses your ambitions, the desire to take control and dominate. Its action can be quite ruthless, like a force of nature that has no regard for human standards of morality and ethics. But people who act like this under the influence of Pluto are often quite tragic.

Having thrown away their humanity, they discover that they can expect no quarter from others who unite to oppose them, and they are brought down. It is essential that you avoid wreaking havoc or even bending the standards of ethics with this transit, for Pluto's energies are too powerful to play games with. Play the game fairly and according to the rules, but continue to pursue your goals. Do not take shortcuts.

If you experience the other side of this transit as altering your life direction, the important idea is not to get discouraged. You may undergo considerable changes during this transit, and you may even feel that you have become a different person, which is probably true. Take all the time you need to find the right course. If you hurry you will only get into another wrong place, and your life will be much less than it could have been, if you had taken enough time to find yourself.

Pluto in the Eleventh House

This will be a period of great changes in your long-range goals and your hopes for the future. Also the kinds of people you have as friends will change. Activities that you once enjoyed may no longer appeal to you now. You may decide that many goals that you once would have pursued are not worth pursuing. Your ideals will change, which will be reflected in a change in the people whom you associate with and the groups or movements you identify with.

You will be looking for quite a different kind of friendship than you have had in the past. Formerly you may have been satisfied simply to spend time with people whom you felt at ease with, but now you seek out people who will provide very intense encounters, emotionally and otherwise. Some of these encounters may not be very pleasant, but that is because you are seeking to confront new dimensions of yourself through them. Friendships now have a purpose in your individual development; they are not the casual encounters that you are used to.

One friendship in particular may change your life at this time. You may meet someone who affects you so strongly that the entire course of your life is changed. But that is what you have been seeking, so this is all for the good. However, avoid associating with individuals just because they are powerful and persuasive. Your desire for intense experiences through others should not lead to friends who will guide your life into paths you shouldn't take. During this transit there is a danger that unconscious compulsions will take over and send you in some direction that you don't really want to go in. But it is equally possible that you will meet someone who can really act as a guide and teacher and send you in a direction that will help you grow.

You may become associated with a group or movement that wants to reform society in some way. Again you should avoid ruthless persons, because with Plutonian energies at work, they could be dangerous. However, if your present interest in positive reform is sincere, you may find others who have the same aims.

Shallow old friendships may end under this transit, and new ones may be formed. In the long run it does not matter, as long as you fulfill the fundamental purposef of this transit, which are transformation through your friendships and regeneration of your goals.

Pluto in the Twelfth House

This transit has many ramifications. In many ways it prepares you for Pluto transiting your first house, in that it clears away old and hidden psychic garbage, which must happen prior to a complete rebuilding of the self.

First and most importantly, the effects of this transit are psychological. It is similar to Pluto's transit through the fourth house in that it brings up aspects of yourself that are deeply buried in your psyche and forces you to confront them. In our interaction with other people we try to hide, both from ourselves and from them, those aspects of ourselves that we have been taught not to approve of. Yet the energies of these hidden characteristics leak out in subversive ways. They undercut our conscious intentions in such a way that we do ourselves in without understanding how or why. Pluto activates these patterns to the point that they can't be ignored. Unconsciously motivated actions can become extremely troublesome at this time. Although you intend to act one way in a particular situation, you suddenly find yourself acting quite differently. During this period it is extremely important to understand these unconscious energies and be willing to confront the aspects of yourself that you have been taught to believe are "bad." You cannot go on through adulthood with subconscious behavior patterns that are clearly childish. You may have to recall and relive the events of your childhood that are affecting you now, and you should feel free to call in any kind of a therapist who seems able to reach inside of you.

This transit activates the hidden side of your nature and makes you understand and control it, but it also activates the hidden side of external elements of your life that you have not faced in the past. These may be relationships that have failed or actions and behavior that you are aware of but do not wish to discuss, even with yourself. The consequences of these actions may come back to haunt you now. You should face up to them honestly and acknowledge them, for only then will they cease to run your life. You may have alienated someone quite unconsciously and even quite blamelessly, who may try to work against you. Older astrology texts refer to such persons as "secret enemies," but usually they are not really unknown to you. It is just that you may have to confront your own feelings of guilt about them, and here again the only course is to bring these feelings out into the open. "Secret" enemies cannot work against you in the open, and if you are completely honest with them, they may have a change of heart toward you.

Whatever your situation, it will be necessary to confront all those hidden and unpleasant aspects of your life and your past. By avoiding them you have created a situation in which they control you. Only by facing them honestly and without guilt can you clear them away and prevent them from having any further influence over you. That is the task of this period in your life.

Pluto Conjunct Sun

This is a time of great change in your life, when you will strive as never before to accomplish your ambitions. You will work harder than ever and not allow obstacles to prevent you from achieving your objectives. If you handle the energies of this transit skillfully, you should be able to go far with it, but you should be aware of certain pitfalls.

Pluto is the planet of death and regeneration, which means the elimination of whatever is old and outworn and the birth of a new, higher order. With Pluto on your Sun, you can be the agent of this process. You can work to remove old outworn structures in your own life and in the lives of those around you, so that all of you can experience a new life. But you must observe two limitations. First, Pluto gives tremendous drive and energy, but only for the elimination of the truly old and outworn, not for doing anything you want. And second, like the other planets beyond Saturn, Pluto is a transcendental planet. Therefore its energies are not easily harnessed to the purposes of unenlightened egotism. What you do with this transit should be for the eventual betterment of everyone around you, not just yourself. You are the steward of this energy, not the owner. If you use the energy that Pluto gives for purely selfish ends, you will provoke such furious opposition that you will eventually be unable to do anything. You may even experience violence at the hands of others who desperately try to stop you. Similarly, if you use this energy to remove structures that are not yet ready to pass away, you will be unable to make progress. Pluto signifies the need to replace an old, inferior state of being with a new and truly superior state. It does not just arbitrarily replace one with another.

The best way to ensure handling the energy of this transit well is to concentrate it on your own life. It is best not to try to dominate others, even "for their own good." Use the energy to transform your own life into a finer expression of yourself. Make every effort to expand your awareness of who and what you are and make that knowledge work in your life at a practical level. And do it in order to express yourself more perfectly, not to satisfy a sense of ambition.

The last point to remember is that you must do something now. You cannot simply sit back and let this transit go by without making some changes. If you do not make them consciously, circumstances will take over for you, probably with unpleasant results. You may have to face some aspects of yourself that you do not like, but that is part of the process, and you will find that those aspects are not really so bad. They only looked bad because you have never given them a place in your conscious personality.

The sweeping changes that take place now may be difficult, but that is because any kind of death is unpleasant. But the birth of something new is as beautiful as the death of the old is fearsome.

Pluto Sextile Sun

During this period subtle energies are at work that can help you make many creative changes in your life. It is a chance to act more effectively than at almost any other time. You may have opportunities to take on more power and to assume authority over others, but this is a subtle influence, and you will not be compelled either by cir-cumstances or your own inner energies to do a great deal. Therefore this transit could go by without significant happenings at all, unless you make a conscious effort to grab the chance. This is a fine time to establish good relations with authority figures such as bosses, employers and other officials, for they can provide opportunities that you can use during this transit.

Another source of creative opportunity may come about through working with groups and organizations, in which you can exercise control and bring about creative reform. With Pluto's energies it is often best to work with groups or agencies, rather than alone as an individual. However, do not fear that your individuality will suffer or be lost within the group. This transit gives you the chance to establish your individuality through working with others.

In your personal life this is also a time of creative change. You can totally rebuild whatever needs rebuilding without the turmoil that you might experience at other times. On the immediate practical level, you may be able to rebuild or repair a house or other material object. At a higher, more psychological level this may mean rebuilding structures within yourself. Great changes can occur that totally alter your objectives in life, largely because your true aims will become more apparent to you. This can be a consciousness-expanding transit in the highest sense of the phrase.

Pluto Square Sun

This transit is a test of your strength and the energy with which you have established yourself in your world. The test may take many forms, but in any form it will require that your sense of personhood be in reasonably good shape; in other words, you should know who and what you are. If you do not really know yourself, this transit is likely to bring about crises that will cause major changes in your life.

One form that it may take is a test of your self-control as you try to get ahead in the world. This transit stimulates your ambition and desire for power out of all proportion. If there is a ruthless side to your personality that will do anything to destroy opposition, it will come out now. But, at the same time, forces in your world will try very hard to stop you. To overcome the forces arrayed against you will require extreme ruthlessness. On the other hand, you may know precisely what you need to succeed and go after just that, being willing to compromise and make your success also the success of others. This is the proper course to take, but unfortunately this kind of accommodating spirit is not often found in Plutonian transits.

If you are of a more retiring disposition, you may experience this transit quite differently. Instead of being the person on a power trip, you may have to contend with someone else who is. Here again you must determine exactly your rights and needs as an individual and stand up for them. The problem here is not that you will overstep your bounds but that someone else will. But you must fight or at least resist. Either of these power struggles is most likely to occur in your profession, quite possibly with someone in authority.

Many people refuse to deal with the energies of Pluto, but this can create problems because the energy will come out, and you won't know where.

It can come out as a physical breakdown. Your body may go through a critical period in which it just has to stop ànd rebuild itself. Certainly if you have any kind of physical crisis during this transit, you should begin a conscientious program of physical exercise and therapy to build your body up again.

Pluto's energy may also surface in the outer expression of your life. You may be surrounded by conditions of breakdown and decay, which are an outward sign of the need to rebuild within.

Under extreme conditions, this transit can release its energy in a single explosive burst as an injury or physical assault. Certainly you should avoid conflicts with others that may lead to physical fighting, because the energies here are quite dangerous.

On the other hand, if you successfully use this transit to establish yourself and make your position in the world clear to yourself and others, without transgressing the bounds of what is rightfully yours, you will be able to accomplish much that will be valuable later.

Pluto Trine Sun

At this time in your life you have a strong sense of having survived heavy challenges in the past and of having reached a level where you can be effective. And indeed you can if you make an effort. This transit can bring you rewards on a silver platter, even if you insist on being totally passive, but it is far better to work positively with the energies that are operating on your behalf.

You are able to express yourself more powerfully and completely to others now than at almost any other time. Others see you as a powerful and effective individual, and they respect you for it.

Obviously this is a good time for personal advancement. You may be given power in an organization, in business or in government to help bring about reforms and changes in the system. Yet you will be seen not as a revolutionary but as someone who can get things done. Your relationships with people in power over you is likely to be excellent, and your advancement may result at least partly from their favor.

On the more personal level, this transit can bring positive change into your life that does not disrupt, but allows you to evolve and grow. You can gain tremendous insights into yourself at this time and make successful efforts to change if you want to.

Your physical body is in good condition under these influences and unusually able to throw off illness and heal itself. You should take advantage of your increased physical vigor and involve yourself in some form of physical education, such as conventional body-building exercises or a discipline like yoga. Yoga is particularly good for you because it involves the mind and spirit as well as the body. You should not compart-mentalize yourself into two units—mind and body—because now you can see your essential unity and can make good use of that insight.

Pluto Opposition Sun

This can be an extrememly difficult period for relationships, both intimate and casual, because you are likely to get involved in power struggles with others. It may be that you will try to force others to take a certain course of action against their will, or others may try to do this for you. In either case you may have to take evasive actions in order to avoid real difficulties. If you are attempting to dominate others, you should stop, no matter what your motives are. You may think you have the best reasons in the world for dominating people, and perhaps you believe that you are only doing it for their own good, but that is probably not really true. It is more likely that you simply cannot leave well enough alone. An excessive desire to meddle and interfere is one of the negative effects of this transit.

If you are the victim of someone else's meddling and interfering, the problem is more difficult. In some way, probably unconsciously, you have given out a signal that you will allow yourself to be treated this way. And having set off this reaction, it is hard for you to stop it. On the other hand, you may gain something by fighting back. It is often useful to experience a test of wills with someone, and it is much less dangerous to you when you are asserting your independence of someone else rather than the other way around. You may need to prove to yourself that you are stronger than your opponent.

One dangerous aspect of this transit is that it may trigger off a conflict with persons in authority over you, such as a boss, a government official or someone in a similar position. These people can do you more harm than most, and you should be very careful.

At its most positive, this transit gives you great energy to accomplish things, provided you can keep down the negative effects so that you don't arouse too much resistance and opposition from others. Your personal ambition is likely to be very high under this transit, and you can succeed, for this is not an "unlucky" transit. It does require you to be careful, because its energies are very powerful. If you arouse people to oppose you, the conflict may result in total defeat unless your real motives, as opposed to your professed ones, are very good. Such a defeat may force you to rethink your entire life plan and make a new beginning. That in itself is not bad, although the circumstances that drive you to it may not be very enjoyable.

Under certain circumstances this transit can have the purely physical effect of causing a health breakdown. It is certainly advisable to treat your body well during this transit, and don't take it for granted.

Pluto Conjunct Moon

This transit signifies a time of extremely powerful emotional change in your life, which can affect your immediate personal surroundings, your home and family, and your inmost psychological development. The feelings evoked by this transit are raw and urgent. You may be surprised at the intensity of some of the internal forces that you will discover, and making yourself deal with these feelings may be the most difficult part of this transit.

Pluto signifies breakdown and reconstruction, while the Moon signifies your innermost personal life, which you usually depend on to be stable, predictable and supportive as you face the external world. Now this aspect of your psyche is in a state of acute transformation, and that is what makes this transit so powerful. The actual experience can vary tremendously because so many different areas of your personal and emotional life can be activated, but here are some typical manifestations.

First of all, on the innermost psychological level, this transit can indicate an enormous emotional change that activates complexes within you that have lain dormant since childhood. You may repeatedly find yourself in situations in which you act as a compuslive child rather than a rational adult. The problem is that your "rational" adulthood has never dealt with these repressed energies, which must be dealt with. You may need psychotherapy or a related technique in order to handle what comes up at this time.

On another level, this transit can transform all your emotionally based relationships, such as those with your spouse, family and parents, particularly your mother. One of these relationships may end completely for any number of reasons, occasionally including death. Relationships with women in general may become particularly intense, regardless of your own sex. For example, you might have an intense emotional involvement at all psychological levels with a woman, or you might be involved in an acute power struggle with a woman close to you who seems to be trying to run your life.

On a more external level this transit can affect your home in a number of ways. You may change your residence, or you may make great changes in your present residence. Repairs may be necessary in order to prevent serious disintegration of a building.

If this transit has a particularly strong emotional effect, you may experience digestive troubles. In this case you should probably consult both a physician and a psychotherapist to help you handle the trouble. But consult the physician first.

Like other Pluto transits, this one may be upsetting now, but in reality it is the preparation for a new stage of development. Keep yourself flexible so that the necessary changes can take place with a minimum of disruption.

Pluto Sextile Moon

At this time you have the chance to get in touch with your innermost psychological being and experience your real emotions. You can understand your real motives and the basis of your unconscious compulsions and drives. You will experience your emotions as profound, real and intense, but not difficult. Because of this you can learn about aspects of your personality that are normally hidden even from yourself. This is an excellent transit for encountering philosophies of human potential and growth. But you won't have to deal with it abstractly, because even in your everyday relationships you will handle people with much more emotional depth and feeling than usual.

This transit can affect your personal and domestic life as well as your innermost psychological nature. It gives the opportunity to make creative changes and reforms in your relationships with the people you see every day, such as your family, relatives and parents. You may make physical changes in your home that reflect the changes taking place within you, so that your immediate surroundings more closely harmonize with your feelings.

But there is little sense of turmoil with this transit. You have a strong sense of belonging, and those who are close to you support the changes that are happening inside you, which makes it easier to progress.

Past conditioning, which often causes difficulties by generating inappropriate behavior, will actually give you a boost now. You have a strong feeling that you have something solid to fall back on, and that whatever you have to do will work out favorably. But you will not be run by past conditioning. Because even as it operates, you can see its actions and understand it.

Pluto Square Moon

This transit produces very intense experiences in your emotional and personal life, and it will test your innermost psychological workings. You may be forced to dig down deeper inside yourself than you have ever done before to get the answers you need at this time.

On the psychological level, this transit dredges up past behavior patterns that may be quite inadequate for the present. Or it may bring up memories from the past that somehow affect the present. Driven by compulsions and irrational drives, you may do things that you would not do if you were entirely clear about yourself. Deep psychological changes are taking place that should not be ignored or swept under the rug. Instead, you should understand them.

In your personal life, this transit can bring an emotional power struggle with someone. Such a struggle can be quite destructive, because the tactics are very subversive, perhaps including manipulation of guilt, jealousy or sense of duty. You will not attempt to wield power directly and nakedly, which your opponent could fight easily. It takes extremely clear perception to see exactly what is happening.

This transit also may signify a relationship in which you feel fascinated by the other person, even though you feel that the relationship is bad for you. You seem unable to get away. Actually you are experiencing a repressed aspect of yourself through the other person.

In your domestic life there may be significant changes, which are external reflections of your inner change. Your most intimate life is the most perfect manifestation of your inner psyche and is therefore most affected. You may find that considerable tension builds up between you and those closest to you, and there may be some very emotional confrontations. Your closest familial relationships are most subject to the kind of emotional power games described earlier; avoid these games, because they can be especially destructive in a family situation, where your most primordial energies are tapped. Parents are particularly likely to be the source of such conflict.

There may be other changes in your domestic life along with or instead of the ones listed above. You may change your residence or make significant changes in your present one, and again these will reflect changes within you.

You can get at a lot of internal refuse under this transit. You can emerge from it psychologically a new person, more emotionally sound and able to deal with the world without being the "victim"of your own unconscious mind. But this will happen only if you are willing to honestly face the changes that occur within you and within your life with a real desire to understand.

Pluto Trine Moon

This is a period of profound experiences, which should be extremely positive and creative for your overall growth and evolution. You are concerned with making your life more profound and emotionally rewarding. No longer satisfied with living at the surface, you want to feel in your heart everything that until now you have understood only with your mind. At the same time your mental understanding will become more profound because it will be based on intuition as well as logic.

This deepening experience of life will affect your relationships as well. In fact it may very well bring about an important new relationship, which may or may not be sexual. In any case you can be sure that it will be emotionally profound and a positive learning experience in which you will discover a great deal about your inner psyche.

Even your existing relationships will now have a great deal more emotional content than they have had and will become the source of much self-discovery. Again you need have little fear for the stability of these relationships.

The most important discovery you will make about yourself during this transit concerns the workings of your subconscious patterns. The Moon rules the unconscious habits and patterns that we carry from our past, and Pluto activates them so that we can get in touch with them. This is an excellent transit for psychotherapy or other consciousness-expanding therapies. It is not that you need them necessarily, but they would be extremely effective at this time.

In your personal and home life you will have a chance to make positive changes. You can make repairs, construct new buildings and generally expand your activities. Your home life should be deeper and more emotionally rewarding now than at other times. This is often a good transit for buying real estate, especially if you plan to live on it.

Pluto Opposition Moon

This transit can denote a period of extreme emotional confrontations with others in which you or they attempt to manipulate each other emotionally. For example, in a love relationship either you or your partner may use various combinations of guilt, jealousy or threats of abandonment to force the other into acting in a particular way. You may be involved in a relationship that is too possessive, in which you or your partner doesn't allow the other any freedom to relate to other people or to be an individual. In such a situation the pressures can build up to the point of explosion, with potentially fatal consequences to the relationship.

Sometimes you are acting from the best motives. You may not even be aware that you are smothering your partner, thinking it's just love, not a suppression of the other's individuality. And the other may not understand what is happening either, except that something is terribly wrong. Then the partner who senses that things are wrong feels very guilty, which can poison the relationship too. And this process is not limited by any means to lovers—it can affect any emotionally based relationship.

The best procedure is to be very honest with everyone with whom you are involved in a relationship and make it clear that you want them to be honest too. Then you can get these pressures and tensions out into the open where you can handle them. If someone is not honest with you, perhaps it would be best to break off the relationship.

This transit can also signify a period of deep inner turmoil. Your unconscious mind may play tricks on you that are quite upsetting, for you become the "victim" of inner compulsions that make no sense in terms of your current experience. They don't make sense because they represent the reactivation of elements from your past that you have never really dealt with. Infantile patterns and childhood "programs" that you thought you had outgrown may surface now to disturb your adult ways of dealing with the world. What you must do is come to an understanding of what these patterns represent in your life. If you recognize them and give them a place in your life, you may find that these energies can be creatively harnessed in adult life. They appear to be "horrible" only because you are programmed to disapprove of them, which distorts your perception.

Be particularly aware of any obsessive ideas or notions. These can be very powerful under this transit and may require therapy to make them a useful rather than a rejected part of your life. Women in particular may become the screen upon which you focus your "projections." If you have trouble with women under this transit, look within yourself for the roots of the problem.

Pluto Conjunct Mercury

In many respects this will be an educational time in your life. Your ideas and opinions on many issues may change radically from what they have been in the past. Or you may become involved in persuading others to adopt your views. In either case, all thought, communication and exchange with others will take on great significance and intensitiy.

Your concern for truth is deepened during this transit. You want to get to the bottom of any issue that concerns you, letting nothing stand in your way. Obviously this is a good transit for any kind of research or investigation, particularly if you are investigating something hidden or secret. Your perception is sharpened so that you can see the facts more clearly and take advantage of your knowledge.

Once you have thoroughly researched your position on any matter, you can tell others what you have learned. As mentioned above, this transit gives you the power to influence people and sway them to your point of view. However, if you try to convince people from a narrow egotistical position, not because of a real concern with truth, you will provoke opposition to your ideas, which could defeat you. Plutonian energies are not easily harnessed to egotistical motives.

Even if you do not try to coerce others with your ideas, others may try to do so with you. Again you have to recognize whether their motives are egotistical or whether they really want to help you learn. Listen to those who want to help you, because they can show you much. The former type will force you to reexamine your own thinking and see where it is weak, but do not automatically surrender to someone else's ideas. Merely question your own.

At its best, this transit can bring you tremendous new understanding about life, if you are flexible enough to learn at all times, even when you are the teacher. Flexibility is very important, because the greatest danger of this transit is that without it you can be victimized by an obsession or fanatical ideal. Then you will only find yourself in furious struggles with others who regard you as a threat that must be curbed.

Pluto Sextile Mercury

This transit is a good time for deep intellectual probing of ideas and beliefs. If you want to or must find out about something, this is an excellent time for it. Your mental powers are sharp and your perception is keen. Also you are in the right frame of mind for working with extreme thoroughness. You are not satisfied with superficial answers and will not be happy until you understand the whole truth.

This is also an excellent time to probe your own mind and see what makes it work. Your desire to explore the secret depths of everything applies even to your own self, so this is a very good time for self-inquiry.

Communications with others take on a heavier tone now. You value significant communication and are uninterested in superficial banter. Your everyday intercourse with the world around you becomes the vehicle for important discoveries that will eventually change your whole way of thinking. You will have a spirit of discovery rather than a feeling that everything is caving in around you, as often happens when you encounter ideas that seem to invalidate your former beliefs. Your burning desire to get at the truth makes every discovery interesting instead of alarming.

And as your depth of mind increases, so will your ability to influence other people. What you say will have greater weight with others. People will believe you because they know you have checked the facts thoroughly and speak with great conviction.

Ideas, concepts and philosophies that are inherently mysterious or that explain the world from an occult point of view are more attractive to you now. This is an excellent time to study occult philosophy, metaphysics or even psychology or psychiatry. Any discipline related to healing the mind will be beneficial at this time.

495

Pluto Square Mercury

This transit can represent a period in which your ideas about the world in general are challenged significantly. Or it can represent a time when your thinking is deepened tremendously, enabling you to deal with ideas that formerly would have been too deep. In this case you will probably try to persuade others of what you believe.

Your routine day-to-day interactions with the world—conversations, letters and other such exchanges—may develop into fairly intense encounters as you try to force your ideals upon others from a fanatical conviction of your own righteousness, or as others try to do the same with you. Once again the issue is knowing precisely what your limits are and what you really think. You also need to learn to allow others' ideas to coexist with yours. It is not good either to automatically bow before someone else's opinions or to demand that others bow to yours. If your experiences seem to invalidate your earlier beliefs, do not try to delude yourself that this isn't so. Face the facts and try to find out what is really happening. This transit can be a learning experience in the most positive sense. While you may find that your internal intellectual structure has to change greatly, the change should be for the better.

On the other hand you may become attracted to new ideas that have very intense emotional overtones. Ideas that are deep and mysterious are very compelling to you now, and you want to plumb the depths of the universe. If you heed one warning, this can do you little harm and can give you new insight and understanding about the universe. But the ideas you are attracted to may convey power in some way, as does the study of magic in the field of the occult. You may become conscious that knowledge is power, but you must be very careful how you use this power. Magic in particular, but all powerful knowledge in general can produce tragic consequences if not handled properly.

Also, when you are teaching others, avoid the temptation to mold them into your own image. Your purpose is to show people the way, not push them down it.

Pluto Trine Mercury

Like other Mercury-Pluto combinations, this transit will help you gain greater intellectual insights and enable you to learn a great deal about whatever you wish to study. At the same time your viewpoints will become deeper and more subtle so that you will really understand ideas that you had grasped only superficially. This is a good time to study a new subject, go to school or take courses on any subject. But you will be most attracted to subjects that explain phenomena in depth, especially the hidden aspects of things. Under this transit you may also meet someone who has a very powerful effect upon your consciousness, perhaps a friend who influences your thinking greatly or a guru figure who opens up the universe to you.

You can be taught under this transit, and you can also teach. Your words carry greater influence at this time because the depth of your perceptions is evident to others. And you should not limit your communication to direct conversations, you should use other media to teach as well. If you have any inclination to write, this is a good time to do it, especially on subjects such as psychotherapy or the occult.

Another aspect of this transit is that Pluto will make you more concerned with studies of hidden and secret things, such as psychology, magic or other occult traditions, or studies of what is hidden in the earth, such as mining, minerology and geology. You want to understand the forces under the surface that cause events to happen.

You will study any subject you choose in depth and with complete single-mindedness, so that you will be able to cover a new discipline completely in a short time. Under this transit you may acquire a new skill in a much shorter time than at other times in the past.

Pluto Opposition Mercury

During this transit communications with others may become quite difficult, if the reason for communicating is to coerce opinions and thinking rather than to inform. Such coercion provokes resistance and then a general breakdown of communication. You must let others be and let them think what they want. And if you are threatened by someone else's coercion, you will be obliged to stand up for your beliefs and fight for them if necessary. First of all, scrutinize your ideas thoroughly so that you know their strengths precisely and can't be caught unprepared in a conflict. And remember that there is nothing wrong with changing your stand if it proves necessary.

Avoid fanatical ideas, that is, opinions that you believe in absolutely and consider worthy of forcing on others. Under this transit you can become totally possessed by convictions that have very little real meaning but that you insist on forcing on others. Also avoid associating with people who are inclined to think this way, because they will force their views upon you. With this transit there is no point in asking for conflict; it will probably come anyway.

Obsessive thinking can take another course also. You may become so obsessed with working out an idea, which may be perfectly valid, that you can't get any peace until you have done so. This can lead to nervous exhaustion or even a nervous breakdown, if you are at all inclined to that. While you are able to do very hard mental work under this transit, you should be careful not to overstrain yourself. Research and other types of mental exploration, especially about occult beliefs or very obscure and hidden matters, are the most dangerous, because they can be very obsessive. Rather than avoiding such work altogether, however, it would be better to exercise restraint in working on them.

Pluto Conjunct Venus

This transit is likely to have a great effect upon your relationships and your sex life. If you have no current sexual relationships, this transit could bring you one that is quite intense but not necessarily smooth. You may become quite obsessed by someone of the opposite sex. This transit combination could be described as love's power, with the emphasis on "power." Any relationship that begins under this influence is not going to be lukewarm. You will either be entirely involved or not at all.

Under this influence you see love not as part of everyday life, but as an experience that can transcend that reality and transform your life completely. Obviously this is a very tall order to fill, but you may very well succeed now. However, the drives that bring about a relationship under this transit are compulsive and not very rational. Unconscious patterns may play a much larger role in who you choose than your sense of what you need in a partner. If you are not careful you may fall for someone who is extremely difficult to get along with, which is precisely why you are attracted to that person. You almost seem to need the experience of a struggle in a relationship at this time. But you may end up in a situation in which you can't live with your partner and can't live without him or her. Fascination with someone who is not very good for you is a great danger with this transit.

However, this effect is not inevitable by any means. A perfectly decent relationship is possible under this transit. The problem is that mainly you are looking for an intense experience, not necessarily a good one. If it happens to be good, it will also be intense, so this transit can signify a very important relationship in your life.

Existing relationships will also be intensified by this transit because your needs are heightened, and you require gratification more urgently. An existing relationship that cannot satisfy your needs may not survive. Certainly the basis of your relationships will change considerably during this time.

If there is no sexual relationship in your life now and this transit does not bring one, this can be a very frustrating time indeed. Your sex drive is very high and needs an outlet. Perhaps it can be sublimated in some kind of creative endeavor, which would be a positive use of the energy. But if you have no outlet at all, you should examine yourself and your entire position on love relationships. You may discover some very severe problems in this area, which you must work on, and now is the time.

Pluto Sextile Venus

This transit deepens your existing relationships and makes them more profound. It may also bring an important new friendship or love relationship that will have an important effect upon your life. In general your personal relationships will become less routine. Through them you will be able to transform your life and aquire greater insight into your own psychology, at least concerning relationships. However, this process is not to be feared because it happens in a relatively gentle manner and heightens your appreciation of your relationships.

Your sense of pleasure and enjoyment is also heightened under this transit. You are able to get far more enjoyment than usual from the things you do for fun. You approach everything with far more emotional intensity.

Any love relationship that comes at this time will have an intensity of feeling that will amaze you. You may not have been aware of the power of your feelings, but now you have the chance to experience them directly and be transformed in the process. This does not necessarily mean that the relationship itself or the other person is in any way extraordinary. It is your own power to feel and love that has grown stronger.

If you have any intrinsic artistic and creative ability, this transit will deepen it and increase the tempo of your artistic activity. Also your work will have a profound quality that it may have lacked, and others will see that your work has a significance beyond the surface appearance. The only negative quality of this transit is that its energies can be abused. If you are so inclined, you can degenerate into a pointless sensualism, in which you are interested only in physical sensations, not in elevating your consciousness and growing as a human being. Love and creativity have the power to transform your life at this time. Don't waste this opportunity.

Pluto Square Venus

Under this transit relationships become a source of challenge and even difficulty, which may point the way for changes that you have to make within yourself. Certainly there will be some significant change in your relationships; an old love relationship may be transformed in some way, or a significant new one may come along. But you will have to deal with several problems at this time.

First of all you have a very strong desire for love now, which you express with urgency and compulsion. But in your haste you may latch on to the first person available and not wait for someone who is good for you. Also you may become so intensely fascinated by that person that you do not see him or her clearly. The problem is that you are under the influence of unconscious drives that are not operating according to your best interest. For example, if you are married, even happily, you might suddenly become fascinated by another person of the opposite sex, which could disrupt your marriage. But avoid the temptation to go with the other person, for this relationship will probably not be long lasting. Wait until the transit is well over before making a commitment to any relationship that comes to you under its influence. Such a relationship is inherently unstable, at least for now. After the transit it *may* settle down to something more reliable.

But an extracurricular affair is not the only challenge to an existing relationship. Strains and stresses that have existed for some time in your love relationships may come to the surface now. Jealousy, possessiveness, unwillingness to grant the partner freedom to be himself or herself—all these may become sources of tension within your relationships. You may be either the perpetrator or the victim of these problems. The best procedure is to deal with these strains and try to communicate honestly about them, even if you feel that what lies at the bottom of the problem is too awful to be discussed. This transit brings both the necesssity and the opportunity to completely transform your relationships. A bad one may end, but a good one will become deeper and more profound.

Pluto Trine Venus

This transit emphasizes the creative and romantic aspects of your life. Venus's ability to bring love and artistic creativity are given great power by the trine from Pluto.

This transit can bring a new relationship or deepen an old one. A new one that comes at this time will be notable for the strength of the feelings involved. It could hardly be described as casual. There is a compulsive quality about the energies that drive you and your partner together, but this is not all negative. It will merely seem to both of you that this relationship was inevitable, and you will both find that it is a learning experience of the best possible kind. You will learn a great deal about the energies within each of you that are at work in a relationship. You may discover that love is less conscious and that you act much more from blind compulsion than you realized. But this realization is the first step toward becoming conscious of your feelings.

Your existing relationships will also enter a period of creative change. Your feelings are stronger now, and again you will both learn more about the way you operate in the relationship.

Your creative energies will be aroused and if you are in any way artistic, you will be able to put deep, feeling energy into your creations as never before. Others will recognize the intensity that has gone into your work, for which you may very well receive considerable recognition.

Art and love will have one element in common during this transit; that is, the experience of them will transport you out of the commonplace into the extraordinary, for that is what you are seeking. Art and love should have considerable impact on your life now and affect your future for many years to come.

Pluto Opposition Venus

This transit can have a variety of effects on the relationships in your life. Sexual relationships in particular are very strongly affected, because both Venus and Pluto are connected with sex, although in different ways.

If you do not have an important existing relationship in your life now, this transit may very well bring one. But you must observe certain cautions about any relationship that begins at this time. First, as with any transit of Pluto, there are strong subconscious forces at work within you that make you "fall in love" with someone at this time. For this reason, the nature of the relationship will probably be determined much more by negative behavior patterns within your psyche than by reason or sense. You may be obsessively, irresistibly attracted to someone, even if you know consciously that he or she is bad for you. If this happens, do not expect very much enjoyment from the relationship, for you are using it unconsciously to get at some aspect of yourself. The relationship itself may not be your real purpose in this case. However, don't assume that any relationship at this time will be negative; it is just that the forces behind its formation are so powerful that any negative forces will be especially troublesome. Any relationship that begins now, whether it is good or bad, will have a powerful effect on your life, so you should try to make sure that it is good.

In an existing sexual relationship, the effects can also be very powerful. At its best, the intensity of feeling may simply deepen so that you and your partner have a more fulfilling relationship. But this transit can create problems of a certain type. One of you, consciously or unconsciously dissatisfied with the other, begins to use love as a device for manipulating the other. The techniques vary, but generally one of you is unwilling to let the other be, perhaps by becoming very possessive and jealous, or by withholding favors, or by using guilt in some way. The tactics are usually subversive rather than those of open confrontation.

In some cases a relationship may end under this transit, because it is not able to withstand the subconscious stresses that are set in motion. All existing relationships will undergo some kind of fundamental transformation, but this is as likely to be positive as negative, if the two of you are willing to be honest with each other. Together you should confront all the issues that you need to know about and understand.

Pluto Conjunct Mars

This is a time of great striving in your life. It can be a time when you overcome all obstacles and triumph in any area of life in which you wish to succeed, but it can also be a time of severe struggle against tremendous obstacles. Although you may be able to overcome them eventually, the struggle will leave you quite exhausted. It is very difficult to tell in advance which of these two extremes you will be closer to.

The energy level of this transit is very high and must be released somehow. If you don't use the power it gives, you are likely to become a victim either of circumstances or of someone else using that kind of power against you. Under extreme circumstances, this transit can signify violent injury or violence at the hands of another person. But this is likely to occur only if you do not use any of this energy yourself.

Mars is an ego planet, whose function is to give you energy and support in maintaining your own separate, individual identity. Under a Pluto transit of this sort, the danger is that you will try to expand your ego in order to dominate others. This transit can produce a ruthless drive to dominate and gain power, or it can signify your struggle to resist such domination by another. However, if you are the one who is dominating, you will only set in motion equally ruthless opposition forces, and you will very likely lose.

But Mars also represents energy in general, which can be harnessed for any type of work. With this transit you can do great things. Work requiring great effort is much easier, because your state of mind makes it seem easy. Hard work is far and away the best use of this energy. And if you are working for the good of others rather than for their domination, it is more likely to work out positively.

Whatever you are doing, this is not a good time to risk any injury. Because of the darker side of the Plutonian energies, its compulsiveness and capacity for ruthlessness, you should avoid all situations in which you might encounter persons of this nature. It is advisable to avoid bad neighborhoods and high crime areas. Physical attacks can occur under this transit, especially if you have not handled the energy in any other way. This is not the most likely manifestation of this transit, but it pays to be careful.

Pluto Sextile Mars

This transit is an opportunity to work and accomplish on a grand scale. Also you are able to influence others and transform a situation in accordance with your views. Your energy level is very high, and you can put out a sustained effort over a long period of time. Consequently you can make great progress in accomplishing the objectives you have set for yourself.

Your ability to accomplish on an individual level is great at this time, but you can make even better use of this transit's energies by working with others to achieve group goals. You need not fear that your own identity will be submerged, because you will emerge as the most significant and important person in the group. Your own identity will actually be strengthened by working in a group.

This transit favors any kind of work that involves making great changes and reforms in your environment. For example, you might reorganize the structure of an office, rebuild or repair a building, or on another level, regenerate and work out your own body. Anything that emphasizes rebuilding is favored.

Any activity you engage in at this time should require you to expend a lot of energy and should not be too limited in scope. You should feel that you can go until you have expended your energies and there is little else to be done. Avoid any situation that would be likely to frustrate or limit you. It is not so much that you would be harmed in such a situation as that you would waste an energy that can be extremely useful. Like all transits by sextile, this one means that you will be given the opportunity to do something, not compelled to do it. If you do not take the opportunity, nothing will happen.

Pluto Square Mars

This transit can have considerable dangers if you do not handle it properly. Its great energies can be used for constructive effort, however, through which you can accomplish a great deal. The problem is that this transit arouses ego energies either in you directly or in another person who can affect you, which can be very difficult if the energies are frustrated.

Taking the first possibility, that you will be affected directly, this transit can stimulate your ambitions and make you want to get ahead at any cost. Positively, this gives you the ability to work incredibly hard for long hours to achieve your objectives. In fact, if you are not careful, you can work so hard that you become physically exhausted, leaving yourself open to illnesses and physical breakdown. You hardly feel fatigue and weariness until it is too late. Use your tremendous energy, but be sure not to overdo it!

A much more dangerous possibility, however, is that you might work toward your personal ends—success, power, fame or whatever—without any regard for those around you. Pluto-Mars energies can be completely egoistic. You may pay no attention to people who disagree with you, whether they oppose you outright or whether they think you are wrong and are trying to set you right. You will lose the benefit of potentially good advice from those who would help you and win the undying hatred of your opponents. Enemies you make at this time will eventually have the power to damage you, even if they don't have it now.

You may find yourself in a fight situation, for the energies of this transit are appropriate to fighting, and you are in a good position to win, especially if you can persuade others to join you. Don't try to go it alone.

Sometimes with this transit the people around you are on a power trip that will affect you. Here again you will have to fight to maintain your position, and you should not hesitate to do so, as long as you have some allies. The problem here is that you may have to be on guard against sneaky tactics and opponents who will not come out into the open.

There is some danger of accidents under this transit, almost always because of frustrated energy within you. For example, you might get angry one day but not express it. Then when you drive off in your car, the frustration may express itself through an accident. Obviously the solution is to express any anger and resentment that you feel and communicate with the people who are important to you about your feelings. Also avoid any situation in which you are exposed to unnecessary risks, for here again the energy may come out in some undesirable way.

Pluto Trine Mars

At this time in your life your energy level is higher than usual, and you are desirous of performing great feats. Often this transit signifies a time when you will make a tremendous drive for success in your profession or in another field of activity that is important to you. You may gain considerable power over others even if you don't seek it, which will allow you to make many changes in the world around you that you have not been able to make before.

Even if you do not gain power in any way, you will have more energy to work than at other times. You will be able to work long, hard and persistently at tasks that would usually tire you out. Because of your high energy, this transit favors physical activities such as athletics. Activities that aim to rebuild your body, the muscles in particular, such as weight-lifting, yoga or another body culture, are especially effective at this time.

This transit also favors any kind of rebuilding, repairing, renovating and restoring, such as working on old furniture or buildings. Pluto, the planet of rebirth, favors the rebuilding of anything, and Mars gives you the energy to do it.

If you have gone through a period of personal crisis in the last several years that has left you feeling discouraged about yourself, this transit will go a long way toward rebuilding your self-confidence. This period prepresents a new birth of energy and ego-drive that will enable you to believe in yourself again. In any case you will be able to proceed in your daily activities with a greater sense of strength and confidence. This is a tremendously reinforcing transit.

Pluto Opposition Mars

This can be a very powerful but somewhat difficult transit to handle, because the energies are so intense that harnessing them creatively may be a problem. But it is not impossible.

The difficulty is that your own or someone else's ego energies and will to dominate are running rampant in your life. If they are someone else's energies, the ultimate purpose is to test the security of your own ego. You will feel great tensions with the people in your life and possibly have serious flare-ups.

First of all, you have to recognize that you have a very strong drive to win, to succeed and, if necessary, to exercise dominion over others in your drive to succeed. These feelings are perfectly all right if you acknowledge them and use them wisely.

If you deny them, you will experience tension within yourself with regard to others and not know the source. You will find that people's actions irritate you greatly and that you are often angry without understanding why. At its worst, the effort to suppress this energy will lead to your becoming the victim of someone else's energy. This can even lead to violence and injury, so avoid taking any serious risks that could lead to accidents during this transit.

If, on the other hand, you let the energy out with no restraint, you may run roughshod over everyone in your way and scramble furiously toward the top. But in doing this you are likely to arouse truly horrendous opposition from people who struggle to the death to prevent you from succeeding. Your actions make it clear to others that you are a threat to them at the deepest psychological or even physical levels of their lives.

But you can use this energy to accomplish much work and make great changes around you. Just don't get so wrapped up in your own ego that you step on everyone else's toes. Try to incorporate others into your work and make it a group effort as much as possible. If you do this well, others will acknowledge you as the leader anyway.

Last of all, avoid using underhanded tactics or becoming involved with subversive and underground elements in society. You cannot count on them, and events may not turn out as you hope. For example, don't borrow money from loan sharks!

If you can really be open with yourself about your needs and drives now, you have the opportunity to transform your ego creatively through confrontation with others, which is not necessarily negative. This transit could help create a new you.

Pluto Conjunct Jupiter

This transit can denote that you will achieve great success in almost any endeavor, or it can mean that people in power will strongly oppose your efforts. It largely depends on what you are trying to accomplish and how.

Most commonly this transit works out well. Under its influence you will experience a rebirth of optimism and hope, which will put you in the proper frame of mind to succeed. Because you expect to succeed, you are likely to. This can apply to any aspect of your life, but it is most likely to be effective if you wish to succeed at something beyond personal glory. You may get your share of glory, but that should not be your primary motive. You should be working to achieve something that will benefit society at large through business, social work or some other means. Pluto designates massive social regeneration and rebirth and aids most those persons and factors in society that work toward that end.

Because Jupiter rules faith and spirit, this transit can signify a rebirth of these elements in your life, a new concern with how you fit into the universe as a whole. You may experience a rebirth of religious concern and a desire to lead others into the knowledge you have gained. Educating the masses to understand the metaphysics of the universe and how it applies to everyone would be one of the highest uses of this transit.

On the other hand, striving in a petty way to succeed at someone else's expense or without recognizing the larger needs of society may lead to trouble. This transit can lead to difficulties with the authorities who are appointed to look after society's needs, if they come to regard you as a threat. Under extreme circumstances, this transit can even indicate arrest.

It is quite possible that even if you are working for a very noble cause, you may arouse opposition from the authorities. However it is likely that you will ultimately win out, if you are really working for a good cause. But if your point of view is limited to yourself, you will have trouble and failure.

Pluto Sextile Jupiter

At this time you may have several chances to get ahead in whatever you are trying to do. This transit favors business and professional interests as well as any other enterprise that involves working with others in groups. In general this is an excellent time to work to actualize any ideal that is at all possible. The power of Pluto can flow through your creative idealism.

And your ideals are higher than usual now. You want to reform and make changes in the world around you. Very often this is expressed in purely personal terms as a drive for personal success, but it may also be expressed as a desire to reform social conditions and correct injustices, either in your personal life, among your immediate friends or in the larger social order.

On a philosophical level also, you will be more idealistic. You are attracted to large systems of thought that explain the society or even the universe as a whole. Consequently this is an excellent time to study law, religion, philosophy or even medicine. Pluto's general concern with healing and regeneration, combined with the nurturing aspect of Jupiter, makes this a good time for the study of healing in any form.

Your interest in ideas that help people understand the world makes you a compelling teacher, because you can enable others to gain understanding and insights as well. And the more you share your insights, the deeper they will become.

On a more mundane level, this is an excellent time for any dealings with the law or with authorities. At work, your relationships with employers will probably be quite good, and they will be of greater assistance than usual.

Pluto Square Jupiter

This transit has great potential for achievement, but you must heed certain dangers. Potentially the basic success drive signified by this transit will enable you to get ahead in all your endeavors, but especially in your work or profession. At its best this transit has a basic optimism that puts you in the right frame of mind to ensure that things will work out as you want.

However, there is the danger that you may overreach yourself, taking on too much and getting too involved. You may find yourself out on a limb when reality catches up with your overinflated expectations. But a far worse result is that you may become arrogant and overbearing in dealing with others. In your self-confidence you may assume an attitude of personal righteousness, a feeling that your aims and goals are much more important than those of anyone around you. It is extremely important that you be willing to compromise and make an effort to understand someone else's position. If you do not, you can be sure that others will make you feel the effects of their power. They will certainly not stand by and let you dominate them. But if you make a reasonable effort to include others in your efforts and in your success, this should not be a problem.

An extreme manifestation of this energy can be legal problems, which could arise if you do not take the needs of others into account, in this case those of society at large. If you are not careful, this transit could even signify arrest.

A related problem is the possibility of being carried away by some religious, meta-physical, spiritual or similar idea. But it is very hard to draw the line here, because at its best this transit makes you very properly concerned with religious and spiritual regeneration. The problem is to maintain your sense of proportion in these matters. Again, do not try to force your ideas upon other people. It is natural and desirable that you want to communicate about these concerns, but let others make their own choices and also listen to what they have to say. Do not become so possessed by an idea that you will not listen to alternatives. There is a struggle here between the openness of Jupiter and the obsessiveness of Pluto. In this situation one can bring real growth, the other only conflict.

Pluto Trine Jupiter

At this time you will seek to make many positive reforms and changes in the world around you. You are concerned with improving conditions so that they are more in accord with your ideals. Your actions are guided by your highest vision of how the world ought to be. You may work within the context of your everyday life, among friends, neighbors, relatives or professional associates, or you make work on a broader scale in the community or society as a whole. No one who comes to you for help will be turned away.

You will be increasingly interested in subjects that encompass a larger view of the world, such as law, religion, philosophy and metaphysics. And you will not be satisfied to learn about them on an intellectual level; you will make them real in the world around you.

This is an extremely favorable time for any dealings with the law or with persons in authority, for they can help you make the kinds of changes that you want to make. They may even assist you in gaining personal power, if that is what you want.

This transit brings a strong drive for power, although it is often motivated by your desire to be in a better position to do good.

Usually this is not an especially egotistical transit. Your generosity is great, and whatever you gain now you want to share with others. You have a strong sense that only what is good for the greater community is good for you.

Pluto Opposition Jupiter

This transit will make you drive yourself and others around you to attain success, excellence or preeminence in some way. It represents the drive to actualize an ideal you hold about how the world ought to be. The danger of this transit is that you may become arrogant and domineering toward those around you, as if you were a kind of superman, above all morality and law except your own. Admittedly that is a rather extreme manifestation, but that is the danger that this transit brings.

Before you try to improve everyone around you, strive to improve yourself, which you can do under this transit. Gain a greater understanding of truth in your world, but do not try to force your views on others. And in pursuing your own conception of excellence, don't try to prevent others from attaining theirs.

In particular, avoid any behavior that could get you into trouble with the law. If you decide to become a law unto yourself, the law of society may have to stop you. Even civil suits should be avoided, if possible, because it will be difficult for you to present a winning case at this time.

You may have a strong desire to manipulate others, not because you want to convince them of your belief in an ideal state of being, but simply because you don't have enough respect for their rights as individuals. Don't proceed as if you had a superiority complex, for that will only cause others to gang up on you and try to destroy you.

It would be a pity to waste this transit on any of its negative manifestations, because it really does give you an opportunity to make yourself over according to your ideals. You can undergo a total spiritual regeneration and achieve a greater understanding of yourself and your place in the universe. And your relations with others will be an integral part of the process. Each new meeting and even encounters with old friends and loved ones will show you more about the path of development that you should take. But if the demands of petty ego drives give you the illusion that you are already "there," you will only dissipate the energy of this transit in needless conflict with others.

Pluto Conjunct Saturn

This transit can denote a rather stressful period in your life. Pluto is the force of inevitable transformation, while Saturn is resistance to such transformation. In several areas of your life you can expect great changes that will come only after considerable difficulty. A typical situation is one in which you are forced to hold on to something for dear life or to persist in some task or project in the face of energies that are trying to make you give up. It must be said that a positive aspect of this transit is that it considerably increases your persistence and tenacity, but unfortunately it also creates the need for these characteristics. In the face of this pressure it is often better to surrender than to take a hard line and hold on. Whatever is being changed usually needs to change, and you will gain little by holding on, except to delay the inevitable.

This transit can also indicate a stage of psychological transformation in which energies within you try to break through the patterns of resistance and tension that you have built up in the course of your life. One psychologist has called these patterns "body armor," referring to the armor-like tensions that they create in your body. Breaking through and free of these patterns can be quite painful, and you will resist the process quite strenuously, but for the most part you would be better off to let it happen.

Ultimately this transit indicates a regeneration of the basic structure of your life as signified by Saturn. Because this structure is so basic to your personality and even to your world, you are likely to experience some disorientation for a while, but this too shall pass.

Things may be taken away from you, such as money or other possessions, relationships or something else that you value perhaps too much. During this transit you must learn to get along with as little as possible, which may be the ultimate lesson of this time. It is certainly a good idea to prepare to deal with scarcity when this transit is coming up. Change your lifestyle so that you don't need as many resources as you have in the past and don't have to be as dependent on others.

Pluto Sextile Saturn

At this time in your life you will be able to get along with very little if necessary, and you will be able to keep plugging away at tasks with tremendous discipline. As a result this is a good time for getting your life ready for hard times, even if this is not an especially difficult period.

However, even if this is a difficult time you can be sure that this transit will help you make it through. It gives you tremendous tenacity and toughness and the ability to apply constant pressure on a situation until it gradually changes. Patience is the watchword of this transit — not that you need patience, but that you have it.

Whatever your objectives, you will keep working at them until you achieve them. In a slow but powerful way, this transit helps you realize your goals, and because you work so slowly, the results you obtain are very lasting indeed.

You will also probably discover that you are changing during this period, not drastically and suddenly, but slowly and at a very profound level of your being. And these changes will make your life more solid and dependable. In general your life is moving from the less solid and abstract to the more solid and real.

You may work alone for the most part now. Saturn is not great for company, but that is not a difficulty. You will probably prefer it that way, at least until you have come somewhere near achieving your goals. This is a very good transit for researching alone, especially when painstaking work is required. Your ability to discipline yourself is extremely high.

Pluto Square Saturn

During this transit you will have to withstand severe challenges to your way of life as it is set up now. As we grow up, we structure our lives to a certain degree, and we come to depend upon this structure for predictability and order. Sometimes, however, the structure is repressive rather than expressive of our true selves. But if it is safe, we tend to keep it regardless of whether we are happy with it. Nevertheless, at some point in our lives the internal energies of this arrangement of our world must evolve or be totally destroyed. Now is such a time in your life. You must adapt to the forces at work during this period *for your own sake!* You may feel like the victim of some massive external force beyond your control that is forcing you to move, but actually the dynamics for change are inherent in your own life structure.

During this transit some circumstance or situation will create forces that seem to push against you. You may feel very pressured to do something that you don't want to do at all, and you will probably put up tremendous resistance. If your life structure is a valid expression of who you are, your efforts to resist will probably be successful. Otherwise you will be forced to change. In either case this period will be characterized by enormous expenditure of energy. If you handle it successfully, you will be able to strive forward and reach new heights as an individual.

As this transit begins, you may find that certain resources — financial, material or otherwise — are no longer available and that you are forced more and more to fall back upon your own devices. This is part of the test of this transit. It is not usually a good time to expand your operations in any field of activity, especially business. Nor is it a good time to spend your energies making everything around you as solid and safe as possible. That should have been done prior to this transit. The best course, which you will be least inclined to take, is to openly and honestly examine all aspects of your life and voluntarily give up whatever you don't really need — those things that make you feel secure but do not aid your personal evolution. If you don't do this voluntarily, circumstances will do it for you. You can expect struggle during this period, but it doesn't have to be a fruitless struggle, unless you try to hold on blindly to everything as it is now.

Pluto Trine Saturn

At this time you will make gradual but very profound changes in your life and create structures that will last a long time. You work at this task with great patience and attention to detail, because you are not working for today only. You are working for tomorrow as well.

This transit confers great endurance, which enables you to work slowly over a long period of time to eliminate those elements of your life that have become unnecessary and limiting, replacing them with structures that are more relevant to your present activities.

This is a period of slow but profound change within yourself also. Certain aspects of your character are changing and taking on a form that will last for many years. This change may be reflected in certain external changes in your work, profession or any other important activity in your life.

You are likely to be very careful about everything that you do under this transit. Because you try not to waste anything, the people around you may think you are excessively conservative. But really you are just acting with great discipline.

Whether or not it is necessary, you are able now to get along with very little in the way of material goods. And you have a phenomenal ability to contend with adversity if you have to. This transit has the effect of toughening you up considerably.

You may also become concerned with social reform in various ways. But it will not be the radical reform associated with Uranus, nor the idealistic kind associated with Jupiter. Rather, your concern is with making the social system work with reasonable fairness and justice on a practical level so that it will work for a long time. In these matters you will bring to bear the same meticulous concern that you display toward the affairs of your personal life.

A related effect is that persons in authority in business or government may give you considerable power to reorganize a structure at some level. They are acknowledging your disciplined, orderly approach to every task, which is characteristic of this transit.

Pluto Opposition Saturn

Under this transit you will experience changing circumstances and situations that may force you to surrender many things — material goods, relationships, principles — that you have previously held on to. You will probably resist these "losses," which is how you will experience them, with great tenacity and stubbornness. You will need great discipline under this transit, because you may not have any resources to waste, and you may be forced to do as much as possible with very little.

Feelings are often suppressed under this transit, as if facing the reality of your present conditions does not permit you the luxury of indulging in emotions. However, this is more apparent than real. You may confuse hardheartedness with hardheadedness and suppress feelings for what you consider to be "practical" reasons. Even if your situation becomes very difficult, you should still keep your heart open to others, or you will bear the scars of this period for the rest of your life as a loss of humanity.

You may feel that you have to work very hard and that nothing ever comes of it. That is true in that the kind of overt success that everyone can clearly recognize is not likely to come now. Your life is in a state of change, and your circumstances are not stable enough to bring anything to the kind of culmination that constitutes success. But you are laying a framework for future success. Your inner structure as a human being is changing, and it is the profound insecurity of such a transformation that is making you hold on to the past so furiously and with such a sense of effort. When this period is over, your life course may be considerably changed. The only reason you aren't getting anywhere now is that there isn't anywhere for you to go in that direction. Remember, the truth works! If it doesn't work for you, it isn't true for you! This may be the most important lesson that you can learn at this time.

Be prepared to let go of whatever you don't really need, even if it is a relationship. Don't take yourself so seriously that every challenge to your current position on any matter seems to be a challenge to life itself. You may not be aware of it, but the physiological reactions that you go through at a time like this were originally intended to deal with a real physical threat to your life. But today we have changed so that our physical existence is not so important as ego-existence, and all of our reactions have to be changed accordingly. Most people have not done so.

Pluto Conjunct Uranus

This transit only occurs in the lives of persons born within approximately seventy years following a conjunction of Uranus and Pluto in the zodiac. The last such conjunction was in 1965, so for the rest of this century everyone who has this transit will be quite young. In the 1970s and 1980s they will not yet be teenagers, and by the end of the century they will be at most seventeen. Consequently this transit affects you in your formative years when you are most vulnerable to long-term transits that can affect your life later on.

The combination of these two planets signifies that you want to break away from circumstances that hold you back. You feel that if things aren't going the way you want, you will make changes in order to get them that way. You are not likely to be very patient at this time, and you may not understand the meaning of discipline. With this transit you are inclined to feel very self-righteous, for you feel that you know what is best, in contrast to the older people around you who seem to be out of touch with what is going on.

However, it would be a shame to waste the energy of this transit in challenging everyone around you or blindly rebelling against all restriction. You can learn a great deal about matters that are really important through the influence of this transit. Since Pluto and Uranus both represent very profound forces within the universe, you should spend your energies learning to know and understand as much as you can about how the universe works. You should not ask yet how you can change it, because you won't understand it very well until after this transit.

The outcome of this transit may very well be that you will be wise beyond your years in your depth of understanding, and through this wisdom you will be in a better position to make conservative and even quite revolutionary changes later on.

Even if you do not feel inclined to rebel or push for changes in your immediate environment, you may find that very tremendous changes are taking place within you. This may be quite upsetting, but try to remain calm and see what is really happening. Here again you have an opportunity to gain an understanding that is considerably beyond your years.

Pluto Sextile Uranus

This is a time of profound but creative change in your life. You will go below the superficial aspects of life to encounter dimensions of living that you never knew existed. And these discoveries will change your life and enable you to live more richly and fully, if you take full advantage of what you learn and do not turn away in fear, for there is no reason to.

The new insights you gain will also bring you the ability to use talents and ingenuity that you may not have known you had. You will be able to make creative changes in your environment as well as within yourself.

This is a favorable time to embark upon any new study, but particularly one that reveals hidden aspects of the universe in a startling, exciting manner. It is a favorable transit for the study of a technical discipline, science, astrology or other branches of the occult, particularly if the discipline is revolutionizing society in some way, as computer technology is now.

If you are inclined toward social reform, this transit may signify that you will join a group or organized movement for that purpose on a large scale. Civil rights organizations and politically moderate as well as more radical reform groups fit this category. And because of the energy of Pluto you are concerned with effective reform and change, not merely with making a lot of noise. Pluto gives greater depth to the Uranian capacity for change.

This is also a favorable period for doing any kind of psychological work, if you feel that it is desirable. You will be able to accomplish much along these lines at this time, and the process will have a permanent effect upon your life.

Pluto Square Uranus

This transit signifies a period of change and even upheaval in your life. But the changes will probably originate, not within your personal sphere, but in larger pressures from society as a whole. Under this influence many individuals feel that little happens in their personal lives but that the changes in the world around them are phenomenal.

The major challenge you will have to face during this period is learning to adapt to changes in the world around you. Rigidity will only make the situation worse, because it is unlikely that you can successfully resist the pressures for change. In fact, if Uranus is strong in your natal chart, you yourself may become an agent for change. If you feel that circumstances have limited you severely, you will probably be attracted to persons and movements that set themselves up as agents of a new order. This may be on a grand political and social scale, or it may be on the much smaller scale of an individual who comes into your life and shows you how to change. Actually, this can be quite a liberating transit, because you are inclined to look toward the future for your strength rather than to the past, so you will probably be able to flow with the changes.

One problem to watch out for is the possibility that you may throw out everything, not just that which needs change. Pluto-Uranus combinations tend to make you overdo revolution, meaning not just social revolution but fundamental changes in your own life that are somewhat unexpected in terms of your past. Try to distinguish what elements of the past have been good and what have not — do not arbitrarily destroy both.

A second warning is that both of these planets are fanatical in nature and not heedful of human feelings and emotions. Do not lose track of feelings in making or experiencing sweeping changes. And because both Pluto and Uranus speak in large social terms, do not lose track of the quality of individuals now. Larger social forces may be behind everything you do or that happens to you, but ultimately those forces are composed of individuals whom you have to deal with as such, not as representatives of some abstraction.

In the long run this transit can be an opportunity to make sweeping changes in your life. The challenge to your humanity is to make them only where appropriate.

Pluto Trine Uranus

This is a time of creative and radical transformation, either in your own life or in the lives of those around you. You will strive to bring about changes that clearly separate this period from the past, not wildly and rebelliously, but with a clear plan in mind and a comprehensive view of the whole. Consequently the changes that you make at this time are lasting as well as thorough.

If you have the opportunity, you may be able to accomplish something quite extraordinary, at least in terms of your normal expectations. The changes you make at this time and the tasks that you undertake will broaden your horizons, and this enables you to do more than usual. Along with this is the fact that during this transit you may become involved in something that is quite unprecedented in your life, which will have this same broadening affect.

You may become interested in completely new kinds of ideas and in the people associated with them. Whether or not you keep your old friends throughout this period, you will certainly gain new friends who will reflect your internal evolution.

Circumstances that used to limit your life, viewpoints that narrowed your perceptions and relationships that were unnecessarily confining may all pass suddenly out of your life at this time. You will not feel a sense of loss, but rather a sense of new birth and freedom. Now you can go on to do all the things that were not possible for you before.

This transit can increase the scope of your life in every way by breaking down all the structures that used to hold you back. This will give you the chance to find out much more about who you are and what your life can really be.

Pluto Opposition Uranus

This transit represents a period of massive changes, which you share with almost everyone of about the same age. Therefore the causes of these changes may be larger social forces that are outside of your personal sphere of life.

The combination of these two planets carries the symbolism of creative revolution; that is, you may be in revolt against many of the factors that have made your life routine and devoid of new challenge and interest. Many elements of your life will pass away suddenly and be gone with little or no warning, even elements that you have felt were a permanent part of your life. This can occur in just about any area of your life, but personal and professional relationships will be very strongly affected.

Your central problem during this transit will be one of attitude. Obviously, the greater your psychological investment in having conditions remain exactly as they are now, the more you will suffer. The more flexible you are, the better off you will be. In fact, if you can look upon this transit as an opportunity to restructure your life creatively, you may be able to take considerable control of the process. If you fight these changes you will be a victim of them to some degree.

You have to understand that although these changes have emerged suddenly in your life, their origins are in the past, and the forces behind them have been at work for many years. And you must recognize that these forces are inherent in the way things have been! Preventing these changes is practically impossible and not even desirable.

You should learn to flow with the great changes that are happening to you now, and you should even make yourself an active agent in bringing them about. Throw away everything that has outlived its purpose in your life; seek changes in your relationships; find ways to make new starts in as many areas as possible. Above all, do not spend your time moping about and wishing for the "good old days." That will only put you out of touch with the world and less and less able to live in it.

Pluto Conjunct Neptune

This transit signifies a period of very deep inward transformation that will be reflected in changed ideals, goals and many other aspects of your world view. You may also work harder than ever to bring about in reality an ideal that you have held for years. However, you will have to give up a great deal to accomplish this, and you will not receive much ego-reinforcement at the time, even if you are successful.

You will find it necessary to question very deeply many beliefs you have held as a matter of course all your life. You may become disoriented as you discover that you have been living under illusions. But at least you will not be alone, for this is one of the transits that affects everyone in one age group at about the same time. In fact, the need to change your ideals may come through your peer group. It would be a good idea to discuss this with someone who is much older or younger who is not suffering the effects of this transit, in order to get a better perspective on what is happening to you. If you begin psychotherapy now, which is quite possible, you should not choose a therapist of your own age. While he or she might understand you, he cannot give you a different perspective.

Many elements of your life — relationships, job situations, places — may pass away now, but this is only a reflection of the profound changes taking place within you. After this transit is over you may find it hard to recognize the person you were before.

Whatever you choose to do, it would be a good idea to study a subject that will give you greater understanding about your life. Astrology, the occult, metaphysics or even depth psychology might serve this purpose. But don't get lost in abstractions! Make sure that what you learn has real consequences in your everyday life, because you have great needs there that should be met. Also your studies should give you very deep understanding. Nothing superficial would help you at this time.

Pluto Sextile Neptune

Because of the current angular relationship between Neptune and Pluto, namely the long-term mutual sextile between them in the zodiac, which extends from the 1940s to the end of the twentieth century, this transit will occur when you are in your fifties or older.

This transit denotes a time when you will become more concerned with mystical and otherworldly ideas and beliefs. You will want to explore the hidden depths of existence and have experiences that are profound and revealing. If you are ready, your experiences may be very enlightening and give you great understanding about your own life and about the lives of others.

Even if you are not inclined to study the occult, this transit will awaken you to the more spiritual dimensions of existence. If you are so inclined, it will involve you in the occult or in a spiritual movement as well. A materialistic view of the universe will no longer seem at all satisfactory, and you will be aware that other elements of existence are in many ways stronger than material concerns.

The mysteries of life and death are not abstractions to you anymore but are directly and immediately relevant to your own life. This does not mean that you have to worry about your own death particularly, but you will refuse to accept any explanation of the world that begs the question of the meaning of life and death.

Pluto Square Neptune

This transit will occur for everyone who is living now when you are in your late sixties and after. As we move into the twenty-first century, the transit will occur progressively later in people's lives. This is because the sextile between transiting Pluto and Neptune will last for the rest of this century.

During this transit you will have to cope with powerful outside forces that seem to take no regard of your individual ego. Your individuality will not be challenged so much as ignored, unless you stand in the way of these forces, in which case you may have some extremely discouraging experiences.

Elements of your life that you have always counted on may begin to pass away in ways that are extremely difficult to understand. There will be no dramatic signs of social struggle and change, but the old order is passing away. What may be most difficult to accept is that there seems to be nothing that you can fight directly. It is as if many circumstances, relationships, possessions and various other conditions of your life have lost their right to be and are withering away. You can waste your time regretting this situation, thereby putting yourself into the same position, or you can come to terms with the new world and become part of it. That is one of the decisions you will have to make, although probably your internal conditioning will determine your decision in advance.

Another side of this transit is that hidden aspects of your unconscious mind may flare up and begin to influence your life now. Elements of your personality that you prefer to keep hidden from others may become so evident that you can no longer avoid them.

The only solution, therefore, is to deal with them. They are probably not as bad as you think anyway. It is not their intrinsic nature but repression that makes them seem bad. Now you must throw away the past conditioning that makes you reject these perfectly valid aspects of yourself.

One response to the above situation may be an increased concern with subjects that reveal the deep, inner, hidden nature of the world, such as psychology, scientific research, the occult, spiritualism or mystical philosophy. The insights you gain from these disciplines could well be the basis of a complete regeneration of yourself. This is in many ways the most positive response to this transit.

Pluto Opposition Neptune

Pluto transiting opposition natal Neptune. This transit has not happened to anyone now alive and will not happen again for at least another century.

Pluto Conjunct Pluto

Pluto transiting conjunct natal Pluto. This transit does not happen to anyone except possibly right after birth.

Pluto Sextile Pluto

During this transit the changes that take place in your life will be part of a creative evolution. You can see that you are moving toward your goals and that you do not need anything else in order to attain them. You will get there simply by allowing the current energies to play themselves out.

At the same time this transit will create additional opportunities for growth that you may or may not choose to take advantage of. This is a period of stability within change.

Quite likely your concerns will become deeper as you become interested in the more profound aspects of your life. You may wish to understand more about your internal psychological workings, and this is a good time to find out without fearing great upsets. The overall gentleness of this transit allows you to discover many things that could be the source of anguish at other times. On another level, this transit will also give you greater concern about the universe as a whole and where you are in relationship to it.

You will probably find that your views about daily life are stabilizing and maturing. Now that the period of rapid change is past, you are arriving at a way of dealing with the world that will not change much more except, hopefully, when future experience invalidates your present views. In other words, this transit doesn't represent settling into rigidity, but stability.

Pluto Square Pluto

Because of Pluto's variable speed, this transit occurs at different times in people's lives, depending upon when in this century you were born. At the earliest, it will occur during your late forties.

This transit signifies a period of general regeneration, which may not be entirely pleasant. Most of us are attached to the past whether or not it is good for us. And this transit will root out precisely those elements of the past that are not good for you, even those aspects that you have forgotten about. Problems that you may have lost track of entirely but which are still working unconsciously in your life may reappear and become active now, usually but not always to your detriment.

Pluto rules forces for change that are inherent within the hidden depths of things. Therefore you should not blame the unpleasant changes that occur now on circumstances or persons in your environment. Look within yourself to see how the groundwork for the present is laid in the past.

Many things may be destroyed at this time, and the destruction will be ruthless if you defend them with rigidity. Pluto's action upon unyielding entities is particularly harsh. Therefore you should simply allow the things of the past to fade and allow the future to be born on their ruins. If you can do this, the potential for positive change with Pluto is very great.

The area of your life where the changes will occur depends upon what houses are involved, but these changes are likely to affect both your home and your professional situation. Relationships that have outlived their creative usefulness may end, especially if they constitute a barrier to future growth.

This transit may also increase your concern about the creative and regenerative processes within the universe and cause you to become interested in the occult. However, certain aspects of the occult, such as magic, are best avoided under this transit, because the energies involved will be difficult to control now. Although your conscious mind may be in control at first, you are likely to find that entirely unconscious forces within you have taken over and are running you completely. This can have disastrous consequences.

You may also get into severe power struggles with people who are trying to prevent the changes in your life or who are trying to expedite changes that you are resisting. Look very carefully to ascertain which category they are in.

Pluto Trine Pluto

In this century, this transit has happened only to people when they are in their eighties and nineties. I have had no opportunity to observe its effects, but I would expect them to be similar to those of Pluto sextile Pluto.

Pluto Opposition Pluto

This transit occurs at a time that is beyond the normal life expectancy.

Pluto Conjunct Midheaven

This is an extremely important transit that will affect the entire course and direction of your life and what you will actually accomplish. It is also a rather long transit, whose effects will be manifested over a period of up to two years.

The central issue here is your life direction. Where are you going? What are you doing? How are you going about it? This is a time of vigorous scrutiny when you will probably examine everything that you have done with your life up until now and ask a number of questions. First, do you really feel that what you have been doing is valid? Don't think solely in terms of your job, although that is certainly an important part of the question. Many people's true vocation consists of what they consider to be an avocation. For example, Sir Isaac Newton's actual job for many years was with the Royal Mint of England. He studied science, his true vocation, on the side, although his mint work left him a great deal of time.

Second, are the means you have used been appropriate to your ends and to your own inner being? This is an extremely important question. With Pluto, what is required is not just success; it must be won properly. If you have had to violate the rules of your game in order to win, this transit is likely to bring you crashing down in failure. And even if this doesn't happen immediately, don't feel that you have gotten away with it, because this effect of the transit continues as long as Pluto is in your natal tenth house.

Your response to this transit depends on your answers to the above questions. If you discover that you are not fulfilling your true calling in your work or another area, Pluto will bring inexorable forces to the surface that will drive you out of your present position. You may leave voluntarily, or you may be forced out by being fired or laid off. If this happens, let your inner feelings guide you in an entirely new direction.

If you have been on the proper course all these years, this transit will give you a massive push to succeed. Only watch out that your push doesn't arouse too much opposition from above that could slow you down. The forces set loose by a Pluto transit are often very difficult to handle. Also be careful about breaking the rules of the game as mentioned above, for this can destroy your efforts.

If you have been on the right course but have not been going about it the right way, you will make big changes in the way you pursue your goals.

Whatever else happens now, there will be many large changes in your life, clearing the way for you to follow your proper life course. There may be significant changes concerning your family or parents that tremendously affect your own life. Things or persons connected with the past may pass out of your life at this time. Do not try to hold on to them, for their departure is part of the clearing process.

Pluto Sextile Midheaven

This transit has widely varying effects upon different people. It can be a time in your career when you make a fundamental change in your objectives. Or it can be a time when you turn inward and evaluate your spiritual progress, with the probable result of a significant change of objectives.

In terms of your career or your life direction, it may be that forces operating behind the scenes, which you probably are not aware of, will give you a chance to exert more personal power for making changes among your fellow workers. The people working on your behalf may have a conscious plan, or you may just happen to fit into a changed circumstance that presents this opportunity.

Sometimes this process may involve a change in jobs or even careers, but usually the change will take place in your present situation.

But there are changes taking place in your personal life also, aimed at increasing your effectiveness in pursuing your life goals. You may improve your immediate living conditions or even change residence for professional reasons. At the same time there will be more emotional intensity in your most intimate relationships with your family.

This process is a reflection of the positive changes taking place within your mind. New psychological pressures are coming to the surface and transforming the way you think about yourself. Quite often emotions associated with past experiences are reactivated at this time, which affect your life very powerfully. This can be a chance to get rid of psychological complexes from your past and to live more freely and with less compulsion.

You may have to look to other people's resources or financial backing to fulfill your current plans. Feel free to do so, because other people may be in a position to help you out tremendously in making changes either in your personal and domestic life or in your career.

Pluto Square Midheaven

At this time you have to be careful not to let your actions stir up resistance from others. Try to avoid acting in ways that say that you are out to change people's lives and habits and that you will not compromise at all. Without even being aware of it, you may become obsessed by achieving certain objectives with an energy out of all proportion to the significance of your goal. This is what scares people and may make them work against you.

On the other hand you may experience this kind of energy from others. Persons or circumstances may attempt to change you against your will. To a certain extent this is a positive encounter, because it forces you to become very conscious of what you are doing so that you can defend yourself against the pressures for change. And indeed it is inevitable that you will change, but the changes can be for the good, if you don't waste all your energies trying to fight them. Your whole conception of yourself and your goals in life will change, and in many ways you will be a new person after this transit.

Your domestic life is particularly likely to change in some regard. Any tensions in your marital and family life will surface at this time, and you will have to do something about them. Do not hope that they will go away, because they won't. But you do have the opportunity to create a whole new relationship out of your present one, if you are willing to face the challenge. Sometimes these pressures for change are manifested externally. You may suddenly need repairs on your house, or appliances may suddenly break down, and as a result the physical health of either you or your family may suffer. This is also a sign that changes are needed, so you should look very intensely for the cause of the difficulty. Perhaps you need to move. Sometimes this transit coincides with a change of residence, which enables you to see what to do more easily because your new surroundings reveal previously hidden problems. You need not expect catastrophe with this transit by any means, but do not shrink from the challenge of change. Only in this way can you keep your life vigorous and challenging.

Pluto Trine Midheaven

During this time gradual changes will take place in your life that will make you more aware of the external and internal forces that make your life move in certain directions. You will gain great psychological insight into yourself and others at this time, and you will go below surface appearances to seek out the fundamental elements of any issue.

This is also a time when you may gain power over others in some way, either in your personal or your professional life. You may be given the authority to direct a project or a group of people working together. However, you should be aware that you are acting as an agent of forces that transcend your own individuality, and that everything you do must be for the common good, or it will be to no avail.

Sometimes the power can take a form that has nothing to do with authority. It may be that your own personality becomes powerful from within, making you a person of moral influence. Without even being aware of the process yourself, you speak with wisdom and others heed what you say. People may be drawn to you, fascinated by your energy and power. Of course this confers the greatest possible responsibility upon you, because you can misuse this power, but the consequences for you would not be good!

Under this transit you may choose to undergo psychotherapy or work with other mind-expanding disciplines in order to increase your self-understanding.

In your professional life you may feel that you have a very significant task to perform at this time, one that is far more important than your usual work. You feel that your work could transform the whole nature of your career, not only for yourself but for others in the same field. You have a much greater sense of purpose in your work than usual. If you take the time to communicate this in detail to others, you can be really effective. But if you assume that your insight is obvious and that everyone else sees what you see, you will become isolated from those who could help, and therefore you will be ineffective.

Pluto Opposition Midheaven

This is a time of great change in your personal and family life and a time of great inner psychological change. The effects of this transit can vary greatly, but it is always an important transit.

On the psychological level, you may encounter certain psychological effects from your past — your childhood and early home life, your relationship with your parents, your hometown or even something from the more distant past of your family or heredity. Psychologists know that the experiences of early life have a strong conditioning affect upon adult behavior, and it is essential to understand the psychological mechanisms created by this experience in order to free yourself from neurotic problems that arise in adulthood. During this transit you can gain such understanding, because the forces within you are much more powerful and near the surface, where they can be observed in action.

On a less profound level, this transit can signify that your personal life will go through great changes as certain things pass away and new things come into existence. Obviously this happens all the time, but the changes are much more dramatic now. There may be great changes within your family, such as divorce, death, a major change of residence or the need for major repairs on a building, to name a few of the changes signified by this transit. The main point is that at some level your personal and domestic life needs to be overhauled so that it can be reconstructed along new lines. Often you need to be liberated from the past, not only at the psychological level but in your everyday practical life as well. This is the time to build a new order in your personal life. However, people often attempt to resist such change, with unpleasant results. The energies merely build up to such a point that they are released through a dramatic or unfortunate incident, such as the breakup of a marriage, sudden damage to property or the like. And resisting the energies of change is a waste of an opportunity to totally regenerate your life from its very roots.

Pluto Conjunct Ascendant

At this time your relationships with others, both intimate and otherwise, will be greatly transformed. Your personality will undergo a period of change that will bring to light some very important but often unacknowledged elements of your psyche, which you will have to deal with. This may be a period of extreme crisis in your life, if you have been attempting to hide certain inner forces from yourself or from others. The psychological changes that take place now may make it desirable for you to undergo psychotherapy or a similar treatment in order to get more in touch with yourself. With this transit it is extremely important that you get more in touch with yourself!

On the purely psychological level, you may find yourself face to face with aspects of your personality that you have chosen to ignore in the past because you thought that they were "evil" or "weak" or otherwise unacceptable. But they are real aspects of yourself, and their energies can only be suppressed for a time, not entirely eliminated. Under this transit the energies will surface.

The process may start with compulsive actions that are hard to understand. Strange drives may emerge that seem to take over your life, without any regard for your conscious intention. Sometimes the compulsions are so subtle that you are not aware of them at all, except that they affect people around you; in fact you may only encounter them when others respond to you. This can be very upsetting, and you may feel that you are being victimized by some outside force, although the force is within you. Even under the best of conditions, you can expect your relationships to change considerably as others encounter the changes within you. A close relationship such as marriage may undergo especially great changes at this time.

Often a tremendous power drive will surface during this transit, as you suddenly want to take control of everything around you. You are not content to be subject to an outside power or to anyone else's will. This can lead you to break away from many restrictions that your life has been subject to in the past. This can be very good, but it can also be dangerous, of course. The worst way to handle it is to not admit it to yourself. Experience has shown that if you do not acknowledge Plutonian energies, someone from the outside is attracted who will act with power and even violence toward you. Granted, you may stir up opposition by trying to take control, but that is better than being surprised by an external agent.

The best tactic with all of these Plutonian effects is to recognize them and try to understand how they fit into your personality. They are there for a reason, and if you understood yourself thoroughly, you would see that they have a positive purpose in your life, if you allow them to be expressed. Now is a chance to release these energies and make them a positive part of your conscious personality. Even if the effects of this transit are a bit difficult, the final purpose is positive.

Pluto Sextile Ascendant

This is a time of positive change and opportunity in your life. You have the chance to remake and reform all your relationships so that they will serve your purposes better. You may also change or reform the life of someone close to you, because in all of your relationships you are exerting more power and having a stronger than usual effect upon others. This means that you have a great responsibility to use this power well and not just for your own narrow ends. Whatever you do to change the life of another must help them as well as yourself.

Contacts with friends and daily associates become more significant at this time. Out of your everyday environment, where you would least expect it, a very intense relationship may emerge that will change the lives of you both. This could be a love affair, but it is more likely to be a powerful friendship. Whatever it is, in this relationship you will encounter each other at a very deep level of emotion. And you will also encounter aspects of yourself that you have kept hidden for years. The most important factor in such a relationship is that it allows you to develop much more of yourself than you have ever known was there. There is as much potential for you to be changed through a significant relationship as there is for you to change a relationship.

Under this transit you could gain a position of authority among your fellow workers or among friends, as in a club or social group. The best way to use this power would be as an agent of reform and improvement. Do not use it for purely personal gain, because that could produce disastrous consequences later on.

During this period you may have experiences that cause you to change your goals. Circumstances and encounters with other people may force you to reevaluate your ideals, and your life may begin to move in a direction quite different from any that you have followed before. This in turn will allow you to develop more fully and experience life more abundantly.

Pluto Square Ascendant

This transit usually provides some very intense encounters with others, which may completely transform the important relationships in your life. The problem is that this transit is not always gentle in its effects. You may feel that each of your important relationships, especially a close personal one such as marriage, is going through a period of upheaval that gives you little peace. A relationship that is in great difficulty or that has outlived its function in your life may end altogether, even though you don't want it to. You can be sure that if a relationship seems to be moving irrevocably to a close now that it is making way for a new life for you. New relationships will replace the old and serve a more constructive purpose. Pluto is the symbol of death and resurrection, which you are experiencing through your relationships at this time.

Persons may enter your life who have a very powerful effect upon your mind and emotions, almost as if they have a magical hold over you. No matter how you strive to escape their influence, you seem to be held by an invisible thread. Such people are holding onto you by a subconscious complex, taking advantage of a weakness or fear within you and using this knowledge to coerce you. They may even be doing this quite inadvertently; their knowledge may be as subconscious as the complex within you that gives them the power. It is important that you learn what part of you is giving someone this power. Do not blame the other person, no matter how culpable he or she seems. Through apparent power struggles with others you will uncover your weaknesses and learn how to deal with them.

In all dealings with other people, be very careful not to resort to underhanded or subversive tactics. Pluto makes some people act ruthlessly or feel that their goals justify any means that will attain them. But this kind of attitude can set forces in motion that are difficult to control and extremely negative in their consequences. These forces can lead to a total breakdown in your relationships, if you allow them to begin.

In many ways you will be a new person after this transit, with new hopes and new potentials. The encounters that take you to that point may not be pleasant, but they are necessary to your life. The best thing to do is to charge right in and get the encounter over with as quickly as possible.

Pluto Trine Ascendant

This is a time of creative change in your relationships. You have the opportunity to be either the agent of the changes or the object of them. Probably you will be both to some extent.

On the one hand you may experience an increase in personal power with this transit. You will have the chance to exert an influence on others either because you are in a position of some power or because your own personal vibration influences people and changes their lives. As with other Pluto transits, it is important to use this power for the general good, for the power of Pluto does not adapt well to purely egoistic purposes.

During this transit you will seek a higher quality and greater intensity in all your experiences. You are not even remotely attracted to superficial qualities, either in people or in experiences. You need to feel with every ounce of your emotion that every encounter changes you at the deepest core of your being.

To this end you may draw people to you who are very intense and who have a very strong effect upon your mind. However, with the trine these relationships are usually quite constructive rather than difficult. Even under the best of conditions, some of what you learn about yourself may not be very pleasant until you learn to accept it, but it usually isn't so bad, even if you think it is.

Under any circumstances the overall effect of these encounters is to broaden your self-understanding and increase your capacity for complete self-expression.

There may be changes in your life at this time, and your relationships may be considerably altered, but this is only so that you may experience a regeneration that will keep your life from becoming stale and dead.

Pluto Opposition Ascendant

Your intimate one-to-one relationships, such as a marriage or other personal relationship, partnership and close encounters with friends and enemies, will be greatly affected by this transit.

In marriage, pressures will surface that indicate that you and your mate need to consider making significant changes in your relationship. Perhaps you have been reluctant to face the forces at work between you, afraid that discussing them would cause a blow-up. And it probably would, but a blow-up is not always a bad thing in a relationship. Now it will become especially urgent that you both lay your cards on the table and work out all the problems in your relationship that are bothering either of you. Otherwise the pressure may build to the breaking point. This transit can cause a marriage to break up, if you do not face your problems honestly.

Very often this transit does not affect the marriage itself but brings about an encounter between you and someone who will be very important to you, someone who may literally transform your life. This may be someone in a professional capacity, such as a psychiatrist, who will help you learn what is making it difficult for you to live the way you want to. Or it may be a friend who affects you more strongly than most. Unfortunately it may also signify a struggle with an enemy who is particularly powerful and disrupts your life. However, even in a confrontation with an enemy there is potential for positive change.

Index